Matrix and Analytical Methods for Performance Analysis of Telecommunication Systems

Valeriy Naumov · Yuliya Gaidamaka ·
Natalia Yarkina · Konstantin Samouylov

Matrix and Analytical Methods for Performance Analysis of Telecommunication Systems

Springer

Valeriy Naumov
Service Innovation Research Institute
(PIKE)
Helsinki, Finland

Yuliya Gaidamaka
Applied Probability and Informatics
Peoples' Friendship University of Russia
(RUDN University)
Moscow, Russia

Natalia Yarkina
Applied Probability and Informatics
Peoples' Friendship University of Russia
(RUDN University)
Moscow, Russia

Konstantin Samouylov
Applied Probability and Informatics
Peoples' Friendship University of Russia
(RUDN University)
Moscow, Russia

ISBN 978-3-030-83134-9 ISBN 978-3-030-83132-5 (eBook)
https://doi.org/10.1007/978-3-030-83132-5

This Springer imprint is published by the registered company Springer Nature Switzerland AG
The registered company address is: Gewerbestrasse 11, 6330 Cham, Switzerland

Dedicated to our teacher Gely Basharin

Foreword

In June 1955, the International Teletraffic Congress (ITC) has been established by the global community of teletraffic scientists and engineers in Copenhagen. After many years of absence, a small delegation of Russian scientists was able to join ITC13, held in Copenhagen in June 1991, once again. This opportunity has been used by the Russian delegates to share their comprehensive knowledge on teletraffic theory which has been generated over decades of the last century. In particular, Gely Basharin's group at Peoples' Friendship University of Russia (RUDN University) in Moscow has been a very active team within the latter teletraffic research community.

In summer 1985, Jean-Jacques Annaud has directed the production of the movie "The Name of the Rose" which is based on Umberto Eco's famous novel "Il Nome Della Rosa" (1980). It tells a dramatic medieval story about a theological disputation in the year 1327 and the search for a famous book of Aristotle which is hidden in an Italian Benedictine monastery. During the production of some scenes in the ancient abbey "Kloster Eberbach" near the river Rhine in Germany, young people including myself have just by chance met the Franciscan friar William of Baskerville alias Sean Connery when he left the Romanesque buildings. But we did not dare to address him. Maybe, we could have asked him to explain us the meaning of a distinguished scene in the book. Therein, the master glazier of the abbey Nicholas of Morimondo says "We no longer have the learning of the ancients, the age of giants is past" and William of Baskerville responds "We are dwarfs, but dwarfs who stand on the shoulders of those giants, and small though we are, we sometimes manage to see farther on the horizon than they". Robert Kelton's book "The Post-Italianate Edition: On the Shoulders of Giants—A Shandean Postscript", University of Chicago Press (1993), includes a foreword written by Umberto Eco. This book reveals the philosophical roots of William of Baskerville's statement that is also related to the assumed OTSOG variant "If I have seen farther, it is by standing on the shoulders of giants" ascribed to Sir Isaac Newton (1643–1727).

Indeed, not only Sir Isaac Newton, but all scientists are standing on the shoulders of giants and they are invited to share their knowledge, ideas, papers, and books. In that summer 1991, the participants of ITC13 have realized once again that their teletraffic research is substantially formed by famous scientists, such as Agner Krarup Erlang, Soren Asmussen, Gely P. Basharin, Pavel P. Bocharov, Jacob W. Cohen, Erol Gelenbe, Boris V. Gnedenko, Arne Jensen, Frank P. Kelly, David G. Kendall, Aleksandr J. Khinchin, Gennadi P. Klimov, Andrey N. Kolmogorov, Igor N. Kovalenko, Guy Latouche, Andrey A. Markov, Debasis Mitra, Marcel F. Neuts, Vaidyanathan Ramaswami, Anatoliy V. Skorohod, Ryszard Syski, Lajos Takàcs, Whard Whitt, and Peter Whittle, to name a few of them. Unexpectedly, one has also realized at that time that new scientific books on matrix-analytic methods could still be withheld at a boundary between states which resembles William of Baskerville's experience at the ancient abbey in 1327.

Nowadays, we have fortunately overcome the enforced isolation of scientific communities by means of personal collaborations on the global scale of Internet and by the assistance of international publishers like Springer.

Reading this book on matrix and analytical methods for the performance analysis of telecommunication systems, you are pursuing again a scientific journey along the unique route of teletraffic theory. Benefitting from research efforts of giants during the last century, it follows the classical path of queueing theory toward the challenges associated with the teletraffic engineering methodologies of our epoch.

Yuliya Gaidamaka, Natalia Yarkina, Valeriy Naumov, and Konstantin Samouylov share with us a comprehensive view on teletraffic modeling and performance analysis techniques for advanced telecommunication systems such a 4G and 5G mobile networks and 5G-mmWave radio access networks. Starting with the classical Erlang's loss and delay systems and moving toward stochastic networks with flexible servers and generalized multi-resource service systems with random resource requirements a refreshed perspective on teletraffic theory is developed. The classical multiclass queueing networks inducing reversible Markov processes, G-networks with positive and negative customers, as well as single and multiple server queues with Poisson or Markovian arrival processes and exponentially, phase-type or generally distributed service times and finite or infinite capacities such as $GI|G|1$, $PH|PH|1|n$, $MAP|PH|1|n$, $MAP|M|\infty$, $\overrightarrow{M}|\overrightarrow{M}|n|n$, $MAP|PH|n|n$, or $\overrightarrow{MAP}|\overrightarrow{PH}|n|m$ enable a probabilistic analysis and yield explicit formulae of the relevant performance indices. Furthermore, they allow the authors to apply matrix-analytic solution methods for Markov chains. The associated explicit analytic and computational solution techniques constitute the theoretical basis of this book. Studying multi-resource service systems with random resource requirements and modeling the resource allocations in loss systems by stochastic lists, the authors substantially extend the existing teletraffic theory and reveal new insights into the insensitivity properties of loss systems. By these means the authors provide tractable mathematical tools to create new efficient resource management techniques and advanced teletraffic engineering methods for next generation communication networks and the future Internet.

We are thankful that we can hold a requested, distinguished book in our hands, in contrast to the experiences of William of Baskerville's fellows in misery. Its unique content describing the teletraffic theory of the twenty-first century is by no means a secret object. Fortunately, we will not be threatened by contamination and death like William if we touch the pages of this book and apply its unique mathematical results.

January 2021

Udo R. Krieger
Universitat Bamberg
Bamberg, Germany

Preface

The global telecommunication network is the largest technological object ever created by human society. It is being constantly enhanced and improved to keep up with our needs to exchange, store and process huge, ever-growing amounts of data. Network performance directly affects the Quality of Service (QoS) of traffic flows and the Quality of Experience (QoE) perceived by users of communication services.

Technologies evolve all the time and new communication systems emerge quickly, whereas it takes much longer to design, deploy, and operate a full-scale network, yet this is when quality of service deficiencies may be revealed. To cover this gap, almost in parallel with new technologies, scholars, and engineers develop new and enhance existing techniques and even theories to analyze performance of emerging communication systems.

User requests for communication services arrive randomly, and session holding times as well as the amounts of network resources per session may also be random. For that reason, communication systems and networks are generally modeled using probability frameworks, and especially queueing systems. For model analysis, however, other mathematical techniques are also widely employed, namely matrix methods of linear algebra.

At the turn of the 2020s, international standardization bodies issued the specifications of 5G wireless networks. Equipment and software have been put on the market, and network operators have launched commercial 5G services. In the preceding 10 years the research community have been developing frameworks and techniques for performance analysis of the new network systems.

In queueing theory, models known *as multi-resource service systems with random resource requirements*, or ReLS (short for resource loss systems), have proved highly relevant, as they reflect particularly well the processes of allocating and sharing radio resources in LTE networks and 5G New Radio (NR) systems operating in millimeter-wave bands (5G mmWave). Moreover, the forecast trends in communication technologies show that such models will remain relevant in the future for performance analysis of terahertz networks. Motivated by the potential of this powerful framework, scholars specializing in mathematical teletraffic theory have laid the foundations of the theory of ReLSes, which is the central theme of this book.

Unlike most textbooks on queueing theory, in particular those dealing with telecommunication applications, the main focus of this volume is indeed on ReLS models. However, before specifically discussing ReLSes in Part III, we provide an overview of the essential prerequisites, from the basic models and techniques in Part I to more sophisticated matrix-analytical methods of queueing theory in Part II.

This book is an advanced graduate textbook intended for postgraduate students and researchers specializing in telecommunication modeling and performance analysis. A rather extensive Part I gives an overview of classical frameworks and techniques prior to ReLS models. We assume that readers are familiar with core mathematical disciplines including the fundamentals of matrix algebra, probability theory, and stochastic processes. Nevertheless, for the sake of completeness and consistency, appendices with reference material are provided.

Part I includes a brief review of mathematical models and theories that have arisen from purely practical problems dealt with by engineers and applied mathematicians as communication systems evolved. However, only the models directly relevant to the main topic of the book are touched on. This is why, in Chap. 1, we review the evolution of the famous Erlang loss formula, from its publication more than a century ago to the present time. In the same chapter, although omitting its application to the communication systems of the first generation, we show how the Erlang formula is used to analyze GSM systems (2G), multiservice networks (3G), and, finally, LTE (4G). It was LTE performance analysis that has clearly revealed the need for loss systems with random resource requirements—ReLSes—which are the main theme of the book.

Since two Erlang's models—loss and delay—are fundamental in the context of this volume, they are specifically treated in Chap. 2. Here, we also discuss the Equivalent Random Traffic (ERT) method to estimate blocking probabilities in loss systems with non-Poisson arrivals and cover major generalizations of Erlang's results: continuous Erlang loss and delay formulas, queueing systems with a sequence of service elements and systems with a fractional number of servers.

An important step in the evolution of Erlang's models are multiservice loss networks, which have a product-form stationary distribution. In Chap. 3, we study multiservice loss networks with two types of communications, unicast and multicast, and derive efficient computational algorithms based upon the product form of the stationary distribution.

Chapter 4, the last in Part I, deals with Markovian arrival processes (MAP). MAPs are specified by several matrices, which permits analyzing service systems with such arrival processes using matrix-analytical methods covered in Part II. To illustrate the application of MAPs, we show how to obtain performance measures of a service system consisting of several single-server queues in series.

Part II is devoted to matrix-analytical methods. Several important results on generator matrices, which were scattered over many books and articles, are brought together in Chap. 5. Special attention is given to systems of equilibrium equations with nonzero right-hand sides, which arise when using the asymptotic method approximation for the arrival process. Also, we show how to solve the equilibrium equations of a lumpable Markov chain using stationary probabilities of the lumped process.

Chapter 6 discusses techniques for solving equilibrium equations with block generator matrices. We explore LU and UL decompositions of block generator matrices and show how they can be used to obtain solutions to equilibrium equations in matrix product and matrix-geometric form. By applying these methods to $MAP|M|\infty$ and $MAP|M|c|c$ service systems, we arrive at matrix generalizations of the Erlang and Wilkinson formulas, namely used in the ERT method.

Chapter 7 deals with matrix-geometrical stationary distributions of quasi birth-and-death processes. We illustrate the application of these results with two matrix-geometrical solutions for the stationary state distribution of a $PH|PH|1|r+1$ queueing system.

In Part III, we deal with ReLSes, which are generalizations of Erlang's loss system to the case when arriving customers demand random amounts of various resources. We allow for negative resource allocations, in which case we consider that the resource amount available to other customers temporarily increases.

Chapter 8 introduces the concepts of stochastic lists and pseudo-lists of resource allocations, the essential tools for ReLS analysis. We show that for a ReLS with Poisson arrivals and exponential service times, lists and pseudo-lists yield the same stationary distribution of the total allocated resource amounts.

Chapter 9 deals with ReLSes in which the service time of a customer depends on its required resource amounts.

In Chap. 10, we discuss a ReLS in which arrivals and departures are governed by a Markov chain and obtain necessary and sufficient conditions for the stationary distribution to have a product form. We also derive a simplified technique to compute the stationary state distribution using Fourier transform.

In Chap. 11, we study resource allocation in multiclass networks having several types of flexible servers and general constraints on the number of servers at each station. We study the maximum network throughput achievable with static resource allocation and propose a solution for the problem of optimal static resource allocation to servers that maximizes network throughput while satisfying constraints on the number of servers at each station.

Finally, in Chap. 12, we discuss some representative examples of ReLSes developed for performance analysis of 5G radio access networks and especially for 5G-mmWave. Among the examples, we study a system with signals, which permits taking into consideration the line-of-sight blocking in mmWave access networks, and the models reflecting resource reservation and multiconnectivity mechanisms of 5G-mmWave.

To study a subject in depth—and that is what this book is for—we strongly encourage further reading. However, to find and properly use the literature on certain topics may prove difficult. To make this challenging task easier, we have placed the main references after each part, while supplementary sources, which are not referenced in the text, are all listed at the end of the volume and split, for convenience, by chapters according to their numbers. As we have mentioned, the book is intended mainly for postgraduate and Ph.D. students, so the provided bibliography can be helpful for writing literature reviews, academic papers, and dissertations.

The volume summarizes the material of a number of courses that have been taught by the authors to postgraduate students at RUDN University for many years. The courses were part of the Technologies Applied Mathematics and Informatics, Mathematics and Computer Sciences, and Fundamental Informatics and Information Technologies study lines, and Theoretical Foundations of Informatics and Mathematical Modeling Ph.D. programs offered by the Physics, Mathematics and Natural Sciences Faculty at a department which is now called Applied Mathematics and Communications Technology Institute.

We are grateful to our colleagues, full and associate professors of RUDN University and Moscow State University, who have been teaching side by side with us courses on probability theory, stochastic processes, queueing theory, mathematical teletraffic theory, multiservice network theory, multiservice network performance analysis, mobile network performance analysis, 5G network modeling and performance analysis. We truly appreciate carrying out research and teaching together during all these years, and gaining invaluable experience in teaching these applied disciplines evolving alongside communication technologies.

We are especially grateful to our two friends, Eduard Sopin and Olli Martikainen, also applied mathematicians, researchers specialized in telecommunications system analysis, our co-authors and colleagues in academic and practical work. Eduard greatly contributed to articles underpinning Chap. 12, and especially to application of ReLSes to performance analysis of 5G wireless networks. Olli, while being the Director Research of Telecom Finland, taught us to comprehend mobile communications and their evolution. He also substantially contributed to articles, on which two chapters of the books are based.

Helsinki, Finland — Valeriy Naumov
Moscow, Russia — Yuliya Gaidamaka
Moscow, Russia — Natalia Yarkina
Moscow, Russia — Konstantin Samouylov

Acronyms and Abbreviations

5G	Fifth Generation
5G NR	5G New Radio
CDF	Cumulative distribution function
CTMC	Continuous-time Markov chain
DFT	Discrete Fourier transform
DTMC	Discrete-time Markov chain
ERT	Equivalent Random Traffic
FFT	Fast Fourier transform
GSM	General System for Mobile communication
LoS	Line-of-sight, unblocked
LTE	Long-Term Evolution
MAP	Markovian arrival process
MC	Markov chain
mmWave	Millimeter wave
nLoS	Non-line-of-sight, blocked
PASTA	Poisson arrivals see time averages
pdf	Probability density function
QBD	Quasi-birth-and-death process
QoS	Quality of service
RAC	Resource allocation problem for a clopen network
RAN	Radio access networks
RAO	Resource allocation problem for an open network
ReLS	Resource loss system with random requirements
RRAO	Relaxed resource allocation problem for an open network
UE	User equipment

Notation

Very little of the general notation is given below. Generally, the particular interpretation of symbols with more than one use is clear from the context.

$\mathbb{N}$	set of natural numbers
$\mathbb{Z}$	set of integers
$\mathbb{R}$	set of real numbers
$\mathsf{P}(A)$	probability of event A
$\mathsf{P}(A\|B)$	conditional probability of A given B
$\mathsf{E}\xi$	expectation of random variable ξ
0	zero constant
$\mathbf{0}$	zero vector
$\mathbf{O}$	zero matrix
$\mathbf{I}$	identity matrix
$\mathbf{u}$	vector of ones, $\mathbf{u} = (1, ..., 1)$
$\mathbf{e}_j$	vector having 1 in the j-th position and zeros elsewhere
$H(a)$	Heaviside step function, $H(a) = \begin{cases} 1, & a > 0 \\ 0, & a \leq 0 \end{cases}$
$*$	convolution
$F^{(n)}(x)$	n-fold convolution of CDF $F(x)$
■	end of proof
$X(t)$	stochastic process at time t
$\mathcal{X}$	state space of process $X(t)$
L	cardinal number of set $\mathcal{L} = \{1, ..., L\}$

Contents

Part I
Preliminaries

Chapter 1
Modeling and Performance Analysis of Telecommunication Systems

Abstract This introductory chapter offers an insight into the techniques of telecommunications performance analysis discussed in the book. Section 1.1 presents a short overview of the Erlang loss formula's evolution, from telephone trunking modeling to 5G radio access performance evaluation. In the remainder of the chapter, we study some illustrative applications of the covered models. In Sect. 1.2, we use the example of GSM to demonstrate the process of probabilistic modeling in telecommunications and study an Erlang's loss model of a GSM cell. In Sect. 1.3, we show how to use a loss network model for performance analysis of multiservice broadband networks. Finally, Sect. 1.4 introduces loss systems with random resource requirements and demonstrates their application to performance analysis of LTE.

1.1 Evolution of the Erlang Formula

At the Onset of the Telecommunications Revolution

It is fair to say that the advent of the celebrate Erlang formula is directly related to the onset of the telecommunications revolution, a process of profound technological and social transformation that has started in 1876—when Alexander Graham Bell patented the first telephone—and has been accelerating ever since.

Agner Krarup Erlang (1878–1929) was the first mathematician and engineer to study telephone networks from the probability perspective. His first article on the subject, "The theory of probability and telephone conversations", appeared in 1909 (Erlang 1909). In 1917, he published his most significant work, "Solution of some problems in the theory of probabilities of significance in automatic telephone exchanges" (Erlang 1917). It is said that a researcher from the Bell Telephone Laboratories even learned Danish in order to read Erlang's papers in the original language.

Since then, Erlang's results have been widely used for performance analysis of telecommunications systems. Moreover, they were substantially extended and generalized following technological advances. This section presents a short overview of the evolution of the Erlang loss formula, from telephone trunking modeling to 5G radio access performance analysis.

V. Naumov et al., *Matrix and Analytical Methods for Performance Analysis of Telecommunication Systems*, https://doi.org/10.1007/978-3-030-83132-5_1

Telephone Trunking Modeling

Trunking is a way to provide network access to multiple users by making them share a group of circuits. Figure 1.1 shows a sample path of a stochastic process modeling telephone trunking. Here, the state of the process, S, corresponds to the number of engaged (busy) circuits; α_1, α_2, ... represent the time intervals between calls, while β_1, β_2, ... represent call durations. An arriving call that finds all circuits busy (three circuits in our example) is blocked and lost.

In terms of queueing theory, the process in Fig. 1.1 can be described by a service (loss) system depicted in Fig. 1.2. The system consists of C servers, each of which is available to an arriving customer whenever it is not busy. Customers arrive according to a Poisson process of rate λ, i.e., interarrival times are independent and have exponential distribution with mean $1/\lambda$. Service times are independent and have exponential distribution with mean $1/\mu$. An arriving customer is blocked and lost if it finds all servers busy.

By studying the above system in 1917, Erlang derived the famous relation now known as the Erlang loss formula, or Erlang B, which gives the probability that a call is lost.

Erlang Loss Formula

Blocking probability can be defined from two perspectives: as *call*-blocking probability and as *time*-blocking probability. Call-blocking probability is the probability that an arriving call finds the system busy, it is obtained as the proportion of lost calls in the long run. Time-blocking probability is the proportion of time when the system is busy.

Fig. 1.1 Stochastic process modeling telephone trunking

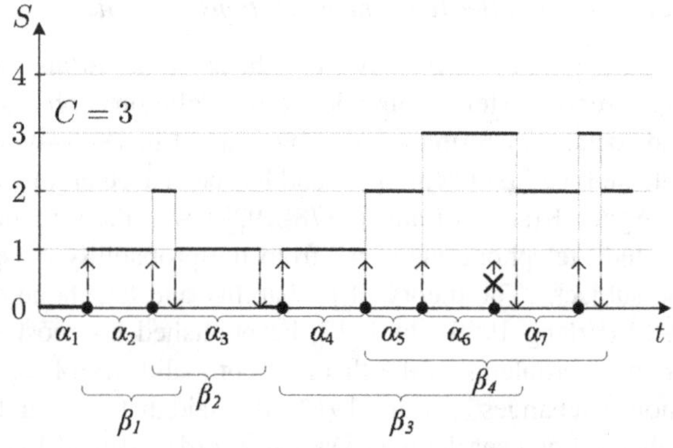

Fig. 1.2 Erlang's loss model

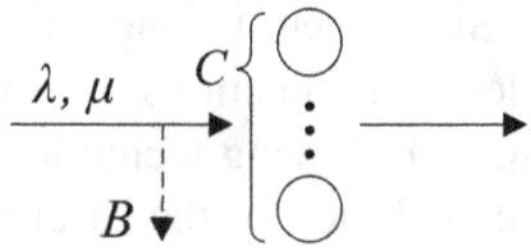

In Chap. 2, we thoroughly study Erlang's loss system and formally derive the famous formula, which gives the time-blocking probability in the system described above:

$$E_C(\rho) = B = \frac{\rho^C}{C!}\left(\sum_{k=0}^{C} \frac{\rho^k}{k!}\right)^{-1}, \tag{1.1}$$

where $\rho = \lambda/\mu$ is the mean number of arrivals during the mean service time, referred to as the *traffic intensity.*

From the PASTA property (Poisson arrivals see time averages), which states that call- and time-blocking probabilities are the same for Poisson arrivals, it follows that the proportion of lost calls in this system is also given by (1.1). Furthermore, a Russian mathematician Boris Sevastyanov proved in 1957 that the Erlang loss formula remains valid if service times have a general distribution (Sevastyanov 1957).

We will see in Sect. 2.1 that formula (1.1) can be computed recursively using the relations

$$E_C(\rho) = \frac{1}{G_C(\rho)}, \; G_0(\rho) = 1, \; G_i(\rho) = 1 + (i/\rho)G_{i-1}(\rho), \; i = 1, 2, \; ..., \; C.$$

Furthermore, several extensions of (1.1) to non-integer C are known, namely the one by Bretschneider (1973)

$$E_C(\rho) = \frac{\rho^C e^{-\rho}}{\int\limits_{\rho}^{\infty} e^{-t} t^C dt},$$

which will prove useful to us in Chap. 2.

Multi-Class Arrivals

So far, we assumed all calls to be alike, but quite often multiple classes of calls have to be considered (e.g. local and long-distance calls). Consider again a C-server loss system, but this time let it be offered two classes of customers arriving according to two independent Poisson processes with rates λ_1 and λ_2. Let the holding times of classes 1 and 2 be independent mutually and from prior arrivals and departures and exponentially distributed with parameters μ_1 and μ_2, respectively. As before, an arriving customer of either class is blocked and lost if it finds all servers busy.

Denote by x the number of class 1 customers in service, and by y the number of class 2 customers. Now, to be a feasible state of the system, a population vector $(x, y) \in \{0, 1, 2, \; ...\}^2$ must satisfy the condition $x + y \leq C$. The transition diagram in Fig. 1.3 shows the transition rates among the central states of the system.

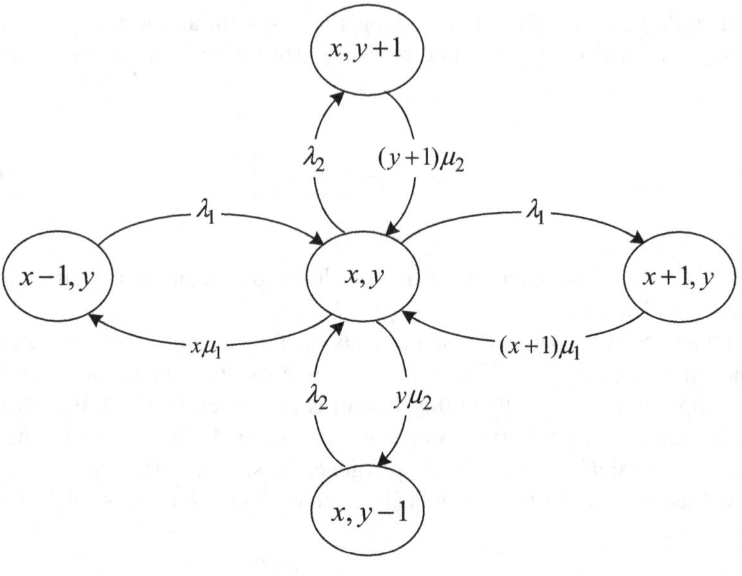

Fig. 1.3 State transition graph of a two-class Erlang's loss model

If we study this system further, we will find that its stationary state distribution is

$$P(x, y) = \frac{\frac{\rho_1^x}{x!}\frac{\rho_2^y}{y!}}{\sum_{i=0}^{C}\sum_{j=0}^{C-i}\frac{\rho_1^i}{i!}\frac{\rho_2^j}{j!}}, x, y \geq 0,\ x + y \leq C, \tag{1.2}$$

and, therefore, the blocking probabilities are given by

$$B_1 = B_2 = \frac{\sum_{i=0}^{C}\frac{\rho_1^i}{i!}\frac{\rho_2^{C-i}}{(C-i)!}}{\sum_{i=0}^{C}\sum_{j=0}^{C-i}\frac{\rho_1^i}{i!}\frac{\rho_2^j}{j!}} = E_C(\rho), \tag{1.3}$$

where $\rho = \rho_1 + \rho_2$.

Now, let us consider a superposition of K independent Poisson processes, which is a Poisson process of rate

$$\lambda = \sum_{k=1}^{K} \lambda_k.$$

In this case, the probability distribution of service times regardless the customer class is a weighted sum of exponential distributions with mean

$$\frac{1}{\mu} = \sum_{k=1}^{K} \frac{\lambda_k}{\lambda} \left(\frac{1}{\mu_k} \right) = \sum_{i=1}^{K} \left(\frac{\lambda_k}{\mu_k} \right) = \frac{1}{\lambda} \sum_{k=1}^{K} \rho_k.$$

Since the Erlang loss formula remains valid if service times have a general distribution, the blocking probability is once again given by $E_C(\rho)$ with

$$\rho = \frac{\lambda}{\mu} = \sum_{k=1}^{K} \rho_k.$$

Generalized Loss Systems

Now, we go one more step further and consider a system having multiple classes of customers with different resource requirements. Let class k customers arrive according to a Poisson process of rate λ_k and have a mean service time of $1/\mu_k$, $k = 1, \ldots, K$. We allow for simultaneous acquisition of multiple servers and let each class k customer in service hold c_k servers simultaneously. The set of feasible states—the state space of the model—is now

$$\mathcal{X} = \{\mathbf{n} \in \mathbb{N}^K : \sum_{k=1}^{K} c_k n_k \leq C\},$$

where n_k corresponds to the number of class k customers in the system.

The stationary state distribution can be obtained similarly to the two-dimensional case, however, the normalization constant has a more general form:

$$p(\mathbf{n}) = \frac{1}{G} \prod_{k=1}^{K} \frac{\rho_k^{n_k}}{n_k!}, \quad \mathbf{n} \in \mathcal{X}, \quad G = \sum_{\mathbf{n} \in \mathcal{X}} \prod_{k=1}^{K} \frac{\rho_k^{n_k}}{n_k!}, \tag{1.4}$$

where $\rho_k = \lambda_k/\mu_k$. Then, the blocking probability for class i customers is given by

$$B_i = 1 - \frac{G_i}{G}, \tag{1.5}$$

where

$$G_i = \sum_{n_1c_1+\ldots+n_Kc_K+c_i \leq C} \prod_{k=1}^{K} \frac{\rho_k^{n_k}}{n_k!}, i = 1, 2, \ldots, K.$$

Generalized loss systems are suitable for modeling multi-rate circuit-switched communications and have proved useful, among other applications, for performance analysis of Time Division Multiplexing (TDM) systems, where multiple time slots can be allocated to reduce delay (see e.g. (Ross 1995)).

Loss Networks

The Erlang formula received further development in application to multiservice broadband networks, which has resulted in a class of models named *loss networks* or *multiservice loss networks* (Kelly 1991; Ross 1995). These models will be discussed in detail in Sect. 1.3 and Chap. 3; here we just point out in what they differ from the previous.

A classical loss network is a general model of a circuit-switched network carrying multi-rate traffic. The model is well suited for bidirectional traffic flows, because the reverse traffic for a given pair of nodes may have different bandwidth requirements.

Let the multi-class loss system considered above have M types of servers. We assume that there are C_m servers of type m, and each class k customer in service holds $c_{k,m}$ servers of type m simultaneously. The stationary state distribution of such a system is also given by (1.4), but with the state space

$$\mathcal{X} = \{\mathbf{n} \in \mathbb{N}^K : \sum_{k=1}^{K} c_{k,m} n_k \leq C_m, m = 1, 2, ..., M\}.$$

The blocking probability is given by (1.5) with constant Gi given by

$$G_i = \sum_{\substack{n_1 c_{1,m} + ... + n_K c_{K,m} + c_{i,m} \leq C_m \\ m = 1, 2, ..., M}} \prod_{k=1}^{K} \frac{\rho_K^{n_k}}{n_k!}, \; i = 1, 2, ..., K.$$

Loss Systems with Random Resource Requirements

Loss systems with random resource requirements (ReLS) conclude our review of the Erlang formula's evolution. Since they will be specifically dealt with in Part III of the book, here we briefly outline the model and provide the expressions for the stationary state distribution to reveal the connection with the Erlang loss formula.

A multi-resource ReLS, depicted in Fig. 1.4, relies on the following assumptions. Let a C-server loss system have M types of resources of capacities given by a vector $\mathbf{R} = (R_1, ..., R_M)$. Class k customers arrive according to a Poisson process of rate λ_k and have a mean service time of $1/\mu_k$, $\rho_k = \lambda_k/\mu_k$, $k = 1, ..., K$.

The ith customer of class k requires an amount $r_{k,m}(i)$ of resources of type m, which is a real-valued random variable. Resource requirements $\boldsymbol{r}_k(i) = (r_{k,1}(i), ..., r_{k,M}(i))$, $i = 1, 2, ...,$ of class k customers are nonnegative random vectors with a Cumulative Distribution Function (CDF) $F_k(\mathbf{x})$. An

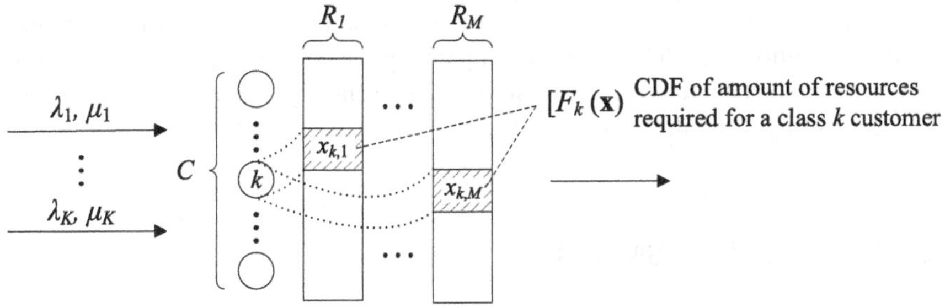

Fig. 1.4 Multi-resource loss system with random resource requirements

arriving customer receives service if it finds at least one server free and the required resource amounts available. Then, the required resource amounts are allocated, and the customer holds them, along with a server, for the duration of its service time. Upon departure, the allocated resources are released.

The state space of the model is given by

$$\mathcal{X} = \{(\mathbf{n}, \boldsymbol{\gamma}_1, ..., \boldsymbol{\gamma}_K) : \mathbf{n} \in \mathbb{N}^K, \boldsymbol{\gamma}_k \in \mathbb{R}_+^M, k = 1, 2, ..., K, \sum_{k=1}^{K} \boldsymbol{\gamma}_k \leq \mathbf{R}, \sum_{k=1}^{K} n_k \leq C\},$$

where $\mathbf{n} = (n_1, ..., n_K)$ is the population vector and $\boldsymbol{\gamma}_k = (\gamma_{k,1}, ..., \gamma_{k,M})$ is the vector of resource allocatons to class k customers in service.

Now, the CDF of the stationary distribution is given by

$$P_{\mathbf{n}}(\mathbf{x}_1, ..., \mathbf{x}_K) = \frac{1}{G} \prod_{k=1}^{K} \frac{\rho_k^{n_k}}{n_k!} F_k^{(n_k)}(\mathbf{x}_k), \ (\mathbf{n}, \mathbf{x}_1, ..., \mathbf{x}_K) \in \mathcal{X},$$

$$G = \sum_{n_1+...+n_K \leq C} (F_1^{(n_1)} * ... * F_K^{(n_K)})(\mathbf{R}) \frac{\rho_1^{n_1} \cdots \rho_K^{n_K}}{n_1! \cdots n_K!}. \tag{1.6}$$

where $*$ denotes convolution, $F_k^{(n_k)}(\mathbf{x})$ denotes the n_k-fold convolution of CDF $F_k(\mathbf{x})$. The blocking probability of class k customers can be obtained by relation (1.5) using the corresponding normalizing constants (1.6) and (1.7),

$$G_k = \sum_{n_1+...+n_K \leq C} (F_1^{(n_1)} * ... * F_k^{(n_k+1)} * ... * F_K^{n_K})(\mathbf{R}) \frac{\rho_1^{n_1} \cdots \rho_K^{n_K}}{n_1! \cdots n_K!}. \tag{1.7}$$

In Chap. 12, we will provide examples of how ReLS models can be applied to performance analysis of 5G radio access networks.

Thus, in our short review, we have covered the principal milestones of the Erlang formula's evolution, which has been accompanying the development of telecommunications from the late nineteenth century to the present day. In the remainder of the chapter, we study some illustrative applications of the discussed models.

1.2 A Model of a GSM Cell

GSM (General System for Mobile Communications) has played a pivotal role in the telecommunications revolution. On the one hand, it is a traditional circuit-switched telephony system, but on the other hand, it was designed so effectively that it provided the basis for the next-generation networks up to Long-Term Evolution (LTE). This is why we begin to study telecommunications modeling with GSM. Similar to the previous section, we focus on call-blocking probabilities due to lack of resources. Not only it is one of the key quality-of-service (QoS) measures of GSM systems but also it permits us to demonstrate the practical application of the Erlang loss formula.

Furthermore, we use the example of GSM to illustrate the whole process of probabilistic modeling in telecommunications. The process usually includes four steps.

i. Study in detail the underlying technology and its application in the network. Choose QoS and performance measures of interest.
ii. Build a system model and determine a set of assumptions—usually simplifying—which would make mathematical modeling feasible.
iii. Build a mathematical model to evaluate QoS and performance measures of interest.
iv. Study the mathematical model, choose or develop a computation method, determine a range of parameters, and conduct the quantitative analysis.

Steps i and iv are beyond the scope of this book, although their importance is hard to overstate. All steps of the process are closely related and the whole process is iterative: sometimes, the quantitative results suggest a modification of the mathematical model, which, on its part, may require a more in-depth study at step i.

Problem Formulation

Although we assume the reader to be familiar with the GMS technology, the section is intentionally written in way to avoid technical details and the need for additional literature. When modeling a mobile network, one has to take into account a multitude of various parameters: from the load intensity to the cell size, which, in its turn, depends on landscape features and buildings, as well as on technical characteristics of base stations and mobile switching centers. Another thing to consider are QoS requirements that must be met by the network services.

A mathematical model is never derived to analyze the entire system, which is hardly possible, but rather to evaluate its performance from an a priori constraint set of measures. When studying a complex system, it is common to decompose it

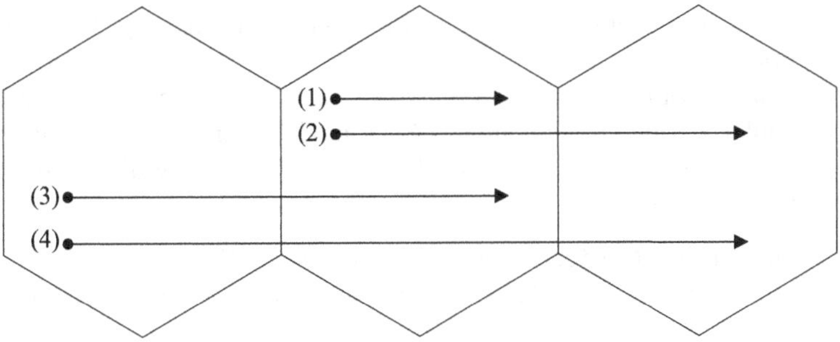

Fig. 1.5 Four types of calls with regard to the middle cell

into parts whose performance can be studied separately. Consider a GSM network and assume that all its cells are identical in size, capacity and QoS requirements. Assume also that the subscribers within the service area of the base station are always uniformly distributed throughout it. Under these assumptions, we can legitimately tackle the performance analysis of a GSM network by studying the behavior of a standalone cell.

The distinctive feature of wireless mobile networks is user mobility, which implies that a call in progress can be handed over between neighboring cells without interrupting the communication. Each network cell is thus offered two types of calls: handover calls and original calls initiated by users in the cell under study. Moreover, if we look further, we can distinguish four types of calls offered to the base station (see Fig. 1.5):

1. original calls initiated and terminated by user in the cell under study,
2. original calls initiated by user in the cell under study and handed over to a neighbor cell,
3. handover calls handed over to the cell under study from a neighbor cell and terminated by user in the cell under study, and
4. handover calls handed over to the cell under study from a neighbor cell and then handed over to a neighbor cell.

In cellular networks, the service areas of neighboring base stations overlap to form so-called handover zones, where a call can be maintained by both base stations. Let us assume that a subscriber that has crossed into a handover zone cannot change direction and return to the cell whose base station is maintaining the connection. Then there are three possibilities:

(a) the call in progress is successfully handed over to the receiving neighbor cell,
(b) the call is user terminated in the handover zone,
(c) the call is force terminated by the receiving base station.

The latter is referred to as the *handover blocking* and occurs if the receiving base station fails to maintain the call in progress when the subscriber leaves the handover zone (e.g., due to lack of free channels). Along with the blocking probability of original calls, the handover blocking probability is one of the main QoS measures of GSM networks.

In the remainder of the section, we study two models of call handling in a GSM cell, one simpler and one more complex. Each model is preceded by simplifying assumptions enabling mathematical modeling. Both models rely on the following assumptions:

(i) Original and handover calls arrive according to two Poisson processes of rates λ_O and λ_H, respectively. Thus, the combined arrival process is also Poisson with rate $\lambda = \lambda_O + \lambda_H$.
(ii) The holding times of the calls terminated by user in the cell under study are exponentially distributed with parameter μ_1, while the holding times of the calls handed over to a neighbor cell (until the handover) are exponentially distributed with parameter μ_2. By consequence, the holding times of all calls regardless the type are exponentially distributed with parameter $\mu = \mu_1 + \mu_2$.
(iii) The number of radio channels in the cell is C.

The following notation is used throughout the section:

$\rho = \lambda/\mu$	- the load intensity offered by all calls;
$\rho_O = \lambda_O/\mu$	- the load intensity offered by original calls;
$\rho_H = \lambda_H/\mu$	- the load intensity offered by handover calls (from all neighbor cells);
B_O	- the blocking probability of original calls;
B_H	- the blocking probability of handover calls;
$X(t)$	- a stochastic process representing the number of calls in progress at time t;
$\mathcal{X}$	- the state space of the process $X(t)$;
$p(n)$	- the stationary state probabilities of the process $X(t)$, $p(n) = \lim_{t\to\infty} \mathsf{P}(X(t) = n),\ n \in \mathcal{X}$.

Baseline Loss Model of a GSM Cell

Let us add two more assumptions:

(iv) There is no handover zone.
(v) No radio channels are reserved for handover calls at the base station (the complete sharing policy is applied).

Under the above assumptions, a GSM cell can be modeled as a C-server loss system with two classes of customers. Such a system is depicted in Fig. 1.6. We are interested in the blocking probabilities B_O and B_H of the original and handover calls, respectively.

Let us introduce a stochastic process $X(t)$ on the state space $\mathcal{X} = \{0, 1, ..., C\}$ representing the number of busy servers in the loss system at time t. In light of assumption (i), we deal with Erlang's loss model, and therefore, the process $X(t)$ has the stationary distribution

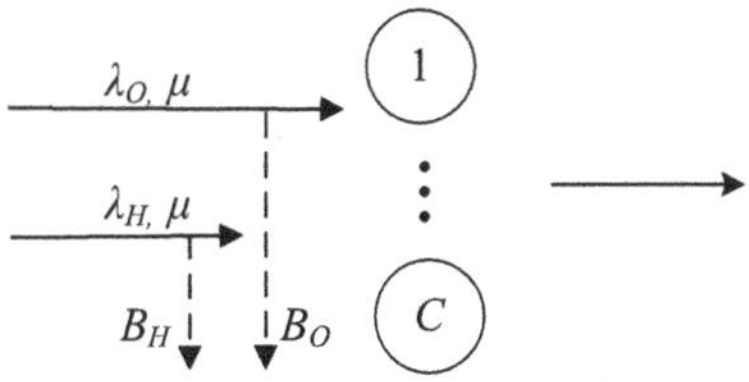

Fig. 1.6 Two-class C-server loss system to model a GSM cell

$$p(n) = \frac{\rho^n}{n!}\left(\sum_{n=0}^{C}\frac{\rho^n}{n!}\right)^{-1}, n = 0, \ldots, C. \tag{1.8}$$

It is clear that arriving customers of either class are lost whenever they find all servers busy. Thus, we have $B_O = p(C)$ and $B_H = p(C)$. In view of the PASTA property mentioned in Sect. 1.1, the blocking probabilities of original and handover calls coincide and are given by the Erlang loss formula (1.1):

$$B_O = B_H = \frac{\rho^C}{C!}\left(\sum_{n=0}^{C}\frac{\rho^n}{n!}\right)^{-1}. \tag{1.9}$$

Loss Model of a GSM Cell with Resource Reservation

Let us now replace assumption (v) by the following:

(vi) At the base station, $g < C$ radio channels are accessible to all calls, while the remaining $C - g$ channels are reserved for handover calls only.

Under assumptions (i)–(iv) and (vi), a GSM cell can be modeled as a two-class C-server loss system with resource reservation, depicted in Fig. 1.7. Once again, we are interested in the blocking probabilities of original and handover calls.

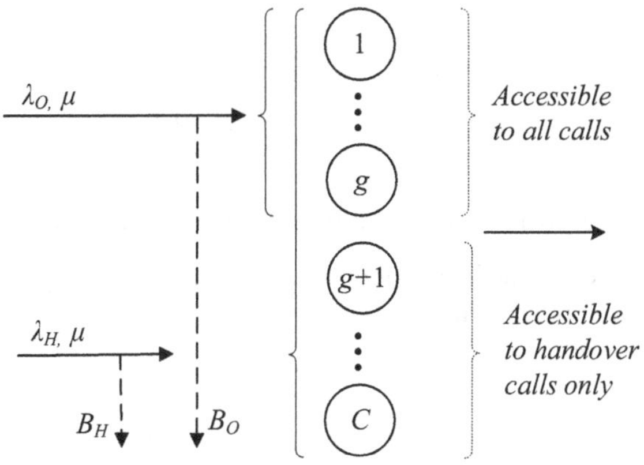

Fig. 1.7 Two-class C-server loss system with resource reservation

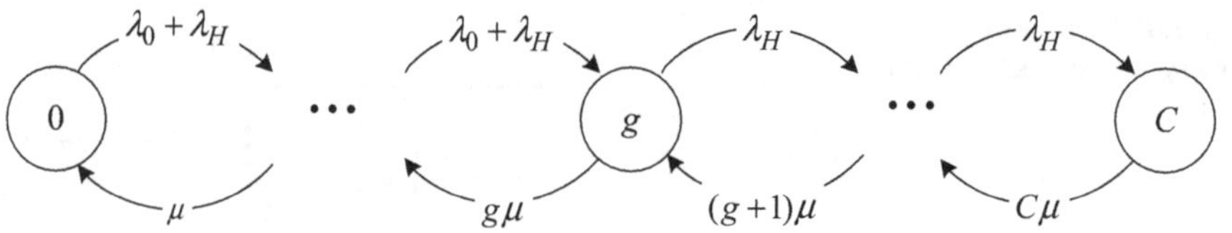

Fig. 1.8 State transition graph of CTMC $X(t)$

Let again $X(t)$ be the number of busy servers at time t. By construction, it is a continuous-time Markov chain (CTMC) (Appendix A2.2) with the state transition graph shown in Fig. 1.8.

The stationary state probabilities $p(n)$, $n = 0, ..., C$, of $X(t)$ satisfy the equilibrium equations

$$\begin{cases} (\lambda_O + \lambda_H)p(0) = \mu p(1), \\ (n\mu + \lambda_O + \lambda_H)p(n) = (\lambda_O + \lambda_H)p(n-1) + (n+1)\mu p(n+1), 1 \le n \le g-1, \\ (g\mu + \lambda_H)p(g) = (\lambda_O + \lambda_H)p(g-1) + (g+1)\mu p(g+1), \\ (n\mu + \lambda_H)p(n) = \lambda_H p(n-1) + (n+1)\mu p(n+1), \quad g+1 \le n \le C-1, \\ C\mu p(C) = \lambda_H p(C-1). \end{cases} \tag{1.10}$$

To solve them, we make use of the detailed balance principle, which yields

$$\begin{cases} (\lambda_O + \lambda_H)p(n-1) = n\mu\, p(n), \ 1 \le n \le g, \\ \lambda_H p(n-1) = n\mu\, p(n), \qquad\qquad g+1 \le n \le C. \end{cases} \tag{1.11}$$

From (1.11), we get that

$$p(n) = \begin{cases} \frac{(\lambda_O+\lambda_H)^n}{n!\mu^n} p(0), \qquad 1 \le n \le g, \\ \frac{(\lambda_O+\lambda_H)^g \lambda_H^{n-g}}{n!\mu^n} p(0), \ g+1 \le n \le C. \end{cases} \tag{1.12}$$

Or, using the notations introduced previously,

$$p(n) = \begin{cases} \frac{\rho^n}{n!} p(0), \qquad 1 \le n \le g; \\ \frac{\rho^g \rho_H^{n-g}}{n!} p(0), \ g+1 \le n \le C, \end{cases} \tag{1.13}$$

where $p(0)$ is determined from the normalization condition $\sum\limits_{n=0}^{C} p(n) = 1$.

Now, an arriving original call is blocked whenever it finds g or more servers busy. The corresponding probability is thus

$$B_O = \sum_{n=g}^{C} p(n). \tag{1.14}$$

An arriving handover call is blocked if it finds all servers busy, and the corresponding probability is then

$$B_H = p(C). \tag{1.15}$$

Unlike in the previous model, here, the handover blocking probabilities are not equal to the blocking probabilities of original calls. Indeed, by substituting the stationary state probabilities, we have

$$B_O = \left(\sum_{n=g}^{C} \frac{\rho^g \rho_H^{n-g}}{n!} \right) \times \left(\sum_{n=0}^{g} \frac{\rho^n}{n!} + \sum_{n=g+1}^{C} \frac{\rho^g \rho_H^{n-g}}{n!} \right)^{-1}, \tag{1.16}$$

$$B_H = \frac{\rho^g \rho_H^{C-g}}{C!} \times \left(\sum_{n=0}^{g} \frac{\rho^n}{n!} + \sum_{n=g+1}^{C} \frac{\rho^g \rho_H^{n-g}}{n!} \right)^{-1}. \tag{1.17}$$

It is easily seen from the above expressions that in the system with channel reservation the handover blocking probability B_H is smaller than the blocking probability of original calls B_O, which makes resource reservation policies attractive in applications.

In conclusion, we note that other modifications of the GSM cell model exist, including models with queues, which will be addressed in Chap. 4.

1.3 A Model of a Multiservice Network

In this section, we briefly introduce an approach to analyzing multi-link multiservice broadband networks, that can be found through books by Frank Kelly (1991) and Keith W. Ross (1995). The framework is commonly referred to as *loss networks* and, in its classical form, represents multi-resource multi-class loss systems with deterministic resource requirements.

A multiservice network is modeled as a multivariate stochastic process whose stationary distribution and session blocking probabilities are derived in explicit product form. The product-form stationary distribution allows for a recursive computation of performance measures. We focus on derivation of such computing techniques in Chap. 3 where we also discuss multiservice networks with unicast (point-to-point) and multicast (point-to-multipoint) communications.

Problem Formulation

Consider a network of arbitrary topology which consists of a number of nodes connected by links. Let L represent the total number of links and $\mathcal{L} = \{1, 2, \ldots, L\}$ be the set of all links numbered arbitrarily. Denote by C_l the capacity of link l, which corresponds to the link's throughput measured in notional capacity units. The value

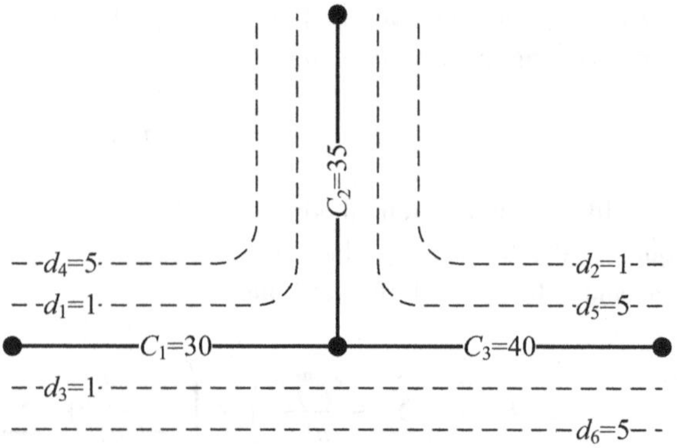

Fig. 1.9 An example of a multiservice network model

of the capacity unit is chosen in each case depending on the data-rate requirements of user sessions. Usually, it is convenient to set the capacity unit equal to the smallest of such requirements. For example, if the capacity unit is set equal to 8 bps then the capacity of 622 Mbps equals ($622 \times 10^3 \div 8 = 77,750$) capacity units.

Point-to-point sessions of several classes can be established in the network in order to transfer data between the nodes. Every session class is characterized by two parameters: the route and the required capacity. The route is the set of links through which data is transferred, while the required capacity is the capacity that must be allocated to the session on each link of its route. Let $\mathcal{K} = \{1, 2, \ldots, K\}$ represent the set of all session classes. For each class k, we denote the route by $\mathcal{L}_k \subseteq \mathcal{L}$ and the required capacity by d_k.

The model considered here is the most natural for applications special case of the general model of a loss network with fixed routing studied in (Kelly 1991). The difference is that in the general model the capacities required by class k sessions on network links are given by a matrix $(d_{kl})_{k\in\mathcal{K}, l\in\mathcal{L}}$, and therefore, the capacity allocated to the same session may differ from one link to another.

To illustrate the introduced notation, Fig. 1.9 depicts a network segment consisting of three links numbered 1, 2, and 3 of capacities 30, 35, and 40, respectively, i.e., $\mathcal{L} = \{1, 2, 3\}$, $C_1 = 30$, $C_2 = 35$, and $C_3 = 40$. Sessions can be established between any two leaf nodes and require either 1 or 5 capacity units on each link of the corresponding route. Thus, we have six classes of sessions $\mathcal{K} = \{1, 2, \ldots, 6\}$, with parameters indicated in the figure. For example, each class 1 session is established through links 1 and 2 and requires 1 capacity unit: $\mathcal{L}_1 = \{1, 2\}$ and $d_1 = 1$.

Now, let us introduce the workload parameters. We assume that sessions are established upon user requests and that requests for establishing class k sessions arrive according to a Poisson process with rate λ_k. We let the holding times of class k sessions be independent of earlier arrival and holding times and exponentially distributed with mean $1/\mu_k$. As previously, we denote $\rho_k = \lambda_k/\mu_k$.

A session is established upon a request if at the time of arrival there is enough free capacity on all links of the corresponding route. Then, the required capacity is allocated to the session for its whole duration. If, conversely, at the time of arrival there is not enough capacity at least on one link of the route, then a blocking occurs and the request is lost.

We turn again to Fig. 1.9. If upon an arrival of a class 4 request ($d_4 = 5, \mathcal{L}_4 = \{1, 2\}$) there are five established (ongoing) sessions of class 6 ($d_6 = 5, \mathcal{L}_6 = \{1, 3\}$) and one session of class 1 ($d_1 = 1, \mathcal{L}_1 = \{1, 2\}$), then the incoming request will be blocked, because link 1 ($C_1 = 30$) has only 4 capacity units available ($30 - 5 \times 5 - 1 \times 1 = 4$), which is less that the required 5 units.

The Stationary State Distribution

Suppose that the capacities of all links are unlimited, i.e., $C_l = \infty, l \in \mathcal{L}$. In such case, all requests for session establishment are accepted and no blocking occurs. Let $\widetilde{X}_k(t)$ denote the number of class k sessions in progress at time t. Then we can model the network's behavior by a multivariate stochastic process

$$\widetilde{\mathbf{X}}(t) = (\widetilde{X}_1(t), \widetilde{X}_2(t), \ \ldots, \widetilde{X}_K(t)), t \geq 0$$

each component of which corresponds to one session class. Since the capacities of the links are infinite, the state space of the process $\widetilde{\mathbf{X}}(t)$ is $\widetilde{\mathcal{X}} = \{0, 1, 2, \ldots\}^K$. One checks easily that $\widetilde{X}_k(t)$ is a birth-and-death process (Appendix A2.2) with the stationary distribution

$$\tilde{p}_k(n_k) = \lim_{t \to \infty} \mathsf{P}\big(\widetilde{X}_k(t) = n_k\big) = \frac{\rho_k^{n_k}}{n_k!} \mathrm{e}^{-\rho_k}, n_k \in \{0, 1, 2, \ldots\}.$$

Due to the unlimited link capacities, the components of the multivariate process $\widetilde{\mathbf{X}}(t)$ are independent from each other, and hence $\widetilde{\mathbf{X}}(t)$ is a reversible CTMC with the product-form stationary distribution

$$\tilde{p}(\mathbf{n}) = \lim_{t \to \infty} \mathsf{P}\big(\widetilde{\mathbf{X}}(t) = \mathbf{n}\big) = \prod_{k \in \mathcal{K}} \frac{\rho_k^{n_k}}{n_k!} \mathrm{e}^{-\rho_k}, \ \ \mathbf{n} \in \widetilde{\mathcal{X}}.$$

Now assume the link capacities to be, again, limited: $C_l < \infty, l \in \mathcal{L}$. For each $l \in \mathcal{L}$, we define the set $\mathcal{K}_l = \{k \in \mathcal{K} : l \in \mathcal{L}_k\}$ of session classes whose routes include link l and a function

$$d_l(\mathbf{n}) = \sum_{k \in \mathcal{K}_l} d_k n_k, \tag{1.18}$$

which corresponds to the number of capacity units occupied on link l when the system is in state $\mathbf{n} \in \widetilde{\mathcal{X}}$. Now, we can express the state space of the system as follows:

$$\mathcal{X} = \big\{\mathbf{n} \in \widetilde{\mathcal{X}} : d_l(\mathbf{n}) \leq C_l, \ l \in \mathcal{L}\big\}. \tag{1.19}$$

We denote by $\mathbf{X}(t)$ the reversible CTMC $\widetilde{\mathbf{X}}(t)$ truncated to the set $\mathcal{X} \subset \widetilde{\mathcal{X}}$. The theorem below follows from the well-known properties of reversible CTMC (see e.g. (Kelly 2011)).

Theorem 1.1 *The stochastic process* $\mathbf{X}(t)$ *is a reversible CTMC and its stationary state distribution is of the product form*

$$p(\mathbf{n}) = \frac{1}{G(\mathcal{X})} \prod_{k \in \mathcal{K}} \frac{\rho_k^{n_k}}{n_k!}, \quad \mathbf{n} \in \mathcal{X}, \tag{1.20}$$

where

$$G(\mathcal{X}) = \sum_{\mathbf{n} \in \mathcal{X}} \prod_{k \in \mathcal{K}} \frac{\rho_k^{n_k}}{n_k!} \tag{1.21}$$

is the normalization constant.

Similar to the Erlang loss formula, the stationary distribution (1.20) is insensitive to the holding time distribution and depends only on its mean (see e.g. (Bonald 2007)). Making use of (1.20) and (1.21), we can derive expressions for many performance measures of interest, including the session blocking probabilities.

Session Blocking Probabilities

As we mentioned previously, if upon a request arrival there is not enough capacity for establishing the corresponding session, then the request will be blocked and lost. Let B_k denote the stationary probability that a class k request is blocked. B_k can be obtained using the state distribution (1.20) as follows:

$$B_k = \sum_{\mathbf{n} \in \mathcal{B}_k} p(\mathbf{n}), \quad k \in \mathcal{K}, \tag{1.22}$$

where $\mathcal{B}_k$ represents the set of all states in which a class k blocking occurs. More specifically, $\mathcal{B}_k$ consists of all states in which there is not enough capacity for establishing a class k session on one or more links of the class k route, i.e.,

$$\mathcal{B}_k = \{\mathbf{n} \in \mathcal{X} : \exists l \in \mathcal{L}_k : d_l(\mathbf{n}) > C_l - d_k\}, \quad k \in \mathcal{K}. \tag{1.23}$$

The complement of $\mathcal{B}_k$ in the state space $\mathcal{X}$ is the admission set

$$\overline{\mathcal{B}}_k = \{\mathbf{n} \in \mathcal{X} : d_l(\mathbf{n}) + d_k \le C_l, l \in \mathcal{L}_k\},$$

consisting of all states in which an incoming class k request will be admitted. Clearly, the admission probability is $\overline{B}_k = \mathrm{P}\left(\mathbf{n} \in \overline{\mathcal{B}}_k\right) = 1 - B_k$.

Referring back to Fig. 1.9, consider, for instance, the state $\mathbf{n} = (4, 3, 1, 2, 3, 3)$. In this state, we have $d_1(\mathbf{n}) = 30$, $d_2(\mathbf{n}) = 32$ and $d_3(\mathbf{n}) = 34$. It is hence a blocking state for all classes but class 2, because link 1 has no free capacity and link 2 has only 3 capacity units available. The state $\mathbf{n}$ is an admission state for class 2. Now, consider, for instance, the set $\mathscr{B}_1$ of class 1 blocking states. It consists of those states of $\mathscr{X}$ in which 30 capacity units are occupied on link 1 or 35 capacity units are occupied on link 2. Thus, besides the state $\mathbf{n}$, $\mathscr{B}_1$ includes the states $(2, 8, 1, 2, 3, 3)$, $(0, 0, 0, 0, 0, 6)$, etc.

Considering how the number of possible states grows with the links' capacities, and the fact that the number of possible routes may increase exponentially with the number of links, it becomes clear that computing blocking probabilities directly by formulas (1.20)–(1.22) may be efficient only in the simplest cases. Moreover, computing the normalization constant directly by formula (1.21) for an arbitrary network topology is an NP-hard problem, meaning that efficient combinatorial algorithms for this do not exist. Therefore, much effort has been spent on developing approximations to compute the system's performance measures for a wide range of models.

Approximations for the type of networks that we have just considered are treated, namely, in Chung (1993). In Chap. 3, we derive a recursive algorithm for estimating blocking probabilities on a single network link. The algorithm plays a central part in those approximations, which belong to the so-called reduced-load or fixed-point approximations.

1.4 A Model of an LTE Cell

The core technology of the fourth generation (4G) cellular networks, LTE (long-term evolution) is substantially different from the radio access technologies of previous generations, in particular from TDMA and CDMA. Put shortly, LTE uses a method of encoding digital data on multiple closely spaced orthogonal carriers known as orthogonal frequency-division multiplexing (OFDM), in which the smallest unit of radio resource allocation is the physical resource block (PRB).

PRBs are allocated to user sessions by schedulers based upon the signal characteristics between the transmitter and receiver. Therefore, the amounts of resources (the number of PRBs) allocated to sessions vary and can be considered as random variables (more precisely, as discrete random variables). In subsequent radio access technologies, such as 5G New Radio (NR) systems operating in a millimeter-wave (mmWave) band, the resource requirement of a session can be represented by a continuous random variable. This is why performance analysis of such systems required another major modification of loss models, giving rise to loss systems with random resource requirements, ReLS, to which this book is largely devoted.

The model of an LTE base station built in this section is referred to as the baseline loss system with random resource requirements. We use it to demonstrate the general

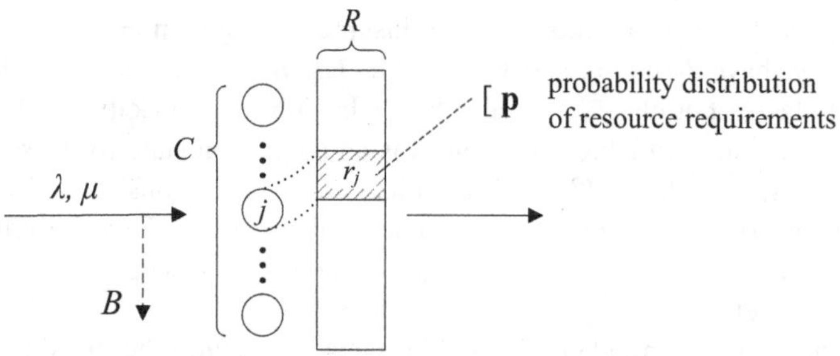

Fig. 1.10 Baseline loss system with random resource requirements

approach to modeling LTE and 5G networks. Later in Chap. 12, more complicated ReLS are considered when addressing 5G NR access networks.

Problem Formulation

Let us consider a standalone LTE base station. As previously, in order to build a model, we first make some simplifying assumptions regarding system operation.

(i) The service area of the base station is such that sessions in progress cannot be interrupted.
(ii) The number of sessions simultaneously in progress can be limited.
(iii) The resource capacity of the system is measured in physical resource blocks and limited.
(iv) The arrival rate of sessions in the service area is constant and known.
(v) The users having sessions in progress are evenly distributed throughout the service area.

Consider a service system with $C \leq \infty$ servers and a resource of a finite capacity R (see Fig. 1.10). Let customers arrive according to a Poisson process of rate λ and have exponentially distributed service times with parameter μ. Each customer in service holds one server and a random amount of resources. For the sake of simplicity, we assume the *resource requirements*—the amounts of resources requested by customers—to be discrete random variables with probability distribution $\mathbf{p} = (p_0, p_1, ...)$, where p_j is the probability that a customer requires a resource amount of j.

If an arriving customer finds all servers busy or the available (unallocated) resource amount is smaller than the resource requirement of the arriving customer, then the customer is blocked. Once service is completed, the customer departs the system and its resource allocation is released. We are interested in the blocking probability due to lack of available resources and the mean of the *allocated total*—the average resource amount allocated to all customers in service combined.

Stationary State Probabilities and Performance Measures

The system's behavior is described by a stochastic process $X_1(t) = (\xi(t), \gamma(t))$, where $\xi(t)$ is the number of customers in service at time t, and $\gamma(t) =$

$(\gamma_1(t), \ldots, \gamma_{\xi(t)}(t))$ is the vector of resource allocations to customers in service with its entries arranged in order of decreasing residual service time.

Let us denote the stationary state probabilities of $X_1(t)$ by

$$Q_k(r_1, \ldots, r_k) = \lim_{t\to\infty} \mathsf{P}(\xi(t) = k, \gamma_1(t) = r_1, \ldots, \gamma_k(t) = r_k),$$
$$0 \le k \le C, r_1 + \ldots + r_k \le R. \tag{1.24}$$

They can be found from the equilibrium equations

$$\lambda Q_0 \sum_{r=0}^{R} p_r = \mu \sum_{r=0}^{R} Q_1(r);$$

$$Q_k(r_1, \ldots, r_k)\left(\lambda \sum_{j=0}^{R-r_1-\ldots-r_k} p_j + n\mu\right) =$$
$$= \frac{\lambda}{k}\sum_{i=1}^{k} Q_{k-1}(r_1, .., r_{i-1}, r_{i+1}, \ldots, r_k)p_{r_i} +$$
$$+ \mu \sum_{i=1}^{k+1} \sum_{j=0}^{R-r_1-\ldots-r_k} Q_{k+1}(r_1, \ldots, r_{i-1}, j, r_i, \ldots, r_k),$$
$$1 \le k \le C-1, r_1 + \ldots + r_k \le R; \tag{1.25}$$

$$C\mu Q_C(r_1, \ldots, r_C) = \tfrac{\lambda}{C}\sum_{i=1}^{C} Q_{C-1}(r_1, .., r_{i-1}, r_{i+1}, \ldots, r_{C-1})p_{r_i},$$
$$r_1 + \ldots + r_C \le R.$$

The system (1.25) has a unique solution satisfying the normalization condition. One checks by substitution that the solution is of the form

$$Q_k(r_1, \ldots, r_k) = Q_0 \frac{\rho^k}{k!} p_{r_1} \ldots p_{r_k}, 1 \le k \le C, \sum_{i=1}^{k} r_i \le R,$$
$$Q_0 = \left(1 + \sum_{k=1}^{C} \sum_{r_1+\ldots+r_k \le R} \frac{\rho^k}{k!} p_{r_1} \ldots p_{r_k}\right)^{-1}, \tag{1.26}$$

where $\rho = \lambda/\mu$ is the load intensity offered to the system.

Note that the state space of the process $X_1(t)$ grows dramatically with C and R, which makes it very hard to compute the stationary probabilities and performance measures despite the explicit formula (1.26). Moreover, the process $X_1(t)$ contains redundant information, which is not needed in most cases. Quite often, to evaluate the model's characteristics it suffices to track only the number of customers in service and the allocated total.

Consider the stationary probabilities of the aggregated (lumped) states

$$P_k(r) = \lim_{t\to\infty} \mathsf{P}\left(\xi(t) = k, \sum_{i=1}^{k} \gamma_i(t) = r\right). \tag{1.27}$$

Then, by summing up the corresponding probabilities (1.26), we have

$$\begin{aligned} P_k(r) &= P_0 \frac{\rho^k}{k!} p_r^{(k)}, \ 1 \le k \le C, r \le R, \\ P_0 &= \left(1 + \sum_{k=1}^{C} \sum_{r=0}^{R} \frac{\rho^k}{k!} p_r^{(k)}\right)^{-1}, \end{aligned} \tag{1.28}$$

where $p_r^{(k)}$ denotes the k-fold convolution of distribution $\mathbf{p} = (p_0, p_1, \ldots)$ and represents the probability that k customers request a total resource amount of r. In practice, it is convenient to calculate discrete convolutions using the recurrence relation

$$p_r^{(k)} = \sum_{i=0}^{r} p_i p_{r-i}^{(k-1)}, k \ge 2, \tag{1.29}$$

where $p_r^{(1)} = p_r, r \ge 0$.

By using the probabilities $P_k(r)$ of the lumped states, one can easily obtain expressions for the characteristics of interest. The blocking probability and the mean value $\mathsf{E}\delta$ of allocated total δ are thus given, respectively, by

$$B = 1 - P_0 \sum_{k=0}^{C-1} \frac{\rho^k}{k!} \sum_{r=0}^{R} p_r^{(k+1)}, \tag{1.30}$$

$$\mathsf{E}\delta = P_0 \sum_{k=1}^{C} \frac{\rho^k}{k!} \sum_{r=1}^{R} r p_r^{(k)} \tag{1.31}$$

ReLS will be studied in depth in Part III. We will also come back to the baseline ReLS model in Chap. 12, where another application example is considered.

References

Bonald, T.: Insensitive traffic models for communication networks. Discrete Event Dyn. Syst. **17**, 405–421 (2007)

Bretschneider, G.: Extension of the equivalent random method to smooth traffics. In: Proceedings of the 7th International Teletraffic Congress, Stockholm (1973)

Chung, S.-P., Ross, K.W.: Reduced load approximations for multirate loss networks. IEEE Trans. Commun. **41**(8), 1222–1231 (1993)

Erlang, A.K.: Løsning af nogle problemer fra sandsynlighedsregningen af betydning for de automatiske telefon-centraler. Elektroteknikeren **13**, 5–13 (1917). (in Danish)

Erlang, A.K.: The theory of probabilities and telephone conversations, Nyt Tidsskrift for Matematik **20**(B), 33–39 (1909)

Kelly, F.P.: Loss networks. Ann. Appl. Probab. **1**(3), 319–378 (1991)

Kelly, F.P.: Reversibility and Stochastic Networks. Cambridge University Press (2011)

Ross, K.W.: Multiservice Loss Models for Broadband Telecommunication Networks. Springer, London (1995)

Sevastyanov, B.A.: Ergodic theorem for Markov processes and its application to telephone systems with failures. Theory of Probab. Appl. **2**(1), 106–116 (1957)

Chapter 2
Erlang's Systems

Abstract This chapter deals with two fundamental models in queueing/teletraffic theory—Erlang's loss and delay systems. We discuss the Equivalent Random Traffic (ERT) method to estimate blocking probabilities in loss systems with non-Poisson arrivals, which uses the overflow process of Erlang's loss system to approximate the original non-Poisson arrival process. Asymptotic relations for the arrival rate and the number of servers in the auxiliary (test) system are derived for a low rate overflow process. Finally, we cover major generalizations of Erlang's results: continuous Erlang B and Erlang C formulas, queueing systems with ordered service elements and systems with a fractional number of servers.

2.1 The Erlang's Loss Model

2.1.1 Problem Formulation

Erlang's loss model was introduced in Sect. 1.1. Here, we explore it in detail, discuss some practical aspects of its application and formally derive its stationary state distribution. For essential notations and concepts of queueing systems, see Appendix A3.

Consider a group of C identical servers operating in parallel (circuits, devices, resource units, etc.), and assume that the group is offered a Poisson stream of customers (calls, messages, service requests, etc.) with a constant rate of λ customers per time unit (see Fig. 2.1). As we have seen previously, the state of such a loss system can be specified by the number n of busy servers, $n \in \mathcal{J} = \{0, 1, \ldots, C\}$. It is assumed that the system has no waiting places (no buffer or queue), and therefore, all customers that arrive in state $n = C$, in which all servers are busy, are blocked.

We assume that blocked customers do not affect the character or rate of the arrival process. From the perspective of applications, this simplifying assumption means either that the blocking probability $E_C(\rho)$ is very small (e.g., of the order of several percent), or that a lost customer seeks service at another loss system and therefore repeated attempts to receive service can be ignored.

V. Naumov et al., *Matrix and Analytical Methods for Performance Analysis of Telecommunication Systems*, https://doi.org/10.1007/978-3-030-83132-5_2

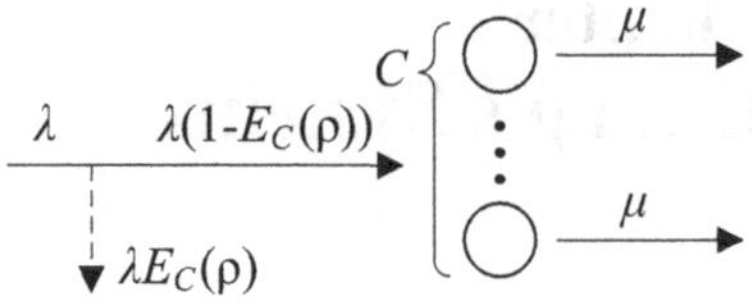

Fig. 2.1 $M|M|C|C$ loss system with a blocking probability $E_C(\rho)$

Each customer that has not been blocked occupies one server and holds it for the duration of its service time, which is assumed exponentially distributed with a parameter μ independent of the arrival process, system state and holding times of other customers. Moreover, incoming customers can occupy free servers in any order—random or not. We will specifically consider server allocation in a particular order in Sect. 2.4.

Recall from Sect. 1.1 that the queueing system described above is commonly called *Erlang's loss model*, after the eminent Danish mathematician and engineer Agner Krarup Erlang (1878–1929), whose works of 1908–1918 have laid the foundations of teletraffic and queueing theories. In Kendall's notation (see Appendix A3.1), it can be represented as $M|M|C|C$, $1 \le C < \infty$, or $M|M|\infty$, where the fourth position is omitted since the number of waiting places is zero.

For a Poisson arrival process (see Appendix A2.3), the average number of arrivals in time τ is $\lambda\tau$, while the average service duration, if service times are exponentially distributed, is $1/\mu$. Therefore, on average, $\rho = \lambda/\mu$ customers arrive in time $1/\mu$. The quantity ρ is independent of the adopted time units and is referred to as the *offered workload, offered traffic intensity,* or *offered traffic load*. In engineering applications, ρ is measured in *Erlangs*. For example, in the queueing system under analysis, a workload of $\rho = 3.5$ Erlangs means either that the mean number of busy servers at any given or arbitrary time is equal to 3.5, or that 3.5 servers are busy on average in the considered time period.

2.1.2 Constructive Definition of a Birth–Death Process

Let now $X(t)$ represent the number of customers in service at time t, $t \ge 0$. Since each customer in service holds one server, the number of customers in service equals the number of busy servers, and $\mathcal{J} = \{0, 1, ..., C\}$, $1 \le C \le \infty$, is the state space of the process $X(t)$, $t \ge 0$. In applications, we are usually interested in cases when resources are limited and therefore set $C < \infty$. However, the following argument and results are valid also for the case of $C = \infty$, which is useful for evaluating delay via the $M|M|\infty$ queueing system.

Since we have assumed the arrival process to be Poisson with parameter λ, for any $t_0 \ge 0$ and $\tau \ge 0$, the number $Y(\tau)$ of customers offered to the system in the time interval $(t_0, t_0 + \tau]$ is Poisson distributed with parameter $\lambda\tau$, i.e.,

$$\mathsf{P}(Y(\tau) = m) = \mathrm{e}^{-\lambda\tau}\frac{(\lambda\tau)^m}{m!}, \ m = 0, 1, \ldots. \tag{2.1}$$

This distribution depends neither on whether arriving customers receive service or not, nor on the holding times of the customers in service. In particular, it follows from (2.1) that

$$\mathsf{P}(\text{no arrivals in } (t_0, t_0 + \tau]) = \mathsf{P}(Y(\tau) = 0) = \mathrm{e}^{-\lambda\tau}, \tag{2.2}$$

i.e., the time between subsequent arrivals is exponentially distributed and independent of t_0, of state $X(t_0)$ and of possible departures in the interval $(t_0, t_0 + \tau]$.

Now let $X(t_0) = n$, $n = 1, \ldots, C$, and denote by $z_1, \ldots, z_n$ the residual holding times of the customers in service. Then, due to the memoryless property of the exponential distribution of the service times and their mutual independence, we have

$$\begin{aligned} &\mathsf{P}(\text{no departures in } (t_0, t_0 + \tau]) = \mathsf{P}(\min(z_1, \ldots, z_n) > \tau) = \\ &= \mathsf{P}(z_1 > \tau, \ldots, z_n > \tau) = \mathsf{P}(z_1 > \tau) \cdots \mathsf{P}(z_n > \tau) = \mathrm{e}^{-n\mu\tau}. \end{aligned} \tag{2.3}$$

Using these facts, one checks easily that $X(t), t \geq 0$, is a homogeneous CTMC. Indeed, in terms of probability, a future state $X(t_0 + \tau)$ is independent of the past $X(s)$, $s < t_0$, given the present $X(t_0)$, and depends on the interval length τ, but not on the time instant t_0 (see Appendix A2.2). Moreover, $X(t)$, $t \geq 0$, is a step Markov process and a birth–death process, because in a small time interval $(t_0, t_0 + \Delta)$, up to $o(\Delta)$, it can either remain unchanged or move up or down by one (see Example A1 in Appendix A2.2).

Using the Heaviside step function,

$$H(x) = \begin{cases} 0, & x \leq 0, \\ 1, & x > 0, \end{cases}$$

for the transition probabilities in time Δ, we have

$$\begin{aligned} P_\Delta(n, n) &= \mathsf{P}(X(t_0 + \Delta) = n | X(t_0) = n) = \\ &= \mathsf{P}(\text{no arrivals in } (t_0, t_0 + \Delta) \text{ and no departures} \\ &\quad \text{from } n \text{ servers} \mid X(t_0) = n\} = \mathrm{e}^{-\lambda H(C-n)\Delta}\mathrm{e}^{-n\mu\Delta} = \\ &= (1 - \lambda H(C - n)\Delta + o(\Delta)) \times (1 - n\mu\Delta + o(\Delta)) = \\ &= 1 - \lambda H(C - n)\Delta - n\mu\Delta + o(\Delta), \quad n = 0, \ldots, C; \end{aligned} \tag{2.4}$$

$$\begin{aligned} P_\Delta(n, n-1) &= \mathsf{P}(X(t_0 + \Delta) = n - 1 | X(t_0) = n) = \\ &= \mathsf{P}(\text{no arrivals in } (t_0, t_0 + \Delta) \\ &\quad \text{and one departure from } n \text{ servers } |X(t_0) = n) = \\ &= \mathrm{e}^{-\lambda\Delta}\tbinom{n}{1}\big(1 - \mathrm{e}^{-\mu\Delta}\big)\mathrm{e}^{-(n-1)\mu\Delta} = n\mu\Delta + o(\Delta), \quad n = 1, \ldots, C; \end{aligned} \tag{2.5}$$

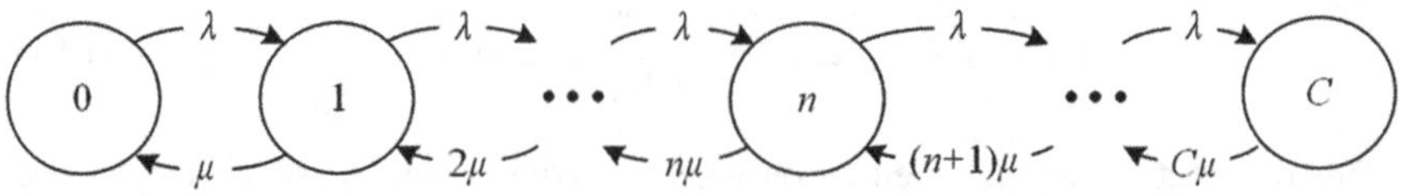

Fig. 2.2 State transition graph of the $M|\,M|\,C|C$ loss system

$$\begin{aligned} P_{\Delta}(n, n+1) &= \mathsf{P}(X(t_0+\Delta) = n+1 | X(t_0) = n) = \\ &= \mathsf{P}(\text{one arrival and no departures} \\ &\quad \text{in } (t_0, t_0+\Delta) \,|\, X(t_0) = n) = \\ &= \left(1 - e^{-\lambda\Delta}\right) e^{-n\mu\Delta} = \lambda\Delta + o(\Delta), \quad n = 0, \ldots, C-1; \end{aligned} \tag{2.6}$$

$$P_{\Delta}(n, m) = 0, |m-n| \geq 2, n, m = 0, \ldots, C. \tag{2.7}$$

It follows from (2.4)–(2.7) that for $n = 0, \ldots, C$ the transition rates are given by

$$\begin{aligned} A(n, n-1) = \mu_n = n\mu; \quad A(n, n+1) = \lambda_n = \lambda H(C-n); \\ a(n) = -A(n, n) = \lambda H(C-n) + n\mu; \\ A(n, m) = 0, |m-n| \geq 2, \end{aligned} \tag{2.8}$$

i.e., $X(t), t \geq 0$, is a birth–death process (Fig. 2.2).

In light of (2.2), (2.3), and (2.8), the sojourn time τ_n in state n is exponentially distributed with mean $1/a(n)$:

$$\mathsf{P}(\tau_n > t) = e^{-(\lambda H(C-n)+n\mu)t}, t \geq 0, n = 0, \ldots, C.$$

Thus, departure times from state n are governed by a Poisson process of rate $a(n)$, while transitions to the neighboring states are determined by the probabilities

$$Q(n, n-1) = \frac{n\mu}{\lambda + n\mu}, n = 1, \ldots, C; \; Q(n, n+1) = \frac{\lambda}{\lambda + n\mu}, n = 0, \ldots, C-1; \tag{2.9}$$

and

$$Q(n, n) = Q(n, m) = 0, |m-n| \geq 2, n, m = 0, \ldots, C. \tag{2.10}$$

We have thus described the behavior of the C-server loss system by the birth–death process $X(t), t \geq 0$, with state space $\mathcal{J} = \{0, 1, \ldots, C\}$, a tridiagonal generator matrix $\mathbf{A} = [A(m, n)]$, $m, n = 1, \ldots, C$, whose elements are given by (2.8), and a bidiagonal stochastic matrix $\mathbf{Q} = [Q(m, n)]$, $m, n = 1, \ldots, C$, given by (2.9)–(2.10).

2.1.3 Stationary State Distribution and the Erlang Loss Formula

The next step of our analysis is to obtain the stationary state distribution of the process $X(t)$, $t \geq 0$, which we denote by $\mathbf{p} = (p(0) ..., p(C))$, $C < \infty$. For a birth–death process with transition rates (2.8), the stationary distribution verifies the global balance equations

$$\begin{gathered} -\lambda p(0) + \mu p(1) = 0; \\ \lambda p(n-1) - (\lambda + n\mu)p(n) + (n+1)\mu p(n+1) = 0, n = 1 ..., C-1; \\ \lambda p(C-1) - C\mu p(C) = 0. \end{gathered} \tag{2.11}$$

By summing up the (2.11) from the zeroth to the $(n-1)$-th, we obtain the detailed balance equations

$$\lambda p(n-1) = n\mu p(n), n = 1 ..., C. \tag{2.12}$$

To explain the physical meaning of (2.12), we turn to Fig. 2.2: the left-hand side gives the probability flow from state $(n-1)$ to state n, while the right-hand side gives the flow from n to $(n-1)$.

By making use of the notation $\rho = \lambda/\mu$, $0 < \rho < \infty$, introduced previously, and applying the normalization condition $\sum_{n=0}^{C} p(n) = 1$, from (2.12), we obtain

$$p(n) = \frac{\frac{\rho^n}{n!}}{\sum_{m=0}^{C} \frac{\rho^m}{m!}}, n = 0 ..., C. \tag{2.13}$$

Note that this result also follows from relations in Appendix A2.2.

Particularly important for designing telecommunication systems is the quantity $p(C)$, which represents the *blocking probability* of the offered traffic. It depends on ρ and is commonly denoted by

$$E_C(\rho) = \frac{\frac{\rho^C}{C!}}{\sum_{m=0}^{C} \frac{\rho^m}{m!}}, 0 \leq \rho < \infty, \tag{2.14}$$

and referred to as the Erlang loss or Erlang B formula. Since its first publication in 1917 (Erlang 1917), this relation has been widely used for designing telecommunication networks of many generations, including the most advanced.

One checks easily that with an unlimited increase in the number of servers the number of busy servers converges to the Poisson distribution,

$$\lim_{C\to\infty} p(n) = e^{-\rho}\frac{\rho^n}{n!}, n = 0, 1, ...$$

By consequence, the distribution $p(n)$, $n = 0 ..., C$, given by (2.13), for $C < \infty$ is the truncated Poisson distribution with parameter ρ.

The blocking probability $E_C(\rho)$ may be easily computed using the recurrence relation

$$E_0(\rho) = 1, E_C(\rho) = \frac{\rho E_{C-1}(\rho)}{C + \rho E_{C-1}(\rho)}, C = 1, 2, ... \tag{2.15}$$

Indeed, by dividing the numerator and the denominator of (2.14) by $\sum_{m=0}^{C-1} \rho^m/m!$, we have

$$E_C(\rho) = \left(\frac{\frac{\rho^C}{C!}}{\sum_{m=0}^{C-1}\frac{\rho^m}{m!}}\right) \cdot \left(\frac{\left(\sum_{m=0}^{C-1}\frac{\rho^m}{m!} + \frac{\rho^C}{C!}\right)}{\sum_{m=0}^{C-1}\frac{\rho^m}{m!}}\right)^{-1} = \frac{\frac{\rho}{C}E_{C-1}(\rho)}{1 + \frac{\rho}{C}E_{C-1}(\rho)}.$$

Moreover, by denoting $\theta_C(\rho) = [E_C(\rho)]^{-1}$, we obtain from (2.15) another recurrence relation:

$$\theta_0(\rho) = 1, \theta_C(\rho) = 1 + \frac{C}{\rho}\theta_{C-1}(\rho), C = 1, 2, ...$$

Both recursions give stable and accurate results, but each of them has a preferable range for ρ and C.

Example problem A telephone exchange has 10^4 subscribers. Each subscriber offers 0.04 Erlang, and 10% of calls are long-distance. Find the number of circuits C for long-distance communications, so that their blocking probability does not exceed 1%.

Solution. Let ρ_1 and ρ_2 denote, respectively, the traffic offered by all calls and long-distance calls. Then,

$$\rho_1 = 10^4 \cdot 0, 04 = 400 \text{ Erlang},$$

$$\rho_2 = 0, 1\rho_1 = 40 \text{ Erlang}.$$

It follows from formula (2.15) and the problem statement that

$$\frac{\rho_2 E_{C-1}(\rho_2)}{C + \rho_2 E_{C-1}(\rho_2)} \leq 0.01.$$

This directly implies that $C \geq 99\rho_2 E_{C-1}(\rho_2)$.

The quantity $E_{C-1}(\rho_2)$ can be found by using the Erlang B recursion (2.15). Finally, we obtain that to keep the blocking probability below 1% for $\rho_2 = 40$, we need $C \geq 53$ circuits.

2.2 Arrival Process Approximation

So far, we have always assumed Poisson arrivals, however, such a simplifying assumption is not always valid. Imagine you have to evaluate performance of a complex service system with some arrival process, but no method for studying such a system with this particular arrival process is available: it does not exist or is too complicated. A possible solution is to approximate the arrival process with another one, chosen so that, on the one hand, the approximation is as accurate as possible, and on the other hand, the analysis of the system with the new arrival process is feasible.

There exist several methods of such approximation. The most straightforward techniques—namely, the stationary-interval and asymptotic methods (Whitt 1982)—neglect the degree to which the arrival process' parameters affect the performance measures of the system. In stationary-interval methods, the original and the approximating arrival processes must have some characteristics of interarrival times identical, for example, the CDFs or several first moments. In asymptotic methods, the two processes must have in common some characteristics of their behavior in long time intervals, for instance, the parameters of the asymptotic expansions for large t of the moments of the number of arrivals in time t.

The hybrid methods, conversely, take account of the degree to which the arrival process' parameters affect the system's performance. For example, in the system with MAP arrivals considered in Sect. 4.3, for any arrival process, the blocking probability is determined only by the values at points μ_1, μ_2 ..., μ_n of the Laplace–Stieltjes transform of the interarrival time CDF. This is why when substituting the arrival process for such a system, these values are better left unchanged.

If we know the parameters of the arrival process to which the system's measures of interest are sensitive, the indirect approach (Whitt 1981) can be used. Here, some test system, similar to the original one but simpler, is first conceived. Then, an approximating arrival process is chosen so that when applied to the test system it yields the same characteristics of interest as the original complicated system.

The best-known method within this approach is the Equivalent Random Traffic method. It was first proposed in 1956 by R. I. Wilkinson (Wilkinson 1956) and G. Bretschneider (Bretschneider 1956) for finding the blocking probability on a multi-circuit link which receives overflow calls from other links. A link comprising infinitely many circuits was used as a test system, while a stream of lost calls from a link with a finite number of circuits was taken as the approximating arrival process.

Consider a $G|M|\infty$ service system with infinitely many servers, general arrival process and queueing times exponentially distributed with mean 1. Let $X(t)$ denote the number of customers in the system at time t. Under rather broad assumptions, there exists a stationary distribution of the process $X(t)$ (Borovkov 1976):

$$p(n) = \lim_{t\to\infty} \mathsf{P}(X(t) = n), n = 0, 1, \ldots. \tag{2.16}$$

Using the probability-generating function $P(z) = \sum_{n=0}^{\infty} p(n)z^n$ of distribution (2.16). The factorial moments of distribution (2.16) are given using the probability-generating function $P(z) = \sum_{n=0}^{\infty} p(n)z^n$ by

$$f_k = \left.\frac{d^k P(z)}{d\, z^k}\right|_{z=1}.$$

The following characteristics of distribution (2.16) are used most often: the mean $m = f_1$, the variance $V = f_2 - f_1^2 + f_1$ and the peakedness $z = \frac{V}{m}$. The Poisson arrival process has peakedness $z = 1$, while the overflow process of $M|M|L|L$ loss system has peakedness $z > 1$.

Consider now a $G|M|N|N$ loss system in Fig. 2.3 whose service times are exponentially distributed with mean 1, and assume its arrival process to be characterized by parameters m and z.

In order to use ERT to estimate the blocking probability $B_N(m, z)$, we need to find a Poisson process of such a rate A that when arriving to an $M|M|L|L$ system it generates an overflow process having mean m and peakedness z. For that, the following identities must hold (Wilkinson 1956):

$$m = AE_L(A), \tag{2.17}$$

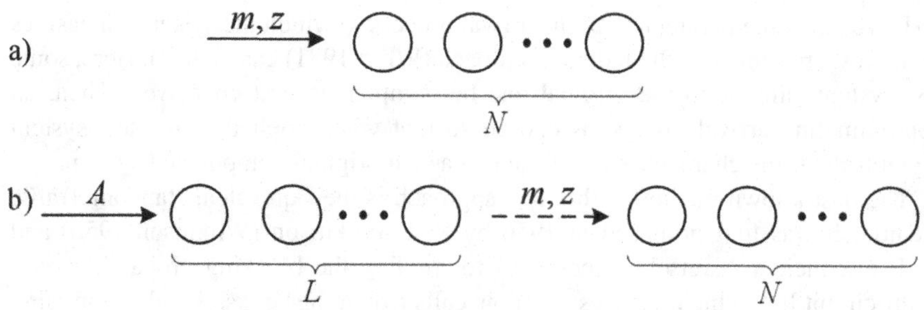

Fig. 2.3. **a** N-server loss system with a general arrival process; **b** Overflow process of an L-server loss system arriving to an N-server loss system

$$z = 1 - m + \frac{A}{L + 1 + m - A}. \tag{2.18}$$

Here, $E_L(A)$ represents the blocking probability of a customer arriving according to a Poisson arrival process of rate A to an L-server loss system, which is given by the Erlang loss formula (2.14). Since the system of (2.17)–(2.18) does not always have a solution such that L is whole, the Erlang loss formula has been extended to non-integer numbers of servers L as follows (Jagerman 1974):

$$E_L(A) = \left(A \int_0^{\infty} e^{-Ax} (1 + x)^L dx \right)^{-1}. \tag{2.19}$$

Equation (2.18) is equivalent to

$$A = q\,(m + L + 1), \tag{2.20}$$

where

$$q = 1 - \frac{1}{m + z}.$$

Thus, if we know one of the parameters A or L, then we can find the other from relation (2.20). Once the system (2.17)–(2.18) is solved, the blocking probability $B_N(m, z)$ for the arrival process characterized by m and z can be found as

$$B_N(m, z) = \frac{E_{N+L}(A)}{E_L(A)}.$$

Parameters A and L are usually calculated by iteration with the initial guess proposed by Y. Rapp (Rapp 1964):

$$A_0 = mz + 3z(z - 1), \tag{2.21}$$

$$L_0 = A_0/q - m - 1. \tag{2.22}$$

However, in practice, very small values of m may occur, and the approximate formulas (2.21)–(2.22) do not work well in such cases. Indeed, for a given z, we have

$$\lim_{m \to 0} A_0 = 3z(z - 1), \ \lim_{m \to 0} L_0 = 3z^2 - 1,$$

whereas from (2.17)–(2.19), it follows that for $z > 1$ the exact values of A and L increase without bound as m becomes small. To obtain more accurate A_0 and L_0, we make use of the following result, which follows from part 3a of Theorem 15 in (Borovkov 1976), p. 226.

Lemma 2.1 *If* $A \to \infty$ *and* $L \to \infty$ *so that* $0 < \varepsilon_1 < \frac{L}{A} - 1 < \varepsilon_2$, *then*

$$E_L(A) \sim \frac{1}{L}\sqrt{\frac{A}{2\pi}}\left(\frac{A}{L}\right)^L e^{L-A}. \tag{2.23}$$

As it follows from (2.20), for a solution $A,\ L$ of (2.17)–(2.19), there exists a limit

$$\lim_{m\to 0}\left(\frac{L}{A} - 1\right) = \frac{1}{z-1}.$$

Therefore, for $z > 1$ and small m, the approximation (2.23) can be used in (2.17) instead of expression (2.19).

Theorem 2.1 *Let* $z > 1$, $Q = 2(q - \ln(q) - 1)$ *and*

$$F = 2(1-q)(1+m) + \ln\left(\frac{q^3}{2\pi m^2 Q}\right) > 1.$$

Then, for $m \to 0$, *a solution* L *to* (2.17)–(2.18) *satisfies the asymptotic relation*

$$L \sim \frac{\psi}{Q}, \tag{2.24}$$

where ψ *is the largest root of the equation*

$$\ln(x) - x + F = 0. \tag{2.25}$$

Proof By substituting the right-hand side of (2.20) for A and the right-hand side of (2.23) for $E_L(A)$ in (2.17), we have.

$$m^2 = \frac{L}{2\pi}\left(\frac{A}{L}\right)^{2L+3} e^{2(L-A)} =$$

$$= \frac{Lq}{2\pi}^3\left(1 + \frac{m+1}{L}\right)^{2L+3} e^{-2q(m+1)} e^{-2L(q-\ln q-1)}.$$

The above identity is equivalent to

$$\begin{aligned} \ln(LQ) - LQ + (2L+3)\ln\left(1 + \tfrac{m+1}{L}\right) - \\ -2q(m+1) + \ln\left(\tfrac{q^3}{2\pi m^2 Q}\right) = 0. \end{aligned} \tag{2.26}$$

As $m \to 0$ and $L \to \infty$, we have

$$(2L+3)\ln\left(1+\frac{m+1}{L}\right) \sim 2(m+1).$$

This and (2.26) yield

$$L \sim \frac{x}{Q}, \tag{2.27}$$

where x is a root of (2.25).

Consider now the function

$$f_c(x) = \ln x - x + c, x > 0.$$

It increases monotonically from $-\infty$ to $c-1$ as x goes from 0 to 1, and then monotonically decreases from $c-1$ to $-\infty$ as x increases from 1 to ∞. Thus, $f_c(x)$ is never zero for $c < 1$. For $c \geq 1$ the equation $f_c(x) = 0$ has two real-valued roots, $0 \leq \varphi \leq 1$ and $\psi \geq 1$, which depend monotonically on c. For $c = 1$, they equal 1 and, as c grows, φ goes to 0, while ψ increases without bound. Since $L \to \infty$ as $m \to 0$, x in (2.27) is the largest root of (2.25). ■

Figure 2.4 plots the exact values of A, which are the solution to (2.17)–(2.18), and their approximations obtained by formula (2.24). The results are close for small m. As m grows, however, the accuracy of (2.24) drops. Finally, for m larger than some $m*$, which depends on z, the relation (2.24) must not be used. In this case, the term F in (2.25) is smaller than one, and the equation has no real-valued roots.

Thus, when choosing the initial guess for the parameters A and L, it is a good practice to compute F first. If $F \leq 1$, Rapp's approximation should be used. If, conversely, $F > 1$, then more accurate values are obtained by (2.20) and (2.24).

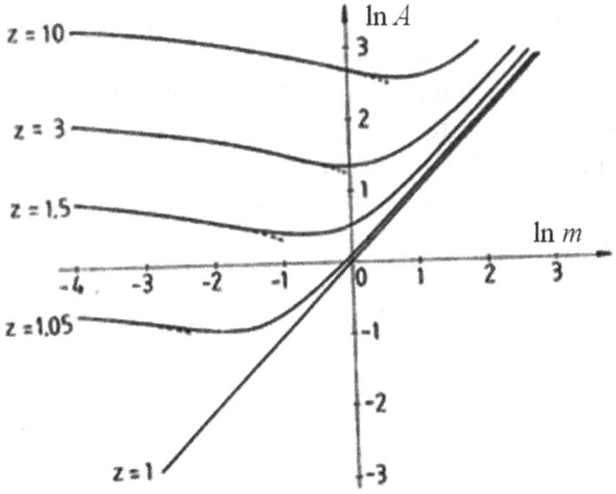

Fig. 2.4 Exact (——) and approximate (·····) values of A

For further properties of the roots of (2.25) and their approximations, see (Naumov 1988).

2.3 The Erlang's Delay Model

2.3.1 Problem Formulation

Consider now C-server queueing system with r waiting places $M|M|C|C+r$, $1 \le C < \infty$, $1 \le r \le \infty$. Let customers arrive according to a Poisson process of a constant rate λ, and the holding times be independent and exponentially distributed with parameter μ.

A service system with waiting places—a queueing system—operates as follows. If an arriving customer finds a free server, it receives service immediately. If, however, upon an arrival, all C servers are busy, then the arriving customer occupies a waiting place (a device or a slot in the buffer memory), i.e., joins the queue until a server is available. Moreover, two options can be considered: the customer vacates the waiting place once service begins or holds it along with a server until service is over. In the former case, the total capacity of the system is $R = C + r$, in the latter, $R = r \ge C$. For the sake of simplicity, we consider the first case only.

The order in which members of the queue are selected for service when a server is available is referred to as the *queue discipline.* The most common queue disciplines are first-in–first-out (FIFO), last-in–last-out (LIFO), service in random order (SIRO), and some others. If the system's engineer or operator considers the blocking probability $p(R)$ to be so small that it can be neglected, then it can be assumed that $r = \infty$ and no blocking occurs. If, however, $r < \infty$ then an arriving customer that finds C customers in service and r more customers in the queue is blocked and lost without affecting future arrivals.

A C-server queueing system with finite queue capacity is depicted in Fig. 2.5. In teletraffic theory, this modification of Erlang's model is also known as Erlang's delay model. Along with the blocking probability, its main performance measures are the waiting (queueing) time and the total time spent in the system (the sojourn time). Note that a long waiting time may cause a customer (a subscriber) to leave without service or to repeat the request, which substantially complicates the model and computations.

Fig. 2.5 $M|M|C|R$ system

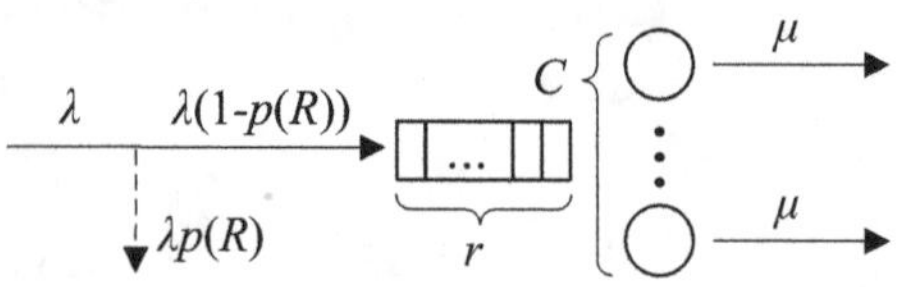

2.3.2 Stationary State Distribution

Let a stochastic process $X(t)$, $t \geq 0$, represent the total number of customers in the system at time t. Then, $\mathcal{J} = \{0, 1 ..., C, C+1 ..., R\}$ is the state space of the process $X(t)$. Since interarrival and service times are exponentially distributed, $X(t)$ is a birth–death step CTMC and its transition rates from state n, $n = 0 ..., R$, are given by

$$\begin{aligned} A(n, n+1) &= \lambda_n = \lambda H(R-n), \\ A(n, n-1) &= \mu_n = \mu \min(n, C), \\ A(n, n) &= -\lambda_n - \mu_n. \end{aligned} \tag{2.28}$$

The transition rates of the process $X(t)$ are illustrated by the state transition graph in Fig. 2.6. Indeed, for the birth–death process $X(t)$, the birth rate λ_n in state $n = 0, ..., R-1$ is constant and equals the rate of the arrival process. In state R, all arriving customers are blocked and therefore the rate of accepted arrivals is zero. The death rate μ_n from state n is equal to $n\mu$ for $n = 0, ..., C$ and to $C\mu$ for $n = C+1, ..., R$.

In view of (2.28), the generator matrix $\mathbf{A}$ of the process $X(t)$ is tridiagonal and is given by Table 2.1.

A raw vector $\mathbf{p} = (p(0), ..., p(R))$ of the sought-for stationary state distribution satisfies the equilibrium equations $\mathbf{pA} = \mathbf{0}$, which, in light of (2.28) and the form of $\mathbf{A}$, are as follows:

$$\begin{gathered} -\lambda p(0) + \mu p(1) = 0; \\ \lambda p(n-1) - (\lambda + n\mu)p(n) + (n+1)\mu p(n+1) = 0, n = 1, ..., C-1; \\ \lambda p(n-1) - (\lambda + C\mu)p(n) + C\mu p(n+1) = 0, n = C, ..., C+r-1; \\ \lambda p(R-1) - C\mu p(R) = 0. \end{gathered} \tag{2.29}$$

By making use of the Heaviside step function, we can rewrite (2.29) in compact form as

$$\begin{aligned} &\lambda p(n-1)H(n) - [\lambda H(R-n) + \mu \min(n, C)]p(n) + \\ &+ \mu \min(n+1, C)p(n+1)H(R-n) = 0, \quad n = 0, ..., R. \end{aligned}$$

By summing the (2.29) from the zeroth to the $(n-1)$-th, we have the detailed balance equations:

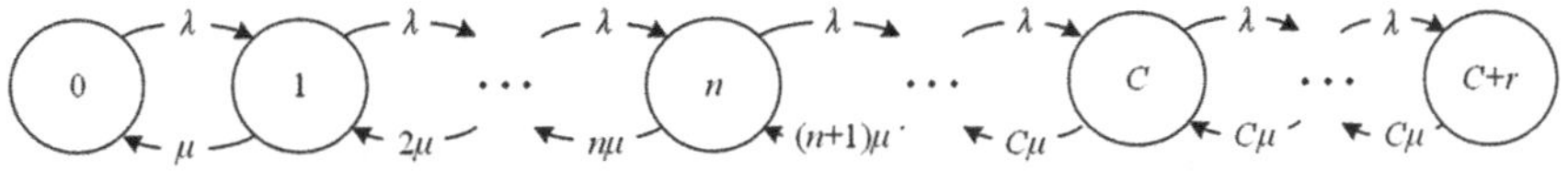

Fig. 2.6 State transition graph of the $M|M|C|C+r$ system

Table 2.1 Generator matrix of the $M|\,M|\,C|C+r$ system

A	0	1	$\cdots$	n	$\cdots$	C	$C+1$	$\cdots$	$C+r-1$	R
0	$-\lambda$	λ	$\cdots$	0	$\cdots$	0	0	$\cdots$	0	0
1	μ	$-\lambda-\mu$	$\ddots$	0	$\cdots$	$\cdots$	$\cdots$	$\cdots$	$\cdots$	0
$\vdots$	$\vdots$	$\ddots$	$\ddots$	$\cdots$	$\cdots$	$\cdots$	$\cdots$	$\cdots$	$\cdots$	$\vdots$
$n-1$	0	$\vdots$	$\ddots$	λ	$\cdots$	$\cdots$	$\cdots$	$\cdots$	$\cdots$	0
n	0	$\vdots$	$\vdots$	$-\lambda-n\mu$	$\ddots$	$\cdots$	$\cdots$	$\cdots$	$\cdots$	0
$n+1$	0	$\vdots$	$\vdots$	$(n+1)\mu$	$\ddots$	$\cdots$	$\cdots$	$\cdots$	$\cdots$	0
$\vdots$	$\vdots$	$\vdots$	$\vdots$	$\vdots$	$\ddots$	$\cdots$	$\cdots$	$\cdots$	$\cdots$	$\vdots$
$C-1$	0	$\vdots$	$\vdots$	$\vdots$	$\vdots$	λ	0	$\cdots$	$\cdots$	0
C	0	$\vdots$	$\vdots$	$\vdots$	$\vdots$	$-\lambda-C\mu$	λ	$\cdots$	$\cdots$	0
$C+1$	0	$\vdots$	$\vdots$	$\vdots$	$\vdots$	$C\mu$	$-\lambda-C\mu$	$\ddots$	$\cdots$	0
$\vdots$	$\vdots$	$\vdots$	$\vdots$	$\vdots$	$\vdots$	$\vdots$	$\ddots$	$\ddots$	$\ddots$	$\vdots$
$C+r-1$	0	$\vdots$	$\vdots$	$\vdots$	$\vdots$	$\vdots$	$\vdots$	$\ddots$	$-\lambda-C\mu$	λ
R	0	0	$\cdots$	0	$\cdots$	0	0	$\cdots$	$C\mu$	$-C\mu$

$$\lambda p(n-1) = n\mu p(n), n = 1, \ldots, C;$$
$$\lambda p(n-1) = C\mu p(n), n = C, \ldots, R,$$

or equivalently

$$\lambda p(n-1) = \min(n, C)\mu p(n), n = 1, \ldots, R. \tag{2.30}$$

For a physical interpretation of the detailed balance equations, we turn to Fig. 2.6. The left-hand side is the probability flow from state $n-1$ to state n, the right-hand side represents the probability flow in the opposite direction. Obviously, this interpretation is valid for both $n = 1, \ldots, C$ and $n = C+1, \ldots, R$.

By denoting $\rho = \lambda/\mu$, we rewrite the recurrence relation (2.30) as $p(n) = \frac{\rho}{\min(n,C)} p(n-1), n = 1, \ldots, R$. Now, we have

$$p(n) = \begin{cases} \dfrac{\rho^n}{n!} p(0), & n = 0, \ldots, C; \\ \left(\dfrac{\rho}{C}\right)^{n-C} p(C) = \dfrac{\rho^n}{C!C^{n-C}} p(0), & n = C, \ldots, R. \end{cases} \tag{2.31}$$

It follows from the normalization condition and (2.31) that

$$\frac{1}{p(0)} = \sum_{n=0}^{C-1} \frac{\rho^n}{n!} + \frac{\rho^C}{C!} \sum_{n=C}^{R} \left(\frac{\rho}{C}\right)^{n-C} = \sum_{n=0}^{C-1} \frac{\rho^n}{n!} + \frac{\rho^C}{C!} \sum_{m=0}^{r} \left(\frac{\rho}{C}\right)^{m} = \\ = \sum_{n=0}^{C-1} \frac{\rho^n}{n!} + \frac{\rho^C}{C!} \frac{1-\left(\frac{\rho}{C}\right)^{r+1}}{1-\frac{\rho}{C}}. \tag{2.32}$$

We have thus proved the following.

Theorem 2.2 *The stationary distribution of the number of customers in Erlang's delay system* $M|M|C|C+r$ *for* $r<\infty$ *and any* $\rho<\infty$ *is given by* (2.31)–(2.32). *For* $r=R=\infty$, *these formulas are valid if*

$$\rho < C,$$

and (2.32) *takes the form*

$$\frac{1}{p(0)} = \sum_{n=0}^{C-1} \frac{\rho^n}{n!} + \frac{\rho^C}{C!} \frac{1}{1-\frac{\rho}{C}}.$$

Using Theorem 2.2 for a one-server queue $M \mid M \mid 1 \mid r+1$, relations (2.31)–(2.32) for $r<\infty$ and any $\rho<\infty$ yield

$$p(n) = \rho^n p(0), n = 0, ..., R; \frac{1}{p(0)} = \frac{1-\rho^{r+2}}{1-\rho}. \tag{2.33}$$

The time-blocking probability is hence given by

$$B = p(R) = \rho^R \frac{1-\rho}{1-\rho^{R+2}}.$$

For $r=R=\infty$ no blocking occurs, yet (2.33) holds if $\rho<1$, and, moreover,

$$p(n) = \rho^n(1-\rho), n = 0, 1, ...$$

Thus, for $C=1$ and $r=\infty$ the distribution (2.31)–(2.32) is geometric with parameter $\rho<1$.

To check the results, we apply (2.31)–(2.32) to Erlang's loss system ($r=0,\ R=C$):

$$p(n) = \frac{\rho^n}{n!} p(0), n = 0, ...C; \frac{1}{p(0)} = \sum_{n=0}^{C} \frac{\rho^n}{n!}. \tag{2.34}$$

Since (2.34) coincides with (2.13), the result is validated. Furthermore, as would be expected, the stationary state distribution for the loss system is a special case of the distribution for the delay system.

2.3.3 Performance Measures and the Erlang Delay Formula

Consider now the random variable X of the number of customers in the system, which has distribution (2.31)–(2.32), and let Y represent the number of customers in service and Z, the number of customers in the queue. Obviously,

$$Y = \min(X, C); Z = (X - C)^+ = \begin{cases} X - C, & X \geq C, \\ 0, & X < C, \end{cases}$$

$$X = Y + Z.$$

Recall that $B = p(R)$ is the time-blocking probability in the system, i.e., the portion of time during the long observation period that system spends in state R. Note, that for finite $M|M|C|R$ systems a time-blocking probability is the same as a call-blocking probability, i.e., the portion of blocked calls during the long observation period. This property for Poisson arrival processes is often referred to as the PASTA property (Poisson Arrivals See Time Averages).

Theorem 2.3 *In the $M|M|C|C+r$ queueing system, for $r < \infty$ and any $\rho < \infty$, the average rate of admitted (non-blocked) traffic equals the average rate of carried traffic, while for $r = \infty$ and $\rho < C$, the average rate of carried traffic equals the average rate of offered traffic.*

Proof By summing up the detailed balance (2.30) for n from 1 to R, we have

$$\lambda(1 - B) = \mu \left[\sum_{n=1}^{C} np(n) + C \sum_{n=C+1}^{R} p(n) \right]. \tag{2.35}$$

The left-hand side represents the admitted traffic for $r < \infty \Leftrightarrow B > 0$ and the offered traffic for $r = R = \infty, \rho < C \Leftrightarrow B = 0$. The right-hand side, in both cases, is the average rate of carried traffic. ■

The identity (2.35) has another useful interpretation.

Corollary 1 *The mean number of busy servers in Erlang's delay system is equal to the average rate of admitted (carried) traffic for $r < \infty$ and to the average rate of offered traffic for $r = \infty$, i.e.,*

$$\mathsf{E}Y = \begin{cases} \rho(1 - B), & r < \infty, \ \rho < \infty, \\ \rho, & r = \infty, \ \rho < C. \end{cases} \tag{2.36}$$

Since $EY \leq C$, (2.36) yields the following physically obvious result.

Corollary 2 *The average rate of admitted traffic cannot exceed the number of servers in the system, i.e.,*

$$\rho(1 - B) \leq C.$$

The stationary state distribution and relation (2.36) permit obtaining expressions for many important performance measures.

In the $M|M|C|C + r$ queueing system, for $r < \infty$ and any $\rho < \infty$, the mean queue length is given by

$$\mathsf{E}Z = p(C)\frac{\rho}{C}\frac{1 + r\left(\frac{\rho}{C}\right)^{r+1} - (r+1)\left(\frac{\rho}{C}\right)^{r}}{\left(1 - \frac{\rho}{C}\right)^2}. \tag{2.37}$$

The mean waiting and sojourn time can be found using Little's law (see Appendix A3.3).

The mean waiting time $\mathsf{E}w$ and the mean sojourn time T for the $M|M|C|C + r$ system with $r < \infty$ is given by

$$\mathsf{E}w = \frac{\mathsf{E}Z}{\lambda(1 - B)}, \quad T = \frac{\mathsf{E}X}{\lambda(1 - B)},$$

where the denominator represents the average rate of admitted traffic.

It is rather rare to be able to derive analytical expressions for stationary state probabilities if interarrival and service times are generally distributed. In some cases, one can use the Pollaczek–Khinchin formula, which gives the probability-generating function of the number of customers in an $M|G|1|\infty$ queueing system via the Laplace–Stieltjes transform $\beta(s)$ of the service time CDF:

$$P(z) = \sum_{n=0}^{\infty} p(n)z^n = (1 - \rho)\frac{(1 - z)\beta(\lambda - \lambda z)}{\beta(\lambda - \lambda z) - z}. \tag{2.38}$$

In particular, (2.38) yields a formula for the mean waiting time in this system (Cooper 1981):

$$\mathsf{E}w = \frac{\rho}{1 - \rho}\left(\frac{\tau}{2} + \frac{\sigma^2}{2\tau}\right), \tag{2.39}$$

where τ and σ^2 are, respectively, the mean and the variance of the service time, and $\rho = \lambda\tau$.

Let now $r = \infty$ and $\rho < C$ and consider the random variable w of the waiting time in the $M|M|C|C + r$ system. Using (2.31)–(2.32), we can find the probability that an arriving customer will have to wait for service as

$$\mathsf{P}(w > 0) = \sum_{n=C}^{\infty} p(n) = p(0)\frac{\rho^C}{C!}\sum_{n\geq C}\left(\frac{\rho}{C}\right)^{n-C} = \frac{\frac{\rho^C}{C!}\frac{C}{C-\rho}}{\sum\limits_{n=0}^{C-1}\frac{\rho^n}{n!}+\frac{\rho^C}{C!}\frac{C}{C-\rho}}.$$

In teletraffic theory, $\mathsf{P}(w > 0)$ is referred to as the Erlang delay formula $D_C(\rho)$, or Erlang C formula, since this quantity can also be regarded as the implicit blocking probability:

$$D_C(\rho) = \frac{\frac{\rho^C}{C!}\frac{C}{C-\rho}}{\sum\limits_{n=0}^{C-1}\frac{\rho^n}{n!}+\frac{\rho^C}{C!}\frac{C}{C-\rho}}. \tag{2.40}$$

It is possible to express $D_C(\rho)$ in terms of $E_C(\rho)$. By dividing the numerator and denominator of (2.40) by $\sum\limits_{n=0}^{C}\frac{\rho^n}{n!}$, after some obvious rearrangements, we have

$$\mathsf{P}(w > 0) = \frac{\frac{\rho^C}{C!}\frac{C}{C-\rho}\left(\sum\limits_{n=0}^{C}\frac{\rho^n}{n!}\right)^{-1}}{\left(\sum\limits_{n=0}^{C-1}\frac{\rho^n}{n!}+\frac{\rho^C}{C!}\frac{C}{C-\rho}\right)\left(\sum\limits_{n=0}^{C}\frac{\rho^n}{n!}\right)^{-1}}$$

$$= \frac{C\cdot E_C(\rho)}{(C-\rho)[1-E_C(\rho)]+CE_v(\rho)} = \frac{C\cdot E_C(\rho)}{C-\rho[1-E_C(\rho)]}.$$

The resulting expression for the Erlang C formula

$$D_C(\rho) = \frac{C\cdot E_C(\rho)}{C-\rho[1-E_C(\rho)]}, \tag{2.41}$$

permits computing $D_C(\rho)$ as function of C and ρ, $\rho < C$, using the tables or the recurrence relations (2.15) to find $E_C(\rho)$.

In the next section, we discuss an important modification of the Erlang loss and delay formulas and the relation between them for a fractional number of servers.

2.4 Modifications of the Erlang Formulas for a Fractional Number of Servers

When studying complex systems using such teletraffic theory techniques as ERT method (Sect. 2.2), one needs to apply the Erlang loss formula to a fractional number of servers. A similar extension of the Erlang delay formula is required, for instance, when applying ERT to queueing systems, or to optimize the arrangement of servers in a multiclass network with flexible servers (Naumov and Martikainen 2011). The analytical extensions of the Erlang formulas proposed in (Bretschneider 1973; Jagers and van Doorn 1991) can be used to calculate values for a fractional number of servers. However, it is not easy because they involve computing incomplete gamma functions. Therefore, in practice, approximations of these extensions are used more frequently (Iversen 2005).

In this section, we consider a family of multi-server queueing systems in which one of the servers operates slower than the others. Each system can be viewed as a generalization of a classical queueing system, such as Erlang's delay system, to a fractional number of servers.

2.4.1 Continued Erlang Formulas

In (Bretschneider 1973), Bretschneider derived the analytical extension of the Erlang loss formula (2.14) for a fractional number of servers s in the form

$$E_s(\rho) = \frac{\rho^s \mathrm{e}^{-\rho}}{\int_\rho^\infty t^s \mathrm{e}^{-t} dt}, \quad s > 0, \tag{2.42}$$

while in (Jagerman 1974) it is proposed to compute function as (2.19).

As we have seen in the previous section, for Erlang's delay system $M|M|s|\infty$ with s servers and an infinite queue, the delay formula (2.40) gives, for $\rho < s$, the probability that an arriving customer finds all servers busy and has to join the queue. In particular, using this probability and Little's law (see Appendix A3.3), the average sojourn time can be easily found as

$$T = \frac{1}{\mu} + \frac{D_s(\rho)}{s\mu - \lambda}, \tag{2.43}$$

where $1/\mu$ is the average service time (Iversen 2005). The extension of the function (2.40) to fractional s, proposed in (Jagers and van Doorn 1991), differs only slightly from the generalized Erlang B formula (2.42):

$$D_s(\rho) = \left(\rho \int_0^\infty \mathrm{e}^{-\rho t} (1+t)^{s-1} t dt\right)^{-1}, s > 0. \tag{2.44}$$

Note that the extended Erlang formulas (2.42) and (2.44), to which, for the sake of brevity, we will refer in the remainder of the chapter as the continued Erlang B formula and continued Erlang C formula, respectively, are still related by (2.41).

Relation (2.41) is useful for calculating the continued Erlang C formula. The continued Erlang B formula can be computed, for instance, using the MATLAB software package (Martinez 2002). For this, it should be first rewritten in the form

$$E_s(\rho) = \frac{f_{s+1}(\rho)}{1 - F_{s+1}(\rho)},$$

where $f_\gamma(x)$ and $F_\gamma(x)$ represent the pdf and CDF of the standard gamma distribution, i.e.,

$$f_\gamma(x) = \frac{1}{\Gamma(\gamma)} x^{\gamma-1} \mathrm{e}^{-x},\ F_\gamma(x) = \frac{1}{\Gamma(\gamma)} \int_0^x t^{\gamma-1} \mathrm{e}^{-t} dt,\ x \geq 0, \gamma > 0.$$

The above can be obtained in MATLAB using the functions $f_\gamma(x) = \text{gampdf}\,(x, \gamma, 1)$ and $F_\gamma(x) = \text{gamcdf}\,(x, \gamma, 1)$.

Chapter 11 shows a fractional number of servers for Erlang's models that arise as a solution to an optimization problem, in particular, the problem of maximizing network throughput or minimizing the time before the network is empty.

2.4.2 *Queuing Systems with a Sequence of Service Elements*

Let us now introduce the concept of a queueing system with ordered service elements. Such a system consists of infinitely many numbered service elements and is specified by three sequences.

1. A nondecreasing sequence of arrival time instants $t_1 \leq t_2 \leq \ldots$.
2. A sequence of positive customer lengths $v_1, v_2, \ldots > 0$, where v_i represents the amount of work corresponding to the i-th customer.
3. A sequence of nonnegative service rates $\delta_1, \delta_2, \ldots \geq 0$, which starts with a positive $\delta_1 > 0$.

Service elements with positive service rates will be called servers, while service elements with zero service rates will be referred to as waiting places. Since we assume $\delta_1 > 0$, there is always at least one server in the system. An arriving customer occupies a free service element with the minimal number. The service by a k-th service element consists in decreasing the remaining length of the customer at a constant rate of δ_k per time unit. As soon as the remaining length of a customer becomes zero, the service is considered completed, the customer departs the system and vacates the server. Once a k-th service element is vacated due to a departure, the customers at service elements $i > k$ move one service element up. When customers switch service elements, their remaining lengths do not change, i.e., they resume service from the interruption point, but possibly with a different rate.

If the service rates are bounded above, it is convenient to assume $0 \leq \delta_k \leq 1$ for all $k = 1, 2, \ldots$. In this case, the parameters δ_k allow for a simple interpretation.

Suppose that the system under study is a subsystem of a more complex system, whose servers serve customers of different subsystems in a time-sharing mode. A k-th server spends time δ_k to serve customers of the given subsystem, while the rest of the time, $1 - \delta_k$, it is busy serving customers of other subsystems. As a result, a k-th server reduces the amount of work offered to the subsystem under study at a constant rate δ_k.

As an illustration, let us consider two systems with a Poisson arrival process of rate λ. We denote by g the average customer length, $\mu = g^{-1}$ and $\rho = \lambda g$.

Example 2.1 A single-server system with ordered servers.

A system with ordered servers that has only one server operates in the same manner as a classical $M|G|1|\infty$ system. The only difference is the parameter $\delta = \delta_1$ specifying the service rate. The remaining length of the customer that holds the server decreases at rate δ until it becomes zero.

Let $G(x)$ denote the CDF of the customer length. Then the CDF of the service time is $F(x) = G(\delta x)$. If $\rho < \delta$, then, using the Pollaczek–Khinchin formula (2.38), we obtain the following expression for the average sojourn time:

$$T = \frac{g}{\delta}\left(1 + \frac{\rho(1 + c^2)}{2(\delta - \rho)}\right).$$

Here, c is the coefficient of variation of the customer length, which coincides with the coefficient of variation of the service time.

Example 2.2 A multi-server system with ordered servers.

Let us consider a system with arbitrary service rates, Poisson arrivals and exponentially distributed with parameter $\mu = g^{-1}$ customer lengths. The number of customers in the system at time t is a birth–death process (App. A2.2) with the birth-and-death rates from state k given, respectively, by

$$\lambda_k = \lambda, \ \mu_k = \mu \sum_{i=1}^{k} \delta_i, \ k = 0, 1, \ldots$$

(where the sum with no terms is assumed zero). Denote

$$\gamma_n = \frac{\rho^n}{\prod\limits_{m=1}^{n} \sum\limits_{k=1}^{m} \delta_k},$$

and consider the Karlin–McGregor conditions (Martinez 2002), which guarantee ergodicity of the process:

$$\sum_{n=0}^{\infty} \gamma_n < \infty, \sum_{n=0}^{\infty} \frac{1}{\lambda_n \gamma_n} = \infty.$$

One checks easily that for the process to be ergodic it is hence necessary and sufficient that

$$\rho < \sum_{i=1}^{\infty} \delta_i.$$

In this case, the stationary distribution of the number of customers in the system is given by a simple expression (Cooper 1981)

$$p(k) = \frac{\gamma_k}{\sum\limits_{n=0}^{\infty} \gamma_n}, k = 0, 1, \ldots$$

To compute the average sojourn time, the following formula for queueing systems with the service rate depending on the number of customers (Lazowska 1984) can be used:

$$T = \sum_{k=1}^{\infty} \frac{k}{\mu_k} p(k-1). \tag{2.45}$$

2.4.3 Systems with a Fractional Number of Servers

Denote by $\lfloor x \rfloor$ the integer part of x, and assume a positive number s and a positive continuous function $R(x)$, $x > 0$, such that

$$\lfloor x \rfloor \leq R(x) < \lfloor x \rfloor + 1, \quad x > 0.$$

Denote $n = \lfloor s \rfloor$, $r = R(s)$, and $\delta = r - n$. Now, consider a system with ordered servers having Poisson arrivals and exponentially distributed customer lengths with mean g. Let the condition $\rho = \lambda g < R(s)$ hold.

Let the service rates be given by

$$\delta_i = \begin{cases} 1, \ 1 \leq i \leq n, \\ \delta, \ i = n+1, \\ 0, \ i \geq n+2. \end{cases} \tag{2.46}$$

The last formula can be interpreted as follows. The system has n fast servers, which operate with unit rate, and one slow server, which has rate $0 \leq \delta < 1$ and becomes a waiting place if $\delta = 0$.

The resulting system, which can be denoted as $M|M|R(s)|\infty$, is a special case of the system in Example 2.2. Its behavior is described by a birth–death process with transition rates $\lambda_k = \lambda$ and

$$\mu_k = \begin{cases} \mu k, & 1 \le k \le n, \\ \mu R(s), & k \ge n+1. \end{cases}$$

The stationary distribution of the number of customers in the system is given by

$$p(0) = \left(\sum_{k=0}^{n} \frac{\rho^k}{k!} + \frac{s\rho^{n+1}}{(s-\rho)rn!} \right)^{-1},$$

$$p(k) = \begin{cases} p(0)\dfrac{\rho^k}{k!}, & 0 \le k \le n, \\ p(0)\dfrac{\rho^n}{n!}\left(\dfrac{\rho}{r}\right)\left(\dfrac{\rho}{s}\right)^{k-n-1}, & k \ge n+1. \end{cases}$$

From (2.45), we obtain the expression for the average sojourn time

$$T = \frac{1}{\mu} + \frac{D_{r,s}(\rho)}{s\mu - \lambda}, \tag{2.47}$$

where

$$D_{r,s}(\rho) = \frac{p(n)}{r(s-\rho)}\big((1-\delta)s^2 + \delta\rho\, s + (s-r)(s-\rho)^2\big). \tag{2.48}$$

Note that the probability $p(n)$ in the above formula can be expressed via the continued Erlang C formula as

$$p(n) = \frac{r(s-\rho)E_n(\rho)}{r(s-\rho) + s\rho E_n(\rho)}.$$

For integer-valued $s = n$, expression (2.48) coincides with (2.40) giving the same probability for the classical $M|M|n|\infty$ system. Therefore, the function $D_{R(s),s}(\rho)$ can be considered as a continuous extension of the Erlang delay formula (2.40) to fractional s, especially since they play a similar role in the expressions for the average sojourn time (2.43) and (2.47).

In fact, we have a whole family of such extensions of the Erlang delay formula, each corresponding to a different function $R(s)$. Let us consider three of them.

Option 1. If we solve the equation $D_{r,s}(\rho) = D_s(\rho)$ with respect to r, then for $r = R_1(s)$ we have

$$R_1(s) = s\frac{E_n(\rho)s + E_n(\rho)(n-\rho)(s-\rho+\rho E_s(\rho))}{E_s(\rho)s + E_n(\rho)(s-\rho)(s-\rho+\rho E_s(\rho))} = s\frac{n-\rho+\frac{D_s(\rho)}{E_s(\rho)}}{s-\rho+\frac{D_s(\rho)}{E_n(\rho)}}.$$

Given such a function $R(x)$, the queueing system with ordered servers and service rates (2.46) has the same average sojourn time and the probability of waiting for service as those calculated by formulas (2.43) and (2.44) using the continued Erlang C formula.

Option 2. In light of the above considerations about servers operating in a time-sharing mode, it makes sense to set $R_2(s) = s$. In this case, the service rate of the slow server is equal to the fractional part of s, i.e., δ. Then, the probability that an arriving customer will wait for service is given by a simple relation

$$D_{s,s}(\rho) = p(n)\left(\frac{s}{s-\rho} - \delta\right).$$

Option 3. The function

$$R_3(s) = n + \frac{\delta\sqrt{s}}{\delta\sqrt{s} + (1-\delta)\sqrt{\rho}},$$

as well as $R_2(s)$, do not require incomplete gamma function calculation. Experiments have shown that $D_{R_3(s),s}(\rho)$ approximate $D_s(\rho)$ better than $D_{R_2(s),s}(\rho)$, except when the probability of waiting is close to 1. This is revealed by Figs. 2.7 and 2.8, which show the probabilities $D_{R_j(s),s}(\rho)$ under light, average and heavy traffic load, calculated for $R(s)$ considered above.

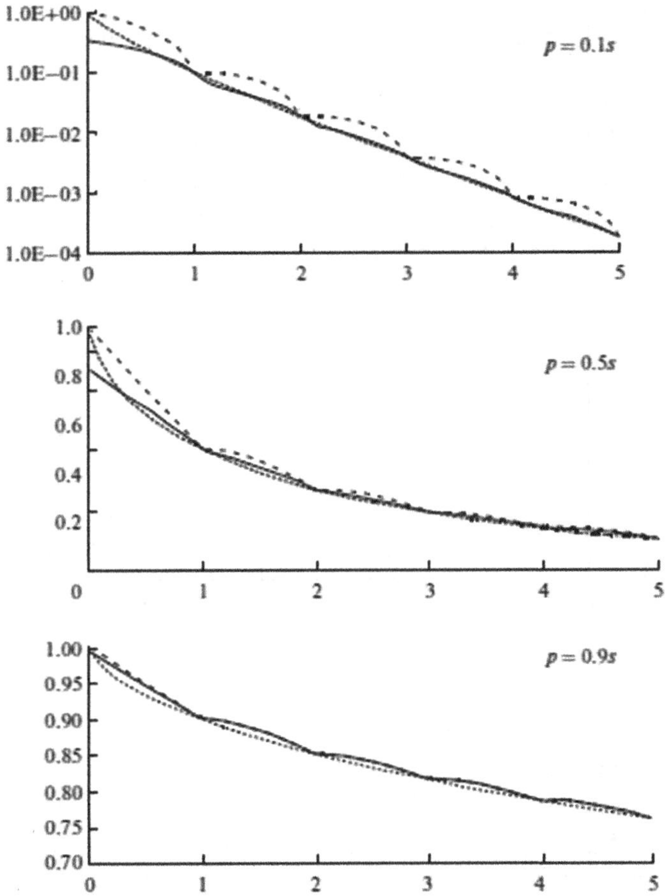

Fig. 2.7 Probabilities of waiting $D_{R_j(s),s}(\rho)$ for $0 < s \leq 5$, ····· R_1, - - - - R_2, — R_3

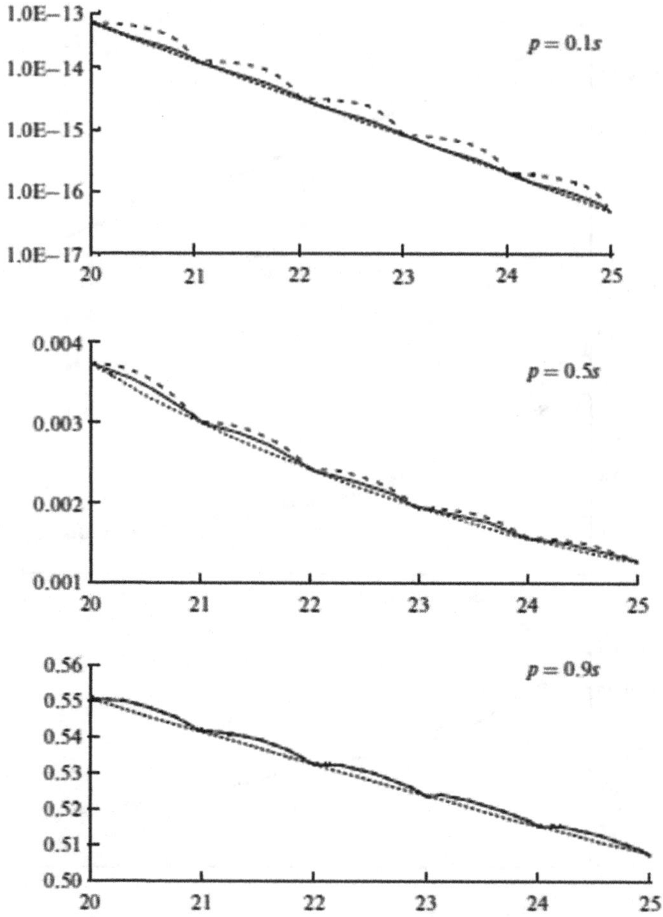

Fig. 2.8 Probabilities of waiting $D_{R_j(s),s}(\rho)$ for $20 \le s \le 25$, ····· R_1, - - - - R_2, — R_3

References

Borovkov, A.A.: Stochastic Processes in Queueing Theory. Springer-Verlag, New York (1976)

Bretschneider, G. De.: Berechnung von Lettungsgruppen fur Uberfiessenden Verkehr in Fernsprechwahlanlangen. Nachrichtentech. «Zeitschrift» **9**, 533–540 (1956)

Bretschneider, G.: Extension of the equivalent random method to smooth traffics, extension of the equivalent random method to smooth traffics. Proc. 7th Int. Teletraffic Congress, Stockholm (1973)

Cooper, R.: Introduction to queueing theory, 2nd edn. Elsevier North Holland, New York (1981)

Erlang, A.K.: Løsning af nogle problemer fra sandsynlighedsregningen af betydning for de automatiske telefon-centraler. Elektroteknikeren **13**, 5–13 (1917)

Iversen, V.B.: Teletraffic Engineering Handbook. ITU-D SG **2**, 16 (2005)

Jagerman, D.L.: Some properties of the Erlang loss function. Bell Syst. Tech. J. **53**(3), 525–551 (1974)

Jagers, A.A., van Doorn, E.A.: Convexity of functions which are generalizations of the Erlang loss function and the Erlang delay function. SIAM Rev. **33**(2), 281–282 (1991)

Lazowska, E.D., Zahorjan, J., Graham, G.S., Sevcik, K.C.: Quantitative system performance computer system analysis using queuing network models. Prentice-Hall, London (1984)

Martinez, W.L., Martinez, A.R.: Computational statistics handbook with MATLAB. Chapman and Hall, New York (2002)

Naumov, V., Martikainen, O.: Method for throughput maximization of multiclass network with flexible servers. ETLA Discussion papers, The Research Institute of the Finnish Economy, Helsinki, 1261 (2011)

Naumov, V.A.: Calculating the real roots of the equation *ln* z - z + c = 0. Numerical methods and informatics, UDN, Moscow, 31–35 (1988) (in Russian)

Rapp, Y.: Planning of junction network in a multiexchange area. Ericsson Technics **20**, 77–130 (1964)

Whitt, W.: Approximating a point process by a renewal process, I: two basic methods. Oper. Res. **30**(1), 125–147 (1982)

Whitt, W.: Approximating a point process by a renewal process: the view through a queue, an indirect approach. Manage. Sci. **27**(6), 619–636 (1981)

Wilkinson, R.I.: Theories for toll traffic engineering in the USA. Bell Syst. Tech. J. **35**(2), 421–514 (1956)

Chapter 3
Multiservice Loss Networks

Abstract The chapter is devoted to loss network models suitable for performance analysis of multiservice broadband networks. We discuss models of multiservice networks with unicast and multicast communications which allow for product-form stationary state distributions. The models are built step by step: first, we consider each type of communications separately, and then combine them in one model. Recursive algorithms are derived to compute blocking probabilities and other stationary characteristics.

3.1 The Single-Link Network with Unicast Communications

A single-link model is an important special case of the network model introduced in Sect. 1.3. Moreover, as we have seen, efficient computation techniques for single-link performance measures can be used for performance evaluation of the whole network. In this section, we discuss a single-link multiservice loss network with unicast (point-to-point) communications and briefly introduce the well-known Kaufman–Roberts algorithm for computing the model performance measures.

Model Formulation

As previously in Sect. 1.3, consider a network of arbitrary topology consisting of L links. Denote by $\mathcal{L} = \{1, 2, \ldots, L\}$ the set of all links and by C_l the capacity of link l. The network supports several classes of unicast sessions, the set of which we denote by $\mathcal{K} = \{1, 2, \ldots, K\}$. Each class k is characterized by a route $\mathcal{L}_k \subseteq \mathcal{L}$ and a capacity requirement (at all links of the route) d_k.

Let now all the network's links except for link l^* be of unlimited capacity. Then, evaluating the blocking probabilities in the network comes down to considering a system consisting of one link l^* of capacity C_{l^*} with the set of session classes $\mathcal{K}_{l^*}$ whose routes include only link l^*: $\mathcal{L}_k = \{l^*\}$, $k \in \mathcal{K}_{l^*}$. For the sake of brevity, *we henceforth omit* the index l^* and write $C = C_{l^*}$, $\mathcal{K} = \mathcal{K}_{l^*}$.

Similar to Sect. 1.3, we assume the sessions of class k to arrive according to a Poisson process of rate λ_k and their holding times to be exponentially distributed

V. Naumov et al., *Matrix and Analytical Methods for Performance Analysis of Telecommunication Systems*, https://doi.org/10.1007/978-3-030-83132-5_3

with parameter μ_k. Thus, each session class is also characterized by its workload intensity $\rho_k = \lambda_k/\mu_k$. The behavior of the system is described by a CTMC $\mathbf{X}(t) = (X_1(t), ..., X_K(t))$, $t \geq 0$, where $X_k(t)$ is the number of active class k sessions at time t. The state space of the process is

$$\mathcal{X} = \left\{\mathbf{n} \in \{0, 1, 2, ...\}^K : d(\mathbf{n}) \leq \mathrm{C}\right\},$$

where $d(\mathbf{n}) = \sum\limits_{k\in\mathcal{K}} d_k n_k$—the number of busy servers in state $\mathbf{n}$, $\mathbf{n} \in \mathcal{X}$. The system satisfies the condition of Theorem 1.1, and therefore its stationary state distribution is given by (3.1) and (3.2), which we reproduce below for convenience of the reader:

$$p(\mathbf{n}) = \frac{1}{G(\mathcal{X})} \prod_{k\in\mathcal{K}} \frac{\rho_k^{n_k}}{n_k!}, \quad \mathbf{n} \in \mathcal{X}, \tag{3.1}$$

where

$$G(\mathcal{X}) = \sum_{\mathbf{n}\in\mathcal{X}} \prod_{k\in\mathcal{K}} \frac{\rho_k^{n_k}}{n_k!}. \tag{3.2}$$

Making use of the above distribution, we derive expressions for the performance measures of interest. The stationary probability that a class k request is blocked is obtained as the sum of the probabilities of the blocking states belonging to the blocking set

$$\mathcal{B}_k = \{\mathbf{n} \in \mathcal{X} : d(\mathbf{n}) > C - d_k\}, \; k \in \mathcal{K}. \tag{3.3}$$

An important performance measure of this system is the link utilization, which can be found via the average occupied capacity, see (1.32). Let the random variable δ represent the occupied capacity of a single link of a unicast network. Then the average occupied capacity is given by

$$\mathsf{E}\delta = \sum_{\mathbf{n}\in\mathcal{X}} d(\mathbf{n}) p(\mathbf{n}). \tag{3.4}$$

Now, we can write the expression for the link utilization factor:

$$U = \frac{\mathsf{E}\delta}{C}. \tag{3.5}$$

The above single-link model is well known in teletraffic theory and is referred to as the basic stochastic knapsack, or the multiservice Erlang's loss system (see e.g., Ross 1995).

Kaufman–Roberts Algorithm

For the single-link model with unicast connections, the exact values of the blocking probabilities and link utilization can be efficiently computed via the Kaufman–Roberts recursive algorithm (Kaufman 1981; Roberts 1981). The algorithm is based upon partitioning the state space according to the occupied capacity, i.e.,

$$\mathcal{C}(n) = \{\mathbf{n} \in \mathcal{X} : d(\mathbf{n}) = n\}, \; n = 0, \ldots, C,$$
$$\mathcal{X} = \bigcup_{n=0}^{C} \mathcal{C}(n); \quad \mathcal{C}(i) \cap \mathcal{C}(j) = \varnothing, \; i \neq j. \tag{3.6}$$

It has been found that the stationary probabilities of the number of occupied capacity units

$$P(n) = \mathrm{P}(\mathbf{n} \in \mathcal{C}(n)) = \sum_{\mathbf{n} \in \mathcal{C}(n)} p(\mathbf{n}) \tag{3.7}$$

are related by the recursion

$$nP(n) = \sum_{k=1}^{K} d_k \rho_k P(n - d_k), \; n = 0, \ldots, C. \tag{3.8}$$

These recursive relations permit deriving a simple and efficient algorithm for computing the measures of interest. Let

$$h(n) = \begin{cases} 0, \; n < 0; \\ 1, \; n = 0; \\ \dfrac{1}{n} \displaystyle\sum_{k=1}^{K} d_k \rho_k h(n - d_k), \; n = 1, \ldots, C. \end{cases} \tag{3.9}$$

Now, the normalization constant (3.2) of the single-link stationary state distribution can be computed as

$$G(\mathcal{X}) = \sum_{n=0}^{C} h(n). \tag{3.10}$$

The blocking probability of a class k request can be obtained as

$$B_k = \frac{\sum\limits_{n=C-d_k+1}^{C} h(n)}{G(\mathcal{X})}, \quad k \in \mathcal{K}. \tag{3.11}$$

The average occupied capacity (3.4) can be computed as

$$\mathsf{E}\delta = \frac{\sum_{n=1}^{C} n \cdot h(n)}{G(\mathcal{X})}. \tag{3.12}$$

If we calculate the normalization constant by (3.10) and compute the function (3.9) recursively, then the computational complexity is of order $O(CK^C)$. If, instead of recursion, we compute the intermediate values of (3.9) successively and store them, then the time complexity is of order $O(CK)$, and hence the time needed to compute the performance measures of the model grows linearly with the capacity of the link.

3.2 The Multiservice Network with Multicast Communications

This section is largely based upon (Gaidamaka and Samouylov 2001) and addresses CTMC modeling of multiservice networks with point-to-multipoint communications (Karvo 2001). We build a model of a multicast network and derive its stationary distribution in an explicit product form. Then, we discuss the analysis of a single link of such a network and derive a recursive algorithm for computing its performance measures.

A Multicast Multiservice Loss Network

Definitions and Notation

We consider a multicast network with multiple data sources and data users, both of which may be connected to any of the network nodes (Gaidamaka and Samouylov 2001, Karvo 2001). Each source provides a finite number of services and sends data to users upon their request. Each network session forms a tree with root at the source's node and leaves at the users' nodes. We refer to such a session as a multicast tree.

The following network model was proposed in (Gaidamaka and Samouylov 2001). We will adopt the same approach later in Sect. 3.3 for modeling a network with unicast and multicast sessions and the following notation will be used throughout both sections. Note that, for the sake of clarity, we write the link number as an upper index.

We will call a *physical path* the sequence of network links from user to source, and denote by.

$\mathcal{L} = \{1, ..., L\}$ the set of all network links;

$\mathcal{S} = \{1, ..., S\}$ the set of all data sources;

$\mathcal{P}_s = \{1, ..., P_s\}$ the set of physical paths to source $s \in \mathcal{S}$;

$\mathcal{M}_s = \{1, ..., M_s\}$ the set of services provided by source $s \in \mathcal{S}$;

$\mathcal{L}_{ps} \subseteq \mathcal{L}$ the set of links of physical path $p \in \mathcal{P}_s$ to source $s \in \mathcal{S}$;

$\mathcal{S}^l = \{s \in \mathcal{S} : \mathcal{P}_s^l \neq \varnothing\}$ the set of sources that provide services through link $l \in \mathcal{L}$;

b_{ms} the capacity required for service $m \in \mathcal{M}_s$;

$\mathcal{P}_s^l = \{p \in \mathcal{P}_s : l \in \mathcal{L}_{ps}\}$ the set of physical paths to source $s \in \mathcal{S}^l$ that use link $l \in \mathcal{L}$;

C_l the capacity of link $l \in \mathcal{L}$.

An example of a multicast network is depicted in Fig. 3.1. The network consists of five links, i.e., $\mathcal{L} = \{1, ..., 5\}$. It has two data sources, $\mathcal{S} = \{1, 2\}$ (cylinders), and four users *a*, *b*, *c*, *d* (triangles). There are physical paths to source 1 from each user, $\mathcal{P}_1 = \{1, ..., 4\}$, such that $\mathcal{L}_{11} = \{2, 1\}$, $\mathcal{L}_{21} = \{3, 1\}$, $\mathcal{L}_{31} = \{4, 3, 1\}$ and $\mathcal{L}_{41} = \{5, 3, 1\}$ (see Fig. 3.2a).

Three paths lead to source 2, since we can consider that user *b* is connected to source 2 directly and and does not use the capacity of network links, thus $\mathcal{P}_2 = \{1, 2, 3\}$ and $\mathcal{L}_{12} = \{2, 3\}$, $\mathcal{L}_{22} = \{4\}$, (see Fig. 3.2b).

Finally, if we look, for instance, at link 3, we see that it has two physical paths to source 1 (from users *c* and *d*) $\mathcal{P}_1^3 = \{3, 4\}$, and one path to source 2, $\mathcal{P}_2^3 = \{1\}$. The multicast trees from each source are depicted in Fig. 3.3.

We refer to the pair (m, s), $m \in \mathcal{M}_s$, $s \in \mathcal{S}$, as a service (m, s) and suppose that service (m, s) requires b_{ms} capacity units on each link of physical path $p \in \mathcal{P}_s$. The

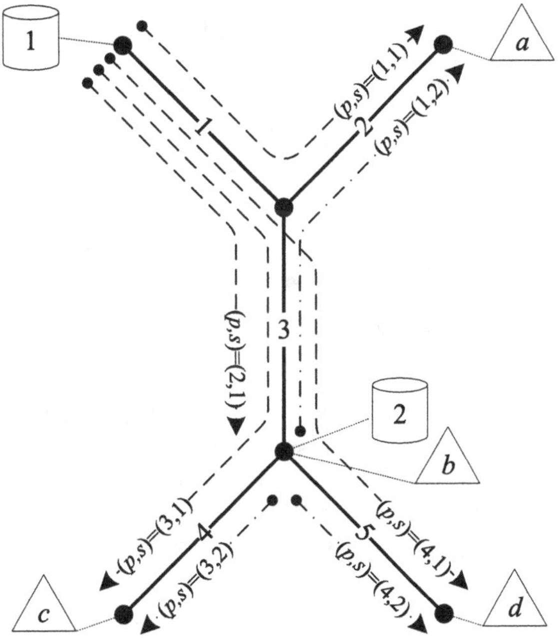

Fig. 3.1 An example of a multicast network

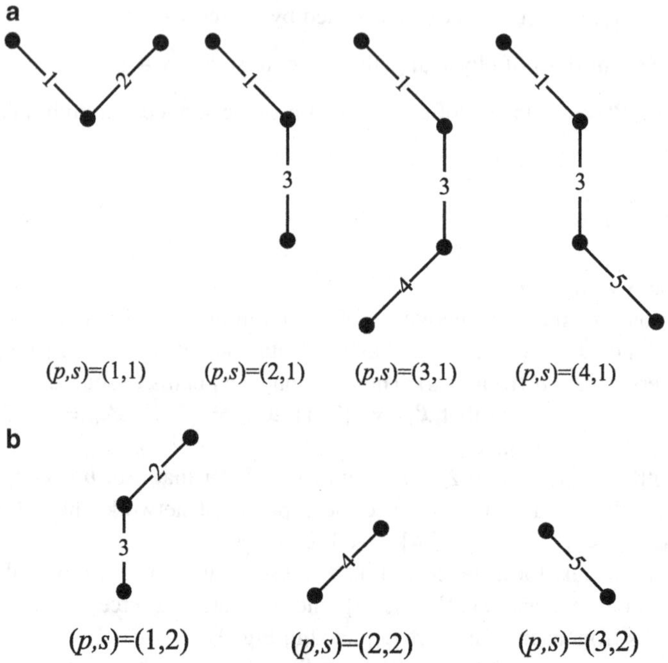

Fig. 3.2 **a** The physical paths to the source 1 in the network of Fig. 3.1. **b** The physical paths to the source 2 in the network of Fig. 3.1

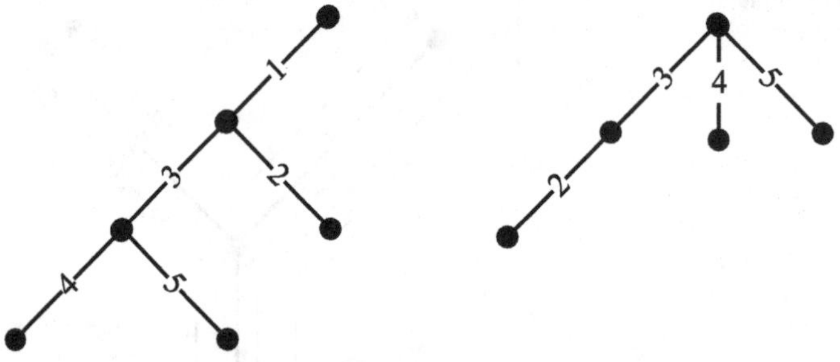

Fig. 3.3 Examples of multicast trees

triple (m, p, s), $m \in \mathcal{M}_s$, $p \in \mathcal{P}_s$, $s \in S$, is called a *logical path*, or simply a *path* (m, p, s). We denote the state of a logical path by x_{mps} and let $x_{mps} = 1$ whenever service (m, s) is being provided to the user linked to source s by physical path p; otherwise, we let $x_{mps} = 0$. Now, we can describe the state of all logical paths in the network by an S-tuple of matrices $\mathbf{x} = (\mathbf{X}_1, ..., \mathbf{X}_s, ..., \mathbf{X}_S)$, where a matrix

$$\mathbf{X}_s = \begin{pmatrix} x_{11s} & \dots & x_{1P_s s} \\ \dots & & \dots \\ x_{M_s 1s} & \dots & x_{M_s P_s s} \end{pmatrix}$$

specifies a detailed state of all logical paths to source $s \in S$. The set of all possible such matrices is denoted by $\widetilde{\mathcal{X}} = \{0, 1\}^{\sum_{s \in S} M_s P_s}$.

State Space and Stationary State Distribution

For each link $l \in \mathcal{L}$, source $s \in S^l$ and network state $\mathbf{x} \in \widetilde{\mathcal{X}}$ we define a function $y^l_{ms}(\mathbf{x}) = H\left(\sum_{p \in \mathcal{P}^l_s} x_{mps}\right)$, which represents the state of service (m, s) on link l. Here $H(a) = \begin{cases} 1, & a > 0 \\ 0, & a \le 0 \end{cases}$ is the Heaviside step function.

Denote by $\mathbf{y}^l(\mathbf{x}) = \left(y^l_{ms}(\mathbf{x})\right)_{m \in \mathcal{M}_s, s \in S^l}$ the state of all services on link l when the logical paths of the network are in state $\mathbf{x} \in \widetilde{\mathcal{X}}$. For $l \in \mathcal{L}$, we define

$$b_l(\mathbf{x}) = \sum_{s \in S^l} \sum_{m \in \mathcal{M}_s} b_{ms} y^l_{ms}(\mathbf{x}), \quad \mathbf{x} \in \widetilde{\mathcal{X}}, \tag{3.13}$$

which represents the number of capacity units occupied on link l whenever the network is in state $\mathbf{x}$. Now, the state space of the network is given by

$$\mathcal{X} = \{\mathbf{x} : b_l(\mathbf{x}) \le C_l,\ l \in \mathcal{L}\}. \tag{3.14}$$

Figure 3.4 depicts the functioning of a logical path (m, p, s) and shows its "life cycles", which include two phases: "on" $\left(x_{mps} = 1\right)$ and "off" $\left(x_{mps} = 0\right)$.

We model the behavior of the network under the simplest assumptions with regard to the logical path's functioning. Let all the logical paths be independent of each other and suppose that requests for establishing path (m, p, s) form a Poisson process with rate λ_{mps}, while its holding time is a random variable exponentially distributed with parameter μ_{mps}.

We represent the behavior of path (m, p, s) by a loss system $M|M|1|1$ with Poisson arrivals of intensity λ_{mps}, exponential service of intensity μ_{mps} and "transparent" customers (Rykov and Samouylov 2000). In such a system, an arrived customer that finds the server free (the logical path is "off") initiates an "on" phase and receives service for the duration of its service time, which also determines the duration of

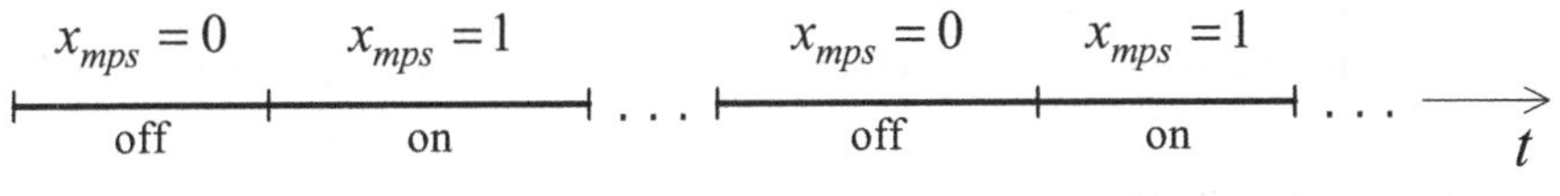

Fig. 3.4 Logical path's functioning

the "on" phase. Any other customer arriving during the "on" phase is neither lost nor put to waiting, but receives service alongside the customer that has initiated the "on" phase. Once the customer that initiated the "on" phase completes service, all the "transparent" customers, which have joined service during this "on" phase, complete their service and depart the system simultaneously. Upon their departure an "off" phase begins.

Let $\xi_{mps}(t)$ represent the number of customers in the system at time $t \geq 0$. The stochastic process $\xi_{mps}(t)$ is a CTMC and, for any $\lambda_{mps} > 0$ and $\mu_{mps} > 0$, possesses a stationary distribution

$$\pi_n = \lim_{t\to\infty} \mathsf{P}\big(\xi_{mps}(t) = n\big), \; n \geq 0,$$

given by

$$\pi_n = \frac{1}{1+\rho_{mps}}\left(\frac{\rho_{mps}}{1+\rho_{mps}}\right)^n, \quad n \geq 0,$$

where

$$\rho_{mps} = \lambda_{mps}/\mu_{mps}. \tag{3.15}$$

Let a CTMC $X_{mps}(t),\; t \geq 0$ represent the state of path (m, p, s) and denote its stationary distribution by

$$p_{mps}\big(x_{mps}\big) = \lim_{t\to\infty} \mathsf{P}\big(X_{mps}(t) = x_{mps}\big), \; x_{mps} \in \{0, 1\}.$$

This distribution is related to the distribution of $\xi_{mps}(t)$ and is given by

$$p_{mps}(0) = \pi_0 = \frac{1}{1+\rho_{mps}},$$
$$p_{mps}(1) = \sum_{n\geq 1} \pi_n = \frac{\rho_{mps}}{1+\rho_{mps}}.$$

Note that the stationary distribution of $X_{mps}(t)$ satisfies the detailed balance equations

$$p_{mps}(0)\lambda_{mps} = p_{mps}(1)\mu_{mps},$$

and the CTMC $X_{mps}(t)$ is hence reversible.

To describe the state of all logical paths, we introduce a multivariate CTMC $\tilde{X}(t) = \big(X_{mps}(t)\big)_{m\in\mathcal{M}_s, p\in\mathcal{P}_s, s\in\mathcal{S}}$, which is reversible by construction on the state space $\widetilde{\mathcal{X}}$ and has a stationary distribution given by

$$\tilde{p}(\mathbf{x}) = \prod_{s\in\mathcal{S}} \prod_{p\in\mathcal{P}_s} \prod_{m\in\mathcal{M}_s} p_{mps}(x_{mps}), \quad \mathbf{x} \in \widetilde{\mathcal{X}}.$$

Note that

$$\tilde{p}(\mathbf{0}) = \prod_{s\in\mathcal{S}} \prod_{p\in\mathcal{P}_s} \prod_{m\in\mathcal{M}_s} \frac{1}{1+\rho_{mps}}.$$

Now, to describe the behavior of a network with limited link capacities, we truncate the CTMC above to the state space $\mathcal{X}$. Let $X(t)$ represent the CTMC $\tilde{X}(t)$ truncated to the set $\mathcal{X} \subseteq \widetilde{\mathcal{X}}$ given by (3.14).

Theorem 3.1 *The stationary distribution* $p(\mathbf{x}) = \lim_{t\to\infty} \mathsf{P}(X(t) = \mathbf{x})$ *of the CTMC* $X(t), t \geq 0$, *has the product form*

$$p(\mathbf{x}) = p(\mathbf{0}) \prod_{s\in\mathcal{S}} \prod_{p\in\mathcal{P}_s} \prod_{m\in\mathcal{M}_s} \rho_{mps}^{x_{mps}}, \ \mathbf{x} \in \mathcal{X},$$

$$p^{-1}(\mathbf{0}) = \sum_{\mathbf{x}\in\mathcal{X}} \prod_{s\in\mathcal{S}} \prod_{p\in\mathcal{P}_s} \prod_{m\in\mathcal{M}_s} \rho_{mps}^{x_{mps}}. \tag{3.16}$$

Proof It follows from the fundamental property of truncated reversible CTMCs (Kelly 2011) that for any state $\mathbf{r}$ of $X(t)$, we have.

$$p(\mathbf{r}) = \frac{\tilde{p}(\mathbf{r})}{\sum\limits_{\mathbf{x}\in\mathcal{X}} \tilde{p}(\mathbf{x})} = \frac{\prod\limits_{s\in\mathcal{S}} \prod\limits_{p\in\mathcal{P}_s} \prod\limits_{m\in\mathcal{M}_s} p_{mps}(r_{mps})}{\sum\limits_{\mathbf{x}\in\mathcal{X}} \prod\limits_{s\in\mathcal{S}} \prod\limits_{p\in\mathcal{P}_s} \prod\limits_{m\in\mathcal{M}_s} p_{mps}(x_{mps})} =$$

$$= \frac{\prod\limits_{s\in\mathcal{S}} \prod\limits_{p\in\mathcal{P}_s} \prod\limits_{m\in\mathcal{M}_s} \frac{\rho_{mps}^{r_{mps}}}{1+\rho_{mps}}}{\sum\limits_{x\in\mathcal{X}} \prod\limits_{s\in\mathcal{S}} \prod\limits_{p\in\mathcal{P}_s} \prod\limits_{m\in\mathcal{M}_s} \frac{\rho_{mps}^{x_{mps}}}{1+\rho_{mps}}} = \frac{\prod\limits_{s\in\mathcal{S}} \prod\limits_{p\in\mathcal{P}_s} \prod\limits_{m\in\mathcal{M}_s} \rho_{mps}^{r_{mps}}}{\sum\limits_{x\in\mathcal{X}} \prod\limits_{s\in\mathcal{S}} \prod\limits_{p\in\mathcal{P}_s} \prod\limits_{m\in\mathcal{M}_s} \rho_{mps}^{x_{mps}}} =$$

$$= p(\mathbf{0}) \prod_{s\in\mathcal{S}} \prod_{p\in\mathcal{P}_s} \prod_{m\in\mathcal{M}_s} \rho_{mps}^{r_{mps}}, \quad \mathbf{r} \in \mathcal{X}.$$

■

Performance Measures

Having found the stationary distribution, we can derive the performance measures of interest. For any subset $\Omega \subseteq \mathcal{X}$, we define a function $G(\Omega)$ as follows

$$G(\Omega) = \sum_{\mathbf{x}\in\Omega} \prod_{s\in\mathcal{S}} \prod_{p\in\mathcal{P}_s} \prod_{m\in\mathcal{M}_s} \rho_{mps}^{x_{mps}}. \tag{3.17}$$

Now, the normalization constant of the distribution (3.16) can be rewritten as

$$p^{-1}(\mathbf{0}) = G(\mathcal{X}).$$

Furthermore, we can use $G(\Omega)$ to express many important performance measures that represent probabilities of events as

$$\mathsf{P}(\mathbf{x} \in \Omega) = \sum_{\mathbf{x} \in \Omega} p(\mathbf{x}) = \frac{G(\Omega)}{G(\mathcal{X})}, \Omega \subseteq \mathcal{X}. \tag{3.18}$$

Among such measures are blocking probabilities and some others, which we will address now.

Let $\mathcal{B}_{mps}$ represent the set of blocking states for path (m, p, s), i.e., the subset of model states in which a request for service (m, s) via physical path $p \in \mathcal{P}_s$ is blocked due to a lack of capacity on the links. In a multicast network for a request to be blocked two conditions must hold simultaneously: first, on one or more links of the corresponding physical path the available capacity must be smaller than b_{ms} and, second, the requested service (m, s) must not be provided via such link to other users. Therefore, the set of blocking states for path (m, p, s) is given by

$$\mathcal{B}_{mps} = \left\{\mathbf{x} \in \mathcal{X} : \exists l \in \mathcal{L}_{ps} : y^l_{ms}(\mathbf{x}) = 0,\ b_l(\mathbf{x}) + b_{ms} > C_l\right\}. \tag{3.19}$$

The corresponding probability $B_{mps} = \mathsf{P}\left(\mathbf{x} \in \mathcal{B}_{mps}\right)$ can be obtained by formula (3.18).

Besides the blocking probabilities, one may be interested in the probability that the service is being provided to the user, and the probability that the service is not provided, yet there is enough capacity for its initialization upon a request. Define for any triple (m, p, s), $m \in \mathcal{M}_s$, $p \in \mathcal{P}_s$, $s \in \mathcal{S}$, events

$$\mathcal{F}_{mps} = \left\{\mathbf{x} \in \mathcal{X} : x_{mps} = 1\right\} \tag{3.20}$$

and

$$\mathcal{H}_{mps} = \left\{\mathbf{x} \in \mathcal{X} : x_{mps} = 0, \forall l \in \mathcal{L}_{ps} b_l(\mathbf{x}) + b_{ms} \le C_l \vee y^l_{ms}(\mathbf{x}) = 1\right\}, \tag{3.21}$$

where $\vee$ denotes logical "or". The corresponding probabilities $F_{mps} = \mathsf{P}\left(\mathbf{x} \in \mathcal{F}_{mps}\right)$ and $H_{mps} = \mathsf{P}\left(\mathbf{x} \in \mathcal{H}_{mps}\right)$ can also be obtained by (3.18). The former is the probability that path (m, p, s) is "on", while the latter is the probability that path (m, p, s) if "off", yet there is enough capacity in the network to switch it "on" if a request arrives.

One checks easily that for, any path (m, p, s), the sets $\mathcal{B}_{mps}$, $\mathcal{F}_{mps}$ and $\mathcal{H}_{mps}$ form a partitioning of the state space $\mathcal{X}$, and therefore the corresponding probabilities sum to 1:

$$B_{mps} + F_{mps} + H_{mps} = 1. \tag{3.22}$$

Lemma 3.1 *For all* (m, p, s), $m \in \mathcal{M}_s$, $p \in \mathcal{P}_s$, $s \in S$, *we have*

$$F_{mps} = \rho_{mps} H_{mps}. \tag{3.23}$$

Proof Let us fix some triple $(\hat{m}, \hat{p}, \hat{s})$, $\hat{m} \in \mathcal{M}_{\hat{s}}$, $\hat{p} \in \mathcal{P}_{\hat{s}}$, $\hat{s} \in S$. By definition of $\mathcal{H}_{mps}$, $x_{\hat{m}\hat{p}\hat{s}} = 0$ for all $\mathbf{x} \in \mathcal{H}_{\hat{m}\hat{p}\hat{s}}$, and for any $l \in \mathcal{L}_{\hat{p}\hat{s}}$, we have

$$\tilde{c} = \sum_{s \in S^l \setminus \{\hat{s}\}} \sum_{m \in \mathcal{M}_s} b_{ms} y^l_{ms}(\mathbf{x}) + \sum_{m \in \mathcal{M}_{\hat{s}} \setminus \{\hat{m}\}} b_{m\hat{s}} y^l_{m\hat{s}}(\mathbf{x}) \le C_l - b_{\hat{m}\hat{s}}.$$

The left-hand side of the inequality above, which we denote by $\tilde{c}$, gives the capacity of link l occupied in state $\mathbf{x}$ not including service $(\hat{m}, \hat{s})$, i.e., $b_l(\mathbf{x}) = \tilde{c}$ if $y^l_{\hat{m}\hat{s}}(\mathbf{x}) = 0$, and $b_l(\mathbf{x}) = \tilde{c} + b_{\hat{m}\hat{s}}$ otherwise.

For any $\mathbf{x} \in \mathcal{H}_{\hat{m}\hat{p}\hat{s}}$, the state $\mathbf{x}' = \left(\mathbf{x} + \mathbf{e}_{\hat{m}\hat{p}\hat{s}}\right)$ belongs to $\mathcal{F}_{\hat{m}\hat{p}\hat{s}}$ (here $\mathbf{e}_{\hat{m}\hat{p}\hat{s}}$ represents a vector whose $(\hat{m}, \hat{p}, \hat{s})$-th entry is 1 and all others are 0). Indeed, $x'_{\hat{m}\hat{p}\hat{s}} = 1$, while for all $l \in \mathcal{L} \setminus \mathcal{L}_{\hat{p}\hat{s}}$, we have $b_l(\mathbf{x}') = b_l(\mathbf{x})$, and for all $l \in \mathcal{L}_{\hat{p}\hat{s}}$, we have

$$\begin{aligned} b_l(\mathbf{x}') &= \sum_{s \in S^l \setminus \{\hat{s}\}} \sum_{m \in \mathcal{M}_s} b_{ms} y^l_{ms}(\mathbf{x}) + \sum_{m \in \mathcal{M}_{\hat{s}} \setminus \{\hat{m}\}} b_{m\hat{s}} y^l_{m\hat{s}}(\mathbf{x}) + b_{\hat{m}\hat{s}} \\ &= \tilde{c} + b_{\hat{m}\hat{s}} \le C_l. \end{aligned}$$

Conversely, for any $\mathbf{x}' \in \mathcal{F}_{\hat{m}\hat{p}\hat{s}}$, we can find $\mathbf{x} \in \mathcal{H}_{\hat{m}\hat{p}\hat{s}}$ such that $\mathbf{x}' = \left(\mathbf{x} + \mathbf{e}_{\hat{m}\hat{p}\hat{s}}\right)$. Thus, the mapping $\mathbf{x}' = \varphi_{\hat{m}\hat{p}\hat{s}}(\mathbf{x}) = \left(\mathbf{x} + \mathbf{e}_{\hat{m}\hat{p}\hat{s}}\right)$ is one-to-one from $\mathcal{H}_{\hat{m}\hat{p}\hat{s}}$ onto $\mathcal{F}_{\hat{m}\hat{p}\hat{s}}$.

Turning to probabilities, we have for all $\mathbf{x}' \in \mathcal{F}_{\hat{m}\hat{p}\hat{s}}$

$$\begin{aligned} p(\mathbf{x}') = G^{-1}(\mathcal{X}) &\prod_{s \in S \setminus \{\hat{s}\}} \prod_{p \in \mathcal{P}} \prod_{m \in \mathcal{M}_s} \rho_{mps}^{x_{mps}} \prod_{p \in \mathcal{P}_{\hat{s}} \setminus \{\hat{p}\}} \prod_{m \in \mathcal{M}_{\hat{s}}} \rho_{mp\hat{s}}^{x_{mp\hat{s}}} \times \\ \times &\prod_{m \in \mathcal{M}_{\hat{s}} \setminus \{\hat{m}\}} \rho_{m\hat{p}\hat{s}}^{x_{m\hat{p}\hat{s}}} \rho_{\hat{m}\hat{p}\hat{s}} = \rho_{\hat{m}\hat{p}\hat{s}}\, p(\mathbf{x}), \end{aligned}$$

where $\mathbf{x} = \left(\mathbf{x}' - \mathbf{e}_{\hat{m}\hat{p}\hat{s}}\right) \in \mathcal{H}_{\hat{m}\hat{p}\hat{s}}$, and finally

$$\begin{aligned} F_{\hat{m}\hat{p}\hat{s}} &= \sum_{\mathbf{x}' \in \mathcal{F}_{\hat{m}\hat{p}\hat{s}}} p(\mathbf{x}') = \sum_{\mathbf{x} \in \mathcal{H}_{\hat{m}\hat{p}\hat{s}}} p\left(\mathbf{x} + \mathbf{e}_{\hat{m}\hat{p}\hat{s}}\right) \\ &= \rho_{\hat{m}\hat{p}\hat{s}} \sum_{\mathbf{x} \in \mathcal{H}_{\hat{m}\hat{p}\hat{s}}} p(\mathbf{x}) = \rho_{\hat{m}\hat{p}\hat{s}} H_{\hat{m}\hat{p}\hat{s}}. \end{aligned}$$

■

Corollary *For any path* (m, p, s), $m \in \mathcal{M}_s$, $p \in \mathcal{P}_s$, $s \in S$, *we have*

$$F_{mps} = \frac{\rho_{mps}}{1 + \rho_{mps}} \left(1 - B_{mps}\right). \tag{3.24}$$

Proof To prove the result, it suffices to use Lemma 3.1 and relation (3.22). ■

A Single-Link Model

Model Formulation

Consider now a multicast network such that for some link $l^* \in \mathcal{L}$ the following relations hold:

$$\sum_{s \in \mathcal{S}^{l^*}} \sum_{m \in \mathcal{M}_s} b_{ms} > C_{l^*},$$

$$\sum_{s \in \mathcal{S}^{l}} \sum_{m \in \mathcal{M}_s} b_{ms} \le C_l, \quad l \in \mathcal{L} \backslash \{l^*\}.$$

This means that all links but l^* have unlimited capacity and we deal with a single-link network. Clearly, the analysis of blocking in a single-link multicast network comes down to analyzing a network that consists of one link $\mathcal{L} = \{l^*\}$ and has one data source $\left(\left|\mathcal{S}^{l^*}\right| = 1\right)$ with the set of services $\mathcal{M} = \bigcup_{s \in \mathcal{S}^{l^*}} \mathcal{M}_s$. Henceforth we omit indices l^* and s for brevity and write $C = C_{l^*}$, $\mathcal{P} = \mathcal{P}^{l^*}$.

We model a single link of a multicast network as a multiclass loss system with C servers. The customers of $M = |\mathcal{M}|$ classes arrive according to M mutually independent Poisson processes with the respective rates $\lambda_1, \ldots, \lambda_M$. If a newly arrived class m customer finds no customers of its class in service then it receives service if there are b_m capacity units free. This capacity will then be allocated to the customer for its service time, which is exponentially distributed with parameter μ_m and independent of the arrival and service times of other classes. All class m customers that arrive during this time interval receive service without allocation of additional capacity and depart the system together once the service time is over; b_m capacity units are then released. An arriving class m customer is lost if it finds no customers of its class in service and less than b_m capacity units available.

Denote $\rho_m = \frac{\lambda_m}{\mu_m}$. As established in Gaidamaka and Samouylov (2001), $\rho_1, \ldots, \rho_M$ are related to the parameters of the corresponding logical paths as follows:

$$\rho_m = \prod_{p \in \mathcal{P}} (1 + \rho_{mp}) - 1, \quad m = 1, \ldots, M, \tag{3.25}$$

where ρ_{mp} is defined as in (3.15) with omitted index s for a network with a single source $\left|\mathcal{S}^{l^*}\right| = 1$.

Let $C = \infty$. In such case, all arriving customers receive service, and no blocking occurs. Let a stochastic process $Y_m(t)$, $t \ge 0$, $m = 1, \ldots, M$, be in state 1 if at time t there is at least one m class customer in service, and in state 0 otherwise. Similar to the CTMC $X_{mps}(t)$ introduced previously, $Y_m(t)$ is a reversible CTMC and has a stationary distribution given by

$$p_m(y_m) = \lim_{t\to\infty} \mathsf{P}(Y_m(t) = y_m) = \frac{\rho_m^{y_m}}{1+\rho_m}, \quad y_m \in \{0, 1\}. \tag{3.26}$$

Consider now the multivariate CTMC $\widetilde{\mathbf{Y}}(t) = (Y_m(t))_{m\in\mathcal{M}},\ t \geq 0$, taking values in the set $\widetilde{\mathcal{Y}} = \{0, 1\}^M$. It is reversible on this set by construction, and it follows from (3.26) that its stationary distribution is given by

$$\tilde{p}(\mathbf{y}) = G^{-1}(\widetilde{\mathcal{Y}}) \prod_{m=1}^{M} \rho_m^{y_m}, \quad \mathbf{y} \in \widetilde{\mathcal{Y}}, \tag{3.27}$$

where $G(\Omega)$ for any $\Omega \subseteq \widetilde{\mathcal{Y}}$ is

$$G(\Omega) = \sum_{\mathbf{y}\in\Omega} \prod_{m=1}^{M} \rho_m^{y_m}. \tag{3.28}$$

It follows from (3.28) that the normalization constant $G(\widetilde{\mathcal{Y}})$ of the distribution of $\widetilde{\mathcal{Y}}(t)$ is given by

$$G(\widetilde{\mathcal{Y}}) = \prod_{m=1}^{M} (1+\rho_m). \tag{3.29}$$

The CTMC $\widetilde{\mathbf{Y}}(t)$ on state space $\widetilde{\mathcal{Y}}$ with the distribution (3.27) describes the behavior of the system for $C = \infty$. Now let $C < \infty$ and hence blocking may occur. We assume that lost customers do not affect the intensity of any arrival process. The behavior of the system is then modeled by a CTMC $\mathbf{Y}(t),\ t \geq 0$, that represents truncated to the set

$$\mathcal{Y} = \{\mathbf{y} \in \widetilde{\mathcal{Y}} : b(\mathbf{y}) \leq C\}, \tag{3.30}$$

where $b(\mathbf{y}) = \sum_{m=1}^{M} b_m y_m$ is the occupied capacity in state $\mathbf{y} \in \widetilde{\mathcal{Y}}$. Since $\mathbf{Y}(t)$ results from truncating a reversible CTMC, it is also reversible, and therefore the following result holds.

Theorem 3.2 *The stationary state distribution of the CTMC $\mathbf{Y}(t),\ t \geq 0$, is of the product form*

$$p(\mathbf{y}) = G^{-1}\mathcal{Y}) \prod_{m=1}^{M} \rho_m^{y_m}, \quad \mathbf{y} \in \mathcal{Y}, \tag{3.31}$$

where $G(\mathcal{Y})$ is the normalization constant

$$G(\mathcal{Y}) = \sum_{\mathbf{y}\in\mathcal{Y}} \prod_{m=1}^{M} \rho_m^{y_m}. \tag{3.32}$$

Performance Measures

Similar to the multi-link network model, the performance measures of a single link can be expressed by using the function $G(\Omega)$ of the corresponding subset of states via the formula (3.18). Among these measures, we find the probability that a customer is blocked, the probability that there is a class m customer in the system, and the probability that there are no m class customers in the system but such a customer will receive service if it arrives.

Recall that the condition for an arriving customer to be lost is twofold: insufficient capacity and the absence of customers of the same class already in service. Therefore, the set of blocking state for class m customers is given by

$$\mathcal{B}_m = \{\mathbf{y} \in \mathcal{Y} : b(\mathbf{y}) + b_m > C,\ y_m = 0\}. \tag{3.33}$$

The set of states in which there are class m customers in service is

$$\mathcal{F}_m = \{\mathbf{y} \in \mathcal{Y} : y_m = 1\}, \tag{3.34}$$

while the set of states in which there are no class m customers in service, but an arriving class m customer will receive service, is given by

$$\mathcal{H}_m = \{\mathbf{y} \in \mathcal{Y} : b(\mathbf{y}) + b_m \le C,\ y_m = 0\}. \tag{3.35}$$

The former event represents the situation in which the data related to service m is being sent over the link under analysis. The latter event is when service m is not being provided but there are enough resources to initiate it upon a user request.

One checks easily that here also for any $m = 1, ..., M$ the sets $\mathcal{B}_m$, $\mathcal{F}_m$ and $\mathcal{H}_m$ constitute a partitioning of the state space $\mathcal{Y}$. The corresponding probabilities hence sum to 1:

$$B_m + F_m + H_m = 1.$$

The following Lemma 3.2 and its Corollary establish an additional relation among these probabilities.

Lemma 3.2 *For any $m = 1, ..., M$ we have*

$$F_m = \rho_m H_m. \tag{3.36}$$

Corollary *For any $m = 1, ..., M$ we have*

$$F_m = \frac{\rho_m}{1+\rho_m}(1 - B_m). \tag{3.37}$$

When analyzing a single link of a multicast network, we are interested in the characteristics of a random variable β representing the occupied capacity in the network link. Then the average occupied capacity can be evaluated as the expectation $\mathsf{E}\beta$ of β, given by

$$\mathsf{E}\beta = \sum_{\mathbf{y}\in\mathcal{Y}} b(\mathbf{y})p(\mathbf{y}). \tag{3.38}$$

Similar to (3.5), $U = \mathsf{E}\beta/C$ represents the link utilization, or utilization factor.

Lemma 3.3 *The average number of busy servers can be computed as*

$$\mathsf{E}\beta = \sum_{m=1}^{M} b_m F_m. \tag{3.39}$$

Proof

$$\sum_{m=1}^{M} b_m F_m = \sum_{m=1}^{M} b_m \sum_{\mathbf{y}\in\mathcal{F}_m} p(\mathbf{y}) = \sum_{m=1}^{M} b_m \sum_{\mathbf{y}\in\mathcal{F}_m} y_m p(\mathbf{y}) =$$

$$= \sum_{m=1}^{M} b_m \left(\sum_{\mathbf{y}\in\mathcal{F}_m} y_m p(\mathbf{y}) + \sum_{\mathbf{y}\in\mathcal{Y}\setminus\mathcal{F}_m} y_m p(\mathbf{y}) \right) =$$

$$= \sum_{m=1}^{M} b_m \sum_{\mathbf{y}\in\mathcal{Y}} y_m p(\mathbf{y}) = \sum_{\mathbf{y}\in\mathcal{Y}} p(\mathbf{y}) \sum_{m=1}^{M} b_m y_m = \sum_{\mathbf{y}\in\mathcal{Y}} b(\mathbf{y})p(\mathbf{y}).$$

■

The next result follows from the relations (3.37) and (3.39).

Lemma 3.4 *The average number of busy servers can be found as*

$$\mathsf{E}\beta = \sum_{m=1}^{M} b_m \frac{\rho_m}{1+\rho_m}(1 - B_m). \tag{3.40}$$

An efficient method for obtaining the above performance measures was proposed in Gaidamaka and Samouylov (2001) and relies upon recursive computation of the normalization constant $G(\mathcal{Y})$.

A Convolution Algorithm

To derive an algorithm for computing the system's performance measures, we first need to explore the properties of $\mathcal{Y}$ and obtain an algorithm for computing the normalization constant $G(\mathcal{Y})$.

For all $m \in \mathcal{M}$ and $n = 0, \ldots, C$, we define the sets

$$\mathcal{Y}(m, n) = \{\mathbf{y}(m) = (y_1, \ldots, y_m) : c(\mathbf{y}(m)) = n\}$$

and extend the definition to $m = 0$ and $n < 0$ as follows:

$$\mathcal{Y}(m, n) = \begin{cases} \mathcal{Y}(m, n), \ m = 1, \ldots, M, \ n = 1, \ldots, C; \\ \{0\}, \ m = 0, \ldots, M, \quad n = 0; \\ \varnothing, \ m = 0, \ n = 1, \ldots, C; \\ \varnothing, \ m = 0, \ldots, M, \ n < 0. \end{cases} \tag{3.41}$$

By construction, $\mathcal{Y}(m, n)$ satisfy

$$\mathcal{Y}(m, n) \cap \mathcal{Y}(m, \tilde{n}) = \varnothing, \ n \neq \tilde{n},$$

for all $m = 0, \ldots, M$, and

$$\mathcal{Y} = \bigcup_{n=0}^{C} \mathcal{Y}(M, n).$$

Furthermore, for all $m = 1, \ldots, M$ and $n = 1, \ldots, C$, the set $\mathcal{Y}(m, n)$ can be expressed as

$$\mathcal{Y}(m, n) = \mathcal{Y}(m-1, n) \times \{0\} \cup \mathcal{Y}(m-1, n-b_m) \times \{1\}. \tag{3.42}$$

We now define a function

$$g(m, n) = \sum_{\mathbf{y}(m) \in \mathcal{Y}(m,n)} \prod_{i=1}^{m} \rho_i^{y_i}$$

and note that

$$G(\mathcal{Y}) = \sum_{n=0}^{C} g(M, n). \tag{3.43}$$

Lemma 3.5 *The function $g(m, n)$ can be computed as*

$$g(m,n)=\begin{cases}0, & m=0,\ n=1,\ \ldots,\ C;\\ 0, & m=0,\ \ldots,\ M,\ n<0;\\ 1, & m=0,\ \ldots,\ M,\ n=0;\\ g(m-1,n)+\rho_m g(m-1,n-b_m), & m=1,\ \ldots,\ M,\ n=1,\ \ldots,\ C.\end{cases} \tag{3.44}$$

Proof The first three rows in (3.44) readily follow from (3.41). We now prove the fourth row. In light of (3.42), we have

$$g(m,n)=\sum_{\mathbf{y}(m)\in\mathcal{Y}(m,n)}\prod_{i=1}^{m}\rho_i^{y_i}=$$

$$=\sum_{\mathbf{y}(m)\in\mathcal{Y}(m-1,n)\times\{0\}}\prod_{i=1}^{m}\rho_i^{y_i}+\sum_{\mathbf{y}(m)\in\mathcal{Y}(m-1,n-b_k)\times\{1\}}\prod_{i=1}^{m}\rho_i^{y_i}=$$

$$=\sum_{\mathbf{y}(m-1)\in\mathcal{Y}(m-1,n)}\prod_{i=1}^{m}\rho_i^{y_i}+\left(\sum_{\mathbf{y}(m-1)\in\mathcal{Y}(m-1,n-b_m)}\prod_{i=1}^{m}\rho_i^{y_i}\right)\rho_m=g(m-1,n)+\rho_m g(m-1,n-b_k).$$

■

Lemma 3.5 along with relation (3.43) defines an algorithm for computing the normalization constant $G(\mathcal{Y})$. Next, the expressions for evaluating the performance measures are derived for the last, M-th service. Generality is not lost since we can always reorder the services so that the service of interest bears number M.

Theorem 3.3 *The stationary performance measures B_M, F_M, H_M and $\mathsf{E}\beta$ of a multicast network link can be computed, respectively, as*

$$B_M=\left(\sum_{n=0}^{C}g(M,n)\right)^{-1}\sum_{n=C-b_M+1}^{C}g(M-1,n), \tag{3.45}$$

$$F_M=\left(\sum_{n=0}^{C}g(M,n)\right)^{-1}\rho_M\sum_{n=0}^{C-b_M}g(M-1,n), \tag{3.46}$$

$$H_M=\left(\sum_{n=0}^{C}g(M,n)\right)^{-1}\sum_{n=0}^{C-b_M}g(M-1,n), \tag{3.47}$$

$$\mathsf{E}\beta=\left(\sum_{n=0}^{C}g(M,n)\right)^{-1}\sum_{n=1}^{C}ng(M,n). \tag{3.48}$$

Proof We only prove (3.45) because the other relations can be proved by a similar argument. The set of blocking states can be written as

$$\mathcal{B}_M = \left\{ \mathbf{y} \in \widetilde{\mathcal{Y}} : C - b_M + 1 \le b(\mathbf{y}) \le C, y_M = 0 \right\} =$$
$$= \{\mathbf{y}(M-1) : C - b_M + 1 \le b(\mathbf{y}(M-1)) \le C\} \times \{0\} \stackrel{not}{=} \widehat{\mathcal{Y}}(M-1) \times \{0\},$$

which yields, using the introduced notation,

$$G(\mathcal{B}_M) = \sum_{\mathbf{y}(M-1)\in\widehat{\mathcal{Y}}(M-1)} \prod_{i=1}^{M-1} \rho_i^{y_i} \cdot 1 = \sum_{n=C-b_M+1}^{C} g(M-1, n).$$

Now, (3.18) and (3.43) yield (3.45).

■

Relations (3.43)–(3.48) define a recursion for computing stationary performance measures of a multicast network link.

3.3 The Multiservice Network with Unicast and Multicast Communications

The straightforward approach to analyzing a network with multicast and unicast communications is to apply a combination of the methods discussed previously. However, one must take into account the more complicated combinatorial structure of the state space, which affects certain aspects of the model. In this chapter we draw on Samouylov and Yarkina (2005), Samouylov et al. (2011) and model a network of arbitrary topology with two types of communications. We derive a recursion for computing performance measures of a tree-shaped network and discuss single-link models and computation techniques.

The Product-Form Stationary State Distribution

Model Formulation

Once again, consider a network of arbitrary topology, which consists of a finite number of nodes connected by links. As in the previous sections, let L denote the total number of links and $\mathcal{L} = \{1, 2, ..., L\}$ represent the set of all links numbered arbitrarily. Denote by C_l the capacity of link. Denote by $\mathcal{S} = \{1, ..., S\}$ the set of all multicast sources and by $\mathcal{M}_s = \{1, ..., M_s\}$ the set of services provided by source s. Let b_{ms} represent the required capacity (in notional capacity units) for service $m \in \mathcal{M}_s$. Denote by $\mathcal{P}_s = \{1, ..., P_s\}$ the set of all physical paths to source s, by $\mathcal{L}_{ps} \subseteq \mathcal{L}$ the set of links that form path p to source s, by $\mathcal{P}_s^l = \{p \in \mathcal{P}_s : l \in \mathcal{L}_{ps}\}$ the set of physical paths to source s that include link l, and by $\mathcal{S}^l = \{s \in \mathcal{S} : \mathcal{P}_s^l \neq \varnothing\}$ the set of sources that provide services over link l.

Unlike multicast communications, unicast sessions may be established between any two network nodes. Denote by $\mathcal{K} = \{1, 2, ..., K\}$ the set of all unicast session classes. As previously, each unicast class is characterized by two parameters: the route, i.e., the set of links over which the session is established, and the required capacity demanded on each route link. Denote by $\mathcal{L}_k \subseteq \mathcal{L}$ the route and by d_k the required capacity of class k session. Finally, let $\mathcal{K}^l = \{k \in \mathcal{K} : l \in \mathcal{L}_k\}$ represent the set of unicast session classes that use link.

An example of such a model is presented in Fig. 3.5, and we will use it to clarify the notation. Here, the network consists of five links, hence $\mathcal{L} = \{1, 2, ..., 5\}$; the capacity of each link is indicated on it. Figure 3.5a shows the parameters of multicast communications. The network has two multicast sources, which are represented by

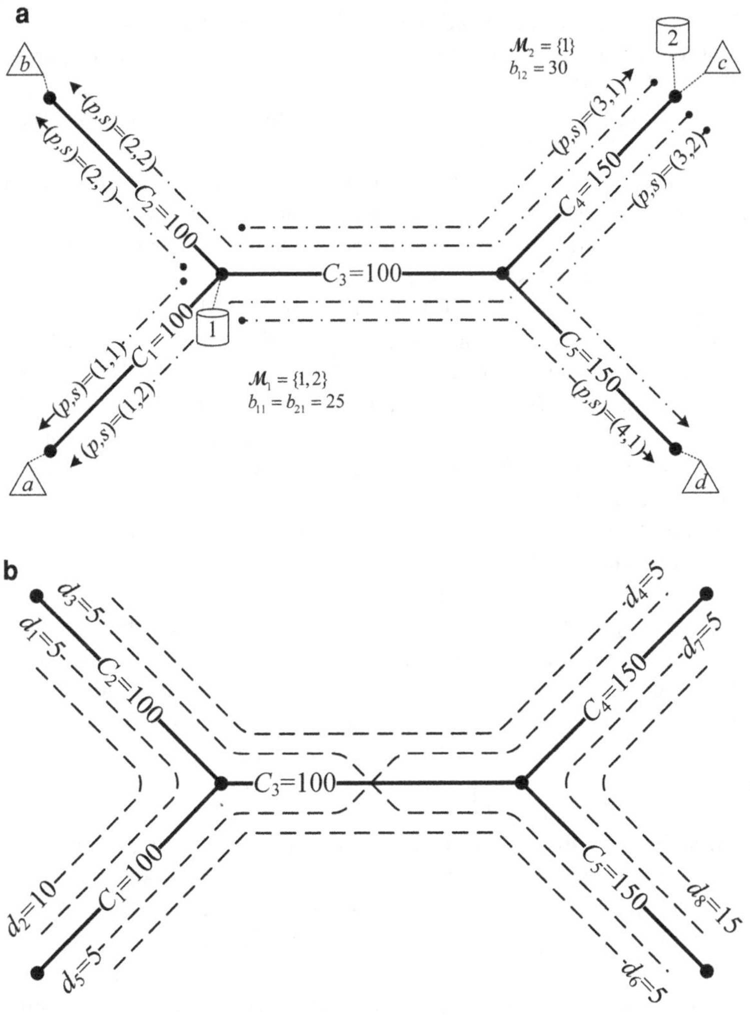

Figure 3.5 **a** The physical paths of the multicast session classes. **b** The routes of the unicast session classes

cylinders, i.e., $\mathcal{S} = \{1, 2\}$, and four user nodes a, b, c, d, which are indicated by triangles. Beside each source, we see the corresponding set of services $\mathcal{M}_s$ and the required capacity for each service, which must be allocated on every link of the corresponding physical path. The physical paths (dash-dotted lines) to source 1 constitute the set $\mathcal{P}_1 = \{1, 2, 3, 4\}$; the sets of their links are $\mathcal{L}_{11} = \{1\}$, $\mathcal{L}_{21} = \{2\}$, $\mathcal{L}_{31} = \{3, 4\}$ and $\mathcal{L}_{41} = \{3, 5\}$. Three physical paths lead to source 2, since we consider user c to be connected to source 2 directly and not by the links of the network. Therefore, we have $\mathcal{P}_2 = \{1, 2, 3\}$, $\mathcal{L}_{12} = \{1, 3, 4\}$, $\mathcal{L}_{22} = \{2, 3, 4\}$ and $\mathcal{L}_{32} = \{4, 5\}$. Finally, if we turn, for instance, to link 3, we see that it is used by two physical paths to source 1, $\mathcal{P}_1^3 = \{3, 4\}$, and two to source 2, $\mathcal{P}_2^3 = \{1, 2\}$.

In Fig. 3.5b, dashed lines represent the routes of the unicast session classes. The required capacity is indicated beside each route. One sees easily that the network has eight classes of unicast sessions, $\mathcal{K} = \{1, 2, ..., 8\}$, with the parameters $\mathcal{L}_1 = \mathcal{L}_2 = \{1, 2\}$, $\mathcal{L}_3 = \{2, 3, 5\}$, etc.; and $d_2 = 10$, $d_8 = 15$ and $d_k = 5$, $k \in \mathcal{K}\backslash\{2, 8\}$. If we turn to link 3 again, we see that the set of unicast session classes that use link 3 is $\mathcal{K}^3 = \{3, 4, 5, 6\}$.

Now we proceed with the model description and make assumptions about the requests for sessions and their duration. We denote the state of path (m, p, s) by $x_{mps} \in \{0, 1\}$ and assume that $x_{mps} = 1$ if source s sends the data corresponding to service m over path p (we say that the path is "on"), and $x_{mps} = 0$ otherwise (in this case we say that the path is "off"). A path can be switched on upon a request if the required resources are available on each link of the route, i.e., on each $l \in \mathcal{L}_{ps}$ either service (m, s) is already being provided to another user (recall the nature of multicasting), or there are b_{ms} capacity units available. Upon session establishment, b_{ms} capacity units are allocated on those links where the service was not being provided. This capacity will be vacated once the service stops being provided on all physical paths going through the link. If upon a request arrival resources are insufficient on at least one link in $\mathcal{L}_{ps}$, then the session establishment is blocked, path (m, p, s) remains "off", and the request is lost.

An arriving request for establishing a unicast session of class k is accepted if it finds d_k capacity units free on each link of the route. Then this capacity gets allocated to the session for its duration and is vacated once the session is terminated. If upon the request arrival resources are insufficient on at least one link of the route, then the session establishment is blocked and the request is lost. We denote by n_k the state of class k, which we define as the number of active sessions of this class, $n_k \in \left\{0, 1, 2, ..., \left\lfloor d_k^{-1} \min_{l \in \mathcal{L}_k} C_l \right\rfloor\right\}$.

Finally, we assume that logical paths and unicast classes are all mutually independent. We let the requests for path (m, p, s) form a Poisson process with rate λ_{mps} and the holding time of the path be independent of the arrivals and exponentially distributed with mean μ_{mps}^{-1}, $\rho_{mps} = \lambda_{mps}/\mu_{mps}$. Similarly, we let the requests for class k sessions arrive according to a Poisson process with rate ν_k and the holding times be independent of the arrival epochs and exponentially distributed with mean κ_k^{-1}, $a_k = \frac{\nu_k}{\kappa_k}$.

The State Space and the Stationary State Distribution

Denote the CTMC representing the behavior of path (m, p, s) and class k of unicast sessions respectively by $X_{mps}(t),\ t \geq 0, m \in \mathcal{M}_s, p \in \mathcal{P}_s, s \in \mathcal{S}$, and $N_k(t),\ t \geq 0$, $k \in \mathcal{K}$. One checks easily that in a network with unlimited link capacities, i.e., such that $C_l = \infty, l \in \mathcal{L}$, these CTMC are reversible with the respective stationary state distributions

$$\lim_{t\to\infty} \mathsf{P}\big(X_{mps}(t) = x_{mps}\big) = \frac{\rho_{mps}^{x_{mps}}}{1+\rho_{mps}}, \quad x_{mps} \in \{0, 1\}, \tag{3.49}$$

and

$$\lim_{t\to\infty} \mathsf{P}(N_k(t) = n_k) = \frac{a_k^{n_k}}{n_k!}\mathrm{e}^{-a_k}, \quad n_k \in \{0, 1, 2, \ ...\}. \tag{3.50}$$

The state of the model is determined by the states of all its logical paths and unicast session classes. Consider a multivariate CTMC

$$\tilde{Z}(t) = \Big(\big(X_{mps}(t)\big)_{m\in\mathcal{M}_s, p\in\mathcal{P}_s, s\in\mathcal{S}},\ (N_k(t))_{k\in\mathcal{K}}\Big),\ t \geq 0,$$

which describes the behavior of all sessions in the network, given that the capacities of all links are unlimited. By construction, this CTMC is reversible on the set

$$\widetilde{\mathcal{Z}} = \widetilde{\mathcal{X}} \times \widetilde{\mathcal{N}},\quad \widetilde{\mathcal{X}} = \{0, 1\}^{\sum_{s\in\mathcal{S}} M_s P_s},\ \widetilde{\mathcal{N}} = \{0, 1, 2, \ ...\}^K, \tag{3.51}$$

and, in light of (3.49) and (3.50), has the stationary distribution

$$p(\mathbf{z}) = p(\mathbf{x}, \mathbf{n}) = G^{-1}(\widetilde{\mathcal{Z}}) \prod_{s\in\mathcal{S}} \prod_{p\in\mathcal{P}_s} \prod_{m\in\mathcal{M}_s} \rho_{mps}^{x_{mps}} \prod_{k\in\mathcal{K}} \frac{a_k^{n_k}}{n_k!},\ \mathbf{z} \in \widetilde{\mathcal{Z}}, \tag{3.52}$$

where the function $G(\Omega)$ for any set $\Omega \subseteq \widetilde{\mathcal{Z}}$ is defined as

$$G(\Omega) = \sum_{\mathbf{z}\in\Omega} \prod_{s\in\mathcal{S}} \prod_{p\in\mathcal{P}_s} \prod_{m\in\mathcal{M}_s} \rho_{mps}^{x_{mps}} \prod_{k\in\mathcal{K}} \frac{a_k^{n_k}}{n_k!}. \tag{3.53}$$

It follows from (3.53) that the normalization constant $G(\widetilde{\mathcal{Z}})$ of the stationary state distribution of $\tilde{Z}(t)$ is given by

$$G(\widetilde{\mathcal{Z}}) = \prod_{s\in\mathcal{S}} \prod_{p\in\mathcal{P}_s} \prod_{m\in\mathcal{M}_s} (1+\rho_{mps})\mathrm{e}^{\sum_{k\in\mathcal{K}} a_k}.$$

For all links $l \in \mathcal{L}$, each source $s \in S^l$ and all states of the logical paths $\mathbf{x} \in \widetilde{\mathcal{X}}$, we define a function $y^l_{ms}(\mathbf{x}) = H\left(\sum_{p \in \mathcal{P}^l_s} x_{mps}\right)$, which represents the state of service (m, s) on link l (as before, $H(\cdot)$ is the Heaviside step function). Let $\mathbf{y}^l(\mathbf{x}) = \left(y^l_{ms}(\mathbf{x})\right)_{m \in \mathcal{M}_s, s \in S^l}$ denote the state of all services on link given that the logical paths of the network are in state $\mathbf{x} \in \widetilde{\mathcal{X}}$, and let $\mathbf{z}^l(\mathbf{z}) = \left(y^l(\mathbf{x}),\ (n_k)_{k \in \mathcal{K}^l}\right)$ denote the state of all sessions on link given the network state $\mathbf{z} \in \widetilde{\mathcal{Z}}$ (unless specified otherwise, vector $\mathbf{z} \in \widetilde{\mathcal{Z}}$ consists of two vector components $\mathbf{x} \in \widetilde{\mathcal{X}}$ and $\mathbf{n} \in \widetilde{\mathcal{N}}$, i.e., $\mathbf{z} = (\mathbf{x}, \mathbf{n})$). Finally, for $l \in \mathcal{L}$, we define

$$\begin{aligned} b_l(\mathbf{x}) &= \sum_{s \in S^l} \sum_{m \in \mathcal{M}_s} b_{ms} y^l_{ms}(\mathbf{x}),\ \ \mathbf{x} \in \widetilde{\mathcal{X}}, \\ d_l(\mathbf{n}) &= \sum_{k \in \mathcal{K}^l} d_k n_k,\ \ \mathbf{n} \in \widetilde{\mathcal{N}}, \end{aligned} \tag{3.54}$$

and

$$c_l(\mathbf{z}) = b_l(\mathbf{x}) + d_l(\mathbf{n}),\ \ \mathbf{z} \in \widetilde{\mathcal{Z}}, \tag{3.55}$$

which represent the capacities occupied on link l by multicast, unicast, and all sessions, respectively, given the network state $\mathbf{z} \in \widetilde{\mathcal{Z}}$.

Now we let $C_l < \infty$, $l \in \mathcal{L}$, and session establishment may be blocked. The state space of the model takes on the shape

$$\mathcal{Z} = \{\mathbf{z} \in \widetilde{\mathcal{Z}} : c_l(\mathbf{z}) \le C_l,\quad l \in \mathcal{L}\}. \tag{3.56}$$

The behavior of a network with limited link capacities is modeled by a CTMC $Z(t),\ t \ge 0$, which represents the truncation of $\tilde{Z}(t)$ to the set $\mathcal{Z}$ given by (3.56). The properties of truncated reversible Markov chains (Kelly 2011) yield the following theorem.

Theorem 3.4 *The CTMC $Z(t),\ t \ge 0$, is reversible and has the stationary state distribution of the product form.*

$$p(\mathbf{z}) = G^{-1}(\mathcal{Z}) \prod_{s \in S} \prod_{p \in \mathcal{P}_s} \prod_{m \in \mathcal{M}_s} \rho_{mps}^{x_{mps}} \prod_{k \in \mathcal{K}} \frac{a_k^{n_k}}{n_k!},\quad \mathbf{z} \in \mathcal{Z}, \tag{3.57}$$

with the normalization constant

$$G(\mathcal{Z}) = \sum_{\mathbf{z} \in \mathcal{Z}} \prod_{s \in S} \prod_{p \in \mathcal{P}_s} \prod_{m \in \mathcal{M}_s} \rho_{mps}^{x_{mps}} \prod_{k \in \mathcal{K}} \frac{a_k^{n_k}}{n_k!} \tag{3.58}$$

and the state space $\mathcal{Z}$ given by (3.56).

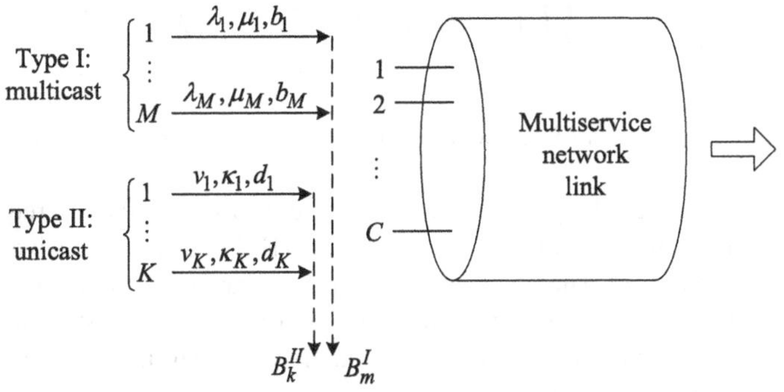

Fig. 3.6 A single-link model with multicast and unicast communications

A Single-Link Model

Problem Formulation

Let all the links in the network have unlimited capacities, except for some link l^*, i.e., let $C_l = \infty$ for $l \in \mathcal{L} \backslash \{l^*\}$. As we have seen previously, performance evaluation of such a network comes down to studying a network that consists of one link l^* and has one multicast source s^* providing the set of services $\mathcal{M} = \bigcup_{s \in S^{l^*}} \mathcal{M}_s$ and the set of unicast session classes $\mathcal{K}^{l^*}$. Henceforth, we omit indices l^* and s^* for brevity and write $C = C_{l^*}$, $\mathcal{K} = \mathcal{K}^{l^*}$.

We model a single network link with unicast and multicast communications as a multiclass multiservice loss system, as shown in Fig. 3.6. Consider a service station with C parallel servers (link capacity units) serving $M = |\mathcal{M}|$ classes of customers of type I and $K = |\mathcal{K}|$ classes of type II. We assume that the corresponding $M + K$ arrival processes are all Poisson and mutually independent.

Type I customers represent requests for multicast communications. If upon arrival of a (I, m)-customer no customer of the same class is being served, then the arriving customer will receive service only if it finds b_m servers (capacity units) free; it will then occupy these servers for a random time interval, which is exponentially distributed with parameter μ_m and independent of the arrival epochs and holding times of other customer classes. All (I, m)-customers that arrive during this time interval receive service without allocation of additional servers and leave the system together once it is over; b_m servers are then vacated. Thus, a customer of type I is lost if upon its arrival there is no same class customer in service and, at the same time, the free capacity is insufficient.

Denote $\rho_m = \frac{\lambda_m}{\mu_m}$, where λ_1, ..., λ_M are the arrival rates of customers in the type I classes. Note that, similarly to the single-link model of a multicast network, ρ_1, ..., ρ_M are related to the traffic intensities of the corresponding logical paths as

$$\rho_m = \prod_{p\in\mathscr{P}^{l^*}} (1+\rho_{mp}) - 1, \ m = 1, ..., M, \tag{3.59}$$

where ρ_{mp} is defined as in (3.15) with omitted index s for a network with a single source.

The arrival processes of type II customers correspond to the arrivals of requests for establishing unicast sessions on link l^*. An arriving (II, k)-customer receives service if it finds d_k servers free. Then it occupies them for a random time interval, which is exponentially distributed with parameter κ_k, and departs the system thereafter, leaving d_k servers free. An arriving customer that finds an insufficient number of free servers is lost. The arrival rates $\nu_1, ..., \nu_K$ of the type II arrival processes coincide with the arrival rates of the corresponding user requests, and we denote $a_k = \nu_k/\kappa_k$.

The State Space and the Stationary State Distribution

First, let $C = \infty$. In such case, all customers receive service and no customer is lost. Let a CTMC $Y_m(t), \ t \geq 0, m = 1, ..., M$, be in state 1 if at time t there is at least one (I, m)-customer in service, and in state 0 otherwise. As we have shown in Sect. 3.2, the CTMC $Y_m(t), \ t \geq 0$, is reversible and has a stationary distribution

$$\lim_{t\to\infty} \mathsf{P}(Y_m(t) = y_m) = \frac{\rho_m^{y_m}}{1+\rho_m}, \quad y_m \in \{0, 1\}. \tag{3.60}$$

We also define a CTMC describing type II customers. Let $N_k(t)$ represent the number of (II, k)-customers in service at time $t \geq 0, k = 1, ..., K$. The CTMC $N_k(t), t \geq 0$, is also reversible and has a stationary distribution given by

$$\lim_{t\to\infty} \mathsf{P}(N_k(t) = n_k) = \frac{a_k^{n_k}}{n_k!}\mathrm{e}^{-a_k}, \quad n_k \in \{0, 1, 2, ...\}. \tag{3.61}$$

Now consider a multivariate CTMC

$$\left\{\widetilde{\mathbf{Z}}(t) = (Y_1(t), ..., Y_M(t), N_1(t), ..., N_K(t)), \ t \geq 0\right\}.$$

By construction, $\widetilde{\mathbf{Z}}(t)$ is reversible on the set $\widetilde{\mathcal{Z}} = \widetilde{\mathcal{Y}} \times \widetilde{\mathcal{N}} = \{0, 1\}^M \times \{0, 1, 2, ...\}^K$ and, in light of (3.7) and (3.8), has a stationary distribution given by

$$\tilde{p}(\mathbf{z}) = G^{-1}(\widetilde{\mathcal{Z}}) \prod_{m=1}^{M} \rho_m^{y_m} \prod_{k=1}^{K} \frac{a_k^{n_k}}{n_k!}, \quad \mathbf{z} = (\mathbf{y}, \mathbf{n}) \in \widetilde{\mathcal{Z}}, \tag{3.62}$$

where the function $G(\Omega)$ for any set $\Omega \subseteq \widetilde{\mathcal{Z}}$ is defined as

$$G(\Omega) = \sum_{\mathbf{z}\in\Omega} \prod_{m=1}^{M} \rho_m^{y_m} \prod_{k=1}^{K} \frac{a_k^{n_k}}{n_k!}. \tag{3.63}$$

The normalization constant $G(\widetilde{\mathcal{Z}})$ of the stationary distribution of $\widetilde{\mathbf{Z}}(t)$ is hence given by

$$G(\widetilde{\mathcal{Z}}) = e^{\sum_{k=1}^{K} a_k} \prod_{m=1}^{M} (1 + \rho_m).$$

The CTMC $\widetilde{\mathbf{Z}}(t)$ with the state space $\widetilde{\mathcal{Z}}$ and the stationary distribution (3.62) models the system under study for $C = \infty$.

Similar to (3.54)–(3.55) let $c(\mathbf{z})$ represent the number of busy servers in state $\mathbf{z} \in \widetilde{\mathcal{Z}}$ and note that it can be written as

$$c(\mathbf{z}) = c(\mathbf{y}, \mathbf{n}) = b(\mathbf{y}) + d(\mathbf{n}) = \sum_{m=1}^{M} b_m y_m + \sum_{k=1}^{K} d_k n_k, \tag{3.64}$$

where $b(\mathbf{y})$ and $d(\mathbf{n})$ are the numbers of servers occupied in state $\mathbf{z} = (\mathbf{y}, \mathbf{n})$ by type I and type II customers, respectively. Now, let $C < \infty$, and customers may be lost. We assume that the lost customers do not affect the arrival processes. Then, the behavior of the system is modeled by a CTMC $\mathbf{Z}(t),\ t \geq 0$ which represents $\widetilde{\mathbf{Z}}(t)$, truncated to the set

$$\mathcal{Z} = \{\mathbf{z} \in \widetilde{\mathcal{Z}} : c(\mathbf{z}) \leq C\}. \tag{3.65}$$

Being a truncated reversible CTMC, it is also reversible and therefore, we have the following result.

Theorem 3.5 *The stationary state distribution of the CTMC $\mathbf{Z}(t),\ t \geq 0$, is of the product form*

$$p(\mathbf{z}) = G^{-1}(\mathcal{Z}) \prod_{m=1}^{M} \rho_m^{y_m} \prod_{k=1}^{K} \frac{a_k^{n_k}}{n_k!}, \quad \mathbf{z} \in \mathcal{Z}, \tag{3.66}$$

where $G(\mathcal{Z})$ is the normalization constant given by

$$G(\mathcal{Z}) = \sum_{\mathbf{z} \in \mathcal{Z}} \prod_{m=1}^{M} \rho_m^{y_m} \prod_{k=1}^{K} \frac{a_k^{n_k}}{n_k!}. \tag{3.67}$$

Performance Measures

Similarly to the model of the whole network, some performance measures of the single link can be found by taking the function $G(\Omega)$ of the corresponding subset of the state space. Among such characteristics are the blocking probabilities of customer classes of both types, the probability that a (I, m)-customer is in service, and the probability that there are no (I, m)-customers in service, yet an arriving customer of this class will receive service.

Recall that an arriving (I, m)-customer is lost only if it finds neither other same-class customers in service, nor enough free servers. The set of blocking states for (I, m)-customers is hence given by

$$\mathcal{B}^I_m = \{\mathbf{z} \in \mathcal{Z} : c(\mathbf{z}) + b_m > C,\ y_m = 0\}. \tag{3.68}$$

Arriving customers of type II are lost if they find an insufficient number of free servers. Thus, the set of blocking states for (II, k)-customers is

$$\mathcal{B}^{II}_k = \{\mathbf{z} \in \mathcal{Z} : c(\mathbf{z}) + d_k > C\}. \tag{3.69}$$

The corresponding probabilities $B^I_m = \mathsf{P}\{\mathbf{z} \in \mathcal{B}^I_m\}$ and $B^{II}_k = \mathsf{P}\{\mathbf{z} \in \mathcal{B}^{II}_k\}$ can be found by (3.66), (3.67); they represent the blocking probabilities of the multicast and unicast sessions, respectively, which correspond to the loss probabilities in the system under study.

The set of such states that there are (I, m)-customers in service (i.e., data related to service m is being sent over the link) is given by

$$\mathcal{F}_m = \{\mathbf{z} \in \mathcal{Z} : y_m = 1\}. \tag{3.70}$$

The set of such states that no (I, m)-customer is being served, yet an arriving (I, m)-customer will receive service (i.e., service m is not provided on the link, yet there is enough capacity to switch it on) is given by

$$\mathcal{H}_m = \{\mathbf{z} \in \mathcal{Z} : c(\mathbf{z}) + b_m \le C,\ y_m = 0\}. \tag{3.71}$$

Similar to the model of the network, in the single-link model the following relation holds for the corresponding probabilities, along with Lemma 3.1 and its corollary:

$$B^I_m + F_m + H_m = 1. \tag{3.72}$$

Lemma 3.6 *For any $m = 1, \ldots, M$ we have*

$$F_m = \rho_m H_m. \tag{3.73}$$

Corollary *For any $m = 1, \ldots, M$ we have*

$$F_m = \frac{\rho_m}{1 + \rho_m}\left(1 - B^I_m\right). \tag{3.74}$$

When studying a single network link, of interest are the characteristics of the random variables β, δ and γ, taking on the values $b(\mathbf{y})$, $d(\mathbf{n})$ and $c(\mathbf{z})$, respectively, $\mathbf{y} \in \widetilde{\mathcal{Y}} = \{0, 1\}^M$, $\mathbf{n} \in \widetilde{\mathcal{N}} = \{0, 1, 2, ...\}^K$, $\mathbf{z} \in \mathcal{Z}$, defined in (3.65). γ represents the random number of busy servers in the loss system, which corresponds to the random number of occupied (by sessions of both types) capacity units in the multiservice network's link. The random variables β and δ are to be interpreted similarly with respect to multicast and unicast sessions. In particular, we can find the average number of busy servers as the mean $\mathsf{E}\gamma$ of γ, i.e.

$$\mathsf{E}\gamma = \sum_{\mathbf{z}\in\mathcal{Z}} c(\mathbf{z})p(\mathbf{z}). \tag{3.75}$$

Similar to (3.5) $U = \mathsf{E}\gamma/C$ represents the link utilization factor.

Lemma 3.7 *The average number of servers occupied by customers of type I can be found as*

$$\mathsf{E}\beta = \sum_{m=1}^{M} b_m F_m. \tag{3.76}$$

Lemma 3.8 *The average number of servers occupied by customers of type I can be as*

$$\mathsf{E}\beta = \sum_{m=1}^{M} b_m \frac{\rho_m}{1+\rho_m}\left(1 - B_m^I\right). \tag{3.77}$$

A Method of Computation

Define a partitioning of the state space $\mathcal{Z}$ according to the number of busy servers:

$$\mathcal{Z}(n) = \{\mathbf{z} \in \mathcal{Z} : c(\mathbf{z}) = n\}, \quad n = 0, ..., C,$$

$$\mathcal{Z} = \bigcup_{n=0}^{C} \mathcal{Z}(n),$$

$$\mathcal{Z}(i) \cap \mathcal{Z}(j) = \varnothing, \ i \neq j, \ i, j = 0, ..., C,$$

and the distribution of the number of busy servers

$$P(n) = \mathsf{P}(\mathbf{z} \in \mathcal{Z}(n)), \quad n = 0, ..., C. \tag{3.78}$$

Then, for the set of blocking states of (II, k)-customers, we can write

$$\mathcal{B}_k^{II} = \bigcup_{n=C-d_k+1}^{C} \mathcal{Z}(n), \quad k = 1, \ldots, K,$$

and their blocking probability is given by

$$B_k^{II} = \sum_{n=C-d_k+1}^{C} P(n), \quad k = 1, \ldots, K.$$

The set $\mathcal{B}_m^I$ of blocking states for (I, m)-customers has a more complicated structure. Define a family of events

$$\mathcal{Z}_m(n) = \{\mathbf{z} \in \mathcal{Z} : c(\mathbf{z}) = n, \; y_m = 0\}, n = 0, \ldots, C, \; m = 1, \ldots, M,$$

and the corresponding probability distribution

$$P_m(n) = \mathsf{P}(\mathbf{z} \in \mathcal{Z}_m(n)), \quad n = 0, \ldots, C, \; m = 1, \ldots, M. \tag{3.79}$$

Now, the set of blocking states for the type I customers can be written as

$$\mathcal{B}_m^I = \bigcup_{n=C-b_m+1}^{C} \mathcal{Z}_m(n), \quad m = 1, \ldots, M,$$

and the blocking probability of a (I, m)-customer is given by

$$B_m^I = \sum_{n=C-b_m+1}^{C} P_m(n), \quad m = 1, \ldots, M.$$

The reader is already familiar with the algorithms for efficient computation of the distributions (3.78) and (3.79) in a system with one type of customers. Thus, if $M = 0$ then $P(n)$ can be computed via the Kaufman–Roberts algorithm, while if $K = 0$, we can calculate $P(n)$ and $P_M(n)$ via the convolution algorithm (3.44) discussed in Sect. 3.2. In the general case (i.e., for $M > 0$, $K > 0$), we apply a combination of the two methods based upon the relation

$$\mathcal{Z}(n) = \bigcup_{i=0}^{n} (\mathcal{Y}(i) \times \mathcal{C}(n-i)), \quad n = 0, \ldots, C,$$

where

$$\mathcal{Y}(n) = \left\{\mathbf{y} \in \widetilde{\mathcal{Y}} : b(\mathbf{y}) = n\right\},$$

$$\mathcal{C}(n) = \left\{\mathbf{n} \in \widetilde{\mathcal{N}} : d(\mathbf{n}) = n\right\}.$$

One checks easily that for any two sets $\Omega \subseteq \widetilde{\mathcal{Y}}$ and $\Upsilon \subseteq \widetilde{\mathcal{N}}$

$$G(\Omega \times \Upsilon) = G(\Omega)G(\Upsilon).$$

Then, in probability form, we have for $n = 0, \ldots, C$

$$P(n) = \frac{G(\mathcal{Z}(n))}{G(\mathcal{Z})} = G^{-1}(\mathcal{Z}) \sum_{i=0}^{n} G(\mathcal{Y}(i))G(\mathcal{C}(n-i)). \tag{3.80}$$

A similar relation holds for $P_m(n)$:

$$\mathcal{Z}_m(n) = \bigcup_{i=0}^{n} (\mathcal{Y}_m(i) \times \mathcal{C}(n-i)), \quad n = 0, \ldots, C,$$

where

$$\mathcal{Y}_m(n) = \left\{\mathbf{y} \in \widetilde{\mathcal{Y}} : b(\mathbf{y}) = n,\ y_m = 0\right\}, \quad n = 0, \ldots, C,$$

or in probability form for $m = 1, \ldots, M$ and $n = 0, \ldots, C$

$$P_m(n) = \frac{G(\mathcal{Z}_m(n))}{G(\mathcal{Z})} = G^{-1}(\mathcal{Z}) \sum_{i=0}^{n} G(\mathcal{Y}_m(i))G(\mathcal{C}(n-i)). \tag{3.81}$$

Lemma 3.9 *Let functions $f_m(i, n)$ be such that for any $n = 0, \ldots, C$*

$$G(\mathcal{Z}(n)) = f_0(M, n),$$

$$G(\mathcal{Z}_m(n)) = f_m(M, n), \quad m = 1, \ldots, M.$$

Then $f_m(i, n)$ can be computed as

$$f_m(i, n) = \begin{cases} 0, \ i = 0, \ldots, M, \ n < 0; \\ h(n), \ i = 0, \ n = 0, \ldots, C; \\ f_m(i-1, n) + (1 - \delta_{im})\rho_i f_m(i-1, n-b_i), \\ \qquad i = 1, \ldots, M, n = 0, \ldots, C \end{cases} \tag{3.82}$$

where the function $h(n)$ is given by (3.9) and δ_{ij} is the Kronecker delta.

Proof The function $f_0(i,n)$ is a convolution of the functions $g(m,n)$ and $h(n)$ defined, respectively, by (3.44) and (3.9):

$$f_0(i,n) = \sum_{j=0}^{n} g(i, n-j)h(j). \tag{3.83}$$

We use the factor $(1-\delta_{im})$ in the third row of (3.82) to omit the m-th entry of vector $\mathbf{y}$ and thus to take into account the condition $y_m = 0$ when computing $P_m(n)$. Since for similar systems with one type of customers, we have

$$G(\mathcal{C}(n)) = h(n),$$

$$G(\mathcal{Y}(n)) = g(M,n),$$

$$G(\mathcal{Y}_M(n)) = g(M-1,n),$$

the result follows from the relations (3.80) and (3.81). ■

The following propositions define an efficient method for computing the performance measures of a network link with two types of communications.

The normalization constant (3.67) can be computed as

$$G(\mathcal{Z}) = \sum_{n=0}^{C} f_0(M,n). \tag{3.84}$$

The blocking probability of a (I, m)-customer can be computed as

$$B_m^I = \frac{\sum\limits_{n=C-b_m+1}^{C} f_m(M,n)}{\sum\limits_{n=0}^{C} f_0(M,n)}, \quad m = 1, \ldots, M. \tag{3.85}$$

The blocking probability of a (II, k)-customer can be computed as

$$B_k^{II} = \frac{\sum\limits_{n=C-d_k+1}^{C} f_0(M,n)}{\sum\limits_{n=0}^{C} f_0(M,n)}, \quad k = 1, \ldots, K. \tag{3.86}$$

The probability that there are no (I, m)-customers in service, yet an arriving (I, m)-customer will receive service can be computed as

$$H_m = \frac{\sum\limits_{n=0}^{C-b_m} f_m(M, n)}{\sum\limits_{n=0}^{C} f_0(M, n)}, \quad m = 1, \ldots, M. \tag{3.87}$$

The average number of busy servers can be computed as

$$\mathsf{E}\gamma = \frac{\sum\limits_{n=1}^{C} n \cdot f_0(M, n)}{\sum\limits_{n=0}^{C} f_0(M, n)}. \tag{3.88}$$

The above results allow for efficient algorithms for computing the performance measures of a single-link multiservice network. Moreover, the computation time of the function $f_m(i, n)$ can be reduced by setting $f_m(i, n) = 1$ for $i = 0, \ldots, M$ and $n = 0$.

A Convolution Algorithm for the Erlang's Model of Multicasting

So far, we have considered the model of multicasting in which the duration of an "on" period is determined by the service time of the "first" customer, i.e., the one that has initiated this "on" period. Once its service is over, all same-class customers that have arrived during the "on" period depart the system simultaneously. In this section, we consider a different service discipline, in which the customers of type I are served on the same servers as previously, but depart the system independently of one another. We refer to such a model as the *Erlang's model of multicasting*, since the distribution of the number of customers in the corresponding loss system $M|M|1|1$ with Poisson arrivals of intensity λ_m, exponential service of intensity μ_m and "transparent" customers is given by

$$\pi_0 = \mathrm{e}^{-\rho_m}, \; \pi_n^{(2)} = \frac{\rho_m^n}{n!}\mathrm{e}^{-\rho_m}, n \geq 1. \tag{3.89}$$

In this subsection, which draws on Boussetta and Beylot (1999), Samouylov et al. (2011), we derive a convolution algorithm for the single-link model with multicast and unicast communications while assuming the Erlang's model of multicasting.

As before in this section, the behavior of the single link is described by the CTMC $\mathbf{Z}(t) = (Y_1(t), \ldots, Y_M(t), N_1(t), \ldots, N_K(t)),\ t \geq 0$, which is reversible on the set $\mathcal{Z} = \{\mathbf{z} \in \tilde{\mathcal{Z}} : c(\mathbf{z}) \leq C\}$ and, as it follows from Samouylov et al. (2011), has a stationary distribution given by

$$p(\mathbf{z}) = G^{-1}(\mathcal{Z}) \prod_{m=1}^{M} (\mathrm{e}^{\rho_m} - 1)^{y_m} \prod_{k=1}^{K} \frac{a_k^{n_k}}{n_k!}, \quad \mathbf{z} = (\mathbf{y}, \mathbf{n}) \in \mathcal{Z}, \tag{3.90}$$

where the normalization constant $G(\mathcal{Z})$ of the distribution of $\mathbf{Z}(t)$ is given by

$$G(\mathcal{Z}) = \sum_{\mathbf{z}\in\mathcal{Z}} \prod_{m=1}^{M} (\mathrm{e}^{\rho_m} - 1)^{y_m} \prod_{k=1}^{K} \frac{a_k^{n_k}}{n_k!}.$$

Note that the right-hand side of (3.90) is a product of three factors: $G(\mathcal{Z})$ is the normalization constant, an $\prod_{m=1}^{M} (\mathrm{e}^{\rho_m} - 1)^{y_m}$ up to a constant factor coincides with the stationary state distribution of states of multicast services, and $\prod_{k=1}^{K} \frac{a_k^{n_k}}{n_k!}$ up to a constant factor coincides with the stationary state distribution of the number of unicast sessions.

It was proved in Samouylov et al. (2011) that the state distribution for the multicast services is insensitive to their holding-time distribution beyond its mean.

Next, we derive a recursive algorithm for computing the performance measures of the model. The following additional notation will be used:

1. $f(c, m)$ is the function up to a constant factor coinciding with the probability that multicast services 1, ..., m and the unicast sessions occupy c capacity units;
2. $f(c, M) = f(c)$;
3. $f_{-m}(c)$ is the function up to a constant factor coinciding with the probability that unicast sessions and multicast services occupy c capacity units and service m is "off".

Now, the normalization constant $G(\mathcal{Z})$ and the blocking probabilities of multicast $\left(B_m^I\right)$ and unicast $\left(B_k^{II}\right)$ sessions can be obtained as

$$G(\mathcal{Z}) = \sum_{c=0}^{C} f(c), \tag{3.91}$$

$$B_m^I = G^{-1}(\mathcal{Z}) \sum_{c=C-b_m+1}^{C} f_{-m}(c),\ m \in \mathcal{M}, \tag{3.92}$$

$$B_k^{II} = G^{-1}(\mathcal{Z}) \sum_{c=C-d_k+1}^{C} f(c),\ k \in \mathcal{K}, \tag{3.93}$$

while the functions $f(c, m)$ and $f_{-m}(c)$ are computed recursively as follows:

$$f(c,m)=\begin{cases}0, & c<0, \quad m=0,1,\ldots,M,\\ 1, & c=0, \quad m=0,1,\ldots,M,\\ \frac{1}{c}\sum_{k=1}^{K}a_k d_k f(c-d_k,0), & c=1,\ldots,C,\ m=0,\\ f(c,m-1)+\varphi_m f(c-b_m,m-1), & c=1,\ldots,C,\ m=1,\ldots,M,\end{cases} \tag{3.94}$$

$$f_{-m}(c)=\begin{cases}0, & c<0,\\ 1, & c=0,\\ f(c)-\varphi_m f_{-m}(c-b_m), & c=1,\ldots,C,\end{cases} \tag{3.95}$$

where $\varphi_m = \mathrm{e}^{\rho_m}-1$.

A scheme of an efficient implementation of the algorithm for computing $G(\mathcal{Z})$ and B_k^{II} is presented in Fig. 3.7, while a scheme of computing B_m^{I} is shown in Fig. 3.8.

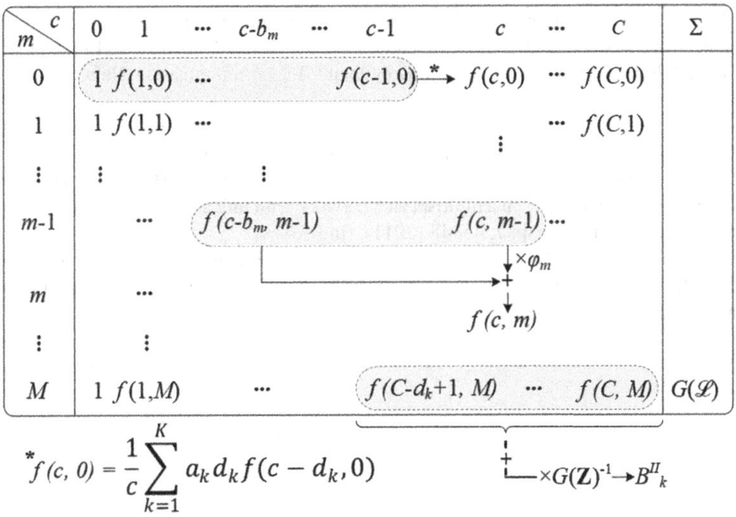

Fig. 3.7 A computation scheme for $G(\mathcal{Z})$ and B_k^{II}

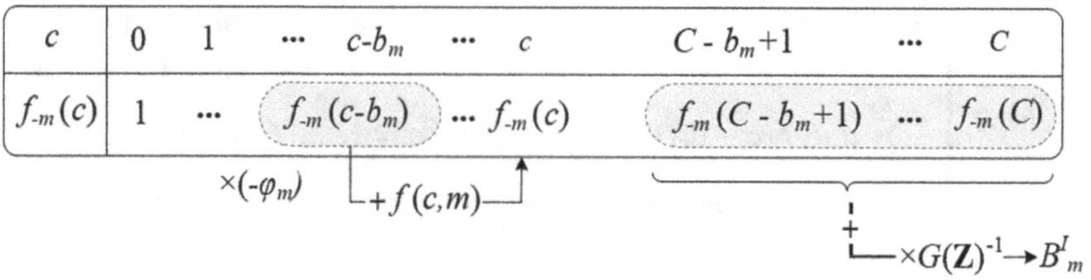

Fig. 3.8 A computation scheme for B_m^I

References

Boussetta, K., Beylot, A.-L.: Multirate resource sharing for unicast and multicast connections. In: International Conference on Broadband Communications, pp. 561–570. Springer, Boston, MA (1999)

Gaidamaka, Y., Samouylov, K.: Analytical model of multicast network and single link performance analysis. In: Proceedings of the 6-th International Conference on Telecommunications, pp. 169–175. Zagreb, Croatia (2001)

Karvo, J., Martikainen, O., Virtamo, J.T., Aalto, S.: Blocking of dynamic multicast connections. Telecommun. Syst. **16**(3–4), 467–481 (2001)

Kaufman, J.S.: Blocking in a shared resource environment. IEEE Trans. Commun. COM **29**(10), 1474–1481 (1981)

Kelly, F.P.: Reversibility and Stochastic Networks. Cambridge University Press (2011)

Roberts, J.W.: A service system with heterogeneous user requirements. In: Performance of Data Communications Systems and Their Applications, North-Holland, pp. 423–431 (1981)

Ross, K.W.: Multiservice Loss Models for Broadband Telecommunication Networks. Springer (1995)

Rykov, V., Samouylov, K.: On the analysis of the probabilities of network resource locks with dynamic multicast connections. Telecommun. Radio Eng. **10**, 27–30 (2000)

Samouylov, K., Gaidamaka, Y., Shchukina, O.: On the application of the Erlang model to the calculation of blocking probabilities in a multiservice network with unicast and multicast connections. T-Comm, Telecommun. Transp. **7**, 45–48 (2011). (in Russian)

Samouylov, K., Yarkina, N.: Blocking probabilities in multiservice networks with unicast and multicast connections. In: Proceedings of the 7-th International Conference on Telecommunications, Zagreb, Croatia, pp. 423–429 (2005)

Chapter 4
Modeling Arrival and Service Processes

Abstract In this chapter, we introduce Markovian arrival processes (MAPs) and their extensions. MAPs appeared when it became clear that the future methods of stochastic system modeling will be computer-based. Indeed, MAPs are specified by several matrices, which makes them convenient to use when analyzing stochastic systems by matrix-analytical methods. At the end of the chapter, we use an example to demonstrate the ease with which a system with a MAP can be studied.

Various models of arrival streams are used when analyzing stochastic systems. Markovian streams of events, or MAPs, constitute a generalization of Markov-modulated Poisson processes, which are formed by transition epochs of a Markov chain, and phase-type renewal processes. The properties of MAPs follow from the general theory of bivariate Markov processes, one of which is a Markov Chain, and another is a counting process of arrivals. Given realization of a Markov Chain, the counting process of a MAP has independent increments. Arrival processes whose counting process has independent increments were called "streams without after-effect" (Khinchin in Theory Prob Appl 1(1):1–15, 1956). This is why, in Russian literature, Markovian arrival processes were referred to as "streams without after-effect, defined on a Markov chain" (Naumov in Analysis of some queues in series. PhD thesis, Peoples' Friendship University, Moscow, 1978), until, at an academic seminar at the Moscow State University, G. Klimov proposed an abbreviated name for this type of arrival processes: MC streams (from "Markov chain"). After M. F. Neuts came up with his model of the MAP (Neuts in A versatile Markovian point process. Tech. report, 1977), (Neuts in J.Appl Probab 16:764–779, 1979), such models became known as N-processes. The term "Markovian arrival process" appeared in 1990, and the unfortunate abbreviation—MAP—has come into use (Lucantoni et al. in Adv Appl Probab 22:676–705, 1990). Unfortunate, because it has been used to designate Markov additive processes, E. Çinlar published his article (Çinlar in Zeitschrift für Wahrscheinlichkeitstheorie und verwandte gebiete 24:85–93, 1972a; Çinlar in Zeitschrift für Wahrscheinlichkeitstheorie und Verwandte Gebiete 24:95–121, 1972b). To avoid confusion, S. Asmussen proposed to abbreviate Markovian arrival processes as MArP in (Asmussen in Applied Probability and Queues. Springer, New York, p 302, 2003), however, the abbreviation MAP has established itself for both Markov additive processes and Markovian arrival process. We denote by $\mathcal{N}^K$ the set of all nonnegative integer-valued vectors of length K,

V. Naumov et al., *Matrix and Analytical Methods for Performance Analysis of Telecommunication Systems*, https://doi.org/10.1007/978-3-030-83132-5_4

$\mathcal{N}_0^k = \mathcal{N}^k \backslash \{\mathbf{0}\}$. Finally, for brevity, instead of writing "n_1 events of type 1, n_2 events of type 2, ..., n_K events of type K", we write "$\mathbf{n}$ events", where $\mathbf{n} = (n_1, n_2, ..., n_K)$.

4.1 Markovian Arrival Processes

4.1.1 Phase-Type Distributions

Phase-type probability distributions are a generalization of the well-known Erlang distribution, introduced in and later named after its author. Phase-type distributions represent the distribution of time until a finite MC ends up in the absorbing state (Neuts 1981). Let $X(t)$, $t \geq 0$, represent a stochastic process on a finite state space $\mathcal{X} = \{1, 2, ..., L\}$, and τ, a nonnegative random variable, $\mathsf{P}(\tau > 0) > 0$. The process $X_0(t) = X(t)\text{Ind}(\tau > t)$ takes on the values $0, 1, 2, ..., L$, with 0 being its absorbing state. Then, τ is said to be a phase-type random variable with phase process $X(t)$ if $X_0(t)$ is a homogeneous Markov process whose transition probabilities

$$P(i, j, t) = \mathsf{P}(X(t) = j, \tau > t | X(0) = i, \tau > 0), i, j \in \mathcal{X},$$

satisfy

$$\lim_{t \to 0} \mathsf{P}(i, j, t) = \delta(i, j), i, j \in \mathcal{X}, \tag{4.1}$$

$$\lim_{t \to \infty} \mathsf{P}(i, j, t) = 0, i, j \in \mathcal{X}. \tag{4.2}$$

Furthermore, in this case there exists an infinitesimal generator matrix τ such that

$$P(i, j, \Delta t) = \delta(i, j) + S(i, j)\Delta t + o(\Delta t), i, j \in \mathcal{X},$$

and the transition probability matrix $\mathbf{P}(t) = [P(i, j, t)]$ satisfies

$$\mathbf{P}(t) = \mathrm{e}^{t\mathbf{S}}. \tag{4.3}$$

It follows from (4.2) and (4.3) that the eigenvalues of matrix $\mathbf{S}$ all have negative real parts. Matrix $\mathbf{S}$ is irreducible and $-\mathbf{S}^{-1}$ nonnegative. Since 0 is the absorbing state of $X_0(t)$, its infinitesimal generator matrix $\mathbf{S}_0$ and transition probability matrix $\mathbf{P}_0(t)$ are of the form

$$\mathbf{S}_0 = \begin{bmatrix} 0 & \mathbf{0} \\ \mathbf{s} & \mathbf{S} \end{bmatrix}, \mathbf{P}_0(t) = \begin{bmatrix} 1 & \mathbf{0} \\ \mathbf{p}(t) & \mathbf{P}(t) \end{bmatrix},$$

where $\mathbf{s} = -\mathbf{S}\mathbf{u}$ and $\mathbf{p}(t) = \mathbf{u} - \mathbf{P}(t)\mathbf{u}$ are column vectors of length L.

The CDF of a phase-type random variable $F(t) = \mathsf{P}(\tau \le t)$ satisfies the relations

$$F(t) = 1 - \mathbf{q}e^{t\mathbf{S}}\mathbf{u}, \tag{4.4}$$

$$F(0) = 1 - \mathbf{q}\mathbf{u}, \quad \frac{d}{dt}F(t) = \mathbf{q}e^{t\mathbf{S}}\mathbf{s}, \, t > 0,$$

where $\mathbf{q} = (q(i))$ is the row vector of initial probabilities. Moreover, a function $F(t)$ given by (4.4) represents a phase-type CDF by definition if $\mathbf{q}$ and $\mathbf{S}$ are such that

$$0 < \sum_{j \in \mathcal{X}} q(j) \le 1, q(i) \ge 0, i \in \mathcal{X}, \tag{4.5}$$

$$\sum_{j \in \mathcal{X}} S(i, j) \le 0, \; S(i, j) \ge 0, \; i \ne j, \; i, j \in \mathcal{X}.$$

The Laplace–Stieltjes transform of $F(x)$,

$$F^*(v) = \int_0^\infty e^{-vx} dF(x) = \mathbf{q}(v\mathbf{I} - \mathbf{S})^{-1}\mathbf{s},$$

can be rewritten as the ratio of two polynomials,

$$F^*(v) = \frac{\mathbf{q}\,\overline{(v\mathbf{I} - \mathbf{S})}\,\mathbf{s}}{\det(v\mathbf{I} - \mathbf{S})},$$

where $\overline{\mathbf{X}}$ denotes the adjoint matrix of $\mathbf{X}$.

Besides, the process $X_0(t)$ with infinitesimal generator $\mathbf{S}_0$ should be able to reach the absorbing state 0 from any other state. For this, it suffices that matrix $\mathbf{S}+\mathbf{s}\,\mathbf{q}$ be irreducible and vector $\mathbf{s}$ nonzero. Phase-type CDFs are matrix-exponential distribution functions; hence, we will elaborate on their properties later, in Sect. 4.2.1.

A phase-type random variable represents a sum of a certain number of random variables distributed exponentially. Thanks to this, Erlang's method of stages can be applied to analyze stochastic systems with such random variables. The use of MAPs permits extending Erlang's method of stages to arrival streams.

4.1.2 Markovian Arrival Processes

Consider a stream $(t_l, \sigma_l), l = 1, 2, ...,$ of batches of heterogeneous events. Here, $0 < t_1 < t_2 < ...$ are the times of arrivals, while $\sigma_l = (\sigma_{l,1}, ..., \sigma_{l,K})$, where $\sigma_{l,k}$ represents the number (batch size) of type k events occurred at time t_l. Let $N_k(t) = \sum_{t_l \leq t} \sigma_{l,k}$ denote the number of type k events occurred during time t, $\mathbf{N}(t) = (N_1(t), N_2(t), ..., N_K(t))$. The stream (t_l, σ_l) is said to be a Markovian arrival process if, for some random process $X(t)$ on a finite state space $\mathcal{X} = \{1, 2, ..., L\}$, the process $\xi(t) = (X(t), \mathbf{N}(t))$ is a homogeneous Markov process and, for any two time instants, $0 \leq s < t$ the vector $\mathbf{N}(t) - \mathbf{N}(s)$ of the numbers of events occurred in the interval $(s, t]$ does not depend, for a given $X(s)$, on the vector $\mathbf{N}(s)$ of events occurred before time s (Pacheco and Parbhu 1995). In other words, for a MAP, the process $\xi(t) = (X(t), \mathbf{N}(t))$ is homogeneous in time and in the second component (Ezhov and Skorokhod 1969a, b).

We assume $\xi(t) = (X(t), \mathbf{N}(t))$ to have right-continuous paths. Its transition probabilities

$$P_{\mathbf{k},\mathbf{n}}(i, j, t) = \mathsf{P}(X(s+t) = j, \mathbf{N}(s+t) = \mathbf{n} | X(s) = i, \mathbf{N}(s) = \mathbf{k}), \;\; A\mathbf{x}(k) = 0 \tag{4.6}$$

are such that

$$P_{\mathbf{k},\mathbf{n}}(i, j, t) = P_{\mathbf{0},\mathbf{n}-\mathbf{k}}(i, j, t), i, j \in \mathcal{X}, \mathbf{k}, \mathbf{n} \in \mathcal{N}^K, \mathbf{k} \leq \mathbf{n}, \tag{4.7}$$

and, therefore, they are uniquely determined by

$$P_{\mathbf{n}}(i, j, t) = P_{\mathbf{0},\mathbf{n}}(i, j, t), i, j \in \mathcal{X}, \mathbf{n} \in \mathcal{N}^K. \tag{4.8}$$

It follows from (4.6)–(4.7) that the transition rates of $\xi(t)$

$$A_{\mathbf{k},\mathbf{n}}(i, j) = \lim_{t \to 0} \frac{1}{t}\big(P_{\mathbf{k},\mathbf{n}}(i, j, t) - \delta(\mathbf{k}, \mathbf{n})\delta(i, j)\big), i, j \in \mathcal{X}, \mathbf{k}, \mathbf{n} \in \mathcal{N}^K, \mathbf{k} \leq \mathbf{n}, \tag{4.9}$$

are of the form

$$A_{\mathbf{k},\mathbf{n}}(i, j) = \begin{cases} A_{\mathbf{n}-\mathbf{k}}(i, j), & \text{if } \mathbf{k} \leq \mathbf{n}, \\ 0, & \text{otherwise}, \end{cases} \tag{4.10}$$

where

$$A_{\mathbf{0}}(i,j) = \lim_{t \to 0} \frac{1}{t}(P_{\mathbf{0}}(i,j,t) - \delta(i,j)), i, j \in \mathcal{X}, \tag{4.11}$$

$$A_{\mathbf{n}}(i,j) = \lim_{t \to 0} \frac{1}{t} P_{\mathbf{n}}(i,j,t), i, j \in \mathcal{X}, \mathbf{n} \in \mathcal{N}_0^K. \tag{4.12}$$

Transition probability matrices $\mathbf{P}_{\mathbf{n}}(t) = [P_{\mathbf{n}}(i,j,t)]$ are uniquely determined by the transition intensity matrices $\mathbf{A}_{\mathbf{n}} = [A_{\mathbf{n}}(i,j)], \mathbf{n} \geq \mathbf{0}$. Indeed, $\mathbf{P}_{\mathbf{n}}(t)$ are the unique solution to the Kolmogorov differential equations

$$\frac{d}{dt}\mathbf{P}_{\mathbf{n}}(t) = \sum_{\substack{\mathbf{i} \in \mathrm{N}^K \\ \mathbf{i} \leq \mathbf{n}}} \mathbf{A}_{\mathbf{i}} \mathbf{P}_{\mathbf{n}-\mathbf{i}}(t), \mathbf{n} \in \mathcal{N}^K, \tag{4.13}$$

with initial conditions

$$\mathbf{P}_{\mathbf{0}}(0) = \mathbf{I}, \mathbf{P}_{\mathbf{n}}(0) = \mathbf{0}, \mathbf{n} \in \mathcal{N}_0^K. \tag{4.14}$$

The solution to (4.13)–(4.14) is given by the recursive relation

$$\mathbf{P}_{\mathbf{0}}(t) = \mathrm{e}^{t\mathbf{A}_{\mathbf{0}}}, \mathbf{P}_{\mathbf{n}}(t) = \sum_{\substack{\mathbf{i} \in \mathcal{N}_0^K \\ \mathbf{i} \leq \mathbf{n}}} \int_0^t \mathbf{P}_{\mathbf{0}}(t-s) \mathbf{A}_{\mathbf{i}} \mathbf{P}_{\mathbf{n}-\mathbf{i}}(s) ds, \mathbf{n} \in \mathcal{N}_0^K. \tag{4.15}$$

It follows from (4.13) that the matrices

$$\mathbf{P}(\mathbf{z}, t) = \sum_{\mathbf{n} \in \mathcal{N}^K} \mathbf{P}_{\mathbf{n}}(t) z_1^{n_1} \cdots z_K^{n_K}, \mathbf{A}(\mathbf{z}) = \sum_{\mathbf{n} \in \mathcal{N}^K} \mathbf{A}_{\mathbf{n}} z_1^{n_1} \cdots z_K^{n_K},$$

where $\mathbf{n} = (n_1, ..., n_K)$, $\mathbf{z} = (z_1, ..., z_K)$, $|z_k| \leq 1$, $k = 1, ..., K$, are related by the simple formula

$$\mathbf{P}(\mathbf{z}, t) = \mathrm{e}^{t\mathbf{A}(\mathbf{z})}. \tag{4.16}$$

The first component of the process $\xi(t) = (X(t), \mathbf{N}(t))$ is itself a homogeneous Markov process (Ezhov and Skorokhod 1969a, b). We refer to $X(t)$ as the phase process of the MAP. The transition probability matrix of $X(t)$ is given by

$$\mathbf{P}(t) = \sum_{\mathbf{n} \in \mathcal{N}^K} \mathbf{P}_{\mathbf{n}}(t). \tag{4.17}$$

Transition rate matrices $\mathbf{A}_{\mathbf{n}}$ have the following properties.

(1) The off-diagonal entries of $\mathbf{A}_{\mathbf{0}}$ are all nonnegative.

(2) Matrices $\mathbf{A_n}, \mathbf{n} \in \mathcal{N}_0^K$, are nonnegative.
(3) Matrix

$$\mathbf{A} = \sum_{\mathbf{n} \in \mathcal{N}^K} \mathbf{A_n} \tag{4.18}$$

is the transition rate matrix (infinitesimal generator matrix) of the phase process $X(t)$.

In what follows we assume that the infinitesimal generator $\mathbf{A}$ is irreducible, $\mathbf{\Lambda} = \mathbf{A} - \mathbf{A_0} \neq \mathbf{0}$, and $\mathbf{p}$ represents the row vector of the stationary distribution of $X(t)$, which is found as the unique solution to the linear equations

$$\mathbf{pA} = \mathbf{0}, \mathbf{pu} = 1. \tag{4.19}$$

There are two common approaches to specifying a MAP. Usually, it is done by specifying the matrices $\mathbf{A_n}, \mathbf{n} \in \mathcal{N}_0^K$. The other method is by construction, via scalars $\gamma(i) > 0, i \in \mathcal{N}$, and nonnegative matrices $\mathbf{\Psi_n} = [\Psi_\mathbf{n}(i, j)], \mathbf{n} \in \mathcal{N}_0^K$, such that

$$\sum_{j \in \mathcal{X}} \sum_{\mathbf{n} \in \mathcal{N}^K} \Psi_\mathbf{n}(i, j) = 1, i \in \mathcal{X}.$$

These parameters specify a homogeneous Markov process in which the sojourn time in state i is exponentially distributed with parameter $\gamma(i)$. Once the sojourn in state i is over, with probability $\Psi_\mathbf{n}(i, j)$, $\mathbf{n}$ events occur and the process moves to state j. If a MAP is specified in this fashion, its matrices $\mathbf{A_n}$ are given by

$$A_\mathbf{n}(i, j) = \gamma(i)(\Psi_\mathbf{n}(i, j) - \delta(\mathbf{n}, \mathbf{0})\delta(i, j)), i, j \in \mathcal{X}, \mathbf{n} \in \mathcal{N}^K. \tag{4.20}$$

Conversely, if matrices $\mathbf{A_n}$ are given, the above parameters of the MAP can be determined as follows. First, $\gamma(i)$ are chosen so that $\gamma(i) \geq -A_0(i, i)$ hold for all i. Then, the transition probabilities $\Psi_\mathbf{n}(i, j)$ are obtained as

$$\Psi_\mathbf{n}(i, j) = \frac{A_\mathbf{n}(i, j)}{\gamma(i)} + \delta(\mathbf{n}, \mathbf{0})\delta(i, j), i, j \in \mathcal{X}, \mathbf{n} \in \mathcal{N}^K. \tag{4.21}$$

The parameters of the constructive definition are clearly not unique and depend upon the choice of $\gamma(i)$. The latter, for instance, can be set $\gamma(i) = \gamma, i \in \mathcal{X}$, where $\gamma \geq \max_i |A_0(i, i)|$. Then, the epochs at which arrivals may occur form a Poisson process of rate γ.

Given the transition probability matrices $\mathbf{P_n}(t)$, one can obtain the joint distribution of the number of events observed in disjoint time intervals

$$p_{\mathbf{k}_1,\mathbf{k}_2,\ldots,\mathbf{k}_m}(x_0, x_1, \ldots, x_m) = \mathsf{P}(\mathbf{N}(\sum_{j=0}^{r} x_j) - \mathbf{N}(\sum_{j=0}^{r-1} x_j) = \mathbf{k}_r, r = 1, 2, \ldots, m) =$$
$$= \boldsymbol{\alpha} \boldsymbol{P}(x_0)\mathbf{P}_{\mathbf{k}_1}(x_1)\mathbf{P}_{\mathbf{k}_2}(x_2)\cdots\mathbf{P}_{\mathbf{k}_m}(x_m)\mathbf{u}, \tag{4.22}$$

$$\mathbf{k}_1, \mathbf{k}_2, \ldots, \mathbf{k}_m \in \mathcal{N}^K, x_0, x_1, \ldots, x_m > 0, m = 1, 2, \ldots,$$

where $\boldsymbol{\alpha} = (\alpha(i))$ is the initial distribution of the phase process, $\alpha(i) = \mathsf{P}(X(0) = i)$. Different initial distributions of the phase process yield different MAPs. If $\boldsymbol{\alpha} = \mathbf{p}$, the process is referred to as the stationary version of the MAP (Pacheco and Prabhu 1995). In this case, the counting process $\mathbf{N}(t)$ has stationary increments, since distribution (4.22) of the numbers of events occurred in intervals of length $x_1, \ldots, x_m$ does not depend upon their starting time x_0. Parameter λ of the stationary version of an MAP and the vector of expected batch sizes $\mathbf{m} = \mathsf{E}\sigma_l$ are given by

$$\lambda = \mathbf{p}\Lambda\mathbf{u}, \mathbf{m} = \frac{1}{\lambda} \sum_{\mathbf{n}\in\mathcal{N}_0^K} (\mathbf{p}\mathbf{a}_\mathbf{n})\mathbf{n}, \tag{4.23}$$

where $\mathbf{a}_\mathbf{n} = \mathbf{A}_\mathbf{n}\mathbf{u}$.

Now, we set $t_0 = 0$ and denote by $\tau_l = t_l - t_{l-1}$, $l = 1, 2, \ldots$, the times between arrivals and by $X_l = X(t_l)$, $l = 1, 2, \ldots$, the states of the phase process at the epochs straight after arrivals. The Markovian arrival process of batches of heterogeneous events is a semi-Markov arrival process since the sequence (X_l, σ_l, τ_l), $l = 1, 2, \ldots$, is a Markov renewal process. For this process, the conditional distribution of the *next state depends only upon the present state of the phase process:*

$$\mathsf{P}(X_l = j, \sigma_l = \mathbf{n}, \tau_l < x | X_{l-1} = i, \sigma_{l-1} = \mathbf{k}, \tau_{l-1} < y) =$$

$$= \mathsf{P}(X_l = j, \sigma_l = \mathbf{n}, \tau_l < x | X_{l-1} = i) = G_\mathbf{n}(i, j, x).$$

The matrices $\mathbf{G}_\mathbf{n}(x) = [G_\mathbf{n}(i, j, x)]$, specifying the renewal process $(X_l, \boldsymbol{\sigma}_l, \tau_l)$ associated with the MAP, and their Laplace–Stieltjes transforms are of the form

$$\mathbf{G}_\mathbf{n}(x) = \int_0^x e^{z\mathbf{A}_0}\mathbf{A}_\mathbf{n} dz = (e^{x\mathbf{A}_0} - \mathbf{I})\mathbf{A}_0{}^{-1}\mathbf{A}_\mathbf{n}, \mathbf{n} \in \mathcal{N}_0^K, \tag{4.24}$$

$$\int_0^\infty e^{-vx} d\mathbf{G}_\mathbf{n}(x) = (v\mathbf{I} - \mathbf{A}_0)^{-1}\mathbf{A}_\mathbf{n}, \mathbf{n} \in \mathcal{N}_0^K. \tag{4.25}$$

By using $\mathbf{G_n}(x)$, we can obtain the joint CDF and the corresponding density function of the numbers of events $\boldsymbol{\sigma}_l$ and the times τ_l between arrivals:

$$F_{\mathbf{k}_1,\mathbf{k}_2,\ldots,\mathbf{k}_m}(x_1, x_2, \ldots, x_m) = \mathsf{P}(\sigma_l = \mathbf{k}_l, \tau_l < x_l, l = 1, 2, \ldots, m) = \\ = \boldsymbol{\alpha} \boldsymbol{G}_{\mathbf{k}_1}(x_1)\mathbf{G}_{\mathbf{k}_2}(x_2)\ldots\mathbf{G}_{\mathbf{k}_m}(x_m)\mathbf{u}, \quad (4.26)$$

$$f_{\mathbf{k}_1,\mathbf{k}_2,\ldots,\mathbf{k}_m}(x_1, x_2, \ldots, x_m) = \\ = \alpha e^{x_1\mathbf{A_0}}\mathbf{A}_{\mathbf{k}_1} e^{x_2\mathbf{A_0}}\mathbf{A}_{\mathbf{k}_2}\ldots e^{x_m\mathbf{A_0}}\mathbf{A}_{\mathbf{k}_m}\mathbf{u}, \\ \mathbf{k}_1, \mathbf{k}_2, \ldots, \mathbf{k}_m \in \mathcal{N}_0^K, x_0, x_1, \ldots, x_m > 0, m = 1, 2, \ldots \quad (4.27)$$

The transition probabilities of the embedded MC $(X_l, \boldsymbol{\sigma}_l)$ depend only upon the state of the phase process after the previous arrival:

$$\mathsf{P}(X_l = j, \boldsymbol{\sigma}_l = \mathbf{n}|X_{l-1} = i, \sigma_{l-1} = \mathbf{k}) = \mathsf{P}(X_l = j, \sigma_l = \mathbf{n}|X_{l-1} = i) = Q_{\mathbf{n}}(i, j),$$

where $Q_{\mathbf{n}}(i, j) = \lim_{x\to\infty} G_{\mathbf{n}}(i, j, x)$. It follows from (4.24) that the transition probability matrix $\mathbf{Q_n} = [Q_{\mathbf{n}}(i, j)]$ of the embedded MC $(X_l, \boldsymbol{\sigma}_l)$ and the transition probability matrix $\mathbf{Q}$ of MC X_l are given by

$$\mathbf{Q} = -\mathbf{A_0}^{-1}\mathbf{\Lambda},\ \mathbf{Q_n} = -\mathbf{A_0}^{-1}\mathbf{A_n}, \mathbf{n} \in \mathcal{N}_0^K. \quad (4.28)$$

The stationary distributions $\mathbf{q} = (q(i))$ and $\mathbf{q_n} = (q_{\mathbf{n}}(i))$, $\mathbf{n} \in \mathcal{N}_0^K$, of MCs X_l and $(X_l, \boldsymbol{\sigma}_l)$, respectively, are related to the stationary distribution $\mathbf{p}$ of the process $X(t)$ as

$$\mathbf{q} = \frac{1}{\lambda}\mathbf{p\Lambda},\ \mathbf{p} = -\lambda\mathbf{q}\mathbf{A_0}^{-1},\ \mathbf{q} = \sum_{\mathbf{n}\in \mathrm{N}_0^K} \mathbf{q_n}\,\mathbf{q} = \sum_{\mathbf{n}\in \mathrm{N}_0^K} \mathbf{q_n}\,\mathbf{n} \in \mathcal{N}_0^K.$$

If the all-ones vector $\mathbf{u}$ is a right eigenvector of each of the matrices $\mathbf{A_n}$ and

$$\mathbf{A_n u} = \lambda_{\mathbf{n}}\mathbf{u}, \mathbf{n} \in \mathcal{N}_0^K, \quad (4.29)$$

then it follows from (4.26) that, for any initial distribution $\boldsymbol{\alpha}$, the MAP is stationary and memoryless. Similarly, if the stationary distribution vector $\mathbf{p}$ is a left eigenvector of $\mathbf{A_n}$ and

$$\mathbf{pA_n} = \lambda_{\mathbf{n}}\mathbf{p}, \mathbf{n} \in \mathcal{N}_0^K, \quad (4.30)$$

then, for the initial distribution $\boldsymbol{\alpha} = \mathbf{p}$, the MAP is stationary and memoryless. In both cases, the arrival times of the MAP form a Poisson process of rate

$$\lambda = \sum_{\mathbf{n} \in \mathcal{N}_0^K} \lambda_{\mathbf{n}} \tag{4.31}$$

and the vectors $\boldsymbol{\sigma}_l$ of the number of events occurred at these time instants are independent and distributed as

$$\mathsf{P}(\sigma_l = \mathbf{n}) = \frac{\lambda_{\mathbf{n}}}{\lambda}, \mathbf{n} \in \mathcal{N}_0^K. \tag{4.32}$$

Various transformations of MAPs, such as superposition, thinning, and linear transformation, are explored in (Pacheco and Prabhu 1995).

4.1.3 *Special Cases of MAPs*

By the simple MAP, we understand a MAP in which exactly one arrival occurs at every arrival epoch and all arrivals are of a single type. Note that in the literature the term Markovian arrival process often refers to this special case. A simple MAP is specified by two matrices $\mathbf{S} = \mathbf{A}_0$ and $\mathbf{R} = \mathbf{A}_1$, while matrices $\mathbf{A}_k$, $k \geq 2$, are zero. Their applications to teletraffic theory problems were considered in (Basharin and Naumov 1984). The process of arrival epochs of any MAP is a simple MAP with $\mathbf{S} = \mathbf{A} - \boldsymbol{\Lambda}$ and $\mathbf{R} = \boldsymbol{\Lambda}$. Phase-type renewal processes are simple MAPs as well. For them, the rank of matrix $\mathbf{R}$ equals 1 and $\mathbf{R} = \mathbf{sq}$.

The simple MAP is semi-Markov since the sequence (X_l, τ_l), $l = 1, 2, ...$, is a Markov renewal process. From (4.24) and (4.25), we follow the expressions for the process's semi-Markov matrix $\mathbf{G}(x) = [G(i, j, x)]$ with entries $G(i, j, x) = \mathsf{P}(X_l = j, \tau_l < x | X_{l-1} = i)$ and for its Laplace–Stieltjes transform

$$\mathbf{G}(x) = \left(\mathrm{e}^{x\mathbf{S}} - \mathbf{I}\right)\mathbf{S}^{-1}\mathbf{R}, \int_0^x \mathrm{e}^{-vx} d\mathbf{G}(x) = (v\mathbf{I} - \mathbf{S})^{-1}\mathbf{R}. \tag{4.33}$$

It follows from (4.27) that the density function of the joint distribution of the time intervals τ_l between arrivals is

$$f(x_1, x_2, ..., x_m) = \boldsymbol{\alpha}\mathrm{e}^{x_1\mathbf{S}}\mathbf{R}\mathrm{e}^{x_2\mathbf{S}}\mathbf{R} \cdots \mathrm{e}^{x_m\mathbf{S}}\mathbf{R}\mathbf{u},$$

$$x_0, x_1, ..., x_m > 0, \; m = 1, 2, ... \tag{4.34}$$

Since the simple MAP is semi-Markov arrival process, when analyzing queueing and loss systems with such arrival processes one can make use of results obtained for systems with semi-Markov arrivals.

Conditions (4.29) and (4.30), which suffice for an MAP to be a Poisson process, in the case of the simple MAP assume the form $\mathbf{Ru} = \lambda\mathbf{u}$ and $\mathbf{pR} = \lambda\mathbf{p}$, respectively, where $\lambda = \mathbf{pRu}$ is the rate of the arrival process. Checking the necessary and sufficient conditions for a simple MAP to be Poisson is more complicated and involves the eigenvectors of matrix $\mathbf{S}$ (Bean et al. 1996).

The counting process $N(t)$ of the stationary version of a simple MAP is asymptotically normal with mean $\mathsf{E}(t) = \lambda t$ and variance

$$\mathbf{t} = (2\mathbf{d}_1\mathbf{s} - \lambda)t + 2(\mathbf{d}_2\mathbf{s} - \lambda) + o(1),$$

where column vectors $\mathbf{d}_1$ and $\mathbf{d}_2$ are the unique solution to the following equilibrium equations with nonzero right parts

$$\mathbf{d}_1\mathbf{A} = \mathbf{p}(\lambda\mathbf{I} - \mathbf{R}),\ \mathbf{d}_1\mathbf{u} = 1 ...\mathbf{d}, 2\mathbf{A} = \mathbf{d}_1 - \mathbf{p},\ \mathbf{d}_2\mathbf{u} = 1.$$

A simple Markovian process of marked arrivals, often abbreviated as MMAP, is a MAP in which exactly one arrival occurs at every arrival epoch and the arrivals can be of K different types. Such a process is specified by $K + 1$ matrices $\mathbf{S} = \mathbf{A_0}$ and $\mathbf{R}_k = \mathbf{A}_{\mathbf{e}_k}$, $k = 1,2, ..., K$, while the other matrices $\mathbf{A_n}$ are zero. Here, the arrivals of one type, say i, form a simple MAP specified by $\mathbf{S}_i = \mathbf{A} - \mathbf{A}_{\mathbf{e}_i}$ and $\mathbf{R}_i$. Simple Markovian processes of marked arrivals were first studied in. It follows from (4.27) that the density of the joint distribution $\mathsf{P}(\omega_l = k_l, \tau_l < x_l, l = 1, 2, ..., m)$ of the types ω_l of arrivals occurred at time t_l and interarrival intervals τ_l is given by

$$f_{k_1,k_2,...,k_m}(x_1, x_2, ..., x_m) =$$

$$= \alpha e^{x_1\mathbf{S}}\mathbf{R}_{k_1} e^{x_2\mathbf{S}}\mathbf{R}_{k_2} \cdots e^{x_m\mathbf{S}}\mathbf{R}_{k_m}\mathbf{u}, \tag{4.35}$$

$$1 \le k_1, k_2, ..., k_m \le K, x_0, x_1, ..., x_m > 0, ...m = 1, 2, ...$$

A *batch MAP* (BMAP) is a MAP in which all arrivals are of a single type and one or more arrivals can occur at any arrival epoch. Such MAPs are defined in terms of matrices $\mathbf{A}_n$ in (Lucantoni 1991).

4.2 Matrix-Exponential Distributions and Arrival Processes

4.2.1 *Matrix-Exponential Distributions*

A CDF $F(t)$ of a nonnegative random variable is said to be matrix-exponential if $F(0) < 1$ and $F(t)$ can be expressed as

$$F(t) = 1 - \mathbf{q}e^{t\mathbf{S}}\mathbf{u} \tag{4.36}$$

for some vector $\mathbf{q}$ and matrix $\mathbf{S}$ whose eigenvalues all have negative real parts.

The idea of matrix-exponential CDFs goes back to (Cox-1, 1955), where it was shown that rational Laplace–Stieltjes transforms of nonnegative CDFs can be written as

$$\tilde{F}(s) = p_0 + \sum_{l=1}^{L} q_0 \cdots q_{l-1} p_l \prod_{i=1}^{l} \frac{\lambda_i}{\lambda_i + s},$$

where $p_i + q_i = 1, i = 1, ..., L,\ p_L = 1$, and $-\lambda_i, i = 1, ..., L$, are the poles of $\tilde{F}(s)$. Such a representation can be rewritten is matrix-exponential form (4.36) by setting

$$\mathbf{q} = (1, 0, ..., 0), \quad \mathbf{S} = \begin{bmatrix} -\lambda_1 & q_1\lambda_1 & 0 & \cdots & 0 \\ 0 & -\lambda_2 & q_2\lambda_2 & \ddots & \vdots \\ 0 & 0 & \ddots & \ddots & 0 \\ \vdots & \ddots & \ddots & -\lambda_{L-1} & q_{L-1}\lambda_{L-1} \\ 0 & \cdots & 0 & 0 & -\lambda_L \end{bmatrix}.$$

For a CDF $F(t)$ of a nonnegative random variable to be matrix-exponential it is necessary and sufficient that the Laplace–Stieltjes transform $\tilde{F}(v)$ of $F(t)$ be rational. The minimal order of $\mathbf{S}$ in the matrix-exponential representation (4.36) equals the number of poles of $\tilde{F}(v)$ with their multiplicity taken into account. A matrix-exponential representation in which matrix $\mathbf{S}$ is of minimal order is said to be minimal.

To highlight the similarity with the exponential CDFs, in some works on matrix-exponential CDFs, such as (Bocharov and Naumov 1977), as well as in book (Bocharov et al. 2004), a representation $F(t) = 1 - \mathbf{q}e^{-t\mathbf{B}}\mathbf{u}$ with the minus sign in front of $t\mathbf{B}$ and a matrix $\mathbf{B}$ whose eigenvalues all have positive real parts is used instead of (4.36). However, at present, only representation (4.36) is widely adopted.

It follows from (4.36) that the moments of the distribution are given by

$$\int_0^\infty t^n dF(t) = n!\mathbf{q}(-\mathbf{S})^{-n}\mathbf{u}, n = 1, 2, ..., \tag{4.37}$$

and the Laplace–Stieltjes transform of $F(t)$ is

$$\tilde{F}(v) = \int_0^\infty \mathrm{e}^{-vt} dF(t) = 1 - \mathbf{qu} + \mathbf{q}(v\mathbf{I} - \mathbf{S})^{-1}\mathbf{s} = 1 - v\mathbf{q}(v\mathbf{I} - \mathbf{S})^{-1}\mathbf{u}, \tag{4.38}$$

where $\mathbf{s} = -\mathbf{Su}$. Besides, matrix-exponential CDFs have the properties as follows.

(1) Let $F_i(t) = 1 - \mathbf{q}_i \mathrm{e}^{t\mathbf{S}_i}\mathbf{u}$, $i = 1, 2$, represent two matrix-exponential CDFs and $p_1 + p_2 = 1$. Then,

$$p_1 F_1(t) + p_2 F_2(t) = 1 - (p_1\mathbf{q}_1, p_2\mathbf{q}_2)\mathrm{e}^{t\begin{bmatrix} \mathbf{S}_1 & \mathbf{O} \\ \mathbf{O} & \mathbf{S}_2 \end{bmatrix}}\mathbf{u}, \tag{4.39}$$

$$(F_1 * F_2)(t) = 1 - (\mathbf{q}_1, F_1(0)\mathbf{q}_2)\mathrm{e}^{t\begin{bmatrix} \mathbf{S}_1 & -\mathbf{S}_1\mathbf{u}\mathbf{q}_2 \\ \mathbf{O} & \mathbf{S}_2 \end{bmatrix}}\mathbf{u}. \tag{4.40}$$

(2) Let τ and γ represent two independent nonnegative random variables with CDFs $F(t)$ and $G(t)$, respectively, and let $F(t)$ be of matrix-exponential form (4.36). Then, the CDF $H(t)$ of the random variable $(\tau - \gamma)^+$ has the matrix-exponential representation

$$H(t) = 1 - \mathbf{qU}\mathrm{e}^{t\mathbf{S}}\mathbf{u}, \tag{4.41}$$

where

$$\mathbf{U} = \int_0^\infty \mathrm{e}^{t\mathbf{S}} dG(t). \tag{4.42}$$

(3) Let $F(t)$ be of matrix-exponential from (4.36) and let $\mathbf{V}$ represent a square matrix whose eigenvalues all have nonnegative real parts. Then

$$\int_0^\infty \mathrm{e}^{-t\mathbf{V}} dF(t) = (1 - \mathbf{qu})\mathbf{I} + (\mathbf{q} \otimes \mathbf{I})\boldsymbol{\Psi}(\mathbf{Su} \otimes \mathbf{I}) = \mathbf{I} - (\mathbf{q} \otimes \mathbf{I})\boldsymbol{\Psi}(\mathbf{u} \otimes \mathbf{V}), \tag{4.43}$$

where $\boldsymbol{\Psi} = (\mathbf{I} \otimes \mathbf{V} - \mathbf{S} \otimes \mathbf{I})^{-1}$.

Note that property (3) can be used for calculating $\mathbf{U}$ in (4.42) for a matrix-exponential CDF $G(t)$.

4.2.2 Rational Arrival Processes

A rational process of batches of heterogeneous (marked) arrivals (t_l, σ_l), $l = 1, 2, \ldots$, can be defined as an arrival process for which the joint distribution of the numbers σ_l of arrivals and the times τ_l between arrival epochs t_l is given by (4.24) and (4.26) with matrices $\mathbf{A_n}$, $\mathbf{n} \in \mathcal{N}^K$, such that:

(1) the real parts of the eigenvalues of $\mathbf{A_0}$ are negative,
(2) the real parts of the eigenvalues of $\mathbf{A} = \sum_{\mathbf{n} \in \mathcal{N}^K} \mathbf{A_n}$ are nonpositive, and
(3) $\mathbf{Au} = \mathbf{0}$.

For the stationary versions of rational arrival processes, it is also required that the initial distribution vector $\boldsymbol{\alpha}$ coincide with the solution $\mathbf{p}$ to the equations $\mathbf{pA} = 0$, $\mathbf{pu} = 1$.

A simple rational process, also called the matrix-exponential process, is a n arrival process in which only one arrival occurs at each arrival epoch and the density of the joint distribution of the interarrival times τ_l is given by (4.34) with matrices $\mathbf{S}$ and $\mathbf{R}$ such that

(a) the real parts of the eigenvalues of $\mathbf{S}$ are negative,
(b) the real parts of the eigenvalues of $\mathbf{S} + \mathbf{R}$ are nonpositive, and
(c) $(\mathbf{S} + \mathbf{R})\mathbf{u} = \mathbf{0}$.

A rational process of marked arrivals is a process of arrivals of various types in which exactly one arrival occurs at each arrival epoch. For such a process, the joint distribution of the types of arrivals ω_l and the interarrival times τ_l is given by (4.35) and matrices $\mathbf{S}$ and $\mathbf{R} = \mathbf{R}_1 + \mathbf{R}_2 + \cdots + \mathbf{R}_K$ satisfy conditions (a)–(c).

Erlang's method of stages has been applied to analysis of stochastic systems for over a century. It has become widely used due to the development of the matrix-exponential representation of phase-type CDFs. These models are well suited for computer-based analysis of stochastic systems, which relies on processing vectors and matrices. As a result, special matrix methods for analyzing stochastic systems have been developed.

The method of fictitious states proposed in (Cox-1, 1955) permitted to extend Erlang's approach to all probability distributions with rational Laplace–Stieltjes transforms. The application of the method of fictitious states is made easier thanks to the matrix-exponential representations of CDFs (Bocharov and Naumov 1977), and arrival processes with arbitrary rational Laplace–Stieltjes transforms (Asmussen and Bladt 1999). A formal application of the method of fictitious states can produce a solution, in which the probabilities corresponding to the fictitious states are negative, larger than 1 or even complex-valued. However, the probabilities associated with real states of the system will be real.

4.3 An Example: Single-Server Queues in Series with MAP Arrivals

The system considered herein was studied in (Bromberg et al. 1977) for a general arrival process. Yet we shall show how the use of Markovian arrival processes can simplify the derivation of results that otherwise would require more complicated methods.

4.3.1 The Single-Server Loss System with MAP Arrivals

Consider a MAP|M|1 loss system with one server and a simple Markovian arrival process $(X(t), N(t))$. Here, $X(t) \in \{1, 2, ..., L\}$ is the phase process with irreducible generator matrix Q and $N(t)$ is the counting process specified by the matrix $\mathbf{R} = [R(i, j)]$ such that

$$\mathsf{P}(X(t+\delta) = j, N(t+\delta) = N(t) + 1 \,|X(t) = i) = R(i, j)\delta + o(\delta).$$

The Laplace–Stieltjes transform $g(s)$ of the CDF of the interarrival times in the stationary mode follows from (4.25) to (4.26):

$$g(s) = \frac{1}{\lambda}\mathbf{qR}(s\mathbf{I} - \mathbf{S})^{-1}\mathbf{Ru} = 1 - \frac{s}{\lambda}\mathbf{qR}(s\mathbf{I} - \mathbf{S})^{-1}\mathbf{u}. \tag{4.44}$$

Here, $\mathbf{q}$ is the stationary distribution of the phase process $X(t)$,

$$\mathbf{qQ} = \mathbf{0}, \ \mathbf{qu} = 1,$$

and $\lambda = \mathbf{qRu}$ is the stationary arrival rate.

We assume that the service times are exponentially distributed with parameter μ. Then the system can be described by a Markov process $Y(t) = (X(t), \xi(t))$, where $\xi(t) \in \{0, 1\}$ is the number of busy servers at time t. The process $Y(t)$ has the state space $\mathcal{Y} = \{(1, 0), (2, 0), ..., (L, 0), (1, 1), (2, 1), ..., (L, 1)\}$, and the block generator matrix

$$\mathbf{A} = \begin{bmatrix} \mathbf{S} & \mathbf{R} \\ \mu\mathbf{I} & \mathbf{Q} - \mu\mathbf{I} \end{bmatrix},$$

where $\mathbf{S} = \mathbf{Q} - \mathbf{R}$. Stationary probability row vector $\mathbf{p} = (\mathbf{p}_0, \mathbf{p}_1)$ of the process $Y(t)$ is the unique solution of the linear system

$$\mathbf{p}_0\mathbf{S} + \mu\mathbf{p}_1 = \mathbf{0}, \tag{4.45}$$

$$\mathbf{p}_0\mathbf{R} + \mathbf{p}_1(\mathbf{Q} - \mu\mathbf{I}) = \mathbf{0}, \tag{4.46}$$

satisfying normalizing condition

$$\mathbf{p}_0\mathbf{u} + \mathbf{p}_1\mathbf{u} = 1. \tag{4.47}$$

The solution to (4.45) – (4.47) is given by

$$\mathbf{p}_0 = \mu\,\mathbf{q}(\mu\mathbf{I} - \mathbf{S})^{-1},\ \mathbf{p}_1 = \mathbf{q}\mathbf{R}(\mu\mathbf{I} - \mathbf{S})^{-1}. \tag{4.48}$$

4.3.2 *The Departure Process of the Single-Server Loss System*

The departure process of a single-server loss system is a simple Markovian arrival process $(Y(t), D(t))$. Its counting process of the number of departures $D(t)$ is characterized by the matrix

$$\mathbf{M} = \begin{bmatrix} \mathbf{O} & \mathbf{O} \\ \mu\mathbf{I} & \mathbf{O} \end{bmatrix}.$$

The stationary probability distribution $\overline{\mathbf{p}}$ of the Markov chain imbedded just after departure times and departure rate $\overline{\lambda}$ can be calculates as

$$\overline{\mathbf{p}} = \frac{1}{\overline{\lambda}}\mathbf{p}\mathbf{M} = \frac{\mu}{\overline{\lambda}}(\mathbf{p}_1, \mathbf{0}),$$

$$\overline{\lambda} = \mathbf{p}\mathbf{M}\mathbf{u} = \mu\mathbf{p}_1\mathbf{u} = \mu\mathbf{q}\mathbf{R}(\mu\mathbf{I} - \mathbf{S})^{-1}\mathbf{u} = \lambda(1 - g(\mu)). \tag{4.49}$$

We use (4.25–4.26) to find the Laplace–Stieltjes transform $\overline{g}(s)$ of the stationary CDF of inter-departure times,

$$\overline{g}(s) = \overline{\mathbf{p}}(s\mathbf{I} - \mathbf{A} + \mathbf{M})^{-1}\mathbf{M}\mathbf{u} = \frac{\mu}{\overline{\lambda}}(\mathbf{p}_1, \mathbf{0})\begin{bmatrix} s\mathbf{I} - \mathbf{S} & -\mathbf{R} \\ \mathbf{O} & (s+\mu)\mathbf{I} - \mathbf{Q} \end{bmatrix}^{-1}\begin{bmatrix} \mathbf{O} & \mathbf{O} \\ \mu\mathbf{I} & \mathbf{O} \end{bmatrix}\mathbf{u} =$$

$$= \frac{\mu^2}{\overline{\lambda}}(\mathbf{p}_1, \mathbf{0})\begin{bmatrix} (s\mathbf{I} - \mathbf{S})^{-1} & (s\mathbf{I} - \mathbf{S})^{-1}\mathbf{R}((s+\mu)\mathbf{I} - \mathbf{Q})^{-1} \\ \mathbf{O} & ((s+\mu)\mathbf{I} - \mathbf{Q})^{-1} \end{bmatrix}\begin{pmatrix} \mathbf{0} \\ \mathbf{u} \end{pmatrix} =$$

$$= \frac{\mu^2}{\overline{\lambda}}\mathbf{q}\mathbf{R}(\mu\mathbf{I} - \mathbf{S})^{-1}(s\mathbf{I} - \mathbf{S})^{-1}\mathbf{R}((s+\mu)\mathbf{I} - \mathbf{Q})^{-1}\mathbf{u} = \tag{4.50}$$

$$= \begin{cases} \frac{\mu^2}{\lambda(\mu^2-s^2)}\mathbf{qR}((s\mathbf{I}-\mathbf{S})^{-1}-(\mu\mathbf{I}-\mathbf{S})^{-1})\mathbf{Ru}, & s \neq \mu, \\ \frac{\mu}{2\lambda}\mathbf{qR}((\mu\mathbf{I}-\mathbf{S})^{-1})^2\mathbf{Ru}, & s = \mu. \end{cases}$$

In the above derivation, we have used the relations

$$((s+\mu)\mathbf{I}-\mathbf{Q})^{-1}\mathbf{u} = \frac{1}{s+\mu}\mathbf{u},$$

$$(\mu\mathbf{I}-\mathbf{S})^{-1}(s\mathbf{I}-\mathbf{S})^{-1} = \frac{1}{\mu-s}((s\mathbf{I}-\mathbf{S})^{-1}-(\mu\mathbf{I}-\mathbf{S})^{-1}), \quad s \neq \mu.$$

Finally, (4.44), (4.49), and (4.50) yield the following relation between the CDFs of the interarrival and inter-departure times in the single-server loss system:

$$\overline{g}(s) = \begin{cases} \frac{\mu^2}{1-g(\mu)}\left(\frac{g(s)-g(\mu)}{\mu^2-s^2}\right), & s \neq \mu, \\ -\frac{\mu}{2(1-g(\mu))} \cdot \left.\frac{dg(s)}{ds}\right|_{s=\mu}, & s = \mu. \end{cases} \tag{4.51}$$

4.3.3 Single-Server Loss Systems in Series with MAP Arrivals

We now consider a n- station loss system $MAP|M|1|1 \to M|1 \to ... \to M|1$ in which each station consists of one server and no waiting places. Customers arrive at the first station according to a simple MAP. Upon completing service at station $k < n$, a customer moves to station $(k+1)$; it receives service if it finds the station free and is lost otherwise. An arriving customer that finds the first station busy is also lost. The service times at station k are independent and exponentially distributed with parameter μ_k.

It follows from (4.51) that the CDF of the inter-departure times from station k depends only on the CDF of the interarrival times at this station and on its service rate.

Let $g_k(s)$ represents the Laplace–Stieltjes transform of the interarrival times at station k. Making use of (4.51), we obtain a relation between $g_k(s)$ and $g_{k+1}(s)$:

$$g_{k+1}(s) = \begin{cases} \frac{\mu_k^2}{1-g_k(\mu_k)}\left(\frac{g_k(s)-g_k(\mu)}{\mu_k^2-s^2}\right), & s \neq \mu_k, \\ -\frac{\mu_k}{2(1-g_k(\mu_k))} \cdot \left.\frac{dg_k(s)}{ds}\right|_{s=\mu_k}, & s = \mu_k. \end{cases} \tag{4.52}$$

The departure rate λ_{k+1} from station k (of customers that have received service) is given by

$$\lambda_{k+1} = \lambda_k(1 - g_k(\mu_k)). \tag{4.53}$$

One can now use (4.52) and (4.53) to derive the probability that a customer arriving to a n-station system will be lost. If μ_k are different from one another, the blocking probability is given by

$$\pi_n = \sum_{k=1}^{n} g_1(\mu_k) \prod_{\substack{i=1 \\ i \neq k}}^{n} \frac{\mu_i^2}{\mu_i^2 - \mu_k^2}. \tag{4.54}$$

If, in contrast, $\mu_k = \mu$ for all k, then

$$\pi_n = \sum_{k=0}^{n-1} (-1)^k \frac{\mu^{2k}}{k!} \cdot \frac{d^k}{ds^k} g_1\left(\sqrt{s}\right)\Big|_{s=\mu^2}. \tag{4.55}$$

Note that it follows from (4.54) that the blocking probability does not depend on the order of the stations.

Note also that the right-hand side of (4.54) is the value for $s = 0$ of the Lagrange interpolating polynomial of the function $g_1\left(\sqrt{s}\right)$ with given values for $s_k = \mu_k^2$, while the right-hand side of (4.55) is the sum of the first n terms of the Maclaurin series for the same function.

References

Asmussen, S., Bladt, M.: Point processes with finite-dimensional conditional probabilities. Stochastic processes and their applications, 82(1):127–142 (1999)

Basharin, G., Naumov, V.: Simple matrix description of peaked and smooth traffic and its applications. In: 3rd ITC Specialist Seminar on Fundamentals of Teletraffic Theory, VINITI, Moscow, 38–44 (1984)

Bean, N.G., Green, D.A., Taylor, P.G.: When is a MAP poisson? In: Proceedings of the Second Australia-Japan Workshop on Stochastic Models in Engineering, Technology and Management, Gold Coast, Australia, 34–43 (1996)

Bocharov, P.P., D'Apice, C., Pechinkin, A.V., Salerno, S.: Queueing Theory. VSP, Boston, Utrecht (2004)

Bocharov, P.P., Naumov, V.A.: On some queuing systems of finite capacity. Probl. Inform. Trans. **13**(4), 314–320 (1977)

Bromberg, M.A., Kokotushkin, V.A., Naumov, V.A.: Queueing system consisting of a chain of devices. Autom. Remote. Control. **38**(3), 351–358 (1977)

Çinlar, E.: Markov additive processes, I. Zeitschrift Für Wahrscheinlichkeitstheorie Und Verwandte Gebiete **24**(2), 85–93 (1972a)

Çinlar, E.: Markov additive processes, II. Zeitschrift Für Wahrscheinlichkeitstheorie Und Verwandte Gebiete **24**(2), 95–121 (1972b)

Cox, D.R.: A use of complex probabilities in the theory of stochastic processes. Mathematical Proceedings of the Cambridge Philosophical Society, 51(2):313–319 (1955)

Ezhov, I.I., Skorokhod, A.V.: Markov processes with homogeneous second component, I. Theory Prob. Appl. **14**(1), 1–13 (1969a)
Ezhov, I.I., Skorokhod, A.V.: Markov processes with homogeneous second component, II. Theory Prob. Appl. **14**(4), 652–667 (1969b)
Khinchin, A.Y.: Sequences of chance events without after-effects. Theory Prob. Appl. **1**(1), 1–15 (1956)
Lucantoni, D.M., Meier-Hellstern, K., Neuts, M.F.: A single-server queue with server vacations and a class of non-renewal arrival processes. Adv. Appl. Prob. **22**(3), 676–705 (1990)
Lucantoni, D.M.: New results on the single server queue with a batch markovian arrival process. Commun. Stat. Stoch. Models **7**(1), 1–46 (1991)
Naumov, V.A.: Analysis of some queues in series. Ph.D. thesis, Peoples Friendship University, Moscow (1978) (in Russian)
Neuts, M.F.: A versatile Markovian point process. Technical Report 77/13, Department of Statistics and Computer Science, University of Delaware, USA (1977)
Neuts, M.F.: A versatile Markovian point process. J. Appl. Probab. **16**(4), 764–779 (1979)
Neuts, M.F.: Matrix-Geometric Solutions in Stochastic Models: An Algorithmic Approach. The John Hopkins University Press, Baltimore (1981)
Pacheco, A., Prabhu, N.U.: Markov-Additive Processes of Arrivals. Advances in Queueing Theory, Methods, and Open Problems, pp. 167–194. CRC Press, Florida (1995)

Part II
Matrix-Analytical Methods

Chapter 5
Generator Matrices

Abstract In this chapter, we discuss the properties of generator matrices, their exponentials, and generalized inverses. We also study homogeneous and nonhomogeneous systems of linear equations with generator matrices and show how lumpability of the matrix can be used to solve the equations.

5.1 Irreducible Generator Matrices

In this chapter, all vectors are column vectors unless stated otherwise. Let **A** and **B** be two rectangular matrices of the same dimensions. We write

$\mathbf{A} \geq \mathbf{B}$ if $A(i, j) \geq B(i, j)$ for all i and j,

$\mathbf{A} \gg \mathbf{B}$ if $A(i, j) > B(i, j)$ for all i and j,

$\mathbf{A} > \mathbf{B}$ if $\mathbf{A} \geq \mathbf{B}$ and $\mathbf{A} \neq \mathbf{B}$.

A matrix **A** is said to be *nonnegative* if $\mathbf{A} \geq \mathbf{0}$, and *positive* if $\mathbf{A} \gg \mathbf{0}$. The same terminology and notation are applicable to vectors. Additionally, a vector $\mathbf{x} > \mathbf{0}$ is said to be *semipositive* if some of its entries are zero. All vectors in this chapter are column.

A nonnegative square matrix **P** of order n is called *substochastic* if

$$\sum_{j=1}^{n} P(i, j) \leq 1, \ \ i = 1, 2, \ ..., n$$

and *stochastic* if

$$\sum_{j=1}^{n} P(i, j) = 1, |i = 1, 2, \ ..., n \, .$$

Stochastic and substochastic matrices appear in the analysis of discrete-time Markov chains. The theory of continuous-time Markov chains largely relies on *generator matrices*, say **A**, whose off-diagonal entries are nonnegative and each row sums up to a nonpositive number:

V. Naumov et al., *Matrix and Analytical Methods for Performance Analysis of Telecommunication Systems*, https://doi.org/10.1007/978-3-030-83132-5_5

$$A(i, j) \geq 0, i \neq j, i, j = 1, 2, \ldots, n,$$

$$\sum_{j=1}^{n} A(i, j) \leq 0, i = 1, 2, \ldots, n.$$

A generator matrix $\mathbf{A}$ is called *conservative* if it satisfies the strict equality $\mathbf{Au} = \mathbf{0}$, where $\mathbf{u} = (1, 1, \ldots, 1)$ is an all-ones column vector of appropriate size.

The fundamental properties of stochastic matrices and generator matrices derive from the general theory of nonnegative and M-matrices (Berman 1979), (Gantmacher 1959). Any generator matrix, say $\mathbf{A}$, satisfies the relations

$$A(i, i) \leq -\sum_{j \neq i} A(i, j) \leq 0, i = 1, 2, \ldots, n.$$

Therefore, the diagonal elements of such matrices are nonpositive, and if some diagonal element is zero then all elements of the corresponding row are zero.

For any scalar $a > 0$ such that$a \geq -\min_j A(j, j)$,matrix $\mathbf{A}$ can be written as $\mathbf{A} = a(\mathbf{P} - \mathbf{I})$, where $\mathbf{P} = \mathbf{I} + a^{-1}\mathbf{A}$ is nonnegative. Matrix $\mathbf{P}$ is substochastic because $\mathbf{Pu} = \mathbf{u} + a^{-1}\mathbf{Au} \leq \mathbf{u}$. Furthermore, $\mathbf{P}$ is stochastic if $\mathbf{A}$ is conservative.

The opposite is also true. Any matrix of the form $\mathbf{A} = a(\mathbf{P} - \mathbf{I})$, where $a > 0$ and $\mathbf{P}$ is substochastic, is a generator matrix. In addition, if $\mathbf{Pu} = \mathbf{u}$ then $\mathbf{Au} = \mathbf{0}$ and, consequently, $\mathbf{A}$ is conservative. Thus, we have proved the following.

Theorem 5.1 *A matrix* $\mathbf{A}$ *is a generator matrix if and only if it can be written in the form* $\mathbf{A} = a(\mathbf{P} - \mathbf{I})$*, where* a *is a positive scalar and* $\mathbf{P}$ *is a substochastic matrix. Furthermore,* $\mathbf{A}$ *is conservative whenever* $\mathbf{P}$ *is stochastic.*

Theorem 5.2 *If* $\mathbf{A}$ *is a generator matrix then from* $\mathbf{Ax} \gg \mathbf{0}$ *it follows that* $\mathbf{x} \ll \mathbf{0}$*. Furthermore,* $\mathbf{A}$ *is nonsingular if and only if from* $\mathbf{Ax} \geq \mathbf{0}$ *it follows that* $\mathbf{x} \leq \mathbf{0}$*.*

Proof Suppose that $\mathbf{A}$ is a generator matrix, $\mathbf{Ax} \gg \mathbf{0}$ and $x(k) = \max_j x(j) \geq 0$. Write $\mathbf{A}$ as $\mathbf{A} = a(\mathbf{P} - \mathbf{I})$, where $a > 0$ and $\mathbf{P}$ is substochastic. Then,

$$\mathbf{Ax}(k) = a\left(\sum_{j=1}^{n} P(k, j)x(j) - x(k)\right) \leq a\left(\sum_{j=1}^{n} P(k, j) - 1\right)x(k) \leq 0,$$

which contradicts the assumption that $\mathbf{Ax} \gg \mathbf{0}$. Thus, $\mathbf{Ax} \gg \mathbf{0}$ implies $\mathbf{x} \ll \mathbf{0}$.

Suppose now that generator matrix $\mathbf{A}$ is nonsingular, $\mathbf{H} = \mathbf{A}^{-1}$ and $\mathbf{Ax} \geq \mathbf{0}$. Then, for any $\varepsilon > 0$, $\mathbf{A}(\mathbf{x} + \varepsilon\mathbf{Hu}) = \mathbf{Ax} + \varepsilon\mathbf{u} \gg \mathbf{0}$. In light of the above discussion, this implies that $\mathbf{x} + \varepsilon\mathbf{Hu} \ll \mathbf{0}$ for any $\varepsilon > 0$, and hence $\mathbf{x} \leq \mathbf{0}$.

Conversely, suppose that for some matrix $\mathbf{A}$ from the inequality $\mathbf{Ax} \geq \mathbf{0}$ it always follows that $\mathbf{x} \leq \mathbf{0}$. If $\mathbf{Ax} = \mathbf{0}$ then the relations $\mathbf{Ax} \geq \mathbf{0}$ and $\mathbf{A}(-\mathbf{x}) \geq \mathbf{0}$ hold simultaneously, and therefore $\mathbf{x} \leq \mathbf{0}$ and $\mathbf{x} \geq \mathbf{0}$. Hence, the equation $\mathbf{Ax} = \mathbf{0}$ has only the zero solution and, consequently, matrix $\mathbf{A}$ is nonsingular. ■

Theorem 5.3 *Let* $\mathbf{A}$ *be a nonsingular generator matrix. Then, the diagonal entries of its inverse* $\mathbf{A}^{-1}$ *are strictly negative and the off-diagonal entries are nonpositive.*

Proof Let $\mathbf{H} = \mathbf{A}^{-1}$ and denote by $\mathbf{h}_j$ the j-th column of $\mathbf{H}$. Further, let $\mathbf{e}_j = (0, ..., 0, 1, 0, ...0)^T$ be a vector whose j-th element is 1 and all the others are zero. Then, $\mathbf{Ah}_j = \mathbf{e}_j \geq \mathbf{0}$ and, by Theorem 5.2, $\mathbf{h}_j \leq \mathbf{0}$. Hence, all the elements of $\mathbf{H}$ are nonpositive. By Theorem 5.1, $\mathbf{A}$ can be written as $\mathbf{A} = a(\mathbf{P}-\mathbf{I})$, where $a > 0$ and $\mathbf{P}$ is a substochastic matrix. It follows from $\mathbf{AH} = \mathbf{I}$ that $a\mathbf{H} = a\mathbf{PH} - \mathbf{I}$ and, moreover, $a\mathbf{PH} \leq \mathbf{0}$. Therefore, the diagonal elements of $\mathbf{H}$ are strictly negative. ■

A square matrix $\mathbf{S}$ is said to be a *permutation matrix* if it has exactly one element of 1 in each column and each row, and 0 elsewhere. An example of a permutation matrix is

$$\mathbf{S} = \begin{bmatrix} 0 & 1 & 0 \\ 0 & 0 & 1 \\ 1 & 0 & 0 \end{bmatrix}.$$

A product of two permutation matrices is a permutation matrix.

To any permutation matrix $\mathbf{S}$ of order n, there corresponds a permutation $\sigma_1, \sigma_2, ..., \sigma_n$ of numbers $1, 2, ..., n$ such that $\sigma_i = j$ if $S(i, j) = 1$. A permutation matrix $\mathbf{S}$ has the following property:

$$\mathbf{SS}^T = \mathbf{S}^T\mathbf{S} = \mathbf{I},$$

that is, its transpose $\mathbf{S}^T$ is also its inverse. Note that the permutation corresponding to $\mathbf{S}^T$ is the inversion (denoted by σ^{-1}) of the permutation σ corresponding to $\mathbf{S}$. Thus, for the example above, we have $\sigma_1 = 2$, $\sigma_2 = 3$, $\sigma_3 = 1$ and $\sigma_1^{-1} = 3$, $\sigma_2^{-1} = 1$, $\sigma_3^{-1} = 2$.

Let a permutation σ correspond to a permutation matrix $\mathbf{S}$. Then, for any matrix $\mathbf{A}$, the multiplication of $\mathbf{A}$ by $\mathbf{S}$ on the left and by $\mathbf{S}^T$ on the right results in the permutation of both rows and columns of $\mathbf{A}$ according to σ:

$$\mathbf{SAS}^T = \begin{bmatrix} A(\sigma_1, \sigma_1) & A(\sigma_1, \sigma_2) & \cdots & A(\sigma_1, \sigma_n) \\ A(\sigma_2, \sigma_1) & A(\sigma_2, \sigma_2) & \cdots & A(\sigma_2, \sigma_n) \\ \cdots & \cdots & \cdots & \cdots \\ A(\sigma_n, \sigma_1) & A(\sigma_n, \sigma_2) & \cdots & A(\sigma_n, \sigma_n) \end{bmatrix}.$$

Recall that a collection of nonempty disjoint sets whose union is a set $\mathcal{X}$ is called a *partition* of the set $\mathcal{X}$. A matrix $\mathbf{A}$ of order n is said to be *irreducible* if $n = 1$

or if $n \geq 2$, and for any partition $\mathcal{Y}$, $\mathcal{Z}$ of the set $\mathcal{X} = \{1, 2, ..., n\}$, there exist $i \in \mathcal{Y}$, $j \in \mathcal{Z}$ such that $A(i, j) \neq 0$. Otherwise, **A** is said to be *reducible*.

Irreducible matrices have at least one nonzero off-diagonal element in every row. Therefore, the diagonal elements of irreducible generator matrices are strictly negative. A matrix **A** is reducible if and only if, for some permutation matrix **S**, matrix $\mathbf{SAS}^T$ is of the form

$$\mathbf{SAS}^T = \begin{bmatrix} \mathbf{B} & \mathbf{O} \\ \mathbf{C} & \mathbf{D} \end{bmatrix}, \tag{5.1}$$

where **B** and **D** are square matrices. In this case $A(i, j) = 0$ for all $i \in \mathcal{Y}$, $j \in \mathcal{Z}$, where $\mathcal{Y} = \{\sigma_k : 1 \leq k \leq m\}$, $\mathcal{Z} = \{\sigma_k | m < k \leq n\}$, and m is the order of **B**. If either of the matrices **B** and **D** is reducible then it can also be written in the form similar to (5.1). This process can be continued until, with appropriate permutation of rows and columns, matrix **A** assumes a block-triangular form

$$\mathbf{PAP}^T = \begin{bmatrix} \mathbf{A}_{11} & & & \mathbf{O} \\ \mathbf{A}_{21} & \mathbf{A}_{22} & & \\ \cdots & \cdots & \ddots & \\ \mathbf{A}_{l1} & \mathbf{A}_{l2} & \cdots & \mathbf{A}_{ll} \end{bmatrix}, \tag{5.2}$$

where the diagonal blocks are irreducible. The resulting block matrix contains isolated diagonal blocks $\mathbf{A}_{ii}$ such that $\mathbf{A}_{ij} = \mathbf{0}$ for all $j \neq i$. By permuting block rows and columns in matrix (5.2), the isolated blocks can be placed first along the main diagonal. Thus, for any reducible matrix **A**, there exists a permutation matrix **Q** such that

$$\mathbf{QAQ}^T = \begin{bmatrix} \mathbf{A}_1 & & & & & & \\ & \mathbf{A}_2 & & & \mathbf{O} & & \\ \mathbf{O} & & \ddots & & & & \\ & & & \mathbf{A}_r & & & \\ \mathbf{A}_{r+1,1} & \mathbf{A}_{r+1,2} & & \mathbf{A}_{r+1,r} & \mathbf{A}_{r+1} & & \\ \cdots & \cdots & \cdots & \cdots & \cdots & \ddots & \\ \mathbf{A}_{l,1} & \mathbf{A}_{l,2} & & \mathbf{A}_{l,r} & \mathbf{A}_{l,r+1} & \cdots & \mathbf{A}_l \end{bmatrix}, \tag{5.3}$$

where $\mathbf{A}_1, \mathbf{A}_2, ..., \mathbf{A}_l$ are irreducible square matrices and each row, $\mathbf{A}_{i1}, \mathbf{A}_{i2}, ..., \mathbf{A}_{i,i-1}$, $i = r+1, r+2, ..., l$, contains at least one nonzero matrix. Matrix (5.3) is said to be *the normal form of the reducible matrix* **A** (Gantmacher 1959).

Theorem 5.4 *A generator matrix* **A** *is reducible if and only if there exists a semipositive vector* **x** *such that* $\mathbf{Ax}(k) = 0$ *for all indices* k*, for which* $x(k) = 0$.

Proof If $\mathbf{A}$ is reducible then there exists a partition $\mathcal{Y}, \mathcal{Z}$ of the set $\mathcal{X} = \{1, 2, ..., n\}$ such that $A(k, j) = 0$ for all $k \in \mathcal{Y}, j \in \mathcal{Z}$. Define a semipositive vector by the relations $x(j) = 0$ for $j \in \mathcal{Y}$ and $x(j) = 1$ for $j \in \mathcal{Z}$. If $x(k) = 0$ then $k \in \mathcal{Y}$ and

$$\mathbf{Ax}(k) = \sum_{j \in \mathcal{Y}} A(k, j)x(j) + \sum_{j \in \mathcal{Z}} A(k, j)x(j) = 0,$$

since $x(j) = 0$ for $j \in \mathcal{Y}$ and $A(k, j) = 0$ for $j \in \mathcal{Z}$.

Conversely, let $\mathbf{x}$ be a semipositive vector and let $\mathbf{Ax}(k) = \mathbf{0}$ for all k such that $x(k) = 0$. Let $\mathcal{Y} = \{i : x(i) = 0\}$ and $\mathcal{Z} = \{i : x(i) > 0\}$. Then, $\mathcal{Y}$ and $\mathcal{Z}$ form a partition of the set $\mathcal{X}$, and for all $i \in \mathcal{Y}$, we have

$$0 = \mathbf{Ax}(i) = \sum_{j \in \mathcal{Y}} A(i, j)x(j) + \sum_{j \in \mathcal{Z}} A(i, j)x(j) = \sum_{j \in \mathcal{Z}} A(i, j)x(j).$$

Since all the terms of the latter sum are nonnegative and $x(j) > 0$ for $j \in \mathcal{Z}$, it follows that $A(i, j) = 0$ for all $i \in \mathcal{Y}, j \in \mathcal{Z}$. Consequently, matrix $\mathbf{A}$ is reducible. ∎

Now, consider *associated graph of a generator matrix* $\mathbf{A}$. It is a directed graph $G(\mathbf{A}) = (\mathcal{X}, \mathcal{V})$ with the set of vertices $\mathcal{X} = \{1, 2, ..., n\}$ and the set of edges $\mathcal{V} \subset \mathcal{X} \times \mathcal{X}$, such that a pair (i, j) forms an edge if $i \neq j$ and $A(i, j) \neq 0$. We assume by convention that for any vertex i there is a path (of length 0) from i to i. A *path* of length $k \geq 1$ from vertex i to vertex j is a sequence $i_0 = i, i_1, ..., i_{k-1}, i_k = j$ of vertices in which every pair of consecutive vertices forms an edge in the graph. A vertex j is said to be *accessible* from a vertex i if in $G(\mathbf{A})$ there exists a path from i to j. A graph $G(\mathbf{A})$ is said to be *strongly connected* if any one of its vertices is accessible from any other vertex.

Theorem 5.5 *A matrix* $\mathbf{A}$ *is irreducible if and only if the graph* $G(\mathbf{A})$ *is strongly connected.*

Proof For matrices of order $n = 1$ the result is obvious. Let $\mathbf{A}$ be an irreducible matrix of order $n \geq 2$. For each vertex i, let $\mathcal{Y}_i$ denote the set of vertices accessible from i. Since $i \in \mathcal{Y}_i$, $\mathcal{Y}_i$ is nonempty. If $\mathcal{Y}_i \neq \mathcal{X}$ then for all $l \in \mathcal{Y}_i$ and $j \in \mathcal{X} \backslash \mathcal{Y}_i$ we have $A(l, j) = 0$, which implies that $\mathbf{A}$ is reducible. Hence, $\mathcal{Y}_i = \mathcal{X}$ and, consequently, $G(\mathbf{A})$ is strongly connected.

Conversely, let $\mathcal{Y}, \mathcal{Z}$ be a partition of $\mathcal{X}$ and $i_0, i_1, ..., i_k$, a path from i to $j, i \in \mathcal{Y}$, $j \in \mathcal{Z}$. Then, at least for one edge (i_{r-1}, i_r) of this path, we have $i_{r-1} \in \mathcal{Y}, i_r \in \mathcal{Z}$, and hence $A(i_{r-1}, i_r) \neq 0$. Consequently, $\mathbf{A}$ is irreducible.

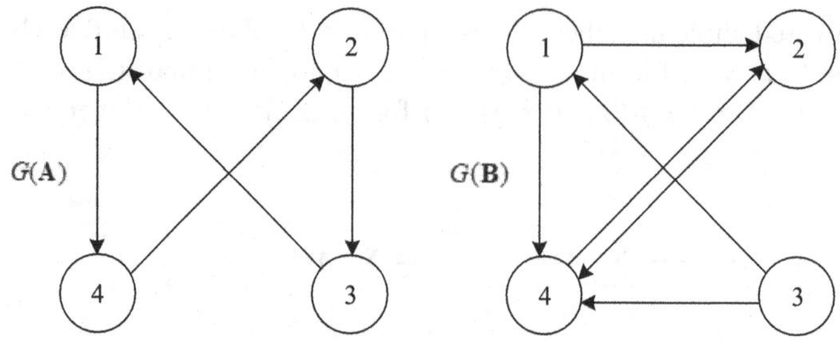

Fig. 5.1. Generator matrices and their associated graphs

Example

$$\mathbf{A} = \begin{bmatrix} -2 & 0 & 0 & 1 \\ 0 & -1 & 1 & 0 \\ 1 & 0 & -1 & 0 \\ 0 & 1 & 0 & -1 \end{bmatrix}, \quad \mathbf{B} = \begin{bmatrix} -2 & 1 & 0 & 1 \\ 0 & -1 & 0 & 1 \\ 1 & 0 & -2 & 1 \\ 0 & 1 & 0 & -1 \end{bmatrix}$$

Matrix **A** is irreducible, whereas **B** is reducible (Fig. 5.1).

5.2 Nonsingular Matrices

Theorem 5.6 *For any generator matrix* **A** *of order n the following are equivalent:*

(a) **A** *is nonsingular;*

(b) $\mathbf{B} = \begin{bmatrix} -n & \mathbf{u}^T \\ -\mathbf{Au} & \mathbf{A} \end{bmatrix}$ *is irreducible;*

(c) $\mathbf{Au} \neq \mathbf{0}$ *and* $\mathbf{C} = \mathbf{A} - \frac{1}{n}\mathbf{Auu}^T$ *is irreducible;*

(d) $\mathbf{A} < \mathbf{Q}$, *where* **Q** *is an irreducible generator matrix.*

Proof Let the rows and columns of the matrix **B** be indexed starting from 0. Suppose that **B** is reducible and let $\mathcal{Y}_i$, $\mathcal{Z}$ be a partition of $\mathcal{X}_0 = \{0, 1, ..., n\}$ such that $B(i, j) = 0$ for all $i \in \mathcal{Y}_i$ and $j \in \mathcal{Z}$. Since the 0-th row of **B** does not contain zero entries, $0 \notin \mathcal{Y}$, and hence $0 \in \mathcal{Z}$.

If $\mathcal{Z} = \{0\}$ then $\mathbf{Au} = \mathbf{0}$ and, consequently, **A** is singular. If, however, $\mathcal{Z} \neq \{0\}$ then we assume, without loss of generality, that $\mathcal{Z} = \{0, 1, ..., r\}$ and $\mathcal{Y}_i = \{r+1, r+2, ..., n\}$, where $1 \leq r < n$. Since $B(i, j) = 0$ for all $i \in \mathcal{Y}_i$ and $j \in \mathcal{Z}$, we have

$$\begin{aligned} \mathbf{Au}(i) &= 0, \; i = r+1, r+2, ..., n, \\ A(i, j) &= 0, \; i = r+1, r+2, ..., n, \; j = 1, 2, ..., r. \end{aligned} \tag{5.4}$$

In this case **A** is of the form

$$\mathbf{A} = \begin{bmatrix} \mathbf{A}_{11} & \mathbf{A}_{12} \\ \mathbf{O} & \mathbf{A}_{22} \end{bmatrix},$$

where $\mathbf{A}_{11}$ and $\mathbf{A}_{22}$ are square, and it follows from (5.4) that $\det(\mathbf{A}_{22}) = 0$. Hence, $\det(\mathbf{A}) = 0$ and $\mathbf{A}$ is singular, which proves that (a) implies (b).

Consider now statement (c). Clearly, $\mathbf{Au} \neq \mathbf{0}$ if $\mathbf{B}$ is irreducible. Suppose that matrix $\mathbf{C}$ is reducible. Then, according to Theorem 5.4, there exists a semipositive vector $\mathbf{x}$ such that $\mathbf{Cx}(i) = 0$ whenever $x(i) = 0$. The vector

$$\mathbf{y} = \begin{bmatrix} \frac{1}{n}\mathbf{u}^T\mathbf{x} \\ \mathbf{x} \end{bmatrix}$$

is semipositive and, moreover, for any zero entry of $\mathbf{y}$ the corresponding entry of the vector

$$\mathbf{By} = \begin{bmatrix} 0 \\ \mathbf{Cx} \end{bmatrix}$$

is also zero. In light of Theorem 5.4, this implies the reducibility of $\mathbf{B}$. Therefore, if $\mathbf{B}$ is irreducible then $\mathbf{C}$ is also irreducible. Thus, (b) implies (c).

Now suppose, conversely, that $\mathbf{A}$ is singular, but $\mathbf{Au} \neq \mathbf{0}$. Let $\mathbf{Ay} = \mathbf{0}$, $\mathbf{y} \neq \mathbf{0}$ and

$$m = \max_i y(i) > 0$$

(otherwise we can take $-\mathbf{y}$ instead of $\mathbf{y}$). Clearly, $\mathbf{x} = m\mathbf{u} - \mathbf{y}$ is semipositive. Moreover, since the off-diagonal entries of $\mathbf{A}$ are nonnegative, we have $\mathbf{Ax}(i) \geq 0$ whenever $x(i) = 0$. On the other hand, $\mathbf{Ax} = m\mathbf{Au} \leq \mathbf{0}$. Therefore, $\mathbf{Ax}(i) = \mathbf{Au}(i) = 0$ for all i such that $x(i) = 0$. For such i, we have

$$\mathbf{Cx}(i) = \mathbf{Ax}(i) - \frac{1}{n}(\mathbf{u}^T\mathbf{x})\mathbf{Au}(i) = 0,$$

which by Theorem 5.4 implies the reducibility of $\mathbf{C}$. Thus, if $\mathbf{A}$ is singular then either $\mathbf{Au} = \mathbf{0}$ or $\mathbf{C}$ is reducible. Therefore, (c) implies (a).

Let us now show that (c) and (d) are equivalent. It can be easily observed that $\mathbf{C}$ is a generator matrix. Moreover, $\mathbf{Au} < \mathbf{0}$ implies $\mathbf{A} < \mathbf{C}$. Therefore, (c) implies (d).

Suppose now that $\mathbf{A} < \mathbf{Q}$, where $\mathbf{Q}$ is an irreducible generator matrix. Then, $\mathbf{Au} < \mathbf{Qu} \leq \mathbf{0}$ and, consequently, $\mathbf{Au} \neq \mathbf{0}$. Compare nonzero entries of $\mathbf{Q}$ and $\mathbf{C}$. If $\mathbf{Au}(i) < 0$ then all entries of the i-th row of $\mathbf{C}$ are nonzero. If, conversely, $\mathbf{Au}(i) = 0$ then all entries of the i-th row of $\mathbf{A}$, $\mathbf{Q}$, and $\mathbf{C}$ coincide. Therefore, $\mathbf{Q}$ has zero entries wherever $\mathbf{C}$ has zero entries, and, since $\mathbf{Q}$ is irreducible, $\mathbf{C}$ is also irreducible. Thus, (d) implies (c). ∎

Corollary *Let generator matrices* $\mathbf{A}$ *and* $\mathbf{B}$ *satisfy* $\mathbf{A} \leq \mathbf{B}$*, and let* $\mathbf{B}$ *be nonsingular. Then,* $\mathbf{A}$ *is nonsingular and* $\mathbf{A}^{-1} \geq \mathbf{B}^{-1}$.

Proof In light of statement (d) of Theorem 5.6, $\mathbf{B} < \mathbf{Q}$, where $\mathbf{Q}$ is an irreducible generator. Since $\mathbf{A} \leq \mathbf{B}$, $\mathbf{A} < \mathbf{Q}$, and hence $\mathbf{A}$ is nonsingular. By Theorem 5.3, $\mathbf{A}^{-1} \leq \mathbf{0}$ and $\mathbf{B}^{-1} \leq \mathbf{0}$, and therefore

$$\mathbf{A}^{-1} - \mathbf{B}^{-1} = (-\mathbf{A}^{-1})(\mathbf{B} - \mathbf{A})(-\mathbf{B}^{-1}) \geq \mathbf{0}.$$

Theorem 5.7 *Let a generator matrix* $\mathbf{A}$ *be irreducible and nonconservative. Then, it is nonsingular and* $\mathbf{A}^{-1} \ll \mathbf{0}$.

Proof If a generator matrix $\mathbf{A}$ of order n is irreducible then matrix $\mathbf{C} = \mathbf{A} - \frac{1}{n}\mathbf{A}\mathbf{u}\mathbf{u}^T$ is also irreducible. If, in addition, $\mathbf{A}\mathbf{u} \neq \mathbf{0}$ then, in light of Theorem 5.6, $\mathbf{A}$ is nonsingular.

By Theorem 5.3, $\mathbf{H} = \mathbf{A}^{-1}$ is nonpositive and its diagonal entries are negative. Suppose that $H(k, j) = 0$ for some k and j and, using the previous notation, let $\mathbf{h}_j$ be the j-th column of $\mathbf{H}$. Then, vector $\mathbf{x} = -\mathbf{h}_j$ is semipositive and $\mathbf{A}\mathbf{x}(k) = -\mathbf{e}_j(k) = \mathbf{0}$ for all k such that $x(k) = 0$. By Theorem 5.4, this implies the reducibility of $\mathbf{A}$. Thus, for $\mathbf{A}$ to be irreducible, all entries of $\mathbf{H}$ should be strictly negative. ■

Theorem 5.8 *Let* $\mathbf{A}$ *be an irreducible generator matrix of order* n *and let* $\mathbf{B}$ *be obtained from* $\mathbf{A}$ *by striking out some* m *rows and* m *columns with the same indices,* $0 < m < n$*. Then,* $\mathbf{B}$ *is a nonsingular generator matrix.*

Proof Let $\mathcal{Y} = \{i_1, ..., i_m\}$ be the set of the removed rows and columns' indices. Set $C(i, j) = A(i, j)$ for $i, j \notin \mathcal{Y}$, $C(i, i) = A(i, i)$ for $i \in \mathcal{Y}$, and $C(i, j) = 0$ otherwise. Then,

$$\det(\mathbf{C}) = \det(\mathbf{B}) \prod_{i \in \mathcal{Y}} A(i, i). \tag{5.5}$$

Since the diagonal entries of an irreducible generator matrix are negative, $\prod_{i \in \mathcal{Y}} A(i, i) \neq 0$. Clearly, $\mathbf{B}$ and $\mathbf{C}$ are generator matrices and, furthermore, $\mathbf{C} < \mathbf{A}$. By Theorem 5.6, $\mathbf{C}$ is nonsingular and, in light of (5.5), $\mathbf{B}$ is also nonsingular. ■

Statement (b) of Theorem 5.6 can be expressed in a convenient form in terms of graphs. Let $\mathbf{A}$ be a generator matrix of order n and consider a *modified associated graph* $G_0(\mathbf{A}) = (\mathcal{X}_0, \mathcal{V}_0)$ with a set of vertices $\mathcal{X}_0$ and a set of edges $\mathcal{V}_0 \subset \mathcal{X}_0 \times \mathcal{X}_0$. Graph $G_0(\mathbf{A})$ is obtained from associated graph $G(\mathbf{A})$ of $\mathbf{A}$, as follows. The set of vertices $\mathcal{X}_0$ consists of all vertices of $G(\mathbf{A})$ (that is, $\mathcal{X} = \{1, 2, ..., n\}$) plus the vertex 0. The edges of $G_0(\mathbf{A})$ include all edges of $G(\mathbf{A})$ and, in addition, the edges to 0 from all vertices $i \neq 0$ such that $\mathbf{A}\mathbf{u}(i) < 0$. That is,

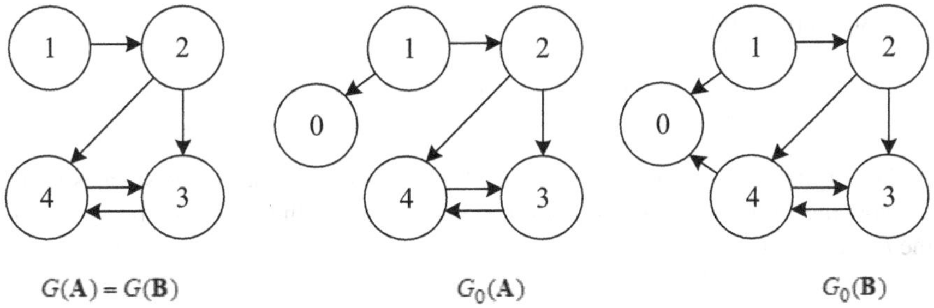

Fig. 5.2. Generator matrices, associated graph, and modified associated graphs

$$\mathcal{X}_0 = \{0, 1, ..., n\},$$

$$\mathcal{V}_0 = \{(i, j) | i, j \in \mathcal{X},\ A(i, j) > 0\} \cup$$

$$\cup \{(i, 0) | i \in \mathcal{X}, \sum_{j=1}^{n} A(i, j) < 0\}.$$

Theorem 5.9 *A generator matrix* **A** *is nonsingular if and only if vertex 0 is accessible from any vertex in* $G_0(\mathbf{A})$.

Proof If the indices of the rows and columns of matrix **B** in Theorem 5.6 start from 0, then $G(\mathbf{B})$ and $G_0(\mathbf{A})$ differ only in that $G(\mathbf{B})$ contains edges from 0 to all other vertices. Clearly, the statement of the theorem is equivalent to strong connectedness of $G(\mathbf{B})$, which, in light of Theorem 5.5, is equivalent to irreducibility of **B**. The latter is equivalent to nonsingularity of **A** (Fig. 5.2). ■

Example

$$\mathbf{A} = \begin{bmatrix} -2 & 1 & 0 & 0 \\ 0 & -3 & 2 & 1 \\ 1 & 0 & -2 & 1 \\ 0 & 0 & 2 & -2 \end{bmatrix}, \quad \mathbf{B} = \begin{bmatrix} -2 & 1 & 0 & 0 \\ 0 & -3 & 2 & 1 \\ 1 & 0 & -2 & 1 \\ 0 & 0 & 1 & -2 \end{bmatrix}.$$

Matrix **A** is singular, whereas matrix **B** is nonsingular (Fig. 5.2).

5.3 Equilibrium Equations

Let $\xi_k,\ k = 0, 1, ...,$ be a homogeneous discrete-time Markov chain with n states. We denote by

$$P(i, j) = P\{\xi_{k+1} = j | \xi_k = i\},\ i, j = 1, 2, ..., n,$$

its transition probabilities and by

$$p_k(j) = P\{\xi_k = j\}, \; j = 1, 2, ..., n,$$

the state probabilities at time k. The transition probability matrix $\mathbf{P}$ is stochastic. If we know the initial distribution $\mathbf{p}_0$ of the Markov chain then the distribution $\mathbf{p}_k$ at time k is given by

$$\mathbf{p}_k^T = \mathbf{p}_0^T \mathbf{P}^k, \; k = 1, 2, ...$$

The initial distribution $\mathbf{p}_0 = \mathbf{q}$ of a discrete-time Markov chain is said to be *stationary* if $\mathbf{p}_k = \mathbf{q}$ for all $k = 0, 1, ...$ Clearly, for this it is necessary and sufficient that $\mathbf{q}$ satisfies the system of linear equations

$$\mathbf{q}^T(\mathbf{P} - \mathbf{I}) = \mathbf{0}^T, \; \mathbf{q}^T\mathbf{u} = 1,$$

which are called the *equilibrium equations for the discrete-time Markov chain.*

Now let $\xi_t, \; t \geq 0$ be a homogeneous continuous-time Markov chain with n states. Denote by

$$P_t(i, j) = \mathsf{P}(\xi_t = j|\xi_0 = i), \; i, j = 1, 2, ..., n, \; t \geq 0,$$

its transition probabilities over time interval t and by

$$p_t(j) = \mathsf{P}(\xi_t = j), \; j = 1, 2, ..., n, \; t \geq 0,$$

the state probabilities at time t. The transition probability matrices $\mathbf{P}_t$ are stochastic. A Markov chain is said to be *stochastically continuous* if

$$\lim_{t \downarrow 0} \mathbf{P}_t = \mathbf{I}.$$

For a stochastically continuous Markov chain, there always exists

$$\mathbf{A} = \lim_{t \downarrow 0} \frac{1}{t}(\mathbf{P}_t - \mathbf{I}),$$

which is called the *generator matrix of the Markov chain.* This matrix uniquely determines the transition probabilities of the Markov chain, since

$$\mathbf{P}_t = e^{\mathbf{A}t}, \; t \geq 0.$$

If the initial distribution $\mathbf{p}_0$ of a Markov chain is known then the distribution $\mathbf{p}_t$ at time t is given by

$$\mathbf{p}_t^T = \mathbf{p}_0^T \mathbf{P}_t, \ t \geq 0.$$

The initial distribution $\mathbf{p}_0 = \mathbf{q}$ of a continuous-time Markov chain is said to be *stationary* if $\mathbf{p}_t = \mathbf{q}$ for all $t \geq 0$. If a Markov chain is stochastically continuous then for the initial distribution to be stationary it is necessary and sufficient that vector $\mathbf{q}$ satisfies the system of linear equations

$$\mathbf{q}^T \mathbf{A} = \mathbf{0}^T, \ \mathbf{q}^T \mathbf{u} = 1,$$

which is called the *system of equilibrium equations for the continuous-time Markov chain.*

One easily checks that for both discrete-time and continuous-time Markov chains the coefficient matrix of the equilibrium equations is a conservative generator matrix.

Theorem 5.10 *For a system of linear equations* $\mathbf{x}^T \mathbf{A} = \mathbf{0}^T$ *with an irreducible conservative generator matrix* $\mathbf{A}$ *there exists a positive solution* $\mathbf{g}$. *Any other solution to this system is a multiple of* $\mathbf{g}$.

Proof By Theorem 5.8, the matrices obtained from $\mathbf{A}$ by striking out a row and a column with the same indices are nonsingular, while $\mathbf{A}$ itself is singular. Consequently, the rank of $\mathbf{A}$ equals $n-1$, and there is not a single solution to $\mathbf{x}^T \mathbf{A} = \mathbf{0}^T$ but a one-dimensional subspace of solutions. Thus, the solution to the system is unique up to a scale factor.

Consider a solution to $\mathbf{g}^T \mathbf{A} = \mathbf{0}^T$ such that $g(k) = \max_i g(i) > 0$. Since $\mathbf{A}$ is irreducible, its k-th row contains a positive element, say $A(k, j)$. Set

$$\mathbf{B} = \mathbf{A} - \frac{1}{2} A(k, j) \mathbf{e}_k \mathbf{e}_j^T,$$

then

$$\mathbf{g}^T \mathbf{B} = -\frac{1}{2} A(k, j) g(k) \mathbf{e}_j^T.$$

It is easy to see that $\mathbf{B}$ is a generator matrix and $\mathbf{Bu} \neq \mathbf{0}$. In light of Theorem 5.7, $\mathbf{B}$ is nonsingular and $\mathbf{B}^{-1} \ll \mathbf{0}$. Therefore,

$$\mathbf{g}^T = -\frac{1}{2} A(k, j) g(k) \mathbf{e}_j^T \mathbf{B}^{-1} \gg \mathbf{0}.$$

■

Corollary *The system of equations* $\mathbf{x}^T\mathbf{A} = \mathbf{0}^T$ *where* $\mathbf{A}$ *is an irreducible conservative generator matrix has a unique solution satisfying the condition* $\mathbf{p}^T\mathbf{u} = 1$. *Furthermore, all elements of* $\mathbf{p}$ *are positive.*

Now let us look at the equilibrium equations with a reducible matrix. For a reducible matrix $\mathbf{A}$, there exists a permutation matrix $\mathbf{Q}$ such that $\mathbf{B} = \mathbf{QAQ}^T$ is of the normal form (5.3). Clearly, a vector $\mathbf{x}$ satisfies $\mathbf{x}^T\mathbf{A} = \mathbf{0}^T$ if and only if $\mathbf{x}^T = \mathbf{y}^T\mathbf{Q}$, where $\mathbf{y}$ is a solution to the system $\mathbf{y}^T\mathbf{B} = \mathbf{0}^T$.

Theorem 5.11 *Let a reducible conservative generator matrix* $\mathbf{B}$ *be of the normal form.*

$$\mathbf{B} = \begin{bmatrix} \mathbf{A}_1 & & & & & & \\ & \mathbf{A}_2 & & & \mathbf{O} & & \\ \mathbf{O} & & \ddots & & & & \\ & & & \mathbf{A}_r & & & \\ \mathbf{A}_{r+1,1} & \mathbf{A}_{r+1,2} & \cdots & \mathbf{A}_{r+1,r} & \mathbf{A}_{r+1} & & \\ \cdots & \cdots & \cdots & \cdots & \cdots & \ddots & \\ \mathbf{A}_{l,1} & \mathbf{A}_{l,2} & \cdots & \mathbf{A}_{l,r} & \mathbf{A}_{l,r+1} & \cdots & \mathbf{A}_l \end{bmatrix},$$

and denote by n_i *the order of matrix* $\mathbf{A}_i$, *and by* $\mathbf{u}_i$ *the all-ones vector of length* n_i *for* $i = 1, 2, ..., l$. *Then, the general solution to the system* $\mathbf{y}^T\mathbf{B} = \mathbf{0}^T$ *is* $\mathbf{y} = (\mathbf{y}_1, \mathbf{y}_2, ..., \mathbf{y}_l)$, *where*

$$\mathbf{y}_i = \begin{cases} c_i\mathbf{p}_i, & 1 \le i \le r, \\ 0, & r < i \le l, \end{cases}$$

is a vector of length n_i, $\mathbf{p}_i$ *is the single solution to the equilibrium equations* $\mathbf{p}_i^T\mathbf{A}_i = \mathbf{0}^T$, $\mathbf{p}_i^T\mathbf{u}_i = 1$, *and* c_i *are some constant factors,* $i = 1, 2, ..., r$.

Proof One checks easily that the diagonal blocks $\mathbf{A}_i$ of $\mathbf{B}$ are irreducible generator matrices. Moreover, $\mathbf{A}_i\mathbf{u}_i = \mathbf{0}$ for $1 \le i \le r$ and $\mathbf{A}_i\mathbf{u}_i < \mathbf{0}$ for $r < i \le l$ since every row $\mathbf{A}_{i1}, \mathbf{A}_{i2}, ..., \mathbf{A}_{ii-1}$ contains a nonzero matrix. Let us write out the system $\mathbf{y}^T\mathbf{B} = \mathbf{0}^T$:

$$\mathbf{y}_l^T\mathbf{A}_l = \mathbf{0}^T, \tag{5.6}$$

$$\mathbf{y}_j^T\mathbf{A}_j = -\sum_{i=j+1}^{l}\mathbf{y}_i^T\mathbf{A}_{ij}, \quad r < j < l, \tag{5.7}$$

$$\mathbf{y}_j^T \mathbf{A}_j = - \sum_{i=r+1}^{l} \mathbf{y}_i^T \mathbf{A}_{ij}, \quad 1 < j < r. \tag{5.8}$$

By Theorem 5.7, matrices $\mathbf{A}_i$, $r < i \leq l$, are nonsingular and (5.6)–(5.7) imply that $\mathbf{y}_i = \mathbf{0}$ for $r < i \leq l$. Therefore, (5.8) assume the form $\mathbf{y}_j^T \mathbf{A}_j = \mathbf{0}^T$, $1 \leq j \leq r$. According to Theorem 5.10 and corollary, every vector $\mathbf{y}_i$ is a multiple of the single solution $\mathbf{p}_i$ to the system of equations $\mathbf{p}_i^T \mathbf{A}_i = \mathbf{0}^T$, $\mathbf{p}_i^T \mathbf{v}_i = 1$. ■

Corollary 1 *Let* **A** *be a conservative generator matrix. Then, the system of equation* $\mathbf{x}^T \mathbf{A} = \mathbf{0}^T$ *has a positive solution if and only if* **A** *can be brought to the form*

$$\mathbf{QAQ}^T = \begin{bmatrix} \mathbf{A}_1 & & \mathbf{O} \\ & \mathbf{A}_2 & \\ & & \ddots & \\ \mathbf{O} & & \mathbf{A}_r \end{bmatrix},$$

where **Q** is some permutation matrix and $\mathbf{A}_i$ are irreducible square matrices.

Corollary 2 *Let* **A** *be a conservative generator matrix. Then, the system of equations* $\mathbf{x}^T \mathbf{A} = \mathbf{0}^T$ *has a unique solution satisfying the condition* $\mathbf{x}^T \mathbf{u} = 1$ *if and only if can be brought to the form*

$$\mathbf{QAQ}^T = \begin{bmatrix} \mathbf{A}_{11} & & & \mathbf{O} \\ \mathbf{A}_{21} & \mathbf{A}_{22} & & \\ \dots & \dots & \ddots & \\ \mathbf{A}_{l1} & \mathbf{A}_{l2} & \cdots & \mathbf{A}_{ll} \end{bmatrix},$$

where **Q** *is some permutation matrix,* $\mathbf{A}_{ii}$ *are irreducible square matrices and, if* $l \geq 2$*, every row*

$$\mathbf{A}_{i1}, \mathbf{A}_{i2}, ..., \mathbf{A}_{ii-1}, \; i = 2, 3, ..., l,$$

contains a nonzero matrix.

5.4 Lumpability of Markov Chains

Let $1 \le m \le n$ and φ be a mapping from $\{1, 2, ..., n\}$ to $\{1, 2, ..., m\}$, $\varphi^{-1}(k) \ne \emptyset$, $k = 1, 2, ..., m$. A generator matrix $\mathbf{A}$ is said to be *φ-lumpable* if for some numbers $A_\varphi(v, w)$, $v, w = 1, 2, ..., m$,

$$\sum_{j \in \varphi^{-1}(r)} A(i, j) = A_\varphi(\varphi(i), r), \ i = 1, 2, ..., n. \tag{5.9}$$

It can be easily seen that vectors $\mathbf{u}_1, \mathbf{u}_2, ..., \mathbf{u}_m$ of length n defined as

$$u_r(j) = \begin{cases} 1, \ \varphi(j) = r, \\ 0, \ \varphi(j) \ne r, \end{cases} \tag{5.10}$$

have the following properties:

$$\mathbf{u}_k > \mathbf{0}, \quad k = 1, 2, ..., m,$$
$$\mathbf{u}_k^T \mathbf{u}_r = 0, \quad k \ne r, \quad k, r = 1, 2, ..., m,$$
$$\sum_{k=1}^{m} \mathbf{u}_k = \mathbf{u}.$$

Every such set of vectors uniquely defines a mapping $\varphi : \{1, 2, ..., n\} \to \{1, 2, ..., m\}$ as follows:

$$\varphi(i) = k \Leftrightarrow u_k(i) > 0.$$

We make use of the vectors $\mathbf{u}_k$ to formulate the condition of lumpability of $\mathbf{A}$ as follows:

$$\mathbf{A}\mathbf{u}_r = \sum_{k=1}^{m} A_\varphi(k, r)\mathbf{u}_k, \ r = 1, 2, ..., m. \tag{5.11}$$

Indeed, in light of (5.9),

$$\mathbf{A}\mathbf{u}_r(i) = \sum_{j \in \varphi^{-1}(r)} A(i, j)u(j) = A_\varphi(\varphi(i), r)u(i) =$$
$$= \sum_{k=1}^{m} A_\varphi(k, r)\delta_{k,\varphi(i)}u(i) = \sum_{k=1}^{m} A_\varphi(k, r)u_k(i).$$

Note that any generator matrix is φ-lumpable if $\varphi(i) = 1, \ i = 1, 2, ..., n$. In this case $m = 1, \ u_1 = u, \ A_\varphi(1, 1) = 0$.

Theorem 5.12 *Let* $\mathbf{A}$ *be a* φ*-lumpable generator matrix. Then,* $\mathbf{A}_{\varphi}$ *is a generator matrix,* $\mathbf{A}_{\varphi}$ *is conservative whenever* $\mathbf{A}$ *is conservative, and* $\mathbf{A}_{\varphi}$ *is irreducible whenever* $\mathbf{A}$ *is irreducible. Furthermore, all the eigenvalues of* $\mathbf{A}_{\varphi}$ *are also eigenvalues of* $\mathbf{A}$.

Proof Set $k = \varphi(i)$. Then, we have

$$A_{\varphi}(k,r) = \sum_{j \in \varphi^{-1}(r)} A(i,j) \geq 0, \ k \neq r,$$
$$\sum_{r=1}^{m} A_{\varphi}(k,r) = \sum_{j=1}^{n} A(i,j) \leq 0.$$

Hence, $\mathbf{A}_{\varphi}$ is a generator matrix and is conservative whenever $\mathbf{A}$ is.

Suppose now that $\mathbf{A}_{\varphi}$ is reducible. By Theorem 5.4, in this case, there exists a semipositive vector $\mathbf{x}$ such that $\mathbf{A}_{\varphi}x(k) = 0$ whenever $x(k) = 0$. One checks easily that a vector $\mathbf{y}$ defined as $y(j) = x(\varphi(j)), j = 1, 2, ..., n$, is semipositive. If $\varphi(i) = k$ then

$$\mathbf{Ay}(i) = \sum_{r=1}^{m} \sum_{j \in \varphi^{-1}(r)} A(i,j)y(j) = \sum_{r=1}^{m} \sum_{j \in \varphi^{-1}(r)} A(i,j)x(r) =$$
$$= \sum_{r=1}^{m} A_{\varphi}(k,r)x(r).$$

This implies that $\mathbf{Ay}(i) = 0$ for all i such that $y(i) = 0$. Then, in light of Theorem 5.4, $\mathbf{A}$ is irreducible. Hence, for an irreducible $\mathbf{A}$, the aggregated matrix $\mathbf{A}_{\varphi}$ is also irreducible.

Now, let $\mathbf{x} \neq \mathbf{0}$ be an eigenvector of $\mathbf{A}_{\varphi}$ corresponding to an eigenvalue γ. Then, for a nonzero vector $\mathbf{y} = \sum_{r=1}^{m} x(r)\mathbf{u}_r$ we have

$$\mathbf{Ay} = \sum_{r=1}^{m} x(r)\mathbf{Au}_r = \sum_{k,r=1}^{m} x(r)A_{\varphi}(k,r)\mathbf{u}_k = \gamma \mathbf{y},$$

that is, γ is the eigenvalue of $\mathbf{A}_{\varphi}$. ■

Theorem 5.13 *Let* $\mathbf{A}$ *be a matrix of order* n*, and* $\mathbf{a}_1, ..., \mathbf{a}_m, \mathbf{b}$ *be vectors of length* n*, and suppose that for some scalars* $\gamma(k,r)$*,* $k, r = 1, 2, ..., m$*,*

$$\mathbf{Aa}_r = \sum_{k=1}^{m} \gamma(k,r)\mathbf{a}_k, \ r = 1, 2, ..., m.$$

Also, let $j_1, j_2, ..., j_m$ be such indices that $a_r(j_r) \neq 0$ and $a_r(j_k) = 0$ for $k \neq r$. Then, a vector $\mathbf{x}$ is a solution of $\mathbf{x}^T\mathbf{A} = \mathbf{b}^T$ if and only if

$$\mathbf{x}^T\mathbf{A}(j) = b(j) \tag{5.12}$$

for all $j \neq j_1, j_2, ..., j_m$ and

$$\sum_{k=1}^{m} (\mathbf{x}^T\mathbf{a}_k)\gamma(k,r) = \mathbf{b}^T\mathbf{a}_r, \ \ r = 1, 2, ..., m. \tag{5.13}$$

Proof Let $\mathbf{x}^T\mathbf{A} = \mathbf{b}^T$, that is, $\mathbf{x}^T\mathbf{A}(j) = b(j)$ for all j. Then, for all r,

$$\sum_{k=1}^{m} (\mathbf{x}^T\mathbf{a}_k)\gamma(k,r) = \mathbf{x}^T\mathbf{A}\mathbf{a}_r = \mathbf{b}^T\mathbf{a}_r.$$

Conversely, suppose that relations (5.13) are true and (5.12) holds for all $j \notin \mathcal{J} = \{j_1, j_2, ..., j_m\}$. Then, since $a_r(j_k) = 0$ for $k \neq r$, we have

$$\mathbf{x}^T\mathbf{A}(j_r)a_r(j_r) = \mathbf{x}^T\mathbf{A}\mathbf{a}_r - \sum_{\substack{j=1\\ j\neq j_r}}^{n} \mathbf{x}^T\mathbf{A}(j)a_r(j) =$$

$$= \sum_{k=1}^{m} (\mathbf{x}^T\mathbf{a}_k)\gamma(k,r) - \sum_{j\notin J} \mathbf{x}^T\mathbf{A}(j)a_r(j) = \mathbf{b}^T\mathbf{a}_r - \sum_{j\notin J} \mathbf{b}(j)a_r(j) =$$

$$= \mathbf{b}^T\mathbf{a}_r - \sum_{\substack{j=1\\ j\neq j_r}}^{n} \mathbf{b}(j)a_r(j) = \mathbf{b}(j_r)a_r(j_r).$$

Since $a_r(j_r) \neq 0$, this implies that (5.12) holds also for $j \in \mathcal{J}$, and hence $\mathbf{x}^T\mathbf{A} = \mathbf{b}^T$. ■

Now let $\mathbf{A}$ represent a φ-lumpable irreducible conservative generator matrix. By Theorem 5.12, the aggregated matrix $\mathbf{A}_\varphi$ is also an irreducible conservative generator matrix and, according to Corollary of Theorem 5.10, there exists a unique solution to the system of the equilibrium equations $\mathbf{p}_\varphi^T\mathbf{A}_\varphi = \mathbf{0}^T$, $\mathbf{p}_\varphi^T\mathbf{u} = 1$. In light of (5.11), vectors $\mathbf{a}_k = \mathbf{u}_k$, defined by (5.10), satisfy the condition of Theorem 5.13 with the elements of $\mathbf{A}_\varphi$ in place of $\gamma(k,r)$.

Theorem 5.14 *Let $\mathbf{A}$ be a φ-lumpable irreducible conservative generator matrix, and indices $j_1, j_2, ..., j_m$ be such that $\varphi(j_k) = k$. Then, a vector $\mathbf{x}$ satisfies the system of the equilibrium equations $\mathbf{x}^T\mathbf{A} = \mathbf{0}^T$, $\mathbf{x}^T\mathbf{u} = 1$ if and only if*

$$\sum_{i=1}^{n} x(i)A(i,j) = 0 \tag{5.14}$$

for all $j \neq j_1, j_2, ..., j_m$ *and*

$$\sum_{i\in\varphi^{-1}(k)} \mathbf{x}(i) = p_{\varphi}(k), |k = 1, 2, ..., m. \tag{5.15}$$

Proof Indeed, in light of Theorem 5.13, a vector $\mathbf{x}$ satisfies $\mathbf{x}^T\mathbf{A} = \mathbf{0}^T$ if and only if it satisfies (5.14) for all $j \neq j_1, j_2, ..., j_m$ and

$$\sum_{k=1}^{m} (\mathbf{x}^T\mathbf{u}_k)A_{\varphi}(k,r) = 0, \ r = 1, 2, ..., m.$$

According to Theorem 5.10, this is equivalent to $\mathbf{x}^T\mathbf{u}_k = cp_{\varphi}(k)$, where c is some constant. However, since $\sum_k \mathbf{x}^T\mathbf{u}_k = \mathbf{x}^T\mathbf{u} = 1$ the constant c equals 1. ■

Thus, if an irreducible conservative generator matrix $\mathbf{A}$ is φ-lumpable and the solution to the aggregated system $\mathbf{p}_{\varphi}^T\mathbf{A}_{\varphi} = \mathbf{0}^T$ is known, then one can remove m equations from the system $\mathbf{x}^T\mathbf{A} = \mathbf{0}^T$—one from each subset of indices $\varphi^{-1}(k)$, $k = 1, 2, ..., m$,—and replace them with (5.15).

Corollary *A system of equations* $\mathbf{x}^T\mathbf{A} = \mathbf{0}^T$, $\mathbf{x}^T\mathbf{u} = 1$ *where* $\mathbf{A}$ *is an irreducible conservative generator matrix, is equivalent to* $\mathbf{x}^T\mathbf{A}_j = \mathbf{e}_j^T$, *where* j *is some index,* $\mathbf{e}_j = (0, ..., 0, 1, 0, ...0)^T$ *is a vector whose* j*-th element is 1 and all the others are zero, and* $\mathbf{A}_j$ *is obtained from* $\mathbf{A}$ *by replacing the* j*-th column by the all-ones vector* $\mathbf{u}$.

To prove this statement, it suffices to consider the trivial aggregation $\varphi(i) = 1, \ i = 1, 2, ..., n$.

5.5 The Maximum Eigenvalue

Let us suppose that among the eigenvalues of a matrix $\mathbf{A}$ there exists a real number σ such that if γ is an eigenvalue of $\mathbf{A}$ different from σ, then $\mathrm{Re}\gamma < \sigma$. In this case, we say that $\mathbf{A}$ has the *maximum eigenvalue*, σ, which we denote by $\sigma(\mathbf{A})$. Obviously, every matrix of order 1 has the maximum eigenvalue $\sigma(\mathbf{A}) = A(1, 1)$.

Theorem 5.15 *Let* $\mathbf{A}$ *be an irreducible matrix of order* $n \geq 2$ *with nonnegative off-diagonal elements. Then* $\mathbf{A}$ *has a maximum eigenvalue.*

$$\sigma(a) > \max_i A(i,i), \tag{5.16}$$

to which there corresponds a positive eigenvector. Furthermore, the eigenvalues of **A** *all lie in the circle in the complex plane*

$$|z - m| \leq \sigma(\mathbf{A}) - m, m = \min_i A(i,i). \tag{5.17}$$

Proof Choose a positive scalar t such that $\mathbf{Au} < t\mathbf{u}$. Then, $\mathbf{A} - t\mathbf{I}$ is an irreducible generator matrix. By Theorem 5.7, matrix $\mathbf{A} - t\mathbf{I}$ is nonsingular and $(\mathbf{A} - t\mathbf{I})^{-1} \ll \mathbf{0}$.

Further, for each vector $\mathbf{x} > \mathbf{0}$ define $\sigma_{\mathbf{x}} = \max\{\gamma : \mathbf{Ax} \geq \gamma\mathbf{x}\}$. One easily checks that

$$\sigma_{\mathbf{x}} = \min_{x(i) \neq 0} \frac{\mathbf{Ax}(i)}{x(i)}.$$

If for some $\mathbf{x} > \mathbf{0}$ the scalar σ_x is larger than t, then $(\mathbf{A} - t\mathbf{I})\mathbf{x} \gg \mathbf{0}$. But, by Theorem 5.2, this is possible only if $\mathbf{x} \ll \mathbf{0}$. Therefore, $\sigma_{\mathbf{x}} \leq t$ for all $\mathbf{x} > \mathbf{0}$. Moreover, function $\sigma_{\mathbf{x}}$ is continuous on the bounded closed set of vectors $\mathbf{x} > \mathbf{0}$, $\mathbf{x}^T\mathbf{u} = 1$. Therefore, it attains its maximum $\sigma = \sigma_{\mathbf{g}} \leq t$ at some vector $\mathbf{g} > \mathbf{0}$, $\mathbf{g}^T\mathbf{u} = 1$. Thus, clearly, $\mathbf{Ag} \geq \sigma\mathbf{g}$.

Let us now show that, in fact, the latter relation is an equality, that is, σ is an eigenvalue of $\mathbf{A}$. Suppose that $\mathbf{Ag} > \sigma\mathbf{g}$ and let $\mathbf{x} = (t\mathbf{I} - \mathbf{A})^{-1}\mathbf{g}$. Then,

$$\mathbf{Ax} - \sigma\mathbf{x} = (\mathbf{A} - \sigma\mathbf{I})(t\mathbf{I} - \mathbf{A})^{-1}\mathbf{g} = (t\mathbf{I} - \mathbf{A})^{-1}(\mathbf{Ag} - \sigma\mathbf{g}) \gg \mathbf{0}.$$

From this it follows that $\sigma_{\mathbf{x}} > \sigma$, which contradicts the definition of σ, and hence $\mathbf{Ag} = \sigma\mathbf{g}$.

Since $\sigma \leq t$ and $t\mathbf{I} - \mathbf{A}$ is nonsingular, $\sigma < t$ and from $(t - \sigma)^{-1}\mathbf{g} = (t\mathbf{I} - \mathbf{A})^{-1}\mathbf{g} \gg \mathbf{0}$ it follows that $\mathbf{g} \gg \mathbf{0}$. Thus, the eigenvector $\mathbf{g}$ corresponding to σ is positive. Furthermore, in every row of the irreducible matrix $\mathbf{A}$ there exists a nonzero off-diagonal element, hence

$$(\sigma - A(i,i))g(i) = \sum_{j \neq i} A(i,j)g(j) > 0,$$

that is, $\sigma > A(i,i)$ for all i.

Finally, let γ be an eigenvalue of $\mathbf{A}$ and $\mathbf{y}$ the corresponding eigenvector. Denote by $|\mathbf{y}|$ a vector with the elements $|y(i)|$. The relation $\mathbf{Ay} = \gamma\mathbf{y}$ implies

$$\mathbf{A}|\mathbf{y}|(i) \geq A(i,i)|y(i)| + \left|\sum_{j\neq i} A(i,j)y(j)\right| =$$
$$= (A(i,i) + |\gamma - A(i,i)|)|y(i)|,$$

hence

$$\sigma_{|\mathbf{y}|} \geq \min_{y(i)\neq 0} (A(i,i) + |\gamma - A(i,i)|).$$

If the inequality $|\gamma - A(i,i)| > \sigma - A(i,i)$ were true for all i, it would follow that $\sigma_{|\mathbf{y}|} > \sigma$, which contradicts the definition of σ. Therefore, at least for one index i, we have $|\gamma - A(i,i)| \leq \sigma - A(i,i)$. Consequently, γ lies in one of the circles

$$|z - A(i,i)| \leq \sigma - A(i,i),\ i = 1, 2, ..., n,$$

all of which lie in the circle (5.17). In particular, no eigenvalue lies in the half-plane Re$z > \sigma$ and none but σ lies on the line Re$z = \sigma$. Hence, σ is the maximum eigenvalue of $\mathbf{A}$. ■

Theorem 5.16 *Let* $\mathbf{A}$ *be a matrix with nonnegative off-diagonal elements. Then, it has a maximum eigenvalue.*

$$\sigma(\mathbf{A}) \geq \max_i A(i,i),$$

to which there corresponds a nonnegative eigenvector. Furthermore, the eigenvalues of $\mathbf{A}$ *all lie in the circle in the complex plane*

$$|z - m| \leq \sigma(\mathbf{A}) - m,\ m = \min_i A(i,i).$$

Proof For any matrix $\mathbf{A}$ with nonnegative off-diagonal elements there exists a permutation matrix $\mathbf{P}$ such that

$$\mathbf{PAP}^T = \begin{bmatrix} \mathbf{A}_{11} & & \mathbf{O} \\ \mathbf{A}_{21} & \mathbf{A}_{22} & \\ \cdots & \cdots & \ddots \\ \mathbf{A}_{l1} & \mathbf{A}_{l2} & \cdots & \mathbf{A}_{ll} \end{bmatrix},$$

where the diagonal blocks are either of order 1 or irreducible with nonnegative off-diagonal entries (see Sect. 5.2). The eigenvalues of the diagonal blocks, and only they, are eigenvalues of $\mathbf{A}$. It follows from Theorem 5.15 that $\sigma = \max_k \sigma(\mathbf{A}_{kk}) \geq \max_i A(i,i)$ is the maximum eigenvalue of $\mathbf{A}$.

Any eigenvalue of $\mathbf{A}$ lies in one of the circles

$$|z - m_k| \leq \sigma(\mathbf{A}_{kk}) - m_k, \; m_k = \min_i A_{kk}(i,i)$$

which are all contained in the circle $|z - m| \leq \sigma(\mathbf{A}) - m, \; m = \min_i A(i,i)$.

For any $\varepsilon > 0$, the off-diagonal elements of matrix $\mathbf{A}_\varepsilon = \mathbf{A} + \varepsilon \mathbf{u}\mathbf{u}^T, \; \mathbf{u} \gg \mathbf{0}$, are all positive and the matrix is irreducible. Let $\mathbf{g}_\varepsilon$ denote a positive eigenvector corresponding to $\sigma(\mathbf{A}_\varepsilon), \; \mathbf{g}_\varepsilon^T\mathbf{u} = 1$. Since the set of vectors $\mathbf{x} > \mathbf{0}, \; \mathbf{x}^T\mathbf{u} = 1$ is bounded and closed, we can choose from the set of vectors $\mathbf{g}_\varepsilon, \; \varepsilon > 0$, a sequence $\mathbf{g}_{\varepsilon_k}, \; k = 1, 2, ...,$ such that, as $\varepsilon_k \to 0$, it converges to some nonnegative vector $\mathbf{g}$.. With that, $\sigma(\mathbf{A}_{\varepsilon_k})$ converges to $\sigma(\mathbf{A})$, and it follows from $\mathbf{A}_{\varepsilon k}\mathbf{g}_{\varepsilon_k} = \sigma(\mathbf{A}_{\varepsilon_k})\mathbf{g}_{\varepsilon_k}$ that $\mathbf{A}\mathbf{g} = \sigma(\mathbf{A})\mathbf{g}$. ■

Corollary *If the off-diagonal entries of a matrix* $\mathbf{A}$ *are nonnegative and, for some positive vector* $\mathbf{f}$, $\mathbf{A}\mathbf{f} \leq \gamma \mathbf{f}$, *then* $\sigma(\mathbf{A}) \leq \gamma$. *In particular,* $\sigma(\mathbf{A}) \leq 0$ *if* $\mathbf{A}$ *is a generator matrix.*

Indeed, if $\mathbf{g}$ is a nonnegative eigenvector of $\mathbf{A}^T$ corresponding to $\sigma(\mathbf{A})$ then $\mathbf{g}^T\mathbf{f} > 0$ and $\sigma(\mathbf{A})\mathbf{g}^T\mathbf{f} = \mathbf{g}^T\mathbf{A}\mathbf{f} \leq \gamma \mathbf{g}^T\mathbf{f}$, that is, $\sigma(\mathbf{A}) \leq \gamma$.

If matrix $\mathbf{A}$ is nonnegative, then the circle $|z - m| \leq \sigma(\mathbf{A}) - m, \; m = \min_i A(i,i)$ is contained in the circle $|z| \leq \sigma(\mathbf{A})$. Therefore, for nonnegative matrices, the eigenvalue $\sigma(\mathbf{A})$ is not only the one with the largest real part, but also the maximum in absolute value.

Theorem 5.17 *Let* $\mathbf{A}$ *be an irreducible matrix of order* $n \geq 2$ *which off-diagonal elements are all nonnegative, and let a matrix* $\mathbf{B}$ *of order* $n - 1$ *be obtained from* $\mathbf{A}$ *by striking out the* j*-th row and the* j*-th column, then* $\sigma(\mathbf{B}) < \sigma(\mathbf{A})$.

Proof Let $\mathbf{B}\mathbf{x} = \sigma(\mathbf{B})\mathbf{x}, \; \mathbf{x} > \mathbf{0}$. Then

$$\sum_{k \neq j} A(i,k)x(k) = \sigma(\mathbf{B})x(i), \; i \neq j, \tag{5.18}$$

$$\sum_{k \neq j} A(j,k)x(k) \geq 0. \tag{5.19}$$

Set $f(i) = x(i)$ for $i \neq j$ and $f(j) = 0$. If we assume equality in (5.19) then for a semipositive vector $\mathbf{f}$ we would have $\mathbf{A}\mathbf{f}(k) = \mathbf{0}$ for all indices k such that $f(k) = 0$. By Theorem 5.4, this would imply reducibility of $\mathbf{A}$, which contradicts the condition of the theorem. Hence, equality holds in (5.19) and $\mathbf{A}\mathbf{f} > \sigma(\mathbf{B})\mathbf{f}$. Further, let $\mathbf{g}$ be a positive eigenvector of $\mathbf{A}^T$ corresponding to $\sigma(\mathbf{A})$. Then, $\mathbf{g}^T\mathbf{f} > 0$ and $\sigma(\mathbf{A})\mathbf{g}^T\mathbf{f} = \mathbf{g}^T\mathbf{A}\mathbf{f} > \sigma(\mathbf{B})\mathbf{g}^T\mathbf{f}$, that is, $\sigma(\mathbf{A}) > \sigma(\mathbf{B})$. ■

Theorem 5.18 *The maximum eigenvalue of an irreducible matrix with nonnegative off-diagonal elements is algebraically simple (algebraic multiplicity equal to 1).*

Proof Let $\mathbf{A}$ be an irreducible matrix of order $n \geq 2$ in which all off-diagonal entries are nonnegative and let $\mathbf{A}_k$ be obtained from $\mathbf{A}$ by striking out the k-th row and the k-th column. Consider the characteristic polynomial $f(s) = \det(s\mathbf{I} - \mathbf{A})$. Differentiating it, we obtain

$$f'(s) = \det(s\mathbf{I} - \mathbf{A}_1) + \det(s\mathbf{I} - \mathbf{A}_2) + ... + \det(s\mathbf{I} - \mathbf{A}_n). \tag{5.20}$$

$\sigma(\mathbf{A}_k)$ is the maximum solution of the polynomial $\det(s\mathbf{I} - \mathbf{A}_k)$. In light of Theorem 5.17, $\sigma(\mathbf{A}_k) < \sigma(\mathbf{A})$. Therefore, if we set $s = \sigma(\mathbf{A})$ then $\det(s\mathbf{I} - \mathbf{A}_k) > 0$ for all k, and from (5.20) we get $f'(\sigma(\mathbf{A})) > 0$. Consequently, $\sigma(\mathbf{A})$ is an algebraically simple root of the characteristic equation. ■

Theorem 5.19 *Let* $\mathbf{Q}$ *be a permutation matrix and*

$$\mathbf{QAQ}^T = \begin{bmatrix} \mathbf{A}_1 & & & & \\ & \mathbf{A}_2 & & \mathbf{O} & \\ \mathbf{O} & & \ddots & & \\ \mathbf{A}_{r+1,1} & \mathbf{A}_{r+1,2} & \cdots & \mathbf{A}_{r+1} & \\ \cdots & \cdots & \cdots & \cdots & \ddots \\ \mathbf{A}_{l,1} & \mathbf{A}_{l,2} & \cdots & \mathbf{A}_{l,r+1} & \cdots \; \mathbf{A}_l \end{bmatrix}$$

be the normal form of a generator matrix $\mathbf{A}$. *Then, the algebraic and geometric multiplicities of the zero eigenvalue of* $\mathbf{A}$ *coincide and equal the number* r *of isolated diagonal blocks.*

Proof In light of Corollary of Theorem 5.16, $\sigma(\mathbf{A}) \leq 0$, and hence the zero eigenvalue of $\mathbf{A}$ is its maximum eigenvalue. By Theorem 5.11, there exists exactly r linearly independent solutions to $\mathbf{x}^T\mathbf{A} = \mathbf{0}^T$. Therefore, the geometric multiplicity of the zero eigenvalue is r. By Theorem 5.7, the matrices $\mathbf{A}_{r+1}, \mathbf{A}_{r+2}, ..., \mathbf{A}_l$ are nonsingular, while, by Theorem 5.18, the algebraic multiplicities of the zero eigenvalue of the matrices $\mathbf{A}_1, \mathbf{A}_2, ..., \mathbf{A}_r$ equal 1. Thus, the algebraic multiplicity of the zero eigenvalue of $\mathbf{QAQ}^T$ and, consequently, of $\mathbf{A}$ is r. ■

Corollary *The zero eigenvalue of a conservative generator matrix is algebraically simple if and only if, for some permutation matrix,*

$$\mathbf{QAQ}^T = \begin{bmatrix} \mathbf{A}_{11} & & \mathbf{O} \\ \mathbf{A}_{21} & \mathbf{A}_{22} & \\ \cdots & \cdots & \ddots \\ \mathbf{A}_{l1} & \mathbf{A}_{l2} & \cdots\ \mathbf{A}_{ll} \end{bmatrix}, \tag{5.21}$$

where $\mathbf{A}_{ii}$ *are irreducible square matrices and, if* $l \geq 2$, *every row*

$$\mathbf{A}_{i1}, \mathbf{A}_{i2}, ..., \mathbf{A}_{ii-1},\ i = 2, 3, ..., l,$$

contains a nonzero matrix.

5.6 Generalized Inverses

A matrix $\mathbf{A}$ is said to be *stable* if its eigenvalues all have strictly negative real parts. Since the maximum eigenvalue of any generator matrix is nonpositive, all nonsingular generator matrices are stable.

Theorem 5.20 *If a matrix* $\mathbf{A}$ *is stable, then*

$$\lim_{t\to\infty} \mathrm{e}^{t\mathbf{A}} = 0, \tag{5.22}$$

$$\int_0^\infty \mathrm{e}^{t\mathbf{A}} dt = -\mathbf{A}^{-1}. \tag{5.23}$$

Proof For $\lim_{k\to\infty} \mathbf{R}^k = 0$, it is necessary and sufficient that the eigenvalues of $\mathbf{R}$ are all smaller than 1 in absolute value. The eigenvalues of $\mathrm{e}^{\mathbf{A}}$ are e^{γ_k}, where γ_k are the eigenvalues of $\mathbf{A}$. Moreover, $|\mathrm{e}^{\gamma_k}| < 1$, since $\mathrm{Re}\gamma_k < 0$. Let $[t]$ denote the whole number part of t. In the right-hand side of $\mathrm{e}^{t\mathbf{A}} = \mathrm{e}^{[t]\mathbf{A}}\mathrm{e}^{(t-[t])\mathbf{A}}$ the matrix $(\mathrm{e}^{\mathbf{A}})^{[t]}$ tends to the zero matrix as $t \to \infty$, while the entries of $e^{(t-[t])\mathbf{A}}$ are all bounded for $t \geq 0$. Therefore, the limit in (5.22) exists. Taking the limit $t \to \infty$ in

$$\int_0^t \mathrm{e}^{x\mathbf{A}} dx = \mathbf{A}^{-1}(\mathrm{e}^{t\mathbf{A}} - \mathbf{I}),$$

we obtain (5.23). ■

Lemma 5.1 Let $\mathbf{f}$ be a vector of length n, $\gamma_1, \gamma_2, \ldots, \gamma_n$ be the eigenvalues of a matrix $\mathbf{A}$ of order n, and γ_1 corresponds to the eigenvector $\mathbf{g}$. Then the eigenvalues of $\mathbf{A} + \mathbf{g}\mathbf{f}^T$ are $\gamma_1 + \mathbf{f}^T\mathbf{g}, \gamma_2, \ldots, \gamma_n$.

Proof Indeed,

$$s\mathbf{I} - \mathbf{A} - \mathbf{g}\mathbf{f}^T = (s\mathbf{I} - \mathbf{A})(\mathbf{I} - \frac{1}{s - \gamma_1}\mathbf{g}\mathbf{f}^T).$$

The determinant of $\mathbf{I} + \mathbf{a}\mathbf{b}^T$ equals $1 + \mathbf{b}^T\mathbf{a}$ for any vectors $\mathbf{a}$ and $\mathbf{b}$. Therefore, the characteristic polynomial of $\mathbf{A} + \mathbf{g}\mathbf{f}^T$ is

$$\det(s\mathbf{I} - \mathbf{A} - \mathbf{g}\mathbf{f}^T) = (1 - \frac{1}{s - \gamma_1}\mathbf{f}^T\mathbf{g}) \det(s\mathbf{I} - \mathbf{A}) =$$

$$= \frac{s - \gamma_1 - \mathbf{f}^T\mathbf{g}}{s - \gamma_1} \prod_{j=1}^{n} (s - \gamma_j) = (s - \gamma_1 - \mathbf{f}^T\mathbf{g}) \prod_{j=2}^{n} (s - \gamma_j).$$

Lemma 5.2 Let $\mathbf{f}^T\mathbf{A} = \mathbf{0}^T$, $\mathbf{A}\mathbf{g} = \mathbf{0}$, and $\mathbf{f}^T\mathbf{g} \neq 0$. Then, for any t, we have

$$e^{t\mathbf{A}} = e^{t(\mathbf{A}+\mathbf{g}\mathbf{f}^T)} + \frac{1}{\mathbf{f}^T\mathbf{g}}(1 - e^{t\mathbf{f}^T\mathbf{g}})\mathbf{g}\mathbf{f}^T.$$

Proof The proof is based upon the relations

$$(\mathbf{A} + \mathbf{g}\mathbf{f}^T)^k = \mathbf{A}^k + (\mathbf{f}^T\mathbf{g})^{k-1}\mathbf{g}\mathbf{f}^T, \ k = 1, 2, \ldots,$$

which follow from the condition of the lemma. Making use of these relations and the definition of the matrix exponential

$$e^{t\mathbf{A}} = \sum_{k=0}^{\infty} \frac{t^k}{k!}\mathbf{A}^k,$$

we obtain the relation to be proved. ■

Now, let us consider conservative generator matrices whose zero eigenvalues are algebraically simple. Such generator matrices are either irreducible or of the normal form (5.21).

Let the zero eigenvalue of a conservative generator matrix $\mathbf{A}$ be algebraically simple and denote its eigenvalues by $\gamma_1 = 0, \gamma_2, \ldots, \gamma_n$. The real parts of $\gamma_2, \ldots, \gamma_n$

are negative because 0 is the maximum eigenvalue of $\mathbf{A}$. According to Corollaries 1 and 2 of Theorem 5.11 and Corollary of Theorem 5.19, there exists a unique solution to the equilibrium equations

$$\mathbf{p}^T\mathbf{A} = \mathbf{0}^T, \ \mathbf{p}^T\mathbf{u} = 1.$$

Now, consider $\mathbf{A} + a\mathbf{u}\mathbf{p}^T$, where a is some scalar. It follows from Lemma 5.1 that the eigenvalues of this matrix are $a, \gamma_2, \dots, \gamma_n$. Moreover,

$$\mathbf{p}^T(\mathbf{A} + a\mathbf{u}\mathbf{p}^T) = a\mathbf{p}^T, \ (\mathbf{A} + a\mathbf{u}\mathbf{p}^T)\mathbf{u} = a\mathbf{u}. \tag{5.24}$$

For any $a \neq 0$, $\mathbf{A} + a\mathbf{u}\mathbf{p}^T$ is nonsingular. The eigenvalues of its inverse $(\mathbf{A} + a\mathbf{u}\mathbf{p}^T)^{-1}$ are $1/a, 1/\gamma_2, \dots, 1/\gamma_n$, while the eigenvalues of the matrices

$$\mathbf{A}_a^{\#} = (\mathbf{A} + a\mathbf{u}\mathbf{p}^T)^{-1} - \frac{1}{a}\mathbf{u}\mathbf{p}^T, \ a \neq 0, \tag{5.25}$$

in light of (5.24) and Lemma 5.1, are $0, 1/\gamma_2, \dots, 1/\gamma_n$.

It follows from Lemma 5.2 that

$$\mathrm{e}^{t\mathbf{A}} = \mathrm{e}^{t(\mathbf{A}+a\mathbf{u}\mathbf{p}^T)} + (1 - \mathrm{e}^{ta})\mathbf{u}\mathbf{p}^T. \tag{5.26}$$

If a is negative then the eigenvalues of $\mathbf{A} + a\mathbf{u}\mathbf{p}^T$ all have negative real parts. Therefore, in the expansion (5.26), as $t \to \infty$, the first term tends to the zero matrix and the second to $\mathbf{u}\mathbf{p}^T$. Thus,

$$\lim_{t\to\infty} \mathrm{e}^{t\mathbf{A}} = \mathbf{u}\mathbf{p}^T.$$

Furthermore, from expansion (5.26) and Theorem 5.20 it follows that

$$\int_0^\infty (\mathrm{e}^{t\mathbf{A}} - \mathbf{u}\mathbf{p}^T)dt = -\mathbf{A}_a^{\#}.$$

Since the left-hand side of this relation does not depend on a, neither does the right-hand side. We summarize these observations in the following.

Theorem 5.21 *Let the zero eigenvalue of a conservative generator matrix* $\mathbf{A}$ *be algebraically simple and* $\mathbf{p}$ *be the solution to the equilibrium equations* $\mathbf{p}^T\mathbf{A} = \mathbf{0}^T$, $\mathbf{p}^T\mathbf{u} = 1$. *Then*

$$\lim_{t\to\infty} \mathrm{e}^{t\mathbf{A}} = \mathbf{u}\mathbf{p}^T, \tag{5.27}$$

$$\int_0^\infty (e^{t\mathbf{A}} - \mathbf{u}\mathbf{p}^T)dt = -\mathbf{A}^\#, \tag{5.28}$$

where

$$\mathbf{A}^\# = (\mathbf{A} + a\mathbf{u}\mathbf{p}^T)^{-1} - \frac{1}{a}\mathbf{u}\mathbf{p}^T, \ a \neq 0, \tag{5.29}$$

does not depend on a.

It follows from (5.24) that

$$\mathbf{p}^T\mathbf{A}^\# = \mathbf{0}^T, \ \mathbf{A}^\#\mathbf{u} = \mathbf{0}. \tag{5.30}$$

Furthermore, from (5.24) and the relation

$$(\mathbf{A} + a\mathbf{u}\mathbf{p}^T)(\mathbf{A} + a\mathbf{u}\mathbf{p}^T)^{-1} = (\mathbf{A} + a\mathbf{u}\mathbf{p}^T)^{-1}(\mathbf{A} + a\mathbf{u}\mathbf{p}^T) = \mathbf{I}$$

follow the below properties of $\mathbf{A}^\#$:

$$\begin{aligned} \mathbf{A}\mathbf{A}^\# &= \mathbf{I} - a\mathbf{u}\mathbf{p}^T(\mathbf{A} + a\mathbf{u}\mathbf{p}^T)^{-1} = \mathbf{I} - \mathbf{u}\mathbf{p}^T, \\ \mathbf{A}^\#\mathbf{A} &= \mathbf{I} - a(\mathbf{A} + a\mathbf{u}\mathbf{p}^T)^{-1}\mathbf{u}\mathbf{p}^T = \mathbf{I} - \mathbf{u}\mathbf{p}^T. \end{aligned} \tag{5.31}$$

Theorem 5.22 *Let the zero eigenvalue of a conservative generator matrix* $\mathbf{A}$ *be algebraically simple. Then, a system of linear equations* $\mathbf{x}^T\mathbf{A} = \mathbf{b}^T$ *has a solution if and only if* $\mathbf{b}^T\mathbf{u} = 0$*. Furthermore,* $\mathbf{x}^T = \mathbf{b}^T\mathbf{A}^\#$ *is its only solution such that* $\mathbf{x}^T\mathbf{u} = 0$.

Proof If there exists a solution to $\mathbf{x}^T\mathbf{A} = \mathbf{b}^T$, then $\mathbf{b}^T\mathbf{u} = \mathbf{x}^T\mathbf{A}\mathbf{u} = 0$.

Conversely, let $\mathbf{b}^T\mathbf{u} = 0$, then, in light of (5.30) and (5.31), we have $\mathbf{b}^T\mathbf{A}^\#\mathbf{u} = 0$ and $\mathbf{b}^T\mathbf{A}^\#\mathbf{A} = \mathbf{b}^T(\mathbf{I} - \mathbf{u}\mathbf{p}^T) = \mathbf{b}^T$. Thus, $\mathbf{x}^T = \mathbf{b}^T\mathbf{A}^\#$ is a solution to $\mathbf{x}^T\mathbf{A} = \mathbf{b}^T$, $\mathbf{x}^T\mathbf{u} = 0$.

Finally, if $\mathbf{y}^T\mathbf{A} = \mathbf{b}^T$ and $\mathbf{y}^T\mathbf{u} = 0$ then $\mathbf{y}^T(\mathbf{A} + \mathbf{u}\mathbf{p}^T) = \mathbf{b}^T$ and, hence, $\mathbf{y}^T = \mathbf{b}^T(\mathbf{A} + \mathbf{u}\mathbf{p}^T)^{-1} = \mathbf{b}^T[(\mathbf{A} + \mathbf{u}\mathbf{p}^T)^{-1} - \mathbf{u}\mathbf{p}^T] = \mathbf{b}^T\mathbf{A}^\#$. ■

Note that the general solution to $\mathbf{x}^T\mathbf{A} = \mathbf{b}^T$ under the condition of Theorem 5.22 is of the form $\mathbf{x}^T = \mathbf{b}^T\mathbf{A}^\# + c\mathbf{p}^T$, where c is some constant scalar and $\mathbf{p}$ is the unique solution to the equilibrium equations $\mathbf{p}^T\mathbf{A} = \mathbf{0}^T$, $\mathbf{p}^T\mathbf{u} = 1$.

It follows from (5.30) and (5.31) that $\mathbf{X} = \mathbf{A}^\#$ satisfies the matrix equations

$$\mathbf{AXA} = \mathbf{A}, \mathbf{XAX} = \mathbf{X}, \ \mathbf{AX} = \mathbf{XA}. \tag{5.32}$$

For any matrix $\mathbf{A}$, the solution $\mathbf{X}$ to these equations, if it exists, is unique and is called *the group generalized inverse* of $\mathbf{A}$. As we have seen, the group generalized inverse of a conservative generator matrix whose zero eigenvalue is algebraically simple is $\mathbf{A}^{\#}$. One can check that any conservative generator matrix has a group generalized inverse. For more information about the group generalized inverse, see Berman (1979) and Meyer (1975).

Another useful generalized inverse is the Moore–Penrose generalized inverse $\mathbf{A}^{+}$, which exists for any matrix $\mathbf{A}$ and is the unique solution to the system of matrix equations

$$\mathbf{AXA} = \mathbf{A},\ \mathbf{XAX} = \mathbf{X},\ (\mathbf{AX})^T = \mathbf{AX},\ (\mathbf{XA})^T = \mathbf{XA}. \tag{5.33}$$

The Moore–Penrose generalized inverse has the following property: for any vector $\mathbf{b}$, vector $\mathbf{x} = \mathbf{A}^{+}\mathbf{b}$ has the smallest norm among all the vectors that minimize the error $\sum_{i=1}^{n} (b(i) - \mathbf{A}x(i))^2$, (Ben-Israel 2003). Note that $(\mathbf{A}^{+})^{+} = \mathbf{A}$ and $(\mathbf{A}^T)^{+} = (\mathbf{A}^{+})^T$.

Following (Paige 1975), let us find $\mathbf{A}^{+}$ for a conservative generator matrix whose zero eigenvalue is algebraically simple.

Lemma 5.3 Let $\overline{\mathbf{A}}$ be the adjoint of a matrix $\mathbf{A}$ of order n and let $\mathbf{f}, \mathbf{g}$ be some vectors of length n. Then

$$\det(\mathbf{A} + \mathbf{f}\mathbf{g}^T) = \det(\mathbf{A}) + \mathbf{g}^T\overline{\mathbf{A}}\mathbf{f}. \tag{5.34}$$

Proof Since $\det(\mathbf{I} + \mathbf{a}\mathbf{b}^T) = 1 + \mathbf{b}^T\mathbf{a}$ and $\mathbf{B}^{-1} = \det(\mathbf{B})^{-1}\overline{\mathbf{B}}$, it follows from

$$\mathbf{A} + \mathbf{f}\mathbf{g}^T - s\mathbf{I} = (\mathbf{A} - s\mathbf{I})[\mathbf{I} + (\mathbf{A} - s\mathbf{I})^{-1}\mathbf{f}\mathbf{g}^T]$$

that

$$\begin{aligned}\det(\mathbf{A} + \mathbf{f}\mathbf{g}^T - s\mathbf{I}) &= \det(\mathbf{A} - s\mathbf{I})(1 + \mathbf{g}^T(\mathbf{A} - s\mathbf{I})^{-1}\mathbf{f}) = \\ &= \det(\mathbf{A} - s\mathbf{I}) + \mathbf{g}^T\overline{(\mathbf{A} - s\mathbf{I})}\mathbf{f}.\end{aligned}$$

By making s tend to 0 in the last relation we obtain (5.34). ■

Theorem 5.23 *Let the zero eigenvalue of a conservative generator matrix* $\mathbf{A}$ *be algebraically simple and* $\mathbf{p}$ *be the solution to the equilibrium equations* $\mathbf{p}^T\mathbf{A} = \mathbf{0}^T$, $\mathbf{p}^T\mathbf{u} = 1$. *Then the Moore–Penrose generalized inverse of* $\mathbf{A}$ *is as follows:*

$$\mathbf{A}^{+} = (\mathbf{A} + \alpha\mathbf{p}\mathbf{u}^T)^{-1} - \alpha\mathbf{u}\mathbf{p}^T, \quad \alpha = \frac{1}{\sqrt{n\,\mathbf{p}^T\mathbf{p}}}. \tag{5.35}$$

Proof From $\mathbf{A}\overline{\mathbf{A}} = \overline{\mathbf{A}}\mathbf{A} = \det(\mathbf{A})\mathbf{I} = \mathbf{0}$, it follows that every column of the adjoint $\overline{\mathbf{A}}$ is a multiple of $\mathbf{u}$, while every row of $\overline{\mathbf{A}}$ is a multiple of $\mathbf{p}$, that is, $\overline{\mathbf{A}} = k\mathbf{u}\mathbf{p}^T$, where k is some constant scalar. One checks easily that the matrix obtained from (5.21) by striking out the first row and the first column is nonsingular, and hence $k \neq 0$. By Lemma 5.3, we have

$$\det(\mathbf{A} + \alpha\mathbf{p}\mathbf{u}^T) = \alpha\mathbf{u}^T\overline{\mathbf{A}}\mathbf{p} = \frac{k}{\alpha} \neq 0.$$

Therefore, $\mathbf{A} + \alpha\mathbf{p}\mathbf{u}^T$ is nonsingular. Further, denote

$$\mathbf{X} = (\mathbf{A} + \alpha\mathbf{p}\mathbf{u}^T)^{-1} - \alpha\mathbf{u}\mathbf{p}^T.$$

From

$$\mathbf{p}^T(\mathbf{A} + \alpha\mathbf{p}\mathbf{u}^T) = \alpha(\mathbf{p}^T\mathbf{p})\mathbf{u}^T, \ \ (\mathbf{A} + \alpha\mathbf{p}\mathbf{u}^T)\mathbf{u} = \alpha n\mathbf{p}$$

it follows that

$$\mathbf{u}^T(\mathbf{A} + \alpha\mathbf{p}\mathbf{u}^T)^{-1} = \frac{1}{\alpha(\mathbf{p}^T\mathbf{p})}\mathbf{p}^T, \ \ (\mathbf{A} + \alpha\mathbf{p}\mathbf{u}^T)\mathbf{p} = \frac{1}{n\alpha}\mathbf{u}.$$

Hence, $\mathbf{u}^T\mathbf{X} = \mathbf{0}^T$ and $\mathbf{X}\mathbf{p} = \mathbf{0}$. From this, in light of

$$(\mathbf{A} + \alpha\mathbf{p}\mathbf{u}^T)(\mathbf{A} + \alpha\mathbf{p}\mathbf{u}^T)^{-1} = (\mathbf{A} + \alpha\mathbf{p}\mathbf{u}^T)^{-1}(\mathbf{A} + \alpha\mathbf{p}\mathbf{u}^T) = \mathbf{I},$$

we have

$$\mathbf{A}\mathbf{X} = \mathbf{I} - \alpha\mathbf{p}\mathbf{u}^T(\mathbf{A} + \alpha\mathbf{p}\mathbf{u}^T)^{-1} = \mathbf{I} - \frac{1}{(\mathbf{p}^T\mathbf{p})}\mathbf{p}\mathbf{p}^T, \tag{5.36}$$

$$\mathbf{X}\mathbf{A} = \mathbf{I} - \alpha(\mathbf{A} + \alpha\mathbf{p}\mathbf{u}^T)^{-1}\mathbf{p}\mathbf{u}^T = \mathbf{I} - \frac{1}{n}\mathbf{u}\mathbf{u}^T. \tag{5.37}$$

Thus, $\mathbf{AX}$ and $\mathbf{XA}$ are symmetric. By multiplying both sides of (5.36) on the right by $\mathbf{A}$ and both sides of (5.37) on the right by $\mathbf{X}$ we obtain, respectively, $\mathbf{AXA} = \mathbf{A}$ and $\mathbf{XAX} = \mathbf{X}$. ■

Note that $\mathbf{p}$ and $\mathbf{u}$ have changed places in brackets in (5.29) and (5.35).

References

Ben-Israel, A., Greville, T.N.E.: Generalized Inverses: Theory and Applications. Springer, New York (2003)

Berman, A., Plemmons, R.J.: Nonnegative Matrices in the Mathematical Sciences. Academic Press, New York (1979)

Gantmacher, F.R.: The Theory of Matrices. AMS Chelsea Publishing (1959)

Gantmacher, F.R.: Applications of the Theory of Matrices. Interscience, New York (1959)

Meyer, C.D., Jr.: The role of the group generalized inverse in the theory of finite Markov chains. SIAM Rev. **17**(3), 443–464 (1975)

Paige, C.C., Styan, G.P., Wachter, P.G.: Computation of the stationary distribution of a Markov chain. J. Stat. Comput. Simul. **4**(3), 173–186 (1975)

Chapter 6
Block Generator Matrices

Abstract In this chapter, we discuss techniques for solving equilibrium equations with block generator matrices. We study LU and UL decompositions of block generator matrices and show how they can be used to obtain solutions to equilibrium equations in matrix product and matrix-geometric form. By applying these methods to MAP$|M|\infty$ and MAP$|M|c|c$ service systems, we arrive at matrix generalizations of the Erlang and Wilkinson formulas, namely, used in the Equivalent Random Traffic (ERT) method.

6.1 Block-Triangular Decompositions

Let $n_0, n_1, ..., n_m$ be some integers such that $n_0, n_1, ..., n_m \geq 1$ and $n_0 + n_1 + \cdots + n_m = n$. A matrix $\mathbf{Q}$ of order n such that

$$\mathbf{Q} = \begin{bmatrix} \mathbf{Q}_{00} & \mathbf{Q}_{01} & \cdots & \mathbf{Q}_{0m} \\ \mathbf{Q}_{10} & \mathbf{Q}_{11} & \cdots & \mathbf{Q}_{1m} \\ \cdots & \cdots & \cdots & \cdots \\ \mathbf{Q}_{m0} & \mathbf{Q}_{m1} & \cdots & \mathbf{Q}_{mm} \end{bmatrix}, \tag{6.1}$$

where $\mathbf{Q}_{ij}$ are $n_i \times n_j$ matrices, is called a block matrix. A block matrix $\mathbf{A}$ is said to be block upper triangular if $\mathbf{Q}_{ij} = 0$ for all $i > j$, and block lower triangular if $\mathbf{Q}_{ij} = 0$ for all $i < j$.

A block-triangular decomposition of matrix $\mathbf{Q}$ refers to a representation of $\mathbf{Q}$ as the product of two matrices, $\mathbf{Q} = \mathbf{BC}$, one of which is block upper triangular and the other, block lower triangular. In such a decomposition, the sizes of the corresponding blocks of matrices $\mathbf{Q}$, $\mathbf{B}$, and $\mathbf{C}$ should coincide. A block-triangular decomposition $\mathbf{Q} = \mathbf{BC}$ is called a block LU decomposition if $\mathbf{B}$ is block lower triangular, and a block UL decomposition if $\mathbf{B}$ is block upper triangular.

Let $\mathbf{Q}^{\Delta}$ denote the block matrix obtained by permuting the centrally symmetric blocks of $\mathbf{Q}$:

V. Naumov et al., *Matrix and Analytical Methods for Performance Analysis of Telecommunication Systems*, https://doi.org/10.1007/978-3-030-83132-5_6

$$\mathbf{Q}^{\Delta} = \begin{bmatrix} \mathbf{Q}_{mm} & \mathbf{Q}_{mm-1} & \cdots & \mathbf{Q}_{m0} \\ \mathbf{Q}_{m-1m} & \mathbf{Q}_{m-1m-1} & \cdots & \mathbf{Q}_{m-10} \\ \cdots & \cdots & \cdots & \cdots \\ \mathbf{Q}_{0m} & \mathbf{Q}_{0m-1} & \cdots & \mathbf{Q}_{00} \end{bmatrix}.$$

It can be easily checked that $(\mathbf{Q}^{\Delta})^{\Delta} = \mathbf{Q}$ and if $\mathbf{Q} = \mathbf{BC}$ is a block LU decomposition of $\mathbf{Q}$ then $\mathbf{Q}^{\Delta} = \mathbf{B}^{\Delta}\mathbf{C}^{\Delta}$ is a block UL decomposition of $\mathbf{Q}^{\Delta}$. By using these properties, the results for block LU decompositions can be easily reformulated for UL decompositions.

Let $\mathbf{Q}_{00}$ be nonsingular. Then we have a block LU decomposition

$$\begin{bmatrix} \mathbf{Q}_{00} & \mathbf{Q}_{01} \\ \mathbf{Q}_{10} & \mathbf{Q}_{11} \end{bmatrix} = \begin{bmatrix} \mathbf{I} & \mathbf{O} \\ \mathbf{Q}_{10}\mathbf{Q}_{00}^{-1} & \mathbf{I} \end{bmatrix} \begin{bmatrix} \mathbf{Q}_{00} & \mathbf{Q}_{01} \\ \mathbf{O} & \mathbf{Q}_{11} - \mathbf{Q}_{10}\mathbf{Q}_{00}^{-1}\mathbf{Q}_{01} \end{bmatrix}. \tag{6.2}$$

Conversely, if $\mathbf{Q}_{11}$ is nonsingular, then we have a block UL decomposition

$$\begin{bmatrix} \mathbf{Q}_{00} & \mathbf{Q}_{01} \\ \mathbf{Q}_{10} & \mathbf{Q}_{11} \end{bmatrix} = \begin{bmatrix} \mathbf{I} & \mathbf{Q}_{01}\mathbf{Q}_{11}^{-1} \\ \mathbf{O} & \mathbf{I} \end{bmatrix} \begin{bmatrix} \mathbf{Q}_{00} - \mathbf{Q}_{01}\mathbf{Q}_{11}^{-1}\mathbf{Q}_{10} & \mathbf{O} \\ \mathbf{Q}_{10} & \mathbf{Q}_{11} \end{bmatrix}. \tag{6.3}$$

This yields a useful relationship:

$$\det(\mathbf{Q}_{00}) \det(\mathbf{Q}_{11} - \mathbf{Q}_{10}\mathbf{Q}_{00}^{-1}\mathbf{Q}_{01}) = \det(\mathbf{Q}_{11}) \det(\mathbf{Q}_{00} - \mathbf{Q}_{01}\mathbf{Q}_{11}^{-1}\mathbf{Q}_{10}),$$

which holds whenever both $\mathbf{Q}_{00}$ and $\mathbf{Q}_{11}$ are nonsingular. In particular, for any nonsingular matrix $\mathbf{Z}$ and matrices $\mathbf{X}$, $\mathbf{Y}$ of corresponding dimensions, we have

$$\det(\mathbf{Z} + \mathbf{XY}) = \det(\mathbf{Z}) \det(\mathbf{I} + \mathbf{YZ}^{-1}\mathbf{X}). \tag{6.4}$$

In the general case, if matrices

$$\mathbf{Q}_{00}, \begin{bmatrix} \mathbf{Q}_{00} & \mathbf{Q}_{01} \\ \mathbf{Q}_{10} & \mathbf{Q}_{11} \end{bmatrix}, \ldots, \begin{bmatrix} \mathbf{Q}_{00} & \mathbf{Q}_{01} & \cdots & \mathbf{Q}_{0l-1} \\ \cdots & \cdots & \cdots & \cdots \\ \mathbf{Q}_{l-10} & \mathbf{Q}_{l-11} & \cdots & \mathbf{Q}_{l-1l-1} \end{bmatrix} \tag{6.5}$$

are nonsingular, then there exists a unique LU decomposition $\mathbf{Q} = \mathbf{BC}$ of matrix (6.1) such that the diagonal blocks of $\mathbf{B}$ are all identity matrices. Alternatively, if matrices

$$\mathbf{Q}_{ll}, \begin{bmatrix} \mathbf{Q}_{l-1l-1} & \mathbf{Q}_{l-1l} \\ \mathbf{Q}_{ll-1} & \mathbf{Q}_{ll} \end{bmatrix}, \ldots, \begin{bmatrix} \mathbf{Q}_{11} & \mathbf{Q}_{12} & \cdots & \mathbf{Q}_{1l} \\ \cdots & \cdots & \cdots & \cdots \\ \mathbf{Q}_{l1} & \mathbf{Q}_{l2} & \cdots & \mathbf{Q}_{ll} \end{bmatrix}, \tag{6.6}$$

are nonsingular, then there exists a unique block UL decomposition $\mathbf{Q} = \mathbf{BC}$ of (6.1) such that the diagonal blocks of $\mathbf{B}$ are identity.

Hereafter, only the block-triangular decompositions $\mathbf{Q} = \mathbf{BC}$ in which the diagonal blocks of $\mathbf{B}$ are identity matrices will be considered. We will write them as $\mathbf{Q} = (\mathbf{I} - \mathbf{T})\mathbf{C}$, where $\mathbf{T}$ is a block-triangular matrix whose diagonal blocks are zero matrices.

By Theorem 5.8, matrices (6.5) and (6.6) are nonsingular if $\mathbf{Q}$ is an irreducible generator matrix. Therefore, such matrices have a unique block LU decomposition $\mathbf{Q} = (\mathbf{I} - \mathbf{S})\boldsymbol{\Psi}$ and a unique block UL decomposition $\mathbf{Q} = (\mathbf{I} - \mathbf{R})\boldsymbol{\Phi}$. The block-triangular decompositions of $\mathbf{Q}$ are of the form

$$\mathbf{Q} = \begin{bmatrix} \mathbf{I} & \mathbf{O} & \cdots & \mathbf{O} \\ -\mathbf{S}_{10} & \mathbf{I} & \ddots & \vdots \\ \vdots & \ddots & \ddots & \mathbf{O} \\ -\mathbf{S}_{m0} & \cdots & -\mathbf{S}_{m-11} & \mathbf{I} \end{bmatrix} \begin{bmatrix} \boldsymbol{\Psi}_{00} & \boldsymbol{\Psi}_{01} & \cdots & \boldsymbol{\Psi}_{0m} \\ \mathbf{O} & \boldsymbol{\Psi}_{11} & \cdots & \boldsymbol{\Psi}_{1m} \\ \vdots & \ddots & \ddots & \vdots \\ \mathbf{O} & \cdots & \mathbf{O} & \boldsymbol{\Psi}_{mm} \end{bmatrix}$$

for the block LU decomposition, and

$$\mathbf{Q} = \begin{bmatrix} \mathbf{I} & -\mathbf{R}_{01} & \cdots & -\mathbf{R}_{0m} \\ \mathbf{O} & \mathbf{I} & \ddots & \vdots \\ \vdots & \ddots & \ddots & -\mathbf{R}_{m-1m} \\ \mathbf{O} & \cdots & \mathbf{O} & \mathbf{I} \end{bmatrix} \begin{bmatrix} \boldsymbol{\Phi}_{00} & \mathbf{O} & \cdots & \mathbf{O} \\ \boldsymbol{\Phi}_{10} & \boldsymbol{\Phi}_{11} & \ddots & \vdots \\ \vdots & \vdots & \ddots & \mathbf{O} \\ \boldsymbol{\Phi}_{m0} & \boldsymbol{\Phi}_{m1} & \cdots & \boldsymbol{\Phi}_{mm} \end{bmatrix}$$

for the block UL decomposition.

In the context of block matrices, we denote by $\mathbf{u}_i$ the vectors of ones of lengths n_i such that $\mathbf{u} = (\mathbf{u}_0, \mathbf{u}_1, \ldots, \mathbf{u}_m)$ is the all-ones vector of length n.

Lemma 6.1 *If*

$$\mathbf{Q} = \begin{bmatrix} \mathbf{Q}_{00} & \mathbf{Q}_{01} \\ \mathbf{Q}_{10} & \mathbf{Q}_{11} \end{bmatrix}$$

is an irreducible generator matrix, then in decomposition (6.2) and (6.3) matrices

$$\mathbf{R}_{01} = -\mathbf{Q}_{01}\mathbf{Q}_{11}^{-1}, \ \mathbf{S}_{10} = -\mathbf{Q}_{10}\mathbf{Q}_{00}^{-1}$$

are nonnegative, and matrices

$$\boldsymbol{\Phi}_{00} = \mathbf{Q}_{00} - \mathbf{Q}_{01}\mathbf{Q}_{11}^{-1}\mathbf{Q}_{10}, \ \boldsymbol{\Psi}_{11} = \mathbf{Q}_{11} - \mathbf{Q}_{10}\mathbf{Q}_{00}^{-1}\mathbf{Q}_{01}$$

are irreducible generator matrices.

Proof We provide the proof for $\mathbf{S}_{10}$ and $\boldsymbol{\Psi}_{11}$ only, since the results for $\mathbf{R}_{01}$ and $\boldsymbol{\Phi}_{00}$ are proved similarly.

By Theorem 5.8, matrix $\mathbf{Q}_{00}$ is a nonsingular generator matrix, while by Theorem 8.3, $\mathbf{Q}_{00}^{-1} \leq 0$. Since the entries of $\mathbf{Q}_{01}$, $\mathbf{Q}_{10}$ and the off-diagonal entries of $\mathbf{Q}_{11}$ are all nonnegative, the entries of $\mathbf{S}_{10} = -\mathbf{Q}_{10}\mathbf{Q}_{00}^{-1}$ and the off-diagonal entries of $\boldsymbol{\Psi}_{11}$ are also all nonnegative. We rewrite the condition $\mathbf{Qu} \leq \mathbf{0}$ as

$$\mathbf{Q}_{00}\mathbf{u}_0 + \mathbf{Q}_{01}\mathbf{u}_1 \leq \mathbf{0}, \tag{6.7}$$

$$\mathbf{Q}_{10}\mathbf{u}_0 + \mathbf{Q}_{11}\mathbf{u}_1 \leq \mathbf{0}. \tag{6.8}$$

Then, by using nonnegativity of $-\mathbf{Q}_{00}^{-1}$ and inequality (6.7), we obtain $-\mathbf{Q}_{00}^{-1}\mathbf{Q}_{01}\mathbf{u}_1 \leq \mathbf{u}_0$. From this and inequality (6.8), it follows that

$$\boldsymbol{\Psi}_{11}\mathbf{u}_1 = \mathbf{Q}_{11}\mathbf{u}_1 - \mathbf{Q}_{10}\mathbf{Q}_{00}^{-1}\mathbf{Q}_{01}\mathbf{u}_1 \leq \mathbf{Q}_{11}\mathbf{u}_1 + \mathbf{Q}_{10}\mathbf{u}_0 \leq \mathbf{0}.$$

Thus, $\boldsymbol{\Psi}_{11}$ is a generator matrix.

Now, suppose that $\boldsymbol{\Psi}_{11}$ is reducible and, in accordance with Theorem 8.4, a semipositive vector $\mathbf{x}$ is such that $\boldsymbol{\Psi}_{11}\mathbf{x}(k) = 0$ whenever $\mathbf{x}(k) = 0$. Then,

$$\mathbf{y} = \begin{bmatrix} -\mathbf{Q}_{00}^{-1}\mathbf{Q}_{01}\mathbf{x} \\ \mathbf{x} \end{bmatrix}$$

is a semipositive vector. If any of its entries is zero, then the corresponding entry of vector

$$\mathbf{Qy} = \begin{bmatrix} \mathbf{0} \\ \boldsymbol{\Psi}_{11}\mathbf{x} \end{bmatrix}$$

is also zero. By Theorem 5.4, this implies reducibility of $\mathbf{Q}$, which contradicts the assumption of the lemma. Hence, $\boldsymbol{\Psi}_{11}$ is irreducible. ■

Theorem 6.1 *Let* $\mathbf{Q} = (\mathbf{I} - \mathbf{S})\boldsymbol{\Psi}$ *be the block LU decomposition of an irreducible generator matrix. Then,* $\mathbf{S}$ *is nonnegative and* $\boldsymbol{\Psi}$ *is a generator matrix. Furthermore, the bottom diagonal block of* $\boldsymbol{\Psi}$ *is irreducible, while the other diagonal blocks of* $\boldsymbol{\Psi}$ *are nonsingular.*

Proof For a matrix $\mathbf{Q} = \mathbf{Q}_{00}$ with a single diagonal block the result is obvious, since in this case $\mathbf{S} = \mathbf{0}$ and $\Psi = \mathbf{Q}$. Now, suppose the result holds for matrices with m diagonal blocks, and let us prove it for matrices with $m + 1$ diagonal blocks.

Rewrite $\mathbf{Q} = (\mathbf{I} - \mathbf{S})\boldsymbol{\Psi}$ in the form

$$\begin{bmatrix} \mathbf{Q}_{00} & \tilde{\mathbf{Q}}_{01} \\ \tilde{\mathbf{Q}}_{10} & \tilde{\mathbf{Q}}_{11} \end{bmatrix} = \begin{bmatrix} \mathbf{I} & \mathbf{O} \\ -\tilde{\mathbf{S}}_{10} & \mathbf{I} - \tilde{\mathbf{S}}_{11} \end{bmatrix} \begin{bmatrix} \boldsymbol{\Psi}_{00} & \tilde{\boldsymbol{\Psi}}_{01} \\ \mathbf{O} & \tilde{\boldsymbol{\Psi}}_{11} \end{bmatrix},$$

where $\widetilde{\mathbf{S}}_{11}$ is a block lower triangular matrix in which diagonal blocks are all zero, and $\tilde{\boldsymbol{\Psi}}_{11}$ is a block upper triangular matrix. This implies

$$\boldsymbol{\Psi}_{00} = \mathbf{Q}_{00}, \ \tilde{\boldsymbol{\Psi}}_{01} = \tilde{\mathbf{Q}}_{01}, \ \tilde{\mathbf{S}}_{10} = \tilde{\mathbf{Q}}_{01}\mathbf{Q}_{00}^{-1} \tag{6.9}$$

$$(\mathbf{I} - \tilde{\mathbf{S}}_{11})\tilde{\boldsymbol{\Psi}}_{11} = \tilde{\mathbf{Q}}_{11} + \tilde{\mathbf{S}}_{10}\boldsymbol{\Psi}_{01} = \tilde{\mathbf{Q}}_{11} + \tilde{\mathbf{Q}}_{10}\mathbf{Q}_{00}^{-1}\tilde{\mathbf{Q}}_{01}. \tag{6.10}$$

Equality (6.10) is the block LU decomposition of matrix $\tilde{\mathbf{Q}}_{11} + \tilde{\mathbf{Q}}_{10}\mathbf{Q}_{00}^{-1}\tilde{\mathbf{Q}}_{01}$, which has l diagonal blocks. According to Lemma 6.1, this matrix is an irreducible generator matrix. By assumption, $\widetilde{\mathbf{S}}_{11}$ is nonnegative and $\tilde{\boldsymbol{\Psi}}_{11}$ is a generator matrix whose bottom diagonal block is irreducible and the others nonsingular.

Relations (6.9) and (6.10) imply that the top diagonal block of $\boldsymbol{\Psi}$ is nonsingular, matrix $\tilde{\boldsymbol{\Psi}}_{11}$ is nonnegative, $\boldsymbol{\Psi}_{00}$ is a generator matrix, and

$$\boldsymbol{\Psi}_{00}\mathbf{u}_0 + \tilde{\boldsymbol{\Psi}}_{01}\mathbf{u}_1 = \mathbf{Q}_{00}\mathbf{u}_0 + \tilde{\mathbf{Q}}_{01}\mathbf{u}_1 \le \mathbf{0}.$$

Therefore, $\boldsymbol{\Psi}$ is a generator matrix. Since $\tilde{\mathbf{Q}}_{01} \ge \mathbf{0}$ and $\mathbf{Q}_{00}^{-1} \le 0$, it follows from (6.10) that $\widetilde{\mathbf{S}}_{10} \ge \mathbf{0}$ and, thus, $\mathbf{S}$ is nonnegative. Hence, the result holds for matrices with $m + 1$ diagonal blocks. ■

Theorem 6.2 *Let* $\mathbf{Q} = (\mathbf{I} - \mathbf{S})\boldsymbol{\Psi}$ *be the block LU decomposition of an irreducible conservative generator matrix. Then, the row vector* $\mathbf{x} = (\mathbf{x}_0, \mathbf{x}_1, \ldots, \mathbf{x}_m)$ *is a solution to the linear system of equilibrium equations* $\mathbf{x}\mathbf{Q} = \mathbf{0}$, *if and only if*

$$\mathbf{x}_m\boldsymbol{\Psi}_{mm} = \mathbf{0},$$
$$\mathbf{x}_k = \sum_{i=k+1}^{m} \mathbf{x}_i\mathbf{S}_{ik}, \quad k = m-1, m-2, \ldots, 0. \tag{6.11}$$

Proof Set a row vector $\mathbf{y} = \mathbf{x}(\mathbf{I} - \mathbf{S})$, that is,

$$\mathbf{y}_m = \mathbf{x}_m, \quad \mathbf{y}_k = \mathbf{x}_k - \sum_{i=k+1}^{m} \mathbf{x}_i\mathbf{S}_{ik}, \quad k = 0, 1, \ldots, m-1. \tag{6.12}$$

The row vector $\mathbf{x}$ is a solution to $\mathbf{x}\mathbf{Q} = \mathbf{0}$, if and only if $\mathbf{y}$ satisfies $\mathbf{y}\boldsymbol{\Psi} = \mathbf{0}$, that is,

$$\mathbf{y}_0\boldsymbol{\Psi}_{00} = \mathbf{0}, \quad \mathbf{y}_k\boldsymbol{\Psi}_{kk} = -\sum_{i=0}^{k-1} \mathbf{y}_i\boldsymbol{\Psi}_{ik}, \quad k = 1, 2, \ldots, m.$$

Since by Theorem 6.1, for $k \ne m$, matrices $\boldsymbol{\Psi}_{kk}$ are nonsingular, the above relations are equivalent to

$$\mathbf{y}_m \boldsymbol{\Psi}_{mm} = \mathbf{0}, \quad \mathbf{y}_k = \mathbf{0}, \quad k = 0, 1, ..., m-1,$$

which, in light of (6.12), yields (6.11). ■

By Theorem 6.1, if $\mathbf{Q}$ is an irreducible conservative generator matrix, then $\boldsymbol{\Psi}_{mm}$ also is a conservative generator matrix. Thus, when solving a linear system of equilibrium equations with an irreducible matrix $\mathbf{Q}$, the block LU decomposition transforms the original system to a system of equilibrium equations with an irreducible matrix $\boldsymbol{\Psi}_{mm}$, which order is smaller. The solution to $\mathbf{x}_m \boldsymbol{\Psi}_{mm} = \mathbf{0}$ can be chosen positive and satisfying, for instance, $\mathbf{x}_m \mathbf{u}_m = 1$. Then, by Theorem 8.10, the whole vector $\mathbf{x} = (\mathbf{x}_0, \mathbf{x}_1, ..., \mathbf{x}_m)$ will be positive. Having found the subvector $\mathbf{x}_m$ of $\mathbf{x}$, we use (6.11) with nonnegative matrix coefficients $\mathbf{S}_{ik}$ to obtain, one by one, the other positive subvectors $\mathbf{x}_{m-1}, \mathbf{x}_{m-2}, ..., \mathbf{x}_0$. Once they are found, it remains to normalize $\mathbf{x} = (\mathbf{x}_0, \mathbf{x}_1, ..., \mathbf{x}_m)$ so that the solution satisfies the condition $\mathbf{xu} = 1$.

The results similar to Theorems 6.1 and 6.2 are true for the UL decomposition.

Theorem 6.3 *Let* $\mathbf{Q} = (\mathbf{I} - \mathbf{R})\boldsymbol{\Phi}$ *be the block UL decomposition of an irreducible generator matrix. Then,* $\mathbf{R}$ *is nonnegative, and* $\boldsymbol{\Phi}$ *is a generator matrix. Furthermore, the top diagonal block of* $\boldsymbol{\Phi}$ *is irreducible and the other diagonal blocks of* $\boldsymbol{\Phi}$ *are nonsingular.*

Theorem 6.4 *Let* $\mathbf{Q} = (\mathbf{I} - \mathbf{R})\boldsymbol{\Phi}$ *be the block UL decomposition of an irreducible conservative generator matrix. Then, the row vector* $\mathbf{x} = (\mathbf{x}_0, \mathbf{x}_1, ..., \mathbf{x}_m)$ *is a solution to* $\mathbf{xQ} = \mathbf{0}$*, if and only if*

$$\mathbf{x}_0 \boldsymbol{\Phi}_{00} = \mathbf{0}, \ \mathbf{x}_k = \sum_{i=0}^{k-1} \mathbf{x}_i \mathbf{R}_{ik}, \quad k = 1, 2, ..., m. \tag{6.13}$$

By equating the blocks in the left-hand and right-hand sides of $\mathbf{Q} = (\mathbf{I} - \mathbf{S})\boldsymbol{\Psi}$, we have the following recursive relations for the blocks of the LU decomposition:

$$\boldsymbol{\Psi}_{rj} = \mathbf{Q}_{rj} + \sum_{k=0}^{r-1} \mathbf{S}_{rk} \boldsymbol{\Psi}_{kj}, \quad r \le j \le m,$$

$$\mathbf{S}_{ir} = -(\mathbf{Q}_{ir} + \sum_{k=0}^{r-1} \mathbf{S}_{ik} \boldsymbol{\Psi}_{kr}) \boldsymbol{\Psi}_{rr}^{-1}, \quad r < i \le m, \quad r = 0, 1, ..., m. \tag{6.14}$$

Similar relations are true for the blocks of the UL decomposition $\mathbf{Q} = (\mathbf{I} - \mathbf{R})\boldsymbol{\Phi}$:

$$\boldsymbol{\Phi}_{rj} = \mathbf{Q}_{rj} + \sum_{k=r+1}^{m} \mathbf{R}_{rk} \boldsymbol{\Phi}_{kj}, \quad 0 \le j \le r,$$

$$\mathbf{R}_{ir} = -(\mathbf{Q}_{ir} + \sum_{k=r+1}^{m} \mathbf{R}_{ik} \boldsymbol{\Phi}_{kr}) \boldsymbol{\Phi}_{rr}^{-1}, \quad 0 \le i < r, \quad r = m, m-1, ..., 0. \tag{6.15}$$

Note that in (6.14) and (6.15) $-\boldsymbol{\Psi}_{rr}^{-1}$ and $-\boldsymbol{\Phi}_{rr}^{-1}$, as well as the summation terms, are all nonnegative matrices.

6.2 Block Hessenberg Matrices

A block matrix $\mathbf{Q}$ is said to be block upper Hessenberg if $\mathbf{Q}_{ij} = 0$ for $i > j+1$, and block lower Hessenberg if $\mathbf{Q}_{ij} = 0$ for $j > i+1$. In the present section, we will consider systems of equilibrium equations with block upper Hessenberg matrices

$$\mathbf{Q} = \begin{bmatrix} \mathbf{Q}_{00} & \mathbf{Q}_{01} & \cdots & \mathbf{Q}_{0m} \\ \mathbf{C}_0 & \mathbf{Q}_{11} & \cdots & \mathbf{Q}_{1m} \\ & \ddots & \ddots & \vdots \\ \mathbf{O} & & \mathbf{C}_{m-1} & \mathbf{Q}_{mm} \end{bmatrix}. \tag{6.16}$$

The following notation will be used:

$$\boldsymbol{\mu}_i = \mathbf{C}_{i-1}\mathbf{u}_{i-1}, \quad \boldsymbol{\lambda}_{ij} = \sum_{k=j}^{m} \mathbf{Q}_{ik}\mathbf{u}_k, \quad 0 \le i < j \le m.$$

It follows from (6.14) that matrix $\mathbf{S}$ in the block LU decomposition $\mathbf{Q} = (\mathbf{I}-\mathbf{S})\boldsymbol{\Psi}$ of an irreducible generator matrix (6.16) is of the form

$$\mathbf{S} = \begin{bmatrix} \mathbf{O} & \cdots & \cdots & \mathbf{O} \\ \mathbf{S}_1 & \ddots & & \vdots \\ & \ddots & \ddots & \vdots \\ \mathbf{O} & & \mathbf{S}_m & \mathbf{O} \end{bmatrix}. \tag{6.17}$$

The nonzero blocks of $\mathbf{S}$ and $\boldsymbol{\Psi}$ satisfy

$$\boldsymbol{\Psi}_{0j} = \mathbf{Q}_{0j}, \; 0 \le j \le m, \tag{6.18}$$

$$\mathbf{S}_r = -\mathbf{C}_{r-1}\boldsymbol{\Psi}_{r-1r-1}^{-1},$$

$$\boldsymbol{\Psi}_{rj} = \mathbf{Q}_{rj} + \mathbf{S}_r\boldsymbol{\Psi}_{r-1j}, \; r \le j \le m, \; r = 1, 2, \ldots, m. \tag{6.19}$$

In consequence, relations (6.11), which yield the solution to the system of equilibrium equations $\mathbf{xQ} = \mathbf{0}$, become substantially simpler. Thus, the row vector $\mathbf{x} = (\mathbf{x}_0, \mathbf{x}_1, \ldots, \mathbf{x}_m)$ with a row vectors $\mathbf{x}_r$, $r = 1, 2, \ldots, m$, as its components, is a solution to $\mathbf{xQ} = \mathbf{0}$, with an irreducible conservative generator matrix of the form (6.16) if and only if

$$\mathbf{x}_m \mathbf{\Psi}_{mm} = \mathbf{0}, \quad \mathbf{x}_k = \mathbf{x}_{k+1}\mathbf{S}_{k+1}, \quad k = m-1, m-2, ..., 0. \tag{6.20}$$

Let us now explore further the case where the blocks of $\mathbf{Q}$ are all of the same size and the subdiagonal blocks of $\mathbf{Q}$ are nonsingular.

Lemma 6.2 *Let* $\mathbf{Q} = (\mathbf{I} - \mathbf{S})\mathbf{\Psi}$ *be the block LU decomposition of an irreducible generator matrix of form (6.16). Then, nonsingularity of the subdiagonal blocks of* $\mathbf{Q}$ *is necessary and sufficient for the subdiagonal blocks of* $\mathbf{S}$ *to be nonsingular. Furthermore, in this case, matrices*

$$\mathbf{H}_0 = \mathbf{I}, \quad \mathbf{H}_k = (\mathbf{S}_k\mathbf{S}_{k-1}...\mathbf{S}_1)^{-1}, \quad 1 \le k \le m, \tag{6.21}$$

satisfy

$$\mathbf{H}_i\mathbf{W}_{ij} = \sum_{k=0}^{i} \mathbf{H}_k\mathbf{Q}_{kj}, \quad 0 \le i \le j \le m, \tag{6.22}$$

$$\mathbf{H}_{j+1} = -\sum_{k=0}^{j} \mathbf{H}_k\mathbf{Q}_{kj}\mathbf{C}_j^{-1}, \quad 0 \le j < m. \tag{6.23}$$

Proof The first statement of the lemma follows directly from (6.16). Let us prove (6.22) and (6.23). One checks easily that the blocks of

$$\mathbf{Y} = (\mathbf{I} - \mathbf{S})^{-1} = \mathbf{I} + \mathbf{S} + \cdots + \mathbf{S}^{m-1} \tag{6.24}$$

are of the form

$$\mathbf{Y}_{ij} = \begin{cases} \mathbf{S}_i\mathbf{S}_{i-1}...\mathbf{S}_{j+1}, & i > j, \\ \mathbf{I}, & i = j, \\ \mathbf{0}, & i < j. \end{cases} \tag{6.25}$$

Since $\mathbf{\Psi} = (\mathbf{I} - \mathbf{S})^{-1}\mathbf{Q} = \mathbf{YQ}$, by equating the corresponding blocks of $\mathbf{YQ}$ and $\mathbf{\Psi}$, we have

$$\sum_{k=0}^{i} \mathbf{Y}_{ik}\mathbf{Q}_{kj} = \mathbf{\Psi}_{ij}, \quad i \le j, \tag{6.26}$$

$$\sum_{k=0}^{j} \mathbf{Y}_{lk}\mathbf{Q}_{kj} + \mathbf{Y}_{lj+1}\mathbf{C}_j = 0, \quad j < m. \tag{6.27}$$

It follows from definition (6.21) of matrices $\mathbf{H}_k$ and from (6.25) that

$$\mathbf{H}_i \mathbf{Y}_{ij} = \mathbf{H}_j, \quad i \geq j. \tag{6.28}$$

By left-multiplying both sides of (6.26) and (6.27) by $\mathbf{H}_i$ and $\mathbf{H}_l$, respectively, and making use of (6.28), we obtain (6.22) and (6.23). ■

Corollary *Let* $\mathbf{Q}$ *be an irreducible generator matrix of the form* (6.16) *with nonsingular subdiagonal blocks, for which*

$$\mathbf{H}_0 = \mathbf{I}, \quad \mathbf{H}_{j+1} = -\sum_{k=0}^{j} \mathbf{H}_k \mathbf{Q}_{kj} \mathbf{C}_j^{-1}, \quad j = 0, 1, \ldots, m-1. \tag{6.29}$$

Then, $\mathbf{H}_k$ are nonsingular and their inverses are nonnegative: $\mathbf{H}_k^{-1} \geq 0$.

Indeed, by Lemma 6.2, the recursive relations (6.26) determine the matrices $\mathbf{H}_k = (\mathbf{S}_k \mathbf{S}_{k-1} \ldots \mathbf{S}_1)^{-1}$, in which, in light of Theorem 6.1, all factors $\mathbf{S}_i$ are nonnegative.

Theorem 6.5 *Let* $\mathbf{Q}$ *be an irreducible conservative generator matrix of the form (6.16) with nonsingular subdiagonal blocks, and matrices* $\mathbf{H}_k$ *be defined by (6.29), and a matrix* $\mathbf{G}$ *be defined as*

$$\mathbf{G} = \sum_{k=0}^{m} \mathbf{H}_k \mathbf{Q}_{kl}. \tag{6.30}$$

Then, $\mathbf{G}\mathbf{u}_l = \mathbf{0}$*, and* $\mathbf{x} = (\mathbf{x}_0, \mathbf{x}_1, \ldots, \mathbf{x}_m)$ *is a solution to the equilibrium equations* $\mathbf{x}\mathbf{Q} = \mathbf{0}$ *if and only if*

$$\mathbf{x}_0 \mathbf{G} = \mathbf{0}, \quad \mathbf{x}_k = \mathbf{x}_0 \mathbf{H}_k, \; 1 \leq k \leq m. \tag{6.31}$$

Proof Let $\mathbf{Q} = (\mathbf{I} - \mathbf{S})\mathbf{\Psi}$ be the block LU decomposition of $\mathbf{Q}$. By Lemma 6.2, $\mathbf{H}_k = (\mathbf{S}_k \mathbf{S}_{k-1} \ldots \mathbf{S}_1)^{-1}$ and $\mathbf{G} = \mathbf{H}_m \mathbf{\Psi}_{mm}$. It follows from $\mathbf{Q}\mathbf{u} = \mathbf{0}$ that $\mathbf{\Psi}\mathbf{u} = \mathbf{0}$ and, in particular, $\mathbf{\Psi}_{mm}\mathbf{u}_m = \mathbf{0}$. Therefore, $\mathbf{G}\mathbf{u}_m = \mathbf{0}$.

By (6.20), vector $\mathbf{x}$ satisfies the system $\mathbf{x}\mathbf{Q} = \mathbf{0}$, if and only if $\mathbf{x}_m \mathbf{\Psi}_{mm} = \mathbf{0}$ and $\mathbf{x}_0 = \mathbf{x}_k \mathbf{S}_k \mathbf{S}_{k-1} \ldots \mathbf{S}_1, \; k = 1, 2, \ldots, m$. For this, it is necessary and sufficient that $\mathbf{x}_k = \mathbf{x}_0 \mathbf{H}_k$, $k = 1, 2, \ldots, m$, and $\mathbf{x}_0 \mathbf{G} = \mathbf{x}_0 \mathbf{H}_m \mathbf{\Psi}_{mm} = \mathbf{x}_m \mathbf{\Psi}_{mm} = \mathbf{0}$. ■

Theorem 6.5 yields a variant of the block Gaussian elimination for linear systems of equilibrium equations, (Golub 1996). Such an algorithm was applied to block tridiagonal generator matrices in Basharin (1978), and then to block Hessenberg matrices in Wikarski (1980).

It follows from (6.15) that matrix $\mathbf{\Phi}$ in the block UL decomposition $\mathbf{Q} = (\mathbf{I} - \mathbf{R})\mathbf{\Phi}$ of an irreducible generator matrix (6.16) is of the form

$$\mathbf{\Phi} = \begin{bmatrix} \mathbf{\Phi}_0 & & & \mathbf{O} \\ \mathbf{C}_0 & \mathbf{\Phi}_1 & & \\ & \ddots & \ddots & \\ \mathbf{O} & & \mathbf{C}_{m-1} & \mathbf{\Phi}_m \end{bmatrix}, \tag{6.32}$$

and, moreover, the subdiagonal blocks of $\mathbf{Q}$ and $\mathbf{\Phi}$ coincide. The diagonal blocks of $\mathbf{\Phi}$ and the blocks of $\mathbf{R}$ can be determined by formulae

$$\mathbf{\Phi}_m = \mathbf{Q}_{mm}, \quad \mathbf{R}_{im} = -\mathbf{Q}_{im}\mathbf{\Phi}_m^{-1}, \quad 0 \le i < m,$$

$$\mathbf{\Phi}_r = \mathbf{Q}_{rr} + \mathbf{R}_{rr+1}\mathbf{C}_r, \tag{6.33}$$

$$\mathbf{R}_{ir} = -(\mathbf{Q}_{ir} + \mathbf{R}_{ir+1}\mathbf{C}_r)\mathbf{\Phi}_r^{-1}, \quad 0 \le i < r, \quad r = m-1, m-2, ..., 0.$$

These relations imply the following useful properties.

Lemma 6.3 *Let* $\mathbf{Q} = (\mathbf{I} - \mathbf{R})\mathbf{\Phi}$ *be the UL decomposition of an irreducible conservative generator matrix of the form (6.16). Then,*

$$\mathbf{\Phi}_0\mathbf{u}_0 = \mathbf{0}, \quad \mathbf{\Phi}_r\mathbf{u}_r = -\boldsymbol{\mu}_r, \quad 1 \le r \le m, \tag{6.34}$$

$$\mathbf{R}_{ir}\boldsymbol{\mu}_r = \boldsymbol{\lambda}_{ir}, \quad i < r, \quad 1 \le r \le m. \tag{6.35}$$

Proof Indeed, $\mathbf{Qu} = \mathbf{0}$ implies $\mathbf{\Phi u} = \mathbf{0}$. Since $\mathbf{\Phi}$ is of the form (6.32), relations (6.34) are true. It follows from (6.33) that

$$\mathbf{R}_{im}\mathbf{\Phi}_m = -\mathbf{Q}_{im}, \quad i < m,$$
$$\mathbf{R}_{ir}\mathbf{\Phi}_r = -(\mathbf{Q}_{ir} + \mathbf{R}_{ir+1}\mathbf{C}_r), \quad i < r, \quad r = m-1, m-2, ..., 0.$$

By right-multiplying both sides of the above equalities by $\mathbf{u}_r$ and making use of (6.34), we have

$$\mathbf{R}_{im}\boldsymbol{\mu}_m = \mathbf{Q}_{im}\mathbf{u}_m, \quad i < m,$$
$$\mathbf{R}_{ir}\boldsymbol{\mu}_r = \mathbf{Q}_{ir}\mathbf{u}_r + \mathbf{R}_{ir+1}\boldsymbol{\mu}_{r+1}, \quad i < r, \quad r = m-1, m-2, ..., 0.$$

These recursive relations imply (6.35). ■

Now, let the subdiagonal blocks of a block Hessenberg matrix $\mathbf{Q}$ have rank one. Linear systems with block tridiagonal matrices that have this property have been solved in Basharin (1983). Relations (6.33) permit to write explicit expressions for the blocks of $\mathbf{R}$ and $\mathbf{\Phi}$ in the UL decomposition of a block Hessenberg matrix.

Theorem 6.6 *Let* $\mathbf{Q} = (\mathbf{I} - \mathbf{R})\boldsymbol{\Phi}$ *be the block UL decomposition of an irreducible conservative generator matrix of the form (6.16) whose subdiagonal blocks are rank-one matrices:*

$$\mathbf{C}_k = \boldsymbol{\mu}_{k+1}\boldsymbol{\beta}_k, \quad k = 0, 1, \ldots, m-1,$$

where $\boldsymbol{\beta}_k \mathbf{u}_k = 1$*. Then,*

$$\boldsymbol{\Phi}_m = \mathbf{Q}_{mm}, \quad \boldsymbol{\Phi}_r = \mathbf{Q}_{rr} + \boldsymbol{\lambda}_{rr+1}\boldsymbol{\beta}_k, 0 \le r < m;$$
$$\mathbf{R}_{im} = -\mathbf{Q}_{im}\boldsymbol{\Phi}_m^{-1}, \quad i < m,$$
$$\mathbf{R}_{ir} = -(\mathbf{Q}_{ir} + \boldsymbol{\lambda}_{ir+1}\boldsymbol{\beta}_r^T)\boldsymbol{\Phi}_r^{-1}, \quad i < r, \quad 0 \le r < m. \tag{6.36}$$

6.3 Block Tridiagonal Matrices

A matrix $\mathbf{Q}$ is said to be block tridiagonal if $\mathbf{Q}_{ij} = \mathbf{0}$ for $|i - j| > 1$. In the present section, we examine systems of equilibrium equations with block tridiagonal matrices

$$\mathbf{Q} = \begin{bmatrix} \mathbf{B}_0 & \mathbf{A}_1 & & \mathbf{O} \\ \mathbf{C}_0 & \mathbf{B}_1 & \ddots & \\ & \ddots & \ddots & \mathbf{A}_m \\ \mathbf{O} & & \mathbf{C}_{m-1} & \mathbf{B}_m \end{bmatrix} \tag{6.37}$$

and use notation

$$\boldsymbol{\mu}_i = \mathbf{C}_{i-1}\mathbf{u}_{i-1}, \quad \boldsymbol{\lambda}_i = \mathbf{A}_{i+1}\mathbf{u}_{i+1}.$$

Also, for $\mathbf{Q}$ such that $\mathbf{Q}\mathbf{u} = \mathbf{0}$, we will write

$$\mathbf{B}_i\mathbf{u}_i = -(\boldsymbol{\lambda}_i + \boldsymbol{\mu}_i).$$

If an irreducible generator matrix is block tridiagonal, then its block LU decomposition has the form

$$\mathbf{Q} = \begin{bmatrix} \mathbf{I} & \mathbf{O} & \cdots & \mathbf{O} \\ -\mathbf{S}_1 & \mathbf{I} & \ddots & \vdots \\ & \ddots & \ddots & \mathbf{O} \\ \mathbf{O} & & -\mathbf{S}_m & \mathbf{I} \end{bmatrix} \begin{bmatrix} \boldsymbol{\Psi}_0 & \mathbf{A}_1 & & \mathbf{O} \\ \mathbf{O} & \ddots & \ddots & \\ \vdots & \ddots & \boldsymbol{\Psi}_{m-1} & \mathbf{A}_m \\ \mathbf{O} & \cdots & \mathbf{O} & \boldsymbol{\Psi}_m \end{bmatrix},$$

and its UL decomposition has the form

$$\mathbf{Q} = \begin{bmatrix} \mathbf{I} & -\mathbf{R}_0 & & \mathbf{O} \\ \mathbf{O} & \ddots & \ddots & \\ \vdots & \ddots & \mathbf{I} & -\mathbf{R}_{m-1} \\ \mathbf{O} & \cdots & \mathbf{O} & \mathbf{I} \end{bmatrix} \begin{bmatrix} \mathbf{\Phi}_0 & \mathbf{O} & \cdots & \mathbf{O} \\ \mathbf{C}_0 & \mathbf{\Phi}_1 & \ddots & \vdots \\ & \ddots & \ddots & \mathbf{O} \\ \mathbf{O} & & \mathbf{C}_{m-1} & \mathbf{\Phi}_m \end{bmatrix}.$$

Such simple forms of block-triangular decompositions follow from (6.14) and (6.15). Those relationships also imply the following recursive relations:

$$\mathbf{\Psi}_0 = \mathbf{B}_0,$$
$$\mathbf{S}_r = -\mathbf{C}_{r-1}\mathbf{\Psi}_{r-1}^{-1}, \quad \mathbf{\Psi}_r = \mathbf{B}_r + \mathbf{S}_r\mathbf{A}_r, \quad r = 1, 2, \ldots, m; \tag{6.38}$$

$$\mathbf{\Phi}_m = \mathbf{B}_m,$$
$$\mathbf{R}_r = -\mathbf{A}_{r+1}\mathbf{\Phi}_{r+1}^{-1}, \quad \mathbf{\Phi}_r = \mathbf{B}_r + \mathbf{R}_r\mathbf{C}_r, \quad r = m-1, m-2\ldots, 0. \tag{6.39}$$

Let now $\mathbf{Q}$ be an irreducible conservative generator matrix. Then, $\mathbf{\Psi}$ and $\mathbf{\Phi}$ in the block-triangular decompositions of $\mathbf{Q}$ are also conservative generator matrices. Therefore, the diagonal blocks of these matrices satisfy

$$\mathbf{\Psi}_m\mathbf{u}_m = \mathbf{0}, \quad \mathbf{\Psi}_r\mathbf{u}_r = -\boldsymbol{\lambda}_r, \quad 0 \le r \le m-1, \tag{6.40}$$

$$\mathbf{\Phi}_0\mathbf{u}_0 = \mathbf{0}, \quad \mathbf{\Phi}_r\mathbf{u}_r = -\boldsymbol{\mu}_r, \quad 1 \le r \le m. \tag{6.41}$$

From the above relations and (6.2), (6.3), it follows that

$$\mathbf{S}_r\boldsymbol{\lambda}_{r-1} = \boldsymbol{\mu}_r, \quad 1 \le r \le m, \tag{6.42}$$

$$\mathbf{R}_r\boldsymbol{\mu}_{r+1} = \boldsymbol{\lambda}_r, \quad 0 \le r \le m-1. \tag{6.43}$$

Consider now a system of equilibrium equations whose matrix is block tridiagonal:

$$\mathbf{x}_0\mathbf{B}_0 + \mathbf{x}_1\mathbf{C}_0 = \mathbf{0}, \tag{6.44}$$

$$\mathbf{x}_{k-1}\mathbf{A}_k + \mathbf{x}_k\mathbf{B}_k + \mathbf{x}_{k+1}\mathbf{C}_k = \mathbf{0}, \ 1 \le k \le m-1, \tag{6.45}$$

$$\mathbf{x}_{m-1}\mathbf{A}_m + \mathbf{x}_m\mathbf{B}_m = \mathbf{0}. \tag{6.46}$$

By using the block-triangular decompositions and Theorems 6.2 and 6.4, its solution can be written in the matrix product form as follows:

$$\mathbf{x}_k = \mathbf{x}_0 \mathbf{R}_0 \mathbf{R}_1 \cdots \mathbf{R}_{k-1}, \quad 1 \le k \le m, \tag{6.47}$$

where $\mathbf{R}_k$ satisfy the recursive relation

$$\mathbf{R}_m = \mathbf{0}, \mathbf{R}_{r-1} = -\mathbf{A}_r(\mathbf{B}_r + \mathbf{R}_r\mathbf{C}_r)^{-1}, \; r = m, m-1, ..., 1, \tag{6.48}$$

or, alternatively,

$$\mathbf{x}_k = \mathbf{x}_m \mathbf{S}_m \mathbf{S}_{m-1} \cdots \mathbf{S}_{k+1}, \quad 0 \le k \le m-1, \tag{6.49}$$

where $\mathbf{S}_k$ satisfy

$$\mathbf{S}_0 = \mathbf{0}, \mathbf{S}_{r+1} = -\mathbf{C}_r(\mathbf{B}_r + \mathbf{S}_r\mathbf{A}_r)^{-1}, \; r = 0, 1, ..., m-1. \tag{6.50}$$

Here, row vectors $\mathbf{x}_0$ and $\mathbf{x}_m$ are, respectively, the unique (up to a constant factor) solutions to the systems of equilibrium equations

$$\mathbf{x}_0(\mathbf{B}_0 + \mathbf{R}_0\mathbf{C}_0) = \mathbf{0}, \quad \mathbf{x}_m(\mathbf{B}_m + \mathbf{S}_m\mathbf{A}_m) = \mathbf{0}. \tag{6.51}$$

It turns out that if nonzero matrices are taken as the initial $\mathbf{R}_m$ and $\mathbf{S}_0$ in (6.48) and (6.50), then the computed matrices $\mathbf{R}_k$ and $\mathbf{S}_k$ can still be used for solving the equilibrium equations. We will discuss this fact in the following section.

6.4 General Vector Difference Equations

In this section, we look into the systems of linear algebraic equations of the form

$$\mathbf{x}_{k-1}\mathbf{A}_k + \mathbf{x}_k\mathbf{B}_k + \mathbf{x}_{k+1}\mathbf{C}_k = \mathbf{b}_k, \; 1 \le k \le m-1, \tag{6.52}$$

with arbitrary $n_{k-1} \times n_k$ matrices $\mathbf{A}_k$, $n_k \times n_k$ matrices $\mathbf{B}_k$, $n_{k+1} \times n_k$ matrices $\mathbf{C}_k$, and vectors $\mathbf{b}_k$ of length n_k. The following notation will be used for matrix products:

$$\prod_{i=k}^{n} \mathbf{H}_i = \begin{cases} \mathbf{H}_k\mathbf{H}_{k+1} \cdots \mathbf{H}_n, & k \le n, \\ \mathbf{I} & k > n, \end{cases}$$

$$\coprod_{i=k}^{n} \mathbf{H}_i = \begin{cases} \mathbf{H}_n\mathbf{H}_{n-1} \cdots \mathbf{H}_k, & k \le n, \\ \mathbf{I} & k > n. \end{cases}$$

Lemma 6.4 *Let matrices* $\mathbf{S}_1, \mathbf{S}_2, ..., \mathbf{S}_m$ *satisfy*

$$\mathbf{S}_{k+1} = -\mathbf{C}_k(\mathbf{B}_k + \mathbf{S}_k\mathbf{A}_k)^{-1}, \quad k = 1, 2, ..., m-1. \tag{6.53}$$

Then, vectors $\mathbf{x}_0, \mathbf{x}_1, ..., \mathbf{x}_m$ *constitute a solution to system (6.52) if and only if there exists a vector* $\mathbf{b}_0$ of length n_0, *such that*

$$\mathbf{x}_k = \mathbf{x}_{k+1}\mathbf{S}_{k+1} - \sum_{i=0}^{k} \mathbf{b}_i\mathbf{W}_i \prod_{j=i+1}^{k} (\mathbf{A}_j\mathbf{W}_j),\ 0 \le k < m, \tag{6.54}$$

where

$$\mathbf{W}_0 = \mathbf{I}, \mathbf{W}_k = -(\mathbf{B}_k + \mathbf{S}_k\mathbf{A}_k)^{-1},\ 0 < k < m. \tag{6.55}$$

Furthermore, necessarily, $\mathbf{b}_0 = \mathbf{x}_1\mathbf{S}_1 - \mathbf{x}_0$.

Proof Let vectors $\mathbf{x}_0, \mathbf{x}_1, ..., \mathbf{x}_m$ be a solution to (6.52). Then, for all $0 < k < m$.

$$(\mathbf{x}_k - \mathbf{x}_{k+1}\mathbf{S}_{k+1})(\mathbf{B}_k + \mathbf{S}_k\mathbf{A}_k) + (\mathbf{x}_{k-1} - \mathbf{x}_k\mathbf{S}_k)\mathbf{A}_k = \mathbf{b}_k$$

which implies the recursive relation

$$\mathbf{x}_k - \mathbf{x}_{k+1}\mathbf{S}_{k+1} = (\mathbf{x}_{k-1} - \mathbf{x}_k\mathbf{S}_k)\mathbf{A}_k\mathbf{W}_k - \mathbf{b}_k\mathbf{W}_k, \quad 0 < k < m.$$

This, in turn, yields (6.54), in which $\mathbf{b}_0 = \mathbf{x}_1\mathbf{S}_1 - \mathbf{x}_0$.

Conversely, if $\mathbf{x}_0, \mathbf{x}_1, ..., \mathbf{x}_m$ satisfy (6.54), then, for all $0 < k < m$,

$$\begin{aligned}\mathbf{x}_{k-1} &= \mathbf{x}_k\mathbf{S}_k - \sum_{i=0}^{k-1} \mathbf{b}_i\mathbf{W}_i \prod_{j=i+1}^{k-1} (\mathbf{A}_j\mathbf{W}_j)\\ &= \mathbf{x}_{k+1}\mathbf{S}_{k+1}\mathbf{S}_k - \left(\sum_{i=0}^{k} \mathbf{b}_i\mathbf{W}_i \prod_{j=i+1}^{k} (\mathbf{A}_j\mathbf{W}_j)\right)\mathbf{S}_k - \sum_{i=0}^{k-1} \mathbf{b}_i\mathbf{W}_i \prod_{j=i+1}^{k-1} (\mathbf{A}_j\mathbf{W}_j).\end{aligned}$$

Therefore, we have

$$\mathbf{x}_{k-1}\mathbf{A}_k + \mathbf{x}_k\mathbf{B}_k + \mathbf{x}_{k+1}\mathbf{C}_k =$$

$$= \left(\mathbf{x}_{k+1}\mathbf{S}_{k+1}\mathbf{S}_k - \left(\sum_{i=0}^{k} \mathbf{b}_i\mathbf{W}_i \prod_{j=i+1}^{k} (\mathbf{A}_j\mathbf{W}_j)\right)\mathbf{S}_k - \sum_{i=0}^{k-1} \mathbf{b}_i\mathbf{W}_i \prod_{j=i+1}^{k-1} (\mathbf{A}_j\mathbf{W}_j)\right)\mathbf{A}_k +$$

$$+\left(\mathbf{x}_{k+1}\mathbf{S}_{k+1}-\sum_{i=0}^{k}\mathbf{b}_i\mathbf{W}_i\prod_{j=i+1}^{k}(\mathbf{A}_j\mathbf{W}_j)\right)\mathbf{B}_k+\mathbf{x}_{k+1}\mathbf{C}_k=$$
$$=\mathbf{x}_{k+1}(\mathbf{S}_{k+1}\mathbf{S}_k\mathbf{A}_k+\mathbf{S}_{k+1}\mathbf{B}_k+\mathbf{C}_k)-\mathbf{b}_k\mathbf{W}_k(\mathbf{S}_k\mathbf{A}_k+\mathbf{B}_k)-$$
$$-\sum_{i=0}^{k-1}\mathbf{b}_i\mathbf{W}_i\left(\prod_{j=i+1}^{k-1}(\mathbf{A}_j\mathbf{W}_j)\right)\mathbf{A}_k[\mathbf{I}+\mathbf{W}_k(\mathbf{B}_k+\mathbf{S}_k\mathbf{A}_k)]=\mathbf{b}_k.$$

Moreover, (6.54) for $k=0$ yields $\mathbf{b}_0=\mathbf{x}_1\mathbf{S}_1-\mathbf{x}_0$. ∎

The following result can be proved by a similar argument.

Lemma 6.5 *Let matrices* $\mathbf{R}_0, \mathbf{R}_1, \ldots, \mathbf{R}_{m-1}$ *satisfy*

$$\mathbf{R}_{k-1}=-\mathbf{A}_k(\mathbf{B}_k+\mathbf{R}_k\mathbf{C}_k)^{-1},\quad k=m-1,m-2,\ldots,1. \tag{6.56}$$

Then, vectors $\mathbf{x}_0, \mathbf{x}_1, \ldots, \mathbf{x}_m$ *constitute a solution to (6.52) if and only if there exists a vector* $\mathbf{b}_m$ *of length* n_m *such that*

$$\mathbf{x}_k=\mathbf{x}_{k-1}\mathbf{R}_{k-1}-\sum_{i=k}^{m}\mathbf{b}_i\mathbf{V}_i\coprod_{j=k}^{i-1}(\mathbf{C}_j\mathbf{V}_j),\ 0<k<m, \tag{6.57}$$

where

$$\mathbf{V}_m=\mathbf{0},\quad \mathbf{V}_k=-(\mathbf{B}_k+\mathbf{R}_k\mathbf{C}_k)^{-1},\ 0<k<m. \tag{6.58}$$

Furthermore, necessarily, $\mathbf{b}_m=\mathbf{x}_{m-1}\mathbf{R}_{m-1}-\mathbf{x}_m$.

One can easily check that for any matrices $\mathbf{S}_k$ and $\mathbf{R}_k$ that satisfy, respectively, (6.53) and (6.56) the following relations hold:

$$\begin{aligned}\mathbf{S}_k\mathbf{A}_k+\mathbf{B}_k+\mathbf{R}_k\mathbf{C}_k&=(\mathbf{I}-\mathbf{R}_k\mathbf{S}_{k+1})(\mathbf{B}_k+\mathbf{S}_k\mathbf{A}_k)=\\&=(\mathbf{I}-\mathbf{S}_k\mathbf{R}_{k-1})(\mathbf{B}_k+\mathbf{R}_k\mathbf{C}_k),\quad 0<k<m.\end{aligned} \tag{6.59}$$

Therefore, if $\mathbf{S}_k\mathbf{A}_k+\mathbf{B}_k+\mathbf{R}_k\mathbf{C}_k$ is nonsingular, so are matrices $\mathbf{I}-\mathbf{R}_k\mathbf{S}_{k+1}$ and $\mathbf{I}-\mathbf{S}_k\mathbf{R}_{k-1}$.

Theorem 6.7 *Let matrices* $\mathbf{S}_1, \ldots, \mathbf{S}_m$ *and* $\mathbf{R}_0, \ldots, \mathbf{R}_{m-1}$ *satisfy (6.53) and (6.56), respectively. Then,*

$$\mathbf{x}_k=\mathbf{g}_k+\sum_{i=0}^{k-1}\mathbf{g}_i\prod_{j=i}^{k-1}\mathbf{R}_j+\sum_{i=k+1}^{m}\mathbf{g}_i\coprod_{j=k+1}^{i}\mathbf{S}_j,\ 0\le k\le m, \tag{6.60}$$

satisfy the system (6.52) if and only if $\mathbf{g}_1, \mathbf{g}_2, \ldots, \mathbf{g}_{m-1}$ *satisfy*

$$\mathbf{g}_k(\mathbf{S}_k\mathbf{A}_k + \mathbf{B}_k + \mathbf{R}_k\mathbf{C}_k) = \mathbf{f}_k, \; 0 < k < m. \tag{6.61}$$

Furthermore, if $\mathbf{S}_k\mathbf{A}_k + \mathbf{B}_k + \mathbf{R}_k\mathbf{C}_k, \; 0 < k < m$, *are nonsingular matrices, then for any solution* $\mathbf{x}_0, \mathbf{x}_1, \ldots, \mathbf{x}_m$ *of* (6.52) *vectors* $\mathbf{g}_0, \mathbf{g}_1, \ldots, \mathbf{g}_m$ *in* (6.60) *are uniquely defined by*

$$\mathbf{g}_0 = (\mathbf{x}_0 - \mathbf{x}_1\mathbf{S}_1)(\mathbf{I} - \mathbf{R}_0\mathbf{S}_1)^{-1}, \tag{6.62}$$

$$\mathbf{g}_k = \mathbf{f}_k(\mathbf{S}_k\mathbf{A}_k + \mathbf{B}_k + \mathbf{R}_k\mathbf{C}_k)^{-1}, \; 0 < k < m, \tag{6.63}$$

$$\mathbf{g}_m = (\mathbf{x}_m - \mathbf{x}_{m-1}\mathbf{R}_{m-1})(\mathbf{I} - \mathbf{S}_m\mathbf{R}_{m-1})^{-1}. \tag{6.64}$$

Proof Let vectors $\mathbf{x}_k$ be given by (6.60). Then,

$$\begin{aligned}
&\mathbf{x}_{k-1}\mathbf{A}_k + \mathbf{x}_k\mathbf{B}_k + \mathbf{x}_{k+1}\mathbf{C}_k = \mathbf{g}_k(\mathbf{S}_k\mathbf{A}_k + \mathbf{B}_k + \mathbf{R}_k\mathbf{C}_k)\\
&+\sum_{i=0}^{k-1}\mathbf{g}_i\left(\prod_{j=i}^{k-2}\mathbf{R}_j\right)(\mathbf{A}_k + \mathbf{R}_{k-1}\mathbf{B}_k + \mathbf{R}_{k-1}\mathbf{R}_k\mathbf{C}_k)\\
&+\sum_{i=k+1}^{m}\mathbf{g}_i\left(\coprod_{j=k+2}^{i}\mathbf{S}_j\right)(\mathbf{S}_{k+1}\mathbf{S}_k\mathbf{A}_k + \mathbf{S}_{k+1}\mathbf{B}_k + \mathbf{C}_k) = \mathbf{g}_k(\mathbf{S}_k\mathbf{A}_k + \mathbf{B}_k + \mathbf{R}_k\mathbf{C}_k)
\end{aligned}$$

for $0 < k < m$. Hence, vectors $\mathbf{x}_k$ satisfy the linear system (6.52) if and only if $\mathbf{g}_1, \mathbf{g}_2, \ldots, \mathbf{g}_{m-1}$ in (6.60) satisfy (6.61).

Now, let $\mathbf{x}_0, \mathbf{x}_1, \ldots, \mathbf{x}_m$ be a solution to (6.52) and $\mathbf{S}_k\mathbf{A}_k + \mathbf{B}_k + \mathbf{R}_k\mathbf{C}_k, \; 0 < k < m$ be nonsingular. Then, in light of (6.56), for $0 < k < m$ matrices $\mathbf{I} - \mathbf{R}_k\mathbf{S}_{k+1}$ and $\mathbf{I} - \mathbf{S}_k\mathbf{R}_{k-1}$ are nonsingular. Matrices $\mathbf{I} - \mathbf{R}_0\mathbf{S}_1$ and $\mathbf{I} - \mathbf{S}_m\mathbf{R}_{m-1}$ are also nonsingular, since

$$(\mathbf{I} - \mathbf{R}_0\mathbf{S}_1)^{-1} = \mathbf{I} + \mathbf{R}_0(\mathbf{I} - \mathbf{S}_1\mathbf{R}_0)^{-1}\mathbf{S}_1,$$

$$(\mathbf{I} - \mathbf{S}_m\mathbf{R}_{m-1})^{-1} = \mathbf{I} + \mathbf{S}_m(\mathbf{I} - \mathbf{R}_{m-1}\mathbf{S}_m)^{-1}\mathbf{R}_{m-1}.$$

Let $\mathbf{V}_k$ and $\mathbf{W}_k$ be given, respectively, by (6.58) and (6.55). Then,

$$\mathbf{R}_{k-1} = \mathbf{A}_k\mathbf{V}_k, \quad \mathbf{S}_{k+1} = \mathbf{C}_k\mathbf{W}_k, \quad 0 < k < m,$$

and the following relations hold:

$$(\mathbf{I}-\mathbf{S}_{k+1}\mathbf{R}_k)\mathbf{C}_k\mathbf{V}_k = \mathbf{C}_k\mathbf{V}_k + \mathbf{S}_{k+1}(\mathbf{I}+\mathbf{B}_k\mathbf{V}_k)$$
$$= \mathbf{C}_k\mathbf{V}_k + \mathbf{S}_{k+1} - (\mathbf{C}_k + \mathbf{S}_{k+1}\mathbf{S}_k\mathbf{A}_k)\mathbf{V}_k = \mathbf{S}_{k+1}(\mathbf{I}-\mathbf{S}_k\mathbf{R}_{k-1}),$$
$$(\mathbf{I}-\mathbf{R}_{k-1}\mathbf{S}_k)\mathbf{A}_k\mathbf{W}_k = \mathbf{A}_k\mathbf{W}_k + \mathbf{R}_{k-1}(\mathbf{I}+\mathbf{B}_k\mathbf{W}_k)$$
$$= \mathbf{A}_k\mathbf{W}_k + \mathbf{R}_{k-1} - (\mathbf{A}_k + \mathbf{R}_{k-1}\mathbf{R}_k\mathbf{C}_k)\mathbf{W}_k = \mathbf{R}_{k-1}(\mathbf{I}-\mathbf{R}_k\mathbf{S}_{k+1}).$$

Therefore, for $0 < k < m$ we have

$$\mathbf{C}_k\mathbf{V}_k = (\mathbf{I}-\mathbf{S}_{k+1}\mathbf{R}_k)^{-1}\mathbf{S}_{k+1}(\mathbf{I}-\mathbf{S}_k\mathbf{R}_{k-1}),$$

$$\mathbf{A}_k\mathbf{W}_k = (\mathbf{I}-\mathbf{R}_{k-1}\mathbf{S}_k)^{-1}\mathbf{R}_{k-1}(\mathbf{I}-\mathbf{R}_k\mathbf{S}_{k+1}).$$

Thus, we can rewrite (6.54) and (6.57) as

$$\mathbf{x}_k = \mathbf{x}_{k+1}\mathbf{S}_{k+1} + \sum_{i=0}^{k}\mathbf{g}_i\prod_{j=i}^{k-1}\mathbf{R}_j(\mathbf{I}-\mathbf{R}_k\mathbf{S}_{k+1}), \quad 0 \le k < m,$$

$$\mathbf{x}_k = \mathbf{x}_{k-1}\mathbf{R}_{k-1} + \sum_{i=k}^{m}\mathbf{g}_i\coprod_{j=k+1}^{i}\mathbf{S}_j(\mathbf{I}-\mathbf{S}_k\mathbf{R}_{k-1}), \quad 0 < k \le m,$$

where $\mathbf{g}_k$ are given by (6.62)–(6.64).

It follows from the above that

$$\mathbf{x}_k = (\mathbf{x}_k\mathbf{R}_k + \sum_{i=k+1}^{m}\mathbf{g}_i\coprod_{j=k+2}^{i}\mathbf{S}_j(\mathbf{I}-\mathbf{S}_{k+1}\mathbf{R}_k))\mathbf{S}_{k+1} + \sum_{i=0}^{k}\mathbf{g}_i\prod_{j=i}^{k-1}\mathbf{R}_j(\mathbf{I}-\mathbf{R}_k\mathbf{S}_{k+1}) =$$
$$= (\mathbf{x}_k\mathbf{R}_k\mathbf{S}_{k+1} + (\sum_{i=0}^{k}\mathbf{g}_i\prod_{j=i}^{k-1}\mathbf{R}_j + \sum_{i=k+1}^{m}\mathbf{g}_i\coprod_{j=k+1}^{i}\mathbf{S}_j)(\mathbf{I}-\mathbf{R}_k\mathbf{S}_{k+1})$$

for $0 \le k < m$, and

$$\mathbf{x}_m = (\mathbf{x}_m\mathbf{S}_m + \sum_{i=o}^{m-1}\mathbf{g}_i\prod_{j=i}^{m-2}\mathbf{R}_j(\mathbf{I}-\mathbf{R}_{m-1}\mathbf{S}_m))\mathbf{R}_{m-1} + \mathbf{g}_m(\mathbf{I}-\mathbf{S}_m\mathbf{R}_{m-1}) =$$
$$= \mathbf{x}_m\mathbf{S}_m\mathbf{R}_{m-1} + \sum_{i=0}^{m}\mathbf{g}_i\prod_{j=i}^{m-1}\mathbf{R}_j(\mathbf{I}-\mathbf{S}_m\mathbf{R}_{m-1}).$$

Since matrices $\mathbf{I}-\mathbf{S}_m\mathbf{R}_{m-1}$ and $\mathbf{I}-\mathbf{R}_k\mathbf{S}_{k+1}$, $0 \le k < m$, are nonsingular, the above relations imply (6.60) for all $0 \le k < m$.

For any $\mathbf{x}_0, \ldots, \mathbf{x}_m$ we can find $\mathbf{g}_0, \ldots, \mathbf{g}_m$ satisfying (6.60), since these vectors are the solution to the linear system $\mathbf{g}^T\mathbf{T} = \mathbf{x}^T$, where $\mathbf{g} = (\mathbf{g}_0, \ldots, \mathbf{g}_m)$, $\mathbf{x} = (\mathbf{x}_0, \ldots, \mathbf{x}_m)$

and $\mathbf{T}$ is of the form

$$\mathbf{T} = \begin{bmatrix} \mathbf{I} & \mathbf{R}_0 & \mathbf{R}_0\mathbf{R}_1 & \cdots & \prod_{i=0}^{m-1}\mathbf{R}_i \\ \mathbf{S}_1 & \mathbf{I} & \mathbf{R}_1 & \cdots & \prod_{i=1}^{m-1}\mathbf{R}_i \\ \mathbf{S}_2\mathbf{S}_1 & \mathbf{S}_2 & \mathbf{I} & \ddots & \vdots \\ \cdots & \cdots & \ddots & \ddots & \mathbf{R}_{m-1} \\ \coprod_{i=1}^{m}\mathbf{S}_i & \coprod_{i=2}^{m}\mathbf{S}_i & \cdots & \mathbf{S}_m & \mathbf{I} \end{bmatrix} = \begin{bmatrix} \mathbf{I} & -\mathbf{R}_0 & & \mathbf{O} \\ \mathbf{O} & \mathbf{I} & \ddots & \\ \vdots & \ddots & \ddots & -\mathbf{R}_{m-1} \\ \mathbf{O} & \cdots & \mathbf{O} & \mathbf{I} \end{bmatrix}^{-1} \times$$

$$\times \begin{bmatrix} \mathbf{I}-\mathbf{R}_0\mathbf{S}_1 & \mathbf{O} & \cdots & \cdots & \mathbf{O} \\ \mathbf{O} & \mathbf{I}-\mathbf{R}_1\mathbf{S}_2 & \ddots & & \vdots \\ \vdots & \mathbf{O} & \ddots & \mathbf{O} & \vdots \\ \vdots & & \ddots & \mathbf{I}-\mathbf{R}_{m-1}\mathbf{S}_m & \mathbf{O} \\ \mathbf{O} & \cdots & \cdots & \mathbf{O} & \mathbf{I} \end{bmatrix} \begin{bmatrix} \mathbf{I} & \mathbf{O} & \cdots & \mathbf{O} \\ -\mathbf{S}_1 & \mathbf{I} & \ddots & \vdots \\ & \ddots & \ddots & \mathbf{O} \\ \mathbf{O} & & -\mathbf{S}_m & \mathbf{I} \end{bmatrix}^{-1}.$$

Matrix $\mathbf{T}$ is nonsingular because all the factors in the right-hand side of the above relation are nonsingular matrices. Thus, vectors $\mathbf{g}_0, \ldots, \mathbf{g}_m$ that satisfy (6.60) are uniquely determined for any given $\mathbf{x}_0, \mathbf{x}_1, \ldots, \mathbf{x}_m$. ■

Corollary *Let* $\mathbf{S}_1, \ldots, \mathbf{S}_m$ *and* $\mathbf{R}_0, \ldots, \mathbf{R}_{m-1}$ *satisfy* (6.53) *and* (6.56), *respectively. Then, vectors* $\mathbf{x}_k$ *defined by* (6.60) *satisfy the homogeneous linear system.*

$$\mathbf{x}_{k-1}\mathbf{A}_k + \mathbf{x}_k\mathbf{B}_k + \mathbf{x}_{k+1}\mathbf{C}_k = \mathbf{0}, \quad 0 < k < m, \tag{6.65}$$

if and only if $\mathbf{g}_1, \mathbf{g}_2, \ldots, \mathbf{g}_{m-1}$ *satisfy*

$$\mathbf{g}_k(\mathbf{S}_k\mathbf{A}_k + \mathbf{B}_k + \mathbf{R}_k\mathbf{C}_k) = \mathbf{0}, \quad 0 < k < m. \tag{6.66}$$

If matrices $\mathbf{S}_k\mathbf{A}_k + \mathbf{B}_k + \mathbf{R}_k\mathbf{C}_k, 0 < k < m$, are nonsingular, then for any solution $\mathbf{x}_0, \mathbf{x}_1, \ldots, \mathbf{x}_m$ to system (6.65) there exist unique vectors

$$\begin{aligned} \mathbf{g}_0 &= (\mathbf{x}_0 - \mathbf{x}_1\mathbf{S}_1)(\mathbf{I} - \mathbf{R}_0\mathbf{S}_1)^{-1}, \ \mathbf{g}_k = \mathbf{0}, \quad 0 < k < m, \\ \mathbf{g}_m &= (\mathbf{x}_m - \mathbf{x}_{m-1}\mathbf{R}_{m-1})(\mathbf{I} - \mathbf{S}_m\mathbf{R}_{m-1})^{-1}, \end{aligned} \tag{6.67}$$

that satisfy (6.60). In this case, the solution to (6.65) is given by

$$\mathbf{x}_k = \mathbf{g}_0 \prod_{j=0}^{k-1}\mathbf{R}_j + \mathbf{g}_m \coprod_{j=k+1}^{m}\mathbf{S}_j, \quad 0 \le k \le m. \tag{6.68}$$

6.5 Homogeneous Vector Difference Equations

Here, we address linear systems of equations for row vectors $\mathbf{x}_k$, $k = 1, 2, \ldots, m-1$, with block tridiagonal matrices

$$\mathbf{x}_{k-1}\mathbf{A} + \mathbf{x}_k\mathbf{B} + \mathbf{x}_{k+1}\mathbf{C} = \mathbf{f}_k, \quad k = 1, 2, \ldots, m-1. \tag{6.69}$$

We assume that there exists a solution $\mathbf{R}$ to the equation

$$\mathbf{A} + \mathbf{XB} + \mathbf{X}^2\mathbf{C} = \mathbf{0}, \tag{6.70}$$

such that matrix $\mathbf{B} + \mathbf{RC}$ is nonsingular, and a solution S to

$$\mathbf{X}^2\mathbf{A} + \mathbf{XB} + \mathbf{C} = \mathbf{0}, \tag{6.71}$$

such that $\mathbf{B} + \mathbf{SA}$ is nonsingular.

By letting

$$\mathbf{U} = -(\mathbf{B} + \mathbf{RC})^{-1}, \quad \mathbf{V} = -(\mathbf{B} + \mathbf{SA})^{-1},$$

we have

$$\mathbf{R} = \mathbf{AU}, \quad \mathbf{S} = \mathbf{CV}. \tag{6.72}$$

Thus, matrices $\mathbf{U}$ and $\mathbf{V}$ satisfy, respectively,

$$\mathbf{U} = -(\mathbf{B} + \mathbf{AUC})^{-1}, \quad \mathbf{V} = -(\mathbf{B} + \mathbf{CVA})^{-1}. \tag{6.73}$$

One checks easily the following relations.

Lemma 6.6 *Let matrices* $\mathbf{U}$ *and* $\mathbf{V}$ *satisfy (6.73). Then,*

(1)

$$\begin{aligned} &\mathbf{I} + \mathbf{UB} + \mathbf{UAUC} = \mathbf{O}, \quad \mathbf{I} + \mathbf{VB} + \mathbf{VCVA} = \mathbf{O}, \\ &\mathbf{I} + \mathbf{BU} + \mathbf{AUCU} = \mathbf{O}, \quad \mathbf{I} + \mathbf{BV} + \mathbf{CVAV} = \mathbf{O}; \end{aligned} \tag{6.74}$$

(2)

$$\begin{aligned} \mathbf{AU}(\mathbf{I} - \mathbf{AUCV}) &= (\mathbf{I} - \mathbf{AUCV})\mathbf{AV}, \\ \mathbf{CV}(\mathbf{I} - \mathbf{CVAU}) &= (\mathbf{I} - \mathbf{CVAU})\mathbf{CU}; \end{aligned} \tag{6.75}$$

(3)

$$\begin{aligned} \mathbf{CVAU} - \mathbf{I} = \mathbf{\Phi U}, \quad \mathbf{AUCV} - \mathbf{I} = \mathbf{\Phi V}, \\ \mathbf{UCVA} - \mathbf{I} = \mathbf{U\Phi}, \quad \mathbf{VAUC} - \mathbf{I} = \mathbf{V\Phi}, \end{aligned} \tag{6.76}$$

where

$$\mathbf{\Phi} = \mathbf{AUC} + \mathbf{B} + \mathbf{CVA} = -(\mathbf{U}^{-1} + \mathbf{B} + \mathbf{V}^{-1}); \tag{6.77}$$

(4)

$$\begin{aligned} \mathbf{A} + s\mathbf{B} + s^2\mathbf{C} = \mathbf{U}^{-1}(s\mathbf{I} - \mathbf{UA})(s\mathbf{UC} - \mathbf{I}) = \\ = (s\mathbf{I} - \mathbf{AU})\mathbf{U}^{-1}(s\mathbf{UC} - \mathbf{I}) = \\ = (s\mathbf{I} - \mathbf{AU})(s\mathbf{CU} - \mathbf{I})\mathbf{U}^{-1}, \end{aligned} \tag{6.78}$$

$$\begin{aligned} s^2\mathbf{A} + s\mathbf{B} + \mathbf{C} = \mathbf{V}^{-1}(s\mathbf{I} - \mathbf{VC})(s\mathbf{VA} - \mathbf{I}) = \\ = (s\mathbf{I} - \mathbf{CV})\mathbf{V}^{-1}(s\mathbf{VA} - \mathbf{I}) \\ = (s\mathbf{I} - \mathbf{CV})(s\mathbf{AV} - \mathbf{I})\mathbf{V}^{-1}. \end{aligned} \tag{6.79}$$

Nonsingularity of $\mathbf{SA} + \mathbf{B} + \mathbf{RC}$ is a stronger condition than nonsingularity of $\mathbf{B} + \mathbf{SA}$ and $\mathbf{B} + \mathbf{RC}$. Indeed,

$$(\mathbf{I} - \mathbf{SR})(\mathbf{B} + \mathbf{RC}) = (\mathbf{I} - \mathbf{RS})(\mathbf{B} + \mathbf{SA}) = \mathbf{SA} + \mathbf{B} + \mathbf{RC}. \tag{6.80}$$

Therefore, nonsingularity of $\mathbf{SA}+\mathbf{B}+\mathbf{RC}$ implies that all four matrices, $\mathbf{B}+\mathbf{RC}$, $\mathbf{B} + \mathbf{SA}$, $\mathbf{I} - \mathbf{SR}$, and $\mathbf{I} - \mathbf{RS}$, are nonsingular.

By setting $\mathbf{\Psi} = -(\mathbf{SA} + \mathbf{B} + \mathbf{RC})^{-1}$, we obtain from (6.80) expressions for $\mathbf{U}$ and $\mathbf{V}$:

$$\mathbf{U} = \mathbf{\Psi}(\mathbf{I} - \mathbf{SR}), \quad \mathbf{V} = \mathbf{\Psi}(\mathbf{I} - \mathbf{RS}). \tag{6.81}$$

The following result follows from Theorem 6.7.

Theorem 6.8 *Let matrices* **S** *and* **R** *be, respectively, solutions to matrix equations.*

$$\mathbf{S} = -\mathbf{C}(\mathbf{B} + \mathbf{SA})^{-1}, \ \mathbf{R} = -\mathbf{A}(\mathbf{B} + \mathbf{RC})^{-1}. \tag{6.82}$$

Then, vectors

$$\mathbf{x}_k = \mathbf{g}_k + \sum_{i=0}^{k-1} \mathbf{g}_i \mathbf{R}^{k-i} + \sum_{i=k+1}^{m} \mathbf{g}_i \mathbf{S}^{i-k}, \quad 0 \le k \le m, \tag{6.83}$$

satisfy the linear system (6.66) if and only if vectors $\mathbf{g}_1, \mathbf{g}_2, \ldots, \mathbf{g}_{m-1}$ *satisfy the systems*

$$\mathbf{g}_k(\mathbf{SA}+\mathbf{B}+\mathbf{RC}) = \mathbf{f}_k, \quad 0 < k < m. \tag{6.84}$$

If matrix $\mathbf{SA} + \mathbf{B} + \mathbf{RC}$ is nonsingular, then for any solution $\mathbf{x}_0, \mathbf{x}_1, ..., \mathbf{x}_m$ of (6.66) there exist unique vectors

$$\mathbf{g}_0 = (\mathbf{x}_0 - \mathbf{x}_1\mathbf{S})(\mathbf{I}-\mathbf{RS})^{-1}, \quad \mathbf{g}_m = (\mathbf{x}_m - \mathbf{x}_{m-1}\mathbf{R})(\mathbf{I}-\mathbf{SR})^{-1}, \tag{6.85}$$

$$\mathbf{g}_k = \mathbf{f}_k(\mathbf{SA}+\mathbf{B}+\mathbf{RC})^{-1}, \quad 0 < k < m, \tag{6.86}$$

that satisfy (6.83).

Corollary *Let matrices* $\mathbf{S}$ *and* $\mathbf{R}$ *be solutions* (6.82). *Then, vectors* $\mathbf{x}_k$ *defined* (6.83) *satisfy the linear system*

$$\mathbf{x}_{k-1}\mathbf{A} + \mathbf{x}_k\mathbf{B} + \mathbf{x}_{k+1}\mathbf{C} = \mathbf{0}, \quad 0 < k < m, \tag{6.87}$$

if and only if vectors $\mathbf{g}_1, \mathbf{g}_2, ..., \mathbf{g}_{m-1}$ *satisfy*

$$\mathbf{g}_k(\mathbf{SA}+\mathbf{B}+\mathbf{RC}) = \mathbf{0}, \quad 0 < k < m. \tag{6.88}$$

If matrix $\mathbf{SA} + \mathbf{B} + \mathbf{RC}$ is nonsingular, then for any solution $\mathbf{x}_0, \mathbf{x}_1, ..., \mathbf{x}_m$ of (6.82) there exist unique vectors

$$\begin{aligned} \mathbf{g}_0 = (\mathbf{x}_0 - \mathbf{x}_1\mathbf{S})(\mathbf{I}-\mathbf{RS})^{-1}, \quad \mathbf{g}_k = \mathbf{0}, \quad 0 < k < m, \\ \mathbf{g}_m = (\mathbf{x}_m - \mathbf{x}_{m-1}\mathbf{R})(\mathbf{I}-\mathbf{SR})^{-1}, \end{aligned} \tag{6.89}$$

which satisfy (6.83). In this case, the solution can be written as

$$\mathbf{x}_k = \mathbf{g}_0\mathbf{R}^k + \mathbf{g}_m\mathbf{S}^{m-k}, \quad 0 \le k \le m. \tag{6.90}$$

In conclusion, we point out that matrix-geometric solutions can be applied to piecewise homogeneous linear systems of the form

$$\mathbf{x}_{k-1}\mathbf{A}_i + \mathbf{x}_k\mathbf{B}_i + \mathbf{x}_{k+1}\mathbf{C}_i = \mathbf{0}, \quad m_{i-1} < k < m_i, \ i = 1, 2, ..., l,$$

where $m_1 < m_2 < \cdots < m_l$ (Krieger 1999).

6.6 Examples

6.6.1 A Matrix Analogue of the Erlang B Formula

Consider a MAP$|M|c|c$ service system with $c \le \infty$ servers and a simple Markovian arrival process $(X(t), N(t))$. Here $X(t) \in \{1, 2, ..., L\}$ is the phase process with an irreducible generator matrix $\mathbf{Q}$ and $N(t)$ is the counting process specified by a matrix $\mathbf{R} = [R(i, j)]$,

$$\mathsf{P}(X(t+\delta)) = j, N(t+\delta) = N(t) + 1 \,|X(t) = i\,) = R(i, j)\delta + o(\delta).$$

We assume that the service times are exponentially distributed with parameter μ. Then, the system can be described by a Markov process $Y(t) = (X(t), \xi(t))$, where $\xi(t)$ is the number of busy servers at time t.

6.6.1.1 $MAP|M|\infty$

First consider the system with an infinite number of servers. In this case, $Y(t) = (X(t), \xi(t))$ is a QBD process with the generator matrix

$$\mathbf{A} = \begin{bmatrix} \mathbf{S} & \mathbf{R} & \mathbf{O} & \mathbf{O} & \cdots \\ \mu\mathbf{I} & \mathbf{S}-\mu\mathbf{I} & \mathbf{R} & \mathbf{O} & \ddots \\ \mathbf{O} & 2\mu\mathbf{I} & \mathbf{S}-2\mu\mathbf{I} & \mathbf{R} & \ddots \\ \mathbf{O} & \mathbf{O} & 3\mu\mathbf{I} & \mathbf{S}-3\mu\mathbf{I} & \ddots \\ \vdots & \ddots & \ddots & \ddots & \ddots \end{bmatrix}, \tag{6.91}$$

where $\mathbf{S} = \mathbf{Q} - \mathbf{R}$. The stationary probability row vector $\mathbf{p} = (\mathbf{p}_0, \mathbf{p}_1, ...)$ of the process $Y(t)$ is the solution to the linear system

$$\mathbf{p}_0\mathbf{S} + \mu\mathbf{p}_1 = \mathbf{0}, \tag{6.92}$$

$$\mathbf{p}_{k-1}\mathbf{R} + \mathbf{p}_k(\mathbf{S} - k\mu\mathbf{I}) + (k+1)\mu\mathbf{p}_{k+1} = \mathbf{0},\ k = 1, 2, ... \tag{6.93}$$

satisfying the normalizing condition

$$\sum_{k=0}^{\infty} \mathbf{p}_k\mathbf{u} = 1. \tag{6.94}$$

Note that

$$\mathbf{q} = \sum_{k=0}^{\infty} \mathbf{p}_k \tag{6.95}$$

is the stationary distribution of the phase process $X(t)$,

$$\mathbf{qQ} = \mathbf{0}, \ \ \mathbf{qu} = 1. \tag{6.96}$$

Denote by $\mathbf{p}(z)$ the probability generating function of the vectors $\mathbf{p}_k$,

$$\mathbf{p}(z) = \sum_{k=0}^{\infty} z^k \mathbf{p}_k,$$

and define vectors $\mathbf{f}_r$ as

$$\mathbf{f}_r = \left. \frac{d^r}{dz^r} \mathbf{p}(z) \right|_{z=1} = \sum_{k=r}^{\infty} \frac{k!}{(k-r)!} \mathbf{p}_k. \tag{6.97}$$

Then $f_r = \mathbf{f}_r\mathbf{u}$ is the r-th factorial moment of the stationary distribution of the number of busy servers.

By multiplying (6.93) by z^k and summing over $k \geq 1$, in light of (6.92), we have

$$z\mathbf{p}(z)\mathbf{R} + \mathbf{p}(z)\mathbf{S} + \mu(1-z)\frac{d}{dz}\mathbf{p}(z) = \mathbf{0}. \tag{6.98}$$

We differentiate (6.98) r times with respect to z and then set $z = 1$, which yields

$$\mathbf{f}_r(\mathbf{S} + \mathbf{R} - r\mu\mathbf{I}) + r\mathbf{f}_{r-1}\mathbf{R} = \mathbf{0}, \ \ r = 1, 2, \ldots \tag{6.99}$$

Since

$$\mathbf{f}_0 = \sum_{k=0}^{\infty} \mathbf{p}_k = \mathbf{q}, \tag{6.100}$$

the vector $\mathbf{f}_0$ is the unique solution of the system (6.96). Due to the part (c) of Theorem 5.6, for an irreducible $\mathbf{Q} = \mathbf{S} + \mathbf{R}$ and $s > 0$, the matrix $\mathbf{Q} - s\mathbf{I}$ is nonsingular. Therefore, once we have found $\mathbf{f}_0$, we can use (6.96) to successively compute $\mathbf{f}_r$, $r = 1, 2, \ldots$, while an explicit expression for $\mathbf{f}_r$ is

$$\mathbf{f}_r = r!\mathbf{q}\mathbf{R}(\mu\mathbf{I} - \mathbf{Q})^{-1}\mathbf{R}(2\mu\mathbf{I} - \mathbf{Q})^{-1}\ldots\mathbf{R}(r\mu\mathbf{I} - \mathbf{Q})^{-1}, \ \ r = 1, 2, \ldots \tag{6.101}$$

Since $\mathbf{Qu} = \mathbf{0}$, we have $(r\mu\mathbf{I} - \mathbf{Q})^{-1}\mathbf{u} = \frac{1}{r\mu}\mathbf{u}$ for $r > 0$. Hence, (6.101) yields the following expression for the factorial moments f_r:

$$\mathbf{f}_r = \frac{1}{\mu}!\mathbf{qR}(\mu\mathbf{I}-\mathbf{Q})^{-1}\mathbf{R}(2\mu\mathbf{I}-\mathbf{Q})^{-1}...((r-1)\mu\mathbf{I}-\mathbf{Q})^{-1}\mathbf{Ru},\ r=1,2,\ ... \tag{6.102}$$

Of the greatest interest are the first two moments, which are used in the so-called Equivalent Random Theory (ERT) method:

$$f_1 = \frac{1}{\mu}\mathbf{qRu},\ f_2 = \frac{1}{\mu}\mathbf{vRu}, \tag{6.103}$$

where the row vector $\mathbf{v} = \mathbf{qR}(\mu\mathbf{I}-\mathbf{Q})^{-1}$ is the unique solution of the linear system

$$\mathbf{v}(\mu\mathbf{I}-\mathbf{Q}) = \mathbf{qR}. \tag{6.104}$$

6.6.1.2 $MAP|M|c|c$

Now consider a $MAP|M|c|c$ loss system with a finite number of servers. The process $Y(t) = (X(t), \xi(t))$ has a block tridiagonal generator matrix,

$$\mathbf{A} = \begin{bmatrix} \mathbf{S} & \mathbf{R} & \mathbf{O} & \cdots & \cdots & \mathbf{O} \\ \mu\mathbf{I} & \mathbf{S}-\mu\mathbf{I} & \mathbf{R} & \ddots & & \vdots \\ \mathbf{O} & 2\mu\mathbf{I} & \mathbf{S}-2\mu\mathbf{I} & \ddots & \mathbf{O} & \vdots \\ \vdots & \mathbf{O} & 3\mu\mathbf{I} & \ddots & \mathbf{R} & \mathbf{O} \\ \vdots & & \ddots & \ddots & \mathbf{S}-(c-1)\mu\mathbf{I} & \mathbf{R} \\ \mathbf{O} & \cdots & \cdots & \mathbf{O} & c\mu\mathbf{I} & \mathbf{Q}-c\mu\mathbf{I} \end{bmatrix}. \tag{6.105}$$

The stationary probability row vector $\mathbf{p} = (\mathbf{p}_0, \mathbf{p}_1, ..., \mathbf{p}_c)$ of the process $Y(t)$ is the solution to the linear system

$$\mathbf{p}_0\mathbf{S} + \mu\mathbf{p}_1 = \mathbf{0}, \tag{6.106}$$

$$\mathbf{p}_{k-1}\mathbf{R} + \mathbf{p}_k(\mathbf{S}-k\mu\mathbf{I}) + (k+1)\mu\mathbf{p}_{k+1} = \mathbf{0},\ k=1,2,\ ...,\ c-1, \tag{6.107}$$

$$\mathbf{p}_{c-1}\mathbf{R} + \mathbf{p}_c(\mathbf{Q}-c\mu\mathbf{I}) = \mathbf{0}, \tag{6.108}$$

satisfying the normalizing condition

$$\sum_{k=0}^{c}\mathbf{p}_k\mathbf{u} = 1. \tag{6.109}$$

Theorem 6.9 *Let matrices* $\mathbf{\Psi}_k$ *be defined as*

$$\mathbf{\Psi}_0 = \mathbf{0},\ \mathbf{\Psi}_k = \left(\mathbf{I} - \frac{1}{k\mu}(\mathbf{S} + \mathbf{\Psi}_{k-1}\mathbf{R})\right)^{-1},\ k = 1, 2, ..., \tag{6.110}$$

Then

(1) $\mathbf{\Psi}_k \geq \mathbf{0},\ k = 1, 2, ...$
(2)

$$\mathbf{\Psi}_k\mathbf{R}\mathbf{u} \leq k\mu\mathbf{u},\ \mathbf{q}\Psi_k \leq \mathbf{q},\ k = 1, 2, ... \tag{6.111}$$

(3) $\mathbf{p}_c = \mathbf{q}(\mathbf{I} - \mathbf{\Psi}_c)$.

Proof The generator matrix **A** satisfies the equality $\mathbf{AU} = \mathbf{UQ}$ with a block column matrix $\mathbf{U} = [\mathbf{I}, \mathbf{I}, ..., \mathbf{I}]$. It simply means that the process $Y(t) = (X(t), \xi(t))$ describing the $MAP|M|L|L$ loss system is lumpable. Its phase process $X(t)$ is a Markov chain with the stationary distribution.

$$\sum_{k=0}^{L} \mathbf{p}_k = \mathbf{q}. \tag{6.112}$$

It follows from Theorem 5.14 that replacing (6.108) in system (6.106)–(6.109) by (6.112) yields a linear system

$$\mathbf{p}\begin{bmatrix} \mathbf{S} & \mathbf{R} & \mathbf{O} & \cdots & \mathbf{O} & \mathbf{I} \\ \mu\mathbf{I} & \mathbf{S} - \mu\mathbf{I} & \mathbf{R} & \ddots & \vdots & \mathbf{I} \\ \mathbf{O} & 2\mu\mathbf{I} & \mathbf{S} - 2\mu\mathbf{I} & \ddots & \mathbf{O} & \vdots \\ \vdots & \mathbf{O} & 3\mu\mathbf{I} & \ddots & \mathbf{R} & \mathbf{I} \\ \vdots & & \ddots & \ddots & \mathbf{S} - (c-1)\mu\mathbf{I} & \mathbf{I} \\ \mathbf{O} & \cdots & \cdots & \mathbf{O} & c\mu\mathbf{I} & \mathbf{I} \end{bmatrix} = \begin{bmatrix} \mathbf{0} \\ \mathbf{0} \\ \vdots \\ \mathbf{0} \\ \mathbf{0} \\ \mathbf{q} \end{bmatrix}, \tag{6.113}$$

which is equivalent to the linear system (6.106)–(6.109). In accordance with Theorem 6.5, the solution of the linear system (6.106)–(6.109) can be found as

$$\mathbf{p}_k = \mathbf{q}(\sum_{i=0}^{c} \mathbf{H}_i)^{-1}\mathbf{H}_k,\ k = 0, 1, ..., c, \tag{6.114}$$

where matrices $\mathbf{H}_k$ are defined by the recursion

$$\mathbf{H}_{-1} = \mathbf{0},\ \mathbf{H}_0 = \mathbf{I},$$

$$\mathbf{H}_k = \frac{1}{k\mu}(\mathbf{H}_{k-1}((k-1)\mu\mathbf{I} - \mathbf{S}) - \mathbf{H}_{k-2}\mathbf{R}), \ k = 1, 2, ..., c. \tag{6.115}$$

Consider a block LU decomposition of the following subgenerator matrix:

$$\begin{bmatrix} \mathbf{S} - \mu\mathbf{I} & \mathbf{R} & & \mathbf{O} \\ \mu\mathbf{I} & \mathbf{S} - 2\mu\mathbf{I} & \ddots & \\ & \ddots & \ddots & \mathbf{R} \\ \mathbf{O} & & c\mu\mathbf{I} & \mathbf{S} - (c+1)\mu\mathbf{I} \end{bmatrix} = \\ = \begin{bmatrix} \mathbf{I} & & & \mathbf{O} \\ -\mathbf{\Psi}_1 & \mathbf{I} & & \\ & \ddots & \ddots & \\ \mathbf{O} & & -\mathbf{\Psi}_c & \mathbf{I} \end{bmatrix} \begin{bmatrix} \mathbf{W}_0 & \mathbf{R} & & \mathbf{O} \\ & \mathbf{W}_1 & \ddots & \\ & & \ddots & \mathbf{R} \\ \mathbf{O} & & & \mathbf{W}_c \end{bmatrix}. \tag{6.116}$$

Nonnegative matrices $\mathbf{\Psi}_k$ are defined by formulae (6.38), and can be computed as

$$\mathbf{\Psi}_0 = \mathbf{0}, \ \mathbf{\Psi}_k = \left(\mathbf{I} - \frac{1}{k\mu}(\mathbf{S} + \mathbf{\Psi}_{k-1}\mathbf{R})\right)^{-1}, \ k = 1, 2, ..., c. \tag{6.117}$$

Let us assume $\mathbf{\Psi}_{k-1}\mathbf{R}\mathbf{u} \leq (k-1)\mu\mathbf{u}$ and show that $\mathbf{\Psi}_k\mathbf{R}\mathbf{u} \leq k\mu\mathbf{u}$. Since $\mathbf{\Psi}_{k-1}\mathbf{R}\mathbf{u} \leq (k-1)\mu\mathbf{u} \leq k\mu\mathbf{u}$ and $\mathbf{R}\mathbf{u} = -\mathbf{S}\mathbf{u}$, we have

$$\mathbf{R}\mathbf{u} \leq k\mu\mathbf{u} - \mathbf{\Psi}_{k-1}\mathbf{R}\mathbf{u} + \mathbf{R}\mathbf{u} = k\mu(\mathbf{I} - \frac{1}{k\mu}(\mathbf{S} + \mathbf{\Psi}_{k-1}\mathbf{R}))\mathbf{u}.$$

By multiplying the left-hand and right-hand sides of this inequality by a nonnegative matrix

$$\mathbf{\Psi}_k = \left(\mathbf{I} - \frac{1}{k\mu}(\mathbf{S} + \mathbf{\Psi}_{k-1}\mathbf{R})\right)^{-1},$$

we obtain the first inequality of (6.111). The second inequality of (6.111) can be proved as follows. Let $\mathbf{q}\Psi_{k-1} \leq \mathbf{q}$. Then,

$$\mathbf{q}\Psi_k = \mathbf{q}(\mathbf{I} - \frac{1}{k\mu}(\mathbf{S} + \mathbf{R}))\mathbf{\Psi}_k \leq \mathbf{q}(\mathbf{I} - \frac{1}{k\mu}(\mathbf{S} + \mathbf{\Psi}_{k-1}\mathbf{R}))\mathbf{\Psi}_k = \mathbf{q}.$$

It remains to prove the last assertion of the theorem. According to Lemma 6.2, for matrices

$$\mathbf{G}_k = (\mathbf{\Psi}_k\mathbf{\Psi}_{k-1}\cdots\mathbf{\Psi}_1)^{-1}, \tag{6.118}$$

we have

$$\mathbf{G}_k = \frac{1}{k\mu}(\mathbf{G}_{k-1}(k\mu\mathbf{I} - \mathbf{S}) - \mathbf{G}_{k-2}\mathbf{R}), k = 1, 2, ..., c, \tag{6.119}$$

where $\mathbf{G}_{-1} = \mathbf{0}$ and $\mathbf{G}_0 = \mathbf{I}$. By comparing recursions (6.115) and (6.119), one easily sees that matrices $\mathbf{H}_k$ in (6.114) can be expressed in terms of $\mathbf{G}_k$ as

$$\mathbf{H}_k = \mathbf{G}_k - \mathbf{G}_{k-1},\ k = 1, 2, ..., c. \tag{6.120}$$

Now, by using (6.114) and (6.120), we obtain

$$\mathbf{p}_c = \mathbf{q}(\sum_{i=0}^{c} \mathbf{H}_i)^{-1}\mathbf{H}_c = \mathbf{q}\mathbf{G}_c^{-1}(\mathbf{G}_c - \mathbf{G}_{c-1}) = \mathbf{q}(\mathbf{I} - \boldsymbol{\Psi}_c). \tag{6.121}$$

■

Corollary 6.1 *The spectral radius of the matrices $\boldsymbol{\Psi}_k$ does not exceed 1.*

Corollary 6.2 *The time-blocking probability E_c that all servers are busy is given by*

$$E_c\ (\rho) = 1 - \mathbf{q}\ \boldsymbol{\Psi}_c\ \mathbf{u}. \tag{6.122}$$

6.6.2 *A Matrix Analogue of Wilkinson Formula*

6.6.2.1 *The Overflow Process of $MAP|M|c|c$*

Consider an $MAP|M|c|c$ loss system with a simple Markovian arrival process with marked arrivals $(X(t), N_1(t), ...N_K(t))$. Here $X(t) \in \{1, 2, ..., L\}$ is the phase process with an irreducible generator matrix $\mathbf{Q}$, while $N_k(t)$ is the counting process of class k customers specified by a matrix $\mathbf{R}_k = [R_k(i, j)]$ defined as

$$\mathsf{P}(X(t+\delta) = j, N_k(t+\delta) = N_k(t) + 1\ |X(t) = i) = R_k(i, j)\delta + o(\delta).$$

We assume that the service times are exponentially distributed with parameter μ for all customer classes and denote by $\xi(t)$ the number of busy servers at time t. Now, the system can be described by a Markov process $Y(t) = (X(t), \xi(t))$ with the generator matrix (6.105) such that

$$\mathbf{R} = \sum_{k=1}^{K} \mathbf{R}_k,\ \ \mathbf{S} = \mathbf{Q} - \mathbf{R}.$$

The overflow process for the $MAP|M|c|c$ loss system is a Markovian arrival process with marked arrivals $(Y(t), C_1(t), ...C_K(t))$ where $C_k(t)$ is the counting process of the k-th overflow process specified by a matrix

$$\mathbf{\Lambda}_k = \begin{bmatrix} \mathbf{O} & \mathbf{O} & \cdots & \mathbf{O} \\ \mathbf{O} & \ddots & \ddots & \vdots \\ \vdots & \ddots & \mathbf{O} & \mathbf{O} \\ \mathbf{O} & \cdots & \mathbf{O} & \mathbf{R}_k \end{bmatrix}. \tag{6.123}$$

Matrix $\mathbf{\Lambda}_k$ is formed by the transition rates of $Y(t)$ from the states in which an arriving class k customer finds the system busy. The k-th overflow process has the stationary rate $\mathbf{p}\Lambda_k\mathbf{u} = \mathbf{p}_c\mathbf{R}_k\mathbf{u}$, where $\mathbf{p} = (\mathbf{p}_0, \mathbf{p}_1, ..., \mathbf{p}_c)$ is the stationary vector of $\mathbf{A}$. The call-blocking probability for class k customers can be computed as the ratio of the rates of the overflow and arrival processes:

$$B_k = \frac{\mathbf{p}_c\mathbf{R}_k\mathbf{u}}{\mathbf{q}\mathbf{R}_k\mathbf{u}} = 1 - \frac{\mathbf{q}\Psi_c\mathbf{R}_k\mathbf{u}}{\mathbf{q}\mathbf{R}_k\mathbf{u}}. \tag{6.124}$$

6.6.2.2 $MAP|M|c|c \rightarrow M|\infty$

Now consider a service system with an infinite number of servers and an arrival process which is the overflow process of an $MAP|M|c|c$ loss system. Assume the service times in both primary and secondary systems to have exponential distribution with parameter μ. The mean m_k and the variance V_k of the number of class k customers in the infinite server (secondary) system can be found using (6.103):

$$m_k = \frac{1}{\mu}\ \mathbf{p}\ \mathbf{\Lambda}_k\ \mathbf{u} = \frac{1}{\mu}\mathbf{p}_c\ \mathbf{R}_k\ \mathbf{u} = \frac{1}{\mu}\mathbf{q}(\mathbf{I} - \mathbf{\Psi}_c)\mathbf{R}_k\ \mathbf{u}, \tag{6.125}$$

$$V_k = \frac{1}{\mu}\mathbf{v}_k\mathbf{\Lambda}_k\mathbf{u} + m_k(1 - m_k), \tag{6.126}$$

where the row vector $\mathbf{v}_k = \mathbf{p}\Lambda_k(\mu\mathbf{I} - \mathbf{A})^{-1}$ is the unique solution of the linear system

$$\mathbf{v}_k(\mu\mathbf{I} - \mathbf{A}) = \mathbf{p}\mathbf{\Lambda}_k. \tag{6.127}$$

Similarly, the variance $V_{i,j}$ of the number of class i and class j customers in the infinite server system is given by

$$V_{i,j} = \frac{1}{\mu}\mathbf{w}_{i,j}(\mathbf{\Lambda}_i + \mathbf{\Lambda}_j)\mathbf{u} + (m_i + m_j)(1 - (m_i + m_j)), \tag{6.128}$$

where

$$\mathbf{w}_{i,j} = \mathbf{p}(\mathbf{\Lambda}_i + \mathbf{\Lambda}_j)(\mu\mathbf{I} - \mathbf{A})^{-1} = \mathbf{v}_i + \mathbf{v}_j. \tag{6.129}$$

From (6.128) and (6.129), we get the following formula for the covariance C_{ij} of the number of class i and class j customers in the infinite server system:

$$C_{ij} = \frac{1}{2}(V_{i,j} - V_i - V_j) = \frac{1}{2\mu}(\mathbf{v}_i\mathbf{\Lambda}_j\mathbf{u} + \mathbf{v}_j\mathbf{\Lambda}_i\mathbf{u}) + m_i m_j. \tag{6.130}$$

Due to the special, sparse structure of matrices $\mathbf{\Lambda}_k$, only the last component $\mathbf{v}_{k,c}$ of each vector $\mathbf{v}_k = (\mathbf{v}_{k,0}, \mathbf{v}_{k,1}, ..., \mathbf{v}_{k,c})$ is required in (6.129) and (6.130), since

$$V_k = \frac{1}{\mu}\mathbf{v}_{k,c}\mathbf{R}_k\mathbf{u} + m_k(1 - m_k) \tag{6.131}$$

and

$$C_{i,j} = \frac{1}{2\mu}(\mathbf{v}_{i,c}\mathbf{R}_j\mathbf{u} + \mathbf{v}_{j,c}\mathbf{R}_i\mathbf{u}) + m_i m_j. \tag{6.132}$$

Vectors $\mathbf{v}_k$ are the unique solution of the linear system (6.127), which we rewrite as

$$\mathbf{v}_{k,1} = \frac{1}{\mu}\mathbf{v}_{k,0}(\mu\mathbf{I} - \mathbf{S}), \tag{6.133}$$

$$\mathbf{v}_{k,i} = \frac{1}{i\mu}(\mathbf{v}_{k,i-1}(i\mu\mathbf{I} - \mathbf{S}) - \mathbf{v}_{k,i-2}\mathbf{R}), \quad i = 2, 3, ..., c, \tag{6.134}$$

$$\mathbf{v}_{k,c}(\mathbf{Q} - (c+1)\mu\mathbf{I}) + \mathbf{v}_{k,c-1}\mathbf{R} = -\mathbf{p}_c\mathbf{R}_k. \tag{6.135}$$

By comparing the recursions (6.119) and (6.134), we see that vectors $\mathbf{v}_{k,i}$ can be calculated as

$$\mathbf{v}_{k,i} = \mathbf{v}_{k,0}\mathbf{G}_i, \quad i = 0, 1, ..., c, \tag{6.136}$$

where matrices $\mathbf{G}_i$ are given by the recursion (6.119) and $\mathbf{v}_{k,0}$ is the unique solution of the linear system

$$\mathbf{v}_{k,0}(\mathbf{G}_c(\mathbf{Q} - (c+1)\mu\mathbf{I}) + \mathbf{G}_{c-1}\mathbf{R}) = -\mathbf{p}_c\mathbf{R}_k. \tag{6.137}$$

By using (6.118) and (6.137) we obtain the following formula for vectors $\mathbf{v}_{k,c}$ required to compute variances (6.131) and covariances (6.132):

$$\mathbf{v}_{k,c} = -\mathbf{p}_c\mathbf{R}_k(\mathbf{G}_c(\mathbf{Q} - (c+1)\mu\mathbf{I}) + \mathbf{G}_{c-1}\mathbf{R})^{-1}\mathbf{G}_c = \\ = \mathbf{q}(\mathbf{I} - \mathbf{\Psi}_c)\mathbf{R}_k((c+1)\mu\mathbf{I} - \mathbf{Q} - \mathbf{\Psi}_c\mathbf{R})^{-1}, \ k = 1, 2, \ldots, K. \tag{6.138}$$

6.6.2.3 Why It Is a Generalization of Erlang and Wilkinson Formula?

Erlang loss formula

$$E_c(\rho) = \frac{\rho^c}{c\,!}\left(\sum_{k=0}^{c}\frac{\rho^k}{k\,!}\right)^{-1}$$

gives the time and call-blocking probability in the $MAP|M|c|c$ loss system as a function of the traffic intensity $\rho = \lambda/\mu$, where λ and μ are, respectively, the arrival and service rates. It can be calculated using the well-known recursion

$$E_0(\rho) = 1, \ \frac{1}{E_c(\rho)} = 1 + \frac{c}{\rho}\frac{1}{E_{c-1}(\rho)}, \ c = 1, 2, \ldots \tag{6.139}$$

Recursion (6.139) can be transformed to obtain the probability that an arriving customer receives service, $\psi_c = 1 - E_c(\rho)$,

$$\psi_0 = 0, \ \psi_c = \left(1 + \tfrac{\rho}{c}(1 - \psi_{c-1})\right)^{-1}, \ c = 1, 2, \ldots \tag{6.140}$$

which is similar to recursion (6.110) for matrices $\mathbf{\Psi}_c$. This analogy becomes even more evident if we compare the properties and expressions for the loss systems with Poisson and Markovian arrival processes shown in Table 6.1.

Table 6.1 Comparison of scalar and matrix variants of Erlang and Wilkinson formula

Poisson process	Markovian arrival process
Properties	
$0 \leq \psi_c \leq 1$	$\boldsymbol{\Psi}_c \geq 0,\ \mathbf{q}\Psi_c \leq \mathbf{q},\ sp(\Psi_c) \leq 1$
Carried traffic	
$\frac{\lambda}{\mu}\psi_c \leq c$	$\frac{1}{\mu}\boldsymbol{\Psi}_c\mathbf{Ru} \leq c\mathbf{u},$
Time-blocking probability	
$E_c(\rho) = 1 - \psi_c$	$E_c(\rho) = 1 - \mathbf{q}\boldsymbol{\Psi}_c\mathbf{u}$
Call-blocking probability	
$B_c(\rho) = 1 - \psi_c$	$B_c(\rho) = \frac{\mathbf{q}(\mathbf{I}-\boldsymbol{\Psi}_c)\mathbf{Ru}}{\mathbf{qRu}}$
Mean and variance of the overflow traffic	
$m = \frac{\lambda}{\mu}(1 - \psi_c)$	$m = \frac{1}{\mu}\mathbf{q}(\mathbf{I} - \boldsymbol{\Psi}_c)\mathbf{Ru}$
$V = \frac{\lambda m}{(c+1)\mu - \lambda\psi_c} + m(1-m)$	$V = \frac{1}{\mu}\mathbf{q}(\mathbf{I} - \boldsymbol{\Psi}_c)\mathbf{R}((c+1)\mu\mathbf{I} - \mathbf{Q} - \boldsymbol{\Psi}_c\mathbf{R})^{-1}\mathbf{Ru} + m(1-m)$

References

Basharin, G.P., Naumov, V.A.: Lösungsmethoden für lineare algebraische Gleichunssysteme stationärer Charakteristiken, Handbuch der Bedienungstheorie, II, pp. 387–430. Academie-Verlag, Berlin (1983)

Basharin, G.P., Gromov, A.I.: A matrix method to find a stationary distribution for some nonstandard servicing systems. Autom. Remote. Control. **39**(1), 20–28 (1978)

Golub, G.H., Van Loan, C.F.: Matrix Computations, 3rd ed. Johns Hopkins University Press (1996)

Krieger, U., Naumov, V.: Analysis of a delay-loss system with a superimposed Markovian arrival process and state-dependent service times. In: Plateau, B., Stewart, W.J., Silva, M. (eds.) Numerical Solution of Markov Chains (NSMC'99), pp. 261–279. Prensas Universitarias de Zaragoza, Zaragoza, Spain (1999)

Wikarski, D.: An algorithm for the solution of linear equation systems with block structure. J. Inf. Process. Cybern. **16**, 615–620 (1980)

Chapter 7
Matrix-Geometric Solutions

Abstract In this chapter, we show how matrix-geometric solutions of the equilibrium equations of finite quasi-birth-and-death processes are related to solutions of matrix quadratic equations. Necessary and sufficient conditions for the existence of solutions to the latter equations are provided and the properties of their minimal nonnegative solutions are studied. We conclude by comparing two matrix-geometric solutions for the stationary state distribution of a *PH*|*PH*|1|*r* + 1 queueing system and determine why computing via minimal nonnegative solutions is more stable.

The book (Neuts 1981) by M. F. Neuts, which appeared in 1981, has laid the foundations of the matrix-geometric methods in queueing theory. The book explores infinite Markov chains of the type $GI|M|1$, which have block lower Hessenberg generator matrices of a special form. Infinite quasi-birth-and-death processes (QBD processes), which have block tridiagonal generator matrices, are a special case of the processes covered in Neuts (1981).

According to Neuts (1981), a positive recurrent Markov chain of the type $GI|M|1$ has a matrix-geometric stationary probability vector $\mathbf{p} = (\mathbf{p}_0, \mathbf{p}_1, \ldots)$ of the form

$$\mathbf{p}_k = \mathbf{p}_0\mathbf{R}^k, k \geq 0,$$

where matrix $\mathbf{R}$ has the spectral radius $\rho < 1$ and is the minimal nonnegative solution of a matrix equation. Recall that for a matrix function of a matrix argument $\mathbf{F}(\mathbf{X})$, a nonnegative matrix $\mathbf{X}$ satisfying the equation $\mathbf{F}(\mathbf{X}) = \mathbf{0}$ is called the *minimal nonnegative solution* of this equation if for any nonnegative solution $\mathbf{Y}$ of $\mathbf{F}(\mathbf{Y}) = \mathbf{0}$, we have $\mathbf{Y} \leq \mathbf{X}$.

V. Naumov et al., *Matrix and Analytical Methods for Performance Analysis of Telecommunication Systems*, https://doi.org/10.1007/978-3-030-83132-5_7

Consider a generator matrix of a finite QBD process

$$\mathbf{Q} = \begin{bmatrix} \mathbf{N}_0 & \mathbf{\Lambda} & \mathbf{O} & \mathbf{O} & \cdots & \mathbf{O} \\ \mathbf{M}_1 & \mathbf{N} & \mathbf{\Lambda} & \mathbf{O} & \cdots & \mathbf{O} \\ \mathbf{O} & \mathbf{M} & \mathbf{N} & \ddots & \ddots & \vdots \\ \mathbf{O} & \mathbf{O} & \ddots & \ddots & \mathbf{\Lambda} & \mathbf{O} \\ \vdots & \vdots & \ddots & \mathbf{M} & \mathbf{N} & \mathbf{\Lambda}_{m-1} \\ \mathbf{O} & \mathbf{O} & \cdots & \mathbf{O} & \mathbf{M} & \mathbf{N}_m \end{bmatrix}.$$

The stationary distribution $\mathbf{p} = (\mathbf{p}_0, \mathbf{p}_1, \dots, \mathbf{p}_m)$ of such a process must satisfy two boundary conditions

$$\mathbf{p}_0\mathbf{N}_0 + \mathbf{p}_1\mathbf{M}_1 = \mathbf{0}, \quad \mathbf{p}_{m-1}\mathbf{\Lambda}_{m-1} + \mathbf{p}_m\mathbf{N}_m = \mathbf{0},$$

and the homogeneous vector difference equation

$$\mathbf{p}_{k-1}\mathbf{\Lambda} + \mathbf{p}_k\mathbf{N} + \mathbf{p}_{k+1}\mathbf{M} = \mathbf{0}, 0 < k < m. \tag{7.1}$$

We have seen in Sect. 6.5 that under certain conditions the solution to this equation can be expressed as a sum of two matrix-geometric terms

$$\mathbf{p}_k = \mathbf{a}\mathbf{R}^k + \mathbf{b}\mathbf{S}^{m-k}, 0 \le k \le m.$$

For QBD processes, the matrices $\mathbf{\Lambda}$ and $\mathbf{M}$ in (7.1) are nonnegative, while $\mathbf{N}$ and $\mathbf{\Lambda} + \mathbf{N} + \mathbf{M}$ are generator matrices. In this chapter, we follow (Naoumov 1996) and study in depth the matrix-geometric solution of (7.1) with such matrices $\mathbf{\Lambda}$, $\mathbf{M}$, and $\mathbf{N}$.

7.1 Quadratic Matrix Equations

This chapter discusses thoroughly the quadratic matrix equations, which arise in *matrix-geometric solutions of equilibrium equations with block tridiagonal matrices. Throughout the chapter, we assume* $\mathbf{P}_{-1}, \mathbf{P}_0, \mathbf{P}_1$ *to be nonnegative square matrices.*

Let $\mathcal{J} = \{-1, 0, 1\}$ and define, for $n \ge 1$, the sets

$$\mathcal{K}_n = \{(\mathcal{K}_1, \dots, k_n) \in \mathcal{J}^n | k_1 \le 0, \quad k_1 + k_2 \le 0, \dots, \\ k_1 + \cdots + k_{n-1} \le 0, \; k_1 + \cdots + k_n = 0\}.$$

We define nonnegative matrices $\mathbf{U}_n$ as

$$\mathbf{U}_0 = \mathbf{I}, \quad \mathbf{U}_n = \sum_{k \in \mathcal{K}_n} \mathbf{P}_{k_1}\mathbf{P}_{k_2} \cdots \mathbf{P}_{k_n}, \quad n = 1, 2, \ldots$$

This definition implies the identities

$$\mathbf{U}_n = \mathbf{U}_{n-1}\mathbf{P}_0 + \sum_{r=0}^{n-2} \mathbf{U}_r\mathbf{P}_{-1}\mathbf{U}_{n-r-2}\mathbf{P}_1, \quad n = 1, 2, \ldots, \tag{7.2}$$

$$\mathbf{U}_n = \mathbf{P}_0\mathbf{U}_{n-1} + \sum_{r=0}^{n-2} \mathbf{P}_{-1}\mathbf{U}_r\mathbf{P}_1\mathbf{U}_{n-r-2}, \quad n = 1, 2, \ldots. \tag{7.3}$$

Finally, we define

$$\mathbf{V}_k = \sum_{n=0}^{k} \mathbf{U}_n, \quad k = 0, 1, \ldots,$$

which are related as

$$\mathbf{0} \le \mathbf{V}_0 \le \mathbf{V}_1 \le \cdots \le \mathbf{V}_k \le \mathbf{V}_{k+1} \le \cdots$$

It follows from identities (7.2) and (7.3) that

$$\mathbf{V}_{k+1} \le \mathbf{I} + \mathbf{V}_k\mathbf{P}_0 + \mathbf{V}_k\mathbf{P}_{-1}\mathbf{V}_k\mathbf{P}, \quad k = 0, 1, \ldots, \tag{7.4}$$

$$\mathbf{V}_{k+1} \le \mathbf{I} + \mathbf{P}_0\mathbf{V}_k + \mathbf{P}_{-1}\mathbf{V}_k\mathbf{P}_1\mathbf{V}_k, \quad k = 0, 1, \ldots \tag{7.5}$$

Indeed, by summing over n from 1 to $k+1$ the left-hand and right-hand sides of (7.2), we obtain

$$\mathbf{V}_{k+1} = \mathbf{I} + \mathbf{V}_k\mathbf{P}_0 + \sum_{r=0}^{k-1} \mathbf{U}_r\mathbf{P}_{-1}\mathbf{V}_{k-r-1}\mathbf{P}_1 \le$$
$$\le \mathbf{I} + \mathbf{V}_k\mathbf{P}_0 + \sum_{r=0}^{k-1} \mathbf{U}_r\mathbf{P}_{-1}\mathbf{V}_k\mathbf{P}_1 \le \mathbf{I} + \mathbf{V}_k\mathbf{P}_0 + \mathbf{V}_k\mathbf{P}_{-1}\mathbf{V}_k\mathbf{P}_1.$$

Inequality (7.5) can be proved in the same way.

Lemma 7.1 *A necessary and sufficient condition for a minimal nonnegative solution of*

$$\mathbf{I} + \mathbf{X}(\mathbf{P}_0 - \mathbf{I}) + \mathbf{X}\mathbf{P}_{-1}\mathbf{X}\mathbf{P}_1 = \mathbf{0} \tag{7.6}$$

and for a minimal nonnegative solution of

$$\mathbf{I} + (\mathbf{P}_0 - \mathbf{I})\mathbf{X} + \mathbf{P}_{-1}\mathbf{X}\mathbf{P}_1\mathbf{X} = \mathbf{0} \tag{7.7}$$

to exist is the convergence of the series

$$\mathbf{U} = \sum_{i=0}^{\infty} \mathbf{U}_i. \tag{7.8}$$

Furthermore, the minimal nonnegative solution of these equations is the sum **U**.

Proof If the series (7.8) converges, then by summing over n from 1 to ∞ the left-hand and right-hand sides of (7.2) and (7.3), we have that a nonnegative matrix **U** satisfies (7.6) and (7.7).

Now, let **Y** represent a nonnegative solution of (7.6). Then,

$$\mathbf{Y} = \mathbf{I} + \mathbf{Y}\mathbf{P}_0 + \mathbf{Y}\mathbf{P}_{-1}\mathbf{Y}\mathbf{P}_1 \geq \mathbf{V}_0,$$

and from (7.4) and $\mathbf{V}_k \leq \mathbf{Y}$ it follows that

$$\mathbf{V}_{k+1} \leq \mathbf{I} + \mathbf{Y}\mathbf{P}_0 + \mathbf{Y}\mathbf{P}_{-1}\mathbf{Y}\mathbf{P}_1 = \mathbf{Y}.$$

Therefore, $\mathbf{V}_k \leq \mathbf{Y}$ for all k. Since the matrix sequence $\mathbf{V}_k$ is nondecreasing, this implies existence of the limit $\lim_{k\to\infty} \mathbf{V}_k = \sum_{i=0}^{\infty} \mathbf{U}_i \leq \mathbf{Y}$. ■

By the same argument, one can show that if there exists a nonnegative solution **Y** of (7.7), then the series (7.8) converges and $\mathbf{U} \leq \mathbf{Y}$.

Corollary *For a nonnegative solution*

$$\mathbf{X} = (\mathbf{I} - \mathbf{P}_0 - \mathbf{P}_{-1}\mathbf{X}\mathbf{P}_1)^{-1} \tag{7.9}$$

to exist it is necessary and sufficient that the series (7.8) converges. Furthermore, its sum **U** *is the minimal nonnegative solution of (7.9).*

Lemma 7.2 *There exists a nonnegative solution to*

$$\mathbf{P}_{-1} + \mathbf{X}(\mathbf{P}_0 - \mathbf{I}) + \mathbf{X}^2\mathbf{P}_1 = \mathbf{0} \tag{7.10}$$

if and only if the series

$$\mathbf{R} = \sum_{i=0}^{\infty} (\mathbf{P}_{-1}\mathbf{U}_i) \tag{7.11}$$

converges. Furthermore, its sum $\mathbf{R}$ *is the minimal nonnegative solution of (7.7).*

Proof If the series (7.11) converges then, by left-multiplying both sides of (7.2) by $\mathbf{P}_{-1}$ and then summing over n, we obtain that the nonnegative matrix $\mathbf{R}$ satisfies (7.1).

Now, let $\mathbf{Y}$ represent a nonnegative solution of (7.7). Then, $\mathbf{P}_{-1}\mathbf{V}_0 \leq \mathbf{P}_{-1} + \mathbf{Y}\mathbf{P}_0 + \mathbf{Y}^2\mathbf{P}_1 = \mathbf{Y}$ and inequalities (7.4) and $\mathbf{P}_{-1}\mathbf{V}_k \leq \mathbf{Y}$ imply

$$\mathbf{P}_{-1}\mathbf{V}_{k+1} \leq \mathbf{P}_{-1} + (\mathbf{P}_{-1}\mathbf{V}_k)\mathbf{P}_0 + (\mathbf{P}_{-1}\mathbf{V}_k)^2\mathbf{P}_1 \leq \mathbf{P}_{-1} + \mathbf{Y}\mathbf{P}_0 + \mathbf{Y}^2\mathbf{P}_1 = \mathbf{Y}.$$

By consequence, $\mathbf{P}_{-1}\mathbf{V}_k \leq \mathbf{Y}$ for all k. Since the matrix sequence $\mathbf{P}_{-1}\mathbf{V}_k$ is nondecreasing, this implies existence of the limit

$$\lim_{k\to\infty} \mathbf{P}_{-1}\mathbf{V}_k = \sum_{i=0}^{\infty} (\mathbf{P}_{-1}\mathbf{U}_i) \leq \mathbf{Y}.$$

■

Similarly, by making use of (7.3) and (7.5), one can check the following result.

Lemma 7.3 *There exists a nonnegative solution to*

$$\mathbf{P}_{-1}\mathbf{X}^2 + (\mathbf{P}_0 - \mathbf{I})\mathbf{X} + \mathbf{P}_1 = \mathbf{0} \tag{7.12}$$

if and only if the series

$$\mathbf{F} = \sum_{i=0}^{\infty} (\mathbf{U}_i\mathbf{P}_1) \tag{7.13}$$

converges. Furthermore, its sum $\mathbf{F}$ *is the minimal nonnegative solution of (7.12).*

Lemma 7.4 *Let (7.12) have a nonnegative solution, let* $\mathbf{F}$ *be the minimal nonnegative solution of (7.12), let* $\mathbf{I} - \mathbf{P}_0 - \mathbf{P}_{-1}\mathbf{F}$ *be a nonsingular matrix and let* $\mathbf{U} = (\mathbf{I} - \mathbf{P}_0 - \mathbf{P}_{-1}\mathbf{F})^{-1} \geq \mathbf{0}$. *Then, there exists a nonnegative solution to (7.7), and matrix* $\mathbf{R} = \mathbf{P}_{-1}\mathbf{U}$ *is the minimal nonnegative solution of (7.7).*

Proof It follows from $(\mathbf{I} - \mathbf{P}_0 - \mathbf{P}_{-1}\mathbf{F})\mathbf{F} = \mathbf{P}_1$ that $\mathbf{F} = \mathbf{U}\mathbf{P}_1$. Hence, $\mathbf{U}$ is a nonnegative solution to (7.9). Now, let $\mathbf{V}$ represent some nonnegative solution to this equation. Then,

$$\mathbf{I} + (\mathbf{P}_0 - \mathbf{I})\mathbf{V} + \mathbf{P}_{-1}\mathbf{V}\mathbf{P}_1\mathbf{V} = \mathbf{0}.$$

By right-multiplying both sides of this identity by $\mathbf{P}_1$, we have that the nonnegative matrix $\mathbf{V}\mathbf{P}_1$ satisfies (7.12). Since $\mathbf{F} = \mathbf{U}\mathbf{P}_1$ is the minimal nonnegative solution of this equation, $\mathbf{U}\mathbf{P}_1 \leq \mathbf{V}\mathbf{P}_1$ is true, and hence

$$\begin{aligned}\mathbf{V}-\mathbf{U} &= (\mathbf{I}-\mathbf{P}_0-\mathbf{P}_{-1}\mathbf{V}\mathbf{P}_1)^{-1}[(\mathbf{I}-\mathbf{P}_0-\mathbf{P}_{-1}\mathbf{U}\mathbf{P}_1)-\\ &\quad -(\mathbf{I}-\mathbf{P}_0-\mathbf{P}_{-1}\mathbf{V}\mathbf{P}_1)](\mathbf{I}-\mathbf{P}_0-\mathbf{P}_{-1}\mathbf{U}\mathbf{P}_1)^{-1}\\ &= \mathbf{V}\mathbf{P}_{-1}(\mathbf{V}\mathbf{P}_1-\mathbf{U}\mathbf{P}_1)\mathbf{U}\geq \mathbf{0}.\end{aligned}$$

By consequence, $\mathbf{U}$ is the minimal nonnegative solution of (7.9). In accordance with Corollary of Lemma 7.1,

$$\mathbf{U}=\sum_{i=0}^{\infty}\mathbf{U}_i,$$

hence, the series (7.11) converges and $\mathbf{R}=\mathbf{P}_{-1}\mathbf{U}$ is the minimal nonnegative solution of (7.7). ■

Lemma 7.5 *Let (7.7) and (7.12) have nonnegative solutions, let* $\mathbf{R}$ *be the minimal nonnegative solution of (7.7), and let* $\mathbf{F}$ *be the minimal nonnegative solution of (7.12). Then,* $\mathbf{R}\mathbf{P}_1=\mathbf{P}_{-1}\mathbf{F}$ *and for any scalar* s

$$\mathbf{P}_{-1}+s(\mathbf{P}_0-\mathbf{I})+s^2\mathbf{P}_1=(s\mathbf{I}-\mathbf{R})\mathbf{T}(\mathbf{I}-s\mathbf{F}), \tag{7.14}$$

where

$$\mathbf{T}=\mathbf{R}\mathbf{P}_1+\mathbf{P}_0-\mathbf{I}=\mathbf{P}_{-1}\mathbf{F}+\mathbf{P}_0-\mathbf{I}.$$

Proof Indeed, by Lemmas 7.2 and 7.3, we have

$$\mathbf{R}\mathbf{P}_1=\sum_{i=0}^{\infty}\mathbf{P}_{-1}\mathbf{U}_i\mathbf{P}_1=\mathbf{P}_{-1}\mathbf{F}.$$

Further,

$$\mathbf{R}\mathbf{T}=\mathbf{R}^2\mathbf{P}_1+\mathbf{R}(\mathbf{P}_0-\mathbf{I})=-\mathbf{P}_{-1},\ \mathbf{T}\mathbf{F}=\mathbf{P}_{-1}\mathbf{F}^2+(\mathbf{P}_0-\mathbf{I})\mathbf{F}=-\mathbf{P}_1,$$

and therefore

$$\begin{aligned}(s\mathbf{I}-\mathbf{R})\mathbf{T}(\mathbf{I}-s\mathbf{F}) &= (s\mathbf{T}+\mathbf{P}_{-1})(\mathbf{I}-s\mathbf{F})=\\ &= s(\mathbf{P}_{-1}\mathbf{F}+\mathbf{P}_0-\mathbf{I})+\mathbf{P}_{-1}+s^2\mathbf{P}_1-s\mathbf{P}_{-1}\mathbf{F}\\ &= \mathbf{P}_{-1}+s(\mathbf{P}_0-\mathbf{I})+s^2\mathbf{P}_1.\end{aligned}$$

■

Corollary *Under the assumptions of Lemma 7.5 the matrix* $\mathbf{T}$ *is nonsingular if and only if, for some scalar s, so is the matrix* $\mathbf{P}_{-1} + s(\mathbf{P}_0 - \mathbf{I}) + s^2\mathbf{P}_1$.

Lemma 7.6 *Let*

$$\mathbf{R}_{k+1} = \mathbf{P}_{-1} + \mathbf{R}_k\mathbf{P}_0 + \mathbf{R}_k^2\mathbf{P}_1, \quad k = 0, 1, \ldots \tag{7.15}$$

Then, $\mathbf{R}_k \leq \mathbf{R}_{k+1}$ for all $k = 0, 1, \ldots$. *There exists a nonnegative solution to* (7.7) *if and only if the limit* $\mathbf{R} = \lim_{k\to\infty} \mathbf{R}_k$ *exists, in which case* $\mathbf{R}$ *is the minimal nonnegative solution of (7.7).*

Proof Clearly, $\mathbf{R}_1 \geq \mathbf{R}_0$, and from $\mathbf{R}_k \geq \mathbf{R}_{k-1}$ it follows that $\mathbf{R}_{k+1} \geq \mathbf{P}_{-1} + \mathbf{R}_{k-1}\mathbf{P}_0 + \mathbf{R}_{k-1}^2\mathbf{P}_1 = \mathbf{R}_k$. Thus, $\mathbf{R}_k \leq \mathbf{R}_{k+1}$ for all $k = 0, 1, \ldots$. If the matrix sequence $\mathbf{R}_k$ converges, then by taking the limit in (7.15) we have that the nonnegative matrix $\mathbf{R}$ solves (7.7).

Now, let $\mathbf{Y}$ represent a nonnegative solution of (7.7). Then, $\mathbf{R}_0 \leq \mathbf{Y}$ and it follows from $\mathbf{R}_k \leq \mathbf{Y}$ that $\mathbf{R}_{k+1} \leq \mathbf{P}_{-1} + \mathbf{Y}\mathbf{P}_0 + \mathbf{Y}^2\mathbf{P}_1 = \mathbf{Y}$. Thus, $\mathbf{R}_k \leq \mathbf{Y}$ for all k. Since the matrix sequence $\mathbf{R}_k$ is nondecreasing, this implies existence of the limit $\mathbf{R} \leq \mathbf{Y}$. ■

By the same argument one can check the following result, which can also be considered a Corollary of Lemma 7.6.

Lemma 7.7 *Let* $\mathbf{F}_0 = \mathbf{0}$,

$$\mathbf{F}_{k+1} = \mathbf{P}_{-1}\mathbf{F}_k^2 + \mathbf{P}_0\mathbf{F}_k + \mathbf{P}_1, \quad k = 0, 1, \ldots \tag{7.16}$$

Then, $\mathbf{F}_k \leq \mathbf{F}_{k+1}$ *for all* $k = 0, 1, \ldots$. *There exists a nonnegative solution to (7.12) if and only if the limit* $\mathbf{F} = \lim_{k\to\infty} \mathbf{F}_k$ *exists, in which case matrix* $\mathbf{F}$ *is the minimal nonnegative solution of (7.12).*

Lemma 7.8 *Let* $\mathbf{g}(\mathbf{P}_{-1} + \mathbf{P}_0 + \mathbf{P}_1) \leq \varepsilon\mathbf{g}$ *for some scalar* $0 \leq \varepsilon \leq 1$ *and a positive row vector* $\mathbf{g}$. *Then, there exists a minimal nonnegative solution* $\mathbf{R}$ *of (7.10) and* $\mathbf{g}\mathbf{R} \leq \varepsilon\mathbf{g}$.

Proof Define a matrix sequence $\mathbf{R}_k$ by relation (7.15). Clearly, $\mathbf{g}\mathbf{R}_0 \leq \varepsilon\mathbf{g}$, and it follows from $\mathbf{g}\mathbf{R}_k \leq \varepsilon\mathbf{g}$ that $\mathbf{g}\mathbf{R}_k \leq \mathbf{g}$ and

$$\mathbf{g}\mathbf{R}_{k+1} \leq \mathbf{g}(\mathbf{P}_{-1} + \mathbf{P}_0 + \mathbf{P}_1) \leq \varepsilon\mathbf{g}.$$

Thus, $\mathbf{g}\mathbf{R}_k \leq \varepsilon\mathbf{g}$ for all k. Since $\mathbf{g}$ is positive and the sequence $\mathbf{R}_k$ is monotonic, this implies existence of the limit $\mathbf{R} = \lim \mathbf{R}_k$ and the inequality $\mathbf{g}\mathbf{R} \leq \varepsilon\mathbf{g}$. By Lemma 7.6, $\mathbf{R}$ is the minimal nonnegative solution of (7.7). ■

Corollary *Under the assumptions of Lemma 7.8 the maximum eigenvalue* $\sigma(\mathbf{R})$ *of* $\mathbf{R}$ *does not exceed* ε.

The following result can be proved by an argument similar to Lemma 7.8.

Lemma 7.9 *Let* $(\mathbf{P}_{-1} + \mathbf{P}_0 + \mathbf{P}_1)\mathbf{f} \leq \varepsilon\mathbf{f}$ *for some scalar* $0 \leq \varepsilon \leq 1$ *and a positive vector* $\mathbf{f}$. *Then, there exists a minimal nonnegative solution* $\mathbf{F}$ *of (7.12) and* $\mathbf{Ff} \leq \varepsilon\mathbf{f}$.

Corollary *Under the assumptions of Lemma 7.9 the maximum eigenvalue* $\sigma(\mathbf{F})$ *of* $\mathbf{F}$ *does not exceed* ε.

Lemma 7.10 *Suppose that* $\mathbf{P} = \mathbf{P}_{-1} + \mathbf{P}_0 + \mathbf{P}_1$ *is irreducible,* $\mathbf{gP} = \mathbf{g}$ *and* $\mathbf{Pf} = \mathbf{f}$ *hold for some positive row vector* $\mathbf{g}$ *and column vector* $\mathbf{f}$, $\mathbf{R}$ *is the minimal nonnegative solution of (7.7), and the matrix* $\mathbf{RP}_1 + \mathbf{P}_0 - \mathbf{I}$ *is nonsingular. Then,* $\sigma(\mathbf{R}) = 1$ *if and only if* $\mathbf{gP}_{-1}\mathbf{f} \geq \mathbf{gP}_1\mathbf{f}$. *Furthermore, any eigenvector of* $\mathbf{R}^T$ *corresponding to the eigenvalue* 1 *is a multiple of* $\mathbf{g}$.

Proof In light of Lemmas 7.8 and 7.9, under the made assumptions, respective minimal nonnegative solutions $\mathbf{R}$ and $\mathbf{F}$ of (7.7) and (7.12) exist and

$$\mathbf{gR} \leq \mathbf{g}, \quad \mathbf{Ff} \leq \mathbf{f}. \tag{7.17}$$

By Lemma 7.5, $\mathbf{RP}_1 = \mathbf{P}_{-1}\mathbf{F}$ and we have the decomposition

$$\mathbf{P} = (\mathbf{I} - \mathbf{R})\mathbf{T}(\mathbf{I} - \mathbf{F}), \tag{7.18}$$

where $\mathbf{T} = \mathbf{RP}_1 + \mathbf{P}_0 - \mathbf{I} = \mathbf{P}_{-1}\mathbf{F} + \mathbf{P}_0 - \mathbf{I}$. Note that $\mathbf{TF} = -\mathbf{P}_1$.

Suppose that $\mathbf{I} - \mathbf{R}$ is singular. Then, for a row vector $\mathbf{h}$

$$\mathbf{h} = \mathbf{g}(\mathbf{I} - \mathbf{R}) > \mathbf{0},$$

and the decomposition (7.18) yields

$$(\mathbf{RP}_1 + \mathbf{P}_0 + \mathbf{P}_1 - \mathbf{I})\mathbf{f} = \mathbf{T}(\mathbf{I} - \mathbf{F})\mathbf{f} = \mathbf{0}. \tag{7.19}$$

It also follows from (7.18) that

$$\mathbf{h}(\mathbf{T} + \mathbf{P}_1) = \mathbf{hT}(\mathbf{I} - \mathbf{F}) = \mathbf{gP} = \mathbf{0}.$$

Since $\mathbf{T}$ is nonsingular, this implies that $\mathbf{hP}_1 \neq \mathbf{0}$ and hence $\mathbf{hP}_1\mathbf{f} > 0$. By making use of (7.19), we have

$$\begin{aligned}\mathbf{gP}_{-1}\mathbf{f} &= \mathbf{g}(\mathbf{I} - \mathbf{P}_0 - \mathbf{P}_1)\mathbf{f} = \mathbf{gRP}_1\mathbf{f} = \\ &= \mathbf{gP}_1\mathbf{f} - \mathbf{g}(\mathbf{I} - \mathbf{R})\mathbf{P}_1\mathbf{f} = \mathbf{gP}_1\mathbf{f} - \mathbf{hP}_1\mathbf{f} < \mathbf{gP}_1\mathbf{f}.\end{aligned}$$

Suppose now that $\mathbf{I} - \mathbf{R}$ is singular and $\mathbf{r}(\mathbf{I} - \mathbf{R}) = \mathbf{0}$, where $\mathbf{r}$ is row vector. As it follows from the decomposition (7.18), in this case $\mathbf{rP} = \mathbf{0}$. Since the maximum eigenvalue of an irreducible matrix $\mathbf{P}$ is algebraically simple, $\mathbf{r} = c\mathbf{g}$, where c is some scalar constant. By applying (7.17), we have

$$\mathbf{gP}_{-1}\mathbf{f} = \mathbf{gRP}_1\mathbf{f} + \mathbf{gP}_{-1}(\mathbf{I} - \mathbf{F})\mathbf{f} = \mathbf{gP}_1\mathbf{f} + \mathbf{gP}_{-1}(\mathbf{I} - \mathbf{F})\mathbf{f} \geq \mathbf{gP}_1\mathbf{f}.$$

■

Lemma 7.11 *Suppose that* $\mathbf{P} = \mathbf{P}_{-1} + \mathbf{P}_0 + \mathbf{P}_1$ *is irreducible,* $\mathbf{gP} = \mathbf{g}$ *and* $\mathbf{Pf} = \mathbf{f}$ *hold for a positive row vector* $\mathbf{g}$ *and a positive column vector* $\mathbf{f}$, $\mathbf{F}$ *is the minimal nonnegative solution of (7.12), and* $\mathbf{P}_{-1}\mathbf{F} + \mathbf{P}_0 - \mathbf{I}$ *is nonsingular. Then,* $\sigma(\mathbf{F}) = 1$ *if and only if* $\mathbf{gP}_1\mathbf{f} \geq \mathbf{gP}_{-1}\mathbf{f}$. *Furthermore, any eigenvector of* $\mathbf{F}$ *corresponding to the eigenvalue* 1 *is a multiple of* $\mathbf{f}$.

This result can be proved by an argument similar to that used in Lemma 7.7.

7.2 Minimal Nonnegative Solutions

Throughout the remainder of this chapter we suppose that $\mathbf{\Lambda} \geq \mathbf{0}$, $\mathbf{M} \geq \mathbf{0}$, and that $\mathbf{N}$ and $\mathbf{H} = \mathbf{\Lambda} + \mathbf{M} + \mathbf{N}$ are generator matrices. We denote $\boldsymbol{\lambda} = \mathbf{\Lambda u}$, $\boldsymbol{\mu} = \mathbf{Mu}$, where $\mathbf{u}$ is the all-ones column vector, and assume a to be some positive scalar such that $\mathbf{N} + a\mathbf{I} \geq \mathbf{0}$.

7.2.1 *Irreducible Matrix* H

In this section, we show that minimal nonnegative solutions $\mathbf{R}$ and $\mathbf{S}$ of the equations $\mathbf{\Lambda} + \mathbf{RN} + \mathbf{R}^2\mathbf{M} = \mathbf{0}$ and $\mathbf{S}^2\mathbf{\Lambda} + \mathbf{SN} + \mathbf{M} = \mathbf{0}$ exist, and derive the conditions for the matrices $\mathbf{N} + \mathbf{RM}$, $\mathbf{N} + \mathbf{S\Lambda}$ and $\mathbf{S\Lambda} + \mathbf{N} + \mathbf{RM}$ to be nonsingular. The following condition D plays a fundamental role in our analysis.

D. The determinant $\det(\mathbf{\Lambda} + s\mathbf{N} + s^2\mathbf{M})$ *is not identically zero.*

The matrices

$$\mathbf{\Lambda} = \begin{bmatrix} 0 & \lambda \\ 0 & 0 \end{bmatrix}, \quad \mathbf{N} = \begin{bmatrix} -\lambda & 0 \\ 0 & -\mu \end{bmatrix}, \quad \mathbf{M} = \begin{bmatrix} 0 & 0 \\ \mu & 0 \end{bmatrix}$$

provide an example where this condition does not hold.

Whenever the condition D holds, $\det(\mathbf{\Lambda} + s\mathbf{N} + s^2\mathbf{M})$ has a finite number k of roots, $1 \leq k \leq 2m$, where m is the order of the matrices $\mathbf{\Lambda}, \mathbf{N}, \mathbf{M}$. Moreover, in this case, the determinant $\det(s^2\mathbf{\Lambda} + s\mathbf{N} + \mathbf{M})$ also is not identically zero.

By the corollary of Theorem 5.16, the maximum eigenvalue $\sigma(\mathbf{H})$ of $\mathbf{H}$ is nonpositive. Condition D holds whenever either of the matrices $\mathbf{\Lambda}$ and M is nonsingular, and also if $\sigma(\mathbf{H}) < 0$, because in this case $\det(\mathbf{\Lambda} + \mathbf{M} + \mathbf{N}) \neq 0$. The following theorem provides a simple sufficient condition for D to hold given that $\mathbf{H}$ is irreducible and conservative.

Theorem 7.1 *Let* $\mathbf{H}$ *be irreducible and let* $\mathbf{pH} = \mathbf{0}$ *for some row vector* $\mathbf{p} \neq \mathbf{0}$. *Then, D holds whenever* $\mathbf{p\lambda} \neq \mathbf{p\mu}$.

Proof In accordance with Theorem 5.16, the entries of $\mathbf{p}$ are all the same sign, and hence $\mathbf{pu} \neq 0$. Thus, without loss of generality, we can assume $\mathbf{pu} = 1$.

Since the eigenvalue $\sigma(\mathbf{H})$ of an irreducible matrix $\mathbf{H}$ is algebraically simple, we can choose respective eigenvectors $\mathbf{g}(s)$ and $\mathbf{f}(s)$ of the matrices $(\mathbf{\Lambda} + s\mathbf{N} + s^2\mathbf{M})^T$ and $\mathbf{\Lambda} + s\mathbf{N} + s^2\mathbf{M},\ s \geq 0$, corresponding to their maximum eigenvalue $\gamma(s)$, such that their entries are continuously differentiable near $s = 1$ and $\mathbf{g}(1) = \mathbf{p},\ \mathbf{f}(1) = \mathbf{u},\quad \mathbf{g}(s)\mathbf{f}(s) = 1$ (Kato 1995). By differentiating the identity

$$\gamma(s) = \mathbf{g}(s)(\mathbf{\Lambda} + s\mathbf{N} + s^2\mathbf{M})\mathbf{f}(s),$$

we have

$$\frac{d}{ds}\gamma(s) = \gamma(s)\left(\frac{d}{ds}\mathbf{g}(s)\right)\mathbf{f}(s) + \gamma(s)\mathbf{g}(s)\left(\frac{d}{ds}\mathbf{f}(s)\right) + \mathbf{g}(s)(\mathbf{N} + 2s\mathbf{M})\mathbf{f}(s).$$

By letting s in the last relation tend to 1, we obtain

$$\frac{d}{ds}\gamma(s)|_{s=1} = \mathbf{pMu} - \mathbf{p\Lambda u}.$$

Thus, whenever $\mathbf{p\lambda} \neq \mathbf{p\mu}$ for some s close to 1, we have $\gamma(s) < \gamma(1) = 0$, and therefore $\mathbf{\Lambda} + s\mathbf{N} + s^2\mathbf{M}$ is nonsingular. ■

Theorem 7.2 *Let* $\mathbf{H}$ *be irreducible and the row vector* $\mathbf{p}$ *represents a positive eigenvector of* $\mathbf{H}$ *corresponding to* $\sigma(\mathbf{H})$. *Then,*

(a) *There exists a minimal nonnegative solution* $\mathbf{R}$ *of*

$$\mathbf{\Lambda} + \mathbf{RN} + \mathbf{R}^2\mathbf{M} = \mathbf{0}. \tag{7.20}$$

(b) $$\mathbf{pR} \leq \left(1 + \frac{\sigma(\mathbf{H})}{a}\right)\mathbf{p}. \tag{7.21}$$

Particularly, the maximum eigenvalue $\sigma(\mathbf{R})$ *of R does not exceed* $1 + \frac{\sigma(\mathbf{H})}{a}$.

(c) *The matrix* $\mathbf{N} + \mathbf{RM}$ *is nonsingular if and only if D holds.*

(d) *Given D,* $\sigma(\mathbf{R}) = 1$ *if and only if* $\sigma(\mathbf{H}) = 0$ *and* $\mathbf{p\lambda} \geq \mathbf{p\mu}$, *in which case the eigenvector of* $\mathbf{R}^T$ *corresponding to the eigenvalue 1 is a multiple of* $\mathbf{p}$.

Proof By setting

$$\mathbf{P}_{-1} = \frac{1}{a}\mathbf{\Lambda},\quad \mathbf{P}_0 = \mathbf{I} + \frac{1}{a}\mathbf{N},\quad \mathbf{P}_1 = \frac{1}{a}\mathbf{M},$$

we obtain nonnegative matrices $\mathbf{P}_{-1}, \mathbf{P}_0, \mathbf{P}_1$ such that

$$\mathbf{p}(\mathbf{P}_{-1} + \mathbf{P}_0 + \mathbf{P}_1) = \varepsilon \mathbf{p}, \quad (\mathbf{P}_{-1} + \mathbf{P}_0 + \mathbf{P}_1)\mathbf{u} \le \mathbf{u},$$

where $\varepsilon = 1 + \frac{\sigma(\mathbf{H})}{a}$. One easily checks that $0 \le \varepsilon \le 1$. In light of Lemmas 7.8 and 7.9, the respective minimal nonnegative solutions $\mathbf{R}$ and $\mathbf{F}$ of $\mathbf{\Lambda} + \mathbf{RN} + \mathbf{R}^2\mathbf{M} = \mathbf{0}$, and $\mathbf{\Lambda F}^2 + \mathbf{NF} + \mathbf{M} = \mathbf{0}$ exist, and (7.21) holds. By Corollary of Lemma 7.5, the condition D is necessary and sufficient for $\mathbf{N} + \mathbf{RM}$ to be nonsingular.

By Corollary of Theorem 5.16, the maximum eigenvalue of $\mathbf{R}^T$, and hence of $\mathbf{R}$, does not exceed $1 + \frac{\sigma(\mathbf{H})}{a}$. In particular, $\sigma(\mathbf{R}) < 1$ whenever $\sigma(\mathbf{H}) < 0$. If $\sigma(\mathbf{H}) = 0$, then it follows from Theorem 5.7 that $\mathbf{Hu} = \mathbf{0}$, and it follows from Lemma 7.7 that, given D, $\sigma(\mathbf{R}) = 1$ if and only if $\mathbf{p}\boldsymbol{\lambda} \ge \mathbf{p}\boldsymbol{\mu}$. Moreover, in this case, the eigenvector of $\mathbf{R}^T$ corresponding to 1 is a multiple of $\mathbf{g}$. ■

The next theorem follows directly from Theorem 7.2.

Theorem 7.3 *Let* $\mathbf{H}$ *be irreducible and the row vector* $\mathbf{p}$ *represent a positive eigenvector of* $\mathbf{H}$ *corresponding to* $\sigma(\mathbf{H})$. *Then,*

(a) *There exists a minimal nonnegative solution* $\mathbf{S}$ *of*

$$\mathbf{S}^2\mathbf{\Lambda} + \mathbf{SN} + \mathbf{M} = \mathbf{0}. \tag{7.22}$$

(b) $$\mathbf{pS} \le \left(1 + \frac{\sigma(\mathbf{H})}{a}\right)\mathbf{p} \tag{7.23}$$

and, in particular, the maximum eigenvalue

$\sigma(\mathbf{S})$ *of* $\mathbf{S}$ *does not exceed* $1 + \frac{\sigma(\mathbf{H})}{a}$.

(c) *The matrix* $\mathbf{N} + \mathbf{S\Lambda}$ *is nonsingular if and only if D holds.*

(d) *Given D,* $\sigma(\mathbf{S}) = 1$ *if and only if* $\sigma(\mathbf{H}) = 0$ *and* $\mathbf{g}\boldsymbol{\lambda} \le \mathbf{g}\boldsymbol{\mu}$, *in which case the eigenvector of* $\mathbf{S}^T$ *corresponding to the eigenvalue 1 is a multiple of* $\mathbf{p}$.

Corollary *Let* $\mathbf{H}$ *be irreducible and let* $\sigma(\mathbf{H}) < 0$. *Then* $\mathbf{N} + \mathbf{RM}$, $\mathbf{N} + \mathbf{S\Lambda}$ *and* $\mathbf{S\Lambda} + \mathbf{N} + \mathbf{RM}$ *are nonsingular.*

Proof Indeed, if $\sigma(\mathbf{H}) < 0$ then D holds and hence the matrices $\mathbf{N} + \mathbf{RM}$ and $\mathbf{N} + \mathbf{S\Lambda}$ are nonsingular. In addition, it follows from (7.21) and (7.23) that

$$\mathbf{p}(\mathbf{S\Lambda} + \mathbf{N} + \mathbf{RM}) \le \mathbf{p}(\mathbf{\Lambda} + \mathbf{M} + \mathbf{N}) = \sigma(\mathbf{H})\mathbf{p}.$$

By Corollary of Theorem 5.16,

$$\sigma(\mathbf{S\Lambda} + \mathbf{N} + \mathbf{RM}) \le \sigma(\mathbf{H}).$$

Hence, $\mathbf{S\Lambda} + \mathbf{N} + \mathbf{RM}$ is nonsingular whenever $\sigma(\mathbf{H}) < 0$. ■

Theorem 7.4 *Let* $\mathbf{H}$ *be irreducible,* $\mathbf{pH} = \mathbf{0}$*,* $\mathbf{pu} = 1$*, and let* $\mathbf{R}$ *and* $\mathbf{S}$ *be the minimal nonnegative solutions of (7.20) and (7.22), respectively. Then, for* $\mathbf{S\Lambda} + \mathbf{N} + \mathbf{RM}$ *to be nonsingular it is necessary that* $\mathbf{p\lambda} \neq \mathbf{p\mu}$*. Moreover, if* $\mathbf{p\lambda} \neq \mathbf{p\mu}$ *and* $\mathbf{S\Lambda} + \mathbf{N} + \mathbf{RM}$ *is irreducible, then it is nonsingular.*

Proof First, note that whenever D holds we have

$$\begin{aligned} \mathbf{pR} &< \mathbf{p}, \quad \mathbf{pS} = \mathbf{p}, \quad \mathbf{if}\ \mathbf{p\lambda} < \mathbf{p\mu}, \\ \mathbf{pR} &= \mathbf{p}, \quad \mathbf{pS} = \mathbf{p}, \quad \mathbf{if}\ \mathbf{p\lambda} = \mathbf{p\mu}, \\ \mathbf{pR} &= \mathbf{p}, \quad \mathbf{pS} < \mathbf{p}, \quad \mathbf{if}\ \mathbf{p\lambda} > \mathbf{p\mu}. \end{aligned}$$

This follows from statements (b) and D of Theorems 7.2 and 7.3.

Relations (7.20) and (7.22) imply the decompositions

$$\mathbf{S\Lambda} + \mathbf{N} + \mathbf{RM} = (\mathbf{I} - \mathbf{SR})(\mathbf{N} + \mathbf{RM}) = (\mathbf{I} - \mathbf{RS})(\mathbf{N} + \mathbf{S\Lambda}). \tag{7.24}$$

Now, if $\mathbf{S\Lambda} + \mathbf{N} + \mathbf{RM}$ is nonsingular, then so is $\mathbf{N} + \mathbf{RM}$ and, by Theorem 7.2, D holds. Moreover, $\mathbf{I} - \mathbf{SR}$ is also nonsingular, and therefore, in light of the above, $\mathbf{p\lambda} \neq \mathbf{p\mu}$.

Conversely, let $\mathbf{p\lambda} \neq \mathbf{p\mu}$. Then, by Theorem 7.1, the condition D holds and, in accordance with Theorems 7.2 and 7.3, the matrices $\mathbf{N} + \mathbf{RM}$ and $\mathbf{N} + \mathbf{S\Lambda}$ are nonsingular. If $\mathbf{p\lambda} < \mathbf{p\mu}$, then $\mathbf{p}(\mathbf{I} - \mathbf{SR}) = \mathbf{p}(\mathbf{I} - \mathbf{R}) \neq \mathbf{0}$ and it follows from (7.24) that $\mathbf{p}(\mathbf{S\Lambda} + \mathbf{N} + \mathbf{RM}) \neq \mathbf{0}$. If $\mathbf{p\lambda} > \mathbf{p\mu}$ then $\mathbf{p}(\mathbf{S\Lambda} + \mathbf{N} + \mathbf{RM}) \neq \mathbf{0}$ and it follows from (7.24) that $\mathbf{p}(\mathbf{I} - \mathbf{RS}) = \mathbf{p}(\mathbf{I} - \mathbf{S}) \neq \mathbf{0}$. Thus, $\mathbf{p}(\mathbf{S\Lambda} + \mathbf{N} + \mathbf{RM}) \neq \mathbf{0}$ whenever $\mathbf{p\lambda} \neq \mathbf{p\mu}$. Moreover,

$$\mathbf{p}(\mathbf{S\Lambda} + \mathbf{N} + \mathbf{RM}) \leq \mathbf{p}(\mathbf{\Lambda} + \mathbf{N} + \mathbf{M}) = \mathbf{0}.$$

Thus, $\mathbf{S\Lambda} + \mathbf{N} + \mathbf{RM}$ is a nonconservative generator matrix. By Theorem 5.7, it is nonsingular if it is irreducible. ■

7.2.2 Reducible Matrix H

Now, let $\mathbf{H}$ be of the normal form

$$\mathbf{H} = \begin{bmatrix} \mathbf{H}_{11} & \mathbf{O} & \cdots & \cdots & \cdots & \cdots & \mathbf{O} \\ \mathbf{O} & \mathbf{H}_{22} & \mathbf{O} & & & & \vdots \\ \vdots & \ddots & \ddots & \ddots & & & \vdots \\ \mathbf{O} & \cdots & \mathbf{O} & \ddots & \ddots & & \vdots \\ \mathbf{H}_{r+11} & \mathbf{H}_{r+12} & \cdots & \mathbf{H}_{r+1r} & \mathbf{H}_{r+1r+1} & \ddots & \vdots \\ \cdots & \cdots & \cdots & \cdots & \cdots & \ddots & \mathbf{O} \\ \mathbf{H}_{l1} & \mathbf{H}_{l2} & \cdots & \mathbf{H}_{lr} & \mathbf{H}_{lr+1} & \cdots & \mathbf{H}_{ll} \end{bmatrix}, \tag{7.25}$$

where $\mathbf{H}_{ii}$ are irreducible generator matrices and, for $l > r$, each row $\mathbf{H}_{i1}, \mathbf{H}_{i2}, ..., \mathbf{H}_{ii-1}$, $i = r+1, r+2, ..., l$, contains a nonzero matrix.

We partition the matrices $\mathbf{\Lambda}, \mathbf{N}, \mathbf{M}$ into blocks in accordance with the partitioning of $\mathbf{H}$. Since the off-diagonal entries of $\mathbf{\Lambda}, \mathbf{N}, \mathbf{M}$ are all nonnegative and $\mathbf{H} = \mathbf{\Lambda} + \mathbf{N} + \mathbf{M}$, the matrices $\mathbf{\Lambda}, \mathbf{N}, \mathbf{M}$ have zero blocks wherever $\mathbf{H}$ has zero blocks. Hence, the matrices $\mathbf{\Lambda}$, $\mathbf{N}$, $\mathbf{M}$ are lower block triangular:

$$\mathbf{\Lambda} = \begin{bmatrix} \mathbf{\Lambda}_{11} & & \mathbf{O} \\ \vdots & \ddots & \\ \mathbf{\Lambda}_{l1} & \cdots & \mathbf{\Lambda}_{ll} \end{bmatrix}, \ \mathbf{N} = \begin{bmatrix} \mathbf{N}_{11} & & \mathbf{O} \\ \vdots & \ddots & \\ \mathbf{N}_{l1} & \cdots & \mathbf{N}_{ll} \end{bmatrix}, \ \mathbf{M} = \begin{bmatrix} \mathbf{M}_{11} & & \mathbf{O} \\ \vdots & \ddots & \\ \mathbf{M}_{l1} & \cdots & \mathbf{M}_{ll} \end{bmatrix}.$$

Theorem 7.5 *There always exists a minimal nonnegative solution* $\mathbf{F}$ *of the equation* $\mathbf{\Lambda F}^2 + \mathbf{NF} + \mathbf{M} = \mathbf{0}$, *and, moreover,* $\mathbf{Fu} \le \left(1 + \frac{\sigma(\mathbf{H})}{a}\right)\mathbf{u}$. *If D holds, then there exists also a minimal nonnegative solution* $\mathbf{R}$ *of the equation* $\mathbf{\Lambda} + \mathbf{RN} + \mathbf{R}^2\mathbf{M} = \mathbf{0}$ *and* $\sigma(\mathbf{R}) \le 1 + \frac{\sigma(\mathbf{H})}{a}$, *in which case* $\mathbf{RM} = \mathbf{\Lambda F}$, *the matrix* $\mathbf{N} + \mathbf{RM}$ *is nonsingular, and we have the decomposition.*

$$\mathbf{\Lambda} + s\mathbf{N} + s^2\mathbf{M} = (s\mathbf{I} - \mathbf{R})(\mathbf{N} + \mathbf{RM})(\mathbf{I} - s\mathbf{F}).$$

Proof Let

$$\mathbf{P}_{-1} = \frac{1}{a}\mathbf{\Lambda}, \quad \mathbf{P}_0 = \mathbf{I} + \frac{1}{a}\mathbf{N}, \quad \mathbf{P}_1 = \frac{1}{a}\mathbf{M}.$$

In light of Lemma 7.9, we conclude that there exists a minimal nonnegative solution $\mathbf{F}$ of the equation

$$\mathbf{\Lambda F}^2 + \mathbf{NF} + \mathbf{M} = \mathbf{0}, \tag{7.26}$$

and

$$\mathbf{F}\mathbf{u} \leq \left(1 + \frac{\sigma(\mathbf{H})}{a}\right)\mathbf{u}. \tag{7.27}$$

Consider the matrix sequence $\mathbf{F}_0 = 0$,

$$\mathbf{F}_{k+1} = \mathbf{F}_k + \frac{1}{a}(\boldsymbol{\Lambda}\mathbf{F}_k^2 + \mathbf{N}\mathbf{F}_k + \mathbf{M}), \quad k = 0, 1, \ldots \tag{7.28}$$

By Lemma 7.7, it converges to $\mathbf{F}$. Since $\boldsymbol{\Lambda}, \mathbf{N}, \mathbf{M}$ are lower block triangular, so are all $\mathbf{F}_k$, and hence so is $\mathbf{F}$. It also follows from relations (7.28) and Lemma 7.7 that the diagonal blocks $\mathbf{F}_{ii}$ of $\mathbf{F}$ are the minimal nonnegative solutions of the equations $\boldsymbol{\Lambda}_{ii}\mathbf{F}_{ii}^2 + \mathbf{N}_{ii}\mathbf{F}_{ii} + \mathbf{M}_{ii} = \mathbf{0}$, $i = 1, 2, \ldots, l$. Here, $\boldsymbol{\Lambda}_{ii} \geq 0$, $\mathbf{M}_{ii} \geq 0$, while $\mathbf{N}_{ii}$, $\mathbf{H}_{ii} = \boldsymbol{\Lambda}_{ii} + \mathbf{N}_{ii} + \mathbf{M}_{ii}$ are generator matrices and $\mathbf{H}_{ii}$ are irreducible. By Theorem 7.2, there exist minimal nonnegative solutions $\mathbf{R}_{ii}$ of the equations

$$\boldsymbol{\Lambda}_{ii} + \mathbf{R}_{ii}\mathbf{N}_{ii} + \mathbf{R}_{ii}^2\mathbf{M}_{ii} = \mathbf{0}, \quad i = 1, 2, \ldots, l.$$

Since the determinant $\det(\boldsymbol{\Lambda} + s\mathbf{N} + s^2\mathbf{M})$ is not identically zero, nor are the determinants $\det(\boldsymbol{\Lambda}_{ii} + s\mathbf{N}_{ii} + s^2\mathbf{M}_{ii})$, $i = 1, 2, \ldots, l$. In accordance with Corollary of Lemma 7.5, the matrices $\mathbf{N}_{ii} + \boldsymbol{\Lambda}_{ii}\mathbf{F}_{ii}$ are nonsingular, as well as the block-triangular matrix $\mathbf{N} + \Lambda\mathbf{F}$.

It follows from (7.27) that $(\mathbf{N} + \boldsymbol{\Lambda}\mathbf{F})\mathbf{u} \leq \mathbf{H}\mathbf{u} \leq \mathbf{0}$. Furthermore, the off-diagonal entries of the nonsingular matrix $\mathbf{N} + \boldsymbol{\Lambda}\mathbf{F}$ are all nonnegative. By Theorem 5.3, $(\mathbf{I} - \mathbf{P}_0 - \mathbf{P}_{-1}\mathbf{F})^{-1} = -a(\mathbf{N} + \boldsymbol{\Lambda}\mathbf{F})^{-1} \geq \mathbf{0}$.

In light of Lemma 7.4, we conclude that there exists a minimal nonnegative solution $\mathbf{R}$ of the equation $\boldsymbol{\Lambda} + \mathbf{R}\mathbf{N} + \mathbf{R}^2\mathbf{M} = \mathbf{0}$. By Lemma 7.5, $\mathbf{R}\mathbf{M} = \boldsymbol{\Lambda}\mathbf{F}$ and we have the decomposition

$$\boldsymbol{\Lambda} + s\mathbf{N} + s^2\mathbf{M} = (s\mathbf{I} - \mathbf{R})(\mathbf{N} + \mathbf{R}\mathbf{M})(\mathbf{I} - s\mathbf{F}).$$

Similarly, to the argument used to establish via Lemma 7.6 that $\mathbf{F}$ is lower block triangular, one can show that $\mathbf{R}$ is also lower block triangular. In light of Theorem 7.2, we can estimate the maximum eigenvalue $\sigma(\mathbf{R})$ of $\mathbf{R}$ as follows:

$$\sigma(\mathbf{R}) = \max_i \sigma(\mathbf{R}_{ii}) \leq \max_i (1 + \frac{\sigma(\mathbf{H}_{ii})}{a}) = 1 + \frac{\sigma(\mathbf{H})}{a}.$$

■

From the above theorem readily follows the next result.

Theorem 7.6 *There always exists a minimal nonnegative solution* $\mathbf{G}$ *of* $\boldsymbol{\Lambda} + \mathbf{N}\mathbf{G} + \mathbf{M}\mathbf{G}^2 = \mathbf{0}$ *and, moreover,* $\mathbf{G}\mathbf{u} \leq (1 + \frac{\sigma(\mathbf{H})}{a})\mathbf{u}$. *Furthermore, if D holds, then there exists also a minimal nonnegative solution* $\mathbf{S}$ *of* $\mathbf{S}^2\boldsymbol{\Lambda} + \mathbf{S}\mathbf{N} + \mathbf{M} = \mathbf{0}$, *and* $\sigma(\mathbf{S}) \leq 1 + \frac{\sigma(\mathbf{H})}{a}$, *in which case* $\mathbf{S}\boldsymbol{\Lambda} = \mathbf{M}\mathbf{G}$, *the matrix* $\mathbf{N} + \mathbf{S}\boldsymbol{\Lambda}$ *is nonsingular, and* *we have the decomposition*

$$s^2\mathbf{\Lambda} + s\mathbf{N} + \mathbf{M} = (s\mathbf{I} - \mathbf{S})(\mathbf{N} + \mathbf{S\Lambda})(\mathbf{I} - s\mathbf{G}).$$

The matrix $\mathbf{\Lambda} + s\mathbf{N} + s^2\mathbf{M}$ is lower block triangular and D holds for it, if it holds for all its diagonal blocks $\mathbf{\Lambda}_{ii} + s\mathbf{N}_{ii} + s^2\mathbf{M}_{ii}$, $i = 1, 2, ..., l$. Since the matrices $\mathbf{H}_{ii} = \mathbf{\Lambda}_{ii} + \mathbf{N}_{ii} + \mathbf{M}_{ii}$ are irreducible, by Theorem 7.1, it is sufficient for this to be true that, for all i, either

(1) $\sigma(\mathbf{H}_{ii}) < 0$, or
(2) $\sigma(\mathbf{H}_{ii}) = 0$ and $\mathbf{p}_i\mathbf{\Lambda}_{ii}\mathbf{u}_i \neq \mathbf{p}_i\mathbf{M}_{ii}\mathbf{u}_i$,

where $\mathbf{p}_i$ is a positive row vector, $\mathbf{p}_i\mathbf{H}_{ii} = \mathbf{0}$, and $\mathbf{u}_i$ is all ones.

By Lemma 7.7, the minimal nonnegative solutions $\mathbf{R}$ and $\mathbf{S}$ of (7.20) and (7.22) are, respectively, the limits of the matrix sequences

$$\mathbf{R}_0 = \mathbf{0}, \quad \mathbf{R}_{k+1} = \mathbf{R}_k + \frac{1}{a}(\mathbf{\Lambda} + \mathbf{R}_k\mathbf{N} + \mathbf{R}_k^2\mathbf{M}), \ k = 0, 1, ..., \tag{7.29}$$

$$\mathbf{S}_0 = \mathbf{0}, \quad \mathbf{S}_{k+1} = \mathbf{S}_k + \frac{1}{a}(\mathbf{S}_k^2\mathbf{\Lambda} + \mathbf{S}_k\mathbf{N} + \mathbf{M}), \quad k = 0, 1, ... \tag{7.30}$$

Since $\mathbf{\Lambda}, \mathbf{N}, \mathbf{M}$ are lower block triangular, so are all $\mathbf{R}_k$ and $\mathbf{S}_k$, and, by consequence, so are $\mathbf{R}, \mathbf{S}$ and $\mathbf{S\Lambda} + \mathbf{N} + \mathbf{RM}$. It follows from (7.29) and (7.30) and Lemma 7.7 that the diagonal blocks of $\mathbf{R}$ and $\mathbf{S}$ are the respective minimal nonnegative solutions of

$$\mathbf{\Lambda}_{ii} + \mathbf{R}_{ii}\mathbf{N}_{ii} + \mathbf{R}_{ii}^2\mathbf{M}_{ii} = \mathbf{0},$$

$$\mathbf{S}_{ii}^2\mathbf{\Lambda}_{ii} + \mathbf{S}_{ii}\mathbf{N}_{ii} + \mathbf{M}_{ii} = \mathbf{0}, i = 1, 2, ..., l,$$

and, moreover, the generator matrices $\mathbf{H}_{ii} = \mathbf{\Lambda}_{ii} + \mathbf{M}_{ii} + \mathbf{N}_{ii}$ are irreducible. By Corollary of Theorem 7.3, the matrices $\mathbf{S}_{ii}\mathbf{\Lambda}_{ii} + \mathbf{N}_{ii} + \mathbf{R}_{ii}\mathbf{M}_{ii}$, which are the diagonal blocks of $\mathbf{S\Lambda} + \mathbf{N} + \mathbf{RM}$, are nonsingular whenever $\sigma(\mathbf{H}_{ii}) < 0$. Thus, $\mathbf{S\Lambda} + \mathbf{N} + \mathbf{RM}$ is nonsingular whenever $\sigma(\mathbf{H}) < 0$.

Conversely, if $\sigma(\mathbf{H}_{ii}) = 0$ for some diagonal blocks of $\mathbf{H}$, then, by Theorem 7.4, for $\mathbf{S\Lambda} + \mathbf{N} + \mathbf{RM}$ to be nonsingular it is necessary that for these blocks $\mathbf{p}_i\mathbf{\Lambda}_{ii}\mathbf{u}_i \neq \mathbf{p}_i\mathbf{M}_{ii}\mathbf{u}_i$, where $\mathbf{p}_i$ is a positive row vector such that $\mathbf{p}_i\mathbf{H}_{ii} = \mathbf{0}$. If this condition holds for any i such that $\sigma(\mathbf{H}_{ii}) = 0$ and $\mathbf{S}_{ii}\mathbf{\Lambda}_{ii} + \mathbf{N}_{ii} + \mathbf{R}_{ii}\mathbf{M}_{ii}$ is irreducible, then $\mathbf{S\Lambda} + \mathbf{N} + \mathbf{RM}$ is nonsingular.

One checks the most easily for which diagonal blocks $\sigma(\mathbf{H}_{ii}) = 0$ and for which $\sigma(\mathbf{H}_{ii}) < 0$ if the generator matrix $\mathbf{H}$ is conservative. In this case

$$\mathbf{H}_{ii}\mathbf{u}_i = 0, \quad i = 1, 2, ..., r,$$

$$\mathbf{H}_{ii}\mathbf{u}_i \le -\sum_{j=1}^{i-1}\mathbf{H}_{ij}\mathbf{u}_j < \mathbf{0}, \quad i = r+1, r+2, \ldots, l.$$

By Theorem 5.7, the matrices $\mathbf{H}_{ii}$, $i > r$, are nonsingular. Hence, $\sigma(\mathbf{H}_{ii}) = 0$ for $i = 1, 2, \ldots, r$ and $\sigma(\mathbf{H}_{ii}) < 0$ for $i = r+1, \ldots, l$.

We sum up the above in the following two theorems.

Theorem 7.7 *Let $\sigma(\mathbf{H}) < 0$. Then D holds, and if $\mathbf{R}$ and $\mathbf{S}$ are the respective minimal nonnegative solutions of (7.20) and (7.22), then $\mathbf{S\Lambda} + \mathbf{N} + \mathbf{RM}$ is nonsingular.*

Theorem 7.8 *Let $\mathbf{Hu} = \mathbf{0}$, $\mathbf{p}_i\mathbf{\Lambda}_{ii}\mathbf{u}_i \neq \mathbf{p}_i\mathbf{M}_{ii}\mathbf{u}_i$ and $\mathbf{p}_i\mathbf{H}_{ii} = \mathbf{0}$, $i = 1, 2, \ldots, r$, where $\mathbf{p}_i$ are positive row vectors. Then, D holds, and, given that $\mathbf{R}$ and $\mathbf{S}$ are the respective minimal nonnegative solutions of (7.20) and (7.22), $\mathbf{S\Lambda} + \mathbf{N} + \mathbf{RM}$ is nonsingular whenever its diagonal blocks $\mathbf{S}_{ii}\mathbf{\Lambda}_{ii} + \mathbf{N}_{ii} + \mathbf{R}_{ii}\mathbf{M}_{ii}$, $i = 1, 2, \ldots, r$, are all irreducible.*

To conclude the section, we note that $\mathbf{S\Lambda} + \mathbf{N} + \mathbf{RM}$ and $\mathbf{MG} + \mathbf{N} + \mathbf{\Lambda F}$ are generator matrices, since their off-diagonal entries are all nonnegative and

$$(\mathbf{S\Lambda} + \mathbf{N} + \mathbf{RM})\mathbf{u} = (\mathbf{MG} + \mathbf{N} + \mathbf{\Lambda F})\mathbf{u} \le \mathbf{Hu} \le \mathbf{0}.$$

7.3 Computing Minimal Nonnegative Solutions

As in the previous section, we assume that $\mathbf{\Lambda} \ge \mathbf{0}$, $\mathbf{M} \ge \mathbf{0}$, and the matrices $\mathbf{N}$ and $\mathbf{H} = \mathbf{\Lambda} + \mathbf{M} + \mathbf{N}$ are generator matrices. Additionally, we suppose that the condition D of Sect. 7.2 holds and the inequality $\mathbf{\Lambda} + \mathbf{M} > \mathbf{0}$ is true.

Let the off-diagonal entries of a matrix $\mathbf{E}$ all be nonnegative and $\mathbf{E} \le \mathbf{N}$. Then $\mathbf{Eu} \le \mathbf{Nu} < \mathbf{Hu} \le \mathbf{0}$ and hence $\mathbf{Eu} < \mathbf{0}$. By Theorem 5.7, $\mathbf{E}$ is nonsingular, while by Theorem 5.3 $\mathbf{E}^{-1} \le \mathbf{0}$. Now let

$$\mathbf{P}_{-1}(\mathbf{E}) = -\mathbf{\Lambda E}^{-1}, \quad \mathbf{P}_0(\mathbf{E}) = (\mathbf{E} - \mathbf{N})\mathbf{E}^{-1}, \quad \mathbf{P}_1(\mathbf{E}) = -\mathbf{ME}^{-1}.$$

One checks easily that the matrices $\mathbf{P}_{-1}(\mathbf{E})$, $\mathbf{P}_0(\mathbf{E})$ and $\mathbf{P}_1(\mathbf{E})$ are all nonnegative, and solutions to

$$\mathbf{P}_{-1}(\mathbf{E}) + \mathbf{X}(\mathbf{P}_0(\mathbf{E}) - \mathbf{I}) + \mathbf{X}^2\mathbf{P}_1(\mathbf{E}) = \mathbf{0} \tag{7.31}$$

also solve $\mathbf{\Lambda} + \mathbf{XN} + \mathbf{X}^2\mathbf{M} = \mathbf{0}$ and vice versa.

Let us define a matrix sequence by the recursive relation

$$\mathbf{R}_0(\mathbf{E}) = \mathbf{0},\ \mathbf{R}_{k+1}(\mathbf{E}) = \mathbf{P}_{-1}(\mathbf{E}) + \mathbf{R}_k(\mathbf{E})\mathbf{P}_0(\mathbf{E}) + \mathbf{R}_k^2(\mathbf{E})\mathbf{P}_1(\mathbf{E}),$$
$$k = 0, 1, \ldots \tag{7.32}$$

Theorem 7.9 *For any matrix* $\mathbf{E} \leq \mathbf{N}$ *whose off-diagonal entries are all nonnegative, the matrix sequence* $\mathbf{R}_k(\mathbf{E})$ *converges monotonically to the minimal nonnegative solution* $\mathbf{R}$ *of the equation.*

$$\mathbf{\Lambda} + \mathbf{RN} + \mathbf{R}^2\mathbf{M} = \mathbf{0}. \tag{7.33}$$

Furthermore, for a matrix $\mathbf{G}$ *whose off-diagonal entries are all nonnegative and such that* $\mathbf{E} \leq \mathbf{G} \leq \mathbf{N}$*, we have* $\mathbf{R}_k(\mathbf{E}) \leq \mathbf{R}_k(\mathbf{G})$ *for all* $k = 0, 1, \ldots$.

Proof Under the assumptions made at the beginning of this section, by Theorem 7.5, there exists a minimal nonnegative solution $\mathbf{R}$ of the equation $\mathbf{\Lambda} + \mathbf{RN} + \mathbf{R}^2\mathbf{M} = \mathbf{0}$. The matrix $\mathbf{R}$ is also the minimal nonnegative solution of (7.20). In accordance with Lemma 7.6, the matrix sequence $\mathbf{R}_k(\mathbf{E})$ converges monotonically to $\mathbf{R}$.

Let the off-diagonal entries of $\mathbf{G}$ all be nonnegative and $\mathbf{E} \leq \mathbf{G} \leq \mathbf{N}$. Then, $\mathbf{R}_0(\mathbf{G}) = \mathbf{R}_0(\mathbf{E})$, and it follows from $\mathbf{R}_k(\mathbf{G}) \geq \mathbf{R}_k(\mathbf{E})$ that

$$\begin{aligned}
-\mathbf{R}_{k+1}(\mathbf{G})\mathbf{G} &= \mathbf{\Lambda} + \mathbf{R}_k(\mathbf{G})(\mathbf{N} - \mathbf{G}) + \mathbf{R}_k^2(\mathbf{G})\mathbf{M} \geq \\
&\geq \mathbf{\Lambda} + \mathbf{R}_k(\mathbf{E})(\mathbf{N} - \mathbf{G}) + \mathbf{R}_k^2(\mathbf{E})\mathbf{M} = \\
&= \mathbf{\Lambda} + \mathbf{R}_k(\mathbf{E})(\mathbf{N} - \mathbf{E}) + \mathbf{R}_k^2(\mathbf{E})\mathbf{M} + \mathbf{R}_k(\mathbf{E})(\mathbf{E} - \mathbf{G}) = \\
&= -\mathbf{R}_{k+1}(\mathbf{E})\mathbf{G} + (\mathbf{R}_{k+1}(\mathbf{E}) - \mathbf{R}_k(\mathbf{E}))(\mathbf{G} - \mathbf{E}) \geq -\mathbf{R}_{k+1}(\mathbf{E})\mathbf{G}.
\end{aligned}$$

Since $(-\mathbf{G})^{-1} \geq \mathbf{0}$, last inequality yields $\mathbf{R}_{k+1}(\mathbf{G}) \geq \mathbf{R}_{k+1}(\mathbf{E})$. Thus, we arrive at $\mathbf{R}_k(\mathbf{E}) \leq \mathbf{R}_k(\mathbf{G})$ for all $k = 0, 1, \ldots$. ■

The above theorem permits to construct a number of matrix sequences that converge to the minimal nonnegative solution of (7.33). The easiest to compute is the sequence $\mathbf{R}_k(\gamma\mathbf{I})$, where $\gamma < 0$ is the smallest diagonal entry of $\mathbf{N}$. The sequence $\mathbf{R}_k(\mathbf{N})$ is the fastest to converge to $\mathbf{R}$, however, it implies calculating the inverse of $\mathbf{N}$. A sensible compromise offers the sequence $\mathbf{R}_k(\mathbf{E})$, in which $\mathbf{E}$ is a triangular matrix whose nonzero entries equal the corresponding entries of $\mathbf{N}$.

Another approach to computing the minimal nonnegative solution $\mathbf{R}$ of (7.33) is based on the identity

$$\mathbf{R} = -\mathbf{\Lambda}(\mathbf{N} + \mathbf{RM})^{-1}.$$

Define a matrix sequence $\overline{\mathbf{R}}_k$ as follows:

$$\overline{\mathbf{R}}_{k+1} = -\mathbf{\Lambda}(\mathbf{N} + \overline{\mathbf{R}}_k\mathbf{M})^{-1}, \quad k = 0, 1, \ldots \tag{7.34}$$

We will now prove the validity of this definition and that $\overline{\mathbf{R}}_k$ converge to $\mathbf{R}$.

Theorem 7.10 *The matrix sequence* $\overline{\mathbf{R}}_k$ *defined by (7.34) converges monotonically to the minimal nonnegative solution* $\mathbf{R}$ *of (7.33). Moreover,* $\mathbf{R}_k(\mathbf{N}) \le \overline{\mathbf{R}}_k$ *for all* $k = 0, 1, \ldots$.

Proof By Theorem 7.2, the matrix $\mathbf{N} + \mathbf{RM}$ is nonsingular. Clearly, $\mathbf{0} = \overline{\mathbf{R}}_0 \le \mathbf{R}$, and in accordance with the Corollary of Theorem 5.6 it follows from $\overline{\mathbf{R}}_k \le \mathbf{R}$ that $\mathbf{N} + \overline{\mathbf{R}}_k\mathbf{M}$ is nonsingular and

$$\overline{\mathbf{R}}_{k+1} = -\boldsymbol{\Lambda}(\mathbf{N} + \overline{\mathbf{R}}_k\mathbf{M})^{-1} \le -\boldsymbol{\Lambda}(\mathbf{N} + \mathbf{RM})^{-1} = \mathbf{R}.$$

Thus, definition (7.33) is valid and $\overline{\mathbf{R}}_k \le \mathbf{R}$ for all $k = 0, 1, \ldots$.

Now, we have $\overline{\mathbf{R}}_1 = -\boldsymbol{\Lambda}\mathbf{N}^{-1} \ge \overline{\mathbf{R}}_0 = \mathbf{0}$ and, by the corollary of Theorem 5.6, $\overline{\mathbf{R}}_k \ge \overline{\mathbf{R}}_{k-1}$ yields

$$\overline{\mathbf{R}}_{k+1} = -\boldsymbol{\Lambda}(\mathbf{N} + \overline{\mathbf{R}}_k\mathbf{M})^{-1} \ge -\boldsymbol{\Lambda}(\mathbf{N} + \overline{\mathbf{R}}_{k-1}\mathbf{M})^{-1} = \overline{\mathbf{R}}_k.$$

The sequence $\overline{\mathbf{R}}_k$ is therefore monotonic and bound above by $\mathbf{R}$. Hence, it converges to some nonnegative matrix $\mathbf{Y} \le \mathbf{R}$, which, in light of (7.33), solves $\boldsymbol{\Lambda} + \mathbf{YN} + \mathbf{Y}^2\mathbf{M} = \mathbf{0}$. Since $\mathbf{R}$ is the minimal solution of this equation, $\mathbf{Y} = \mathbf{R}$.

We will show now that $\overline{\mathbf{R}}_k$ converges to $\mathbf{R}$ faster than $\mathbf{R}_k(\mathbf{N})$. Clearly, $\overline{\mathbf{R}}_0 = \mathbf{R}_0(\mathbf{N})$, and, since $\overline{\mathbf{R}}_k$ is monotonic, $\overline{\mathbf{R}}_k \ge \mathbf{R}_k(\mathbf{N})$ yields

$$\begin{aligned}\overline{\mathbf{R}}_{k+1} &= -\boldsymbol{\Lambda}\mathbf{N}^{-1} - \overline{\mathbf{R}}_{k+1}\overline{\mathbf{R}}_k\mathbf{M}\mathbf{N}^{-1} = \mathbf{P}_{-1}(\mathbf{N}) + \overline{\mathbf{R}}_{k+1}\mathbf{R}_k\mathbf{P}_1(\mathbf{N})\\ &\ge \mathbf{P}_{-1}(\mathbf{N}) + \overline{\mathbf{R}}_k^2\mathbf{P}_1(\mathbf{N}) \ge \mathbf{P}_{-1}(\mathbf{N}) + \mathbf{R}_k^2(\mathbf{N})\mathbf{P}_1(\mathbf{N}) = \mathbf{R}_{k+1}(\mathbf{N}).\end{aligned}$$

Hence, $\overline{\mathbf{R}}_k \ge \mathbf{R}_k(\mathbf{N})$ for all $k = 0, 1, \ldots$. ■

It should be noted that (7.20) and (7.22) can be solved by various iterative algorithms, the fastest of which is the logarithmic reduction algorithm (Latouche and Ramaswami 1993). This algorithm was modified in Krieger et al. (1998) and Bini et al. (1999) in a way that both rate matrices can be found in one pass.

7.4 Irreducibility of the Matrix $\mathbf{S}\boldsymbol{\Lambda} + \mathbf{N} + \mathbf{RM}$

Once again, we assume that $\boldsymbol{\Lambda} \ge \mathbf{0}$, $\mathbf{M} \ge \mathbf{0}$, and the matrices $\mathbf{N}$ and $\mathbf{H} = \boldsymbol{\Lambda} + \mathbf{M} + \mathbf{N}$ are generator matrices. In addition, we assume that the condition D of Sect. 7.2 holds.

Let $\mathbf{R}$ and $\mathbf{S}$ represent the respective minimal nonnegative solutions of $\boldsymbol{\Lambda} + \mathbf{RN} + \mathbf{R}^2\mathbf{M} = \mathbf{0}$ and $\mathbf{S}^2\boldsymbol{\Lambda} + \mathbf{SN} + \mathbf{M} = \mathbf{0}$. One can check whether

$\mathbf{S}\boldsymbol{\Lambda} + \mathbf{N} + \mathbf{R}\mathbf{M}$ is irreducible without knowing the solutions $\mathbf{R}$ and $\mathbf{S}$. This can be done by observing the graph $G(\mathbf{A})$ of the infinite in both directions of block tridiagonal matrix

$$\mathbf{A} = \begin{bmatrix} \ddots & \ddots & \ddots & & & \\ & \ddots & \mathbf{N} & \boldsymbol{\Lambda} & \mathbf{O} & \\ & \ddots & \mathbf{M} & \mathbf{N} & \boldsymbol{\Lambda} & \ddots \\ & & \mathbf{O} & \mathbf{M} & \mathbf{N} & \ddots \\ & & & \ddots & \ddots & \ddots \end{bmatrix}.$$

The set of vertices of $G(\mathbf{A})$ is

$$\mathcal{X}_* = \bigcup_{k=-\infty}^{\infty} \mathcal{X}_k,$$

where $\mathcal{X}_k = \{(k,i) : i \in \mathcal{X}\}$, $\mathcal{X} = \{1, 2, \ldots, m\}$, and m is the order of $\boldsymbol{\Lambda}, \mathbf{M}, \mathbf{N}$. We will refer to the subsets $\mathcal{X}_k$ as levels. In $G(\mathbf{A})$, edges exist only between vertices of the same level or adjacent levels. More specifically, there exists an edge from (k,i) to (k,j) if $N(i,j) > 0$, from (k,i) to $(k+1,j)$ if $\Lambda(i,j) > 0$, and from (k,i) to $(k-1,j)$ if $M(i,j) > 0$.

Theorem 7.11 *The matrix* $\mathbf{S}\boldsymbol{\Lambda} + \mathbf{N} + \mathbf{R}\mathbf{M}$ *is irreducible if and only in* $G(\mathbf{A})$ *there exists a path from any vertex of level* $\mathcal{X}_0$ *to any other vertex of level* $\mathcal{X}_0$.

Proof By Theorem 7.5, matrix $\mathbf{N} + \mathbf{R}\mathbf{M}$ is nonsingular, while by Theorem 5.3 $(\mathbf{N} + \mathbf{R}\mathbf{M})^{-1} \leq \mathbf{0}$. Let $\mathbf{U} = -(\mathbf{N} + \mathbf{R}\mathbf{M})^{-1}$, then it follows from $\boldsymbol{\Lambda} + \mathbf{R}(\mathbf{N} + \mathbf{R}\mathbf{M}) = \mathbf{0}$ that $\mathbf{R} = \boldsymbol{\Lambda}\mathbf{U}$. $\mathbf{U}$ is therefore a nonnegative solution of

$$\mathbf{U} = -(\mathbf{N} + \boldsymbol{\Lambda}\mathbf{U}\mathbf{M})^{-1}. \tag{7.35}$$

If $\mathbf{Y}$ is another nonnegative solution of this equation, then the nonnegative matrix $\boldsymbol{\Lambda}\mathbf{Y}$ solves $\boldsymbol{\Lambda} + \mathbf{X}\mathbf{N} + \mathbf{X}^2\mathbf{M} = \mathbf{0}$ and therefore $\boldsymbol{\Lambda}\mathbf{Y} \geq \mathbf{R}$. In accordance with Corollary of Theorem 5.6,

$$\mathbf{Y} = -(\mathbf{N} + \boldsymbol{\Lambda}\mathbf{Y}\mathbf{M})^{-1} \geq -(\mathbf{N} + \mathbf{R}\mathbf{M})^{-1} = \mathbf{U},$$

i.e., $\mathbf{U}$ is the minimal nonnegative solution of (7.35).

Let $\alpha > 0$ represent some scalar such that $\mathbf{N} + \alpha\mathbf{I} \geq \mathbf{0}$, and let $\mathbf{P}_{-1} = \frac{1}{\alpha}\boldsymbol{\Lambda}$, $\mathbf{P}_0 = \mathbf{I} + \frac{1}{\alpha}\mathbf{N}$, $\mathbf{P}_1 = \frac{1}{\alpha}\mathbf{M}$. Then $\mathbf{U}$ is the minimal nonnegative solution of $\mathbf{U} = (\mathbf{I} - \mathbf{P}_0 - \mathbf{P}_{-1}\mathbf{U}\mathbf{P}_1)^{-1}$, and by Corollary of Lemma 7.1 $\mathbf{U}$ is of the form

$$\mathbf{U} = \mathbf{I} + \sum_{n=1}^{\infty} \sum_{k \in K_n} \mathbf{P}_{k_1} \mathbf{P}_{k_2} \cdots \mathbf{P}_{k_n},$$

where

$$K_n = \{(k_1, k_2, \ldots, k_n) \in \{-1, 0, 1\}^n : k_1 \le 0,\ k_1 + k_2 \le 0,\ \ldots$$
$$\ldots, k_1 + \ldots + k_{n-1} \le 0,\ k_1 + \ldots + k_n = 0\}, \quad n = 1, 2, \ldots$$

This implies that $U(i, j) \neq 0$ if and only if in $G(\mathbf{A})$ there exists a path from $(1, i)$ to $(1, j)$ which includes vertices of levels $\mathcal{X}_1, \mathcal{X}_2, \ldots$ and does not include any vertices of levels $\mathcal{X}_0, \mathcal{X}_{-1}, \mathcal{X}_{-2}, \ldots$.

Similarly, if $\mathbf{S}$ is the minimal nonnegative solution of $\mathbf{S}^2\boldsymbol{\Lambda} + \mathbf{SN} + \mathbf{M} = \mathbf{0}$, then $\mathbf{S} = \mathbf{MV}$, where $\mathbf{V} = -(\mathbf{N} + \mathbf{S}\boldsymbol{\Lambda})^{-1}$ is the minimal nonnegative solution of

$$\mathbf{V} = -(\mathbf{N} + \mathbf{MV}\boldsymbol{\Lambda})^{-1}. \tag{7.36}$$

For $V(i, j) \neq 0$ it is necessary and sufficient that in $G(\mathbf{A})$ there exists a path from $(-1, i)$ to $(-1, j)$ which includes vertices of levels $\mathcal{X}_{-1}, \mathcal{X}_{-2}, \ldots$ and does not include any vertices of levels $\mathcal{X}_0, \mathcal{X}_1, \mathcal{X}_2, \ldots$.

Let

$$\boldsymbol{\Phi} = \mathbf{S}\boldsymbol{\Lambda} + \mathbf{N} + \mathbf{RM} = \mathbf{MV}\boldsymbol{\Lambda} + \mathbf{N} + \boldsymbol{\Lambda}\mathbf{UM}$$

and consider the graph $G(\boldsymbol{\Phi})$. Clearly, $i \neq j$ and $\Phi(i, j) \neq 0$ if and only if $N(i, j) \neq 0$ or $(\boldsymbol{\Lambda}\mathbf{UM})(i, j) \neq 0$ or $(\mathbf{MV}\boldsymbol{\Lambda})(i, j) \neq 0$. In light of the above, this is equivalent to the fact that in $G(\mathbf{A})$ there exists a path from $(0, i)$ to $(0, j)$ which does not include any other vertices of level $\mathcal{X}_0$. In particular, if in $G(\boldsymbol{\Phi})$ there exists a path from i to j, then in $G(\mathbf{A})$ there exists a path from $(i, 0)$ to $(j, 0)$.

If in $G(\mathbf{A})$ there exists a path from $(i, 0)$ to $(j, 0)$, then it consists of one or several parts, each of which starts and ends in vertices of level $\mathcal{X}_0$ but does not include other vertices of $\mathcal{X}_0$. To these parts correspond the edges of $G(\boldsymbol{\Phi})$ which form a path from i to j. Thus, the condition of Theorem 7.11 is equivalent to strong connectedness of $G(\boldsymbol{\Phi})$. ■

7.5 Eigenvalues of Minimal Nonnegative Solutions

As in the previous sections, we assume that $\boldsymbol{\Lambda} \ge \mathbf{0}$, $\mathbf{M} \ge \mathbf{0}$, and the matrices $\mathbf{N}$ and $\mathbf{H} = \boldsymbol{\Lambda} + \mathbf{M} + \mathbf{N}$ are generator matrices. We denote $\boldsymbol{\lambda} = \boldsymbol{\Lambda}\mathbf{u}$, $\boldsymbol{\mu} = \mathbf{Mu}$, where $\mathbf{u}$ is the all-ones column vector, and α is some positive scalar such that $\mathbf{N} + \alpha\mathbf{I} \ge \mathbf{0}$. We assume also that the condition D of Sect. 7.2 holds.

Let $\mathbf{S}, \mathbf{R}, \mathbf{F}, \mathbf{G}$ represent the respective minimal nonnegative solutions of the equations

$$\mathbf{S}^2\mathbf{\Lambda} + \mathbf{SN} + \mathbf{M} = \mathbf{0}, \quad \mathbf{\Lambda} + \mathbf{RN} + \mathbf{R}^2\mathbf{M} = \mathbf{0},$$
$$\mathbf{\Lambda F}^2 + \mathbf{NF} + \mathbf{M} = \mathbf{0}, \quad \mathbf{\Lambda} + \mathbf{NG} + \mathbf{MG}^2 = \mathbf{0}. \tag{7.37}$$

In accordance with Theorems 7.5 and 7.6, the eigenvalues of $\mathbf{S}, \mathbf{R}, \mathbf{F}, \mathbf{G}$ all lie in the disk $|s| \leq 1 + \frac{\sigma(\mathbf{H})}{\alpha}$, the matrices $\mathbf{N} + \mathbf{RM}$ and $\mathbf{N} + \mathbf{S\Lambda}$ are nonsingular and we have the decompositions

$$\mathbf{\Lambda} + s\mathbf{N} + s^2\mathbf{M} = (s\mathbf{I} - \mathbf{R})(\mathbf{N} + \mathbf{RM})(\mathbf{I} - s\mathbf{F}), \tag{7.38}$$

$$\mathbf{\Lambda} + s\mathbf{N} + s^2\mathbf{M} = (\mathbf{I} - s\mathbf{S})(\mathbf{N} + \mathbf{S\Lambda})(s\mathbf{I} - \mathbf{G}). \tag{7.39}$$

Consider the first of these decompositions. The polynomial $\det(s\mathbf{I} - \mathbf{R})$ is of degree m, while the degree r of $\det(\mathbf{I} - \mathbf{sF})$ is bound by $0 \leq r \leq m$. Therefore, the degree $k = m + r$ of the polynomial $\Delta(s) = \det(\mathbf{\Lambda} + s\mathbf{N} + s^2\mathbf{M})$ is $m \leq k \leq 2m$. The roots of $\Delta(s)$ include m eigenvalues of $\mathbf{R}$, which lie in the disk $|s| \leq 1 + \frac{\sigma(\mathbf{H})}{\alpha}$, and $r = k - m$ reciprocals of the nonzero eigenvalues of $\mathbf{F}$. The absolute values of the latter r eigenvalues of $\Delta(s)$ are larger or equal to $\left(1 + \frac{\sigma(\mathbf{H})}{\alpha}\right)^{-1}$.

If the degree r of the polynomial $\det(\mathbf{I} - s\mathbf{F})$ is smaller than m, then we can write the characteristic polynomial of $\mathbf{F}$ as $\det(s\mathbf{I} - \mathbf{F}) = s^{m-r}\left[s^r \det\left(\mathbf{I} - \frac{1}{s}\mathbf{F}\right)\right]$. In the last expression, enclosed in square brackets is a polynomial of degree r, whose constant term equals the coefficient at s^r of the polynomial $\det(\mathbf{I} - s\mathbf{F})$ and hence is nonzero. Therefore, for $r < m$, the matrix $\mathbf{F}$ has zero eigenvalue of multiplicity $m - r = 2m - k$.

It follows from (7.39) that the degree of $\det(\mathbf{I} - s\mathbf{S})$ equals $k - m = r$. The roots of $\Delta(s)$ comprise m eigenvalues of $\mathbf{G}$, which lie in the disk $|s| < 1 + \frac{\sigma(\mathbf{H})}{\alpha}$, and r reciprocals of the nonzero eigenvalues of $\mathbf{S}$, for which $|s| \geq \left(1 + \frac{\sigma(\mathbf{H})}{\alpha}\right)^{-1}$. For $r < m$, the matrix $\mathbf{S}$ has zero eigenvalue of multiplicity $m - r$.

Let $\sigma(\mathbf{H}) < 0$. Then, in the range $|s| < 1$ lie exactly m roots of $\Delta(s)$ which are the eigenvalues of $\mathbf{R}$ and, at the same time, the eigenvalues of $\mathbf{G}$. Hence, the characteristic polynomials of $\mathbf{R}$ and $\mathbf{G}$ coincide. In the range $|s| > 1$ lie exactly r roots of $\Delta(s)$ which are reciprocal of the nonzero eigenvalues of $\mathbf{F}$ and, at the same time, reciprocal of the nonzero eigenvalues of $\mathbf{S}$. If $r < m$ then $\mathbf{F}$ and $\mathbf{S}$ both have zero eigenvalue of multiplicity $m - r$. Hence, the characteristic polynomials of $\mathbf{F}$ and $\mathbf{S}$ also coincide.

If, conversely, $\sigma(\mathbf{H}) = 0$, then consider the minimal nonnegative solutions $\mathbf{S}_\varepsilon, \mathbf{R}_\varepsilon, \mathbf{F}_\varepsilon, \mathbf{G}_\varepsilon$ of the equations

$$\mathbf{S}_\varepsilon^2\mathbf{\Lambda} + \mathbf{S}_\varepsilon(\mathbf{N} - \varepsilon\mathbf{I}) + \mathbf{M} = \mathbf{0}, \quad \mathbf{\Lambda} + \mathbf{R}_\varepsilon(\mathbf{N} - \varepsilon\mathbf{I}) + \mathbf{R}_\varepsilon^2\mathbf{M} = \mathbf{0},$$

$$\mathbf{\Lambda F}_\varepsilon^2 + (\mathbf{N} - \varepsilon\mathbf{I})\mathbf{F}_\varepsilon + \mathbf{M} = \mathbf{0}, \quad \mathbf{\Lambda} + (\mathbf{N} - \varepsilon\mathbf{I})\mathbf{G}_\varepsilon + \mathbf{M}\mathbf{G}_\varepsilon^2 = \mathbf{0},$$

where $\varepsilon > 0$. Since $\sigma(\mathbf{\Lambda} + \mathbf{N} - \varepsilon\mathbf{I} + \mathbf{M}) = -\varepsilon < 0$, the characteristic polynomial of $\mathbf{R}_\varepsilon$ coincides with that of $\mathbf{G}_\varepsilon$, and the characteristic polynomial of $\mathbf{S}_\varepsilon$ coincides with that of $\mathbf{F}_\varepsilon$. As $\varepsilon \to 0$ the matrices $\mathbf{S}_\varepsilon$, $\mathbf{R}_\varepsilon$, $\mathbf{F}_\varepsilon$ and $\mathbf{G}_\varepsilon$ tend, respectively, to $\mathbf{S}$, $\mathbf{R}$, $\mathbf{F}$ and $\mathbf{G}$. Hence, for $\sigma(\mathbf{H}) = 0$ also the characteristic polynomials of $\mathbf{R}$ and $\mathbf{G}$ coincide, as well as the ones of $\mathbf{S}$ and $\mathbf{F}$.

It follows from the above that under the assumptions made at the beginning of this section the following result is true.

Theorem 7.12 *Let* $\mathbf{R}, \mathbf{S}, \mathbf{F}, \mathbf{G}$ *represent the respective minimal nonnegative solutions of (7.37). Then the characteristic polynomial of* $\mathbf{R}$ *coincides with that of* $\mathbf{F}$*, while the characteristic polynomial of* $\mathbf{S}$ *coincides with that of* $\mathbf{F}$*. The degree* k *of the polynomial* $\Delta(s) = \det(\mathbf{\Lambda} + s\mathbf{N} + s^2\mathbf{M})$ *is bound by* $m \le k \le 2m$*. This polynomial has* m *roots which are the eigenvalues of* $\mathbf{R}$ *and* $\mathbf{G}$ *and* $k - m$ *roots which are the reciprocals of the nonzero eigenvalues of* $\mathbf{S}$ *and* $\mathbf{F}$*. If* $k < 2m$*, then* $\mathbf{S}$ *and* $\mathbf{F}$ *have zero eigenvalue of multiplicity* $2m - k$*.*

This theorem permits to obtain all eigenvalues of $\mathbf{R}$ and $\mathbf{S}$, if we know two disjoint subsets of the complex plane in which lie, respectively, the eigenvalues of $\mathbf{R}$ and the reciprocals of the nonzero eigenvalues of $\mathbf{S}$. In the case considered above, when $\sigma(\mathbf{H}) < 0$, such subsets are the inside and outside of the disk $|s| < 1$.

Now let $\sigma(\mathbf{H}) = 0$, assume $\mathbf{H}$ to be irreducible and let $\mathbf{pH} = 0$, where $\mathbf{p}$ is a positive row vector. If $\mathbf{p\lambda} < \mathbf{p\mu}$ then, in light of Theorems 7.2 and 7.3, $\sigma(\mathbf{R}) < 1$, while $\sigma(\mathbf{S}) = 1$. Therefore, the eigenvalues of $\mathbf{R}$ all lie inside the disk $|s| < 1$, while the reciprocals of the nonzero eigenvalues of $\mathbf{S}$ lie outside. If, conversely, $\mathbf{p\lambda} > \mathbf{p\mu}$ then $\sigma(\mathbf{R}) = 1$, while $\sigma(\mathbf{S}) < 1$. Therefore, for the eigenvalues of $\mathbf{R}$ we have $|s| \le 1$, while for the reciprocals of the nonzero eigenvalues of $\mathbf{S}$, $|s| > 1$.

7.6 Matrix-Geometric Solutions

In this section, we assume that $\mathbf{\Lambda} \ge \mathbf{0}$, $\mathbf{M} \ge \mathbf{0}$, and that $\mathbf{N}$ and $\mathbf{H} = \mathbf{\Lambda} + \mathbf{N} + \mathbf{M}$ are generator matrices, and denote $\mathbf{\lambda} = \mathbf{\Lambda u}$, $\mathbf{\mu} = \mathbf{Mu}$. We also assume that $\det(\mathbf{\Lambda} + s\mathbf{N} + s^2\mathbf{M}) \ne 0$ for some s, the generator matrix $\mathbf{H}$ is irreducible, $\mathbf{Hu} = \mathbf{0}$ and denote $\mathbf{p}$ a solution of the linear system $\mathbf{pH} = \mathbf{0}$, $\mathbf{pu} = 1$.

7.6.1 General Case

According to Theorems 7.2 and 7.3, there exist minimal nonnegative solutions $\mathbf{R}$ and $\mathbf{S}$ of the equations

$$\mathbf{\Lambda} + \mathbf{RN} + \mathbf{R}^2\mathbf{M} = \mathbf{0}, \tag{7.40}$$

$$\mathbf{S}^2\mathbf{\Lambda} + \mathbf{SN} + \mathbf{M} = \mathbf{0}, \tag{7.41}$$

which have spectral radii satisfying $sp(\mathbf{R}) \leq 1$, $sp(\mathbf{S}) \leq 1$. According to Theorems 7.5 and 7.6, there exist minimal nonnegative solutions **F** and **G** of the equations

$$\mathbf{\Lambda F}^2 + \mathbf{NF} + \mathbf{M} = \mathbf{0}, \tag{7.42}$$

$$\mathbf{\Lambda} + \mathbf{NG} + \mathbf{MG}^2 = \mathbf{0}, \tag{7.43}$$

which satisfy $\mathbf{Fu} \leq \mathbf{u}$, $\mathbf{Gu} \leq \mathbf{u}$. Matrices $\mathbf{N} + \mathbf{RM}$ and $\mathbf{N} + \mathbf{S\Lambda}$ are nonsingular and matrices $\mathbf{V} = -(\mathbf{N} + \mathbf{RM})^{-1}$ and $\mathbf{W} = -(\mathbf{N} + \mathbf{S\Lambda})^{-1}$ are nonnegative. The following equalities hold for these matrices:

$$\mathbf{R} = \mathbf{\Lambda V}, \mathbf{S} = \mathbf{MW}, \tag{7.44}$$

$$\mathbf{RM} = \mathbf{\Lambda F}, \mathbf{S\Lambda} = \mathbf{MG}. \tag{7.45}$$

Matrix $\mathbf{\Phi}$, defined as

$$\mathbf{\Phi} = \mathbf{MV\Lambda} + \mathbf{N} + \mathbf{\Lambda VM}, \tag{7.46}$$

satisfies equalities

$$\mathbf{R\Phi} = \mathbf{\Phi F}, \mathbf{S\Phi} = \mathbf{\Phi G}, \tag{7.47}$$

$$\mathbf{\Phi} = (\mathbf{I} - \mathbf{SR})(\mathbf{N} + \mathbf{\Lambda VM}) = (\mathbf{I} - \mathbf{RS})(\mathbf{N} + \mathbf{MW\Lambda}), \tag{7.48}$$

$$\mathbf{\Phi} = (\mathbf{N} + \mathbf{\Lambda VM})(\mathbf{I} - \mathbf{GF}) = (\mathbf{N} + \mathbf{MW\Lambda})(\mathbf{I} - \mathbf{FG}). \tag{7.49}$$

The form of the matrix-geometric solution of the linear system

$$\mathbf{x}_{k-1}\mathbf{\Lambda} + \mathbf{x}_k\mathbf{N} + \mathbf{x}_{k+1}\mathbf{M} = \mathbf{0}, 0 < k < m, \tag{7.50}$$

is determined by the properties of the matrix $\mathbf{\Phi}$.

Theorem 7.13 *For any solution* $\mathbf{x}_0, \mathbf{x}_1, \ldots, \mathbf{x}_m$ *of the linear system (7.50) there exist vectors.*

$$\mathbf{f} = \mathbf{x}_0(\mathbf{N} + \mathbf{MW\Lambda}) + \mathbf{x}_1\mathbf{M}, \mathbf{g} = \mathbf{x}_m(\mathbf{N} + \mathbf{\Lambda VM}) + \mathbf{x}_{m-1}\mathbf{\Lambda}, \tag{7.51}$$

such that $\mathbf{x}_0, \mathbf{x}_1, \ldots, \mathbf{x}_m$ *satisfy linear system*

$$\mathbf{x}_k\mathbf{\Phi} = \mathbf{f}\mathbf{F}^k + \mathbf{g}\mathbf{G}^{m-k}, 0 \le k \le m. \tag{7.52}$$

Proof First, notice that according to Lemmas 6.4 and 6.5 any solution of (7.50) satisfies

$$\mathbf{x}_k = \mathbf{x}_{k+1}\mathbf{S} + \boldsymbol{\alpha}(\mathbf{\Lambda}\mathbf{W})^k, 0 \le k < m,$$

$$\mathbf{x}_k = \mathbf{x}_{k-1}\mathbf{R} + \boldsymbol{\beta}(\mathbf{M}\mathbf{V})^{m-k}, 0 < k \le m,$$

with $\boldsymbol{\alpha} = \mathbf{x}_0 - \mathbf{x}_1\mathbf{S}$ and $\boldsymbol{\beta} = \mathbf{x}_m - \mathbf{x}_{m-1}\mathbf{R}$. It implies that for $0 \le k < m$ the following equalities are valid:

$$\begin{aligned}\mathbf{x}_k &= (\mathbf{x}_k\mathbf{R} + \boldsymbol{\beta}(\mathbf{M}\mathbf{V})^{m-k-1})\mathbf{S} + \boldsymbol{\alpha}(\mathbf{\Lambda}\mathbf{W})^k = \\ &= \mathbf{x}_k\mathbf{R}\mathbf{S} + \boldsymbol{\alpha}\mathbf{W}^{-1}(\mathbf{W}\mathbf{M})^k\mathbf{W} + \boldsymbol{\beta}\mathbf{V}^{-1}(\mathbf{V}\mathbf{M})^{m-k}\mathbf{W}.\end{aligned}$$

Hence,

$$\mathbf{x}_k\mathbf{\Phi} = \mathbf{x}_k(\mathbf{I} - \mathbf{R}\mathbf{S})(\mathbf{N} + \mathbf{M}\mathbf{W}\mathbf{\Lambda}) = -\mathbf{x}_k(\mathbf{I} - \mathbf{R}\mathbf{S})\mathbf{W}^{-1} = \mathbf{f}\mathbf{F}^k + \mathbf{g}\mathbf{G}^{m-k}$$

with

$$\mathbf{f} = -\boldsymbol{\alpha}\mathbf{W}^{-1} = \mathbf{x}_0(\mathbf{N} + \mathbf{M}\mathbf{W}\mathbf{\Lambda}) + \mathbf{x}_1\mathbf{M},$$

$$\mathbf{g} = -\boldsymbol{\beta}\mathbf{V}^{-1} = \mathbf{x}_m(\mathbf{N} + \mathbf{\Lambda}\mathbf{V}\mathbf{M}) + \mathbf{x}_{m-1}\mathbf{\Lambda}.$$

Besides, for $k = m$ we have

$$\mathbf{x}_m = (\mathbf{x}_m\mathbf{S} + \boldsymbol{\alpha}(\mathbf{\Lambda}\mathbf{W})^{m-1})\mathbf{R} + \boldsymbol{\beta} = \mathbf{x}_m\mathbf{S}\mathbf{R} + \boldsymbol{\alpha}\mathbf{W}^{-1}(\mathbf{W}\mathbf{\Lambda})^m\mathbf{V} + \boldsymbol{\beta},$$

and hence

$$\mathbf{x}_m\mathbf{\Phi} = \mathbf{x}_m(\mathbf{I} - \mathbf{S}\mathbf{R})(\mathbf{N} + \mathbf{\Lambda}\mathbf{V}\mathbf{M}) = -\mathbf{x}_m(\mathbf{I} - \mathbf{S}\mathbf{R})\mathbf{V}^{-1} = \mathbf{f}\mathbf{F}^m + \mathbf{g}.$$

Therefore, any solution $\mathbf{x}_0, \mathbf{x}_1, \ldots, \mathbf{x}_m$ of the linear system (7.50) satisfy (7.52).

7.6.2 The Case of Nonsingular Matrix $\boldsymbol{\Phi}$

According to Theorem 7.4, for matrix $\boldsymbol{\Phi}$ to be nonsingular it is necessary that $\mathbf{p}\boldsymbol{\lambda} \neq \mathbf{p}\boldsymbol{\mu}$. Moreover, if $\mathbf{p}\boldsymbol{\lambda} \neq \mathbf{p}\boldsymbol{\mu}$ and $\boldsymbol{\Phi}$ is irreducible, then it is nonsingular.

Let matrix $\boldsymbol{\Phi}$ be nonsingular. It follows from Theorem 7.13 that vectors $\mathbf{x}_0, \mathbf{x}_1, \ldots, \mathbf{x}_m$ satisfy linear system (7.52) if and only if they could be expressed as

$$\mathbf{x}_k = (\mathbf{f}\mathbf{F}^k + \mathbf{g}\mathbf{G}^{m-k})\boldsymbol{\Phi}^{-1}, 0 \le k \le m. \tag{7.53}$$

Since $\mathbf{F}\boldsymbol{\Phi}^{-1} = \boldsymbol{\Phi}^{-1}\mathbf{R}$ and $\mathbf{G}\boldsymbol{\Phi}^{-1} = \boldsymbol{\Phi}^{-1}\mathbf{S}$, representation (7.53) is equivalent to the following:

$$\mathbf{x}_k = \mathbf{a}\mathbf{R}^k + \mathbf{b}\mathbf{S}^{m-k}, 0 \le k \le m, \tag{7.54}$$

where $\mathbf{a} = \mathbf{f}\boldsymbol{\Phi}^{-1}$ and $\mathbf{b} = \mathbf{g}\boldsymbol{\Phi}^{-1}$.

7.6.3 The Case of Singular Matrix $\boldsymbol{\Phi}$

Here we consider the case of singular irreducible matrix $\boldsymbol{\Phi}$, which is possible only if $\mathbf{p}\boldsymbol{\lambda} = \mathbf{p}\boldsymbol{\mu}$. In this case, $\mathbf{p}\mathbf{R} = \mathbf{p}$, $\mathbf{p}\mathbf{S} = \mathbf{p}$, matrices $\mathbf{F}$, and $\mathbf{G}$ are stochastic, matrix $\boldsymbol{\Phi}$ is generator matrix and $\mathbf{p}$ is its stationary probability vector. Matrices $\boldsymbol{\Lambda}$ and $\mathbf{M}$ cannot be simultaneously equal to $\mathbf{0}$, since $\det(\boldsymbol{\Lambda} + \mathbf{N} + \mathbf{M}) = \mathbf{0}$, but $\det(\boldsymbol{\Lambda}+s\mathbf{N}+s^2\mathbf{M}) \neq 0$ for some s. Therefore, we have $\mathbf{p}\boldsymbol{\lambda} = \mathbf{p}\boldsymbol{\mu} \neq 0$. We denote $\boldsymbol{\Phi}^{\#}$ generalized group inverse of $\boldsymbol{\Phi}$. Since $\boldsymbol{\Phi}$ is irreducible, we have $\boldsymbol{\Phi}^{\#}\boldsymbol{\Phi} = \Phi\Phi^{\#} = \mathbf{I} - \mathbf{up}$.

Since matrices $\mathbf{F} = \mathbf{W}\mathbf{A}$ and $\mathbf{G} = \mathbf{V}\mathbf{C}$ are stochastic, and $\Phi\mathbf{u} = \mathbf{0}$, vectors $\mathbf{f}$ and $\mathbf{g}$ in (7.52) satisfy equality

$$\mathbf{f}\mathbf{u} + \mathbf{g}\mathbf{u} = 0. \tag{7.55}$$

Notice that $\mathbf{N}\mathbf{u} = -(\boldsymbol{\lambda} + \boldsymbol{\mu})$ and any solution of linear system (7.50) satisfies

$$\mathbf{x}_{k-1}\boldsymbol{\lambda} + \mathbf{x}_k\mathbf{N}\mathbf{u} + \mathbf{x}_{k+1}\boldsymbol{\mu} = 0, 0 < k < m. \tag{7.56}$$

It follows from (7.54) that

$$\mathbf{x}_k\boldsymbol{\mu} - \mathbf{x}_{k-1}\boldsymbol{\lambda} = \mathbf{x}_{k+1}\boldsymbol{\mu} - \mathbf{x}_k\boldsymbol{\lambda}, 0 < k < m, \tag{7.57}$$

and from (7.51) that $\mathbf{fu} = \mathbf{x}_1\boldsymbol{\mu} - \mathbf{x}_0\boldsymbol{\lambda}$. Therefore, for any solution of linear system (7.50), we have

$$\mathbf{x}_k\boldsymbol{\mu} - \mathbf{x}_{k-1}\boldsymbol{\lambda} = \mathbf{fu}, 0 < k \leq m. \tag{7.58}$$

Theorem 7.14 *Let matrix $\boldsymbol{\Phi}$ be singular and irreducible. Then vectors $\mathbf{x}_0, \mathbf{x}_1, \ldots, \mathbf{x}_m$ satisfy linear system (7.50) if and only if there exist unique vectors $\mathbf{f}$ and $\mathbf{g}$, satisfying $\mathbf{fu} + \mathbf{gu} = 0$, and unique constant h_0 such that*

$$\mathbf{x}_k = \mathbf{y}_k + (\mathbf{p}\boldsymbol{\mu})^{-1}h_k\mathbf{p}, 0 \leq k \leq m. \tag{7.59}$$

Here vectors $\mathbf{y}_k$ are defined as

$$\mathbf{y}_k = (\mathbf{fF}^k + \mathbf{gG}^{m-k})\boldsymbol{\Phi}^{\#}, 0 \leq k \leq m, \tag{7.60}$$

and constants h_k are given by

$$h_k = h_{k-1} + \mathbf{fu} + \mathbf{y}_{k-1}\boldsymbol{\lambda} - \mathbf{y}_k\boldsymbol{\mu}, 0 < k \leq m. \tag{7.61}$$

Proof Let $\mathbf{x}_0, \mathbf{x}_1, \ldots, \mathbf{x}_m$ be a solution of linear system (7.50). By Theorem 7.13, there exist unique vectors $\mathbf{f}$ and $\mathbf{g}$ such that $\mathbf{x}_0, \mathbf{x}_1, \ldots, \mathbf{x}_m$ satisfy linear systems (7.52). Vectors $\mathbf{f}$ and $\mathbf{g}$ are given by (7.51) and satisfy equality (7.56). Since matrix $\boldsymbol{\Phi}$ is irreducible and $\mathbf{p}\boldsymbol{\Phi} = \mathbf{0}$, any solution $\mathbf{x}_k$ of (7.52) could be expressed as $\mathbf{x}_k = \mathbf{y}_k + c_k\mathbf{p}$, where c_k is a constant and vector $\mathbf{y}_k$ is given by (7.60). It follows from (7.58) that $c_k = (\mathbf{p}\boldsymbol{\mu})^{-1}h_k$, with h_k satisfying recursion (7.61). ■

7.7 Matrix-Geometric Solutions for the $PH|PH|1|r+1$ Queue

Probability distribution of phase type is the simplest matrix-analytical model for inter-arrival and service time distributions; however, they can fairly closely approximate less tractable distributions (Okamura and Dohi 2016). Explicit matrix-geometric solution for single server $PH|PH|1|r+1$ queue with finite buffer, in which inter-arrival and service times have the phase-type distributions, was obtained in Bocharov and Naumov (1984). But later it was found this solution suffers from low accuracy when buffer size is large. Stationary distribution of system states may also be found applying general matrix-geometric solution for finite QBD processes (Naoumov 1996; Akar and Sohraby 1997). It is expressed in terms of two rate matrices, which are the minimal nonnegative solutions of matrix quadratic equations. We will call such a solution as iterative matrix geometric, since matrix quadratic equations are usually solved by iterative methods. In this chapter, we compare two matrix-geometric solutions for finite $PH|\,PH|\,1|r+1$ queue and explain unstable behavior of explicit matrix-geometric solution.

7.7.1 *Iterative Matrix-Geometric Solution for the $PH|\,PH|\,1|r+1$ Queue*

Consider single server $PH|\,PH|\,1|r+1$ queue with finite buffer of size r and phase-type service and inter-arrival times. The customer arrived at the full buffer is lost and does not return to the system. Let probability distribution function $F(x)$ of inter-arrival times has irreducible PH representation $(\boldsymbol{\alpha}, \boldsymbol{\Lambda})$ of order n with mean $\tau_F = -\boldsymbol{\alpha}\boldsymbol{\Lambda}^{-1}\mathbf{u}$, and probability distribution function $G(x)$ of service times has irreducible PH representations $(\boldsymbol{\beta}, \mathbf{M})$ of order m with mean $\tau_G = -\boldsymbol{\beta}\mathbf{M}^{-1}\mathbf{u}$. We denote $\boldsymbol{\lambda} = -\boldsymbol{\Lambda}\mathbf{u}$, $\boldsymbol{\mu} = -\mathbf{M}\mathbf{u}$, and $\mathbf{q}$ the stationary probability vector of the generator matrix $\boldsymbol{\Lambda} + \boldsymbol{\lambda}\boldsymbol{\alpha}$. The Laplace–Stieltjes transforms $F^*(s)$ of $F(x)$ and $G^*(s)$ of $G(x)$ are given by

$$F^*(s) = \frac{\boldsymbol{\alpha}\overline{(s\mathbf{I}-\boldsymbol{\Lambda})}\boldsymbol{\lambda}}{\det(s\mathbf{I}-\boldsymbol{\Lambda})},\; G^*(s) = \frac{\boldsymbol{\beta}\overline{(s\mathbf{I}-\mathbf{M})}\boldsymbol{\mu}}{\det(s\mathbf{I}-\mathbf{M})}, \tag{7.62}$$

with the matrix $\overline{\mathbf{X}}$ adjoint to $\mathbf{X}$. It is assumed that these PH representations are minimal in sense that numerator and denominator polynomials in formulae (7.62) do not have common zeros.

The system is described by a finite QBD process $X(t)$ state space $\mathcal{X} = \bigcup_{l=0}^{r+1} \mathcal{X}_l$, with subsets

$$\mathcal{X}_0 = \{(i, 0)|i = 1, 2, \ldots, n\},$$

$$\mathcal{X}_k = \{(i, j, k)|i = 1, 2, \ldots, n,\; j = 1, 2, \ldots, m\}, k = 1, 2, \ldots, r+1,$$

corresponding to the number of customers in the system. The generator matrix of the QBD process has a block tridiagonal structure given by

$$\mathbf{Q} = \begin{bmatrix} \mathbf{B}_1 & \mathbf{B}_0 & \mathbf{O} & \cdots\cdots & & \mathbf{O} \\ \mathbf{B}_2 & \mathbf{A}_1 & \mathbf{A}_0 & \mathbf{O} & & \vdots \\ \mathbf{O} & \mathbf{A}_2 & \mathbf{A}_1 & \ddots & \ddots & \vdots \\ \vdots & \mathbf{O} & \ddots & \ddots & \mathbf{A}_0 & \mathbf{O} \\ \vdots & & & \ddots & \mathbf{A}_2 \; \mathbf{A}_1 & \mathbf{A}_0 \\ \mathbf{O} & \cdots\cdots & & \mathbf{O} & \mathbf{A}_2 & \mathbf{A}_1 + \mathbf{A}_0 \end{bmatrix},$$

where

$$\mathbf{A}_0 = \boldsymbol{\lambda\alpha} \otimes \mathbf{I}, \mathbf{A}_1 = \boldsymbol{\Lambda} \otimes \mathbf{I} + \mathbf{I} \otimes \mathbf{M}, \mathbf{A}_2 = \mathbf{I} \otimes \boldsymbol{\mu\beta},$$

$$\mathbf{B}_0 = \boldsymbol{\lambda\alpha} \otimes \boldsymbol{\beta}, \mathbf{B}_1 = \boldsymbol{\Lambda}, \mathbf{B}_2 = \mathbf{I} \otimes \boldsymbol{\mu}.$$

Here we use standard notation $\otimes$ for the Kronecker product of two matrices.

Let $\mathbf{R}$ and $\mathbf{S}$ be the minimal nonnegative solutions of the matrix equations

$$\mathbf{A}_0 + \mathbf{R}\mathbf{A}_1 + \mathbf{R}^2\mathbf{A}_2 = \mathbf{0}, \mathbf{S}^2\mathbf{A}_0 + \mathbf{S}\mathbf{A}_1 + \mathbf{A}_2 = \mathbf{0}, \tag{7.63}$$

and $\mathbf{p} = (\mathbf{p}_0, \mathbf{p}_1, ..., \mathbf{p}_{r+1})$ be the stationary probability vector of the process $X(t)$. It follows from Sect. 7.6.2, if $\tau_F \neq \tau_G$ the vectors $\mathbf{p}_i$ are expressed as a sum of forward and backward matrix-geometric terms:

$$\mathbf{p}_{k+1} = \mathbf{f}\mathbf{R}^k + \mathbf{g}\mathbf{S}^{r-k}, 0 \leq k \leq r. \tag{7.64}$$

Vectors $\mathbf{f}$, $\mathbf{g}$ and $\mathbf{p}_0$ are unique solutions of the following linear system:

$$\mathbf{p}_0\mathbf{B}_1 + (\mathbf{f} + \mathbf{g}\mathbf{S}^r)\mathbf{B}_2 = \mathbf{0}, \tag{7.65}$$

$$\mathbf{p}_0\mathbf{B}_0 + (\mathbf{f} + \mathbf{g}\mathbf{S}^r)\mathbf{A}_1 + (\mathbf{f}\mathbf{R} + \mathbf{g}\mathbf{S}^{r-1})\mathbf{A}_2 = \mathbf{0}, \tag{7.66}$$

$$(\mathbf{f}\mathbf{R}^{r-1} + \mathbf{g}\mathbf{S})\mathbf{A}_0 + (\mathbf{f}\mathbf{R}^r + \mathbf{g})(\mathbf{A}_0 + \mathbf{A}_1) = \mathbf{0}, \tag{7.67}$$

$$(\mathbf{p}_0 + \mathbf{f}\sum_{k=0}^{r}\mathbf{R}^k + \mathbf{g}\sum_{k=0}^{r}\mathbf{S}^k)\mathbf{u} = 1. \tag{7.68}$$

7.7.2 Explicit Matrix-Geometric Solution for the $PH|PH|1|r+1$ Queue

Now consider explicit solution of the linear system $\mathbf{pQ} = \mathbf{0}, \mathbf{pu} = 1$, for the stationary probability vector $\mathbf{p} = (\mathbf{p}_0, \mathbf{p}_1, ..., \mathbf{p}_{r+1})$, which we rewrite as

$$\mathbf{p}_0\boldsymbol{\Lambda} + \mathbf{p}_1(\mathbf{I} \otimes \boldsymbol{\mu}) = \mathbf{0}, \tag{7.69}$$

$$\mathbf{p}_0(\boldsymbol{\lambda\alpha} \otimes \boldsymbol{\beta}) + \mathbf{p}_1(\boldsymbol{\Lambda} \otimes \mathbf{I} + \mathbf{I} \otimes \mathbf{M}) + \mathbf{p}_2(\mathbf{I} \otimes \boldsymbol{\mu\beta}) = \mathbf{0}, \tag{7.70}$$

$$\mathbf{p}_{k-1}(\boldsymbol{\lambda\alpha} \otimes \mathbf{I}) + \mathbf{p}_k(\boldsymbol{\Lambda} \otimes \mathbf{I} + \mathbf{I} \otimes \mathbf{M}) + \mathbf{p}_{k+1}(\mathbf{I} \otimes \boldsymbol{\mu\beta}) = \mathbf{0}, 2 \le k \le r, \tag{7.71}$$

$$\mathbf{p}_r(\boldsymbol{\lambda\alpha} \otimes \mathbf{I}) + \mathbf{p}_{r+1}((\boldsymbol{\Lambda} + \boldsymbol{\lambda\alpha}) \otimes \mathbf{I} + \mathbf{I} \otimes \mathbf{M}) = \mathbf{0}, \tag{7.72}$$

$$\sum_{k=0}^{r+1} \mathbf{p}_k\mathbf{u} = 1. \tag{7.73}$$

Multiplying both sides of equalities (7.70)–(7.72) from the right by the matrix $\mathbf{I} \otimes \mathbf{u}$, we obtain

$$\mathbf{p}_0\boldsymbol{\lambda\alpha} + \mathbf{p}_1(\boldsymbol{\Lambda} \otimes \mathbf{u} - \mathbf{I} \otimes \boldsymbol{\mu}) + \mathbf{p}_2(\mathbf{I} \otimes \boldsymbol{\mu}) = \mathbf{0}, \tag{7.74}$$

$$\mathbf{p}_{k-1}(\boldsymbol{\lambda\alpha} \otimes \mathbf{u}) + \mathbf{p}_k(\boldsymbol{\Lambda} \otimes \mathbf{u} - \mathbf{I} \otimes \boldsymbol{\mu}) + \mathbf{p}_{k+1}(\mathbf{I} \otimes \boldsymbol{\mu}) = \mathbf{0}, 2 \le k \le r, \tag{7.75}$$

$$\mathbf{p}_r(\boldsymbol{\lambda\alpha} \otimes \mathbf{u}) + \mathbf{p}_{r+1}((\boldsymbol{\Lambda} + \boldsymbol{\lambda\alpha}) \otimes \mathbf{u} - \mathbf{I} \otimes \boldsymbol{\mu}) = \mathbf{0}. \tag{7.76}$$

Summing up all equalities (7.74)–(7.76) and (7.69) we obtain

$$\left(\mathbf{p}_0 + \sum_{k=1}^{r+1} \mathbf{p}_k(\mathbf{I} \otimes \mathbf{u})\right)(\boldsymbol{\Lambda} + \boldsymbol{\lambda\alpha}) = \mathbf{0}. \tag{7.77}$$

After multiplying both sides of equalities (7.69), (7.74) and (7.75) from the right by the vector $\mathbf{u}$, we obtain

$$\mathbf{p}_0\boldsymbol{\lambda} - \mathbf{p}_1(\mathbf{u} \otimes \boldsymbol{\mu}) = \mathbf{0},$$

$$\mathbf{p}_0\boldsymbol{\lambda} - \mathbf{p}_1(\boldsymbol{\lambda} \otimes \mathbf{u} + \mathbf{u} \otimes \boldsymbol{\mu}) + \mathbf{p}_2(\mathbf{u} \otimes \boldsymbol{\mu}) = \mathbf{0},$$

$$\mathbf{p}_{k-1}(\boldsymbol{\lambda} \otimes \mathbf{u}) - \mathbf{p}_k(\boldsymbol{\lambda} \otimes \mathbf{u} + \mathbf{u} \otimes \boldsymbol{\mu}) + \mathbf{p}_{k+1}(\mathbf{u} \otimes \boldsymbol{\mu}) = \mathbf{0}, 2 \le k \le r.$$

From this, we obtain the balance equations

$$\mathbf{p}_1(\mathbf{u} \otimes \boldsymbol{\mu}) = \mathbf{p}_0\boldsymbol{\lambda}, \; \mathbf{p}_{k+1}(\mathbf{u} \otimes \boldsymbol{\mu}) = \mathbf{p}_k(\boldsymbol{\lambda} \otimes \mathbf{u}), \; 1 \leq k \leq r. \tag{7.78}$$

Multiplying both sides of equalities (7.70) and (7.71) from the right by the matrix $\mathbf{I} \otimes (\mathbf{u}\boldsymbol{\beta} - \mathbf{I})$, we obtain

$$\mathbf{p}_1(\boldsymbol{\Lambda} \otimes \mathbf{I} + \mathbf{I} \otimes \mathbf{M})(\mathbf{I} \otimes (\mathbf{u}\boldsymbol{\beta} - \mathbf{I})) = \mathbf{0},$$

$$\mathbf{p}_{k-1}(\boldsymbol{\lambda}\boldsymbol{\alpha} \otimes (\mathbf{u}\boldsymbol{\beta} - \mathbf{I})) + \mathbf{p}_k(\boldsymbol{\Lambda} \otimes \mathbf{I} + \mathbf{I} \otimes \mathbf{M})(\mathbf{I} \otimes (\mathbf{u}\boldsymbol{\beta} - \mathbf{I})) = \mathbf{0}, \; 2 \leq k \leq r.$$

From this, taking into account equality (7.69) and balance equations (7.78), we obtain

$$\mathbf{p}_1\widetilde{\mathbf{M}} = \mathbf{p}_1(\mathbf{I} \otimes \boldsymbol{\mu}\boldsymbol{\beta}) = -\mathbf{p}_0(\boldsymbol{\Lambda} \otimes \boldsymbol{\beta}), \tag{7.79}$$

$$\begin{aligned}\mathbf{p}_k\widetilde{\mathbf{M}} &= \mathbf{p}_k(\mathbf{I} \otimes \boldsymbol{\mu}\boldsymbol{\beta}) + \mathbf{p}_{k-1}(\boldsymbol{\lambda}\boldsymbol{\alpha} \otimes \mathbf{I}) - \mathbf{p}_{k-1}(\boldsymbol{\lambda}\boldsymbol{\alpha} \otimes \mathbf{u}\boldsymbol{\beta}) \\ &= \mathbf{p}_k(\mathbf{I} \otimes \boldsymbol{\mu}\boldsymbol{\beta}) + \mathbf{p}_{k-1}(\boldsymbol{\lambda}\boldsymbol{\alpha} \otimes \mathbf{I}) - \mathbf{p}_k(\mathbf{u}\boldsymbol{\alpha} \otimes \boldsymbol{\mu}\boldsymbol{\beta}), \quad 2 \leq k \leq r,\end{aligned} \tag{7.80}$$

where

$$\widetilde{\mathbf{M}} = \boldsymbol{\Lambda} \otimes (\mathbf{u}\boldsymbol{\beta} - \mathbf{I}) - \mathbf{I} \otimes \mathbf{M}. \tag{7.81}$$

Multiplying both sides of (7.70) and (7.71) from the right by the matrix $(\mathbf{u}\boldsymbol{\alpha} - \mathbf{I}) \otimes \mathbf{I}$, we obtain

$$\mathbf{p}_k(\boldsymbol{\Lambda} \otimes \mathbf{I} + \mathbf{I} \otimes \mathbf{M})((\mathbf{u}\boldsymbol{\alpha} - \mathbf{I}) \otimes \mathbf{I}) + \mathbf{p}_{k+1}((\mathbf{u}\boldsymbol{\alpha} - \mathbf{I}) \otimes \boldsymbol{\mu}\boldsymbol{\beta}) = \mathbf{0}.$$

This implies that

$$\mathbf{p}_k\widetilde{\boldsymbol{\Lambda}} = \mathbf{p}_k(\boldsymbol{\lambda}\boldsymbol{\alpha} \otimes \mathbf{I}) + \mathbf{p}_{k+1}((\mathbf{I} - \mathbf{u}\boldsymbol{\alpha}) \otimes \boldsymbol{\mu}\boldsymbol{\beta}), \tag{7.82}$$

where

$$\widetilde{\boldsymbol{\Lambda}} = (\mathbf{u}\boldsymbol{\alpha} - \mathbf{I}) \otimes \mathbf{M} - \boldsymbol{\Lambda} \otimes \mathbf{I}. \tag{7.83}$$

Finally, from (7.79), (7.80), (7.82), and (7.72), it follows that

$$\mathbf{p}_1\widetilde{\mathbf{M}} = -\mathbf{p}_0(\boldsymbol{\Lambda} \otimes \boldsymbol{\beta}), \tag{7.84}$$

$$\mathbf{p}_k\widetilde{\mathbf{M}} = \mathbf{p}_{k-1}\widetilde{\boldsymbol{\Lambda}}, \; 2 \leq k \leq r, \tag{7.85}$$

$$\mathbf{p}_{r+1}((\mathbf{\Lambda}+\boldsymbol{\lambda\alpha})\otimes\mathbf{I}+\mathbf{I}\otimes\mathbf{M}) = -\mathbf{p}_r(\boldsymbol{\lambda\alpha}\otimes\mathbf{I}). \tag{7.86}$$

It can be shown that matrices $\widetilde{\mathbf{M}}$ and $((\mathbf{\Lambda}+\boldsymbol{\lambda\alpha})\otimes\mathbf{I}+\mathbf{I}\otimes\mathbf{M})$ are nonsingular. See (Bocharov and Naumov 1984) or (Bocharov et al. 2004). Therefore, we may introduce matrices

$$\mathbf{W}_0 = -(\mathbf{\Lambda}\otimes\boldsymbol{\beta})\widetilde{\mathbf{M}}^{-1},\ \mathbf{W} = \widetilde{\mathbf{\Lambda}}\widetilde{\mathbf{M}}^{-1},$$
$$\mathbf{W}_r = -(\boldsymbol{\lambda\alpha}\otimes\mathbf{I})((\mathbf{\Lambda}+\boldsymbol{\lambda\alpha})\otimes\mathbf{I}+\mathbf{I}\otimes\mathbf{M})^{-1},$$

$$\mathbf{V} = \mathbf{I}+\mathbf{W}_0\left(\sum_{k=0}^{r-1}\mathbf{W}^k+\mathbf{W}^{r-1}\mathbf{W}_r\right)(\mathbf{I}\otimes\mathbf{u}).$$

It follows from (7.84)–(7.86) and (7.76) that the stationary probability vector of the process $X(t)$ has matrix-geometric form given by

$$\mathbf{p}_{k+1} = \begin{cases} \mathbf{p}_0\mathbf{W}_0, & k=0, \\ \mathbf{p}_0\mathbf{W}_0\mathbf{W}^k, & 0<k<r, \\ \mathbf{p}_0\mathbf{W}_0\mathbf{W}^k\mathbf{W}_r & k=r, \end{cases} \tag{7.87}$$

with vector $\mathbf{p}_0$ satisfying the linear system $\mathbf{p}_0\mathbf{V} = \mathbf{q}$.

7.7.3 *Eigenvalues of the Rate Matrices* R *and* S

According to Theorem 7.12, eigenvalues of the rate matrices **R** and **S** are zeros of the polynomials

$$f(s) = \det(\mathbf{A}_0 + s\mathbf{A}_1 + s^2\mathbf{A}_2) = \det((s\mathbf{\Lambda}+\boldsymbol{\lambda\alpha})\oplus s(\mathbf{M}+s\boldsymbol{\mu\beta})),$$

$$g(s) = \det(s^2\mathbf{A}_0 + s\mathbf{A}_1 + \mathbf{A}_2) = \det(s(\mathbf{\Lambda}+s\boldsymbol{\lambda\alpha})\oplus(s\mathbf{M}+\boldsymbol{\mu\beta})).$$

Matrices **R** and **S** have rank *m* and *n,* respectively (Bini et al. 1999). If $\rho_1, \rho_2, \ldots, \rho_m$ are nonzero eigenvalues of **R** and $\sigma_1, \sigma_2, \ldots, \sigma_n$ are nonzero eigenvalues of **S**, then

$$s_1 = \rho_1,\ \ldots,\ s_m = \rho_m,\quad s_{m+1} = \frac{1}{\sigma_1},\ \ldots,\ s_{m+n} = \frac{1}{\sigma_n},$$

are zeros of the polynomial $f(s)$. Maximal eigenvalues (spectral radii) of $\mathbf{R}$ and $\mathbf{S}$ satisfy $sp(\mathbf{R})$, $sp(\mathbf{S}) \leq 1$, moreover $sp(\mathbf{R}) = 1$ if and only if $\tau_A \leq \tau_B$, and $sp(\mathbf{S}) = 1$ if and only if $\tau_A \geq \tau_B$.

Maximal eigenvalues of the rate matrices are important characteristics describing asymptotic behavior of the system. Let w be the steady-state waiting time and q be the steady-state number of customers in the system with infinite buffer, and $\tau_A > \tau_B$. Then the following approximations are valid:

$$\mathsf{P}(w > x) \approx a e^{-\xi x}, \mathsf{P}(q = k) \approx b\eta^k$$

for suitably large x and k, where a and b are constants. The exponential decay rate ξ is the smallest positive root of the equation

$$F^*(z)G^*(-z) = 1, \tag{7.88}$$

and the geometric decay rate η is given by $\eta = sp(\mathbf{R}) = F^*(\xi)$ (Neuts 1981).

All roots of (7.88) with $\mathrm{Re}(z) = 0$ are equal to 0. If $\tau_A \neq \tau_B$ then (7.88) has exactly one root equal to 0. If $\tau_A > \tau_B$, it has $n - 1$ roots with $\mathrm{Re}(z) < 0$ and m roots with $\mathrm{Re}(z) > 0$. If $\tau_A < \tau_B$, it has n roots with $\mathrm{Re}(z) < 0$ and $m - 1$ roots with $\mathrm{Re}(z) > 0$. We show that every root of (7.88) corresponds to a nonzero eigenvalue of either $\mathbf{R}$ or $\mathbf{S}$ (Naumov 2003).

Theorem 7.15 *Polynomial $f(s)$ has $n + m$ zeros given by*

$$s_i = F^*(z_i) = \frac{1}{G^*(-z_i)}, i = 1, 2, \ldots, n + m, \tag{7.89}$$

where $z_1, z_2, \ldots, z_{n+m}$ are the roots of (7.88), and other zeros of $f(s)$ are equal to 0.

Proof If a matrix $\mathbf{X}$ is nonsingular, then

$$\det(\mathbf{X} + \mathbf{YZ}) = \det(\mathbf{X}) \det(I + \mathbf{ZX}^{-1}\mathbf{Y}). \tag{7.90}$$

Applying this equality, the characteristic polynomial of the matrix $s\boldsymbol{\Lambda} + \boldsymbol{\lambda\alpha}$ can be expressed as

$$\begin{aligned}\det(x\mathbf{I} - s\boldsymbol{\Lambda} - \boldsymbol{\lambda\alpha}) &= \det(x\mathbf{I} - s\boldsymbol{\Lambda})(1 - \boldsymbol{\alpha}(x\mathbf{I} - s\boldsymbol{\Lambda})^{-1}\boldsymbol{\lambda}) = \\ &= \det(x\mathbf{I} - s\boldsymbol{\Lambda}) - \boldsymbol{\alpha}\overline{(x\mathbf{I} - s\boldsymbol{\Lambda})}\boldsymbol{\lambda} \\ &= \left(1 - \frac{1}{s}F^*\left(\frac{x}{s}\right)\right)\det(x\mathbf{I} - s\boldsymbol{\Lambda}),\end{aligned}$$

and the characteristic polynomial of the matrix $\mathbf{M} + s\boldsymbol{\mu\beta}$ can be expressed as

$$\det(y\mathbf{I}-\mathbf{M}-s\boldsymbol{\mu}\boldsymbol{\beta}) = \det(y\mathbf{I}-\mathbf{M})(1-s\boldsymbol{\beta}(y\mathbf{I}-\mathbf{M})^{-1}\boldsymbol{\mu}) =$$
$$= \det(y\mathbf{I}-\mathbf{M}) - s\boldsymbol{\beta}\overline{(y\mathbf{I}-\mathbf{M})}\boldsymbol{\mu}$$
$$= (1-sG^*(y))\det(y\mathbf{I}-\mathbf{M}).$$

Matrix $(s\boldsymbol{\Lambda}+\boldsymbol{\lambda}\boldsymbol{\alpha}) \oplus s(\mathbf{M}+s\boldsymbol{\mu}\boldsymbol{\beta})$ has the eigenvalue 0 if and only if s is a zero of $f(s)$. It is known, eigenvalues of the Kronecker sum of two matrices are sums of eigenvalues of these matrices. Since numerator and denominator polynomials in (7.62) do not have common zeros, $s_i \neq 0$ is a zero of polynomial $f(s)$ if and only if there exist an eigenvalue x_i of the matrix $s_i\boldsymbol{\Lambda}+\boldsymbol{\lambda}\boldsymbol{\alpha}$ and an eigenvalue y_i of the matrix $\mathbf{M}+s_i\boldsymbol{\mu}\boldsymbol{\beta}$ such that

$$x_i + s_i y_i = 0,\ F^*\left(\frac{x_i}{s_i}\right) = s_i,\ G^*(y_i) = \frac{1}{s_i},$$

i.e., $s_i = F^*(z_i)$, $F^*(z_i)G^*(-z_i)) = 1$, with $z_i = \frac{x_i}{s_i}$. Thus, $f(s)$ has exactly $n+m$ zeros $s_i \neq 0$ given by (7.89) and other zeros must be equal to 0, completing the proof.

■

Corollary *Let* $z_1, z_2, \ldots, z_m$ *be roots of (7.88) with* $\mathrm{Re}(z) \geq 0$ *and* $z_{m+1}, z_{m+2}, \ldots, z_{m+n}$ *be roots with* $\mathrm{Re}(z) \leq 0$. *Then matrix* $\mathbf{R}$ *has eigenvalue* 0 *with multiplicity* $nm-m$ *and* m *nonzero eigenvalues* $\rho_i = F^*(z_i)$, $i = 1, 2, \ldots, m$. *Matrix* $\mathbf{S}$ *has eigenvalue* 0 *with multiplicity* $mn-n$ *and* n *nonzero eigenvalues* $\sigma_i = G^*(-z_{m+i})$, $i = 1, 2, \ldots, n$.

Therefore, to find eigenvalues of two rate matrices there is no need to compute zeros of polynomials $f(s)$ of order $nm+n$ and $g(s)$ of order $nm+m$. It is enough to find only $n+m$ roots of (7.88).

7.7.4 Eigenvalues of the Matrix W in the Explicit Matrix-Geometric Solutions

Since,

$$\det(s\mathbf{I}-\mathbf{W}) = \det(s\mathbf{I}-\widetilde{\boldsymbol{\Lambda}}\widetilde{\mathbf{M}}^{-1}) = \frac{\det(s\widetilde{\mathbf{M}}-\widetilde{\boldsymbol{\Lambda}})}{\det(\widetilde{\mathbf{M}})},$$

eigenvalues of the matrix $\mathbf{W}$ are zeros of the polynomial $\det(s\widetilde{\mathbf{M}}-\widetilde{\boldsymbol{\Lambda}})$ of order nm.

Theorem 7.16

$$\det(s\widetilde{\mathbf{M}}-\widetilde{\boldsymbol{\Lambda}}) = \frac{(-1)^{nm-n}(s-1)^{nm-n-m}}{s^{nm-m}} f(s). \tag{7.91}$$

Proof It follows from (7.90) that

$$\left(\mathbf{I}-\frac{1}{1-s}\mathbf{u}\boldsymbol{\alpha}\right)^{-1}=\left(\mathbf{I}-\frac{1}{s}\mathbf{u}\boldsymbol{\alpha}\right),\left(\mathbf{I}+\frac{s}{1-s}\mathbf{u}\boldsymbol{\beta}\right)^{-1}=(\mathbf{I}-s\mathbf{u}\boldsymbol{\beta}),\qquad(7.92)$$

$$\det\left(\mathbf{I}-\frac{1}{1-s}\mathbf{u}\boldsymbol{\alpha}\right)=\frac{s}{s-1},\ \det\left(\mathbf{I}+\frac{s}{1-s}\mathbf{u}\boldsymbol{\beta}\right)=\frac{1}{1-s}.\qquad(7.93)$$

Using equalities (7.92) matrix $s\widetilde{\mathbf{M}}-\widetilde{\mathbf{\Lambda}}$ can be expressed as

$$\begin{aligned}
s\widetilde{\mathbf{M}}-\widetilde{\mathbf{\Lambda}} &= (1-s)\left(\mathbf{\Lambda}\otimes\left(\mathbf{I}+\frac{s}{1-s}\mathbf{u}\boldsymbol{\beta}\right)+\left(\mathbf{I}-\frac{1}{1-s}\mathbf{u}\boldsymbol{\alpha}\right)\otimes\mathbf{M}\right)=\\
&= (1-s)\left(\mathbf{\Lambda}\left(\mathbf{I}-\frac{1}{s}\mathbf{u}\boldsymbol{\alpha}\right)\otimes\mathbf{I}+\mathbf{I}\otimes\mathbf{M}(\mathbf{I}-s\mathbf{u}\boldsymbol{\beta})\right)\times\\
&\times\left(\left(\mathbf{I}-\frac{1}{1-s}\mathbf{u}\boldsymbol{\alpha}\right)\otimes\left(\mathbf{I}+\frac{s}{1-s}\mathbf{u}\boldsymbol{\beta}\right)\right)=\\
&= \frac{(1-s)}{s}((s\mathbf{\Lambda}+\boldsymbol{\lambda}\boldsymbol{\alpha})\otimes\mathbf{I}+s\mathbf{I}\otimes(\mathbf{M}+s\boldsymbol{\mu}\boldsymbol{\beta}))\times\\
&\times\left(\left(\mathbf{I}-\frac{1}{1-s}\boldsymbol{\alpha}\right)\otimes\left(\mathbf{I}+\frac{s}{1-s}\mathbf{u}\boldsymbol{\beta}\right)\right).
\end{aligned}$$

Then we use equalities (7.93) and the equality $\det(\mathbf{X}\otimes\mathbf{Y})=\det(\mathbf{X})^m\det(\mathbf{Y})^n$ that is valid for any $n\times n$ matrix $\mathbf{X}$ and $m\times m$ matrix $\mathbf{Y}$. As a result, we get

$$\begin{aligned}
\det(s\widetilde{\mathbf{M}}-\widetilde{\mathbf{\Lambda}}) &= \left(\frac{1-s}{s}\right)^{nm}\left(\frac{s}{s-1}\right)^{m}\left(\frac{1}{1-s}\right)^{n}\times\\
&\times\det((s\mathbf{\Lambda}+\boldsymbol{\lambda}\boldsymbol{\alpha})\otimes\mathbf{I}+s\mathbf{I}\otimes(\mathbf{M}+s\boldsymbol{\mu}\boldsymbol{\beta}))=\\
&= \frac{(-1)^{nm-n}(s-1)^{nm-n-m}}{s^{nm-m}}\times\\
&\times\det((\boldsymbol{\lambda}\boldsymbol{\alpha}\otimes\mathbf{I})+s(\mathbf{\Lambda}\otimes\mathbf{I}+\mathbf{I}\otimes\mathbf{M})+s^2(\mathbf{I}\otimes\boldsymbol{\mu}\boldsymbol{\beta})).
\end{aligned}$$

Thus, formula (7.91) is valid, completing the proof. ∎

Corollary *Each eigenvalue of the matrix* **W** *is either an eigenvalue of* **R** *or inverse to an eigenvalue of* **S**.

Hence, the matrix **W** in explicit solution (7.87) may have the eigenvalues less, equal, and greater than one. This fact explains loss of accuracy of the explicit solution for the system with large buffer. In contrast, the rate matrices are nonnegative and have eigenvalues inside unit circle that lead to stable exponentiation.

References

Akar, N., Sohraby, K.: Finite and infinite QBD chains: a simple and unifying algorithmic approach. In: Proceedings of INFOCOM, vol. 3, pp. 1105–1113. IEEE (1997)
Bini, D., Chakravarthy, S., Meini, B.: A new algorithm for the design of finite capacity service units. In: Numerical Solution of Markov Chains, pp. 247–260 (1999)
Bocharov, P.P., Naumov, V.A.: Matrix-geometric stationary distribution for the PH/PH/1R queue. RR-0304, INRIA (1984)
Bocharov, P.P., D'Apice, C., Pechinkin, A.V., Salerno, S.: Queueing Theory. VSP, Utrecht, Boston (2004)
Kato, T.: Perturbation theory for linear operators. Classics in Mathematics, Berlin (1995)
Krieger, U.R., Naoumov, V., Wagner, D.: Analysis of a finite FIFO buffer in an advanced packet-switched network. IEICE Trans. Commun. **E81-B**(5), 937–947 (1998)
Latouche, G., Ramaswami, V.: A logarithmic reduction algorithm for quasi-birth-death processes. J. Appl. Probab. **30**(3), 650–674 (1993)
Naoumov, V.A.: Matrix-multiplicative approach to quasi-birth-and-death processes analysis. In: Matrix-Analytic Methods in Stochastic Models, pp. 87–106 (1996)
Naumov, V.: Spectral properties of finite buffers with phase type service and interarrival times. In: Teletraffic Science and Engineering, vol. 5, pp. 611–619. Elsevier (2003)
Neuts, M.F.: Matrix-Geometric Solutions in Stochastic Models: An Algorithmic Approach. Johns Hopkins University Press, Baltimore (1981)
Okamura, H., Dohi, T.: Fitting phase-type distributions and Markovian arrival processes: algorithms and tools. In: Principles of Performance and Reliability Modeling and Evaluation, pp. 49–75. Springer, Cham (2016)

Part III
Resource Queueing Systems

Chapter 8
Stochastic Lists of Resource Allocations

Abstract The chapter introduces the concepts of stochastic lists and pseudo-lists of resource allocations for modeling loss systems in which random amounts of resources of multiple types are allocated to customers for the total duration of their service times and then released. In such systems, once service is completed, a customer releases the exact amounts of resources that have been allocated to it upon arrival. Thus, for each customer in service we must "remember" its resource allocation, which greatly complicates the stochastic processes that model the behavior of such systems. The analysis can be substantially simplified by using pseudo-lists. In this approach, we deal with an otherwise same service system, but the resource amounts released upon a departure are assumed random. We will show that for a loss system with Poisson arrivals and exponential service times, lists and pseudo-lists yield the same stationary distribution of the allocated totals.

Lists are widely used in programming (Knuth 1997) and when defining computer and communication systems (Le Boudec 2010). In this chapter, we show how lists can be adopted in queueing theory to study multi-resource loss systems with random resource requirements (multi-resource ReLS), in which random amounts of resources of multiple types are allocated to customers for the total duration of their service and and then released.

In such systems, an arriving customer that does not find the totality of the required resource amounts available is lost. Once service is completed, the customer releases the exact amounts of resources that were allocated to it upon arrival. Thus, for each customer in service we must "remember" its allocated resource amounts, which greatly complicates the stochastic processes that model the behavior of such systems. Incidentally, here lies the main distinction from the stochastic storage models, in which the input and output processes are inherently different from each other.

The analysis of these complicated systems can be substantially simplified by using what we will call *pseudo-lists*. In this approach, we deal with an otherwise same service system, but the resource amounts released upon a departure are assumed random and may differ from the amounts allocated to the departing customer upon its arrival. We assume that given the *totals* of allocated resources—i.e., for each resource type, the resource amount held by all customers combined—and the number of

V. Naumov et al., *Matrix and Analytical Methods for Performance Analysis of Telecommunication Systems*, https://doi.org/10.1007/978-3-030-83132-5_8

customers in service, the resource amounts released upon a departure are independent of the system's behavior prior to the departure instant and have an easily calculable CDF. Stochastic processes representing the behavior of such simplified systems are easier to study since there is no need to remember the resource amounts held by each customer: the totals of allocated resources suffice. We will show that for a system with Poisson arrivals and exponential service times, lists and pseudo-lists yield the same stationary distribution of the allocated totals.

We allow the resource amounts requested by customers to be positive or negative. While an allocation of a positive resource amount reduces the available amount of the resource, an allocation of a negative amount, on the contrary, increases the available amount of the resource for the duration of the customer's service time.

The concept of positive and negative customers was introduced in (Gelenbe 1991). Positive customers can represent resource requests, whereas negative customers can increase the amount of available resources by cancelling some requests. In our analysis, the behavior of negative customers is slightly different: instead of request cancellation, negative customers temporarily increase the amount of resources available to positive customers. Queueing systems with positive and negative resource demands can be used to model standalone wireless access points whose capacity can be dynamically increased, or to study heterogeneous networks in which mobile users (or vehicles) can provide their network capacity to nearby users and take it back when leaving the area.

8.1 Stochastic Lists and Lists of Resource Allocations

8.1.1 Stochastic Lists

Let S represent a nonempty measurable set. We will refer to the elements of S^k as *lists* of length k of items from S. The set of all lists of items from S will be denoted by $\bar{S} = \bigcup_{k=0}^{L} S^k$, where $L \le \infty$ represents the maximum list length. The set S^0 is assumed to consist of a single list () of zero length.

Let us denote by $|\xi|$ the length of list $\xi \in \bar{S}$ and introduce two list operations. The operation of *deleting* the i-th item from a list $\xi = (s_1, s_2, ..., s_k)$ results in the list $\mathrm{Del}_i(\xi) = (s_1, ..., s_{i-1}, s_{i+1}, ..., s_k)$, $1 \le i \le k$. The operation of *inserting* $u \in S$ as a j-th item yields the list $\mathrm{Ins}_j(\xi, u) = (s_1, ..., s_{j-1}, u, s_j, ..., s_k)$, $1 \le j \le k+1$.

Now, let $\xi(t) \in \bar{S}$, $t \ge 0$, be a right-continuous jump stochastic process with jumps at random times $0 < \tau_1 < \tau_2 < ....$ We let $\tau_0 = 0$ and denote $\xi_n = \xi(\tau_n)$, $n \ge 0$. The process $\xi(t)$ is said to be a *stochastic list* if, for any $n \ge 1$, the values of the process before and after time τ_n are related as either.

(1) $\xi_n = \mathrm{Del}_j(\xi_{n-1})$ for some index j, $1 \le j \le |\xi_{n-1}|$, or
(2) $\xi_n = \mathrm{Ins}_j(\xi_{n-1}, u)$ for some $u \in S$ and j, $1 \le j \le |\xi_n|$.

Put simply, a jump process $\xi(t) \in S$ is a stochastic list if each of its states is obtained from the previous one either through insertion or deletion of an item.

8.1.2 Lists of Resource Allocations

In classical queueing systems, servers and waiting spaces play the role of resources required for serving customers. However, sometimes, besides these, customers may require additional resources. A customer may use the capacity of some additional resource while waiting for service, while in service, or both. As an example, consider a hairdressing salon. Arriving customers may have a seat in the waiting room, but may also hang their coats on a rack. While the seat will be freed once the customer proceeds to the hairdresser, the hook on the coat rack will remain occupied until the customer leaves the salon.

Usually, the total service capacities of resources are limited, and an arriving customer is lost if the system does not have the required amounts of resources available. In multi-resource systems with deterministic resource requirements, such as loss networks discussed in Chap. 3, the amounts of occupied and available resources are uniquely determined by the number of customers in service. This is not so, however, if resource requirements are random. Going back to our hairdresser example, a waiting customer may or may not use the coat rack, or may take one, two, or more magazines while waiting. In this case, we cannot tell how many hooks on the coat rack are occupied or how many magazines are left available just from the number of customers in the waiting room. Moreover, we cannot tell how many of them will be freed once a customer leaves the salon, unless we keep track of resource allocations. This is why when studying ReLSes, we use stochastic lists to store the information about resources allocated to customers in service.

From now on, we will only consider lists whose items are real-valued vectors of size M, i.e., the set S of items is a measurable subset of $\mathbb{R}^M$. Let $\mathbf{v} \in \mathbb{R}^M$ be some nonnegative vector of size M. The elements of vector $\mathbf{v}$ can be interpreted as the capacities of resources of different types in a system with M types of resources. Now, a stochastic list $\xi(t) = (\boldsymbol{\zeta}_1(t), \boldsymbol{\zeta}_2(t), ..., \boldsymbol{\zeta}_{n(t)}(t))$ of length $n(t) = |\xi(t)| \le L \le \infty$, where $\boldsymbol{\zeta}_k(t) = (\zeta_{1,k}(t), \zeta_{2,k}(t), ..., \zeta_{M,k}(t)) \in \mathbb{R}^M$, is said to be a *list of resource allocations* of capacity $\mathbf{v}$ if at any time t we have $\boldsymbol{\sigma}(t) = \boldsymbol{\zeta}_1(t) + \boldsymbol{\zeta}_2(t) + ... + \boldsymbol{\zeta}_{n(t)}(t) \le \mathbf{v}$. We refer to the list items $\boldsymbol{\zeta}_k(t)$ as *resource allocations*, and to $\boldsymbol{\sigma}(t)$ as the *vector of allocated totals* at time t. The difference $\mathbf{v} - \boldsymbol{\sigma}(t)$ represents a vector of idle resources available to arriving customers.

Note that the constraint on the list length $n(t) \le L$ can be easily integrated into the list itself by adding a zeroth component equal to 1 to each resource allocation vector, $\tilde{\boldsymbol{\zeta}}_k(t)(t) = \big(1, \zeta_{1,k}(t), ..., \zeta_{M,k}(t)\big)$, and a zeroth component equal to L to the capacity vector, $\tilde{v} = (L, v_1, ..., v_M)$. This is illustrated by an example in Fig. 8.1, where the list shown in Fig. 8.1b is equivalent to the list in Fig. 8.1a with the length constraint integrated into the list.

$$\overbrace{\left(\begin{bmatrix}1\\3\\2\end{bmatrix},\begin{bmatrix}5\\2\\1\end{bmatrix},\dots,\begin{bmatrix}4\\3\\4\end{bmatrix}\right)}^{L}\quad\begin{bmatrix}v_1\\v_2\\v_3\end{bmatrix}$$

a)

$$\left(\begin{bmatrix}1\\1\\3\\2\end{bmatrix},\begin{bmatrix}1\\5\\2\\1\end{bmatrix},\dots,\begin{bmatrix}1\\4\\3\\4\end{bmatrix}\right)\quad\begin{bmatrix}L\\v_1\\v_2\\v_3\end{bmatrix}$$

b)

Fig. 8.1 Examples of lists of resource allocations with separate (**a**) and integrated (**b**) length constraint

Let us denote by a_k, $k = 1, 2, \dots$, the insertion times, i.e., such times that $n(a_k) = n(a_k - 0) + 1$, and by b_k, $k = 1, 2, \dots$, the deletion times, i.e., such times that $n(b_k) = n(b_k - 0) - 1$. The item being inserted at time a_k is denoted by $\mathbf{r}_k = \sigma(a_k) - \sigma(a_k - 0)$. If the i-th element $r_k(i)$ of $\mathbf{r}_k$ is positive, then the amount of idle resources of type i decreases when $\mathbf{r}_k$ is inserted and increases when $\mathbf{r}_k$ is deleted. If, on the contrary, $r_k(i) < 0$ then the amount of idle type i resources increases when $\mathbf{r}_k$ is inserted and decreases upon its deletion. Thus, vectors with negative entries, while present in a list, increase the capacity of resources of the corresponding types. In our hairdresser example, a negative allocation can represent a customer bringing some extra magazines and making them available to other customers in the waiting room. The extra magazines are, however, taken away once the customer who has brought them leaves the salon.

Let α_k represent the index of the position at which, at time a_k, an item $\mathbf{r}_k$ is inserted, $1 \le \alpha_k \le n(a_k - 0) + 1$, and let β_k represent the index of the position at which, at time b_k, an item is deleted, $1 \le \beta_k \le n(b_k - 0)$. Parameters α_k and β_k determine the positions of inserted and deleted list items. For example, under the first-in-first-out (FIFO) discipline, we would insert each element at the last position, i.e., $\alpha_k = n(a_k - 0) + 1$, and always delete the first element, i.e., $\beta_k = 1$. Conversely, under the last-in-first-out (LIFO) discipline, we would insert each element last, i.e., $\alpha_k = n(a_k - 0) + 1$, but we would also delete the last element, i.e., $\beta_n = n(b_n - 0)$.

Since $\sigma(t) \le \mathbf{v}$ for all t and the maximum length of the list is $L \le \infty$, for an insertion to occur at time a_k we must have $n(a_k - 0) < L$ and $\sigma(a_k - 0) + \mathbf{r}_k \le \mathbf{v}$, i.e., the list length after insertion cannot exceed L and the item to be inserted cannot make the allocated totals exceed the capacity. The conditions for a deletion at time b_k are $n(b_k - 0) > 0$ and $\sigma(b_k - 0) - \boldsymbol{\zeta}_{\beta_k}(b_k - 0) \le \mathbf{v}$, i.e., the list before deletion cannot be empty and, again, the allocated totals after deletion cannot exceed the capacity. The latter is possible if the allocation to be deleted contains negative elements.

The process $\sigma(t)$ is similar to the stochastic storage processes studied in (Prabhu 1998), with a major difference that only the items that are present in the list can be deleted. Consequently, only vectors that have been previously added to $\sigma(t)$ are subtracted. This is why even if we are interested only in the totals of allocated resources, to describe their dynamics we still have to deal with all items in the list.

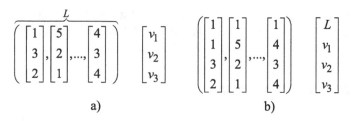

8.2 Pseudo-Lists of Resource Allocations

Stochastic lists of resource allocations $\xi(t)$ fully describe the system under study but are hard to work with. To evaluate the totals of allocated resources, instead of $\xi(t)$, one can use a simpler jump process $(\kappa(t), \boldsymbol{\vartheta}(t))$, which we will refer to as the *pseudo-list of resource allocations* of capacity $\mathbf{v}$. This process has an integer component $\kappa(t) \in \mathbb{N}$, which we will call the pseudo-list's *length*, and a vector component $\boldsymbol{\vartheta}(t) \in \mathbb{R}^M$, called the pseudo-list's *volume*. At any transition of the pseudo-list process, its length $\kappa(t)$ either increases by 1 or decreases by 1. The pseudo-list's volume cannot exceed its capacity, i.e., $\boldsymbol{\vartheta}(t) \leq \mathbf{v}$.

The behavior of a pseudo-list of resource allocations is defined by the sequences of

— insertion times a_k, $k = 1, 2, ...,$ when the length increases, i.e., such that $\kappa(a_k) = \kappa(a_k - 0) + 1$;

— deletion times $b_k, k = 1, 2, ...,$ when the length decreases, i.e., such that $\kappa(b_k) = \kappa(b_k - 0) - 1$;

— vectors $\mathbf{r}_k = \boldsymbol{\vartheta}(a_k) - \boldsymbol{\vartheta}(a_k - 0)$ by which the volume $\boldsymbol{\vartheta}(t)$ increases at times a_k; and

— vectors $\boldsymbol{\delta}_k = \boldsymbol{\vartheta}(b_k - 0) - \boldsymbol{\vartheta}(b_k)$ by which the volume $\boldsymbol{\vartheta}(t)$ decreases at times b_k.

Vector $\boldsymbol{\delta}_k$ corresponds to the item $\boldsymbol{\zeta}_{\beta_k}(b_k - 0)$ of the list of resource allocations $\xi(t)$, deleted from it at time b_k, $k = 1, 2, ...$ However, since pseudo-lists, unlike lists, do not keep track of each resource allocation, $\boldsymbol{\delta}_k$ can only be determined probabilistically, using the probability distribution of $\mathbf{r}_k$.

Assume $\mathbf{r}_k$ to be independent and identically distributed random vectors with a CDF $F(\mathbf{x})$. The CDF $F^{(n)}(\mathbf{x})$ of the sum $\mathbf{r}_1 + \mathbf{r}_2 + ... + \mathbf{r}_n$, which represents the n-fold convolution of the distribution $F(\mathbf{x})$, can be obtained via the recurrence relation

$$F^{(1)}(\mathbf{x}) = F(\mathbf{x}), \; F^{(n)}(\mathbf{x}) = \int\limits_{\mathbf{y} \in \mathbb{R}^M} F^{(n-1)}(\mathbf{x} - \mathbf{y}) F(d\mathbf{y}), \; n > 1.$$

If there exists a pdf $f(\mathbf{x})$ of the CDF $F(\mathbf{x})$, then the CDFs $F^{(n)}(\mathbf{x})$ have pdfs $f^{(n)}(\mathbf{x})$, which are related as follows:

$$f^{(1)}(\mathbf{x}) = f(\mathbf{x}), \; f^{(n)}(\mathbf{x}) = \int\limits_{\mathbf{y} \in \mathbb{R}^M} f^{(n-1)}(\mathbf{x} - \mathbf{y}) f(\mathbf{y}) d\mathbf{y}, \; n > 1.$$

Define now conditional CDFs $F_k(\mathbf{x}|\mathbf{y})$ as

$$F_k(\mathbf{x}|\mathbf{y}) = \mathsf{P}(\boldsymbol{r}_k \leq \mathbf{x} | \mathbf{r}_1 + \mathbf{r}_2 + ... + \mathbf{r}_k = \mathbf{y}), \quad k \geq 1. \tag{8.1}$$

$F_1(\mathbf{x}|\mathbf{y})$ is a CDF of a constant vector $\mathbf{y}$, and it follows from the definition of the conditional probability (Gikhman 1969) that for $k \geq 2$ the function $F_k(\mathbf{x}|\mathbf{y})$ solves

$$\int\limits_{\mathbf{z}\leq\mathbf{y}} \int\limits_{\mathbf{w}\geq\mathbf{z}-\mathbf{x}} F_k(d\mathbf{w}|\mathbf{z})F^{(k)}(d\mathbf{z}) = \int\limits_{\mathbf{z}\leq\mathbf{x}} F(\mathbf{y}-\mathbf{z})F^{(k-1)}(d\mathbf{z}), \ \mathbf{x}, \mathbf{y} \in \mathbb{R}^M. \qquad (8.2)$$

Since $\mathbf{r}_1 + ... + \mathbf{r}_{k-1} \leq \mathbf{x}$ and $\mathbf{r}_k \geq \mathbf{r}_1 + ... + \mathbf{r}_k - \mathbf{x}$ are equivalent, the left-hand and right-hand sides of (8.2) both equal the probability $\mathsf{P}(\mathbf{r}_1 + ... + \mathbf{r}_{k-1} \leq \mathbf{x}, \mathbf{r}_1 + ... + \mathbf{r}_{k-1} \leq \mathbf{y})$. If there exists a pdf $f(\mathbf{x})$ of the CDF $F(\mathbf{x})$, then for such $\mathbf{y}$ that $f^{(k)}(\mathbf{y}) \neq 0$ the CDF $F_k(\mathbf{x}|\mathbf{y})$ has a pdf

$$f_k(\mathbf{x}|\mathbf{y}) = f(\mathbf{x})\frac{f^{(k-1)}(\mathbf{y}-\mathbf{x})}{f^{(k)}(\mathbf{y})}, \ \mathbf{x}, \mathbf{y} \in \mathbb{R}^M. \qquad (8.3)$$

Now, given the state $(n, \mathbf{y})$ of the pseudo-list before deletion time b_k, we assume vector $\boldsymbol{\delta}_k$ to be independent of the pseudo-list's behavior prior to b_k and have the CDF

$$\mathsf{P}(\boldsymbol{\delta}_k \leq \mathbf{x} : \kappa(b_k - 0) = n, \boldsymbol{\vartheta}(b_k - 0) = y) = F_n(\mathbf{x}|\mathbf{y}).$$

Since $F_1(\mathbf{x}|\mathbf{y})$ is the CDF of a constant vector equal to $\mathbf{y}$, $\boldsymbol{\vartheta}(t) = 0$ whenever $\kappa(t) = 0$.

Thus, a pseudo-list of resource allocations $(\kappa(t), \boldsymbol{\vartheta}(t))$ defined above imitates the behavior of the allocated totals $\boldsymbol{\sigma}(t)$ in a list of resource allocations, but, instead of previously inserted vectors $\mathbf{r}_k$, we subtract from $\boldsymbol{\vartheta}(t)$ random vectors $\boldsymbol{\delta}_k$ distributed with the CDFs $F_n(\mathbf{x}|\mathbf{y})$. The latter depend on the pseudo-list's length n and volume $\mathbf{y}$ and are obtained as a solution of (8.2).

The probability distribution of $\boldsymbol{\delta}_k$ can be made simpler, if we discretize the resource allocations as follows. Let vectors $\mathbf{r}_j$ assume, with positive probability, only values of the form $\mathbf{Dk} = (k_1\Delta_1, k_2\Delta_2, ..., k_M\Delta_M)$, where $\mathbf{k} = (k_1, k_2, ..., k_M)$ is an integer-valued vector and $\mathbf{D}$ is a diagonal matrix of order M with diagonal entries $\Delta_i > 0$. The latter gives the value of the allocation unit for type i resources. For example, if $\Delta_i = 0.1$, then only amounts $k\times 0.1$, $k \in \mathbb{Z}$, of type i resources can be requested and allocated.

Denote $p(\mathbf{i}) = \mathsf{P}\big(\mathbf{r}_j = \mathbf{Di}\big)$ and

$$p^{(k)}(\mathbf{j}) = \mathsf{P}(\mathbf{r}_1 + ... + \mathbf{r}_k = \mathbf{Dj}) = \sum_{\mathbf{i}\in\mathbb{Z}^M} p^{(k-1)}(\mathbf{j}-\mathbf{i})p(\mathbf{i}), \quad \mathbf{j} \in \mathbb{Z}^M.$$

Then, for such $\mathbf{j} \in \mathbb{Z}^M$ that $p^{(k)}(\mathbf{j}) > 0$, the conditional probabilities $p_k(\mathbf{i}|\mathbf{j}) = \mathsf{P}(\mathbf{r}_k = \mathbf{Di} : \mathbf{r}_1 + \mathbf{r}_2 + ... + \mathbf{r}_k = \mathbf{Dj})$ are given by

$$p_k(\mathbf{i}|\mathbf{j}) = p(\mathbf{i})\frac{p^{(k-1)}(\mathbf{j}-\mathbf{i})}{p^{(k)}(\mathbf{j})}, \quad \mathbf{i}, \mathbf{j} \in \mathbb{Z}^M. \tag{8.4}$$

8.3 Two Models of a Multi-Resource Loss System with Random Resource Requirements

Consider a ReLS with L servers, a Poisson arrival process of rate λ and service times exponentially distributed with parameter μ. Assume the system to possess M types of resources, each of which has a limited service capacity. Let each customer require a random, possibly negative, amount of each resource. A customer is lost if upon its arrival the idle service capacity of some resource is less than the amount requested. If the customer is admitted for service, it is allocated the requested resource amounts for the duration of its service time, which makes the idle service capacity of each resource decrease by the same amount. When the customer departs the system, resource allocations are released.

Denote by v_m the total service capacity of type m resources, $\mathbf{v} = (v_1, v_2, ..., v_M)$, and by $\mathbf{r}_j = (r_{j,1}, r_{j,2}, ..., r_{j,M})$ the vector of resource amounts requested by the j-th customer (numbered in order of arrival), $j = 1, 2, ...$ We assume the resource requirement vectors $\mathbf{r}_j$ independent (mutually and of the arrival and service processes) and identically distributed with a CDF $F(\mathbf{x})$, $F(\mathbf{v}) > 0$. Lastly, we denote by S the support of $F(\mathbf{x})$, i.e., the smallest closed set to which vectors $\mathbf{r}_j$ belong with probability 1.

8.3.1 Modeling by a List of Resource Allocations

When modeling a ReLS by a list of resource allocations, we assume that the exact amounts of allocated resources are released upon a departure. In other words, once service is completed, the idle service capacity of each resource increases by the amount of this resource that has been allocated to the departing customer upon its arrival. The state of the system at time t is described by a list of resource allocations $\xi(t) = (\boldsymbol{\zeta}_1(t), \boldsymbol{\zeta}_2(t), ..., \boldsymbol{\zeta}_{n(t)}(t))$ of capacity $\mathbf{v}$, which consists of vectors $\boldsymbol{\zeta}_i(t)$ representing the resource amounts allocated to customers in service. The length $n(t)$ of the list equals the number of customers in service. The items of the list are numbered in the order of decreasing residual service times of the corresponding customers.

The stochastic process $\xi(t)$ is a jump Markov process (Gikhmans 1969). The set of states of the process $\xi(t)$ consists of all vectors $(\mathbf{x}_1, ..., \mathbf{x}_n) \in \bar{S} = \bigcup_{k=0}^{L} S^k$ satisfying the inequality $\mathbf{x}_1 + ... + \mathbf{x}_n \leq \mathbf{v}$. Transitions of $\xi(t)$ can only occur at times τ_i of either arrivals or departures. Consider an interval between consecutive transitions (τ_{i-1}, τ_i)

and let in this interval $\xi(t) = (\mathbf{c}_1,...,\mathbf{c}_k)$. The length of the interval is exponentially distributed with parameter $\lambda + k\mu$. Once it is over, either an arrival occurs with probability $\frac{\lambda}{\lambda+k\mu}$, or a departure with probability $\frac{k\mu}{\lambda+k\mu}$.

Let us first consider the case when τ_i is an arrival time. Let $\mathbf{r}$ represent the resource requirement of the arriving customer and denote by $\mathbf{c}$ the vector of allocated totals at this time instant: $\mathbf{c} = \mathbf{c}_1 + \mathbf{c}_2 + ... + \mathbf{c}_k$. Since the residual service times and the service time of the arriving customer are mutually independent and identically exponentially distributed, the arriving customer, if admitted, can receive one of $k+1$ possible index numbers with equal probability. If the arriving customer finds less than L customers in service and $\mathbf{c} + \mathbf{r} \leq \mathbf{v}$, then it receives service, and the process $\xi(t)$, with probability $\frac{1}{k+1}$, jumps into one of $k+1$ states: $(\mathbf{r}, \mathbf{c}_1, \mathbf{c}_2, ..., \mathbf{c}_k)$, $(\mathbf{c}_1, \mathbf{r}, \mathbf{c}_2, ..., \mathbf{c}_k)$, ..., $(\mathbf{c}_1, \mathbf{c}_2, ..., \mathbf{c}_k, \mathbf{r})$. If, conversely, either $k = L$ or the inequality $\mathbf{c} + \mathbf{r} \leq \mathbf{v}$ is violated, the customer is lost and the process state remains unchanged.

Now, let τ_i be a departure time. Since the customers in service are numbered in the order of decreasing residual service times, the departing customer has the largest number. Then, if $\mathbf{c} - \mathbf{c}_k \leq \mathbf{v}$, the customer departs the system, and the process $\xi(t)$ jumps to state $(\mathbf{c}_1, \mathbf{c}_2, ..., \mathbf{c}_{k-1})$. Otherwise, no transition occurs at time τ_i.

We assume that the times of customer arrival to the empty system are the regeneration points of the process $\xi(t)$. Due to exponential distribution of the idle period, the cycle length has nonlattice distribution. In such case, there exists the limiting distribution of $\xi(t)$ (Asmussen 2003):

$$p_0 = \lim_{t\to\infty} \mathsf{P}(n(t) = 0),$$

$$P_k(\mathbf{x}_1, \mathbf{x}_2, ..., \mathbf{x}_k) = \lim_{t\to\infty} \mathsf{P}(\mathrm{n}(t) = k, \zeta_1(t) \leq \mathbf{x}_1, \zeta_2(t) \leq \mathbf{x}_2, ..., \zeta_k(t) \leq \mathbf{x}_k),$$

$$\mathbf{x}_1, \mathbf{x}_2, ..., \mathbf{x}_k \in \mathbb{R}^M, \ \sum_{i=1}^{k} \mathrm{x}_i \leq \mathbf{v}, \ 1 < k \leq L.$$

It follows from the transitions of the process, which we have studied above, that the limiting distribution of $\xi(t)$ solves the system of equilibrium equations:

$$\lambda F(\mathbf{v}) p_0 = \mu P_1(\mathbf{v}); \tag{8.5}$$

$$\lambda \int\limits_{\mathbf{y}_1 \leq \mathbf{x}_1} F(\mathbf{v} - \mathbf{y}_1) P_1(d\mathbf{y}_1) + \mu P_1(\mathbf{x}_1) =$$

$$= \lambda F(\mathbf{x}_1) p_0 + 2\mu \int\limits_{\substack{\mathbf{y}_1 \leq \mathbf{x}_1 \\ \mathbf{y}_2 \leq \mathbf{v} - \mathbf{y}_1}} P_2(d\mathbf{y}_1, d\mathbf{y}_2), \mathbf{x}_1 \leq \mathbf{v};$$

(8.6)

$$\lambda \int\limits_{\substack{\mathbf{y}_i \le \mathbf{x}_i,\ i=1,2,\ \dots,k+ \\ \mathbf{y}_1+\dots+\mathbf{y}_k \le \mathbf{v}}} F(\mathbf{v}-\mathbf{y}_1-\mathbf{y}_2-\dots-\mathbf{y}_k)P_k(d\mathbf{y}_1, d\mathbf{y}_2, \dots, d\mathbf{y}_k)+$$

$$+\ k\mu \int\limits_{\substack{\mathbf{y}_i \le \mathbf{x}_i,\ i=1,2,\dots,k \\ \mathbf{y}_1+\dots+\mathbf{y}_{k-1} \le \mathbf{v}}} P_{k+1}(d\mathbf{y}_1,\ \dots, d\mathbf{y}_{k-1}, d\mathbf{y}_k) = \tag{8.7}$$

$$= \frac{\lambda}{k}\sum_{i=1}^{k} P_{k-1}(\mathbf{x}_1,\ \dots, \mathbf{x}_{i-1}, \mathbf{x}_{i+1},\ \dots, \mathbf{x}_k)F(\mathbf{x}_i)+$$

$$+\ (k+1)\mu \int\limits_{\substack{\mathbf{y}_i \le \mathbf{x}_i,\ i=1,2,\ \dots,k \\ \mathbf{y}_{k+1} \le \mathbf{v}-\mathbf{y}_1-\dots-\mathbf{y}_k}} P_{k+1}(d\mathbf{y}_1,\ \dots, d\mathbf{y}_k, d\mathbf{y}_{k+1}),$$

$$L\mu \int\limits_{\substack{\mathbf{y}_i \le \mathbf{x}_i,\ i=1,2,\dots,L \\ \mathbf{y}_1+\dots+\mathbf{y}_{L-1} \le \mathbf{v}}} P_{k+1}(d\mathbf{y}_1, \dots, d\mathbf{y}_{L-1}, d\mathbf{y}_L) =$$

$$= \frac{\lambda}{L}\sum_{i=1}^{L} P_{L-1}(\mathbf{x}_1, \dots, \mathbf{x}_{i-1}, \mathbf{x}_{i+1}, \dots, \mathbf{x}_L)F(\mathbf{x}_i),\ \sum_{i=1}^{L}\mathbf{x}_i \le \mathbf{v}. \tag{8.8}$$

One checks by substitution that the solution of this system that satisfies the normalizing condition

$$p_0 + \sum_{k=1}^{L} \int\limits_{\mathbf{x}_1+\mathbf{x}_2+\dots+\mathbf{x}_k \le \mathbf{v}} P_k(d\mathbf{x}_1, d\mathbf{x}_2,\ \dots, d\mathbf{x}_k) = 1$$

is of the form

$$p_0 = \left(1 + \sum_{k=1}^{L} F^{(k)}(\mathbf{v})\frac{\rho^k}{k!}\right)^{-1}, \tag{8.9}$$

$$P_k(\mathbf{x}_1, \mathbf{x}_2,\ \dots, \mathbf{x}_k) = p_0\frac{\rho^k}{k!}F(\mathbf{x}_1)F(\mathbf{x}_2)\dots F(\mathbf{x}_k), \tag{8.10}$$

$$\mathbf{x}_1, \mathbf{x}_2,\ \dots, \mathbf{x}_k \in \mathbb{R}^M,\ \sum_{i=1}^{k}\mathbf{x}_i \le \mathbf{v},\ 1 < k \le L,$$

where $\rho = \lambda/\mu$.

Now, denote by $\boldsymbol{\sigma}(t) = \sum\limits_{i=1}^{n(t)} \boldsymbol{\zeta}_i(t)$ the vector of the allocated totals at time t. It follows from (8.10) that the process $X(t) = (n(t), \boldsymbol{\sigma}(t))$ has the stationary distribution

$$Q_k(\mathbf{x}) = \lim_{t\to\infty} \mathsf{P}(n(t) = k\,;\ \boldsymbol{\sigma}(t) \le \mathbf{x}) = p_0 F^{(k)}(\mathbf{x})\frac{\rho^k}{k!}, \tag{8.11}$$

$$\mathbf{x} \in \mathbb{R}^M, \quad \mathbf{x} \le \mathbf{v}, \quad 1 \le k \le L.$$

By using the above, we can compute the blocking probability as

$$B = 1 - p_0 \sum_{k=0}^{L-1} F^{(k+1)}(\mathbf{v})\frac{\rho^k}{k!} \tag{8.12}$$

and the mean of the allocated totals as

$$\mathbf{b} = p_0 \sum_{k=1}^{L} \mathbf{b}_k \frac{\rho^k}{k!}, \quad \mathbf{b}_k = \int_{\mathbf{x}\le\mathbf{v}} \mathbf{x} F^{(k)}(d\mathbf{x}). \tag{8.13}$$

Note also that if a pdf $f(\mathbf{x})$ of the CDF $F(\mathbf{x})$ exists, then the k-fold convolution $F^{(k)}(\mathbf{x})$ has a pdf $f^{(k)}(\mathbf{x})$ and, consequently, there exist pdfs of the distributions $P_k(\mathbf{x}_1, \mathbf{x}_2, ..., \mathbf{x}_k)$ and $Q_k(\mathbf{x})$.

8.3.2 Modeling by a Pseudo-List of Resource Allocations

Let us now show how the same loss system can be described using a pseudo-list of resource allocations. When modeling a loss system by a pseudo-list $Y(t) = (\kappa(t), \boldsymbol{\vartheta}(t))$, it is assumed that, at a departure time τ_i, the pseudo-list's volume $\boldsymbol{\vartheta}(t)$, representing the allocated totals in the system under study, decreases by a random vector $\boldsymbol{\delta}_i = (\delta_{i,1}, \delta_{i,2}, ..., \delta_{i,M})$. Given the number of customers in service and the allocated totals, $\boldsymbol{\delta}_i$ is independent of the system's behavior prior to τ_i and has a CDF

$$\mathsf{P}(\boldsymbol{\delta}_i \le \mathbf{x} | \kappa(\tau_i - 0) = k\,;\ \boldsymbol{\vartheta}(\tau_i - 0) = y) = F_k(\mathbf{x}|\mathbf{y})$$

that solves (8.2).

We assume that the times of customer arrival to the state $(0, \mathbf{0})$ are the regeneration points of the process $Y(t)$. Due to exponential distribution of the idle period, the cycle length has nonlattice distribution. In such case, there exists the limiting distribution of $Y(t)$ (Asmussen 2003):

$$\tilde{p}_0 = \lim_{t\to\infty} \mathsf{P}(\kappa(t) = 0),$$

$$\tilde{Q}_k(x) = \lim_{t\to\infty} \mathsf{P}(\kappa(t) = k;\ \boldsymbol{\vartheta}(t) \leqslant \mathbf{x}),\ \mathbf{x} \in \mathbb{R}^M,\ 1 \leqslant k \leqslant L.$$

In our case, the limiting distribution of the pseudo-list $(\kappa(t), \boldsymbol{\vartheta}(t))$ solves the system of equilibrium equations

$$\lambda F(\mathbf{v})\tilde{p}_0 = \mu \tilde{Q}_1(\mathbf{v}); \tag{8.14}$$

$$\begin{gathered}\lambda \int\limits_{\mathbf{y}\leq\mathbf{x}} F(\mathbf{v}-\mathbf{y})\tilde{Q}_1(d\mathbf{y}) + \mu\tilde{Q}_1(\mathbf{x}) = \\ \lambda F(\mathbf{x})\tilde{p}_0 + 2\mu \int\limits_{\substack{\mathbf{y}\leq\mathbf{v}\\ \mathbf{y}-\mathbf{z}\leq\mathbf{x}}} F_2(d\mathbf{z}|\mathbf{y})\tilde{Q}_2(d\mathbf{y}), \quad \mathbf{x}\leq\mathbf{v};\end{gathered} \tag{8.15}$$

$$\begin{aligned}&\lambda \int\limits_{\mathbf{y}\leq\mathbf{x}} F(\mathbf{v}-\mathbf{y})\tilde{Q}_k(d\mathbf{y}) + k\mu \int\limits_{\substack{\mathbf{y}\leq\mathbf{v}\\ \mathbf{y}-\mathbf{z}\leq\mathbf{x}}} F_k(d\mathbf{z}|\mathbf{y})\tilde{Q}_k(d\mathbf{y}) = \lambda \int\limits_{\mathbf{y}\leq\mathbf{x}} F(\mathbf{x}-\mathbf{y})\tilde{Q}_{k-1}(d\mathbf{y}) \\ &+ \ (k+1)\mu \int\limits_{\substack{\mathbf{y}\leq\mathbf{v}\\ \mathbf{y}-\mathbf{z}\leq\mathbf{x}}} F_{k+1}(d\mathbf{z}|\mathbf{y})\tilde{Q}_{k+1}(d\mathbf{y}), \quad \mathbf{x}\leq\mathbf{v}, \quad 1<k<L,\end{aligned} \tag{8.16}$$

$$L\mu \int\limits_{\substack{\mathbf{y}\leq\mathbf{v}\\ \mathbf{y}-\mathbf{z}\leq\mathbf{x}}} F_L(d\mathbf{z}|\mathbf{y})\tilde{Q}_L(d\mathbf{y}) = \lambda \int\limits_{\mathbf{y}\leq\mathbf{x}} F(\mathbf{x}-\mathbf{y})\tilde{Q}_{L-1}(d\mathbf{y}), \ \mathbf{x}\leq\mathbf{v}. \tag{8.17}$$

By substituting in the above identities p_0 for $\tilde{p}_0$ and $Q_k(\mathbf{x})$ for $\tilde{Q}_k(\mathbf{x})$, where p_0 and $Q_k(\mathbf{x})$ are given, respectively, by (8.9) and (8.11), and then by making use of (8.2) with $\mathbf{y} = \mathbf{v}$, we obtain that $\tilde{p}_0 = p_0$ and $\tilde{Q}_k(\mathbf{x}) = Q_k(\mathbf{x})$ solve (8.14–8.17).

Thus, we have proved that, when modeling a loss system using lists and pseudo-lists of resource allocations, the stationary distributions of the allocated totals coincide and are given by (8.9) and (8.11).

References

Asmussen, S.: Applied probability and queues, 2nd edn. Springer-Verlag, New York (2003)

Gelenbe, E.: Product-form queuing networks with negative and positive customers. J. App. Prob. 28(3), 656–663 (1991)

Gelenbe, E., Glynn, P., Sigman, K.: Queues with negative arrivals, J. App. Prob. 28, 245–250 (1991)

Gikhman, I.I., Skorokhod, A.V.: Introduction to the theory of random processes. Dover Publications, New York (1969)

Knuth, D.E.: The art of computer programming: fundamental algorithms, 3rd edn. Addison-Wesley, Berkeley (1997)

Le Boudec, J.-Y.: Performance evaluation of computer and communication systems. EPFL Press, Lausanne (2010)
Prabhu, N.U.: Stochastic storage processes: queues, insurance risk, dams, and data communication, 2nd edn. Springer-Verlag, New York (1998)

Chapter 9
The Multi-Resource Service System with Service Times Dependent on the Required Amounts of Resources

Abstract In this chapter, we show how multi-class loss networks can be used to study ReLS in which the service time of a customer depends on its required resource amounts. We demonstrate that for each such loss system there exists a loss system having the same stationary distribution but whose service times are exponentially distributed and independent of resource requirements.

9.1 An Auxiliary Loss Network

Consider a loss network (Naumov 2017) consisting of multiple nodes connected by links. Denote by M the total number of links and by $c(m)$ the capacity of link m, $\mathbf{c} = (c(1), c(2), ..., c(M))$. User sessions of $h = h_1 + ... + h_K$ different classes can be established between the network's nodes. Every session class (k, l), $l = 1, ..., h_k$, $k = 1, ..., K$, is characterized by its capacity requirements $\mathbf{c}_{k,l} = (c_{k,l}(1), c_{k,l}(2), ..., c_{k,l}(M))$, where $c_{k,l}(m)$ is the number of capacity units (channels) required by a class (k, l) session on link m. We assume that requests for establishing class (k, l) sessions arrive according to a Poisson process with rate $\lambda_{k,l}$, while the mean session duration is $m_{k,l}$. If an arriving request for establishing a session finds an insufficient number of idle channels on some link, or the maximum number L of simultaneously established sessions is reached, then the request is blocked and lost.

Denote by $\nu_{k,l}(t)$ the number of established class (k, l) sessions at time t, $\boldsymbol{\nu}(t) = (\nu_{1,1}(t), ..., \nu_{1,h_1}(t), ..., \nu_{K,1}(t), ..., \nu_{K,h_K}(t))$. The state space S of the process $\boldsymbol{\nu}(t)$ contains all nonnegative integer-valued vectors $\mathbf{n} = (n_{1,1}, ..., n_{1,h_1}, ..., n_{K,1}, ..., n_{K,h_K})$ such that

$$\sum_{k=1}^{K}\sum_{l=1}^{h_k} n_{k,l} \le L, \quad \sum_{k=1}^{K}\sum_{l=1}^{h_k} n_{k,l}\mathbf{c}_{k,l} \le \mathbf{c}.$$

The stationary state distribution $q(n_{1,1}, ..., n_{1,h_1}, ..., n_{K,1}, ..., n_{K,h_K})$ of $\boldsymbol{\nu}(t)$ depends on the probability distribution of session durations only through their means

V. Naumov et al., *Matrix and Analytical Methods for Performance Analysis of Telecommunication Systems*, https://doi.org/10.1007/978-3-030-83132-5_9

and is given by the relations (Ross 1995)

$$q(n_{1,1},\ ...,n_{1,h_1},\ ...,n_{K,1},\ ...,n_{K,h_K}) = \frac{1}{Q}\prod_{k=1}^{K}\prod_{l=1}^{h_k}\frac{\rho_{k,l}^{n_{k,l}}}{n_{k,l}!}, \tag{9.1}$$

$$(n_{1,1},\ ...,n_{1,h_1},...,n_{K,1},\ ...,n_{K,h_K}) \in \mathbf{S},$$

where $\rho_{k,l} = \lambda_{k,l}m_{k,l}$ and

$$Q = \sum_{(n_{1,1},...,n_{1,h_1},...,n_{K,1},...,n_{K,h_K})\in S}\prod_{k=1}^{K}\prod_{l=1}^{h_k}\frac{\rho_{k,l}^{n_{k,l}}}{n_{k,l}!}. \tag{9.2}$$

Now, define a class k of sessions as a union of classes $(k, l), l = 1,\ ...,h_k$. Denote by $n_k(t) = \nu_{k,1}(t)+...+\nu_{k,h_k}(t)$ the number of established sessions of the combined class k and let $\boldsymbol{\theta}_k(t) = \nu_{k,1}(t)\mathbf{c}_{k,1} + ... + \nu_{k,h_k}(t)\mathbf{c}_{k,h_k}$ represent the vector of link capacities allocated to class k sessions at time t. Also, let $\rho_k = \rho_{k,1} + ... + \rho_{k,h_k}$, $\mathcal{C}_k = \{\mathbf{c}_{k,1},\ ...,\mathbf{c}_{k,h_k}\}$ and

$$\mathcal{Z}_{k,n}(\mathbf{i}) = \{(z_1,\ ...,z_{hk}) \in \mathbb{N}^{h_k} : z_1 + ... + z_{h_K} = n, z_1c_{k,1} + ... + z_{h_k}c_{k,h_k} = \mathbf{i}\}.$$

The stationary distribution of the aggregated process $X(t) = (n_1(t),\ ...,n_K(t); \boldsymbol{\theta}_1(t),\ ...,\boldsymbol{\theta}_K(t))$,

$$p_{n_1,...,n_K}(\mathbf{i}_1,\ ...,\mathbf{i}_K) = \lim_{t\to\infty}\mathsf{P}\{n_1(t) = n_1,\ ...,n_K(t) =$$

$$= n_K; \boldsymbol{\theta}_1(t) = \mathbf{i}_1,\ ...,\boldsymbol{\theta}_K(t) = \mathbf{i}_K), \tag{9.3}$$

$$n_1,\ ...,n_K \in \mathbb{N},\ \ n_1 + ... + n_K \le L,\ \ \mathbf{i}_1,\ ...,\mathbf{i}_K \in \mathbb{N}^M,\ \mathbf{i}_1 + ... + \mathbf{i}_K \le \mathbf{c}, \tag{9.4}$$

is related to the distribution (9.1)–(9.2) of the original process $\boldsymbol{\nu}(t)$ as

$$p_{n_1,...,n_K}(\mathbf{i}_1,\ ...,\mathbf{i}_K) = \sum_{\substack{(n_{1,1},...,n_{1,h_1},...,n_{K,1},...,n_{K,h_K})\in S\\ (n_{1,1},...,n_{1,h_1})\in\mathcal{Z}_{1,n_1}(\mathbf{i}_1),\ ...,\\ (n_{K,1},...,n_{K,h_K})\in\mathcal{Z}_{K,n_K}(\mathbf{i}_K)}} q(n_{1,1},\ ...,n_{1,h_1},\ ...,n_{K,1},\ ...,n_{K,h_K}). \tag{9.5}$$

For $n_1,\ ...,n_K$ and $\mathbf{i}_1,\ ...,\mathbf{i}_K$ that satisfy constraints (9.4), vector $(n_{1,1},\ ...,n_{1,h_1},\ ...,n_{K,1},\ ...,n_{K,h_K})$ belongs to the set S whenever $(n_{1,1},\ ...,n_{1,h_1}) \in \mathcal{Z}_{1,n_1}(\mathbf{i}_1),\ ...,(n_{K,1},\ ...,n_{K,h_K}) \in \mathcal{Z}_{K,n_K}(\mathbf{i}_K)$. The condition $(n_{1,1},\ ...,n_{1,h_1},\ ...,n_{K,1},\ ...,n_{K,h_K}) \in S$ in (9.5) can hence be omitted. Thus, we have

$$p_{n_1,\ldots,n_K}(\mathbf{i}_1,\ \ldots,\mathbf{i}_K)Q = \sum_{\substack{(n_{1,1},\ldots,n_{1,h_1})\in\mathcal{Z}_{1,n_1}(\mathbf{i}_1),\ \ldots,\\ (n_{K,1},\ldots,n_{K,h_K})\in\mathcal{Z}_{K,n_K}(\mathbf{i}_K)}} \prod_{k=1}^{K}\left(\frac{\rho_{k,1}^{n_{k,1}}}{n_{k,1}!}\cdots\frac{\rho_{k,h_k}^{n_{k,h_k}}}{n_{k,h_k}!}\right) =$$

$$= \sum_{\substack{(n_{1,1},\ldots,n_{1,h_1})\in\mathcal{Z}_{1,n_1}(\mathbf{i}_1),\ldots,\\ (n_{K,1},\ldots,n_{K,h_K})\in\mathcal{Z}_{K,n_K}(\mathbf{i}_K)}} \prod_{k=1}^{K}\left(\frac{n_k!}{n_{k,1}!\cdots n_{k,h_k}!}\left(\frac{\rho_{k,1}}{\rho_k}\right)^{n_{k,1}}\cdots\left(\frac{\rho_{k,h_k}}{\rho_k}\right)^{n_{k,h_k}}\frac{\rho_k^{n_k}}{n_k!}\right) =$$

$$= \sum_{\substack{(n_{1,1},\ldots,n_{1,h_1})\in\mathcal{Z}_{1,n_1}(\mathbf{i}_1),\ldots,\\ (n_{K,1},\ldots,n_{K,h_K})\in\mathcal{Z}_{K,n_K}(\mathbf{i}_K)}} \left(\frac{n_1!}{n_{1,1}!\cdots n_{1,h_1}!}\left(\frac{\rho_{1,1}}{\rho_1}\right)^{n_{1,1}}\cdots\left(\frac{\rho_{1,h_1}}{\rho_1}\right)^{n_{1,h_1}}\frac{\rho_1^{n_1}}{n_1!}\right)\times\ldots$$

$$\times\left(\frac{n_K!}{n_{K,1}!\cdots n_{K,h_K}!}\left(\frac{\rho_{K,1}}{\rho_K}\right)^{n_{k,1}}\cdots\left(\frac{\rho_{K,h_K}}{\rho_K}\right)^{n_{K,h_K}}\frac{\rho_K^{n_K}}{n_K!}\right) =$$

$$= \left(\sum_{(n_{1,1},\ldots,n_{1,h_1})\in\mathcal{Z}_{1,n_1}(\mathbf{i}_1)} \frac{n_1!}{n_{1,1}!\cdots n_{1,h_1}!}\left(\frac{\rho_{1,1}}{\rho_1}\right)^{n_{1,1}}\cdots\left(\frac{\rho_{1,h_1}}{\rho_1}\right)^{n_{1,h_1}}\frac{\rho_1^{n_1}}{n_1!}\right)\times\ldots$$

$$\times\left(\sum_{(n_{K,1},\ldots,n_{K,h_K})\in\mathcal{Z}_{K,n_K}(\mathbf{i}_K)} \frac{n_K!}{n_{K,1}!\cdots n_{K,h_K}!}\left(\frac{\rho_{K,1}}{\rho_K}\right)^{n_{k,1}}\cdots\left(\frac{\rho_{K,h_K}}{\rho_K}\right)^{n_{K,h_K}}\frac{\rho_K^{n_K}}{n_K!}\right) =$$

$$= \prod_{k=1}^{K}\pi_k^{(n_k)}(\mathbf{i}_k)\frac{\rho_k^{n_k}}{n_k!},$$

where

$$\pi_k^{(n)}(\mathbf{i}) = \sum_{(z_1,\ldots,z_{h_k})\in\mathcal{Z}_{k,n}(\mathbf{i})} \frac{n!}{z_1!\cdots z_{h_k}!}\left(\frac{\rho_{k,1}}{\rho_k}\right)^{z_1}\cdots\left(\frac{\rho_{k,h_k}}{\rho_k}\right)^{z_{h_k}}. \tag{9.6}$$

Similarly, we can rewrite (9.2) for the normalization constant Q:

$$Q = \sum_{(n_{1,1},\ldots,n_{1,h_1},\ldots,n_{K,1},\ldots,n_{K,h_K})\in S}\ \prod_{k=1}^{K}\prod_{l=1}^{h_k}\frac{\rho_{k,l}^{n_{k,l}}}{n_{k,l}!} =$$

$$= \sum_{\substack{n_1,\ldots,n_K\in\mathbb{N}\\ n_1+\ldots+n_K\le L}}\ \sum_{\substack{\mathbf{i}_1,\ldots,\mathbf{i}_K\in\mathbb{N}^M\\ \mathbf{i}_1+\ldots+\mathbf{i}_K\le\mathbf{c}}}\ \prod_{k=1}^{K}\pi_k^{(n_k)}(\mathbf{i}_k)\frac{\rho_k^{n_k}}{n_k!}.$$

Thus, we have proved the following theorem for the joint distribution of the numbers of established sessions and allocated link capacities.

Theorem 9.1 *The stationary distribution of the stochastic process* $X(t) = (n_1(t), ..., n_K(t); \boldsymbol{\theta}_1(t), ..., \boldsymbol{\theta}_K(t))$ *is given by*

$$p_{n_1,...,n_K}(\mathbf{i}_1, ..., \mathbf{i}_K) = \frac{1}{Q} \prod_{k=1}^{K} \pi_k^{(n_k)}(\mathbf{i}_k) \frac{\rho_k^{n_k}}{n_k!}, \tag{9.7}$$

$$n_1, ..., n_K \in \mathbb{N}, n_1 + ... + n_K \le L, \ \mathbf{i}_1, ..., \mathbf{i}_K \in \mathbb{N}^M, \ \mathbf{i}_1 + ... + \mathbf{i}_K \le \mathbf{c},$$

where

$$Q = \sum_{\substack{n_1,...,n_K \in \mathbb{N} \\ n_1+...+n_K \le L}} \sum_{\substack{\mathbf{i}_1,...,\mathbf{i}_K \in \mathbb{N}^M \\ \mathbf{i}_1+...+\mathbf{i}_K \le c}} \prod_{k=1}^{K} \pi_k^{(n_k)}(\mathbf{i}_k) \frac{\rho_k^{n_k}}{n_k!}. \tag{9.8}$$

Now, let a random vector $\boldsymbol{\xi}_k$ takes values $\mathbf{c}_{k,1}, \mathbf{c}_{k,2}, ..., \mathbf{c}_{k,h_k}$ with probabilities $\frac{\rho_{k,1}}{\rho_k}, \frac{\rho_{k,2}}{\rho_k}, ..., \frac{\rho_{k,h_k}}{\rho_k}$, respectively, and let π_k represent its probability distribution

$$\pi_k(\mathbf{i}) = \begin{cases} \frac{\rho_{k,l}}{\rho_k}, & \mathbf{i} = \mathbf{c}_{k,l}, \\ 0, & \mathbf{i} \notin \mathfrak{C}_k. \end{cases} \tag{9.9}$$

Then, $\pi_k^{(n)}$ in (9.6) is the n-fold convolution of the distribution π_k.

9.2 The Multi-Resource System with Service Times Dependent on the Required Amounts of Resources

Consider a multi-resource service system with M types of resources and K customer classes. Let L represent the maximum number of customers that can be in service simultaneously. We assume class k customers to arrive according to a Poisson process of rate λ_k, $\lambda = \lambda_1 + ... + \lambda_K$. Denote by $v(m)$ the total service capacity of the type m resource, $\mathbf{v} = (v(1), v(2), ..., v(M))$. A j-th arriving customer of class k is characterized by its service time $s_{k,j}$ and its resource requirements $\mathbf{r}_{k,j} = (r_{k,j}(1), r_{k,j}(2), ..., r_{k,j}(M))$. Random vectors $(s_{k,j}, \mathbf{r}_{k,j})$ are independent mutually and of the arrival process and have a joint CDF $H_k(t, \mathbf{x}) = \mathsf{P}(s_{k,j} \le t, \mathbf{r}_{k,j} \le \mathbf{x})$, the same for all class k customers. Denote by $F_k(\mathbf{x}) = \mathsf{P}(\mathbf{r}_{k,j} \le \mathbf{x})$ the CDF of the required resource amounts of class k customers and by $B_k(t) = \mathsf{P}(s_{k,j} \le t)$ the CDF of their service times. Let $b_k < \infty$ represent the mean service time and denote $\rho_k = \lambda_k b_k$.

Define a CDF $G_k(\mathbf{x})$ as

$$G_k(\mathbf{x}) = \frac{1}{b_k} \int\limits_{\mathbf{y} \le \mathbf{x}} \int\limits_0^{\infty} t H_k(dt, d\mathbf{y}). \tag{9.10}$$

In order to clarify this definition, consider the conditional mean service time of class k customers given that the vector of required resource amounts equals $\mathbf{x}$. We can define it as a function $b_k(\mathbf{x})$ that satisfies the equation

$$\int\limits_{\mathbf{y} \le \mathbf{x}} \int\limits_0^{\infty} t H_k(dt, d\mathbf{y}) = \int\limits_{\mathbf{y} \le \mathbf{x}} b_k(\mathbf{y}) F_k(d\mathbf{y}) \tag{9.11}$$

for any $\mathbf{x}$, $\mathbf{0} \le \mathbf{x} \le \mathbf{v}$ (Appendix A1.1). Now, by using (9.11) we can rewrite the expression (9.10) for the function $G_k(\mathbf{x})$ as

$$G_k(\mathbf{x}) = \frac{1}{b_k} \int\limits_{\mathbf{y} \le \mathbf{x}} b_k(\mathbf{y}) F_k(d\mathbf{y}). \tag{9.12}$$

Let $n_k(t)$ represent the number of class k customers in service at time t and let $\boldsymbol{\sigma}_k(t)$ be the vector of the total resource amounts allocated to class k customers. We are interested in the limiting distribution of the process $Y(t) = (n_1(t), ..., n_K(t), \boldsymbol{\sigma}_1(t), ..., \boldsymbol{\sigma}_K(t))$:

$$p_0 = \lim_{t \to \infty} \mathsf{P}(n_1(t) = 0, ..., n_K(t) = 0), \tag{9.13}$$

$$P_{n_1,...,n_K}(\mathbf{x}_1, ..., \mathbf{x}_K) = \lim_{t \to \infty} \mathsf{P}(n_1(t) = n_1, ..., n_K(t) = n_K,$$

$$\boldsymbol{\sigma}_1(t) \le \mathbf{x}_1, ..., \boldsymbol{\sigma}_K(t) \le \mathbf{x}_K), \tag{9.14}$$

$$n_1, ..., n_K \in \mathbb{N},\ n_1 + ... + n_K \le L, \quad \mathbf{x}_1 \ge \mathbf{0}, ..., \mathbf{x}_K \ge \mathbf{0}, \quad \mathbf{x}_1 + ... + \mathbf{x}_K \le \mathbf{v}.$$

We will derive these distributions for the case of arithmetic CDFs $F_k(\mathbf{x})$. Then vectors of resource amounts can be written in the form $\mathbf{r}_{k,j} = \mathbf{D}\mathbf{u}_{k,j}$, where $\mathbf{D}$ is a diagonal matrix whose diagonal elements are all positive and $\mathbf{u}_{k,j}$ are nonnegative integer-valued random vectors.

Theorem 9.2 *Let the CDFs $F_k(\mathbf{x})$of the required resource amounts be arithmetic. Then, the stationary distribution of the stochastic process $Y(t)$is of the form*

$$P_{n_1,...,n_K}(\mathbf{x}_1, ..., \mathbf{x}_K) = \frac{1}{Q} \frac{\rho_1^{n_1}}{n_1!} ... \frac{\rho_K^{n_K}}{n_K!} G_1^{(n_1)}(\mathbf{x}_1) \cdots G_K^{(n_K)}(\mathbf{x}_K), \tag{9.15}$$

$$n_1, \ldots, n_K \in N,\ n_1 + \cdots + n_K \le L, \quad \mathbf{x}_1 \ge \mathbf{0}, \ldots, \mathbf{x}_K \ge \mathbf{0}, \quad \mathbf{x}_1 + \cdots + \mathbf{x}_K \le \mathbf{v}.$$

Here, $G_k^{(n)}(\mathbf{x})$is the n-fold convolution of the CDF $G_k(\mathbf{x})$, and

$$Q = \sum_{\substack{n_1, \ldots, n_K \in \mathrm{N} \\ n_1 + \ldots + n_K \le L}} \frac{\rho_1^{n_1}}{n_1!} \cdots \frac{\rho_K^{n_K}}{n_K!} \left(G_1^{(n_1)} * \ldots * G_K^{(n_K)} \right)(\mathbf{v}), \tag{9.16}$$

where $*$ denotes the convolution of the CDFs.

Proof Let the CDFs $F_k(\mathbf{x})$ of the required amounts of resources $\mathbf{r}_{k,j}$ be arithmetic functions with coordinate increments $\Delta(1), \Delta(2), \ldots, \Delta(M) > 0$. Then, vectors $\mathbf{r}_{k,j}$ almost surely assume values of the form $\mathbf{Di} = (i(1)\Delta(1), i(2)\Delta(2), \ldots, i(M)\Delta(M))$, where $\mathbf{i} = (i(1), i(2), \ldots, i(M))$ is a integer-valued vector and $\mathbf{D}$ is a diagonal matrix with diagonal elements $\Delta(m)$. We will refer to $\Delta(m)$ as the unit of service capacity of resource m and denote by $c(m)$ the quotient of dividing $v(m)$ by $\Delta(m)$, $\mathbf{c} = (c(1), c(2), \ldots, c(M))$. Then, the vectors $\mathbf{r}_{k,j}$ and $\boldsymbol{\sigma}_k(t)$ can be written as $\mathbf{r}_{k,j} = \mathbf{D}\mathbf{u}_{k,j}$ and $\boldsymbol{\sigma}_k(t) = \mathbf{D}\boldsymbol{\theta}_k(t)$, where $\mathbf{u}_{k,j}$ and $\boldsymbol{\theta}_k(t)$ are nonnegative integer-valued random vectors that represent, respectively, the required resource amounts and the totals of allocated resources expressed in resource service capacity units.

Denote by $f_k(\mathbf{i})$ the probability that a j-th customer of class k requires a vector $\mathbf{u}_{k,j} = \mathbf{i}$ of resource units. Denote by $m_k(\mathbf{i}) = b_k(\mathbf{Di})$ the conditional mean service time of a class k customer given $\mathbf{u}_{k,j} = \mathbf{i}$. Let us index the elements of the set $\mathfrak{C}_k = \{\mathbf{i} \in \mathbb{N}^M : f_k(\mathbf{i}) > 0\}$ and denote by $\mathbf{c}_{k,l} = \left(c_{k,l}(1), c_{k,l}(2), \ldots, c_{k,l}(M)\right)$ its l-th element, $l = 1, 2, \ldots, h_k$. Using these notations, we can rewrite the CDFs $F_k(\mathbf{x})$ and $G_k(\mathbf{x})$ as

$$F_k(\mathbf{x}) = \sum_{\substack{\mathbf{i} \in \mathfrak{C}_k \\ \mathbf{Di} \le \mathbf{x}}} f_k(\mathbf{i}), \quad G_k(x) = \frac{1}{b_k} \sum_{\substack{\mathbf{i} \in \mathfrak{C}_k \\ \mathbf{Di} \le \mathbf{x}}} f_k(\mathbf{i}) m_k(\mathbf{i}). \tag{9.17}$$

Partition each class k of customers into h_k subclasses so that a class k customer belongs to subclass (k, l) if it requires $\mathbf{u}_{k,l} = \mathbf{c}_{k,l}$ of resources. Class (k, l) customers arrive according to a Poisson process of rate $\lambda_{k,l} = \lambda_k f_k(\mathbf{c}_{k,l})$, while their mean service time is $m_{k,l} = m_k\left(\mathbf{c}_{k,l}\right)$. Now, the limiting distribution of the process $X(t) = (n_1(t), \ldots, n_K(t); \boldsymbol{\theta}_1(t), \ldots, \boldsymbol{\theta}_K(t))$,

$$\begin{aligned} p_{n_1, \ldots, n_K}(\mathbf{i}_1, \ldots, \mathbf{i}_K) = \lim_{t \to \infty} \mathsf{P}(n_1(t) = n_1, \ldots, n_K(t) = n_K; \\ \boldsymbol{\theta}_1(t) = \mathbf{i}_1, \ldots, \boldsymbol{\theta}_K(t) = \mathbf{i}_K), \\ n_1, \ldots, n_K \in \mathbb{N},\ n_1 + \ldots + n_K \le L, \end{aligned} \tag{9.18}$$

$$\mathbf{i}_1, \ldots, \mathbf{i}_K \in \mathbb{N}^M,\ \mathbf{i}_1 + \ldots + \mathbf{i}_K \le \mathbf{c},$$

is given by Theorem 9.1 with the following parameter values in (9.7):

$$\rho_{k,l} = \lambda_{k,l} m_{k,l} = \lambda_k f_k(\mathbf{c}_{k,l}) m_k(\mathbf{c}_{k,l}),$$

$$\rho_k = \sum_{l=1}^{h_k} \lambda_{k,l} m_{k,l} = \lambda_k \sum_{l=1}^{h_k} f_k\left(\mathbf{c}_{k,l}\right) m_k\left(\mathbf{c}_{k,l}\right) = \lambda_k b_k.$$

By using (9.7) we obtain the distribution (9.13):

$$P_{n_1,\ldots,n_K}(\mathbf{x}_1, \ldots, \mathbf{x}_K) = \sum_{\substack{\mathbf{i}_1,\ldots,\mathbf{i}_K \in \mathbb{N}^M \\ \mathbf{D}\mathbf{i}_1 \le \mathbf{x}_1,\ldots,\mathbf{D}\mathbf{i}_K \le \mathbf{x}_K}} p_{n_1,\ldots,n_K}(\mathbf{i}_1, \ldots, \mathbf{i}_K) =$$

$$= \frac{1}{Q} \sum_{\substack{\mathbf{i}_1,\ldots,\mathbf{i}_K \in \mathbb{N}^M \\ \mathbf{D}\mathbf{i}_1 \le \mathbf{x}_1,\ldots,\mathbf{D}\mathbf{i}_K \le \mathbf{x}_K}} \prod_{k=1}^{K} \pi_k^{(n_k)}(i_k) \frac{\rho_k^{n_k}}{n_k!}$$

$$= \frac{1}{Q} \prod_{k=1}^{K} \left(\frac{\rho_k^{n_k}}{n_k!} \sum_{\substack{\mathbf{i}_k \in \mathbb{N}^M \\ \mathbf{D}\mathbf{i}_k \le \mathbf{x}_k}} \pi_k^{(n_k)}(\mathbf{i}_k) \right) =$$

$$= \frac{1}{Q} \prod_{k=1}^{K} \left(\frac{\rho_k^{n_k}}{n_k!} \sum_{\substack{\mathbf{i} \in \mathbf{c}_k \\ \mathbf{D}\mathbf{i} \le \mathbf{x}_k}} \pi_k^{(n_k)}(\mathbf{i}) \right). \tag{9.19}$$

Here, $\pi_k^{(n)}$ is the n-fold convolution of a discrete probability distribution of a random vector $\boldsymbol{\xi}_k$ that assumes values $\mathbf{c}_{k,l}$, $l = 1, 2, \ldots, h_k$, with probabilities

$$\pi_k\left(\mathbf{c}_{k,l}\right) = \frac{\rho_{k,l}}{\rho_k} = \frac{f_k\left(\mathbf{c}_{k,l}\right) m_k\left(\mathbf{c}_{k,l}\right)}{b_k}.$$

This and (9.17) yield the following relations for the CDF of ξ_k :

$$\sum_{\substack{\mathbf{i} \in \mathbf{c}_k \\ \mathbf{D}\mathbf{i} \le \mathbf{x}}} \pi_k(\mathbf{i}) = \frac{1}{b_k} \sum_{\substack{\mathbf{i} \in \mathbf{c}_k \\ \mathbf{D}\mathbf{i} \le \mathbf{x}}} f_k(\mathbf{i}) m_k(\mathbf{i}) = G_k(\mathbf{x}). \tag{9.20}$$

By substituting (9.20) in (9.19) we obtain (9.15). A similar argument proves the relation (9.16) for the normalizing constant Q. ∎

The blocking probabilities can be derived as the complementary probabilities of receiving service.

Corollary *The blocking probability for class k customers is given by*

$$B_k = 1 - \frac{1}{Q} \sum_{\substack{n_1, \dots, n_K \in \mathbb{N} \\ n_1 + \dots + n_K < L}} \frac{\rho_1^{n_1}}{n_1!} \cdots \frac{\rho_K^{n_K}}{n_K!} \left(G_1^{(n_1)} * \dots * G_K^{(n_K)} * F_k \right)(\mathbf{v}). \tag{9.21}$$

Note that for a system under study whose service times and resource requirements are interdependent, there exists a corresponding service system with exponential service times that has the same stationary joint distribution of the number of customers in service and the total amounts of allocated resources. It is a multi-resource queuing system with K Poisson arrival processes of rates $\lambda_1, \dots, \lambda_K$, exponential service times with means $b_1, \dots, b_K$, and resource requirements having CDFs $G_1(\mathbf{x}), \dots, G_K(\mathbf{x})$ which are independent of the service times. In such a system, the stationary joint distribution of the number of customers in service and the totals of allocated resources is also given by (9.15)–(9.16).

Let us see what happens if we merge the arrival streams into one stream of rate $\lambda = \lambda_1 + \dots + \lambda_K$. Each customer of the combined stream belongs to class k with probability λ_k/λ. For the service system with the combined arrival stream we therefore have the joint CDF of the service time and the required resource amounts

$$H(t, \mathbf{x}) = \sum_{k=1}^{K} \frac{\lambda_k}{\lambda} H_k(t, \mathbf{x}),$$

the CDF of the required resource amounts

$$F(\mathbf{x}) = \sum_{k=1}^{K} \frac{\lambda_k}{\lambda} F_k(\mathbf{x}),$$

the CDF of the service times

$$B(t) = \sum_{k=1}^{K} \frac{\lambda_k}{\lambda} B_k(t),$$

and the mean service time

$$b = \sum_{k=1}^{K} \frac{\lambda_k}{\lambda} b_k.$$

All these characteristics are weighted sums of the corresponding class characteristics with weights λ_k/λ. However, for the CDF $G(\mathbf{x})$, which gives the stationary distribution of the total amounts of allocated resources, we have

$$G(\mathbf{x}) = \frac{1}{b} \int\limits_{\mathbf{y} \le \mathbf{x}} \int\limits_{0}^{\infty} t H(dt, d\mathbf{y}) = \frac{1}{\sum\limits_{k=1}^{K} \frac{\lambda_k}{\lambda} b_k} \int\limits_{\mathbf{y} \le \mathbf{x}} \int\limits_{0}^{\infty} t \sum_{k=1}^{K} \frac{\lambda_k}{\lambda} H_k(dt, d\mathbf{y}) =$$

$$= \frac{1}{\sum\limits_{k=1}^{K} \lambda_k b_k} \sum_{k=1}^{K} \frac{\lambda_k b_k}{b_k} \int\limits_{\mathbf{y} \le \mathbf{x}} \int\limits_{0}^{\infty} t H_k(dt, d\mathbf{y}) = \sum_{k=1}^{K} \frac{\rho_k}{\rho} G_k(\mathbf{x}),$$

where $\rho = \rho_1 + \ldots + \rho_K$. Thus, $G(\mathbf{x})$ is a weighted sum of $G_k(\mathbf{x})$ with weights ρ_k / ρ.

References

Ross, K.W.: Multiservice loss models for broadband telecommunication networks. Springer-Verlag (1995)

Naumov, V., Samouylov, K.: Analysis of multi-resource loss system with state dependent arrival and service rates. Probab. Eng. Inf. Sci. **31**(4), 413–419 (2017)

Chapter 10
Markovian Systems with Random Resource Requirements

Abstract In this chapter, we begin by studying a ReLS model whose arrival and service rates depend on the number of customers in service. Then, we consider a ReLS in which arrivals and departures are governed by a Markov chain and obtain the necessary and sufficient conditions for the stationary distribution to have a product form. Finally, a simplified technique to compute the stationary state distribution using Fourier transform is derived.

10.1 Multi-resource Loss Systems with State-Dependent Arrival and Service Rates

10.1.1 System Description

Consider a multi-resource loss system with random resource requirements (ReLS) and K classes of customers. Whenever there are n_k customers of class k in service, class k arrivals form a Poisson process of rate $\lambda_k(n_k)$. An admitted customer begins service immediately, and class k receives service at rate $\mu_k(n_k)$, which is equally shared among the customers of the class. We denote the maximum number of customers allowed in the system simultaneously by L and, for each class k, assume $\mu_k(0) = 0$ and $\lambda_k(n) = 0$ for $n \geq L$.

Let the system have M types of resources of capacities $v_1, v_2, \ldots, v_M$, and let real-valued vectors $\mathbf{r}_j = (r_{j1}, r_{j2}, \ldots, r_{jM})$ denote the resource amounts requested by a customer arriving at time $a_j, j = 1, 2, \ldots$. We assume that the resource requirement vectors $\mathbf{r}_j$ are independent of the arrival and service processes, mutually independent, and, for class k customers, are identically distributed with a CDF $F_k(\mathbf{x})$, $F_k(\mathbf{v}) > 0$. Let S_k denote the support of $F_k(\mathbf{x})$, i.e., the smallest closed set that almost surely contains all resource requests $\mathbf{r}_j$ of class k.

The system behavior can be described by a jump Markov process $\boldsymbol{\xi}(t) = (\boldsymbol{\zeta}_1(t), \boldsymbol{\zeta}_2(t), \ldots, \boldsymbol{\zeta}_K(t))$, where a list of resource allocations $\boldsymbol{\zeta}_k(t) = (\boldsymbol{\zeta}_{k,1}(t), \boldsymbol{\zeta}_{k,2}(t), \ldots, \boldsymbol{\zeta}_{k,n_k(t)}(t))$ contains the vectors of resource allocations to class k customers at time t in the order of their arrival. The length $n_k(t)$ of list $\boldsymbol{\zeta}_k(t)$ is equal to the number of class k customers in service. Let

V. Naumov et al., *Matrix and Analytical Methods for Performance Analysis of Telecommunication Systems*, https://doi.org/10.1007/978-3-030-83132-5_10

$\sigma_k(t) = \zeta_{k,1}(t) + \zeta_{k,2}(t) + \cdots + \zeta_{k,n_k(t)}(t)$ represent the vector of resources occupied by all class k customers in service, and denote $\boldsymbol{n}(t) = (n_1(t), ..., n_K(t))$ and $\sigma(t) = \sigma_1(t) + \cdots + \sigma_K(t)$.

The system operates as follows. At time $t = 0$ the system is empty and $\sigma(0) = \mathbf{0}$. A customer arriving at time a_j receives service only if the total number of customers already in service is less than L and all required resource amounts can be provided, i.e., $\sigma(a_j - 0) + \mathbf{r}_j \le \mathbf{v}$, where $\mathbf{v} = (v_1, v_2, ..., v_M)$. If this is the case, the resource amounts specified by vector $\mathbf{r}_j = (r_{j1}, r_{j2}, ..., r_{jM})$ are allocated to the customer and the process $\sigma(t)$ takes the value $\sigma(a_j) = \sigma(a_j - 0) + \mathbf{r}_j$.

Since we allow for negative resource allocations, we also put constraints on customer departures. We say that the departure of a customer j is *enabled* at time t if $\sigma(t) - \mathbf{r}_j \le \mathbf{v}$, otherwise the customer's departure is *disabled*. If the customer's departure is enabled at the time of service completion, then the customer leaves the system, otherwise the customer restarts service. Upon departure of a customer, the resources allocated to it are released and the corresponding vector $\mathbf{r}_i$ is subtracted from the vector of allocated totals $\sigma(t)$. Thus, the vector of allocated totals $\sigma(t)$ always satisfies the constraint $\sigma(t) \le \mathbf{v}$.

Let $|\mathbf{n}| = n_1 + \cdots + n_K$ denote the sum of the components of a vector $\mathbf{n} = (n_1, n_2, ..., n_K)$, and $\mathcal{J}$ denote the set of all vectors $\mathbf{n} = (n_1, n_2, ..., n_K)$ from $\mathbb{N}^K$ such that $0 < |\mathbf{n}| \le L$. A set $S(\mathbf{n})$ of all possible states of the process $\xi(t)$ depends on the population vector $\mathbf{n} = \boldsymbol{n}(t)$. If $\mathbf{n} = \mathbf{0}$ then the set $S(\mathbf{n})$ consists of the empty list () only. If $|\mathbf{n}| > 0$ then it consists of all row vectors $\mathbf{y} = (\mathbf{y}_{1,1}, ..., \mathbf{y}_{1,n_1}, ..., \mathbf{y}_{K,1}, ..., \mathbf{y}_{K,n_K}) \in S_1^{n_1} \times \cdots \times S_K^{n_K}$ of length $|\mathbf{n}|$ satisfying $\mathbf{y}\mathbf{U} \le \mathbf{v}$, where $\mathbf{U}$ is a block matrix of the form

$$\mathbf{U} = \begin{bmatrix} \mathbf{I} \\ \mathbf{I} \\ \vdots \\ \mathbf{I} \end{bmatrix} \tag{10.1}$$

consisting of $|\mathbf{n}|$ identity matrices $\mathbf{I}$ of order M.

10.1.2 Stationary State Distribution and Performance Measures

We assume that the times of customer arrivals to an empty system are the regeneration points of the process $\xi(t)$. Due to the exponential distribution of the idle period, the cycle length has a nonlattice distribution. In such a case, there exists a limiting distribution of $\xi(t)$ (Asmussen 2003)

$$p_0 = \lim_{t\to\infty} \mathsf{P}(n(t) = \mathbf{0}),$$
$$P_{\mathbf{n}}(\mathbf{x}) = \lim_{t\to\infty} \mathsf{P}(\boldsymbol{n}(t) = \mathbf{n}, \boldsymbol{\xi}(t) \le \mathbf{x}), \quad \mathbf{x} \in S(\mathbf{n}), \quad \mathbf{n} \in \mathcal{J}, \tag{10.2}$$

The following theorem gives the stationary state distribution of the ReLS with state-dependent arrival and service rates.

Theorem 10.1 *Let $F_k^{(n)}(\mathbf{x})$ be the n-fold convolution of the CDF $F_k(\mathbf{x})$ and let functions $\Phi_{\mathbf{n}}(\mathbf{x})$ be defined by*

$$\Phi_{\mathbf{n}}(\mathbf{x}) = \int\limits_{\substack{\mathbf{y}\le\mathbf{x}\\ \mathbf{y}\mathrm{U}\le\mathbf{v}}} F_1(d\mathbf{y}_{1,1})...F_1(d\mathbf{y}_{1,n_1})...F_K(d\mathbf{y}_{K,1})...F_K(d\mathbf{y}_{K,n_K}),$$
$$\mathbf{x} \in \mathbb{R}^{M\,|\mathbf{n}|}, \quad \mathbf{n} \in \mathcal{J}. \tag{10.3}$$

Then, the stationary probability distribution of the process $X(t) = (\boldsymbol{n}(t), \boldsymbol{\xi}(t))$ is given by

$$p_0 = \left(1 + \sum_{\mathbf{n}\in J} (F_1^{(n_1)} * F_2^{(n_2)} * ... * F_K^{(n_K)})(\mathbf{v}) \prod_{k=1}^{K}\prod_{j=1}^{n_k} \frac{\lambda_k(j-1)}{\mu_k(j)}\right)^{-1}, \tag{10.4}$$

$$P_{\mathbf{n}}(\mathbf{x}) = p_0 \Phi_{\mathbf{n}}(\mathbf{x}) \prod_{k=1}^{K}\prod_{j=1}^{n_k} \frac{\lambda_k(j-1)}{\mu_k(j)}, \mathbf{x} \in \mathbb{R}^{M\,|\mathbf{n}|}, \quad \mathbf{n} \in \mathcal{J}. \tag{10.5}$$

Proof The system's state can change only at times t_i, when either an arrival occurs, or the service of one of the customers in the system is completed. Consider the sojourn of the process $\boldsymbol{\xi}(t)$ in state $(\mathbf{y}_1, ..., \mathbf{y}_K)$, where $\mathbf{y}_k = (\mathbf{y}_{k,1}, ..., \mathbf{y}_{k,n_k})$, $k = 1, 2, ..., K$. Each sojourn time of $\boldsymbol{\xi}(t)$ in this state is exponentially distributed with parameter.

$$\gamma(\mathbf{n}) = \sum_{k=1}^{K} \lambda_k(n_k) + \sum_{k=1}^{K} \mu_k(n_k).$$

At the end of such a sojourn, either with probability $\lambda_k(n_k)/\gamma(\mathbf{n})$ an arrival of a class k customer occurs, or with probability $\mu_k(n_k)/\gamma(\mathbf{n})$ the service of a class k customer completes. In the latter case, any class k customer may complete its service with probability $1/n_k$.

Upon a class k customer arrival, process $\boldsymbol{\xi}(t)$ jumps to state $(\mathbf{n}_k+\mathbf{e}_k, \mathbf{y}_1, \ldots, \mathbf{y}_{k-1}, \overline{\mathbf{y}}_k, \mathbf{y}_{k+1}, \ldots, \mathbf{y}_K)$, where $\overline{\mathbf{y}}_k = (\mathbf{y}_{k,1}, ..., \mathbf{y}_{k,n_k}, \mathbf{y}_{k,n_k+1})$. Upon a class k customer departure, process $\boldsymbol{\xi}(t)$ jumps to state $(\mathbf{n}_k - \mathbf{e}_k, \mathbf{y}_1, ..., \mathbf{y}_{k-1}, \tilde{\mathbf{y}}_k, \mathbf{y}_{k+1}, ..., \mathbf{y}_K)$, where vector $\tilde{\mathbf{y}}_k$ is obtained from $\mathbf{y}_k$ by deleting the subvector of resource allocations of one of the enabled class k customers.

The state transitions of the process $\boldsymbol{\xi}(t)$ uniquely determine its infinitesimal transition rates (Gikhman and Skorokhod 1969) and yield the following system of equations for the stationary probability distribution:

$$p_0 \sum_{k=1}^{K} \lambda_j(0) F_j(\mathbf{v}) = \sum_{k=1}^{K} \mu_j(1) P_{\mathbf{e}_j}(\mathbf{v});$$

$$\lambda_k(1) \int\limits_{\mathbf{y}\le\mathbf{x}} F_k(\mathbf{v}-\mathbf{y}) P_{\mathbf{e}_k}(d\mathbf{y}) + \sum_{\substack{i=1\\ i\ne k}}^{K} \lambda_i(0) \int\limits_{\mathbf{y}\le\mathbf{x}} F_i(\mathbf{v}-\mathbf{y}) P_{\mathbf{e}_k}(d\mathbf{y}) + \mu_k(1) P_{\mathbf{e}_k}(\mathbf{x}) =$$

$$= \lambda_k(0) F_k(\mathbf{x}) p_0 + \frac{\mu_k(2)}{2} \Big(\int\limits_{\substack{\mathbf{y}\le\mathbf{x}\\ \mathbf{y}\le\mathbf{v}}} P_{2\mathbf{e}_k}(d\mathbf{y}, d\mathbf{z}) + \int\limits_{\substack{\mathbf{y}\le\mathbf{x}\\ \mathbf{y}\le\mathbf{v}}} P_{2\mathbf{e}_k}(d\mathbf{z}, d\mathbf{y}) \Big) +$$

$$+ \sum_{i=1}^{k-1} \mu_j(1) \int\limits_{\substack{\mathbf{y}\le\mathbf{x}\\ \mathbf{y}\le\mathbf{v}}} P_{\mathbf{e}_k+\mathbf{e}_i}(d\mathbf{y}, d\mathbf{z}) + \sum_{i=k+1}^{K} \mu_j(1) \int\limits_{\substack{\mathbf{y}\le\mathbf{x}\\ \mathbf{y}\le\mathbf{v}}} P_{\mathbf{e}_k+\mathbf{e}_i}(d\mathbf{z}, d\mathbf{y}),$$

$$\mathbf{x} \in \mathbb{R}^M, \quad 1 \le k \le K;$$

$$\sum_{i=1}^{K} \lambda_i(n_i) \int\limits_{\mathbf{y}\le\mathbf{x}} F_i(\mathbf{v}-\mathbf{y}\mathbf{U}) P_{\mathbf{n}}(d\mathbf{y}_{1,1}, \ldots, d\mathbf{y}_{1,n_1}, \ldots, d\mathbf{y}_{K,1}, \ldots, d\mathbf{y}_{K,n_K}) +$$

$$+ \sum_{\substack{i=1\\ n_i\ne 0}}^{K} \frac{\mu_i(n_i)}{n_i} \sum_{j=1}^{n_i} \int\limits_{\substack{\mathbf{y}\le\mathbf{x}\\ \mathbf{y}\mathbf{U}-\mathbf{y}_{i,j}\le\mathbf{v}}} P_{\mathbf{n}}(d\mathbf{y}_{1,1}, \ldots, d\mathbf{y}_{1,n_1}, \ldots, d\mathbf{y}_{K,1}, \ldots, d\mathbf{y}_{K,n_K}) =$$

$$= \sum_{i=1}^{K} \lambda_i(n_i - 1) \int\limits_{\substack{\mathbf{y}\le\mathbf{x}\\ \mathbf{y}\mathbf{U}\le\mathbf{v}}} P_{\mathbf{n}-\mathbf{e}_i}(d\mathbf{y}_{1,1}, \ldots, d\mathbf{y}_{1,n_1}, \ldots, d\mathbf{y}_{i,1}, \ldots, d\mathbf{y}_{i,n_i-1}, \ldots,$$

$$\ldots, d\mathbf{y}_{K,1}, \ldots, d\mathbf{y}_{K,n_K}) F_i(d\mathbf{y}_{i,n_i}) +$$

$$+ \sum_{i=1}^{K} \frac{\mu_i(n_i+1)}{n_i+1} \sum_{j=1}^{n_i+1} \int\limits_{\substack{\mathbf{y}\le\mathbf{x}\\ \mathbf{y}\mathbf{U}\le\mathbf{v}}} P_{\mathbf{n}+\mathbf{e}_i}(d\mathbf{y}_{1,1}, \ldots, d\mathbf{y}_{1,n_1}, \ldots$$

$$\ldots, d\mathbf{y}_{i,1}, \ldots, d\mathbf{y}_{i,j-1}, d\mathbf{z}, d\mathbf{y}_{i,j}, \ldots, d\mathbf{y}_{i,n_k}, \ldots, d\mathbf{y}_{K,1}, \ldots, d\mathbf{y}_{K,n_K}),$$

$$\mathbf{x} \in \mathbb{R}^{M|\mathbf{n}|}, \quad \mathbf{n} \in \mathcal{J}, 1 \le |\mathbf{n}| < L,$$

$$\sum_{\substack{i=1\\ n_i\ne 0}}^{K} \frac{\mu_i(n_i)}{n_i} \sum_{j=1}^{n_i} \int\limits_{\substack{\mathbf{y}\le\mathbf{x}\\ \mathbf{y}\mathbf{U}-\mathbf{y}_{i,j}\le\mathbf{v}}} P_{\mathbf{n}}(d\mathbf{y}_{1,1}, \ldots, d\mathbf{y}_{1,n_1}, \ldots, d\mathbf{y}_{K,1}, \ldots, d\mathbf{y}_{K,n_K}) =$$

$$= \sum_{i=1}^{K} \lambda_i(n_i - 1) \int\limits_{\substack{\mathbf{y} \le \mathbf{x} \\ \mathbf{y}\mathbf{U} - \mathbf{y}_{i,j} \le \mathbf{v}}} P_{\mathbf{n}-\mathbf{e}_i}(d\mathbf{y}_{1,1}, \ldots, d\mathbf{y}_{1,n_1}, \ldots, d\mathbf{y}_{i,1}, \ldots, d\mathbf{y}_{i,n_i-1}, \ldots$$

$$\ldots, d\mathbf{y}_{K,1}, \ldots, d\mathbf{y}_{K,n_K}) F_i(d\mathbf{y}_{i,n_i}), \mathbf{x} \in \mathbb{R}^{ML}, \quad \mathbf{n} \in \mathcal{J}, \ |\mathbf{n}| = L.$$

Now, one can verify by substitution that the solution of these equations that satisfies the normalization condition is given by formulas (10.4)–(10.5). ■

Corollary *The joint stationary probability distribution of the numbers of customers in service* $\boldsymbol{n}(t)$ *and the vectors of allocated totals to classes* $\boldsymbol{\sigma}_1(t), \ldots, \boldsymbol{\sigma}_K(t)$ *is given by*

$$Q_{\mathbf{n}}(\mathbf{x}_1, \ldots, \mathbf{x}_K) = p_0 \Psi_{\mathbf{n}}(\mathbf{x}_1, \ldots, \mathbf{x}_K) \prod_{k=1}^{K} \prod_{j=1}^{n_k} \frac{\lambda_k(j-1)}{\mu_k(j)}, \tag{10.6}$$

$$\mathbf{x}_1, \ldots, \mathbf{x}_K \in \mathbb{R}^M, \quad \mathbf{n} \in \mathcal{J},$$

where functions $\Psi_{\mathbf{n}}(\mathbf{x}_1, \ldots, \mathbf{x}_K)$ *are defined by*

$$\Psi_{\mathbf{n}}(\mathbf{x}_1, \ldots, \mathbf{x}_K) = \int\limits_{\substack{\mathbf{y}_k \le \mathbf{x}_k, k=1, \ldots, K \\ \mathbf{y}_1 + \cdots + \mathbf{y}_K \le \mathbf{v}}} F_1^{(n_1)}(d\mathbf{y}_1) \ldots F_K^{(n_K)}(d\mathbf{y}_K),$$

$$\mathbf{x}_1, \ldots, \mathbf{x}_K \in \mathbb{R}^M, \quad \mathbf{n} \in \mathcal{J} \tag{10.7}$$

Formulas (10.4)–(10.7) permit computing various stationary characteristics of the system. For example, it follows from (10.5) that the blocking probability of class k customers is given by

$$B_k = 1 - \frac{h_k}{g_k},$$

where

$$h_k = p_0 \sum_{\mathbf{n} \in \mathcal{J}} \lambda_k(n_k)(F_1^{(n_1)} * F_2^{(n_2)} * \ldots * F_K^{(n_K)})(\mathbf{v}) \prod_{i=1}^{K} \prod_{j=1}^{n_i} \frac{\lambda_i(j-1)}{\mu_i(j)}$$

is the mean arrival rate, and g_k is the mean acceptance rate of class k customers,

$$g_k = p_0 \sum_{\mathbf{n} \in \mathcal{J}} \lambda_k(n_k)(F_1^{(n_1)} * \cdots * F_{k-1}^{(n_{k-1})} * F_k^{(n_k+1)} * F_{k+1}^{(n_{k+1})} * \cdots * F_K^{(n_K)})(\mathbf{v}) \times$$

$$\times \prod_{i=1}^{K} \prod_{j=1}^{n_i} \frac{\lambda_i(j-1)}{\mu_i(j)} =$$

$$= p_0 \sum_{\mathbf{n} \in \mathcal{J}} \mu_k(n_k)(F_1^{(n_1)} * F_2^{(n_2)} * \cdots * F_K^{(n_K)})(\mathbf{v}) \prod_{i=1}^{K} \prod_{j=1}^{n_i} \frac{\lambda_i(j-1)}{\mu_i(j)}.$$

Note that formulas for functions (10.3) and (10.7) can be simplified for some particular values of the arguments. Thus, we have

$$\Phi_{\mathbf{n}}(\mathbf{x}) = F_1(\mathbf{x}_{1,1}) \cdots F_1(\mathbf{x}_{1,n_1}) \cdots F_K(\mathbf{x}_{K,1}) \cdots F_K(\mathbf{x}_{K,n_K}),$$

whenever $\mathbf{xU} \leq \mathbf{v}$, and

$$\Psi_{\mathbf{n}}(\mathbf{x}_1, \ldots, \mathbf{x}_K) = F_1^{(n_1)}(\mathbf{x}_1) \cdots F_K^{(n_K)}(\mathbf{x}_K),$$

whenever $\sum_{k=1}^{K} \mathbf{x}_k \leq \mathbf{v}$.

10.1.3 Positive and Negative Customers

Assume now that the set of customer classes $\mathcal{K} = \{1, 2, \ldots, K\}$ is partitioned into two disjoint subsets $\mathcal{K}_-$ and $\mathcal{K}_+$ such that the vectors of resource requirements of customers of classes belonging to $\mathcal{K}_-$ are nonpositive, whereas the vectors of resource requirements of customers of classes in $\mathcal{K}_+$ are nonnegative. Then, two types of customers can be considered: positive customers, which belong to classes in $\mathcal{K}_+$, and negative customers belonging to classes in $\mathcal{K}_-$.

The inequality $\boldsymbol{\sigma}(t) \leq \mathbf{v}$ holds for all t, and at the time of arrival of a negative customer we always have $\boldsymbol{\sigma}(a_j - 0) + \mathbf{r}_j \leq \mathbf{v}$. Therefore, if upon a negative customer arrival the system is not full, i.e., $|\mathbf{n}| < L$, then the customer cannot be blocked. Similarly, at a time t of service completion of a positive customer we always have $\boldsymbol{\sigma}(t) - \mathbf{r}_j \leq \mathbf{v}$. Therefore, the departure of a positive customer cannot be disabled and positive customers always depart the system upon service completion.

We can rewrite the inequality $\boldsymbol{\sigma}(t) \leq \mathbf{v}$ as

$$\sum_{k \in \mathcal{K}_+} \boldsymbol{\sigma}_k(t) \leq \mathbf{v} - \sum_{k \in \mathcal{K}_-} \boldsymbol{\sigma}_k(t). \tag{10.8}$$

The left-hand side of (10.8) is the vector of resource amounts allocated to positive customers. It is bounded above by the sum of the vector of resource capacities, $\mathbf{v}$, and the vector of resource amounts allocated to negative customers taken with the opposite sign. Hence, an arrival of a negative customer temporarily increases the amount of resources available to positive customers. If upon service completion of a negative customer the resources brought by it to the system are being used by positive customers, then the departure of the negative customer is disabled and the customer restarts service. The negative customer will be able to depart the system only if its departure becomes enabled after re-servicing.

10.2 Markovian Systems with Random Resource Requirements

10.2.1 Description of a Markovian Loss System

Consider a ReLS which can be described by such a stochastic process $X(t)$ over a finite state space $\mathcal{X}$ that its sample paths are continuous on the right and have limits on the left. Customers arrive and depart the system one by one. Denote by $0 < a_1 < a_2 < ...$ the arrival times and by $0 < b_1 < b_2 < \cdots$ the instants of service completion. We assume that the process $X(t)$ describes the system's behavior in such a way that for any of its states $i \in \mathcal{X}$ it is possible to determine the number $\kappa(i)$ of customers in service. We denote the maximum number of customers allowed in the system simultaneously by L, partition the state space $\mathcal{X}$ into disjoint subsets $\mathcal{X}_k = \{i \in \mathcal{X} : \kappa(i) = k\}$, $k = 0, 1, ..., L$, and denote by l_k the number of elements in subset $\mathcal{X}_k$. In what follows, the notation $\mathbf{x} \succ \mathbf{y}$ means that at least for one component the strict inequality $x_m > y_m$ holds.

Let the system have resources of M types. Denote by v_m the service capacity of type m resources, $\mathbf{v} = (v_1, v_2, ..., v_M)$, and by $\mathbf{r}_n = (r_{n,1}, r_{n,2}, ..., r_{n,M})$ the vector of resource amounts requested by an n-th customer. We assume that the resource requirement vectors $\mathbf{r}_n$, $n = 1, 2, ...$, are mutually independent and identically distributed with a CDF $F(\mathbf{x})$.

All customers in the system are numbered. If a customer arriving at time a_n is accepted for service, it is assigned a number φ_n in the interval $1 \le \varphi_n \le \kappa(X(a_n - 0)) + 1$. The customers with numbers $\varphi_n, \varphi_n + 1, ..., \kappa(X(a_n - 0))$, assigned prior to time a_n, will then have their numbers increased by one. Conversely, if at a service completion time d_n a customer number ψ_n leaves the system, then the customers with numbers $\psi_n + 1, \psi_n + 2, ..., \kappa(X(d_n - 0))$, prior to time d_n, will have their numbers reduced by one.

Information about resource allocations at time t is stored as a list $\boldsymbol{\xi}(t) = (\boldsymbol{\zeta}_1(t), \boldsymbol{\zeta}_2(t), ..., \boldsymbol{\zeta}_k(t))$ of length $k = \kappa(X(t))$, where $\boldsymbol{\zeta}_i(t) \in \mathbb{R}^M$ is the vector of resource allocations to the customer with the assigned number i. Although the resource amounts allocated to customers may be negative, the allocated totals $\boldsymbol{\sigma}(t) = \boldsymbol{\zeta}_1(t)+\boldsymbol{\zeta}_2(t)+\cdots+\boldsymbol{\zeta}_{\kappa(X(t))}(t)$ must meet the resource constraints $\mathbf{0} \le \boldsymbol{\sigma}(t) \le \mathbf{v}$ at any time. Note that, in addition to the resource constraint $\boldsymbol{\sigma}(t) \le \mathbf{v}$ considered previously, here we also assume the allocated totals to be bounded below by zero.

We denote by $S_k = \{(\mathbf{x}_1, ..., \mathbf{x}_k) : \mathbf{x}_1, ..., \mathbf{x}_k \in \mathbb{R}^M\}$ the set of lists of resource allocations to k customers, and by f_k and g_k the following probabilities

$$f_k = \mathsf{P}(\mathbf{0} \le \mathbf{r}_1 + \cdots + \mathbf{r}_k \le \mathbf{v}), \quad 1 \le k \le L, \tag{10.9}$$

$$g_k = \mathsf{P}(\mathbf{0} \le \mathbf{r}_1 + \cdots + \mathbf{r}_{k-1} \le \mathbf{v}, \mathbf{0} \le \mathbf{r}_1 + \cdots + \mathbf{r}_k \le \mathbf{v}), \quad 2 \le k \le L. \tag{10.10}$$

An arriving customer is blocked if it finds L customers in service. In addition, arriving customers are blocked if their acceptance for service results in a resource constraint violation. Let $\boldsymbol{\xi}(a_n - 0) = (\mathbf{x}_1, \mathbf{x}_2, ..., \mathbf{x}_k)$ be the state of the list of resource allocations before an arrival with resource requirement $\mathbf{r}_n$. If either $\mathbf{0} \succ \mathbf{r}_n + \mathbf{x}_1 + \mathbf{x}_2 + \cdots + \mathbf{x}_k$ or $\mathbf{r}_n + \mathbf{x}_1 + \mathbf{x}_2 + \cdots + \mathbf{x}_k \succ \mathbf{v}$, then we say that resource constraints are violated upon an arrival. In this case, the arriving customer is lost and the list of resource allocations remains unchanged. If, conversely, $\mathbf{0} \le \mathbf{r}_n + \mathbf{x}_1 + \mathbf{x}_2 + \cdots + \mathbf{x}_k \le \mathbf{v}$ then the customer is accepted for service, and the vector of resource requirements $\mathbf{r}_n$ is inserted into the list $\boldsymbol{\xi}(a_n) = (\mathbf{x}_1, ..., \mathbf{x}_{\varphi_n - 1}, \mathbf{r}_n, \mathbf{x}_{\varphi_n}, ..., \mathbf{x}_k)$ in position φ_n.

Similarly, suppose that right before the service completion of a customer with the assigned number ψ_n the list of resource allocations is in state $\boldsymbol{\xi}(d_n - 0) = (\mathbf{x}_1, \mathbf{x}_2, ..., \mathbf{x}_k)$. If either $\mathbf{0} \succ \mathbf{x}_1 + \cdots + \mathbf{x}_{\psi_n - 1} + \mathbf{x}_{\psi_n + 1} + \cdots + \mathbf{x}_k$ or $\mathbf{x}_1 + \cdots + \mathbf{x}_{\psi_n - 1} + \mathbf{x}_{\psi_n + 1} + \cdots + \mathbf{x}_k \succ \mathbf{v}$, then we say that resource constraints are violated upon a service completion. In this case, the customer with number ψ_n restarts service and the list of resource allocations does not change. Conversely, if $\mathbf{0} \le \mathbf{x}_1 + \cdots + \mathbf{x}_{\psi_n - 1} + \mathbf{x}_{\psi_n + 1} + \cdots + \mathbf{x}_k \le \mathbf{v}$, then the customer with number ψ_n departs the system, its resource allocation is deleted from the list and the list jumps to state $\boldsymbol{\xi}(d_n) = (\mathbf{x}_1, ..., \mathbf{x}_{\psi_n - 1}, \mathbf{x}_{\psi_n + 1}, ..., \mathbf{x}_k)$. Note that resource constraints cannot be violated upon the service completion of a single customer, i.e., if $\kappa(X(d_n - 0)) = 1$.

10.2.2 The Markovian System Model

Assume that $Y(t) = (X(t), \boldsymbol{\xi}(t))$ is a homogeneous Markov jump process with the state space $\mathcal{Y} = \{(i, \mathbf{x}) | i \in \mathcal{X}, \mathbf{x} \in S_{\kappa(i)}\}$. Its sojourn time in each state $(i, \mathbf{x})$ has an exponential distribution whose parameter depends only on the state i of the system. Additionally, the list of resource allocations $\boldsymbol{\xi}(t)$ can change only upon customer arrivals and departures. The following parameters characterize a Markovian ReLS:

$a(i)$ the arrival rate when the system is in state i, $a(i) = 0$ if $\kappa(i) = L$;

$\alpha_\varphi(i, j)$ the conditional probability that an arriving customer is assigned number φ, $1 \le \varphi \le \kappa(i) + 1$, and the process moves from state i to state j such that $\kappa(j) = \kappa(i) + 1$, given that the resource constraints are not violated upon arrival, $a_\varphi(i, j) = a(i)\alpha_\varphi(i, j)$;

$\zeta(i, j)$ the conditional probability to move, upon an arrival, from state i to state j such that $\kappa(j) = \kappa(i)$, given that the resource constraints are violated upon arrival, $\pi(i, j) = a(i)\zeta(i, j)$;

$b_\psi(i)$ the service rate of customers with the assigned number ψ when the system is in state i, $1 \le \psi \le \kappa(i)$;

$\beta_\psi(i, j)$ the conditional probability that, upon service completion of a customer with the assigned number ψ, the process moves from state i to state j such that $\kappa(j) = \kappa(i) - 1$, given that the resource constraints are not violated upon service completion, $b_\psi(i, j) = b_\psi(i)\beta_\psi(i, j)$;

$\eta_\psi(i, j)$ the conditional probability that, upon service completion of a customer with the assigned number ψ, the process moves from state i to state j such that $\kappa(j) = \kappa(i)$, given that the resource constraints are violated upon service completion, $\theta_\psi(i, j) = b_\psi(i)\eta_\psi(i, j)$;

$c(i, j)$ the transition rate from state i to state j such that $j \neq i$ and $\kappa(j) = \kappa(i)$ unrelated to customer arrivals or service completions, and $c(i, i) = -(a(i)+b(i)+c(i))$, where

$$b(i) = \sum_{\psi=1}^{\kappa(i)} b_\psi(i), \quad c(i) = \sum_{\substack{j\neq i,\\ \kappa(j)=\kappa(i)}} c(i, j).$$

In what follows, we will need rectangular matrices $\mathbf{A}_{k,\varphi} = [a_\varphi(i, j)]$, $i \in \mathcal{X}_k$, $j \in \mathcal{X}_{k+1}$, of size $l_k \times l_{k+1}$, $\mathbf{B}_{k,\psi} = [b_\psi(i, j)]$, $i \in \mathcal{X}_k$, $j \in \mathcal{X}_{k-1}$, of size $l_k \times l_{k-1}$,

$$\mathbf{A}_k = \sum_{\varphi=1}^{k+1} \mathbf{A}_{k,\varphi}, \quad \mathbf{B}_k = \sum_{\psi=1}^{k} \mathbf{B}_{k,\psi},$$

and square matrices $\mathbf{C}_k = [c(i, j)]$, $i, j \in \mathcal{X}_k$, $\mathbf{\Pi}_k = [\pi(i, j)]$, $i, j \in \mathcal{X}_k$, $\mathbf{\Theta}_{k,\psi} = [\theta_\psi(i, j)]$, $i, j \in \mathcal{X}_k$, of order l_k,

$$\mathbf{\Theta}_k = \sum_{\psi=1}^{k} \mathbf{\Theta}_{k,\psi}.$$

We assume that there exists a the state $(i^*, \mathbf{0})$, $i^* \in \mathcal{X}_0$, which is the regeneration state of the process $Y(t)$. In such a case, there exists a limiting distribution of $Y(t)$ (Asmussen 2003)

$$p(i) = \lim_{t\to\infty} \mathsf{P}\{X(t) = i\},\ i \in \mathcal{X}_0,$$
$$P(i, \mathbf{x}) = \lim_{t\to\infty} \mathsf{P}\{X(t) = i, \boldsymbol{\xi}(t) \leq \mathbf{x}\}, \quad i \in \mathcal{X}_k,\ \mathbf{x} \in \mathbf{S}_k, 0 < k \leq L,$$

and row vectors

$$\mathbf{p}_0 = (p(i)), \quad i \in \mathcal{X}_0,$$
$$\mathbf{p}_k(\mathbf{x}) = (P(i, \mathbf{x})), \quad i \in \mathcal{X}_k, \quad \mathbf{x} \in \mathbf{S}_k, \quad 0 < k \leq L.$$

The equilibrium equations for the stationary probabilities can be written in matrix form as

$$\mathbf{p}_0\mathbf{C}_0 + (1 - \int\limits_{\mathbf{0}\le\mathbf{y}\le\mathbf{v}} F(d\mathbf{y}))\,\mathbf{p}_0\mathbf{\Pi}_0 + \mathbf{p}_1(\mathbf{v})\mathbf{B}_1 = \mathbf{0}; \tag{10.11}$$

$$\begin{aligned}
&\int\limits_{\mathbf{0}\le\mathbf{y}_1\le\mathbf{x}_1} F(d\mathbf{y}_1)\,\mathbf{p}_0\mathbf{A}_{0,1} + \mathbf{p}_1(\mathbf{w}_1)\mathbf{C}_1 + [\mathbf{p}_1(\mathbf{x}_1) - \\
&\quad - \int\limits_{\substack{\mathbf{0}\le\mathbf{y}_1+\mathbf{y}_2\le\mathbf{v},\\ \mathbf{0}\le\mathbf{y}_1\le\mathbf{x}_1}} F(d\mathbf{y}_2)\mathbf{p}_1(d\mathbf{y}_1)]\mathbf{\Pi}_1 + \\
&\quad + \int\limits_{\substack{\mathbf{0}\le\mathbf{y}_1+\mathbf{y}_2\le\mathbf{v},\\ \mathbf{0}\le\mathbf{y}_1\le\mathbf{x}_1}} \mathbf{p}_2(d\mathbf{y}_2, d\mathbf{y}_1)\mathbf{B}_{2,1} + \\
&\quad + \int\limits_{\substack{\mathbf{0}\le\mathbf{y}_1+\mathbf{y}_2\le\mathbf{v},\\ \mathbf{0}\le\mathbf{y}_1\le\mathbf{x}_1}} \mathbf{p}_2(d\mathbf{y}_1, d\mathbf{y}_2)\mathbf{B}_{2,2} = \mathbf{0}, \quad \mathbf{x}_1 \in S_1;
\end{aligned} \tag{10.12}$$

$$\begin{aligned}
&\sum_{\varphi=1}^{k} \int\limits_{\substack{\mathbf{0}\le\mathbf{y}_1+\cdots+\mathbf{y}_{k-1}\le\mathbf{v},\\ \mathbf{0}\le\mathbf{y}_1+\cdots+\mathbf{y}_k\le\mathbf{v},\\ \mathbf{y}_i\le\mathbf{x}_i, i=1,\dots,k}} F(d\mathbf{y}_\varphi)\,\mathbf{p}_{k-1}(d\mathbf{y}_1, \dots, d\mathbf{y}_{\varphi-1}, d\mathbf{y}_{\varphi+1}, \dots, d\mathbf{y}_k)\mathbf{A}_{k-1,\varphi} + \\
&\quad + \mathbf{p}_k(\mathbf{x}_1, \dots, \mathbf{x}_k)\mathbf{C}_k + \\
&+ [\mathbf{p}_k(\mathbf{x}_1, \dots, \mathbf{x}_k) - \int\limits_{\substack{\mathbf{0}\le\mathbf{y}_1+\cdots+\mathbf{y}_{k+1}\le\mathbf{v},\\ \mathbf{0}\le\mathbf{y}_1+\cdots+\mathbf{y}_k\le\mathbf{v},\\ \mathbf{y}_i\le\mathbf{x}_i, i=1,\dots,k}} F(d\mathbf{y}_{k+1})\mathbf{p}_k(d\mathbf{y}_1, \dots, d\mathbf{y}_k)]\mathbf{\Pi}_k + \\
&\quad + \mathbf{p}_k(\mathbf{x}_1, \dots, \mathbf{x}_k)\mathbf{C}_k - \\
&- \sum_{\psi=1}^{k} \int\limits_{\substack{\mathbf{0}\le\mathbf{y}_1+\cdots+\mathbf{y}_{k-1}\le\mathbf{v},\\ \mathbf{0}\le\mathbf{y}_1+\cdots+\mathbf{y}_k\le\mathbf{v},\\ \mathbf{y}_i\le\mathbf{x}_i, i=1,\dots,k}} \mathbf{p}_k(d\mathbf{y}_1, \dots, d\mathbf{y}_{\psi-1}, d\mathbf{y}_k, d\mathbf{y}_\psi, \dots, d\mathbf{y}_{k-1})]\mathbf{\Theta}_{k,\psi} + \\
&+ \sum_{\psi=1}^{k+1} \int\limits_{\substack{\mathbf{0}\le\mathbf{y}_1+\cdots+\mathbf{y}_{k+1}\le\mathbf{v},\\ \mathbf{0}\le\mathbf{y}_1+\cdots+\mathbf{y}_k\le\mathbf{v},\\ \mathbf{y}_i\le\mathbf{x}_i, i=1,\dots,k}} \mathbf{p}_{k+1}(d\mathbf{y}_1, \dots, d\mathbf{y}_{\psi-1}, d\mathbf{y}_{k+1}, d\mathbf{y}_\psi, \dots, d\mathbf{y}_k)\mathbf{B}_{k+1,\psi} = \mathbf{0}, \\
&\quad (\mathbf{x}_1, \dots, \mathbf{x}_k) \in S_k, \quad 1 < k < L;
\end{aligned} \tag{10.13}$$

$$\sum_{\varphi=1}^{L} \int\limits_{\substack{\mathbf{0}\le \mathbf{y}_1+\dots+\mathbf{y}_{L-1}\le \mathbf{v},\\ \mathbf{0}\le \mathbf{y}_1+\dots+\mathbf{y}_L\le \mathbf{v},\\ \mathbf{y}_i\le \mathbf{x}_i, i=1,\dots,L}} F(d\mathbf{y}_\varphi)\,\mathbf{p}_{L-1}(d\mathbf{y}_1,\ \dots,\ d\mathbf{y}_{\varphi-1}, d\mathbf{y}_{\varphi+1},\ \dots,\ d\mathbf{y}_L)\mathbf{A}_{L-1,\varphi}+$$

$$+\mathbf{p}_L(\mathbf{x}_1,\ \dots\mathbf{x}_L)\mathbf{C}_L + [\mathbf{p}_L\mathbf{x}_1 \dots,\ \mathbf{x}_L -$$

$$-\sum_{\psi=1}^{L} \int\limits_{\substack{\mathbf{0}\le \mathbf{y}_1+\dots+\mathbf{y}_{L-1}\le \mathbf{v},\\ \mathbf{0}\le \mathbf{y}_1+\dots+\mathbf{y}_L\le \mathbf{v},\\ \mathbf{y}_i\le \mathbf{x}_i, i=1,\dots,L}} \mathbf{p}_L(d\mathbf{y}_1,\ \dots,\ d\mathbf{y}_{\psi-1}, d\mathbf{y}_L, d\mathbf{y}_\psi,\ \dots,\ d\mathbf{y}_{L-1})]\mathbf{\Theta}_{L,\psi} = \mathbf{0},$$

$$(\mathbf{x}_1,\ \dots,\ \mathbf{x}_L) \in S_L. \tag{10.14}$$

In addition to these equations, the stationary probabilities of the process $Y(t)$ satisfy the normalizing condition

$$\mathbf{p}_0\mathbf{u}_0 + \sum_{k=1}^{L} \int\limits_{S_k} \mathbf{p}_k(d\mathbf{y})\mathbf{u}_k = 1, \tag{10.15}$$

where $\mathbf{u}_k$ are columns vectors of ones of length l_k.

10.2.3 Product-Form Stationary Probability Distribution

Assume provisionally that the resource constraints do not affect the system's behavior. For example, if all vectors of requested resources $\mathbf{r}_n$ are nonnegative and bounded above by the vector $\frac{1}{L}\mathbf{v}$, then the resource constraints cannot be violated because at any time the inequalities $\mathbf{0} \le \sigma(t) \le \mathbf{v}$ are met. In this case, $X(t)$ is a homogeneous Markov process with a block-tridiagonal generator matrix

$$\mathbf{Q} = \begin{bmatrix} \mathbf{C}_0 & \mathbf{A}_0 & \mathbf{O} & \cdots & \mathbf{O} \\ \mathbf{B}_1 & \mathbf{C}_1 & \ddots & \ddots & \vdots \\ \mathbf{O} & \ddots & \ddots & \ddots & \mathbf{O} \\ \vdots & \ddots & \ddots & \ddots & \mathbf{A}_{L-1} \\ \mathbf{O} & \cdots & \mathbf{O} & \mathbf{B}_L & \mathbf{C}_L \end{bmatrix}. \tag{10.16}$$

We assume that the matrix $\mathbf{Q}$ is irreducible. Then, the stationary probability vector $\mathbf{q} = (\mathbf{q}_0,\ \dots,\ \mathbf{q}_L)$ of the process $X(t)$ is the unique solution of the linear system

$$\begin{aligned} \mathbf{q}_0\mathbf{C}_0 + \mathbf{q}_1\mathbf{B}_1 &= \mathbf{0}, \\ \mathbf{q}_{k-1}\mathbf{A}_{k-1} + \mathbf{q}_k\mathbf{C}_k + \mathbf{q}_{k+1}\mathbf{B}_{k+1} &= \mathbf{0}, \ 1 \le k \le L-1, \\ \mathbf{q}_{L-1}\mathbf{A}_{L-1} + \mathbf{q}_L\mathbf{C}_L &= \mathbf{0}, \end{aligned} \tag{10.17}$$

and satisfies the normalizing condition

$$\sum_{k=0}^{L} \mathbf{q}_k\mathbf{u}_k = 1. \tag{10.18}$$

Now, consider the general case. We are interested in conditions that guarantee the following product form of the stationary probability distribution of $Y(t)$:

$$\begin{gathered} p(i) = Cq(i), i \in \mathcal{X}_0, \\ P(i, (\mathbf{x}_1, ..., \mathbf{x}_k)) = Cq(i)F_k(\mathbf{x}_1, ..., \mathbf{x}_k), \ \ i \in \mathcal{X}_k, \ \ (\mathbf{x}_1, ..., \mathbf{x}_k) \in S_k, \ \ 0 < k \le L. \end{gathered} \tag{10.19}$$

Here

$$F_k(\mathbf{x}_1, ..., \mathbf{x}_k) = \int\limits_{\substack{\mathbf{0} \le \mathbf{y}_1 + \cdots + \mathbf{y}_k \le \mathbf{v}, \\ \mathbf{y}_i \le \mathbf{x}_i, i=1, ..., k}} F(d\mathbf{y}_1) \cdots F(d\mathbf{y}_k), \, (\mathbf{x}_1, .., \mathbf{x}_k) S_k, \ \ 1 \le k \le L,$$

probabilities $q(i)$, $i \in \mathcal{X}$, are the stationary state distribution for the system with no resource constraint violation, obtained as the solution of the linear system (10.15)–(10.17), and C is the normalization constant,

$$C = (\mathbf{q}_0\mathbf{u}_0 + \sum_{k=1}^{L} f_k \mathbf{q}_k \mathbf{u}_k)^{-1}.$$

Let functions $G_k(\mathbf{w}_1, ..., \mathbf{w}_k)$ and $H_k(\mathbf{w}_1, ..., \mathbf{w}_k)$ be defined for $(\mathbf{w}_1, ..., \mathbf{w}_k) \in S_k$ by the probabilities of the following events

$$\begin{aligned} G_k(\mathbf{w}_1, ..., \mathbf{w}_k) = \mathsf{P}(&\mathbf{0} \le \mathbf{r}_1 + \cdots + \mathbf{r}_{k-1} \le \mathbf{v}, \mathbf{0} \le \mathbf{r}_1 + \cdots + \mathbf{r}_k \le \mathbf{v}, \\ &\mathbf{r}_i \le \mathbf{w}_i, i = 1, ..., k), \\ H_k(\mathbf{w}_1, ..., \mathbf{w}_k) = \mathsf{P}(&\mathbf{0} \le \mathbf{r}_1 + \cdots + \mathbf{r}_{k+1} \le \mathbf{v}, \mathbf{0} \le \mathbf{r}_1 + \cdots + \mathbf{r}_k \le \mathbf{v}, \\ &\mathbf{r}_i \le \mathbf{w}_i, i = 1, ..., k). \end{aligned}$$

Theorem 10.2 *For the stationary probability distribution of the process $Y(t)$ to have the product form (10.19), it is necessary and sufficient that*

$$(1 - f_1)(\mathbf{q}_0\mathbf{\Pi}_0 - \mathbf{q}_1\mathbf{B}_1) = \mathbf{0}, \tag{10.20}$$

$$(f_1 - g_2)(\mathbf{q}_1\mathbf{\Pi}_1 - \mathbf{q}_2\mathbf{B}_2) = \mathbf{0}, \tag{10.21}$$

$$(f_L - g_L)(\mathbf{q}_L\Theta_L - \mathbf{q}_{L-1}\mathbf{A}_{L-1}) = \mathbf{0}, \tag{10.22}$$

and also either both

$$\mathbf{x}_k = (f_k - g_k)(\mathbf{q}_k\Theta_k - \mathbf{q}_{k-1}\mathbf{A}_{k-1})$$

and

$$\mathbf{y}_k = (f_k - g_{k+1})(\mathbf{q}_k\mathbf{\Pi}_k - \mathbf{q}_{k+1}\mathbf{B}_{k+1})$$

be zero vectors, or $\mathbf{x}_k \neq \mathbf{0}$, $\mathbf{y}_k \neq \mathbf{0}$, $\mathbf{x}_k + \mathbf{y}_k = \mathbf{0}$, *and equality*

$$\begin{aligned}(f_k - g_{k+1})(F_k(\mathbf{w}_1, \ldots, \mathbf{w}_k) - G_k(\mathbf{w}_1, \ldots, \mathbf{w}_k)) = \\ = (f_k - g_k)(F_k(\mathbf{w}_1, \ldots, \mathbf{w}_k) - H_k(\mathbf{w}_1, \ldots, \mathbf{w}_k))\end{aligned} \tag{10.23}$$

be valid for all vectors $(\mathbf{w}_1, \ldots, \mathbf{w}_k) \in S_k$, $1 < k < L$.

Proof At first, we substitute the expressions (10.19) into the (10.11)–(10.14) and eliminate the vectors $\mathbf{q}_k\mathbf{C}_k$ from the obtained expressions using (10.17). As a result, after some elementary transformations, we obtain the following equations which are necessary and sufficient for the product form of the stationary distribution of $Y(t)$:

$$(1 - f_1)(\mathbf{q}_0\mathbf{\Pi}_0 - \mathbf{q}_1\mathbf{B}_1) = \mathbf{0}; \tag{10.24}$$

$$(F_1(\mathbf{w}_1) - H_1(\mathbf{w}_1))(\mathbf{q}_1\mathbf{\Pi}_1 - \mathbf{q}_2\mathbf{B}_2) = \mathbf{0}, \mathbf{w}_1 \in S_1; \tag{10.25}$$

$$\begin{aligned}(F_k(\mathbf{w}_1, \ldots, \mathbf{w}_k) - G_k(\mathbf{w}_1, \ldots, \mathbf{w}_k))(\mathbf{q}_k\Theta_k - \mathbf{q}_{k-1}\mathbf{A}_{k-1}) + \\ +(F_k(\mathbf{w}_1, \ldots, \mathbf{w}_k) - H_k(\mathbf{w}_1, \ldots, \mathbf{w}_k))(\mathbf{q}_k\mathbf{\Pi}_k - \mathbf{q}_{k+1}\mathbf{B}_{k+1}) = \mathbf{0}, \\ (\mathbf{w}_1, \ldots, \mathbf{w}_k) \in S_k, \ 1 < k < L;\end{aligned} \tag{10.26}$$

$$\begin{aligned}(F_L(\mathbf{w}_1, \ldots, \mathbf{w}_L) - G_L(\mathbf{w}_1, \ldots, \mathbf{w}_L))(\mathbf{q}_L\Theta_L - \mathbf{q}_{L-1}\mathbf{A}_{L-1}) = \mathbf{0}, \\ (\mathbf{w}_1, \ldots, \mathbf{w}_L) \in S_L.\end{aligned} \tag{10.27}$$

There is a simple relationship between the probabilities f_k, g_k introduced in (10.9)–(10.10) and the following integrals:

$$\int\limits_{S_k} F_k(d\mathbf{w}_1, \ldots, d\mathbf{w}_k) = \mathsf{P}(\mathbf{0} \leq \boldsymbol{r}_1 + \cdots + \boldsymbol{r}_k \leq \mathbf{v}) = f_k, \tag{10.28}$$

$$\int_{S_k} G_k(d\mathbf{w}_1, \ldots, d\mathbf{w}_k) = \\ = \mathsf{P}(\mathbf{0} \le \mathbf{r}_1 + \cdots + \mathbf{r}_{k-1} \le \mathbf{v}, \mathbf{0} \le \mathbf{r}_1 + \cdots + \mathbf{r}_k \le \mathbf{v}) = g_k, \tag{10.29}$$

$$\int_{S_k} H_k(d\mathbf{w}_1, \ldots, d\mathbf{w}_k) = \\ = \mathsf{P}(\mathbf{0} \le \mathbf{r}_1 + \cdots + \mathbf{r}_{k+1} \le \mathbf{v}, \mathbf{0} \le \mathbf{r}_1 + \cdots + \mathbf{r}_k \le \mathbf{v}) = g_{k+1}. \tag{10.30}$$

Let us show that for $1 < k \le L$ the equality $f_k = g_k$ is equivalent to the fact that $F_k(\mathbf{w}_1, \ldots, \mathbf{w}_k) = G_k(\mathbf{w}_1, \ldots, \mathbf{w}_k)$ for any vector $(\mathbf{w}_1, \ldots, \mathbf{w}_k) \in S_k$. Consider the events $\Phi_k = \{\mathbf{0} \le \mathbf{r}_1 + \cdots + \mathbf{r}_k \le \mathbf{v}\}$ and $\Psi_k(\mathbf{w}_1, \ldots, \mathbf{w}_k) = \{\mathbf{r}_i \le \mathbf{w}_i,\ i = 1, \ldots, k\}$. With $f_k = g_k$ the equality $\mathsf{P}(\Phi_{k-1}\Phi_k) = \mathsf{P}(\Phi_k)$ holds. Hence

$$\mathsf{P}(\overline{\Phi}_{k-1}\Phi_k) = \mathsf{P}(\Phi_k) - \mathsf{P}(\Phi_{k-1}\Phi_k) = 0$$

and

$$0 = \mathsf{P}(\overline{\Phi}_{k-1}\Phi_k) \ge \mathsf{P}(\overline{\Phi}_{k-1}\Phi_k\Psi_k(\boldsymbol{w}_1, \ldots, \boldsymbol{w}_k)) \ge 0$$

Thus $\mathsf{P}(\overline{\Phi}_{k-1}\Phi_k\Psi_k(\mathbf{w}_1, \ldots, \mathbf{w}_k)) = 0$ for any vector $(\mathbf{w}_1, \ldots, \mathbf{w}_k) \in S_k$, and so equalities

$$F_k(\mathbf{w}_1, \ldots, \mathbf{w}_k) = \mathsf{P}(\Phi_k\Psi_k(\mathbf{w}_1, \ldots, \mathbf{w}_k)) = \mathsf{P}(\Phi_{k-1}\Phi_k\Psi_k(\mathbf{w}_1, \ldots, \mathbf{w}_k)) + \\ + \mathsf{P}(\overline{\Phi}_{k-1}\Phi_k\Psi_k(\mathbf{w}_1, \ldots, \mathbf{w}_k)) = \mathsf{P}(\Phi_{k-1}\Phi_k\Psi_k(\mathbf{w}_1, \ldots, \mathbf{w}_k)) = G_k(\mathbf{w}_1, \ldots, \mathbf{w}_k)$$

are valid. The opposite is also true. If $F_k(\mathbf{w}_1, \ldots, \mathbf{w}_k) = G_k(\mathbf{w}_1, \ldots, \mathbf{w}_k)$ for any vector $(\mathbf{w}_1, \ldots, \mathbf{w}_k) \in S_k$, then from (10.28) and (10.29) it follows that $f_k = g_k$. In exactly the same way it can be proved that for $1 \le k < L$ the equality $f_k = g_{k+1}$ is equivalent to the fact that $F_k(\mathbf{w}_1, \ldots, \mathbf{w}_k) = H_k(\mathbf{w}_1, \ldots, \mathbf{w}_k)$ for any vectors $(\mathbf{w}_1, \ldots, \mathbf{w}_k) \in S_k$. Now it is clear that (10.25) and (10.27) are equivalent to (10.21) and (10.22).

If $\mathbf{x}_k = \mathbf{0}$ and $\mathbf{y}_k = \mathbf{0}$ for some $1 < k < L$, then we have the equality (10.26). Let $\mathbf{x}_k \ne \mathbf{0}$, $\mathbf{y}_k \ne \mathbf{0}$, and $\mathbf{x}_k + \mathbf{y}_k = \mathbf{0}$. By multiplying pairwise the left-hand and right-hand sides of the equations $\mathbf{x}_k = -\mathbf{y}_k$ and (10.23) we obtain

$$(f_k - g_k)(f_k - g_{k+1})(F_k(\mathbf{w}_1, \ldots, \mathbf{w}_k) - G_k(\mathbf{w}_1, \ldots, \mathbf{w}_k))(\mathbf{q}_k\Theta_k - \mathbf{q}_{k-1}\mathbf{A}_{k-1}) = \\ = -(f_k - g_k)(f_k - g_{k+1})(F_k(\mathbf{w}_1, \ldots, \mathbf{w}_k) - H_k(\mathbf{w}_1, \ldots, \mathbf{w}_k))(\mathbf{q}_k\mathbf{\Pi}_k - \mathbf{q}_{k+1}\mathbf{B}_{k+1}).$$

Therefore, since $f_k \ne g_k$ and $f_k \ne g_{k+1}$, the equality (10.26) holds in this case.

The opposite is also true. Let (10.26) hold for all $(\mathbf{w}_1, \ldots, \mathbf{w}_k) \in S_k$. Integrating functions in (10.26) over all $(\mathbf{w}_1, \ldots, \mathbf{w}_k) \in S_k$, we obtain the equality $\mathbf{x}_k + \mathbf{y}_k = \mathbf{0}$. It follows that if one of the vectors $\mathbf{x}_k$ and $\mathbf{y}_k$ is equal to 0, then the other vector is also zero. If both of these vectors are nonzero, then in order for the equality $\mathbf{x}_k + \mathbf{y}_k = \mathbf{0}$ and (10.26) to hold simultaneously, it is necessary that in these relationships the coefficients at the vectors $\mathbf{q}_k\Theta_k - \mathbf{q}_{k-1}\mathbf{A}_{k-1}$ and $\mathbf{q}_k\mathbf{\Pi}_k - \mathbf{q}_{k+1}\mathbf{B}_{k+1}$ satisfy (10.23). This completes the proof of the theorem. ∎

Corollary 1 *The following equalities are necessary and sufficient for the stationary probability distribution of $Y(t)$ to have a product form for any function $F(\mathbf{x})$:*

$$\begin{aligned} \mathbf{q}_k\mathbf{A}_k &= \mathbf{q}_{k+1}\Theta_{k+1}, \quad 1 \le k < L, \\ \mathbf{q}_k\mathbf{B}_k &= \mathbf{q}_{k-1}\mathbf{\Pi}_{k-1}, \quad 1 \le k \le L. \end{aligned} \tag{10.31}$$

Corollary 2 *Let all resource requirement vectors $\mathbf{r}_n$ be nonnegative. Then, the following equalities are necessary and sufficient for the stationary probability distribution of the process $Y(t)$ to have a product form:*

$$\begin{aligned} (1 - f_1)(\mathbf{q}_0\pi_0 - \mathbf{q}_1\mathbf{B}_1) &= \mathbf{0}, \\ (f_k - g_{k+1})(\mathbf{q}_k\pi_k - \mathbf{q}_{k+1}\mathbf{B}_{k+1}) &= \mathbf{0}, \quad 1 \le k \le L. \end{aligned} \tag{10.32}$$

Indeed, in the case of nonnegative resource requirements, the event Φ_k implies the event Φ_{k-1}. Therefore, $f_k = g_k$ and the vector $\mathbf{x}_k$ in Theorem 10.2 is always zero, hence the vector $\mathbf{y}_k$ must be zero.

10.2.4 An Example: The MAP|M|L|L Loss System

The stationary probability distribution of an L-server ReLS with Poisson arrival process and exponentially distributed service times, studied in Chap. 8, has a product form for any CDF $F(\mathbf{x})$ of resource requests. The results of this section allow to verify whether the stationary probability distribution of the same system but with a Markovian arrival process (MAP) has the same property.

Let $N(t) = \sup\{n : a_n \le t\}$ be the counting process of MAP and $X(t)$ be a random process with a finite state space X such that $(X(t), N(t))$ is a homogeneous Markov process with a homogeneous second component. In this case, for all $i, j \in \mathcal{X}$, $n \ge k$, and $h, t > 0$, we have

$$\mathsf{P}(X(h+t) = j, N(h+t) = n | X(h) = i, N(h) = k) = P_{i,j}(n-k, t),$$

and the process $X(t)$ is also a homogeneous Markov process with transition probabilities

$$P_{i,j}(t) = \mathsf{P}(X(h+t) = j | X(h) = i) = \sum_{n=0}^{\infty} p_{i,j}(n, t).$$

For a simple MAP, also called the MC-stream, the probability of more than one arrival during an interval of length ε is $o(\varepsilon)$. The simple MAP is characterized by two matrices: $\mathbf{S} = [s_{i,j}]$, $i, j \in \mathcal{X}$, and $\mathbf{R} = [r_{i,j}]$, $i, j \in \mathcal{X}$, whose elements are defined by

$$s_{i,j} = \lim_{\varepsilon \to 0} \frac{1}{\varepsilon}(p_{i,j}(0, \varepsilon) - \delta_{i,j}), \ \ r_{i,j} = \lim_{\varepsilon \to 0} \frac{1}{\varepsilon} p_{i,j}(1, \varepsilon), \ \ i, j \in \mathcal{X},$$

and whose sum $\mathbf{A} = \mathbf{S}+\mathbf{R}$ is the generator of the phase process $X(t)$. We assume that the generator $\mathbf{A}$ is irreducible and denote by p the stationary probability distribution of $X(t)$.

The generator of the Markov process describing the ReLS under study has the form (10.16) with blocks $\mathbf{A}_k = \mathbf{R}$, $k = 0, 1, ..., L-1$; $\mathbf{B}_k = k\mu\mathbf{I}$, $k = 1, 2, ..., L$; $\mathbf{C}_k = \mathbf{S} - k\mu\mathbf{I}$, $k = 0, 1, ..., L-1$; $\mathbf{C}_L = \mathbf{A} - L\mu\mathbf{I}$, where $\mathbf{I}$ is the identity matrix, and μ is the service rate. If upon an arrival the resource constraints are violated, then the phase process changes its state in accordance with the rate matrices $\mathbf{\Pi}_k = \mathbf{R}$, but the number of customers in the system remains unchanged. If upon a service completion the resource constraints are violated, then neither the phase process nor the number of customers in the system change, and the rate matrices $\mathbf{\Theta}_k$ are given by $\mathbf{\Theta}_k = k\mu\mathbf{I}$.

Therefore, the conditions of Corollary 1 of Theorem 2 assume the form $\mathbf{q}_k\mathbf{R} = (k+1)\mu\mathbf{q}_{k+1}$, $k = 0, 1, ..., L-1$. It follows from this and relationships (10.17) that conditions (10.31) are equivalent to the equalities

$$\mathbf{q}_k\mathbf{A} = \mathbf{0}, \ \ k = 0, 1, ..., L. \tag{10.33}$$

Since the matrix $\mathbf{A}$ is irreducible, the solutions of (10.33) are given by $\mathbf{q}_k = c_k\mathbf{p}$, where c_k are some constants. However, such a product form of the stationary distribution $\mathbf{q}$ is possible only if the arriving MAP is Poisson (Naumov 1976). Thus, the stationary probability distribution of a MAP|M|L|L loss system with random resource requirements has the product form (10.19) only in the case when the arrival process is Poisson.

10.3 Computing Stationary Distributions via the Fourier Transform

10.3.1 Computing Stationary Distributions of Loss Systems with Random Resource Requirements

Consider a single-resource L-server loss system modeled by a homogeneous jump Markov process $\xi(t) = (X(t), \sigma(t))$, where $X(t) \in \mathcal{X}$ is the state of the system and $\sigma(t)$ is the total amount of resources occupied by the customers at time t, $0 \le \sigma(t) \le V$. We suppose that the state space $\mathcal{X}$ of the process $X(t)$ is discrete and characterizes the system at a rather detailed level so that for any state $i \in \mathcal{X}$ one can determine the number $v(i)$ of customers currently in service.

For the loss systems with random resource requirements discussed in this chapter, the stationary distribution

$$P(i,x) = \lim_{t\to\infty} \mathsf{P}(X(t) = i, \sigma(t) \le x) \tag{10.34}$$

of $X(t)$ is of the product form

$$P(i,x) = cq(i)G^{*v(i)}(x), \quad x \in \mathcal{X}, 0 \le x \le V. \tag{10.35}$$

Here $q(i)$, $i \in \mathcal{X}$, are the stationary probabilities of the system states in the case of unlimited resources, $G^{*k}(x)$ is the k-fold convolution of the resource requirement CDF $G(x)$, and c is the normalizing constant,

$$c = \left(\sum_{i\in\mathcal{X}} q(i)G^{*v(i)}(V)\right)^{-1}. \tag{10.36}$$

In order to find the stationary distribution (10.35)–(10.36) of the ReLS, one should compute a series of convolutions $G^{*n}(x)$, $n = 2, 3, ..., L$, in the interval $0 \le x \le V$. These functions are related by the following recursion formula:

$$G^{*0}(x) = 1, \quad G^{*n}(x) = \int_0^x G^{*(n-1)}(x-t)dG(t), \quad n = 1, 2, ..., L, \quad 0 \le x \le V. \tag{10.37}$$

For computing $G^{*n}(x)$ we approximate $G(x)$ by some step function $F(x)$ with jumps of size f_k at τk, $k = 0, 1, 2, ..., K$, where $\tau K = V$. The convolutions $F^{*n}(x)$ are also step functions and their jumps f_k^{*n} at τk are related by the recursion formula

$$f_k^{*0} = \delta_{k,0}, \quad f_k^{*n} = \sum_{i=0}^{k} f_{k-i}^{*(n-1)} f_i, \quad n = 1, 2, ..., L, \quad 0 \le k \le K. \tag{10.38}$$

Thus, the task of computing approximately the integrals in (10.37) depends on computing the convolution powers $f^{*n} = (f_k^{*n})$ of the sequence $f = (f_k)$.

10.3.2 Computing Convolutions via DFT

The method for computing convolutions by means of the forward and inverse discrete Fourier transforms (DFT) is well known (Nussbaumer 1990). Let $a = (a_i,\ i = 0, 1, \ldots, I)$, and $b = (b_j,\ j = 0, 1, \ldots, J)$ be two finite sequences. Choose a whole number $M > I + J$ and let $A = (A_m)$ and $B = (B_m)$ denote the DFTs of the sequences a and b over the range from 0 to $M - 1$:

$$A_m = \sum_{r=0}^{I} a_r e^{2\pi jmr/M},\quad B_m = \sum_{r=0}^{J} b_r e^{2\pi jmr/M},\quad m = 0, 1, \ldots, M-1,$$

where $j = \sqrt{-1}$. Elements c_k of the convolution $c = a * b$ can be found by the inverse DFT:

$$c_k = \frac{1}{M}\sum_{m=0}^{M-1} A_m B_m e^{-2\pi jmk/M},\quad k = 0, 1, \ldots, I+J,$$

$$c_k = \frac{1}{M}\sum_{m=0}^{M-1} A_m B_m e^{-2\pi jmk/M},\quad k = 0, 1, \ldots, I+J.$$

10.3.3 Computing Truncated Convolutions

The procedure described above allows computing consecutively the convolutions (10.38). This requires the calculation of the DFTs $\Phi^{(n)} = (\Phi_m^{(n)})$ of the convolution f^{*n},

$$\Phi_m^{(n)} = \sum_{r=0}^{nK} f_r^{*n} e^{2\pi jmr/M_n},\quad m = 0, 1, \ldots, M_n - 1,$$

over the range of length $M_n > nK$, which increases with n.

Equation (10.38) can be quickened further in the following way. Note that there is no need to calculate the values of f_k^{*n} for $k > K$ since they are not present in (10.37) and (10.38). For any given sequence $a = (a_0, a_1, \ldots, a_w)$ of length $w \geq K$, let $Tr(a) = (a_0, a_1, \ldots, a_K)$ denote the sequence of its first $K + 1$ members. Obviously, the probabilities in (10.35) will remain unchanged if we replace f^{*n} with their truncations $g^{(n)} = Tr(f^{*n})$ in (10.35) and (10.36). It follows from (10.38) that the truncated sequences $g^{(n)}$ satisfy the recursion relation

$$g^{(1)} = Tr(f),\ g^{(n)} = Tr(g^{(n-1)} * g^{(1)}),\ n = 2, 3, \ldots, L. \tag{10.39}$$

There are two options for calculating truncated convolution powers f^{*n}, $n = 2, 3, ..., L$: the calculation of the convolution powers using the recursion of (10.38) with their subsequent truncation, and the calculation of the truncated convolution powers using the recursion of (10.39). In the first case the forward and inverse DFTs deal with sequences of length $M_n > nK$, $n = 2, 3, ..., L$, while in the second case DFTs deal with sequences of size M_2. For large L it radically decreases computational time because the total length $(L-1)M_2$ of sequences $g^{(n)}$, $n = 2, 3, ..., L$, is much smaller than the total length $M_2 + M_3 + \cdots + M_L$ of sequences f^{*n}, $n = 2, 3, ..., L$. Moreover, the computation time of sequences $g^{(n)}$ can be substantially reduced further using fast Fourier Transform (FFT) with M_2 set equal to a power of 2 (Nussbaumer 1990), for example,

$$M_2 = 2^m, m = 1 + [\log_2(1+K)]. \tag{10.40}$$

10.3.4 Computing a Stationary Distribution

It follows from the above that one can compute the stationary distribution of a ReLS via FFT in the following steps.

1. Choose a whole number K and a discretization step size $\tau = V/K$.
2. Choose a step function $F(x)$ with jumps of size f_k at τk, $k = 0, 1, ..., K$ that would approximate CDF $G(x)$.
3. Apply FFT and compute the sequences $g^{(n)} = (f_0^{*n}, f_1^{*n}, ..., f_K^{*n})$, $n = 2, 3, ..., L$, using formulas (10.39).
4. Define the functions

$$F^{*n}(x) = \sum_{k=0}^{\left[\frac{x}{\tau}\right]} f_k^{*n}, 0 \le x \le V, \ n = 2, 3, ..., L.$$

5. Obtain the stationary state probabilities $q(i)$, $i \in \mathcal{X}$, of the system with unlimited resources.
6. Use distribution $q(i)$, $i \in \mathcal{X}$, and the approximations $G^{*n}(x) \approx F^{*n}(x)$ given by (10.35) and (10.37) to compute the stationary distribution of the system with limited resources.

10.3.5 Numerical Examples

To approximate the resource requirement CDF $G(x)$, it is convenient to use one of the following functions (see Fig. 10.1):

$$F_1(x) = G\left(\left[\tfrac{x}{\tau}\right]\tau\right),$$

$$F_2(x) = G\left(\left[\tfrac{x}{\tau}\right]\tau + \tau\right),$$

$$F_3(x) = G\left(\left[\tfrac{x}{\tau}\right]\tau + 0.5\tau\right), 0 \le x < V.$$

We use $F_3(x)$ because it approximates $G(x)$ closer than $F_1(x)$ and $F_2(x)$. We also consider the following approximation:

$$F_4(V) = G(V),\ F_4(x) = \tfrac{1}{4\tau}(G(k\tau) + 2G((k+0.5)\tau) + G((k+1)\tau)),$$

$$k\tau \le x < (k+1)\tau, k = 0, \ldots, K-1.$$

In the interval $k\tau \le x < (k+1)\tau$, $F_4(x)$ equals the average value of $G(x)$ obtained approximately using the trapezoidal rule (Davis and Rabinowitz 1984):

$$\tfrac{1}{\tau}\int_{k\tau}^{(k+1)\tau} G(t)dt \approx \tfrac{1}{4\tau}(G(k\tau) + 2G((k+0.5)\tau) + G((k+1)\tau)).$$

The plot of $F_4(x)$ is similar to $F_3(x)$ and, therefore, not shown in Fig. 10.1.

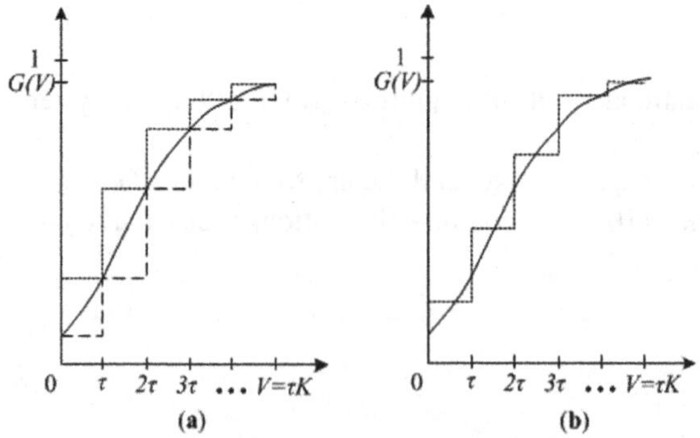

Fig. 10.1 The resource requirement CDF $G(x)$ (solid line) and its approximations: **a** dashed line—$F_1(x)$, dotted line—$F_2(x)$; **b** dotted line—$F_3(x)$

To verify the accuracy of the proposed method, it is necessary to compare the obtained approximate values of the truncated convolution powers with their exact values $G^{*n}(x), 0 \le x < V$. The gamma distribution

$$\Gamma_{\alpha,\beta}(x) = \frac{1}{\Gamma(\alpha)} \int\limits_{0}^{\beta x} e^{-t} t^{\alpha-1} dt$$

is well suited for these purposes because it has a useful property facilitating computation of exact values of convolution powers:

$$\Gamma^{*n}_{\alpha,\beta}(x) = \Gamma_{n\alpha,\beta}(x).$$

We compare the exact values of $G^{*n}(x) = \Gamma^{*n}_{\alpha,\beta}(x)$ with their approximations $F_3^{*n}(x)$ and $F_4^{*n}(x)$ obtained using the method proposed in Sect. 10.3.4. The gamma distribution was calculated via the incog procedure from (Zhang and Jin 1996), and the convolutions were found via FFT using the ffako procedure from (Engeln-Müllges and Uhlig 1996).

Now we consider the case where the total amount of system resources is $V = 100$ and the interval $[0, V]$ is divided into $K = 10^5$ subintervals. Figure 10.2 shows the approximation errors

$$\varepsilon_i^{(n)} = \max_{1 \le k \le K} |G^{*n}(k\tau) - F_i^{*n}(k\tau)|, \ i = 3, 4,$$

as functions of n for various values of the mean $m = \alpha/\beta$ and the square of the coefficient of variation $s = 1/\alpha$ of the resource requirements. The time needed to compute the series of truncated convolutions of length 250 on a PC with an Intel i5-7200 2.5 GHz processor did not exceed 20 min. The proposed discretization technique via function $F_4(x)$ yields better or similar results as via function $F_3(x)$. For $s < 1$, the approximation errors $\varepsilon_3^{(n)}$ and $\varepsilon_4^{(n)}$ were under 0.0001 and the difference between them was negligible. Therefore, only the results for $s > 1$ are shown in Fig. 10.2. The computational errors grew with the coefficient of variation and have their maximum value mainly for small n. Table 10.1 shows the maximum computational errors for the cases depicted in Fig. 10.2.

All in all, FFT permits computing long series of truncated convolution powers with sufficient accuracy.

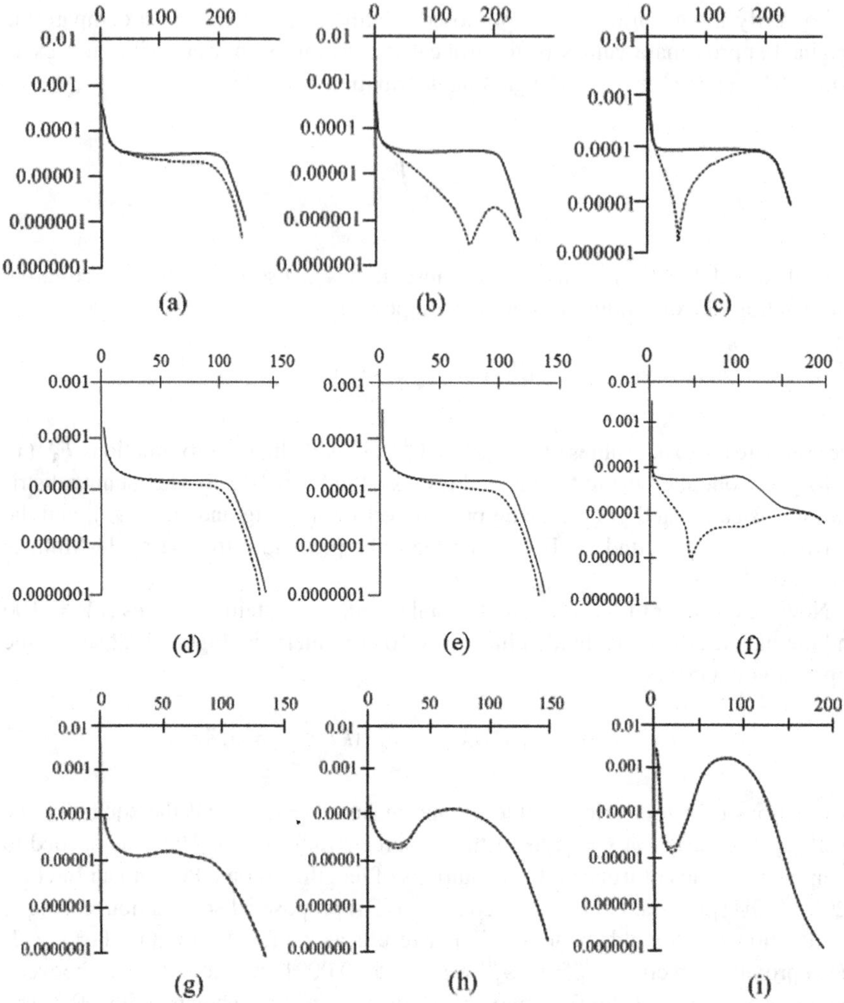

Fig. 10.2 The approximation errors $\varepsilon_3^{(n)}$ (solid lines) and $\varepsilon_4^{(n)}$ (dashed lines) as functions of n **a** $m = 0.5,\ s = 1.5$; **b** $m = 0.5,\ s = 2.0$; **c** $m = 0.5,\ s = 3.0$; **d** $m = 1.0,\ s = 1.5$; **e** $m = 1.0,\ s = 2.0$; **f** $m = 1.0,\ s = 3.0$; **g** $m = 2.0,\ s = 1.5$; **h** $m = 2.0,\ s = 2.0$; **i** $m = 2.0,\ s = 3.0$

Table 10.1 Maximum computational errors when calculating the convolutions for $s = 3$

	m	$n = 2$	$n = 3$	$n = 4$	$n = 5$
$\varepsilon_3^{(n)}$	0.5	0.006027	0.000468	0.000196	0.000154
	1	0.003797	0.000234	0.000097	0.000076
	2	0.002392	0.000117	0.000048	0.000037
$\varepsilon_4^{(n)}$	0.5	0.004003	0.000275	0.000165	0.000126
	1	0.002522	0.000142	0.000084	0.000065
	2	0.001589	0.000073	0.000043	0.000033

References

Asmussen, S.: Applied Probability and Queues, 2nd edn. Springer-Verlag, New York (2003)

Davis, P.J., Rabinowitz, P.: Methods of Numerical Integration, 2nd edn. Academic Press. Orlando, Florida, United States (1984)

Engeln-Müllges, G., Uhlig, F.: Numerical Algorithms with Fortran. Springer-Verlag, Berlin, Germany (1996)

Gikhman, I.I., Skorokhod, A.V.: Introduction to the Theory of Random Processes. Dover Publications, New York (1969)

Naumov, V.A.: On the independent work of the subsystems of a complex system. In: Gnedenko, B.V., Gromak, Yu.I., Chepurin, E.V. (eds.) Queueing Theory, pp. 169–177. Moscow: MSU Press, in Russian (1976)

Nussbaumer, H.J.: Fast Fourier Transform and Convolution Algorithms, 2nd edn. Springer, Berlin, Germany (1990)

Zhang, S., Jin, J.: Computation of Special Functions. Wiley-Interscience, New York (1996)

Chapter 11
Stochastic Networks with Flexible Servers

Abstract In this chapter, we study resource allocation in multi-class networks having several types of flexible servers and general constraints on the number of servers at each station. Each customer class is characterized by the station where the customer is processed and by the amount of work allocated to that station upon customer arrival. Servers may have different working efficiency and resource requirements. We study the maximum network throughput achievable with static resource allocation. We propose a solution for the problem of optimal static resource allocation to servers that maximize network throughput while satisfying constraints on the number of servers at each station.

11.1 Flexible Servers with Deterministic Resource Requirements

There are extensive lists of papers analyzing throughput of systems with flexible servers. Linear programming model was proposed in Andradottir et al. (2003) to determine the optimal allocation of a given number of flexible servers in a multi-class network. In Down and Karakostas (2008), this linear programming model was extended to study server allocation under a constraint on the number of servers at each station. We consider a network composed of N stations, K classes of customers, and M types of servers. The stations represent the customer processing stage, and each station consists of an infinite buffer and several servers that work in parallel. A customer's class uniquely identifies the customer's station, and a given customer can change class after each processing stage. We use $\mathcal{J}(n)$ to denote the set of customer classes processed at station n. Figure 11.1 shows the relation between network components and parameters. Upon the completion of service, a customer in class i is either routed to class j with probability p_{ij} or leaves the network with probability $1 - \sum_{j=1}^{K} p_{ij}$. The transition from class i to class j may correspond to a transition of the customer from one station to another, or it may represent the customer's transition to another class within the same station. We assume that the matrix $\mathbf{I} - \mathbf{P}$ is nonsingular which implies that each customer class has a finite expected time to leave the network. A network is open if customers are allowed to

V. Naumov et al., *Matrix and Analytical Methods for Performance Analysis of Telecommunication Systems*, https://doi.org/10.1007/978-3-030-83132-5_11

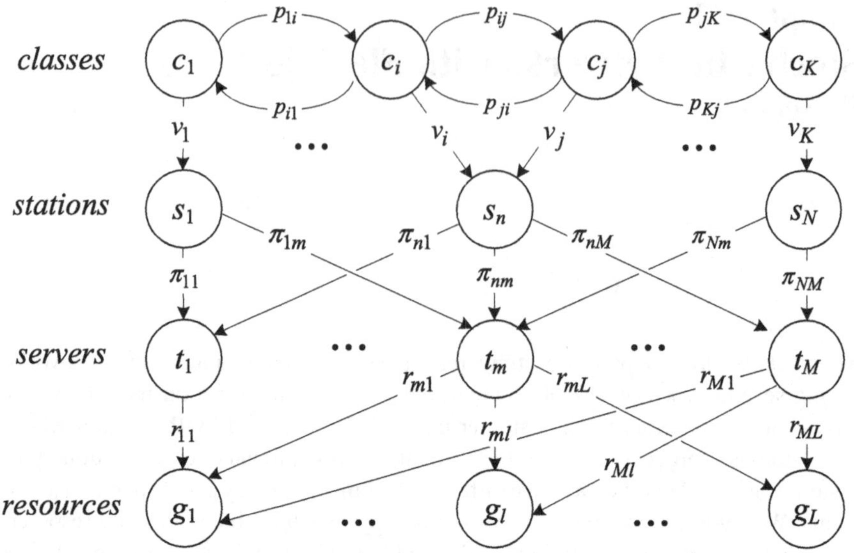

Fig. 11.1 Network components and parameters

both enter and leave the system. We will call a network *clopen* if there are no arrivals, so that customers can only leave the system.

A customer transmits to a station some volume of work that must be performed by servers. We assume these volumes of work to be independent, exponentially distributed random variables. We denote by v_j the expected volume of work that each customer of class j brings to a station. We consider networks having multi-skilled servers that are split into M types according to their functionality. Each server type is characterized by server productivity and its resource quantities required for operation. The sets of stations where servers operate may overlap, and each server can be allocated to any station where the server is operational. Server allocation can be described by an integer $N \times M$-matrix $\mathbf{X} = [x_{nm}]$, where x_{nm} is the number of servers of type m allocated to station n.

A server's productivity is represented by a constant value that describes the volume of work that the server is able to process at a station per unit of time. We denote the productivity of type m servers at station n by π_{nm}. Servers of type m having zero productivity (i.e., $\pi_{nm} = 0$) imply that these servers are not operational at station n. Thus, a server can receive customers at a given station only if its productivity at the station is positive. For that matter, a server can be allocated to any station where it is operational. For example, servers of type 1 may be operational only at stations 1, 2, and 3, whereas servers of type 2 may be operational only at stations 2, 3, and 4. The $N \times M$-matrix $\mathbf{\Pi} = [\pi_{nm}]$ will be called the productivity matrix. The resulting skill matrix $\mathbf{\Sigma} = [\sigma_{nm}]$ is defined by setting $\sigma_{nm} = 1$ if $\pi_{nm} > 0$ and by setting $\sigma_{nm} = 0$ if $\pi_{nm} = 0$. If the elements of the productivity matrix are required to be either 0 or 1, the productivity matrix coincides with the skill matrix.

Let's say that there are L types of resources and that the resources of each type are limited and fixed in quantity. We denote the quantity of type l resources required for a type m server to operate by r_{ml}. For each resource of type l, the server allocation matrix $\mathbf{X}$ must satisfy the following constraints:

$$\sum_{n=1}^{N}\sum_{m=1}^{M} x_{nm} r_{ml} \leq R_l, l = 1, \ldots, L, \tag{11.1}$$

where R_l is the total quantity of type l resources.

The quantity of available resources of type l, u_l, is the difference between the total quantity and allocated quantity of type l resources, i.e.,

$$u_l = R_l - \sum_{n=1}^{N}\sum_{m=1}^{M} x_{nm} r_{ml}.$$

Let $\mathcal{U} = \{l | u_l = 0\}$ be the set containing the types of missing resources. We say that a nonnegative vector $\boldsymbol{\theta} = (\theta_1, \theta_2, \ldots, \theta_M)$ is *the composition vector for the server of type* k if $\boldsymbol{\theta}$ satisfies the following properties:

1. $r_{kl} \leq \sum_{j=1}^{M} \theta_j r_{jl}$, for all $l \in \mathcal{U}$;
2. If numbers ξ_j satisfy inequalities $0 \leq \xi_j \leq \theta_j$ for all $j = 1, \ldots, M$, and $r_{kl} \leq \sum_{j=1}^{M} \xi_j r_{jl}$ for all $l \in \mathcal{U}$, then $\xi_j = 0$, for all $j = 1, \ldots, M$.

Note that the set of composition vectors depends on both the server resource requirements and the types of missing resources, which, in turn, depend on the server allocation $\mathbf{X}$.

We assume that servers cooperate in the sense that if there are multiple servers allocated to a station, they pool their efforts, so that the aggregated productivity of all servers allocated to station n can be calculated as

$$\eta_n(\mathbf{X}) = \sum_{m=1}^{M} \pi_{nm} x_{nm}, n = 1, 2, \ldots, N. \tag{11.2}$$

Let $\mathcal{N} = \{1, 2, \ldots, N\}$ represent the set of all stations, and $\mathcal{G} = \{S_1, S_2, \ldots S_K\}$ denote a collection of nonempty subsets of $\mathcal{N}$. We assume that for each set of stations $S_i \in \mathcal{G}$ a positive number B_i is specified serving as an upper limit for the number of servers allocated to stations belonging to the set $S_i \in \mathcal{G}$. Therefore, only those server allocations are feasible that satisfy the constraints

$$\sum_{n \in S_i}\sum_{m=1}^{M} x_{nm} \leq B_i, i = 1, 2, \ldots, K. \tag{11.3}$$

For example, if $\mathcal{G} = \{\{1\}, \{2\}, ..., \{N\}, \mathcal{N}\}$, then the number of servers at station n has upper bound B_n, $n = 1, 2, ..., N$, whereas the total number of servers in the network cannot exceed B_{N+1}.

11.2 Upper Bounds for the Maximum Throughput

11.2.1 Open Networks

Assume that arriving customers are routed to class j with probability α_j, where $\sum_{j=1}^{K} \alpha_j = 1$. The expected number of visits γ_j to class j, called the visiting ratio, can be uniquely determined by solving the following linear system:

$$\gamma_j = \alpha_j + \sum_{i=1}^{K} \gamma_i p_{ij}, \ j = 1, 2, ..., K.$$

The total expected workload at station n, which is the expected volume of work that each customer places in station n during the customer's lifetime, is given by

$$w_n = \sum_{j \in \mathcal{J}(n)} \gamma_j v_j. \tag{11.4}$$

We assume that w_n is positive for each station n, i.e., that the system does not have superfluous stations.

The total expected service time required for processing a customer at a station n over all that customer's visits to the station can be calculated as

$$\tau_n(\mathbf{X}) = \frac{w_n}{\eta_n(\mathbf{X})}, \tag{11.5}$$

and the saturation rate of station n can be calculated as

$$\mu_n(\mathbf{X}) = \frac{\eta_n(\mathbf{X})}{w_n}. \tag{11.6}$$

At each station of a stable network, the customer arrival rate a cannot exceed the saturation rate (Denning 2008). Therefore, a customer arrival rate a is feasible only if it satisfies the inequality $a \leq \lambda(\mathbf{X})$, where the network throughput $\lambda(\mathbf{X})$ is defined as

$$\lambda(\mathbf{X}) = \min_{1 \leq n \leq N} \mu_n(\mathbf{X}).$$

Equivalently, the customer arrival rate a must satisfy the following constraints:

$$aw_n \le \eta_n(\mathbf{X}), n = 1, 2, \ldots, N.$$

These constraints demand that the total expected amount of work placed into each station per unit of time does not exceed the total productivity of the servers allocated to the station. These inequalities compose a necessary but not a sufficient condition for network stability. Necessary and sufficient conditions for the stability of various stochastic networks can be found in Bramson (2008).

For any arrival rate satisfying $a \le \lambda(\mathbf{X})$, the utilization of station n can be calculated as

$$\rho_n(\mathbf{X}) = \frac{a}{\mu_n(\mathbf{X})}. \tag{11.7}$$

A bottleneck station is defined to be any station n for which the saturation rate $\mu_n(\mathbf{X})$ attains its minimum value $\lambda(\mathbf{X})$ (Denning 2008). It follows from (11.7) that bottleneck stations have the highest utilization in the system. We define the utilization of type m servers, $\alpha_m(\mathbf{X})$, and type l resources, $\beta_l(\mathbf{X})$, as

$$\alpha_m(\mathbf{X}) = \begin{cases} \frac{1}{x_m} \sum\limits_{n=1}^{N} \rho_n(\mathbf{X}) x_{nm}, & x_m > 0, \\ 0, & x_m = 0, \end{cases} \tag{11.8}$$

$$\beta_l(\mathbf{X}) = \frac{1}{R_l} \sum_{m=1}^{M} \alpha_m(\mathbf{X}) x_m r_{ml} = \frac{1}{R_l} \sum_{n=1}^{N} \sum_{m=1}^{M} \rho_n(\mathbf{X}) x_{nm} r_{ml}, \tag{11.9}$$

where $x_m = \sum\limits_{n=1}^{N} x_{nm}$ is the total number of type m servers. It is easy to see that server and resource utilizations cannot exceed the utilization of a bottleneck station. In a balanced network, all stations are equally utilized, and as a result, in (11.8) and (11.9), we have that $\rho_n(\mathbf{X}) = \rho(\mathbf{X})$ for all $n = 1, 2, \ldots, N$. In this case, all servers are also equally utilized:

$$\alpha_m(\mathbf{X}) = \rho(\mathbf{X}), m = 1, 2, \ldots, M,$$

and for resource utilization, we have the following equation:

$$\beta_l(\mathbf{X}) = \frac{\rho(\mathbf{X})}{R_l} \sum_{m=1}^{M} x_m r_{ml}, l = 1, \ldots, L.$$

Let $\mathbb{N}$ denote the set of natural numbers. We formulate the resource allocation problem for an open network (RAO) as the following integer programming problem:

RAO:

maximize

$$\lambda(\mathbf{X}) = \min_{1 \le n \le N} \frac{1}{w_n} \sum_{m=1}^{M} \pi_{nm} x_{nm}, \tag{11.10}$$

subject to:

$$\sum_{n=1}^{N} \sum_{m=1}^{M} x_{nm} r_{ml} \le R_l, \; l = 1, \; ..., \; L, \tag{11.11}$$

$$\sum_{n \in S_i} \sum_{m=1}^{M} x_{nm} \le B_i, i = 1, 2, \; ..., \; K, \tag{11.12}$$

$$x_{nm} \in \mathbb{N}, n = 1, 2, \; ..., \; N, m = 1, 2, \; ..., \; M. \tag{11.13}$$

For the solution $\widetilde{\mathbf{X}}$ of RAO, the value of $\lambda(\widetilde{\mathbf{X}})$ gives the maximum throughput that can be achieved with static server allocation given by $\widetilde{\mathbf{X}}$.

11.2.2 Clopen Networks

Now consider a clopen network, for which at time $t = 0$ there are q_i class i customers for $j = 1, 2, \; ..., \; K$. Let $Q(t)$ represent the number of customers in service within the network at time t and $\Theta = \inf_{t \ge 0} \{Q(t) = 0\}$ denote the time until the network is empty, or time-to-empty. We want to find an allocation of servers that minimizes the expected time-to-empty, $\theta = \mathsf{E}\Theta$.

The expected number of visits of servers entering class j from class i, γ_{ij}, can be uniquely determined by solving the linear system

$$\gamma_{ij} = \delta_{ij} + \sum_{k=1}^{K} \gamma_{ik} p_{kj}, \quad i, j = 1, 2, \; ..., \; K.$$

Considering the initial state of the network, the expected number of class j customers processed by the network before it becomes empty can be calculated as

$$Q_j = \sum_{k=1}^{K} q_k \gamma_{kj}. \tag{11.14}$$

This value also can be determined directly from the linear system

$$Q_j = q_j + \sum_{k=1}^{K} Q_k p_{kj}, \quad j = 1, 2, \ldots, K.$$

Therefore, the expected volume of work placed to the station n can be calculated as

$$W_n = \sum_{j \in \mathcal{J}(n)} Q_j v_j, \tag{11.15}$$

and the total expected service time over all visits of all customers at station n can be calculated as

$$T_n(\mathbf{X}) = \frac{W_n}{\eta_n(\mathbf{X})}. \tag{11.16}$$

Because the network time-to-empty cannot be less than any given station's time-to-empty, we deduce the following bound for the expected network time-to-empty:

$$\frac{1}{\theta} \leq \min_{1 \leq n \leq N} \frac{1}{W_n} \sum_{m=1}^{M} \pi_{nm} x_{nm}. \tag{11.17}$$

Therefore, we can formulate the resource allocation problem for a clopen network (RAC) as the problem of maximizing the right side of inequality (11.17), as follows:

RAC:

maximize

$$\Lambda(\mathbf{X}) = \min_{1 \leq n \leq N} \frac{1}{W_n} \sum_{m=1}^{M} \pi_{nm} x_{nm} \tag{11.18}$$

subject to:

$$\sum_{n=1}^{N} \sum_{m=1}^{M} x_{nm} r_{ml} \leq R_l, \ l = 1, \ldots, L, \tag{11.19}$$

$$\sum_{n \in S_i} \sum_{m=1}^{M} x_{nm} \leq B_i, i = 1, 2, ..., K, \tag{11.20}$$

$$x_{nm} \in \mathbb{N}, n = 1, 2, ..., N, m = 1, 2, ..., M. \tag{11.21}$$

Note that the formulations of the server allocation problem for open and clopen networks are similar. However, the implied meaning of the corresponding objective functions is different. For the optimal allocation of servers specified by the solution $\widetilde{\mathbf{X}}$ to the RAC, the value of $\theta = \Lambda(\widetilde{\mathbf{X}})^{-1}$ gives the minimum expected network time-to-empty that can be achieved with static server allocation.

11.2.3 Upper Bounds for the Maximum Throughput

The solution of the RAO and RAC, both of which rely on integer programming, presents a difficult task, but some simplifications may help to estimate the optimal solution. Below we give an upper bound for the throughput of open networks. Similar results can be obtained for clopen networks by substituting $\lambda(\mathbf{X})$ and w_n with $\Lambda(\mathbf{X})$ and W_n, respectively.

The case $\boldsymbol{\pi_{nm} = \pi_n}$ *for all n and m.*

Let $\mathbf{X}^*$ be a solution to a RAO, and assume that server productivities are independent of the server type, i.e., assume that

$$\pi_{nm} = \pi_n > 0 \tag{11.22}$$

for all n and m. Then for all stations n we have that

$$\lambda(\mathbf{X}^*) \frac{w_n}{\pi_n} \leq \sum_{m=1}^{M} x^*_{nm}, \tag{11.23}$$

and it follows from (11.23) that for each set $S_i \in \mathcal{G}$ the following inequality is valid:

$$\lambda(\mathbf{X}^*) \sum_{n \in S_i} \frac{w_n}{\pi_n} \leq \sum_{n \in S_i} \sum_{m=1}^{M} x^*_{nm} \leq B_i.$$

Therefore, the maximum throughput of the network is given by the following upper bound:

$$\lambda(\mathbf{X}^*) \leq \min_{1 \leq i \leq K} \frac{B_i}{\sum_{n \in S_i} \frac{w_n}{\pi_n}}. \tag{11.24}$$

Note that the denominator in (11.24) is the total expected service time required for processing a customer over all its visits to the set of stations S_i.

In addition to assumption (11.22), let resource requirements also be independent of the server type, i.e., suppose that for all m and l,

$$r_{ml} = r_l > 0. \tag{11.25}$$

In this case, due to (11.11), the total quantity of allocated servers satisfies the following inequality:

$$\sum_{n=1}^{N}\sum_{m=1}^{M} x_{nm}^{*} \leq \frac{R_l}{r_l}. \tag{11.26}$$

Furthermore, another bound for the network throughput follows from (11.23):

$$\lambda(\mathbf{X}^{*}) \leq \frac{\min\limits_{1\leq l\leq L} \frac{R_l}{r_l}}{\sum\limits_{n=1}^{N} \frac{w_n}{\pi_n}}. \tag{11.27}$$

General case

In the general case, a relaxation of the constraints in (11.21) can be used to evaluate the maximum throughput $\lambda(\mathbf{X})$. Consider the following Relaxed RAO (RRAO).

RRAO:

maximize

$$\lambda(\mathbf{X}) = \min_{1\leq n\leq N}\left(\frac{1}{w_n}\sum_{m=1}^{M} \pi_{nm} x_{nm}\right) \tag{11.28}$$

subject to:

$$\sum_{n=1}^{N}\sum_{m=1}^{M} x_{nm} r_{ml} \leq R_l,\ l = 1,\ ...,\ L, \tag{11.29}$$

$$\sum_{n\in S_i}\sum_{m=1}^{M} x_{nm} \leq B_i,\ i = 1, 2,\ ...,\ K, \tag{11.30}$$

$$x_{nm} \geq 0, n = 1, 2,\ ...,\ N, m = 1, 2,\ ...,\ M. \tag{11.31}$$

The only difference between RRAO and RAO is that in RRAO the unknown variables x_{nm} may take on any nonnegative real values. Because the search space in RRAO is larger than in RAO, the value of the objective function $\lambda(\widetilde{\mathbf{X}})$ for a solution $\widetilde{\mathbf{X}}$ to RRAO yields an upper bound for the maximum network throughput $\lambda(\mathbf{X}^*)$ provided by the solution $\mathbf{X}^*$ from RAO.

For any solution $\mathbf{Y}$ to the RRAO, there exists a balanced solution $\mathbf{X}$ giving the same throughput as $\mathbf{Y}$ and satisfying the following equalities:

$$\mu_n(\mathbf{X}) = \lambda(\mathbf{Y}), n = 1, 2, ..., N. \tag{11.32}$$

For example, the matrix $\mathbf{X}$ defined by

$$x_{nm} = y_{nm} \frac{\lambda(\mathbf{Y})}{\mu_n(\mathbf{Y})}$$

satisfies conditions (11.29)–(11.32).

The RRAO problem has an equivalent linear programming formulation.

LRAO:

maximize λ

subject to:

$$\begin{aligned}
\lambda w_n &\le \sum_{m=1}^{M} \pi_{nm} x_{nm}, n = 1, 2, ..., N, \\
\sum_{n=1}^{N} \sum_{m=1}^{M} x_{nm} r_{ml} &\le R_l, l = 1, ..., L, \\
\sum_{n \in S_i} \sum_{m=1}^{M} x_{nm} &\le B_i, i = 1, 2, ..., K, \\
x_{nm} &\ge 0, n = 1, 2, ..., N, m = 1, 2, ..., M.
\end{aligned}$$

We prefer the formulation given in (11.28)–(11.31) because it helps to understand the idea underlying the server allocation procedure presented in the next section. This procedure uses server composition vectors to determine stations with an excess of resources and balances the network by allocating it to the bottleneck station.

11.3 Solution of the Relaxed Throughput Maximization Problem

Starting with some initial server allocation, we can consistently increase network throughput by moving servers from non-bottleneck stations to bottleneck stations. Figure 11.2 illustrates the resource allocation procedure for a simplified RRAO in

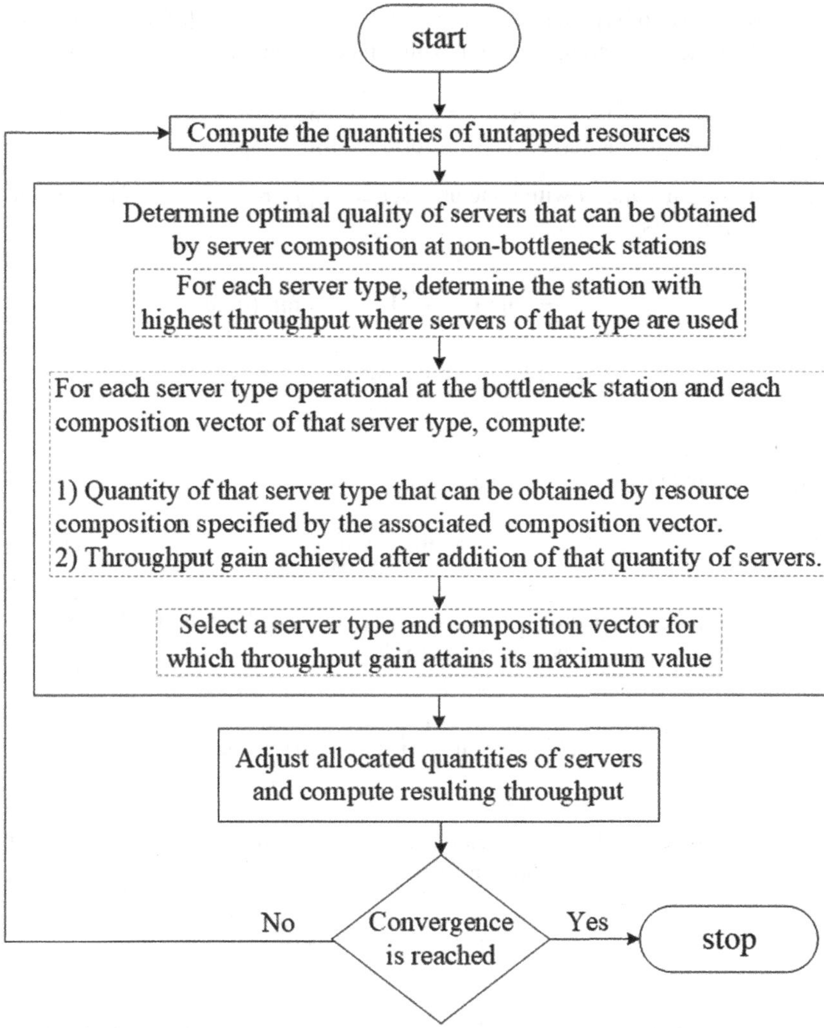

Fig. 11.2 Resource allocation procedure for simplified RRAO

which the constraints from (11.30) have been omitted. This procedure is iterative and converges to a solution with required accuracy ε, where $0 < \varepsilon \ll 1$, while undertaking the following steps:

1. For each resource of type l, compute the quantity of available resources of type l, u_l.
2. Compute the saturation rate of each station and determine a permutation $q(1), q(2), ..., q(N)$ of the indices $1, 2, ..., N$ that will place the saturation rates into nondecreasing order, $\mu_{q(1)} \leq \mu_{q(2)} \leq \cdots \leq \mu_{q(N)}$.

3. For each server of type j, compute v_j as follows. If $x_{q(i)j} = 0$ for all i, then set $v_j = 0$. Otherwise, compute the maximal index i such that $x_{q(i)j} > 0$, and set $v_j = q(i)$.
4. For each server of type k having $\pi_{q(1)k} > 0$ and each composition vector $\boldsymbol{\theta}$ corresponding to this server type, perform the following steps.

   (a) For each station i with nonempty set $\mathcal{Z}_i = \{j : \theta_j > 0, v_j = i\}$, compute parameters a_i, b_i, and c_i as

$$a_i = \min_{j \in \mathcal{Z}_i} \left(\frac{x_{q(i)j}}{\theta_j} \right), \quad c_i = \min(a_i, b_i),$$

$$b_i = \frac{\mu_{q(i)} - \mu_{q(1)}}{\frac{\pi_{q(1)k}}{w_{q(1)}} + \frac{1}{w_{q(i)}} \sum_{j \in \mathcal{Z}_i} \pi_{q(i)j} \theta_j}.$$

   (b) Compute parameter $\delta_k(\boldsymbol{\theta})$ as

$$\delta_k(\boldsymbol{\theta}) = \min_{i:\mathcal{Z}_i \neq \emptyset} c_i. \tag{11.33}$$

   (c) Compute the quantity of type k servers that can be obtained by resource composition as specified by vector $\boldsymbol{\theta}$:

$$\Delta_k(\boldsymbol{\theta}) = \min_{l:r_{kl}>0} \frac{1}{r_{kl}} \left(u_l + \delta_k(\boldsymbol{\theta}) \sum_{j=1}^{K} \theta_j r_{jl} \right). \tag{11.34}$$

   (d) Compute the throughput gain achieved after addition of $\Delta_k(\boldsymbol{\theta})$ units of type k servers to the bottleneck station as

$$g_k(\boldsymbol{\theta}) = \Delta_k(\boldsymbol{\theta}) \frac{\pi_{q(1)k}}{w_{q(1)}}. \tag{11.35}$$

5. Select servers of type $k = \hat{k}$ and take the composition vector $\boldsymbol{\theta} = \hat{\boldsymbol{\theta}}$ for which the throughput gain $g_k(\boldsymbol{\theta})$, achieved after the addition of $\Delta_k(\boldsymbol{\theta})$ units of type k servers to the bottleneck station, attains its maximum value.
6. Adjust the allocated quantities of servers by adding $\Delta_{\hat{k}}(\hat{\boldsymbol{\theta}})$ servers of type $\hat{k}$ to station $q(1)$ and removing $\hat{\theta}_j \delta_{\hat{k}}(\hat{\boldsymbol{\theta}})$ servers of type j from station v_j, i.e., set

$$\begin{aligned} x_{q(1),\hat{k}} &:= x_{q(1),\hat{k}} + \Delta_{\hat{k}}(\hat{\boldsymbol{\theta}}), \\ x_{v_j,j} &:= x_{v_j,j} - \hat{\theta}_j \delta_{\hat{k}}(\hat{\boldsymbol{\theta}}),\ j = 1, 2, \ldots, K. \end{aligned} \tag{11.36}$$

7. Compute the throughput $\lambda(\mathbf{X})$.
8. If $\Delta_{i^*k^*} < \varepsilon\lambda(\mathbf{X})$, then convergence has been obtained, and terminate the server allocation procedure; otherwise, return to the step 1.

Before each iteration, there is a group of bottleneck stations having the same saturation rate. At each iteration, the saturation rate of a bottleneck station in the group increases, and after increasing the saturation rate of the last bottleneck station in the group, a new group of bottleneck stations arises. The saturation rate in the new group of bottleneck stations is higher than that of the previous group of bottleneck stations. Therefore, the sequence of network throughputs calculated at each iteration is a nondecreasing, bounded, and convergent sequence. When convergence is reached, $\lambda(\mathbf{X})$ gives the highest throughput that can be achieved with available resources.

11.4 Examples

Consider an open two-station network processing three classes of customers. External arrivals belong to either class 1, with probability 0.8, or class 2, with probability 0.2. The first station serves class 1 and 2 customers. After service, class 1 customers leave the network, while class 2 customers arrive at the second station as class 3 customers. The quantity of resources and the number of servers at the second stations are limited by $R_1 = 5$, $R_2 = 3$, and $b_2 = 2$. Server productivity and resource requirements are presented in Fig. 11.3, which also depicts external arrivals and customer class distribution.

Table 11.1 gives network throughput and server allocation for different values of b_1 limiting the maximum number of servers at the first station. Utilization of stations, servers, and resources for the arrival rate $a = 0.6$ are given in Table 11.2. To calculate the performance metrics of the stations with a fractional number of servers for the optimized system one can use formulas from Sect. 2.4.3.

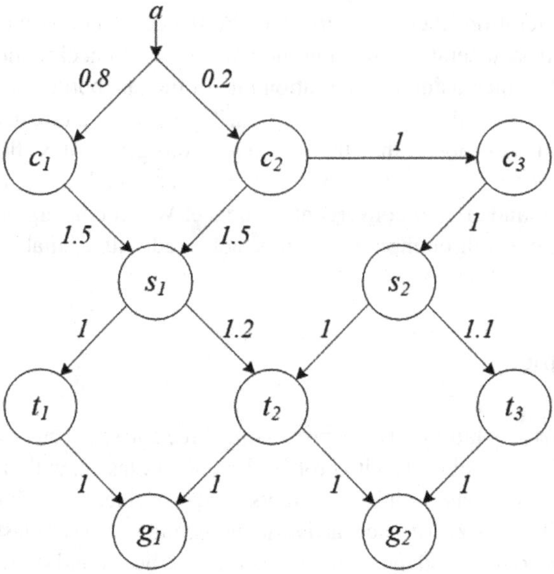

Fig. 11.3 Components and parameters of example network

Table 11.1 Network throughput and resource allocation

	Network throughput	Server allocation			
		Station	Quantities of type 1 servers	Quantities of type 2 servers	Quantities of type 3 servers
$b_1 = 1$	0.800	1	0.000	1.000	0.000
		2	0.000	0.000	0.364
$b_1 = 2$	1.600	1	0.000	2.000	0.000
		2	0.000	0.000	0.727
$b_1 = 3$	2.250	1	1.125	1.875	0.000
		2	0.000	0.000	1.023
$b_1 = 4$	2.883	1	2.375	1.625	0.000
		2	0.000	0.000	1.311
$b_1 = 5$	3.500	1	3.750	1.250	0.000
		2	0.000	0.000	1.591
$b_1 = 6$	3.500	1	3.750	1.250	0.000
		2	0.000	0.000	1.591

Table 11.2 Utilization of network components for arrival rate $a = 0.6$

Capacity of station 1	Station		Server type			Resource type	
	1	2	1	2	3	1	2
$b_1 = 1$	0.750	0.750	0.000	0.750	0.750	0.150	0.341
$b_1 = 2$	0.375	0.375	0.000	0.375	0.375	0.150	0.341
$b_1 = 3$	0.267	0.267	0.267	0.267	0.267	0.160	0.258
$b_1 = 4$	0.208	0.208	0.208	0.208	0.208	0.166	0.207
$b_1 = 5$	0.171	0.171	0.171	0.171	0.171	0.171	0.162
$b_1 = 6$	0.171	0.171	0.171	0.171	0.171	0.171	0.162

References

Andradottir, S., Ayhan, H., Down, D.G.: Dynamic server allocation for queueing networks with flexible servers. Oper. Res. **51**(6), 952–968 (2003)

Bramson, M.: Stability of queueing networks, pp. 77–138. Springer, Berlin, Heidelberg (2008)

Denning, P.J: Throughput. In: Wiley Encyclopedia of Computer Science and Engineering. Wiley-Interscience (2008)

Down, D.G., Karakostas, G.: Maximizing throughput in queueing networks with limited flexibility. Eur. J. Oper. Res. **187**(1), 98–112 (2008)

Chapter 12
Application Examples and Case Studies

Abstract In this chapter we study some representative examples of loss systems with random resource requirements (ReLS) developed for performance analysis of 5G radio access networks and especially 5G mmWave communications. The main difference of ReLS from classical service systems is that a customer, beside a server, demands a random amount of some limited resources, which is held for the duration of its service time and then released. The resulting models can thus reflect the fact that user session requirements for the radio resources of a base station vary due to random spectral efficiency of the transmission channel. A shortcut approach to model analysis which substantially simplifies the derivations, yet yields the same stationary results as the straightforward solution is proposed. Among the examples, we study a system with signals, which permits taking into consideration the line-of-sight blocking in mmWave access networks, and the models reflecting resource reservation and multiconnectivity mechanisms in 5G mmWave communications.

In this chapter, we study some examples of loss systems with random resource requirements (ReLS) which have enabled performance analysis of 5G radio access networks (RAN) with due regard to the dynamics of user sessions' arrivals and departures. As we have seen in previous chapters, the main difference of ReLS from classical service systems is that, in order to be served, a customer, beside a server, demands a random amount of some limited resources. The resulting models can thus reflect the fact that user session requirements for the radio resources of a base station vary due to random user positioning, and, as a consequence, to random spectral efficiency of the transmission channel.

We do not intend to give a complete review of the applications of ReLS here, but rather discuss some representative example models, most often used for analyzing 5G RAN and especially 5G mmWave communications. We do not touch on the technical aspects of 5G RAN design and operation. The interested reader may refer to numerous other publications, which cover the technology to various degrees of detail. This chapter relies on the baseline ReLS model introduced in Chap. 1, in Sects. 1.1 and 1.4.

Section 12.1 presents the general model assumptions and parameters (Samouylov et al. 2015, 2019). In Sect. 12.2 we discuss a shortcut approach to model analysis

V. Naumov et al., *Matrix and Analytical Methods for Performance Analysis of Telecommunication Systems*, https://doi.org/10.1007/978-3-030-83132-5_12

which substantially simplifies the derivations, yet yields the same results as the straightforward solution (Naumov et al. 2014, 2015, 2016; Samouylov et al. 2018). In Sect. 12.3 we study a ReLS model with signals, which permits taking into consideration the line-of-sight blocking in mmWave access networks. Sections 12.4 and 12.5 study the models reflecting resource reservation and multiconnectivity (Petrov et al. 2017).

12.1 General Model Assumptions

Queueing theory has traditionally played a central role in modeling communication systems characterized by random call arrivals. With the emergence of wireless packet-switched access networks, beside the random session patterns, we must take into account the randomness of resource requirements due to the user's position relative to the base station and other factors.

Unlike LTE, 5G RANs are specifically fitted for bandwidth-greedy applications, such as high-resolution video streaming and augmented and virtual reality. Another distinction is that in such applications traffic is not elastic and a constant bit rate is often required for the whole duration of a session.

A possible approach to modeling the user service process in 5G RANs is to combine the stochastic geometry and queueing theory frameworks. The stochastic geometry techniques permit us to take into account the random positions of arriving users and the dynamics of propagation path obstruction, as well as to characterize the random requests for resources. The queueing theory models combine the above factors with the random arrivals and departures of user sessions.

Consider a C-server system in which each customer requires one server. Customers arrive to the system according to a Poisson process of rate λ. The service times are exponentially distributed with parameter μ. Beside the servers, the system has associated resources of capacity R.

We assume there exists a minimal indivisible resource unit of size Δ, corresponding, for instance, to the minimum size of the 5G New Radio (NR) resource block. Let the customers' resource requirements be independent identically distributed discrete nonnegative random variables, independent of the arrival and departure processes and specified by a probability distribution $\{p_r\}_{r\geq 0}$. If upon an arrival the system does not have the required resource amount available, the arriving customer is blocked.

The resource requirements of the customers in service may change during their service time. We assume that each customer in service is associated with a Poisson process of signals of rate α. Upon signal, the customer vacates all resources that have been allocated to it and generates a new resource requirement with the same distribution $\{p_r\}_{r\geq 0}$. If the new resource requirement exceeds the available resource amount, the customer is blocked and dropped.

The above procedure permits reflecting a distinctive aspect of 5G access networks: the user equipment (UE) may change states between LoS (Line-of-Sight, or unblocked direct path from the source to the receiver) and nLoS (non-Line-of-Sight, or blocked direct path from the source to the receiver) due to signal propagation path obstruction between the UE and the base station. Among possible scenarios, one can consider a base station with certain coverage area, given by its radius, and fixed and/or mobile users in a field of fixed or moving line-of-sight blockers within this area. Note that if both users and blockers are fixed, there is no need to add a signaling process since no UE state change occurs.

To specify the model we need to define the following parameters: (a) the base station coverage radius for the given transmission power, along with the transmitter and receiver configuration, (b) the resource requirement distribution $\{p_r\}_{r\geq 0}$, and (c) the rate α of the UE state change. Note that this is a convenient yet relevant way to represent the radio component of the system by just three parameters.

We are interested in evaluating both network performance and QoS measures. In particular, a major network performance characteristic of interest to the network operator is the resource utilization, i.e., the average ratio of allocated resources. Among QoS measures, we point out the blocking probability of an arriving user session and the dropping probability of an ongoing session.

12.2 A Shortcut Approach to ReLS Analysis

Recall that in Sect. 1.4 we have derived a baseline ReLS model by means of a stochastic list and have formulated a major result giving its stationary distribution. In this section we go on studying this system using a shortcut approach which relies on pseudo-lists of resource allocations. For details on stochastic lists and pseudo-lists, see Chap. 8.

12.2.1 A Simplified ReLS Model

As in Sect. 1.4, we consider a service system with $C \leq \infty$ servers and resources of a finite capacity R. Customers arrive according to a Poisson process of rate λ and have exponentially distributed service times with parameter μ. Each customer in service holds one server and a random amount of resources. Customer resource requirements are distributed according to $\{p_r\}_{r\geq 0}$.

Consider a pseudo-list process $X_2(t) = (\xi(t), \delta(t))$ in which, unlike in the process $X_1(t)$ studied in Sect. 1.4, the second component $\delta(t)$ represents the total resource amount allocated to all customers in service. Such a simplification, on the one hand, reduces the size of the state space, but on the other hand, results in loosing some important information about the process.

Indeed, we cannot say exactly how much resources a customer will vacate upon departure. However, we can address this by adopting a probability approach as follows. Suppose the system is in state (k, r) right before a departure. Then the probability that the departing customer vacates a resource amount of j can be found by Bayes' rule as $\frac{p_j p_{r-j}^{(k-1)}}{p_r^{(k)}}$, where p_j is the probability that a customer requires a resource amount of j, and $p_j^{(k)}$ is the probability that k customers together require a resource amount of j, found as the k-fold convolution of distribution $\{p_r\}_{r\geq 0}$.

Let us now derive the equilibrium equations for the stationary probabilities $q_k(r)$ of the process $X_2(t)$:

$$\begin{aligned} &\lambda q_0 \sum_{r=0}^{R} p_r = \mu \sum_{r=0}^{R} q_1(r), \\ &q_k(r)\left(\lambda \sum_{r=0}^{R-r} p_r + k\mu\right) = \lambda \sum_{j=0}^{r} q_{k-1}(j)p_{r-j} + \\ &+ (k+1)\mu \sum_{j=0}^{R-r} q_{k+1}(r+j)\frac{p_j p_r^{(k)}}{p_{r+j}^{(k+1)}}, 1 \leq k \leq C-1, 0 \leq r \leq R, \\ &C\mu q_C(r) = \lambda \sum_{j=0}^{r} q_{C-1}(j)p_{r-j}, 0 \leq r \leq R. \end{aligned} \tag{12.1}$$

By substituting into (12.1) the expressions for $P_k(r)$ given by (1.28) in Sect. 1.4, one checks, that (1.28) verifies these equations. Thus, the stationary probabilities of the simplified process $X_2(t)$ coincide with the probabilities $P_k(r)$ of the aggregated (lumped) states of the original process $X_1(t)$.

This fact will be crucial for more complex systems studied in further sections. The reason is that for more complex systems, usually, one fails to derive an analytical expression for the stationary probabilities and the equilibrium equations have to be solved numerically. The proposed shortcut approach hence permits obtaining the performance measures of the system numerically in a reasonable time.

Note, however, that for more complex systems, it has not been proved that the aggregated states' probabilities of the original process equal the stationary probabilities of the corresponding simplified process. We can reasonably believe that such a simplification provides a good approximation, with an acceptable error. When applied in practice, however, this assumption is to be verified, for instance through simulation.

12.2.2 A Multi-class ReLS Model

Consider now a ReLS with multiple customer classes. Unlike the system discussed above, this system receives L Poisson arrival processes of rates λ_l, $l = 1, 2, ..., L$. The service times of l-class customers are exponentially distributed with rate μ_l, while their resource requirements have a probability distribution $\{p_{l,r}\}_{r\geq 0}$.

For such a system, the stationary probabilities $Q_{k_1,...,k_L}(r_1, ..., r_L)$ that k_1 class 1 customers in service are allocated a total resource amount of r_1, k_2 class 2 customers in service are allocated a total resource amount of r_2, etc., and k_L class L customers in service are allocated a total resource amount of r_L is given by

$$Q_{k_1,\dots,k_L}(r_1,\dots,r_L) = Q_0 \frac{\rho_1^{k_1}}{k_1!} \cdots \frac{\rho_L^{k_L}}{k_L!} p_{1,r_1}^{(k_1)} \cdots p_{L,r_L}^{(k_L)}, \quad \sum_{l=1}^{L} k_l \le C, \sum_{l=1}^{L} r_l \le R$$
$$Q_0 = \left(1 + \sum_{1 \le k_1+\dots+k_L \le C} \; \sum_{0 \le r_1+\dots+r_L \le R} Q_{k_1,\dots,k_L}(r_1,\dots,r_L)\right)^{-1}. \tag{12.2}$$

Here, $\rho_l = \lambda_l / \mu_l$, $l = 1, 2, \dots, L$.

Note that the expressions (12.2) are hardly suitable for straightforward computation. We will show next that the stationary probabilities of a ReLS with L customer classes are equal to the state probabilities of a single-class system receiving an aggregated arrival process and having the weighted average distribution of resource requirements.

For all positive integers k, define a sequence $G_{L,k,r}$, $r \ge 0$, as

$$G_{L,k,r} = \sum_{\substack{k_1,\dots,k_L \ge 0 \\ k_1+\dots+k_L = k}} \frac{\rho_1^{k_1}}{k_1!} \cdots \frac{\rho_L^{k_L}}{k_L!} \sum_{\substack{r_1,\dots,r_L \ge 0 \\ r_1+\dots+r_L = r}} p_{1,r_1}^{(k_1)} \cdots p_{L,r_L}^{(k_L)}. \tag{12.3}$$

Consider the generating function of the sequence $G_{L,k,r}$, which is given by

$$G_{L,k}(z) = \sum_{r=0}^{\infty} z^r \sum_{\substack{k_1,\dots,k_L \ge 0 \\ k_1+\dots+k_L = k}} \frac{\rho_1^{k_1}}{k_1!} \cdots \frac{\rho_L^{k_L}}{k_L!} \sum_{\substack{r_1,\dots,r_L \ge 0 \\ r_1+\dots+r_L = r}} p_{1,r_1}^{(k_1)} \cdots p_{L,r_L}^{(k_L)}. \tag{12.4}$$

Denote by $P_l(z)$ the generating function of the resource requirement distribution of class l customers. Then, using the properties of generating functions, we have

$$G_{L,k}(z) = \sum_{\substack{k_1,\dots,k_L \ge 0 \\ k_1+\dots+k_L = k}} \frac{\rho_1^{k_1}}{k_1!} \cdots \frac{\rho_L^{k_L}}{k_L!} P_1^{k_1}(z) \dots P_L^{k_L}(z). \tag{12.5}$$

Finally, by denoting $\rho = \rho_1 + \dots + \rho_L$ and using the multinomial theorem, we obtain

$$G_{L,k}(z) = \frac{\rho^k}{k!} \sum_{\substack{k_1,...,k_L \geq 0 \\ k_1+...+k_L=k}} \frac{k!}{k_1!...k_L!}\left(\frac{\rho_1}{\rho}\right)^{k_1}...\left(\frac{\rho_L}{\rho}\right)^{k_L} P_1^{k_1}(z)...P_L^{k_L}(z) = \tag{12.6}$$
$$= \frac{\rho^k}{k!}\left(\frac{\rho_1}{\rho}P_1(z)+...+\frac{\rho_L}{\rho}P_L(z)\right)^k.$$

It follows from the above, that a multi-class ReLS has the same joint distribution of the total number of customers in service and total amount of allocated resources as a single-class system having a weighted average distribution of resource requirements. In other words, the stationary probabilities $Q_k(r)$ that there are k customers in service (all classes combined) and the resource amount allocated to them is r are given by

$$Q_k(r) = Q_0\frac{\rho^k}{k!}\overline{p}_r^{(k)},\quad 1 \leq k \leq C, r \leq R,$$
$$Q_0 = \left(1+\sum_{k=1}^{C}\sum_{r=0}^{R} Q_k(r)\right)^{-1}, \tag{12.7}$$

where $\rho = \rho_1 + \rho_2 + ... + \rho_L$ and

$$\overline{p}_r = \sum_{l=1}^{L}\frac{\rho_l}{\rho}p_{l,r}. \tag{12.8}$$

Now, the mean allocated total $\mathsf{E}\delta$ can be found by the formula

$$\mathsf{E}\delta = Q_0\sum_{k=1}^{C}\frac{\rho^k}{k!}\sum_{r=1}^{R} r\overline{p}_r^{(k)}$$

similar to (1.31) in Sect. 1.4, while the blocking probability of a class l customer is given by

$$B_l = 1 - \sum_{k=0}^{C-1}\sum_{r=0}^{R} Q_k(r)p_{l,R-r}. \tag{12.9}$$

12.2.3 An Algorithm for Computing Performance Measures

Computing the characteristics of a ReLS model directly, using the analytical expressions for the stationary probabilities, is complicated by the necessity to calculate the multiple convolutions of the resource requirement distribution. To reduce the computational complexity, we derive a recursive algorithm for calculating the normalization constant, which permits obtaining the model performance measures without calculating the stationary probabilities.

Define $G(n, r) = \sum_{k=0}^{n} \frac{\rho^k}{k!} \sum_{j=0}^{r} p_j^{(k)}$ for all nonnegative integers n and r. In accordance with this definition and formulas (12.7), the normalization constant, which represents the probability that the system is empty, is given by $Q_0 = G(C, R)^{-1}$. Using the properties of the sums, one checks easily that the functions $G(n, r)$ satisfy the recurrence relation

$$G(n, r) = G(n-1, r) + \frac{\rho}{n} \sum_{j=0}^{r} p_j (G(n-1, r-j) - G(n-2, r-j)), \tag{12.10}$$

with the initial conditions

$$G(0, r) = 1, \quad G(1, r) = 1 + \sum_{j=0}^{r} p_j, \quad r \geq 0. \tag{12.11}$$

The functions $G(n, r)$ can be used to compute many performance measures of the system. For instance, the blocking probability B and the mean allocated total $\mathsf{E}\delta$ can be expressed as

$$B = 1 - \frac{1}{G(C, R)} \sum_{j=0}^{R} p_j G(C-1, R-j), \tag{12.12}$$

$$\mathsf{E}\delta = R - \frac{1}{G(C, R)} \sum_{j=1}^{R} G(C, R-j). \tag{12.13}$$

12.3 A ReLS Model with Signals

In this section we consider a ReLS model with signals, which permits taking into account the line-of-sight blocking in 5G mmWave RAN. The signals represent an external stream of events corresponding to a line-of-sight state change and, by consequence, may result in a change of the required amount of time–frequency resources.

Let us extend the model considered in the previous section as follows. Let each customer in service generate a Poisson process of signals with rate α. Upon signal, the customer vacates the allocated resources and generates a new resource requirement with the same probability distribution. If the reallocation attempt fails the customer is dropped. Other assumptions of the baseline model remain unchanged.

For model analysis we will use the shortcut approach introduced previously. The system's behavior is described by a stochastic process $X(t) = (\xi(t), \delta(t))$ in which, once again, the first component represents the number of customers in service at time t, while the second component represents the total amount of resources allocated to all customers in service at time t.

The system's state space is given by

$$\Psi = \bigcup_{k=0}^{C} \Psi_k, \quad \Psi_k = \left\{(k, r) : 0 \le r \le R,\, p_r^{(k)} > 0\right\}. \tag{12.14}$$

We reorder the states in the sets Ψ_k so that the amount of allocated resources increases, and let $I(k, r)$ represent the index of state (k, r) in the set Ψ_k.

12.3.1 Stationary Probabilities

We first introduce an additional notation which will facilitate understanding of this and further sections. Let $\theta_i(k, r)$ represent the conditional probability that one customer is allocated a resource amount of i given that k customers are allocated a total resource amount of r. Then, by Bayes' rule, we have

$$\theta_i(k, r) = \frac{p_i p_{r-i}^{(k-1)}}{p_r^{(k)}}. \tag{12.15}$$

To derive the generator matrix of the process $X(t)$, let us examine possible transitions among the system's states. Let the system be in state (k, r) at some time instant. With probability p_j a customer arrives and demands a resource amount of j. If $j \le R - r$ then the system jumps to state $(k + 1, r + j)$. Upon a customer departure, a resource amount i is released with probability $\theta_i(k, r)$. In this case the system jumps to state $(k - 1, r - i)$.

Upon a signal arrival, one of the customers in service first releases a resource amount of i with probability $\theta_i(k, r)$ and then demands a resource amount of j with probability p_j. If $j \le i$ then the customer is sure to remain in service. However, if $j < i$, then the system jumps to state $(k, r - i + j)$ with probability $\theta_i(k, r)p_j$, while if $j = i$ the state remains unchanged. On the other hand, if the new resource requirement exceeds the previous one, then the customer remains in service only if $j \le R - r + i$. Otherwise, the customer is dropped and the system jumps to state $(k - 1, r - i)$.

The generator $\mathbf{A}$ of the process $X(t)$ is block tridiagonal with diagonal blocks $\mathbf{D}_0, \mathbf{D}_1, ..., \mathbf{D}_C$, upper diagonal blocks $\mathbf{\Lambda}_1, ..., \mathbf{\Lambda}_C$ and lower diagonal blocks $\mathbf{M}_0, ..., \mathbf{M}_{C-1}$:

$$\mathbf{A} = \begin{pmatrix} \mathbf{D}_0 & \mathbf{\Lambda}_1 & \mathbf{O} & \dots & & \mathbf{O} \\ \mathbf{M}_0 & \mathbf{D}_1 & \mathbf{\Lambda}_2 & & & \mathbf{O} \\ \mathbf{O} & \ddots & \ddots & & \ddots & \dots \\ \dots & & \mathbf{M}_{C-2} & & \mathbf{D}_{C-1} & \mathbf{\Lambda}_C \\ \mathbf{O} & \dots & \mathbf{O} & & \mathbf{M}_{C-1} & \mathbf{D}_C \end{pmatrix}. \tag{12.16}$$

Its first blocks are given by

$$\mathbf{D}_0 = -\lambda \sum_{j=0}^{R} p_j, \tag{12.17}$$

$$\mathbf{\Lambda}_1 = (\lambda p_0, ..., \lambda p_R), \tag{12.18}$$

$$\mathbf{M}_0 = (\mu, ..., \mu)^T, \tag{12.19}$$

and we must remove zero elements from $\mathbf{\Lambda}_1$, so that its number of columns, as well as the number of rows in $\mathbf{M}_0$, equals the number of states in Ψ_1. The other blocks are given by the following expressions:

$$\mathbf{D}_n(I(n,i),(n,j)) = \begin{cases} -\left(\lambda \sum\limits_{j=0}^{R-i} p_j + n\mu + n\alpha(1 - \sum\limits_{m=0}^{i} \theta_m(n,i)) p_m\right), i = j, \\ n\alpha \sum\limits_{m=0}^{i} \theta_m(n,i) p_{j-i+m}, \ i < j, \\ n\alpha \sum\limits_{m=i-j}^{i} \theta_m(n,i) p_{j-i+m}, \ i > j, \end{cases}$$
$$(n,i),(n,j) \in \Psi_n, \quad 1 \le n \le C-1; \tag{12.20}$$

$$\mathbf{D}_C(I(C,i),(C,j)) = \begin{cases} -\left(C\mu + C\alpha(1 - \sum\limits_{m=0}^{i} \theta_m(C,i)) p_m\right), \ i = j, \\ C\alpha \sum\limits_{m=0}^{i} \theta_m(C,i) p_{j-i+m}, \ i < j, \\ C\alpha \sum\limits_{m=i-j}^{i} \theta_m(C,i) p_{j-i+m}, \ i > j, \end{cases} \tag{12.21}$$
$$(C,i),(C,j) \in \Psi_C;$$

$$\mathbf{\Lambda}_n(I(n-1,i),(n,j)) = \begin{cases} \lambda p_{j-i}, & i \le j \le R, \\ 0, & j < i, \end{cases} \tag{12.22}$$
$$(n-1,i) \in \Psi_{n-1}, (n,j) \in \Psi_n, \quad 2 \le n \le C;$$

$$\mathbf{M}_n(I(n+1,i),(n,j)) = \begin{cases} (n+1)\mu\theta_{i-j}(n+1,i), & j \le i \le R, \\ 0, & j > i, \end{cases} \tag{12.23}$$
$$(n+1,i) \in \Psi_{n+1}, (n,j) \in \Psi_n, \quad 1 \le n \le C-1.$$

The stationary probabilities $Q_k(r)$ of the process $X(t)$ are the unique solution to the equilibrium equations with the normalization condition, given, in the matrix form, by

$$\mathbf{QA} = \mathbf{0}, \quad \mathbf{Qu} = 1, \tag{12.24}$$

where $\mathbf{Q}$ is the stationary probability row vector, and $\mathbf{u}$ is a column vector of ones of a corresponding size. The system of linear equations (12.24) can be solved by any numerical method, including those that make use of the particular block structure of the considered generator matrix.

12.3.2 System Performance Measures

We now proceed to the system performance measures, which include, as before, the blocking probability B of an arriving customer and the mean allocated total $\mathsf{E}\delta$. Note that resource utilization can then be obtained as $\mathsf{E}\delta/R$. These characteristics can be found directly using the stationary probabilities:

$$B = 1 - \sum_{k=0}^{C-1}\sum_{r=0}^{R} Q_k(r) \sum_{j=0}^{R-r} p_r, \tag{12.25}$$

$$\mathsf{E}\delta = \sum_{k=0}^{C}\sum_{r=0}^{R} r Q_k(r). \tag{12.26}$$

Besides, we may be interested in the probability B_{drop} that a customer in service is dropped due to a resource reallocation failure upon a signal arrival. Recall that a customer in service is dropped whenever, upon signal, the new resource requirement exceeds the available (unallocated) resource amount. Therefore, the dropping rate is given by

$$\kappa = \alpha \mathsf{E}\xi \sum_{k=1}^{C}\sum_{r=0}^{R} Q_k(r) \sum_{j=0}^{r} \theta_j(k,r)\left(1 - \sum_{i=0}^{R-r+j} p_i\right), \tag{12.27}$$

where $\mathsf{E}\xi$ is the mean number of customers in service,

$$\mathsf{E}\xi = \sum_{k=1}^{C}\sum_{r=0}^{R} kQ_k(r). \tag{12.28}$$

Now, the probability B_{drop} can be found as the limit of the ratio of the number of dropped customers in time T to the number of admitted customers in time T as T goes to infinity. Thus, we have

$$B_{drop} = \lim_{T\to\infty} \frac{\kappa T}{\lambda(1-B)T} = \frac{\kappa}{\lambda(1-B)}. \tag{12.29}$$

Note that the dropping probability is the most critical among the aforementioned performance measures. This is why in the further sections we will address the mechanisms that permit reducing this probability.

To conclude this section, let us remind that for a ReLS model with signals the proposed shortcut approach, which keeps track of the allocated totals instead of per-customer allocations, provides an approximate solution and not the exact one. When using this technique in applications, one must check that the relative error for the given parameter range is acceptable.

12.4 A ReLS Model with Resource Reservation

Reserving some network capacity to maintain sessions that require more resources due to line-of-sight blocking is a way to improve session-continuity-related QoS in mmWave RANs. If this mechanism is employed, only a share of the system's resources is available to arriving sessions, while the remainder is reserved for maintaining ongoing sessions only. In this section we discuss a ReLS with signals modeling such a mechanism for a 5G NR base station and derive its performance measures. We adopt the same model assumptions as in Sect. 1.4 and apply the shortcut approach proposed in Sect. 12.2.

12.4.1 Model Description

We consider an C-server system with a finite resource amount of R, only a fraction of which, $R_0 = (1-\gamma)R$, $0 < \gamma < 1$, is available to arriving customers. Here, γ is a reservation parameter representing the resource share reserved for maintaining customers in service. The system's behavior is described by a stochastic process $X(t) = (\xi(t), \delta(t))$, where $\xi(t)$ is the number of customers in service and $\delta(t)$ is the allocated total. The system's state space Ψ is given by (12.14).

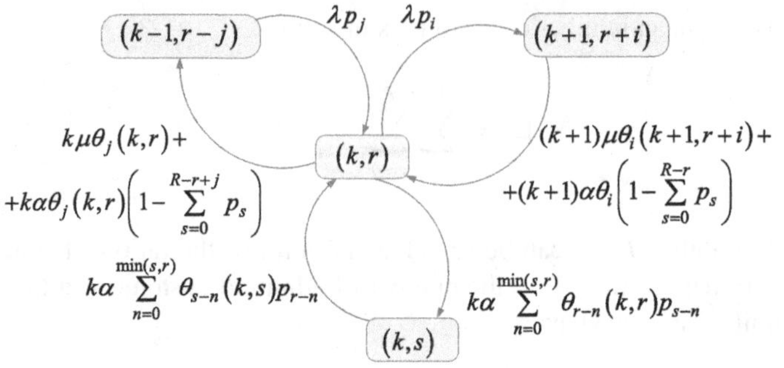

Fig. 12.1 Transition diagram for a central system state

Unlike in the system studied in Sect. 12.3, only resource amount $R_0 < R$ is accessible to arriving customers. Let the system be in state (k, r) and a customer arrive with a resource requirement of j. Then, (1) if $r > R_0$, then any arriving customer is blocked, (2) if $r \le R_0$ and $j > R_0 - r$, then the arriving customer is blocked, and (3) if $r \le R_0$ and $j \le R_0 - r$, then the arriving customer receives service.

When resources are reallocated to a customer upon signal, then the total resource amount R becomes accessible. In other words, if upon a signal arrival in state (k, r), the corresponding customer releases resource amount i and demands resource amount j, then the customer is dropped only if $j > R - r + i$.

Beside from that, the system operates similarly to the one in Sect. 12.3. The transition diagram in Fig. 12.1 shows the transition intensities for the most general, central system state.

12.4.2 Equilibrium Equations

Using the notation introduced previously and the relation

$$\theta(R_0 - j) = \begin{cases} 0, & j > R_0, \\ 1, & j \le R_0, \end{cases} \tag{12.30}$$

we can write the equilibrium equations of the system as follows:

$$\lambda Q_0 \sum_{j=0}^{R_0} p_j = \mu \sum_{j:(1,j)\in\Psi_1} Q_1(j) + \alpha \sum_{j:(1,j)\in\Psi_1} Q_1(j)\left(1 - \sum_{s=0}^{R} p_s\right),$$

$$\left(\theta(R_0 - j)\lambda \sum_{j=0}^{R_0-r} p_j + k\mu + k\alpha\right) Q_k(r) =$$
$$= \theta(R_0 - j)\lambda \sum_{j\geq 0:(k-1,r-j)\in\Psi_{k-1}} Q_{k-1}(r-j)p_j +$$
$$+ (k+1)\mu \sum_{j\geq 0:(k+1,r+j)\in\Psi_{k+1}} Q_{k+1}(r+j)\theta_j(k+1, j+r) +$$
$$+ (k+1)\alpha\left(1 - \sum_{s=0}^{R-r} p_s\right) \sum_{j\geq 0:(k+1,r+j)\in\Psi_{k+1}} Q_{k+1}(r+j)\theta_j(k+1, j+r) +$$
$$+ k\alpha \sum_{j\geq 0:(k,j)\in\Psi_k} Q_k(j) \sum_{i=0}^{min(j,r)} \theta_{j-i}(k+1, j+r)p_{r-i},$$
$$1 \leq n \leq C-1, 0 \leq r \leq R,$$

(12.31)

$$C(\mu+\alpha)Q_C(r) = \theta(R_0 - j)\lambda \sum_{j\geq 0:(C-1,j)\in\Psi_{C-1}} Q_{C-1}(r-j)p_j +$$
$$+ C\alpha \sum_{j\geq 0:(C,j)\in\Psi_C} Q_C(j) \sum_{i=0}^{min(j,r)} \theta_{j-i}(C, j)p_{r-i}, 1 \leq r \leq R.$$

The stationary probabilities can be found as the solution to the (12.31) with the normalization condition. The infinitesimal generator of the process can be obtained from the equations by an argument similar to the one in Sect. 12.3.1. We leave this to the reader as an exercise.

12.4.3 System Performance Measures

Since the system under consideration differs from the one in Sect. 12.3 only in the new customer admission algorithm, only the expression for the blocking probability needs modification, and we have

$$B = 1 - \sum_{k=0}^{C-1} \sum_{r=0}^{R_0} Q_k(r) \sum_{j=0}^{R_0-r} p_r. \tag{12.32}$$

The mean allocated total and the dropping probability can be found, respectively, by (12.26) and (12.29).

12.5 A ReLS Model with Multiconnectivity and Resource Reservation

Another way to increase user session continuity in mmWave RAN is the multiconnectivity, which implies that a mobile UE is connected to multiple access points simultaneously. If this is the case, only one link is used to transfer data at any specific time, but if this link gets blocked due to line-of-sight obstruction, the UE instantaneously switches to a link to another access point.

In this section we address a system with both multiconnectivity and resource reservation. Unlike in previous sections, here we consider a set of base stations, each of which is accessible to every user, with a possible scenario being several base stations located around the perimeter of a city square.

12.5.1 *Multiconnectivity Model Description*

Consider a K-node service network in which node k is a C_k-server ReLS having a resource amount of $R_{k,1}$ and receiving a Poisson process of customers with rate λ_k, $k = 1, 2, ..., K$. Denote $\lambda = \sum_{k=1}^{K} \lambda_k$. The resource requirements of all arriving customers have the same probability distribution, which we denote by $\{p_{0,r}\}_{r\geq 0}$.

Not all the resource capacity of a node is accessible to arriving customers, but only its fraction given by $R_{k,0} = R_{k,1}(1 - \gamma)$, $0 < \gamma < 1$. As before, an arriving customer is blocked and lost if it finds all servers busy or the available resource amount insufficient. We assume the service times at all nodes exponentially distributed with the same parameter μ.

Each customer in service at node k generates a Poisson process of signals of rate α_k, $k = 1, 2, ..., K$, which represents the channel changing states between LoS and nLoS. Upon a signal arrival, a customer releases the resource amount allocated to it previously and generates a new resource requirement according to a distribution $\{p_{1,r}\}_{r\geq 0}$. Otherwise, assuming that $K > 1$, the customer leaves node k and attempts to resume service at any other node with probability $1/(K - 1)$ with a new resource requirement generated according to distribution $\{p_{1,r}\}_{r\geq 0}$. We will refer to such resuming customers as *secondary*, in contrast to newly arriving customers, which will be called *primary*. The number of transitions among the nodes will be referred to as the *level* of a secondary customer. At each node k, secondary customers form an additional Poisson process of rate φ_k, $k = 1, 2, ..., K$. We denote $\varphi = \sum_{k=1}^{K} \varphi_k$.

The whole resource amount of the node is accessible to secondary customers. However, if the node to which a secondary customer has moved does not have a free server and enough available resources, the customer is dropped. Note that due to the memoryless property of the exponential distribution, the remaining service time of a secondary customer is also exponentially distributed with parameter μ.

Fig. 12.2 A ReLS network

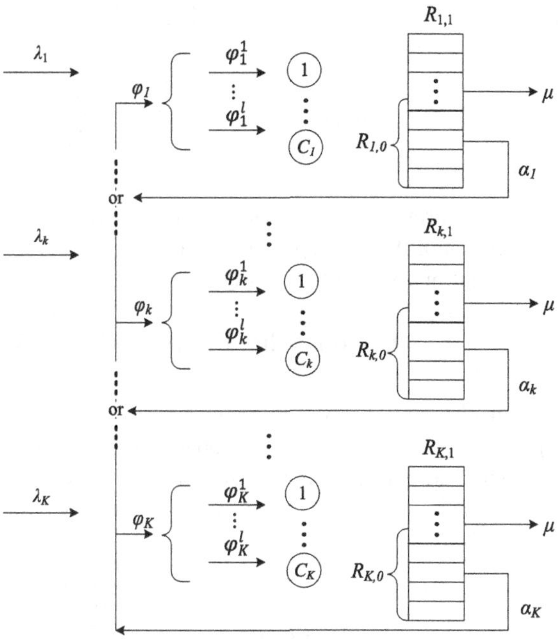

A scheme of the ReLS network under consideration is depicted in Fig. 12.2.

To analyze the model performance, we suggest using the decomposition method, which is commonly employed when dealing with complex service networks. The key assumption here is that the service process at each node is independent of the service processes at other nodes. In the next subsection we address the service process at a single node of the network, while in Sect. 12.5.3 an algorithm for computing the performance measures of the whole network is derived.

12.5.2 A Single Node Model

Consider a node of the ReLS network introduced above, say k. The node receives two Poisson processes: of primary customers with rate λ_k and of secondary customers with rate φ_k. In view of the properties of the exponential distribution, the holding times at the node are exponentially distributed with parameter $\mu + \alpha_k, \ \ k = 1, 2, ..., K$.

Once again, we employ the shortcut approach and keep track of the total allocated resource amount only. Then, since we need to consider both the arriving and resuming customers, we describe the system's behavior by a trivariate process $X(t) = (\xi_1(t), \xi_2(t), \delta(t))$, where $\xi_1(t)$ and $\xi_2(t)$ represent, respectively, the numbers of primary and secondary customers in service at time t, while $\delta(t)$ represents the total allocated resource amount. The state space of the process is given by

$$\Psi = \bigcup_{0 \le n_1+n_2 \le C} \Psi_{n_1,n_2},$$
$$\Psi_{n_1,n_2} = \left\{ (n_1, n_2, r) : 0 \le r \le R_1, \sum_{i=0}^{\min(r,R_0)} p_{0,i}^{(n_1)} p_{1,r-i}^{(n_2)} > 0 \right\}, \tag{12.33}$$

where, as previously, an upper index in brackets, say n, indicates the n-fold convolution of the corresponding distribution.

The stationary probabilities $Q_{n_1,n_2}(r)$ of states $(n_1, n_2, r) \in \Psi$ are defined as

$$Q_{n_1,n_2}(r) = \lim_{t\to\infty} \mathsf{P}(\xi_1(t) = n_1, \xi_2(t) = n_2, \delta(t) = r). \tag{12.34}$$

Consider now a resource amount released by a departing customer. Denote by $\beta_{0,j}(n_1, n_2, r)$ the conditional probability that upon a primary customer departure a resource amount of j is released given that the system is in state (n_1, n_2, r). For $r \le R_0$ the probabilities $\beta_{0,j}(n_1, n_2, r)$ are easily obtained using Bayes' rule:

$$\beta_{0,j}(n_1, n_2, r) = \frac{p_{0,j} \sum_{i=0}^{r-j} p_{0,i}^{(n_1-1)} p_{1,r-j-i}^{(n_2)}}{\sum_{i=0}^{r} p_{0,i}^{(n_1)} p_{1,r-i}^{(n_2)}}. \tag{12.35}$$

Similarly, denote by $\beta_{1,j}(n_1, n_2, r)$ the conditional probability that a departing secondary customer releases a resource amount of j given that the system is in state (n_1, n_2, r). This probability is given by

$$\beta_{1,j}(n_1, n_2, r) = \frac{p_{1,j} \sum_{i=0}^{r-j} p_{0,i}^{(n_1)} p_{1,r-j-i}^{(n_2-1)}}{\sum_{i=0}^{r} p_{0,i}^{(n_1)} p_{1,r-i}^{(n_2)}}. \tag{12.36}$$

It is much harder to evaluate $\beta_{0,j}(n_1, n_2, r)$ and $\beta_{1,j}(n_1, n_2, r)$ for $r > R_0$. We notice that these probabilities depend on the arrival order of the primary and secondary customers, which cannot be recovered from the system state. However, since primary and secondary arrivals are mutually independent and we know how many customers of each type are in service, we can consider all their permutations in time to be equally likely. The probability that the last primary customer arrived in the k-th position is

$$\binom{k-1}{n_1-1} \Big/ \binom{n_1+n_2}{n_1}, \tag{12.37}$$

where $\binom{k-1}{n_1-1}$ is the number of possibilities to place $n_1 - 1$ (indistinguishable) primary customers in the first $k - 1$ positions (because the last one takes the k-th position), and $\binom{n_1+n_2}{n_1}$ is the number of possibilities to place n_1 primary customers. The probability that n_1 primary and $k - n_1$ secondary customers are allocated a resource amount of $i \leq R_0$ is given by the convolution

$$\sum_{s=0}^{i} p_{0,s}^{(n_1)} p_{1,i-s}^{(k-n_1)}, \tag{12.38}$$

Now, the conditional probability that n_1 primary and n_2 secondary customers combined are allocated a resource amount of r given that the last primary customer arrived in the k-th position is given by

$$\sum_{i=0}^{\min(r,R_0)} p_{1,r-i}^{(n_2+n_1-k)} \sum_{s=0}^{i} p_{0,s}^{(n_1)} p_{1,i-s}^{(k-n_1)}. \tag{12.39}$$

Finally, the unconditional probability that n_1 primary and n_2 secondary customers combined are allocated a resource amount of r is

$$\sum_{k=n_1}^{n_1+n_2} \frac{\binom{k-1}{n_1-1}}{\binom{n_1+n_2}{n_1}} \sum_{i=0}^{\min(r,R_0)} p_{1,r-i}^{(n_2+n_1-k)} \sum_{s=0}^{i} p_{0,s}^{(n_1)} p_{1,i-s}^{(k-n_1)}. \tag{12.40}$$

The resulting expressions for $\beta_{0,j}(n_1, n_2, r)$ and $\beta_{1,j}(n_1, n_2, r)$ are too lengthy to reproduce here, and the complete derivation is left to the reader. Moreover, using these formulas for $r > R_0$ is a hard computational task. Therefore, to reduce the computational complexity we suggest using the approach of (12.35) and (12.36) for all r and ignore the order of arrivals. This yields

$$\begin{aligned} \beta_{0,j}(n_1, n_2, r) &= \frac{p_{0,j} \sum_{i=0}^{\min(r-j,R_0-j)} p_{0,i}^{(n_1-1)} p_{1,r-j-i}^{(n_2)}}{\sum_{i=0}^{\min(r,R_0)} p_{0,i}^{(n_1)} p_{1,r-i}^{(n_2)}}, \\ \beta_{1,j}(n_1, n_2, r) &= \frac{p_{1,j} \sum_{i=0}^{\min(r-j,R_0)} p_{0,i}^{(n_1)} p_{1,r-j-i}^{(n_2-1)}}{\sum_{i=0}^{\min(r,R_0)} p_{0,i}^{(n_1)} p_{1,r-i}^{(n_2)}}. \end{aligned} \tag{12.41}$$

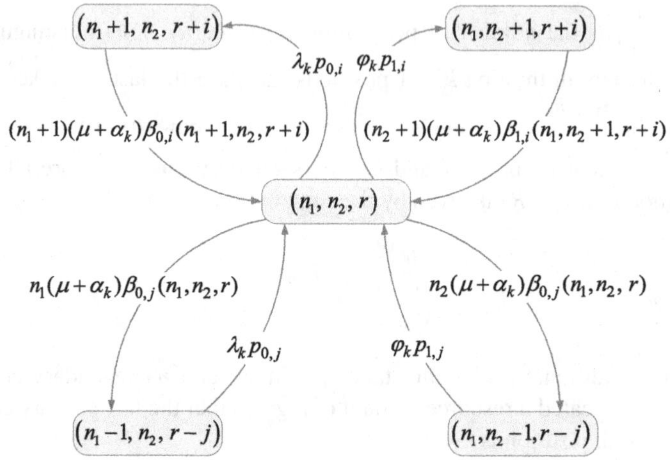

Fig. 12.3 Transition rates to and from a central state

Experiments show that for a reserved resource share of $\gamma < 0.2$ such an approach does not result in significant errors.

Having the probabilities $\beta_{0,j}(n_1, n_2, r)$ and $\beta_{1,j}(n_1, n_2, r)$, we can proceed to derive the equilibrium equations of the process $X(t)$. Its transition to and from a central state are depicted in Fig. 12.3. As for the equilibrium equations, we have

$$Q_0\left[\lambda_k \sum_{j=0}^{R_0} p_{0,j} + \varphi_k \sum_{j=0}^{R_1} p_{1,j}\right] = \\ = (\mu+\alpha_k)\left[\sum_{j:(1,0,j)\in\Psi_{1,0}} Q_{1,0}(j) + \sum_{j:(0,1,j)\in\Psi_{0,1}} Q_{0,1}(j)\right]. \tag{12.42}$$

$$Q_{n_1,n_2}(r)\left[\lambda_k \sum_{j=0}^{R_0-r} p_{0,j} + \varphi_k \sum_{j=0}^{R_1-r} p_{1,j} + (n_1+n_2)(\mu+\alpha_k)\right] = \\ = \lambda_k \sum_{j:(n_1-1,n_2,r-j)\in\Psi_{n_1-1,n_2}} p_{0,j} Q_{n_1-1,n_2}(r-j) + \\ + \varphi_k \sum_{j:(n_1,n_2-1,r-j)\in\Psi_{n_1,n_2-1}} p_{1,j} Q_{n_1,n_2-1}(r-j) + \\ + (n_1+1)(\mu+\alpha_k) \sum_{j:(n_1+1,n_2,r+j)\in\Psi_{n_1+1,n_2}} Q_{n_1+1,n_2}(r+j)\beta_{0,j}(n_1+1, n_2, r+j) + \\ + (n_2+1)(\mu+\alpha_k) \sum_{j:(n_1,n_2+1,r+j)\in\Psi_{n_1,n_2+1}} Q_{n_1,n_2+1}(r+j)\beta_{1,j}(n_1, n_2+1, r+j), \\ n_1+n_2 < C, r \le R_0.$$

$$Q_{n_1,n_2}(r)\left[\varphi_k \sum_{j=0}^{R_1-r} p_{1,j} + (n_1+n_2)(\mu+\alpha_k)\right] =$$
$$= \varphi_k \sum_{j:(n_1,n_2-1,r-j)\in\Psi_{n_1,n_2-1}(r-j)} p_{1,j} Q_{n_1,n_2-1}(r-j) +$$
$$+ (n_1+1)(\mu+\alpha_k) \sum_{j:(n_1+1,n_2,r+j)\in\Psi_{n_1+1,n_2}} Q_{n_1+1,n_2}(r+j)\beta_{0,j}(n_1+1,n_2,r+j) +$$
$$+ (n_2+1)(\mu+\alpha_k) \sum_{j:(n_1,n_2+1,r+j)\in\Psi_{n_1,n_2+1}} Q_{n_1,n_2+1}(r+j)\beta_{1,j}(n_1,n_2+1,r+j),$$
$$n_1+n_2 < C, r > R_0.$$

$$(n_1+n_2)(\mu+\alpha_k)Q_{n_1,n_2}(r) = \lambda_k \sum_{j:(n_1-1,n_2,r-j)\in\Psi_{n_1-1,n_2}} p_{0,j} Q_{n_1-1,n_2}(r-j) +$$
$$+\varphi_k \sum_{j:(n_1,n_2-1,r-j)} p_{1,j} Q_{n_1,n_2-1}(r-j),\ n_1+n_2 = C,\ r \le R_0,$$

$$(n_1+n_2)(\mu+\alpha_k)Q_{n_1,n_2}(r) = \varphi_k \sum_{j:(n_1,n_2-1,r-j)\in\Psi_{n_1,n_2-1}} p_{1,j} Q_{n_1,n_2-1}(r-j),$$
$$n_1+n_2 = C,\ r > R_0.$$

The above equations are derived by the following argument.

1. In the left-hand side of the first equation, $\lambda_k \sum_{j=0}^{R_0} p_{0,j} + \varphi_k \sum_{j=0}^{R_1} p_{1,j}$ represents the transition rate from state (0, 0, 0). In the right-hand side, $(\mu+\alpha_k)$ is the transition rate from any state of the form (1, 0, j) or (0, 1, j) to state (0, 0, 0), which occurs when a customer departs the network upon service completion or moves to another node.
2. The second equation holds for $n_1+n_2 < C$, $r \le R_0$. In the left-hand side, $\lambda_k \sum_{j=0}^{R_0-r} p_{0,j} + \varphi_k \sum_{j=0}^{R_1-r} p_{1,j} + (n_1+n_2)(\mu+\alpha_k)$ is the transition rate from state (n_1, n_2, r). In the right-hand side, the first term $\lambda_k \sum_{j:(n_1-1,n_2,r-j)\in\Psi_{n_1-1,n_2}} p_{0,j} Q_{n_1-1,n_2}(r-j)$ corresponds to moving from $(n_1-1, n_2, r-j)$ to (n_1, n_2, r) due to a primary arrival to node k, the second term corresponds to a transition due to a secondary arrival, while the last two terms describe transitions due to departures of primary and secondary customers.
3. The third equation holds for $n_1+n_2 < C$ and $r > R_0$ and is structured in the same manner.
4. The fourth equation describes transitions for $n_1+n_2 = C$, $r \le R_0$. In the left-hand side, $(n_1+n_2)(\mu+\alpha_k)$ is the transition rate from (n_1, n_2, r) to $(n_1-1, n_2, r-j)$ or $(n_1, n_2-1, r-j)$ resulting from a departure due to service completion or a signal arrival. In the right-hand side, the first term corresponds to transitions to state (n_1, n_2, r) due to primary arrivals, the second, to secondary arrivals.
5. The fifth equation is similar and holds for $n_1+n_2 = C$, $r > R_0$.

Equation (12.42) can be solved numerically. Since the number of equations in the system can reach $C(C+1)R_1/2$, we suggest using sparse matrix libraries and functions to deal with the generator matrix, and employ iterative methods for linear equations, for instance, the Gauss–Seidel method.

12.5.3 An Iterative Algorithm for Computing the Performance Measures of the Network

The network's performance measures can be evaluated via an iterative algorithm based upon the aforementioned decomposition method. The computation process is iterative because at each iteration a level of secondary customers is added. The procedure is completed as soon as the required accuracy for the performance measures is reached.

At the first iteration, set the secondary arrival rates at all nodes equal to zero: $\varphi_k = 0,\ k = 0, 1, ..., K$. Then, proceed as follows:

1. Using parameters λ_k, μ, α_k, φ_k and the distributions $\{p_{0,j}\}_{j\geq 0}$ and $\{p_{1,j}\}_{j\geq 0}$, compute the performance measures of each node separately. Obtain the blocking probability of a primary customer, the probability $B_{1,k}$ that a transition to another node of a secondary customer fails, the mean number of customers in service $\mathrm{E}\xi_k$ and the mean allocated resource amount $\mathrm{E}\delta_k$.
2. Compute the performance measures of the whole network: the blocking probability of a primary customer B_0, the probability B_1 that a transition to another node of a secondary customer fails, and the average amount of allocated resources $\mathrm{E}\delta$.
3. If the required accuracy is reached, the algorithm stops. Otherwise, compute the arrival rates of the secondary customers of the next level, φ_k^{v+1}, and reiterate.

The performance measures can be obtained using the following expressions. The probabilities $B_{0,k}$ and $B_{1,k}$ at node k are given, respectively, by

$$
\begin{aligned}
B_{0,k} &= 1 - \sum_{0\leq n_1+n_2\leq C-1}\ \sum_{r\leq R_{k,0}:(n_1,n_2,r)\in\Psi_{n_1,n_2}} Q_{n_1,n_2}(r) \sum_{j=0}^{R_{k,0}-r} p_{0,j},\\
B_{1,k} &= 1 - \sum_{0\leq n_1+n_2\leq C-1}\ \sum_{r:(n_1,n_2,r)\in\Psi_{n_1,n_2}} Q_{n_1,n_2}(r) \sum_{j=0}^{R_{k,1}-r} p_{1,j}.
\end{aligned}
\tag{12.43}
$$

The arrival rates of secondary customers are found as

$$\varphi_k = \sum_{v=1}^{\infty} \varphi_k^v,$$

$$\varphi_k^1 = \sum_{i=1}^{K} \lambda_i (1 - B_{0,i}) \frac{\alpha_i}{\mu + \alpha_i} \varphi_{i,k}, \tag{12.44}$$

$$\varphi_k^v = \sum_{i=1}^{K} \varphi_i^{v-1} (1 - B_{1,i}) \frac{\alpha_i}{\mu + \alpha_i} \varphi_{i,k}, \; v > 1,$$

where v denotes the level of a secondary customer and $\varphi_{i,k}$ is the probability of redirection from node i to node k, which is equal to 0, if $i = k$, and $1/(K-1)$ otherwise in the considered scenario.

The performance measures for the whole network, i.e., the blocking probability of a primary customer B_0, the probability B_1 that a transition to another node of a secondary customer fails, are as following:

$$B_0 = \sum_{k=1}^{K} \frac{\lambda_k}{\lambda} B_{0,k}, \quad B_1 = \sum_{k=1}^{K} \frac{\varphi_k}{\varphi} B_{1,k}. \tag{12.45}$$

Another important network performance measure is the probability that a customer that has been admitted in service is dropped. It can be obtained as

$$B_{drop} = \lim_{t \to \infty} \frac{\varphi B_1 t}{\lambda(1 - B_0)t} = \frac{\varphi B_1}{\lambda(1 - B_0)}, \tag{12.46}$$

where the numerator represents the average number of dropped customers in time t, while the denominator is the number of customers admitted in service in time t.

References

Naumov, V.A., Samouylov, K.E., Samuilov, A.K.: On the total amount of resources occupied by serviced customers. Autom. Remote Control **77**(8), 1419–1427 (2016)

Naumov, V., Samouylov, K., Sopin, E., Andreev, S.: Two approaches to analyzing dynamic cellular networks with limited resources. In: 6th International Congress on Ultra Modern Telecommunications and Control Systems and Workshops (ICUMT) Proceedings, St. Petersburg, pp. 485–488 (2014)

Naumov, V., Samouylov, K., Yarkina, N., Sopin, E., Andreev, S., Samuylov, A.: LTE performance analysis using queuing systems with finite resources and random requirements. In: 7th Congress on Ultra Modern Telecommunications and Control Systems ICUMT-2015, pp. 100–103. IEEE (2015)

Petrov, V., Solomitckii, D., Samuylov, A., Lema, M.A., Gapeyenko, M., Moltchanov, D., Andreev, S., Naumov, V., Samouylov, K., Dohler, M., Koucheryavy, Y.: Dynamic multi-connectivity performance in ultra-dense urban mmWave deployments. IEEE J. Sel. Areas Commun. **35**(9), 2038–2055 (2017)

Samouylov, K., Gaidamaka, Yu., Sopin, E.: Simplified analysis of queueing systems with random requirements. Stat. Simul. **231**, 381–390 (2018)

Samouylov, K., Sopin, E., Vikhrova, O.: Analyzing blocking probability in LTE wireless network via queuing system with finite amount of resources. Communications in Computer and Information Science, 564, 393–403 Springer (2015)

Samuylov, A., Beschastnyi, V., Moltchanov, D., Ostrikova, D., Gaidamaka, Y., Shorgin, V.: Modeling coexistence of unicast and multicast communications in 5G New Radio systems. In: 2019 IEEE 30th Annual International Symposium on Personal, Indoor and Mobile Radio Communications (PIMRC), pp. 1–6. IEEE (2019)

Appendix

A1. Random Elements

A1.1. Probability Space

A measurable space is a pair $(\Omega, \mathcal{F})$, where Ω is a nonempty set and $\mathcal{F}$ is a σ-algebra on Ω, i.e., a set of subsets of Ω such that

(i) $\Omega \in \mathcal{F}$,
(ii) $A \in \mathcal{F} \Rightarrow \overline{A} \in \mathcal{F}$,
(iii) $A_1, A_2, \ldots \in \mathcal{F} \Rightarrow \bigcup\limits_{n=1}^{\infty} A_n \in \mathcal{F}$.

Elements of $\mathcal{F}$ are called *events*.

A probability measure on $(\Omega, \mathcal{F})$ is a mapping $\mathrm{P} : \mathcal{F} \to [0, 1]$ that satisfies

(a) $\mathsf{P}(\varnothing) = 0$ and $\mathsf{P}(\Omega) = 1$,
(b) $\mathsf{P}\left(\bigcup\limits_{n \in \mathcal{J}} A_n\right) = \sum\limits_{n \in \mathcal{J}} \mathsf{P}(A_n)$

for any countable family of mutually exclusive events $A_n, n \in \mathcal{J}$. The triple $(\Omega, \mathcal{F}, \mathsf{P})$ is called *the probability space*.

Let $(\boldsymbol{S}, \mathcal{B})$ be a measurable space. A random element with values in $\boldsymbol{S}$ is a function $\xi : \Omega \to \boldsymbol{S}$ such that $\{\omega \in \Omega | \xi(\omega) \in B\} \in \mathcal{F}$ for each $B \in \mathcal{B}$. Distribution $F(B)$ of a random element ξ is a probability measure on $(\boldsymbol{S}, \mathcal{B})$ defined by $F(B) = \mathsf{P}(\omega \in \Omega | \xi(\omega) \in B)$. For brevity it is customary to write $\{\xi \in B\}$ instead of $\{\omega \in \Omega | \xi(\omega) \in$

V. Naumov et al., *Matrix and Analytical Methods for Performance Analysis of Telecommunication Systems*, https://doi.org/10.1007/978-3-030-83132-5

$B\}$, so that $F(B) = \mathsf{P}(\xi \in B)$. The conditional probability $\mathsf{P}(A|\xi = s)$ is a function satisfying equations

$$\int_B \mathsf{P}(A|\xi = s)F(ds) = \mathsf{P}(A \cap \{\xi \in B\}),\ B \in \mathcal{B}.$$

The conditional probability of A given B is defined as $\mathsf{P}(A|B) = \mathsf{P}(A|\chi_B = 1)$, where χ_B is the indicator function of B. It satisfies the equality

$$\mathsf{P}(A|B)\mathsf{P}(B) = \mathsf{P}(A \cap B).$$

Two events A and B are said to be *independent* if

$$\mathsf{P}(A \cap B) = \mathsf{P}(A)\mathsf{P}(B).$$

This implies $\mathsf{P}(A|B) = \mathsf{P}(A)$ and $\mathsf{P}(B|A) = \mathsf{P}(B)$.

If

(a) $A_i \cap A_j = \varnothing$ for $i \neq j$,
(b) $\mathsf{P}(A_i) > 0$ for $i = 1, 2, ..., n$,
(c) $A_1 \cup A_2 \cup ... \cup A_n = \Omega$,

then

(1) $\mathsf{P}(B) = \sum_{i=1}^{n} \mathsf{P}(A_i)\mathsf{P}(B|A_i)$ (*the total probability formula*),
(2) $\mathsf{P}(A_j|B) = \frac{\mathsf{P}(A_j)\mathsf{P}(B|A_j)}{\sum_{i=1}^{n} \mathsf{P}(A_i)\mathsf{P}(B|A_i)}$ (*Bayes' rule*).

A1.2. Random Variables

A real-valued *random variable* ξ is a mapping $\xi : \Omega \to \mathbb{R}$ such that $\{\omega \in \Omega|\xi(\omega) \leq x\} \in \mathcal{F}$ for all $x \in \mathbb{R}$. The function $F_\xi(x) = \mathsf{P}(\xi \leq x)$ is called *the cumulative distribution function* of ξ. It satisfies the properties:

(1) $\lim_{x\to-\infty} F_\xi(x) = 0$,
(2) $\lim_{x\to+\infty} F_\xi(x) = 1$,
(3) $F_\xi(x) \leq F_\xi(y)$, if $x \leq y$ (nondecreasing),
(4) $\lim_{\varepsilon\to 0} F_\xi(x + \varepsilon^2) = F_\xi(x)$ (right continuous).

Discrete random variables: A random variable is *discrete* if it takes values only in a countable (finite or infinite) set $\mathcal{X} = \{x_1, x_2, ..., x_i, ...\}$. The distribution function $F_\xi(x)$ of a discrete random variable ξ can be given by a table with $p_i = \mathsf{P}(\xi = x_i)$.

x_1	x_2	...	x_i	...
p_1	p_2	...	p_i	...

We have

(a) $p_i \geq 0$,
(b) $\sum_i p_i = 1$,
(c) $F_\xi(y) = \sum_{x_i \leq y} p_i$,
(d) $p_i = F_\xi(x_i) - F_\xi(x_i - 0)$.

Properties (a) and (b) mean that $\mathbf{p} = (p_1, p_2, ..., p_i, ...)$ is a *probability vector* (Fig. A.1).

Continuous random variables: A random variable is *continuous* if there exists a nonnegative function $f_\xi(x)$ called the *probability density function*, such that

$$F_\xi(x) = \int_{-\infty}^{x} f_\xi(y)dy \text{ for all } x \in \mathbb{R}.$$

We have

(a) $f_\xi(x) \geq 0$,
(b) $\int_{-\infty}^{+\infty} f_\xi(x)dx = 1$,
(c) if $f_\xi(x)$ is continuous at $x = x_0$, then $f_\xi(x) = \frac{dF_\xi(x)}{dx}$ (Fig. A.2).

The joint cumulative distribution function of random variables $\xi_1, \xi_2, ..., \xi_n$ is defined as $F_{\xi_1,...,\xi_n}(x_1, ..., x_n) = \mathsf{P}(\xi_1 \leq x_1, ..., \xi_n \leq x_n)$. A joint cumulative distribution function satisfies the properties:

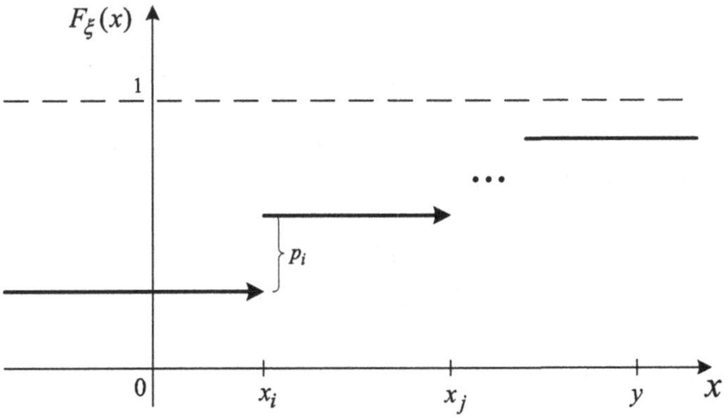

Fig. A.1 Distribution function $F_\xi(x)$ of a discrete random variable ξ

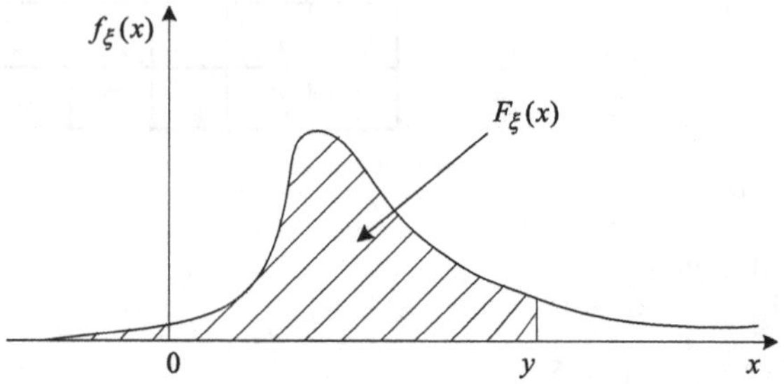

Fig. A.2 Cumulative distribution function $F_\xi(x)$ and the probability density function $f_\xi(x)$ of a continuous random variable ξ

(1) $\lim\limits_{x_i \to -\infty} F_{\xi_1,\ldots,\xi_n}(x_1, \ldots, x_n) = 0,$

(2) $\lim\limits_{x_i \to +\infty} F_{\xi_1,\ldots,\xi_n}(x_1, \ldots, x_n) = F_{\xi_1,\ldots,\xi_{i-1},\xi_{i+1},\ldots,\xi_n}(x_1, \ldots, x_{i-1}, x_{i+1}, \ldots, x_n),$

(3) $F_{\xi_1,\ldots,\xi_n}(x_1, \ldots, x_n) \le F_{\xi_1,\ldots,\xi_n}(y_1, \ldots, y_n)$ if $x_1 \le y_1, \ldots, x_n \le y_n,$

(4) $\lim\limits_{\varepsilon \downarrow 0} F_{\xi_1,\ldots,\xi_n}\left(x_1, \ldots, x_{i-1}, x_i + \varepsilon^2, x_{i+1}, \ldots, x_n\right) =$
$= F_{\xi_1,\ldots,\xi_n}(x_1, \ldots, x_{i-1}, x_i, x_{i+1}, \ldots, x_n).$

Random variables $\xi_1, \xi_2, \ldots, \xi_n$ are *independent* if

$$F_{\xi_1,\ldots,\xi_n}(x_1, \ldots, x_n) = \prod_{i=1}^{n} F_{\xi_i}(x_i)$$

for arbitrary $x_1, x_2, \ldots, x_n$.

A1.3. Expectation

For a discrete random variable ξ, if $\sum\limits_i |g(x_i)| p_i < \infty$, then the *expectation* of $g(\xi)$ is defined by

$$\mathsf{E}g(\xi) = \sum_i g(x_i) p_i.$$

For a continuous random variable ξ, if $\int_{-\infty}^{+\infty} |g(x)| f_\xi(x) dx < \infty$, then the *expectation* of $g(\xi)$ is defined by

$$\mathsf{E}g(\xi) = \int_{-\infty}^{+\infty} g(x) f_\xi(x) dx.$$

$m_k = \mathsf{E}\xi^k$ is called the k-th *moment* of ξ, $v_k = \mathsf{E}(\xi - m_1)^k$ is called the k-th *central moment* of ξ, $m_l = \mathsf{E}\xi$ is the *expectation* or *mean of* ξ, $\mathsf{Var}(\xi) = \mathsf{E}(\xi - m_1)^2 = m_2 - m_1^2$ is the *variance* of ξ.

Suppose that α and β are random variables such that $\mathrm{E}\alpha$ and $\mathsf{E}\beta$ exist, and let c be a real number. Then

(a) $\mathsf{E}c = c$ and $\mathsf{E}(c\alpha) = c \times \mathrm{E}\alpha$,
(b) $\mathsf{E}(\alpha + \beta) = \mathsf{E}\alpha + \mathsf{E}\beta$,
(c) if α and β are independent, then $\mathsf{E}(\alpha\beta) = (\mathsf{E}\alpha)(\mathsf{E}\beta)$.

Suppose that α and β are random variables such that $\mathsf{E}\alpha^2$ and $\mathsf{E}\beta^2$ exist, and let c be a real number. Then

(a) $\mathsf{Var}(c) = 0$ and $\mathsf{Var}(c\alpha) = c^2\mathsf{Var}(\alpha)$,
(b) $\mathsf{Var}(\alpha + \beta) = \mathsf{Var}(\alpha) + \mathsf{Var}(\beta) + 2\mathsf{Cov}(\alpha, \beta)$, with the *covariance* of α and β defined by $\mathsf{Cov}(\alpha, \beta) = \mathsf{E}(\alpha\beta) - (\mathsf{E}\alpha)(\mathsf{E}\beta)$.

A2. Markov Chains

A Stochastic process ξ_t with a discrete state space $\mathcal{X}$ is called a (*homogeneous*) *Markov chain* if there exists a function $P_t(x, y)$, such that

$$\mathsf{P}(\xi_r = y|\xi_{s_1} = x_1, ..., \xi_{s_n} = x_n, \xi_s = x) = P_{r-s}(x, y)$$

for all states $x_1, \cdots, x_n, x, y \in \mathcal{X}$, whenever $s_1 < s_2 < \cdots < s_n < s < r$.

The probability $P_t(x, y) = \mathsf{P}(\xi_{s+t} = y|\xi_s = x)$ is called the *probability of a transition* from state x to state y in time t. Transition probabilities satisfy the following properties:

$$P_t(x, y) \geq 0, x, y \in \mathcal{X},$$

$$\sum_{y \in \mathcal{X}} P_t(x, y) = 1, \ x \in \mathcal{X},$$

$$\sum_{y \in \mathcal{X}} P_t(x, y) P_h(y, z) = P_{t+h}(x, z), x, z \in \mathcal{X}.$$

Similarly, the *transition probability matrix* $\mathbf{P}_t = [P_t(x, y)]$ has the following properties

$$\mathbf{P}_t \geq 0, \ \mathbf{P}_t\mathbf{u} = \mathbf{u}, \ \mathbf{P}_t\mathbf{P}_h = \mathbf{P}_{t+h}.$$

Let $p_t(x)$ be the probability that process ξ_t is in state x at time t, i.e., $p_t(x) = \mathsf{P}(\xi_t = x)$. The row vector $\mathbf{p}_t = (p_t(x), p_t(y), p_t(z), ...)$, $x, y, z, ... \in \mathcal{X}$, is called *the distribution of* ξ_t *at time* t. It satisfies equality

$$\mathbf{p}_t \mathbf{P}_h = \mathbf{p}_{t+h}.$$

The vector $\mathbf{p}_0$ is called the *initial distribution* of ξ_t. Probability vector $\mathbf{q}$ is a *stationary distribution* of ξ_t if $\mathbf{q}\mathbf{P}_t = \mathbf{q}$ for all t. If the initial distribution $\mathbf{p}_0$ of ξ_t is stationary, then ξ_t has the same distribution $\mathbf{p}_t = \mathbf{p}_0$ at any time t. A probability vector $\mathbf{q}$ is a *limiting distribution* of ξ_t, if $\mathbf{q} = \lim_{t \to \infty} \mathbf{p}_t$. If the a limiting distribution of a Markov chain exists, it is its stationary distribution.

State x is called *absorbing* if $P_t(x, x) = 1$ for all t. State y is said to be *accessible* from state x if for some t $P_t(x, y) > 0$. Two states x and y, each accessible from the other, are said *to communicate.* Markov chain is *irreducible* if all states communicate with each other. A state x is *recurrent* if starting from state x, the probability of returning to state x after some finite time is equal to one. If x is recurrent and x communicates with y, then y is recurrent.

A nonrecurrrent state is said to be *transient.* A recurrent state is called *positive recurrent* if the expectation of the return time exists. Otherwise, it is called *null recurrent.* All states of an irreducible finite Markov chain are positive recurrent. All states of an irreducible Markov chain are positive recurrent if its stationary distribution exists. The stationary distribution of an irreducible Markov chain is unique if it exists.

A2.1. Discrete-Time Markov Chains

The transition probability matrix $\mathbf{P}_t$ of a discrete-time Markov chain (DTMC) satisfies the equation $\mathbf{P}_t = \mathbf{P}^t$ for all $t = 0, 1, ...,$ with $\mathbf{P} = \mathbf{P}_1$. Matrix $\mathbf{P} = [P(x, y)]$ is called the *one-step transition probability matrix.*

The straightforward approach to calculating matrix $\mathbf{X} = \mathbf{P}^k$ by the formula

$$\mathbf{P}^j = (\mathbf{P}^{j-1})\mathbf{P}, \quad j = 2, 3, ..., k,$$

involves $k - 1$ matrix multiplications. A more efficient algorithm is based upon the binary representation of the index of power k. If $k = \sum_{j=0}^{m} i_j 2^j, m = \lfloor \log_2 k \rfloor$, is the binary representation of k, then

$$\mathbf{X} = \mathbf{P}^{\sum_{j=0}^{m} i_j 2^j} = \prod_{j=0}^{m} (\mathbf{P}^{2^j})^{i_j} = \prod_{j=0}^{m} \mathbf{Y}_j^{i_j},$$

where $\mathbf{Y}_0 = \mathbf{P}, \quad \mathbf{Y}_j = \mathbf{Y}_{j-1}^2, \quad j = 1, 2, ..., m$. In total, m matrix multiplications are needed to compute matrices $\mathbf{Y}_j$, and $\sum_{j=0}^{m} i_j - 1$ multiplications of $\mathbf{Y}_j$ to compute

X. The total number of matrix multiplications thus does not exceed $2m = 2[\log_2 k]$, and one never has to multiply more than $(k-1)$ matrices.

The stationary distribution $\mathbf{p} = (p(x), p(y), p(z), ...)$, $x, y, z, ... \in \mathcal{X}$, of a discrete-time Markov chain satisfies the linear system

$$p(x) = \sum_{y \in \mathcal{X}} p(y)P(y, x), x \in \mathcal{X},$$

and the *normalization condition*

$$\sum_{x \in \mathcal{X}} p(x) = 1.$$

For any discrete-time Markov chain with a finite stochastic matrix **P** there exists a stochastic matrix **Q** such that

$$\lim_{n \to \infty} \frac{1}{n} \sum_{m=1}^{n} \mathbf{P}^m = \mathbf{Q}.$$

Moreover, $\mathbf{QP} = \mathbf{PQ} = \mathbf{Q}$ and $\mathbf{Q}^2 = \mathbf{Q}$. Particularly, each row of **Q** is a stationary distribution of the Markov chain.

The *state transition graph*$G(\mathbf{P})$ of a discrete-time Markov chain has the set of vertices $\mathcal{X}$ and an edge leads from x to y if $P(x, y) > 0$. An edge from x to y is labeled with $P(x, y)$.

Example A1 Markov chain with the state transition graph in Fig. A.3, where $\alpha + \beta = 1$, has one-step transition probability matrix

$$\mathbf{P} = \begin{bmatrix} 0 & \alpha & \beta & 0 \\ 0 & 0 & 0 & 1 \\ 0 & 0 & 0 & 1 \\ 1 & 0 & 0 & 0 \end{bmatrix}.$$

It is irreducible, and its unique stationary distribution satisfies the linear system

$$p(1) = p(4),\ p(2) = p(1)\alpha,\ p(3) = p(1)\beta,\ p(4) = p(2) + p(3),$$
$$p(1) + p(2) + p(3) + p(4) = 1.$$

Hence, we have

$$p(1) = p(4) = \tfrac{1}{\alpha+\beta+2},\ p(2) = \tfrac{\alpha}{\alpha+\beta+2},\ p(3) = \tfrac{\beta}{\alpha+\beta+2}.$$

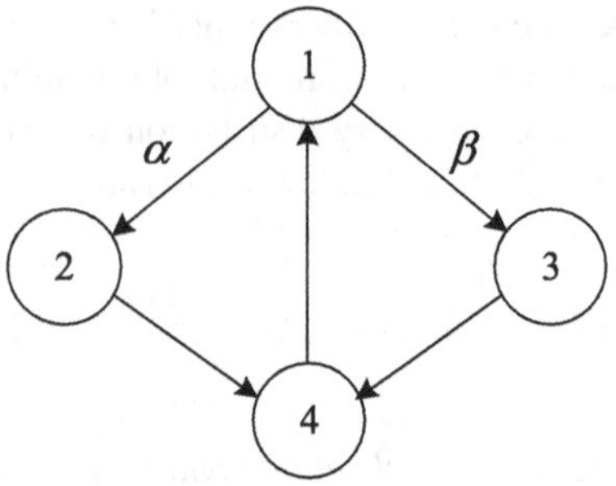

Fig. A.3 State transition graph for Example A1

A2.2. Continuous-Time Markov Chains

We assume that the continuous-time Markov chain has no absorbing states, and all its realizations are right continuous.

Then for all $x, y \in \mathcal{X}$ the following limits exist

$$A(x,x) = \lim_{t\to 0} \frac{P_t(x,x)-1}{t} < 0,\ A(x,y) = \lim_{t\to 0} \frac{P_t(x,y)}{t} \geq 0,\ x \neq y.$$

The quantities $A(x, y)$ satisfy the property

$$\sum_{y\in\mathcal{X}} A(x,y) = 0, \text{ for all } x \in \mathcal{X},$$

and have the following interpretation. When the Markov chain is in state x then the rate at which it departs from state x is $a(x) = -A(x, x)$, and the rate at which it moves from state x to state y, $x \neq y$, is $A(x, y)$.

The sequence $\zeta_0, \zeta_1, \ldots,$ of successive different values of a continuous-time Markov chain ξ_t is a discrete-time Markov chain with the one-step transition

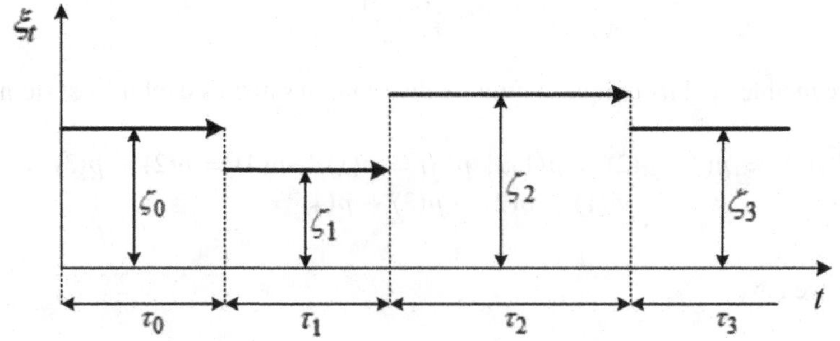

Fig. A.4 A CTMC realization

probabilities

$$P(x, y) = \begin{cases} \frac{A(x,y)}{a(x)}, & x \neq y, \\ 0, & x = y. \end{cases}$$

It is called the *embedded Markov chain*. The sojourn time in state ζ_n has the exponential distribution

$$\mathsf{P}(\tau_n \leq t \mid \zeta_n = x) = 1 - \mathrm{e}^{-a(x)t}, t \geq 0.$$

The matrix $\mathbf{A} = [A(x, y)]$ is called the *transition rate matrix* or *generator*.

The stationary distribution $\mathbf{p}$ of a continuous-time Markov chain satisfies the linear system called the *equilibrium equations*:

$$p(x)a(x) = \sum_{y \neq x} p(y)A(y, x), x \in \mathcal{X}.$$

It also has to satisfy the *normalization condition*

$$\sum_{x \in \mathcal{X}} p(x) = 1.$$

The *state transition graph*$G(\mathbf{A})$ of a continuous-time Markov chain has the set of vertices $\mathcal{X}$, and an edge leads from x to y if $A(x, y) > 0$. An edge from x to y is labeled with $A(x, y)$.

The transition probability matrix $\mathbf{P}_t$ of a continuous-time Markov chain is given by

$$\mathbf{P}_t = \mathrm{e}^{\mathbf{A}t}$$

for all $t \geq 0$. Here matrix $\mathrm{e}^{\mathbf{B}}$ is defined by

$$\mathrm{e}^{\mathbf{B}} = \sum_{k=0}^{\infty} \tfrac{1}{k!} \mathbf{B}^k.$$

For a finite Markov chain, let us denote $a(x) = -A(x, x)$, $a = \max_x a(x)$, and

$$\mathbf{R}_t = \mathbf{I} + \frac{t}{\lceil a\, t \rceil} \mathbf{A}.$$

Then we have

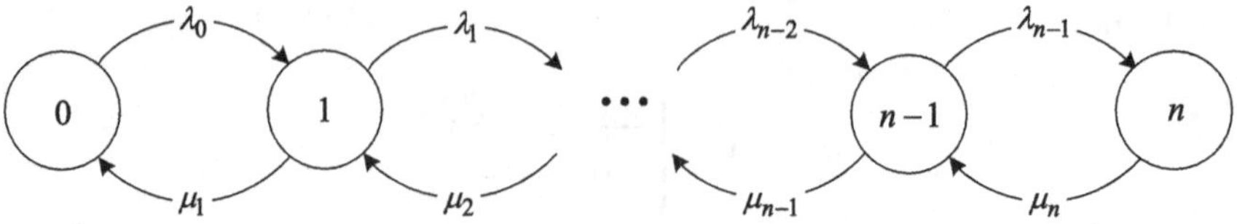

Fig. A.5 The state transition graph of a finite BDP

$$\mathbf{P}_t = e^{\mathbf{A}t} = e^{\lceil a\,t \rceil (\mathbf{R}_t - \mathbf{I})} = \mathbf{S}_t^{\lceil a\,t \rceil},$$

where

$$\mathbf{S}_t = e^{-1} e^{\mathbf{R}_t} = \frac{1}{e} \sum_{k=0}^{\infty} \frac{1}{k!} \mathbf{R}_t^k.$$

The matrices $\mathbf{R}_t$ and $\mathbf{S}_t$ are stochastic. This is why the series to compute $\mathbf{S}_t$ converges fast. In order to find the matrix of transition probabilities in time t, one has to raise $\mathbf{S}_t$ to an integer-valued power $\lceil a\,t \rceil$. After that, by raising $\mathbf{P}_t$ to powers, one can obtain matrices $\mathbf{P}_{2t}$, $\mathbf{P}_{3t}$, ...

Example A2 *A Finite Birth-and-Death Process* (BDP) is a continuous-time Markov chain with $\mathcal{X} = \{1, 2, \ldots, n\}$ and the state transition graph in Fig. A.5.

The system of equilibrium equations

$$\begin{gathered} p(0)\lambda_0 = p(1)\mu_1, \\ p(k)(\lambda_k + \mu_k) = p(k-1)\lambda_{k-1} + p(k+1)\mu_{k+1}, 0 < k < n, \\ p(n)\mu_n = p(n-1)\lambda_{n-1} \end{gathered}$$

has the solution

$$p(k) = C \prod_{i=1}^{k} \tfrac{\lambda_{i-1}}{\mu_i}, 0 \le k \le n,$$

with the normalization constant

$$C = \left(\sum\nolimits_{k=0}^{n} \prod\nolimits_{i=1}^{k} \tfrac{\lambda_{i-1}}{\mu_i} \right)^{-1}.$$

A2.3. Jump Processes

Let $(\boldsymbol{S}, \mathcal{B})$ be a measurable space. A continuous-time stochastic process ξ_t with the state space $\boldsymbol{S}$ is a *jump process* if all its realizations are right-continuous step functions with a finite number of jumps in any finite time interval. It can be represented by sequences ζ_n, $n = 0, 1, \ldots$, and t_n, $n = 0, 1, \ldots$, where $\zeta_n = \xi_{t_n}$, $t_0 = 0$, and for $n \geq 1$, t_n is the time instant of the n-th jump. The difference $\tau_n = t_{n+1} - t_n$ is the time spent by the jump process in state ζ_n (see Fig. A.4).

A Markov *renewal process* is a sequence (ζ_n, τ_n), $n = 0, 1, \ldots$ such that

$$\mathsf{P}(\zeta_{r+1} \in \mathcal{B}, \tau_r < x | \tau_0 = x_0, \ldots, \tau_{r-1} = x_{r-1}, \zeta_0 = s_0, \ldots, \zeta_{r-1} = s_{r-1}, \zeta_r = s,) = H_s(x, \mathcal{B}).$$

If this is the case, the jump process ξ_t is called a *semi-Markov process.* For a semi-Markov process ξ_t the sequence ζ_n,$n = 0, 1, \ldots$ is a homogeneous Markov chain with a transition kernel

$$P(s, B) = \mathsf{P}(\zeta_{n+1} \in \mathcal{B} | \zeta_n = s) = \lim_{x \to \infty} H_s(x, \mathcal{B}),$$

and the CDF of the sojourn time of ξ_t in state s is given by

$$H_s(x) = \mathsf{P}(\tau_n \leq x | \zeta_n = s) = H_s(x, \boldsymbol{S}).$$

A semi-Markov process with transition probabilities

$$H_s(x, \mathcal{B}) = (1 - \mathrm{e}^{-x\lambda(s)}) P(s, \mathcal{B})$$

is called a *(homogeneous) Markov jump process.* Each sojourn time of the Markov jump process ξ_t in state s is exponentially distributed with parameter $\lambda(s)$. At the end of such a sojourn, the process jumps into a set $\mathcal{B}$ with probability $P(s, \mathcal{B})$. The stationary distribution $p(\mathcal{B})$ of the Markov jump process is the solution of the equilibrium equations

$$\int_{\mathcal{A}} \lambda(s) p(ds) = \int_{S} Q(s, \mathcal{A}) p(ds), \mathcal{A} \in \mathcal{B},$$

where $Q(s, \mathcal{A}) = \lambda(s) P(s, \mathcal{A})$ is the transition rate kernel.

A3. Queueing Systems

A3.1. Kendall's Notation

A *Queueing system* consists of servers and a waiting room (or buffer) of finite or infinite capacity. *Customers* (or *calls*) from an external source enter the queueing system to receive service. Upon arrival a customer joins the waiting room if all servers are busy. When a customer has completed service, it leaves the queueing system.

A special notation, called *Kendall's notation,* is used to describe a queueing system. The notation has the form $A|\,B|\,n|m$ where

- A describes the interarrival time distribution;
- B describes the service time distribution;
- n is the number of servers;
- m is the total capacity of the system, including servers and waiting places.

The symbols traditionally used for A and B are

- M for exponential distribution;
- D for deterministic distribution;
- G (or GI) for general (general independent) distribution.

When the system capacity is infinite one simply writes $A|B|n$, for example $M|\,M|1$, $M|\,G|n$, $GI|\,M|\infty$.

Example A3 The poisson process.

An arrival process is called a renewal process if its interarrival times are independent and identically distributed random variables.

A renewal process is called the *Poisson process* of rate λ if interarrival times have the exponential CDF

$$F(x) = 1 - \mathrm{e}^{-\lambda x}, \ x \geq 0.$$

The poisson process is a stationary process with *independent increments*, i.e.,

$$\mathsf{P}\left(a\left(\sum_{i=0}^{k} h_i\right) - a\left(\sum_{i=0}^{k-1} h_i\right) = j_k, 1 \leq k \leq n\right) = \prod_{k=1}^{n} \frac{(\lambda h_k)^{j_k}}{j_k!}\mathrm{e}^{-\lambda h_k},$$

for all $h_0, \ldots, h_n > 0, j_1, \ldots, j_n \geq 0$, and $n \geq 1$.

Particularly, the probability of i arrivals in $(t, t + h]$

$$\mathsf{P}(a(t + h) - a(t) = i) = \frac{(\lambda h)^i}{i!}\mathrm{e}^{-\lambda h}$$

does not depend on t:

$$\begin{aligned}\mathsf{P}(a(t+h) = a(t)) &= 1 - \lambda h + o(h),\\ \mathsf{P}(a(t+h) = a(t) + 1) &= \lambda h + o(h),\\ \mathsf{P}(a(t+h) \geq a(t) + 2) &= o(h).\end{aligned}$$

A3.2. The M|M|1 Queue

Let $X(t)$ be the number of customers in the $M|M|1$ queueing system with arrival rate λ and service rate μ. The continuous-time Markov chain $X(t)$ has the state transition graph depicted in Fig. A.6.

The system of equilibrium equations has the probability solution p_0, p_1, ... if the stability condition

$$\rho = \frac{\lambda}{\mu} < 1$$

holds. Then we have

$$p_n = (1-\rho)\rho^n, n = 0, 1, \dots\dots$$

Generalized $M|M|1$**queue (infinite Birth and Death Process).** Consider a single server queueing system with the waiting room of infinite size and both arrival and service rates depending on the number of customers in the system. Assume that

$$\begin{aligned}&\mathsf{P}(X(t+h) = n+1 | X(t) = n) = \lambda_n h + o(h), \text{ for } n \geq 0,\\ &\mathsf{P}(X(t+h) = n-1 | X(t) = n) = \mu_n h + o(h), \text{ for } n \geq 1,\\ &\mathsf{P}(|X(t+h) - X(t)| \geq 2) = o(h).\end{aligned}$$

Parameters λ_n and μ_n are called the *birth rates* and *death rates,* respectively.

We assume that the following *regularity condition* holds

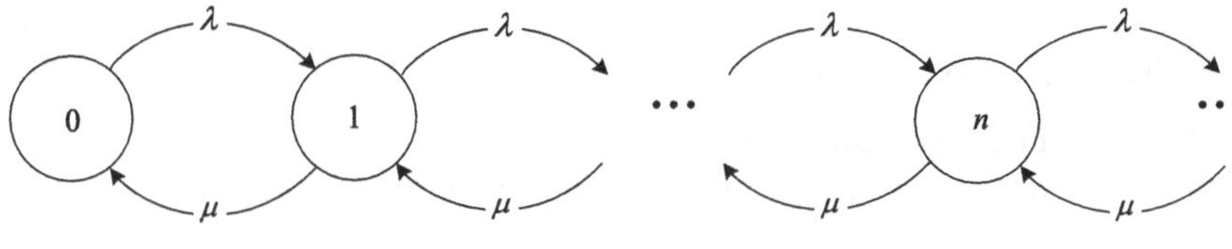

Fig. A.6 State transition graph for the $M|M|1$ queue

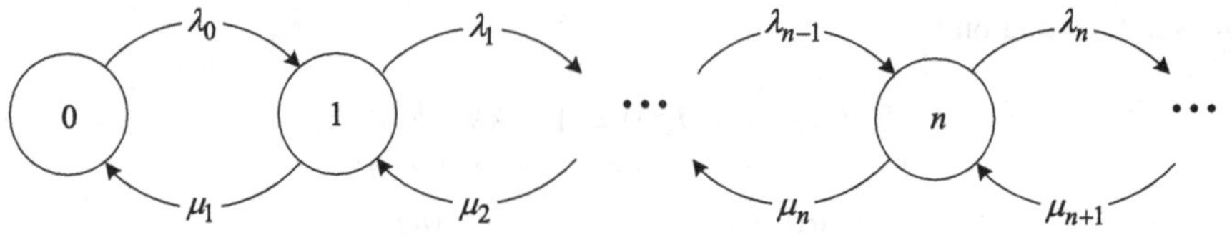

Fig. A.7 State transition graph of an infinite BDP

$$\sum_{n=0}^{\infty} \pi_n \sum_{k=0}^{n} \frac{1}{\lambda_k \pi_k} = \infty,$$

where

$$\pi_0 = 1, \pi_n = \frac{\lambda_0 \lambda_1 \ldots \lambda_{n-1}}{\mu_1 \mu_2 \ldots \mu_n}, n \geq 1.$$

It guarantees the existence of a continuous-time Markov Process $X(t)$ with given birth and death rates, and with the right-continuous realizations. This process is called a *birth-and-death process* (BDP).

A BDP has the state transition graph depicted in Fig. A.7.

The stationary distribution of a BDP exists if the *stability condition* holds

$$C = \sum_{n=0}^{\infty} \pi_n < \infty.$$

In this case the stationary state probabilities are given by

$$p_n = \frac{\pi_n}{C}, n \geq 0.$$

A3.3. Little's Law

Let us introduce some notations:

$a(t)$—the number of customer arrivals by time t,
$\alpha_t = \frac{a(t)}{t}$—the average number of arrivals per unit of time by time t,

$$\delta_k(t) = \begin{cases} 1, \text{ if the } k \text{ - th customer is in the system at time } t, \\ 0, \text{ otherwise,} \end{cases}$$

$v(t) = \sum_{k=1}^{\infty} \delta_k(t)$—the number of customers in the system at time t,

$d_k(t) = \int_0^t \delta_k(x)dx$—the time spent by the k-th customer in the system by time t,

$b(t) = \int_0^t v(x)dx = \int_0^t \sum_{k=1}^{\infty} \delta_k(x)dx = \int_0^t \sum_{k=1}^{\alpha(t)} \delta_k(x)dx = \sum_{k=1}^{\alpha(t)} d_k(t)$—the total time spent in the system by all customers during $(0, t)$,

$l_t = \frac{b(t)}{t}$—the average number of customers in the system during $(0, t)$,

$\Delta_t = \frac{b(t)}{\alpha(t)}$—the average time spent in the system during $(0, t)$ by customers arriving in $(0, t)$.

Then, we have

$$l_t = \alpha_t \Delta_t.$$

If l_t, α_t and Δ_t have limits l, α and Δ, respectively, then the following formula, called *Little's Law*, is valid:

$$l = \alpha \Delta.$$

It can be applied to a large variety of systems.

Example A4 A queueing system $G|G|n$ with mean arrival rate λ and mean service time b satisfying *stability condition*$\rho = \lambda b < n$.

- Mean queue length is given by $\lambda \times \mathsf{E}w$, where $\mathsf{E}w$ is the mean waiting time.
- Mean number of busy servers is equal to ρ.

Supplementary References

Part I

Akimaru, H., Kawashima, K.: Teletraffic. Theory and Applications. Springer, London (1993)

Alfa, A.S.: Queueing Theory for Telecommunications: Discrete Time Modelling of a Single Node System. Springer Science & Business Media (2010)

Artalejo, J.R., Gómez-Corral, A.: Markovian arrivals in stochastic modelling: a survey and some new results. Stat. Oper. Res. Trans. **34**(2), 101–144 (2010)

Asmussen, S., Bladt, M.: Renewal Theory and Queueing Algorithms for Matrix-Exponential Distributions, pp. 313–341. Matrix-Analytic Methods in Stochastic Models, Marcel Dekker, New York (1996)

Asmussen, S., O'Cinneide, C.A.: Matrix-Exponential Distributions, p. 3. Encyclopedia of Statistical Sciences, Wiley, Hoboken (2006)

Basharin, G.P., Langville, A.N., Naumov, V.A.: The life and work of AA Markov. Linear algebra and its applications. (2004)

Basharin, G., Naumov, V., Samouylov, K.: On Markovian modelling of arrival processes. Stat. Pap. **59**(4), 1533–1540 (2018)

Basharin, G.P., Gaidamaka, Yu.V., Samouylov, K.E.: Mathematical theory of teletraffic and its application to the analysis of multiservice communication of next generation networks. Autom. Control. Comput. Sci. **47**(2), 62–69 (2013)

Basharin, G.P., Kokotushkin, V.A., Naumov, V.A.: Equivalent random traffic in teletraffic theory. Itogi Nauki i Tekhniki. VINITI **2**, 82–123 (1980)

Basharin, G.P., Samouylov, K.E., Yarkina, N.V., Gudkova, I.A.: A new stage in mathematical teletraffic theory. Autom. Remote Control **70**(12), 1954–1964 (2009)

Basharin, G.P.: Lectures on the mathematical theory of teletraffic, 3rd edn. RUDN, Moscow (2009).(in Russian)

Bladt, M., Nielsen, B.F.: Matrix-Exponential Distributions in Applied Probability, p. 81. Springer, New York (2017)

Bocharov, P.P., D'Apice, C., Pechinkin, A.V., Salerno, S.: Queueing Theory (2003)

Buchholz, P., Kriege, J., Felko, I.: Input Modeling with Phase-Type Distributions and Markov Models: Theory and Applications. Springer (2014)

Daigle, J.N.: Queueing Theory with Applications to Packet Telecommunication. Springer Science & Business Media (2005)

Daley, D.J., Vere-Jones, D.: An Introduction to the Theory of Point Processes, vol. 1: Elementary Theory and Methods. Verlag New York Berlin Heidelberg, Springer (2002)

V. Naumov et al., *Matrix and Analytical Methods for Performance Analysis of Telecommunication Systems*, https://doi.org/10.1007/978-3-030-83132-5

Daley, D.J., Vere-Jones, D.: An Introduction to the Theory of Point Processes, vol. II. Springer, General Theory and Structure (2008)
Dudin, A.N., Klimenok, V.I., Vishnevsky, V.M.: The Theory of Queuing Systems with Correlated Flows. Springer (2020)
Erlang, A.K.: Solution of some problems in the theory of probabilities of significance in automatic telephone exchanges. Trans. Danish Acad. Tech. Sci. **2**, 138–155 (1948)
Fiche, G., Hebuterne, G.: Communicating Systems & Networks: Traffic & Performance. Kogan Page (2004)
Gnedenko, B.V., König, D.: Handbuch der Bedienungstheorie II: Formeln und andere Ergebnisse. Akademie-Verlag, Berlin (1984)
Gnedenko, B.V., König, D.: Handbuch der bedienungstheorie I: Grundlagen und Methoden. Akademie-Verlag, Berlin (1983)
Häggström, O.: Finite Markov Chains and Algorithmic Applications. Cambridge University Press (2002)
Iversen, V.B.: Teletraffic engineering and network planning. Technical University of Denmark (2011)
Logothetis, M., Moscholios I.: Efficient multirate teletraffic lvoss models beyond Erlang. John Wiley & Sons Ltd (2019)
Kelly, F.: Reversibility and Stochastic Networks. Wiley, New York (1979)
Kemeny, J.G., Snell, J.L., Knapp, A.W., Griffeath, D.S.: Denumerable Markov Chains. Graduate Texts in Mathematics (1976)
Kemeny, J.G., Snell, J.L.: Finite Markov chains. Undergraduate Texts in Mathematics (1976)
Kijima, M.: Markov Processes for Stochastic Modeling. Chapman & Hall, London (1997)
Kleinrock, L.: Queueing Systems, vol. I: Theory, A Wiley-Interscience Publication, Wiley (1976)
Kleinrock, L.: Queueing Systems: Volume II: Computer Applications. A Wiley-Interscience Publication, Wiley (1976)
Kleinrock, L., Gail, R.: Queueing Systems: Problems and Solutions. Wiley (1996)
Lakatos, L., Szeidl, L., Telek, M.: Introduction to Queueing Systems with Telecommunication Applications, 2nd edn. Springer (2019)
Mazumdar, R.R.: Performance modeling, loss networks, and statistical multiplexing. Synth. Lect. Commun. Netw. **2**(1), 1–151 (2009)
Naumov, V.A., Samouylov, K.E.: On relationship between queuing systems with resources and Erlang networks. Inf. Appl. **10**(3), 9–14 (2016)
Ng, C.H., Boon-Hee, S.: Queueing Modelling Fundamentals: With Applications in Communication Networks. Wiley (2008)
Riordan, J.: Stochastic Service Systems. Wiley, New York (1962)
Ross, I.W.: Multiservice Loss Models for Broadband Telecommunication Networks (1995)
Scourias, J.: Overview of the global system for mobile communications. University of Waterloo, 4 (1995)
Shiryaev, A.: Probability. Springer Science & Business Media (2013)
Zukerman, M.: Introduction to Queueing Theory and Stochastic Teletraffic Model. City University of Hong Kong (2020)

Part II

Andersen, A.T.: Modelling of packet traffic with matrix analytic methods: Ph.D. thesis. Technical University of Denmark (DTU) (1995)
Berman, A., Plemmons, R.J.: Nonnegative Matrices in the Mathematical Sciences. Academic Press, New York (1979)

Bini, D.A., Latouche, G., Meini, B.: Numerical Methods for Structured Markov Chains. Oxford University Press on Demand (2005)
Breuer, L., Baum, D.: An Introduction to Queueing Theory and Matrix-Analytic Methods. Springer Science & Business Media (2005)
Gantmacher, F.R.: The Theory of Matrices. Reprinted by American Mathematical Society, AMS Chelsea Publishing (2000)
He, Q.M.: Fundamentals of Matrix-Analytic Methods. Springer, New York (2014)
Krieger, U.R., Naoumov, V., Wagner, D.: Analysis of a versatile multi-class delay-loss system with a superimposed Markovian arrival process. Eur. J. Oper. Res. **108**(2), 425–437 (1998)
Krieger, U.R., Naumov, V.: Analysis of a Versatile Queueing Model with State-dependent Service Times. In: Messung, Modellierung und Bewertung von Rechensystemen (MMB '99). D. Baum, N.Th. Müller, R. Rödler (Hrsg.). VDE Verlag: Berlin (1999)
Krieger, U.: Numerical solution methods for large finite Markov chains. In: Marie, R., Haring, G., Kotsis, G. (eds.) Performance and Reliability Evaluation, pp. 267–318. R. Oldenbourg Verlag, Wien (1994)
Latouche, G., Ramaswami, V.: Introduction to matrix analytic methods in stochastic modeling. Society for Industrial and Applied Mathematics (1999)
Li, Q.-L.: Constructive Computation in Stochastic Models with Applications. Springer, Berlin Heidelberg (2010)
Lipsky, L.: Queueing Theory. A Linear Algebraic Approach. Springer, New York (2009)
Naoumov V., Krieger U.R., Wagner D.: Analysis of a Multi-Server Delay-Loss System with a General Markovian Arrival Process. In: Chakravarthy, S., Alfa, A.S. (eds.) Matrix-Analytic Methods in Stochastic Models, pp. 87–106. Marcel Dekker (1996)
Neuts, M.F.: Algorithmic Probability: A Collection of Problems. CRC Press (1995)
Neuts, M.F.: Matrix-Geometric Solutions in Stochastic Models. The John Hopkins University Pres, An algorithm approach (1981)
Neuts, M.F.: Structured Stochastic Matrices of M/G/1 Type and Their Applications. Marcel Dekker, New York and Basel (1989)
Ramaswami, V.: Matrix analytic methods: a tutorial overview with some extensions and new results, in Matrix Analytic Methods in Stochastic Models. Marcel Dekker, New York (1997)
Seneta, E.: Non-negative Matrices and Markov Chains. Springer Science & Business Media (2006)
Stasiak, M., Glabowski, M., Wisniewski, A., Zwierzykowski, P.: Modeling and Dimensioning of Mobile Wireless Networks: From GSM to LTE. Wiley (2010)
Stewart, W.J.: Probability, Markov Chains, Queues, and Simulation: The Mathematical Basis of Performance Modeling. Princeton University Press (2009)

Part III

Melikov, A.Z.: Computation and optimization methods for multiresource queues. Cybern. Syst. Anal. **32**(6), 821–836 (1996)
Moiseev, A., Moiseeva, S., Lisovskaya, E.: Infinite–server queueing tandem with MMPP arrivals and random capacity of customers. In: 31st European Conference on Modelling and Simulation Proceedings, pp. 673–679. Budapest (2017)
Naumov, V.A., Gaidamaka, Y.V., Samouylov, K.E.: Computing the stationary distribution of queueing systems with random resource requirements via fast Fourier transform. Mathematics **8**(5), 772 (2020)
Naumov, V.A., Samouylov, K.E.: Analysis of networks of the resource queuing systems. Autom. Remote. Control. **79**, 822–829 (2018)
Naumov, V., Martikainen, O.: Method for throughput maximization of multiclass networks with flexible servers. ETLA Discuss. Pap. **1261**, 1–27 (2011)

Naumov, V., Samouylov, K.: Analysis of multi-resource loss system with state-dependent arrival and service rates. Probab. Eng. Inf. Sci. **31**(4), 413–419 (2017)

Naumov, V., Samouylov, K.: Product-form Markovian queueing systems with multiple resources. Probability in the Engineering and Informational Sciences, pp. 1–9 (2019)

Pechinkin, A.V.: M|G|1|n system with LIFO discipline and constrained total amount of items. Autom. Remote. Control. **4**, 545–553 (1998)

Petrov, V., Solomitckii, D., Samuylov, A., Lema, M.A., Gapeyenko, M., Moltchanov, D., Andreev, S., Naumov, V., Samouylov, K., Dohler, M., Koucheryavy, Y.: Dynamic multi-connectivity performance in ultra-dense urban mmWave deployments. IEEE J. Sel. Areas Commun. **35**(9), 2038–2055 (2017)

Samouylov, K., Sopin, E., Vikhrova, O.: Analysis of queueing system with resources and signals. Communications in Computer and Information Science, vol. 800, pp. 358–369. Springer (2017)

Samuylov, A., Moltchanov, D., Kovalchukov, R., Pirmagomedov, R., Gaidamaka, Y., Andreev, S., Koucheryavy, Y., Samouylov, K.: Characterizing resource allocation trade-offs in 5G NR serving multicast and unicast traffic. IEEE Trans. Wireless Commun. **19**(5), 3421–3434 (2020)

Sengupta, B.: The spatial requirement of an M/G/1 queue, or: How to design for buffer space. Modelling and performance evaluation methodology, vol. 60, pp. 545–562. Berlin, Heidelberg. Springer (1984)

Sopin, E.S., Ageev, K.A., Markova, E.V., Vikhrova, O.G., Gaidamaka, Y.V.: Performance analysis of M2M traffic in LTE network using queuing systems with random resource requirements. Autom. Control. Comput. Sci. **52**(5), 345–353 (2018)

Sopin, E., Samouylov, K., Vikhrova, O., Kovalchukov, R., Moltchanov, D., Samuylov, A.: Evaluating a case of downlink uplink decoupling using queuing system with random requirement, vol. 9870, pp. 440–450. Lecture Notes in Computer Science. Springer (2016)

Sopin, E., Samouylov, K.: On the analysis of the limited resources queuing system under MAP arrivals. International Conference on Applied Mathematics, Computational Science and Systems Engineering **16**, 01008 (2018)

Sopin, E., Vikhrova, O., Samouylov K.: LTE network model with signals and random resource requirement. 9th International Congress on Ultra Modern Telecommunications and Control Systems and Workshops (ICUMT), pp. 101–106 (2017)

Teng, Y., Liu, M., Yu, F.R., Leung, V.C.M., Song, M., Zhang, Y.: Resource allocation for ultra-dense networks: a survey, some research issues and challenges. IEEE Commun. Surv. Tutorials **21**(3), 2134–2168 (2018)

Tikhonenko, O.M.: Distribution of the total volume of messages in a single-server queueing system with group arrival. Autom. Remote Control **46**, 1412–1416 (1985)

Tikhonenko, O.M.: Generalized Erlang problem for queueing systems with bounded total size. Problems Inform. Transm. **41**(3), 243–253 (2005)

Tikhonenko, O.M., Klimovich, K.G.: Analysis of queuing systems for random-length arrivals with limited cumulative volume. Problems Inform. Transm. **37**(1), 70–79 (2001)

Tikhonenko, O.M.: Queuing system with processor sharing and limited resources. Autom. Remote Control **71**(5), 803–815 (2010)

Vishnevsky, V., Samouylov, K., Naumov, V., Krishnamoorty, A., Yarkina, N.: Multiservice queieing system with map arrivals for modelling LTE cell with H2H and M2M communications and M2M aggregation. Communications in Computer and Information Science, vol. 700, pp. 63–74. Springer (2017)

Printed in the United States
by Baker & Taylor Publisher Services